Jesus and Judgment

JESUS AND JUDGMENT

The Eschatological
Proclamation
in Its Jewish Context

Marius Reiser
Translated by
Linda M. Maloney

Fortress Press   Minneapolis

JESUS AND JUDGMENT
The Eschatological Proclamation in Its Jewish Context

English translation first published by Fortress Press in 1997.

Translated from *Die Gerichtspredigt Jesu: Eine Untersuchung zur eschatologischen Verkündigung Jesu und ihrem frühjüdischen Hintergrund*, Neutestamentliche Abhandlungen, Neue Folge, Band 23, published by Aschendorff, Münster, Germany. Copyright © 1990 Aschendorffsche Verlagsbuchhandlung GmbH & Co.

Fortress Press edition copyright © 1997 Augsburg Fortress.

Cover design by David Meyer

Library of Congress Cataloging-in-Publication Data
Reiser, Marius.
    [Gerichtspredigt Jesu. English]
    Jesus and judgment : The eschatological proclamation in its Jewish context / Marius Reiser; translated by Linda M. Maloney.
        p.   cm.
    Includes bibliographical references (p.   ) and indexes.
    ISBN 0-8006-2623-0 (alk. paper)
    1. Judgment—Biblical teaching.   2. Jesus Christ—Teachings.   3. Bible.   N.T.   Gospels—Criticism, interpretation, etc.   4. Bible. O.T.—Criticism, interpretation, etc.   I. Title.
BS2417.J83R4513   1997
236'—dc21   97-13241
                                                                                                            CIP

The paper used in this publication meets the minimum requirements of the American National Standard for Information Sciences—Permanence of Paper for Printed Library Materials, ANSI Z329.48-1948.   ∞

Manufactured in the U.S.A.   AF 1-2623

01   00   99   98   97   1   2   3   4   5   6   7   8   9

Contents

PART ONE
JUDGMENT IN THE ESCHATOLOGICAL THOUGHT
OF SECOND TEMPLE JUDAISM

PART TWO
JUDGMENT IN THE PREACHING OF
JOHN THE BAPTIZER

PART THREE
JUDGMENT IN THE PREACHING OF JESUS

Preface to the Fortress Press Edition

The German original of this book appeared in 1990. The English-language edition contains a number of corrections and minor changes, as well as additional bibliographic notices and a few expansions of the text. A complete revision was not possible. Instead, I have added a section, "The Question in Contemporary Scholarship" (pp. 1–16), that incorporates recent literature on the historical Jesus, especially with an eye to the state of the discussion in America. I there also describe some of my hermeneutical presuppositions and respond to a few of the reactions to my theses that were published in the interim.

I am delighted that a book on this neglected topic will appear in English as well. An examination of the theme of judgment should not only aid us in understanding some of the hotly contested aspects of Jesus' preaching, but also clarify the ways in which Christian eschatology is rooted in Jewish eschatological thought, thereby bringing into focus an essential element of Jewish-Christian continuity. My thanks are due to Fortress Press and especially to the translator, Dr. Linda Maloney, without whose energy and abilities this edition would not have been possible.

Preface

Judgment is a topic that has been neglected, and even avoided, both by theological research and church preaching, for some time. The present investigation is devoted to the theme of judgment in the preaching of Jesus. It was accepted by the faculty of Catholic theology of the Eberhard-Karls-Universität, Tübingen, in the winter semester of 1989 as a *Habilitationsschrift*, and has been revised for publication. The first section, on the ideas of judgment in Second Temple Judaism, was originally planned as a brief introduction to Jesus' preaching of judgment, but because there has been no recent and comprehensive investigation of the topic, it expanded into a separate study. However, this independent treatment of early Jewish eschatology proved to be especially fruitful for understanding both Jesus' eschatology and that of John the Baptizer.

The theme of eschatological judgment has become for me more than simply material for an interesting historical investigation. I received the initial suggestion from my highly respected teacher, Professor Gerhard Lohfink. He accompanied the work with his own critical judgment and invaluable advice until its completion, and for this I owe him immense gratitude. My thanks go also to Professor H. P. Rüger for his assistance, and to Professor Martin Hengel for the inspiration I received at the evening gatherings of the "New Testament Society" in his house. Further thanks go to Professors Walter Groß, Harald Schweizer, and Michael Theobald, and also to Professor Joachim Gnilka. To these and to all the others who contributed to the success of this undertaking, I extend my heartfelt thanks.

Abbreviations

Abbreviations of ancient Jewish and rabbinic literature follow those in the *Hermeneia* style sheet; the same is true of the abbreviations of the titles of periodicals, monograph series, and standard works. Abbreviations of ancient Greek and Latin authors follow those in the *TDNT.* In addition to, or differing from the above, are the following abbreviations used in the text:

BD   Blass, F., and Debrunner, A., *Grammatik des neutestamentlichen Griechisch* (with an additional volume by D. Tabachowitz). Göttingen, 13th ed. 1970.

H./v.S.   Hoffmann, E. G., and Siebenthal, H. von, *Griechische Grammatik zum Neuen Testament.* Riehen (Switzerland), 1985.

KG   Kühner, R., and Gerth, G., *Ausführliche Grammatik der griechischen Sprache.* 2 vols. Hannover and Leipzig, 3rd ed. 1898, 1904; repr. 1976.

SNTU   Studien zum Neuen Testament und seiner Umwelt

THAT   E. Jenni, with C. Westermann, eds., *Theologisches Handwörterbuch zum Alten Testament.* 2 vols. Munich, 1984.

ThLL   *Thesaurus Linguae Latinae.* Leipzig, 1900ff.

Quotations of sources from Hebrew, Aramaic, Greek, and Latin texts have been newly prepared by the author with the assistance of the existing translations. In this way, a degree of consistency in the use of important concepts, formulas, and expressions has been achieved. For Syrian and Ethiopic texts I have relied primarily on the translations of Kautzsch and those in the JSHRZ. The Hebrew Old Testament is quoted according to the *Biblia Stuttgartensia;* the LXX from Rahlfs's edition; and the New Testament from the 26th edition by Nestle-Aland.

The Question in Contemporary Scholarship

The Vanishing Judgment

In preaching and catechesis within the churches today, the general consensus is that Jesus' message was *good news, not grim news,* as the handy formula would have it.* A Jesus who threatens a city with "you will be brought down to Hades!"[1] does not fit the popular picture of Jesus, the friend of humanity, who proclaimed a God who forgives without measure. How could Jesus' Abba judge a human being?[2]

But it is not only in preaching that the serious side of Jesus' message is neglected; it also receives little attention among scholars. Those who study Jesus' eschatology generally restrict themselves to the aspect of salvation, treating it under the topic of "reign of God." That theme continues to produce an undiminished flood of literature, but there is a remarkable silence regarding

---

* Translator's note: the German contrast between "Drohbotschaft" (threat) and "Frohbotschaft" (good news) cannot be reproduced in English.

1. Luke 10:15//Matt. 11:23. See below, 221–30.

2. The thesis inspired by Joachim Jeremias, that "Abba" was a childish endearment like our "papa" or "daddy," still has great influence on preaching, even though it was long ago shown to be false (cf. J. Barr, "Abba"; G. Schelbert, "Abba, Vater!"; G. Vermes, *Religion,* 180–83). Unfortunately, however, the popular misconception continues to be propagated in scholarly publications: e.g., M. Görg, art. "Abba," *NBL* 1 (1991): 2–3; P. Stuhlmacher, *Biblische Theologie* 1: 87.

1

Jesus' proclamation of judgment.[3] Hans Conzelmann could still write: "The idea of judgment is internally consistent with that of the reign [of God]"[4] but it appears that, for the most part, that insight has been lost today.[5] The Jewish scholar Geza Vermes recently published a book entitled *The Religion of Jesus the Jew*. In a work with that title one would certainly expect to find a chapter on Jesus' ideas about judgment, but there is nothing on that subject in the entire book.[6] Joachim Gnilka's Jesus book represents a major exception to this overall picture. He has a separate chapter on the topic of "The Reign of God and the Judgment."[7]

A recent book entitled *Studying the Historical Jesus*[8] typifies the present situation in scholarship—at least in North America. It is presented as a comprehensive review of research. It does contain an article on "The Kingdom of God in Recent Discussion," but apparently the editors considered a corresponding article on the topic of judgment to be superfluous. Why? Because there has been no recent discussion of that theme? But in that case, why is there no survey of the much-discussed problem of the Son of man?

This situation may be connected with an amazing shift in opinion that is broadly represented in American exegesis. According to Marcus J. Borg, the consensus that existed at midcentury has been shattered, and now "only a mi-

---

3. This is, in principle, true also of the collection entitled *Weltgericht und Weltvollendung*, edited by H.-J. Klauck. It contains essays on judgment in early Judaism, in Q, in Paul and John; but there is none treating Jesus' preaching of judgment. In J. Schlosser's contribution dealing with Jesus' eschatology, the primary focus is on the transcendent, "heavenly" character of salvation. Also noteworthy is S. H. Travis's book, *Christ and the Judgment of God*. It treats Paul, the Synoptics, and John, but does not attempt a reconstruction of Jesus' preaching of judgment. However, cf. Travis's article, "Judgment," in *Dictionary of Jesus and the Gospels*, ed. Joel B. Green et al. (Leicester, 1992), 408–11.

4. H. Conzelmann, art. "Jesus Christus," *RGG*[3] 3 (1959): 619–53, at 645.

5. It can still be found in Ben F. Meyer, art. "Jesus Christ," *ABD* 3 (1992): 773–96, at 784. H. Stegemann, *Die Essener*, 332, also emphasizes this connection against the background of Essene ideas.

6. It is true that Vermes refers to the logion about the Gentiles as table companions of the ancestors in the reign of God (Matt. 8:11-12 par.) in connection with the sayings about the reign of God (*Religion*, 141–42). But because he sees that logion not as a warning, but as a statement of the final rejection of Israel, he considers the saying to be a construction of the church. The same argument is found in *The Five Gospels*, 348.

7. J. Gnilka, *Jesus*, 157–65. In this chapter he treats only the sayings about individual judgment; the judgment sayings concerning Israel receive a chapter of their own (ibid., 194–203). P. Stuhlmacher, on the other hand, devotes only a short section to the topic of judgment in Jesus' preaching (*Biblische Theologie*, 95–96).

8. B. Chilton and C. A. Evans, eds., *Studying the Historical Jesus. Evaluations of the State of Current Research*. NTTS 19 (Leiden, 1994).

nority of Jesus scholars active in North America" believes "that Jesus was eschatological."[9] What is so astonishing is not the change in opinion as such, but the way in which it came about. If I see the matter correctly, it did not happen as a result of scholarly discussion of the subject, but instead because certain aspects of eschatology, including judgment, were silently dropped from consideration. The effect is that, even if we set aside the Son of man sayings, a substantial portion of the traditional material is almost completely neglected.[10]

It is true that many scholars today, without extensive discussion, have come to consider this part of the traditional material nonauthentic. The same is true of the judgment sayings that I have treated at length in this book. They are all printed in black in *The Five Gospels,* indicating that the members of the Jesus seminar consider them not to be authentic. The principal reason for that conclusion seems to be the one that is given in the commentary on the double saying about the Queen of the South and the Ninevites (Matt. 12:41-42//Luke 11:31-32): "The vindictive tone of these sayings is uncharacteristic of Jesus."[11] This represents the popular judgment mentioned at the outset. Everyone knows what is characteristic of Jesus. The only question is: how?[12]

The major Jesus book by John Dominic Crossan appears to me also typical of this type of silent fade-out. Many people consider it a model and pathbreaking work, especially as regards its method.[13] Crossan hopes not only to place historical Jesus scholarship on a broad footing with regard to sources, including noncanonical sources such as the Gospel of Thomas; he also attempts to devise a better method of historical analysis of his source material by using a formal classification or, more precisely, a "stratification" of the sources, which is presented in the appendix to the book. There, each individual source is located within a hierarchy of strata, and Crossan indicates the number of independent witnesses each source has. The traditions from the first (oldest)

---

9. M. J. Borg, "Reflections," 21; idem, *Jesus in Contemporary Scholarship,* 59–60. Cf. W. R. Telford, "Major Trends," 43.

10. See below, chap. 9.

11. R. S. Funk, R. W. Hoover, and The Jesus Seminar, *The Five Gospels,* 188. Cf. M. J. Borg, *Jesus in Contemporary Scholarship,* 166. Regarding the way in which the Jesus Seminar makes its decisions about the authenticity or nonauthenticity of Jesus-sayings, I can only say (with apologies to Shakespeare): Though the procedure be arbitrary, there is method in it.

12. This represents the same *petitio principii* that I criticize below (chap. 8).

13. Thus Marcus Borg writes: "I think his approach will itself become a model" ("Reflections," 23; cf. idem, 25–26). "It could be the most important book on the historical Jesus since Albert Schweitzer's *Quest of the Historical Jesus*" (Borg, *Jesus in Contemporary Scholarship,* 33). On the contrary, James H. Charlesworth and C. A. Evans have criticized the book sharply ("Jesus in the Agrapha," 532–33).

layer have the best chance of being authentic, and the more independent witnesses the tradition has, the greater its chance of authenticity.[14] At this stage, the principle is: "everything is original until it is argued otherwise."[15]

What does that mean as far as Jesus' preaching of judgment is concerned? According to Crossan, there was none. In his appendix of sources, all the judgment sayings I have treated are designated as nonauthentic, even though (with the exception of Luke 13:1-5) they are all included within Crossan's first stratum. One of them, the saying about acknowledging or not acknowledging Jesus (Luke 12:8-9), is supported by four independent witnesses; two other logia have two independent witnesses each.[16] According to his own methodical principle, Crossan can only set aside these sayings after thorough discussion, but such a discussion appears nowhere in the book.[17] Had Crossan decided otherwise, it would scarcely have been possible for him to present Jesus as a Jewish Cynic and his proclamation of the reign of God as a kind of party program.

Or would he? Marcus J. Borg represents Jesus as a charismatic and the head of a socially critical movement, in whose political program sayings and parables about judgment also have a place. According to Borg, the judgment Jesus preached was the social catastrophe that would be the inevitable result of a failed social policy. Thus the judgment has no eschatological character at all. It is true that Jesus shared his contemporaries' belief in a final judgment, but he did not expect it to happen immediately, and his belief in it had no particular influence on his message.[18] This interpretation does justice neither to the reality of early Jewish eschatology, within whose tradition Jesus stood, nor to his understanding of his mission. Only by means of violent reinterpretations can one present Jesus as a socially engaged politician in modern format.

Truth and Method

Crossan's example reveals once again how much in the realm of scholarship depends on methodical and hermeneutical presuppositions. One of my col-

---

14. However, as Crossan himself admits, in two-thirds of all cases there is only a single independent witness (*Jesus*, xxxiii).

15. Ibid., xxxii.

16. Matt. 7:1-2 par. (prohibition of judging); Luke 13:28a par. (gnashing of teeth).

17. Crossan discusses only Luke 12:8-9 in connection with the Son of man sayings (*Jesus*, 247–49). He also classifies the reconstructed Q version as a "sentence of holy law" from the early church, without giving any reason other than a reference to Ernst Käsemann.

18. Marcus J. Borg, *Jesus*, 157, 168; idem, "The Teaching of Jesus," *ABD* 3 (1992): 804–12, at 809–11; idem, *Jesus in Contemporary Scholarship*, 54.

leagues admitted to me that he had read my methodical principle, according to which the burden of proof is on the one who wishes to deny that Jesus uttered a particular saying, and that he was shocked.[19] The historian of antiquity Helga Botermann holds precisely the opposite opinion. She wrote not long ago that "I have for years been shocked by the way New Testament scholars treat their sources." She formulates the following basic principle for historical criticism: "To begin with, the source has a fundamental claim to be trusted. The burden of proof is on the critic."[20]

It is true that even the best method and the finest principle do not produce complete objectivity. There is no objective standpoint. Only God is capable of an unprejudiced point of view that leaves nothing out of consideration. Every human scholar, by contrast, has prejudices, and it is right that he or she should have them. In one case they may be more church oriented, in another less so; in every case the convictions one brings to the work will influence the research, including one's assessment of the sources. This, too, is not a bad thing, as long as the scholar is aware of his or her own prejudices. Our goal cannot be a scholarship free of prejudice or a complete impartiality; what is important, instead, is that we constantly make our assumptions clear, and that we are always prepared to correct the judgments we have made in light of new evidence. Otherwise, progress in scholarship is impossible.

Historical Jesus research has elaborated special criteria for determining authentic Jesus traditions, over and above the generally valid principles of historical research. There has been general acceptance of the so-called criterion of "dissimilarity" or "nonderivability."[21] This means that a tradition can most probably be traced to the pre-Easter Jesus if it does not fit either within earlier Judaism or in early Christianity. Of course, this criterion can reach only what is absolutely unique and original with Jesus, and not the things that relate him to the one tradition or the other. On the basis of this consideration we can formulate the following rule: No image of Jesus and his proclamation can be accurate if it shows him as being in complete or even far ranging discontinuity with the principal currents of early Judaism. It is equally true that no image of

---

19. Among those who reviewed my book, B. Chilton (144) and L. Oberlinner (383) also expressed some uneasiness on this point. Both were apparently disturbed by the statement that "It is not the genuineness of a document that must be proven, but its falsity" (see chap. 6 below). There may be a slight misunderstanding at issue here: The statement refers to documents in the juridical sense, not to the New Testament, which can only be called a "document" in a figurative sense. J. C. O'Neill calls my principle a "reasonable assumption" (231).

20. H. Botermann, "Der Heidenapostel," 64, 66.

21. Cf. W. R. Telford, "Major Trends," 66–68.

Jesus and his proclamation can be accurate that portrays him in complete or even far ranging discontinuity with the major currents in early Christianity. But if this is valid, Crossan's picture of the Jewish Cynic without an eschatological message is as distant from the historical Jesus as Borg's image of the social critic without an eschatological message. The noneschatological Jesus is a phantom and a product of wishful thinking. If one result of Albert Schweitzer's research has been repeatedly confirmed, it is this: A Jesus who seems altogether modern cannot be historical.

Types and Models

In order to be able to make a better detailed judgment regarding continuity and discontinuity in eschatology, I have made an effort to prepare a classification of eschatological ideas. Despite differences in detail, we can recognize the same pattern throughout. The whole body of eschatological ideas can easily be classified in two basic types or fundamental models: One is a historical conception which sees the eschaton as the final reversal in the history of Israel and the nations (historical eschatology); the other is a model conceived quite apart from history, regarding the eschaton of death as the ultimate reversal in the existence of each individual (eschatology of the hereafter). Since the first model tends to speak in temporal categories (now/then), systematic theologians prefer to speak of it as a "horizontal" conception, while the second, which is more inclined to think in spatial categories (above/below), is called a "vertical" conception. There are also two basic notions of the judgment that is associated with the final reversal: One type conceives the judgment as a great action of punishment and destruction, while the other sees it as a kind of judicial procedure followed by the imposition and carrying out of the sentence. In both cases, what is at stake is that God creates justice where human beings have been unable or unwilling to bring it about. The true purpose of the judgment is thus not the elimination of sinners or the punishment of those condemned, but the salvation of the righteous, the poor, and the weak that is thereby made possible. That is why devout believers hope for God's judgment and pray, as in the psalms, that God will intervene as judge.

The creation of such a classification for systematic purposes is an obvious enough procedure. However, it is only sensible and illuminating when it is developed on the basis of the textual evidence. In that case, it can help us to a better understanding of the text in its uniqueness, and aid us in relating it to particular traditions.

In a study of the eschatology of 1 Peter[22] I have attempted to show that the classification I have suggested, with its various additions, not only applies to early Jewish texts, the preaching of the Baptizer and of Jesus, but also aids in understanding the unique features of early Christian eschatology. When we separate the early Jewish and specifically Christian elements in the system of this eschatology we find that only one element appears that is really new and also genuinely Christian: the resurrection of Jesus. However, this new element results in an essential change in the fundamental eschatological model: With the resurrection of Jesus, the new age begins within the old, without bringing it to an end. Such a situation was not envisioned in any of the early Jewish models, but in a certain sense it is anticipated in the preaching of the pre-Easter Jesus. That is to say, Jesus, with a boldness heretofore unknown, asserted the presence of eschatological salvation in his own person, his deeds, and his actions,[23] but without surrendering his conviction of the future character of that very salvation.[24] Thus Jesus' proclamation reveals the same paradox of already and not yet that we find in early Christian preaching, and in both cases the conviction about the presence of eschatological salvation is based on a miraculous event *in* and *through* the person of Jesus. Here I see a remarkable continuity between the proclamation of Jesus and that of early Christianity precisely in what is uniquely theirs.

Egon Brandenburger has suggested a different classification of types of judgment from that here proposed.[25] He distinguishes four basic types: (1) the "wrath of God"; (2) the "judgment of redemption or salvation"; (3) the "judgment of destruction"; and (4) the "judicial process before the throne of judgment."[26] The third and fourth basic types in this list are clearly justified by the material evidence; not so the first and second. The "wrath of God" is not a type of judgment, but a motif that can be associated with various types.[27] In

---

22. Marius Reiser, "Die Eschatologie des 1. Petrusbriefs." Unfortunately, a misleading error crept into the graphics in the appendix to the article: numbers 4 and 5 have been switched; the text printed with no. 4 belongs with no. 5, and vice versa.
23. Cf., e.g., Luke 7:22 par.; 11:20 par.; Matt. 13:16-17 par.
24. "Your kingdom come!" (Luke 11:2 par.). Cf. G. Lohfink, "Die Not der Exegese."
25. E. Brandenburger, "Gerichtskonzeption." In the first sections (5–22), this essay presents an outstanding critical introduction to the problems and deficiencies in previous research.
26. Ibid., 22–30.
27. Brandenburger himself speaks of the "motif of divine wrath" (ibid., 25, 31) and writes on p. 42, contradicting his previous remarks, that the descriptions of eschatological judgment in apocalyptic literature are "almost, if not totally, restricted to two or three types of judgment," namely, the "judgment of redemption or salvation" and the "judgment of destruction or condemnation."

the other case, the phrase "judgment of redemption or salvation" is in itself confusing, if not sheer nonsense, because the final judgment, in any event, leads to the salvation of some and the damnation of others. What Brandenburger intends by this designation is the idea of God's "coming" for judgment,[28] but this conception does not constitute a type of judgment as such; the types of judgment associated with the "coming" of God are the usual two: either a judgment of punishment and destruction or a juridical process.[29] Brandenburger's terminology is inexact, and therefore inappropriate.

Karlheinz Müller recommends in a recent essay that the idea of "judgment" itself be restricted to those eschatological concepts and texts that present juridical metaphors and the idea of judicial process.[30] However, this restriction would correspond neither to early Jewish nor to New Testament and Christian usage, and Müller himself does not hold to it; otherwise he could not speak of a "judgment of destruction."[31]

Like Brandenburger, Müller proposes that the universal judgment of the world appears first in the New Testament, because early Christian preaching created the preconditions for such a concept.[32] However, the idea of such a universal world judgment is also attested in the Fourth Sibyl and the Testament of Abraham.[33] The idea is anticipated in statements like that in Isaiah 66:16: "For by fire will the Lord execute judgment, and by his sword, *on all flesh*" (NRSV). *Jubilees* 23:18 expressly says that the judgment of destruction will fall upon every living thing.

Müller also expresses the opinion that my description overstates "the position and theological status of God's 'judgment' on the early Jewish scene."[34] But is it really possible to disparage that theological status by reference to exceptional figures like Philo and Josephus, in whose work eschatology plays only a marginal role? Philo represents only a small class of Jewish "intellectuals," and Josephus deliberately eliminated apocalyptic from his work. He did so with the purest of motives, and thereby, in describing Judaism for a largely non-Jewish audience, he accomplished more or less what some authors today have done with Jesus and his gospel in order to bring them to the attention of

28. Ibid., 24–26.
29. See below, chap. 4.
30. K. Müller, "Gott als Richter," 25–30. His previous essays are now collected in: K. Müller, *Studien zur frühjüdischen Apokalyptik.*
31. "Gott als Richter," 40, and frequently elsewhere.
32. Ibid., 48–49; E. Brandenburger, "Gerichtskonzeptionen," 30.
33. See below, 100–102, 123–29.
34. K. Müller, "Gott als Richter," 36; cf. ibid., 23–25.

a particular audience. In the estimation of the importance of eschatology in the thought of Second Temple Judaism, and of the position of the idea of judgment within that body of thought, references to Philo and Josephus do not take us very far.

"Simplified Theories" and "Comforting Generalizations"?

J. C. O'Neill gave my book an extensive and friendly review.[35] Like other reviewers, he agrees with the main thesis, "that as judgement was the most important element in early Jewish eschatology, so judgement was also necessarily central to the preaching of John the Baptist and Jesus."[36] What he finds missing is a bolder assault on the "scholarly establishment" and a more frequent disassociation from the general scholarly consensus. He repeatedly complains of my clinging to old prejudices and "comforting propositions that can be taught easily to students."[37] In his opinion, these include "simplified theories" such as: that early Jewish eschatology is derived from the idea of the Day of YHWH; that historical eschatology is genuinely Jewish, while eschatology of the hereafter reveals Hellenistic influence; that the idea of an eschatological judgment of condemnation is older than the notion of a judgment in the form of a judicial process, but that the latter acquired increasing influence;[38] that judgment falls only on sinners, and the idea of a judgment on both sinners and the righteous emerged only at a very late period; and that these two notions of judgment are logically irreconcilable. Finally, he adds "the old prejudice" that the Baptizer placed judgment in the foreground of his preaching, while Jesus gave pride of place to salvation.[39] O'Neill notes with satisfaction some places in which such "prejudices" are refuted, and regrets only that there are not more of them.

Here I must make a confession: I am reluctant to deviate from a *communis opinio* of the world of scholarship. Where there exist acknowledged or broadly accepted results of scholarship, I begin with the idea that it is right that they should be accepted. I oppose them only if my findings, or new points of view, urgently demand that I do so. Critical research—that is, the readiness to call everything into question—should, in my opinion, not lead us to a heedless presentation of new hypotheses, as original as possible if not aberrant, and an

---

35. J. C. O'Neill, *JThS*, n.s., 44 (1993): 228–35.
36. Ibid., 232.
37. Ibid., 229.
38. On this, cf. now the striking exposition by K. Müller, "Gott als Richter," 30–34.
39. O'Neill, *JThS*, n.s., 44 (1993): 229–30.

immediate popularization of such hypotheses—something that, unfortunately, happens more and more frequently. Where our fund of sources does
not permit us to make clear assertions, we should admit it and leave open the
things that cannot be decided. Far too seldom do we read: "We do not know."

Regarding the old "prejudices" listed above, I not only saw no compelling
reasons to surrender them; my further observations tended rather to support
them. Let me refer, for example, to the importance of the idea of an eschatological "day," which points to a continuity between the prophetic eschatology
of the Old Testament and that of early Judaism.[40]

O'Neill objects to my insistence on the contradictory nature of certain eschatological concepts that are, nevertheless, found in combination, by saying
that those who handed them on in the tradition evidently thought them thoroughly compatible. He is correct, and I myself emphasized that fact.[41] But
O'Neill goes farther, and questions the justification of systematic classifications
such as those I have used; in his opinion they are "oversimplifications."[42]

It appears to me that this represents a fundamental distrust of the application of systematic distinctions in historical and philosophical investigations,
something I find more and more common. Behind it lies the fear that systematic categories can obscure the living variety of the phenomena, and sweep
aside or separate things that belong together in life.[43] Undoubtedly, that danger
exists, but equally so the other: that in viewing the full number and variety we
lose the broad view, and fail to see the forest for the trees. Anyone who does
not apply considered categories works with categories that are unconsidered.
But when we deliberately collect certain matters, phenomena, and ideas, and
assign them to individual "conceptions," "types," "models," "traditions," or
"currents" within a culture, it does not mean that these collectives existed in
and of themselves, leading their own independent lives.[44] We have no intention, in this way, of separating what life (of an author, or a text) has joined,
nor do we wish to join what life had separated. But we do desire to distinguish
between one idea and another within a group, and to trace the individual

40. See below, chap. 4.
41. See below, chaps. 3–4.
42. O'Neill, *JThS*, n.s., 44 (1993): 230.
43. I see this same fear behind a remark of Rudolf Schnackenburg in his review of
my book. He says of my distinctions: "These are useful parameters for a general evaluation of early Jewish ideas of judgment; but they cannot really separate the flowing currents themselves" (258).
44. According to O'Neill, that is a "common assumption," and he suspects it of me
as well (p. 230).

ideas, themes, and motifs, as well as their various combinations, through history—in particular, the history of ideas—and also, where possible, to pay attention to those who handed on the tradition and their motives in passing that tradition along or in creating new traditions. In retrospect, we will discern connections of which the authors of our texts and the people they portray may not even have been aware. The Baptizer and his preaching stand within a particular tradition of Judaism; he uses traditional concepts and well-worn ideas, even if this may not have been clear to him. On the other hand, he also placed himself consciously within a particular tradition when he appeared as a prophet. Systematic categories and classifications then help us to understand a subject if they are not brought in from outside, but developed inductively from the given materials themselves. Does not a major part of our understanding consist in mental organization and association?

Connected with these questions is another difficulty that O'Neill addresses. He apparently sees a contradiction between my saying that eschatology of the hereafter and historical eschatology cannot be combined without internal contradiction, and then, nevertheless, adducing reasons why it was entirely sensible to retain both of them.[45] This is not altogether an unusual case. There are many paradoxes in life, not because we are fond of contradictions, but because some realities can only be grasped and preserved in a unity of irreconcilables. We are all familiar with the *docta ignorantia*, the *felix culpa, sobria ebrietas*, and vanilla ice cream with hot raspberry sauce (or baked alaska). Every metaphor is constituted by the trinitarian unity of three paradoxes.[46] The church's fundamental christological dogma is a paradox. Another such paradox—related to this last—is the association and combination of the already and the not yet, the old and the new, the present and future age that marks even the preaching of Jesus.

Certainly, we must ask whether there is not some philosophical solution that permits the combination, without contradiction, of the two concepts of eschatology of the hereafter and historical eschatology. In this, the problem of linear time that is basic to the historical model may play a significant role. This kind of time exists only within the earthly conditions of space-time. Only under these conditions can there be a problem such as the "interval" (between

---

45. See below, p. 21; on this, see O'Neill, p. 229.
46. (1) An expression used metaphorically simultaneously means and does not mean something. (2) It is both compatible and incompatible with its context. (3) The recipient understands it both in its proper and in its transferred sense. Cf. A. Horn, "Zur Paradoxie der Metapher," *Colloquium Helveticum* 5 (1987): 9–28.

individual death and the Last Day) and the "intermediate condition."[47] If we could solve this problem, there would be no obstacle to a noncontradictory combination of the two models. Such a solution could be something like this: At death, the individual human being enters the eschaton and thus arrives immediately at the point in world history that history as a whole will attain only after the passage of a certain length of "time." The work of the systematic theologian begins at this point.

The Baptizer's Preaching of Judgment

There is, at the present time, a remarkable interest in the person and message of John the Baptizer. A number of extensive studies on this topic have been published in the last several years.[48] Almost simultaneously with my book appeared R. L. Webb's sociohistorical study of *John the Baptizer and Prophet.* In a situation like today's, when in many areas of our field of scholarship we stand face-to-face with an increasingly impenetrable forest of hypotheses that one is reluctant to make still more opaque by adding to it, it is gratifying to see that a colleague can arrive at the same or similar results independently of one's own research.[49] This is true, for example, of John's baptism, its power to forgive sins, and its function as initiation into the true Israel.[50] It should be said that in this connection Webb avoids speaking of a sacramental character of John's baptism.

I see an important agreement in his identification of the figure of the judge, whom the Baptizer preached in a remarkably vague fashion. German scholarship continues to be dominated by a tendency to interpret this figure as the Son of man. Joachim Gnilka, for example, sees only two alternatives—Son of man or God—and decides for the Son of man as the judge expected by the Baptizer.[51] In this way, it is thought, one can more easily explain why Jesus

47. See below, Introduction.
48. Beyond those cited, let me mention just three recent German monographs: K. Backhaus, *Die "Jüngerkreise" des Täufers*; J. Ernst, *Johannes der Täufer, der Lehrer Jesu?*; M. Tilly, *Johannes der Täufer.* Let me refer also to R. L. Webb's review of research in "John the Baptist and His Relationship to Jesus."
49. Incidentally, the same is true of J. S. Kloppenborg's investigation of Q, the German edition of which I had missed. It turned out that he had come to the same conclusions as I had in all the important questions. Hence I needed only to insert the corresponding references.
50. R. L. Webb, *John the Baptizer,* 190–202. Cf. below, chap. 5.
51. J. Gnilka, *Jesus,* 81–82. Peter Stuhlmacher also decides in favor of the Son of man (*Biblische Theologie* 1: 61–62). Rudolf Schnackenburg refuses to be persuaded by

talked about a Son of man. At the same time, there is no agreement about whether the sayings about the Son of man can really be traced to the pre-Easter Jesus.[52] Scarcely any attention has been paid to the fact that in early Jewish tradition other figures, such as the Messiah or the archangel Michael, could appear as eschatological judges. Now Webb has emphatically pointed this out. He traces the individual figures and asks in each case whether or not this could have been the one expected by the Baptizer. In doing so, he applies five criteria that could be regarded as characteristic marks of the judge proclaimed by the Baptizer and the judgment with which he is associated.

> Among these criteria is the "coming" of the one announced. This criterion would have been more helpful if Webb had defined it more precisely: It is not just any (eschatological) coming that is at stake, but the coming *for judgment* (see below, chap. 5). Another criterion Webb applies is baptism "with holy spirit and fire." He regards baptism with spirit as an original element in the Baptizer's preaching (*John the Baptizer*, 272–77). I incline rather to see this as a Christian addition (see below, chap. 5). Webb lists as further criteria for the identification of the figure of the judge that "his activities include judgment and restoration," "he is mighty," and "his judgment and restoration is portrayed employing threshing-floor imagery." (221)

Initially, Webb concludes positively that the judge announced by the Baptizer can only be God.[53] But he goes on to say that there are indications that the Baptizer did not expect God to come for judgment; instead, he expected a (human) representative.[54] These indications are: (1) the peculiar image of service in connection with the sandals;[55] (2) the fact that the Baptizer does not simply call the Coming One "strong," but "stronger than I," which seems highly inappropriate with reference to God; (3) the Baptizer's asking Jesus whether he is "the one who is to come" (Luke 7:18-19 par.). Webb thinks that the Baptizer deliberately spoke in vague terms about the "Coming One" because he did not want to commit himself. The arguments mentioned, espe-

---

my solution and simply says: "However, the author introduces a number of reasons for his opinion" (*BZ*, n.s. 35 [1991]: 258).

52. Only recently A. Vögtle, in a thorough study of the saying about acknowledging and denying (Luke 12:8-9), has again defended the thesis that talk about the "Son of man" appeared only after Easter (*Die "Gretchenfrage" des Menschensohnproblems*).

53. Ibid., 222–60.

54. Ibid., 284–88; idem, "John the Baptist," 200–202.

55. Cf. chap. 5 below.

cially the second and third, should be taken very seriously. It may be that further research will bring other new insights.

> However, in one detail regarding the similitude of the winnowing I am decidedly of a different opinion. Webb accepts the idea that the image is not about the winnowing of the threshed grain, but the removal of the grain and the "cleansing" of the threshing floor (*John the Baptizer,* 295–300; idem, "Activity"). Webb's presentation of the philosophical and material evidence is not entirely adequate: ἅλων can mean the grain lying on the threshing floor; (δια)καθαίρειν is attested in the sense of "winnowing"; and πτύον is known to us only in its function as a winnowing shovel (see below, chap. 5). Hence we should hold to the previous interpretation.

Webb ends his most recent article by saying: "We may conclude at the historical level what the early Christians concluded at a theological level: John the Baptist was the forerunner of Jesus."[56] I believe we can go further, especially with regard to the judge expected by the Baptizer. If Jesus was the one whom Christian faith holds him to be, we can also regard the Baptizer as the forerunner of Jesus on the theological level. If we must all, in fact, expect to answer for our lives before Christ's judgment seat, as Paul says (2 Cor. 5:10), then he was and is the "Coming One" proclaimed by John the Baptizer.

Bibliography for The Question in Contemporary Scholarship

Backhaus, Knut. *Die "Jüngerkreise'" des Täufers Johannes: eine Studie zu den religionsgeschichtlichen Ursprungen des Christentums.* PThSt 19. Paderborn, 1991.

Barr, James. "Abba Isn't Daddy," *JThS,* n.s., 39 (1988): 28–47.

Borg, Marcus J. "A Temperate Case for a Non-Eschatological Jesus," *Forum* 2/3 (1986): 81–102.

———. *Jesus: A New Vision.* San Francisco, 1991.

———. "Reflections on a Discipline: A North American Perspective," 9–31 in Bruce Chilton and Craig A. Evans, eds., *Studying the Historical Jesus.*

———. *Jesus in Contemporary Scholarship.* Valley Forge, Pa., 1994.

Botermann, Helga. "Der Heidenapostel und sein Historiker. Zur historischen Kritik der Apostelgeschichte," *ThBeitr* 24 (1993): 62–84.

Brandenburger, Egon. "Gerichtskonzeptionen im Urchristentum und ihre Voraussetzungen. Eine Problemstudie," *SNTU* 16 (1991): 5–54. Also pp. 289–338 in his

---

56. R. L. Webb, "John the Baptist," 229. Webb concluded his book with a similar, though more cautiously formulated, statement.

Studien zur Geschichte und Theologie des Urchristentums. SBAB.NT 15. Stuttgart, 1993.

Charlesworth, James H., and Evans, Craig A. "Jesus in the Agrapha and Apocryphal Gospels," 479–533 in Bruce Chilton and Craig A. Evans, eds., *Studying the Historical Jesus.*

Chilton, Bruce. Review of Marius Reiser, *Gerichtspredigt Jesu. JBL* 111 (1992): 143–44.

Chilton, Bruce, and Evans, C. A., eds. *Studying the Historical Jesus. Evaluation of the State of Current Research.* NTTS 19. Leiden, 1994.

Crossan, John Dominic. *The Historical Jesus. The Life of a Mediterranean Jewish Peasant.* San Francisco, 1991.

Ernst, Josef. *Johannes der Täufer, der Lehrer Jesu?* Freiburg, 1994.

Funk, Robert W., Hoover, Roy W., and The Jesus Seminar. *The Five Gospels: The Search for the Authentic Words of Jesus. New Translation and Commentary.* New York, 1993.

Gnilka, Joachim. *Jesus von Nazareth. Botschaft und Geschichte.* HThK Suppl. 3. Freiburg, 1990.

Klauck, Hans-Josef, ed. *Weltgericht und Weltvollendung. Zukunftsbilder im Neuen Testament.* QD 150. Freiburg, 1994.

Lohfink, Gerhard. "Die Not der Exegese mit der Reich-Gottes-Verkündigung Jesu," *ThQ* 168 (1988): 1–15. Also pp. 383–402 in his *Studien zum Neuen Testament.* SBA.NT 5. Stuttgart, 1989.

Meyer, Ben F. *The Aims of Jesus.* London, 1979.

———. "Jesus's Scenario of the Future," *DR* 109 (1991): 1–15.

Müller, Karlheinz. *Studien zur frühjüdischen Apokalyptik.* SBAB.NT 11. Stuttgart, 1991.

———. "Gott als Richter und die Erscheinungsweisen seiner Gerichte in den Schriften des Frühjudentums. Methodische und grundsätzliche Vorüberlegungen zu einer sachgemäßeren Einschätzung," 23–53 in H.-J. Klauck, ed., *Weltgericht und Weltvollendung.*

Oberlinner, Lorenz. Review of Marius Reiser, *Gerichtspredigt Jesu. ThR* 88 (1992): 382–84.

O'Neill, John C. Review of Marius Reiser, *Gerichtspredigt Jesu. JThS,* n.s., 44 (1993): 228–35.

Reiser, Marius. "Die Eschatologie des 1. Petrusbriefs," 164–81 in H.-J. Klauck, ed., *Weltgericht und Weltvollendung.*

Schelbert, G. "Abba, Vater! Stand der Frage," *FZPhTh* 40 (1993): 259–81.

Schlosser, J. "Die Vollendung des Heils in der Sicht Jesu," 54–84 in H.-J. Klauck, ed., *Weltgericht und Weltvollendung.*

Schnackenburg, Rudolf. Review of Marius Reiser, *Gerichtspredigt Jesu. BZ,* n.s., 35 (1991): 257–59.

Stegemann, Hartmut. *Die Essener, Qumran, Johannes der Täufer und Jesus.* Freiburg, 1993.

Stuhlmacher, Peter. *Biblische Theologie des Neuen Testaments. Vol. 1: Grundlegung. Von Jesus zu Paulus.* Göttingen, 1992.

Telford, William R. "Major Trends and Interpretive Issues in the Study of Jesus," 33–74 in B. Chilton and C. A. Evans, eds., *Studying the Historical Jesus.*

Tilly, Michael. *Johannes der Täufer und die Biographie der Propheten. Die synoptische Täuferüberlieferung und das jüdische Prophetenbild zur Zeit des Täufers.* BWANT 137. Stuttgart, 1994.

Travis, Stephen H. *Christ and the Judgment of God: Divine Retribution in the New Testament.* London, 1986.

Vermes, Geza. *The Religion of Jesus the Jew.* London and Minneapolis, 1993.

Vögtle, Anton. *Die "Gretchenfrage" des Menschensohnproblems: Bilanz und Perspektive.* QD 152. Freiburg, 1994.

Webb, Robert L. *John the Baptizer and Prophet: A Socio-Historical Study.* JSNT.SS 62. Sheffield, 1991.

———. "The Activity of John the Baptist's Expected Figure at the Threshing Floor (Matthew 3.12 = Luke 3.17)," *JSNT* 43 (1991): 103–11.

———. "John the Baptist and His Relationship to Jesus," 179–229 in Bruce Chilton and Craig A. Evans, eds., *Studying the Historical Jesus.*

PART ONE

Judgment in the Eschatological Thought of Second Temple Judaism

—————————— CHAPTER ONE ——————————

Introduction

In order to understand the uniqueness of Jesus' preaching of judgment, it is necessary to see it against the background of Old Testament and early Jewish ideas about eschatological judgment. Therefore the first part of this study contains a survey of those ideas and the imagery connected with them. But since judgment represents only a *single* incident within the whole of the eschatological event, we must always consider it within the framework of the overall eschatological conception of each of the texts or authors under investigation. To avoid an inappropriate systematizing and harmonizing of different concepts we will, so far as possible, treat individual literary units, writings, and groups of writings separately.

> This is a conscious deviation from the method employed in the indispensable work of Paul Volz, which is admirable for the mass of materials collected in it. It is true that in the first section (pp. 4–62) Volz gives an overview of the writings he is using and their eschatology, and in the second part (pp. 63–134) attempts to trace "the development of the idea and atmosphere of eschatology" (section title) in terms of certain themes. But then, in the principal section (pp. 135–421) he presents the whole of the material within a systematic framework, so that what emerges is a kind of dogmatic tract on the last things. More historically oriented and far more easily grasped is the section on eschatology in J. J. Bonsirven, *Judaïsme* 1: 307–541, and the corresponding section by Wilhelm Bousset and Hugo Gressman (*Religion*, 202–301) still repays reading. Paul Billerbeck amassed an enormous quantity of material on this theme, especially in Excursuses 29–33 (Str.-B. 4: 799–1212). It is not altogether easy to come to terms with all this or to make a critical selection from it.

It is true that the difficulties in dating, as well as the conditions of transmission of early Jewish literature, especially the collection and editing of related texts from different epochs (e.g., *1 Enoch* or the *Sibylline Oracles*) permit only a very general chronological arrangement. It quickly became apparent that

19

there was no need to separate writings of the Hellenistic diaspora from Palestinian documents. There are no essential differences in their eschatology.

The selection of writings presented here may be regarded as representative for our theme and purpose. It is true that further sources from the period under consideration, such as the Apocalypse of Abraham, Syrian Baruch, or Slavic Enoch, would increase the number of examples and offer variations in detail, but they would change nothing in the overall picture.

At this point it is necessary to say something about the concepts of eschatology and apocalyptic, and their different definitions.[1] Both were in use within the Jewish-Christian milieu, and therefore the following definitions are also presented in light of Jewish-Christian intellectual history, especially the literature treated in this book.

With the word *eschatology,* I am speaking primarily of a salvation-historical concept, the expectation of a definitive change to be wrought by God in the direction of historical events and the course of world history, and followed by an enduring time of salvation in which the righteous need no longer suffer at the hands of sinners.

Sigmund Mowinckel offers a definition I find appropriate:

> Eschatology is a doctrine or a complex of ideas about "the last things," which is more or less organically coherent and developed. Every eschatology includes in some form or other a dualistic conception of the course of history, and implies that the present state of things and the present world order will suddenly come to an end and be superseded by another of an essentially different kind. As a rule this new order has the character of a fresh beginning, a *restitutio in integrum,* a return to the origins, without the corruption which subsequently overtook and deformed the original creation. Eschatology also includes the thought that this drama has a universal, cosmic character. The universe itself, heaven and earth, is thrown into the melting pot. It follows that this is not brought about by human or historical forces, or by any immanent, evolutionary process. The trans-

---

1. It is not possible to enter into a full discussion here. Instead, let me refer to H. D. Preuss, ed., *Eschatologie im Alten Testament,* especially the editor's introduction (pp. 4–8) and the contribution by Gunther Wanke, "'Eschatologie.' Ein Beispiel theologischer Sprachverwirrung," 342–60; also Klaus Koch, "Ratlos," 15–33; Philipp Vielhauer, "Einleitung"; J. M. Schmidt, *Apokalyptik* passim, esp. 46–48, 77–79, 91–95, 101–103, 120–22, 148–49, 171–89, 215–39, 277–94, 312–17; John J. Collins, "Apocalyptic Eschatology"; idem, ed., *Apocalypse;* idem, *Apocalyptic Imagination,* 1–32; James Barr, "Apocalyptic"; Goswin Habets, "Eschatologie"; Marie-Theres Wacker, *Weltordnung,* 18–30; Jean Carmignac, "Les dangers de l'eschatologie"; idem, "Qu'est-ce que l'apocalyptique?"; Odil Hannes Steck, "Überlegungen"; K. Koch and J. M. Schmidt, eds., *Apokalyptik;* Werner Zager, *Apokalyptik.*

formation is definitely catastrophic in character, and is brought about by super-
natural, divine, or demonic powers. In Christian terms, the new situation is the
work of God: it is God's will that is accomplished, and his plan for the world
which reaches its fulfillment. Later Judaism had an eschatology of this kind
which is presupposed by the preaching of Jesus. (*He That Cometh,* 125–26)

Alongside this *historical eschatology,* which ultimately found conceptual expression in the schema of the two ages, but the substance of which appears
early in the postexilic period, we encounter also a type of *eschatology of the
hereafter* that focuses on the differing fates of the righteous and sinners after
death.[2] However, this eschatology of the hereafter appears to be connected in
almost all the texts with historical eschatology, although in what from one
point of view is a contradictory manner: that is, the latter seems also to expect
a day of general judgment that not only puts an end to the course of the earthly
history of evil, but also brings the dead to a judgment (strictly considered, a
second judgment). This appears unnecessary, considering that the dead are
already separated into righteous and sinners and, as such, have already received
their reward or punishment immediately after death. The significance and
function of this general judgment in addition to the one already presupposed
by the eschatology of the hereafter must be examined and clarified as a separate
issue. Christian tradition and dogmatic theology have "inherited" this problem from the Jewish tradition. Here the question is: What is the relationship
between the special and the general, or last, judgment? Is there an "intermediate condition" of souls between the death of the individual and the last judgment, and in that case, what about the problem of time?[3]

When the adjectives *eschatological* or *final* refer to events, I am speaking of
those events that, within the framework of a historical eschatology, introduce
the time of salvation ("travails of the end time," judgment). These can also
designate the gifts of that time (eternal life, peace, joy, light, salvation, community with the angels, etc.). As in Qumran, they can be experienced as being

2. "Hereafter" in this book always refers to the state after death, in sharp contrast
to the future age of historical eschatology that, if it contemplates such a hereafter at all,
thinks of it only as a preliminary place for the preservation of the souls of the dead
until the general judgment.
3. For this problem in Christian tradition and dogmatic theology, cf. T. F. Glasson,
Appearing, 72–75, 86–87; Paul Althaus, *Die letzten Dinge,* 141–59; Peter Müller–
Goldkuhle, *Eschatologie,* 74–76; Michael Schmaus, *Dogmatik* IV/2, 445; Karl Rahner,
"'Zwischenzustand'"; Hans Urs von Balthasar, *Theodramatik* 4: 315–28. The normative
solution to date is formulated in *STh* Suppl. 88, 1 ad 1. Cf. chap. 4 below.

given even in the present, in a kind of anticipation of the end. In such a case, it makes sense to distinguish between future and present eschatology.

The adjective *messianic,* which especially in older literature was often used to mean the same thing as *eschatological,* should be applied only to those eschatological constructs in which the Messiah or a comparable figure plays a part. It is absurd to speak of a messianic time without a Messiah.

The concept of *"eschatological judgment"* or *"final judgment"* incorporates two different models that, if possible, should be kept separate: the eschatological judgment as a court of punishment and destruction, or as a forensic judgment. The former idea is fundamental to all the texts when they speak of the "execution of judgment." Unfortunately, the translations are often ambiguous and render the corresponding expressions as "judging." Whenever the texts permit, I have attempted to give an unambiguous translation. For the general eschatological judgment considered as forensic, I will also use the expression found in Christian tradition: "last judgment."

Individual judgment immediately after death is also considered as forensic: this is the "special judgment" in Christian tradition. However, this idea first appears in Jewish and Christian texts near the end of the period under investigation, even though the eschatology of the hereafter in texts like *1 Enoch* 22 or the book of Wisdom really implies such a judgment.

For further clarifications and a graphic representation of the eschatological models and concepts I am attempting to distinguish here, the reader is referred to the summary in chapter 4.

Apocalyptic is even more difficult to define than *eschatology*.[4] Apocalyptic is a more developed form of prophetic eschatology found primarily in apocalyptic literature. However, even the definition of what is to be regarded as an apocalypse is disputed. There does exist a general agreement about certain typical features and characteristics of apocalyptic literature such as pseudonymity, symbolism, fondness for secrets and revelations, reports of visions, periodizing overviews of history with a description of the "end" (usually conceived as imminent), its preliminary signs, and so on. It is scarcely possible to

---

4. "Anyone who uses the concept of apocalyptic should be aware of the fact that no one has yet succeeded in defining it satisfactorily" (G. von Rad, *Theologie* 2: 316). That is still true. Hartmut Stegemann remarks that at the Uppsala Congress on "Apocalypticism in the Mediterranean World and the Near East," there was much controversy over the definition of apocalyptic. "There was not even the hint of a beginning of unanimity on the part of the participants" ("Qumranfunde," 526). There is a helpful overview of the problems in Michael E. Stone, "Apocalyptic Literature," in idem, *Jewish Writings,* 383–94.

highlight a single characteristic, whether of content or form, as the principal feature of apocalyptic. The best candidate would be the eschatological judgment as a primary theme. For that reason, I will not attempt to give a more precise definition here.[5] In my opinion it is impossible to produce a set of characteristics of an "apocalyptic writer" that would even approach clarity and precision.

Literary-critical and tradition-historical distinctions certainly have their own hermeneutical functions for us at the present time; they help us to distinguish individual concepts and traditions and to trace their history. But we must not forget that Jesus and his contemporaries neither saw these literary units and layers that we discover or postulate, nor were they interested in the history and interweaving of individual ideas, traditions, and concepts. They regarded all of Sacred Scripture as the word of God and would only have shaken their heads in incomprehension at our operations on the text and the interest that lies behind them. For that reason I have restrained myself from making literary-critical distinctions, particularly in the Old Testament texts, and instead have made an effort to read the texts with the eyes of Jesus' contemporaries, to the extent that such a thing is possible.

In this, the history of interpretation of Old Testament texts and motifs can be most helpful to us. We must indeed proceed on the fundamental assumption that Jesus also encountered Sacred Scripture with the preunderstanding of his own time. At the same time, we must not exclude the possibility that, in certain instances, Jesus could use the Old Testament in a sovereign manner and interpret it against the usual understanding. This is even explicitly, and no doubt correctly, attested in Mark 1:22, 27.

This sovereign interpretation of the Torah (ἐξεπλήσσοντο!), so alarming—at least at the outset—to those present in the synagogue at Capernaum, is what is meant when Mark 1:22 tells us: ἦν γὰρ διδάσκων αὐτοὺς ὡς ἐξουσίαν ἔχων καὶ οὐχ ὡς οἱ γραμματεῖς. Unfortunately, ἐξουσία ("right, ability, authority, absolute power, freedom of choice, warrant") is almost always translated into German as *Vollmacht*, a term borrowed from legal language and easily misunderstood. English and French translations usually render it with "authority" (*auto-*

---

5. Hartmut Stegemann calls for what seems to me an unhelpful restriction: "Genres, modes of thought, materials and motifs are 'apocalyptic' only within the framework of apocalypses, not elsewhere" ("Qumranfunde," 499). Writings that are outside the genre of apocalypse can also contain typically apocalyptic motifs and passages. Cf. Florentino García-Martínez, "Encore l'Apocalyptique," 229–30; E. J. C. Tigchelaar, "Apocalyptic."

rité). What is intended could probably best be reproduced in German with "*Souveränität*" or "*absolute Souveränität*" ("sovereignty, absolute sovereignty [or: superiority]"). Note also the construction ὡς with the participle, which gives a subjective impression (in this case: "he acts as if he could teach with absolute sovereignty"), and leaves open the question whether this also corresponds to an objective reality (in this case, whether Jesus also has a right to exercise this sovereignty). Thus a translation of Mark 1:22 should rightly be something like: "And they were amazed at his teaching, because he taught them as if he had absolute sovereignty, and not as the scribes." On this subject, see especially Martin Hengel, *The Charismatic Leader and His Followers*, 67–71 ("The unique 'messianic' authority of Jesus"). On p. 70 he speaks accurately of Jesus' "simply *sovereign attitude . . . towards the Law of Moses*," and on p. 67 refers correctly to Mark 1:22, 27 par. as an instance of this.

In the time of Jesus, exegetical preconceptions were strongly shaped by eschatological ideas, so that an eschatological interpretation of many Old Testament passages was simply a matter of course. Unfortunately, so far as I am aware there are no monographs on this subject. The LXX deserves a study of its own from this point of view. That cannot be done here, but it is scarcely possible to deny that there is an eschatologizing tendency in that translation. It is apparent, for example, when בְּאַחֲרִיתֶךָ, "in the end," "at last," in Deut. 8:16 is rendered with ἐπ᾽ ἐσχάτων τῶν ἡμερῶν σου.[6] The same is true of the translation of the expression בְּאַחֲרִית הַיָּמִים, "in days to come," "in the future." While in passages like Isa. 2:2; Mic. 4:1; Hos. 3:5; Ezek. 38:16 the Hebrew text may already suggest an eschatological meaning,[7] it is certainly present in the LXX, which translates this expression with ἐπ᾽ ἐσχάτων τῶν ἡμερῶν (Gen. 49:1; Hos. 3:5; Mic. 4:1; Ezek. 38:16); ἐπ᾽ ἐσχάτου / ἐπ᾽ ἐσχάτῳ τῶν ἡμερῶν (Num. 24:14; Deut. 4:30), ἐν ταῖς ἐσχάταις ἡμέραις (Isa. 2:2), and similar phrases.[8] And there can be no doubt that the translators of the LXX understood the "day of visitation" (ἡμέρα τῆς ἐπισκοπῆς) in Isa. 10:3 and the "time of visitation" (καιρὸς ἐπισκοπῆς) in Jer. 6:15; 10:15 eschatologically,[9] and saw

---

6. Similarly in Deut. 32:20 (B). Cf. also the differing representations of Dan. 2:29, 45 in the LXX and Theodotion.

7. Horst Seebaß, *TDOT* 1: 211–12. On the contrary, Ernst Jenni, *THAT* 1:116–17. In Dan. 10:14 this expression should be translated "at the end of days," equivalent to קֵץ הַיָּמִין in Dan. 12:13. Cf. Pierre Grelot, "Histoire," 73; Gerhard Delling, *TDNT* 8: 53.

8. Cf. Pierre Grelot, "Histoire," 72–73. Jean Carmignac, however, rejects an eschatological significance in all these cases ("Notion d'eschatologie," 20–22). Cf. also Deut. 31:29.

9. Cf. Wis. 3:7; 1 Pet. 2:12.

the theophany described in Mic. 1:2-4 as did the author of *1 Enoch* 1:3b-6 as a depiction of the end time *parousia* of God for judgment. The future verb forms alone indicate this. It is true that they are, for the most part, occasioned by Hebrew imperfects: the LXX usually reflects Hebrew perfects with the aorist or imperfect. And yet it can even violate this rule by translating Hebrew perfects in a future sense, for example, in Isa. 3:13: ἀλλὰ νῦν καταστήσεται εἰς κρίσιν κύριος καὶ στήσει εἰς κρίσιν τὸν λαὸν αὐτοῦ ("But now the Lord will stand up for judgment, and will enter into judgment with his people"). This translation can only be accounted for by an eschatological interpretation of the passage. We will find it again in the rabbinic writings.[10] Isaiah 26:19, ἀναστήσονται οἱ νεκροί, καὶ ἐγερθήσονται οἱ ἐν τοῖς μνημείοις ("The dead shall rise, and they that are in the tombs shall be raised"), undoubtedly refers, both in the LXX and in the Targum, to the resurrection at the end.

We therefore find that an inclination toward an eschatological interpretation of the Old Testament, as we see it fully developed in the early Jewish writings (especially Qumran) and in the rabbinic authors, is also to be presumed for the LXX and should be taken into account wherever the LXX is cited.[11]

---

10. See below, chap. 3.
11. Cf. Robert Hanhart, "Bedeutung," 45–46; Odo Camponovo, *Königtum,* 377–400, esp. 398–99. For the rabbinic writings, see below, chap. 3. For Qumran, see F. García Martínez, "Escatologización."

CHAPTER TWO

Judgment in the Hebrew Bible

The "Day of YHWH" in the Prophets

The prophets' proclamation of the approaching "day of YHWH" had a decisive influence on later ideas about the final judgment.[1] The postexilic prophets, at any rate, understand that "day" primarily as an eschatological day when "the skies [shall] roll up like a scroll" (Isa. 34:4). Gloomy images are associated with it, because it is a "day of wrath" and of the "fierce anger" of YHWH,[2] a "day of distress" and of "calamity,"[3] of "visitation" (Isa. 10:3) and of "vengeance" (Isa. 34:8; Jer. 46:10), a day "of ruin and devastation" (Zeph. 1:15), of "clouds and thick darkness" (Ezek. 34:12; Joel 2:2; Zeph. 1:15), of "darkness . . . and gloom" (Amos 5:20; Joel 2:2; Zeph. 1:15). In Mal. 3:2 it is very pointedly described as "the day of his [i.e., YHWH's] coming." The announcement of YHWH's approach is formulaic: קָרוֹב יוֹם יְהוָה, ἐγγὺς ἡμέρα κυρίου.[4] To those with sharp ears it can already be heard, like the noise of an approaching army (Zeph. 1:14-16; cf. Isa. 13:4). On that day, YHWH will judge with fire and

---

1. On this, see R. H. Charles, *Eschatology*, 86–123; S. Mowinckel, *Psalmenstudien* 2: 268–76; M. Sæbø, *TDOT* 6: 26–32; H. Wildberger, *Jesaja* 1: 91, 105–6; 2: 499; G. von Rad, *TDNT* 2: 943–47; idem, *Theologie* 2: 129–33; H.-P. Müller, *Ursprünge*, 72–85; J. Bourke, "Jour"; J. H. Grönbæk, "Eschatologie," 11–14; K.-D. Schunk, "Strukturlinien," idem, "'Tag Jahwes'"; O. Loretz, *Regenritual und Jahwetag.* L. Köhler writes: "The idea of the judgment that God will hold when [God's] great and fearful day comes is the basic framework of the prophetic preaching" (*Theologie*, 212).
2. Isa. 13:13; Ezek. 7:19; Zeph. 1:15, 18; 2:2, 3. The motif of wrath and burning anger is also encountered in connection with this day in Isa. 10:4; 13:3, 9; 34:2; Ezek. 7:3, 8, 12, 14; 30:15; Nah. 1:6; Hab. 3:12.
3. Obad. 1:12, 14; Nah. 1:7; Hab. 3:16; Zeph. 1:15.
4. Cf. Isa. 13:6; Ezek. 7:7; 30:3; Joel 1:15; 3:14 [HB 4:14] (cf. 2:1); Obad. 1:15; Zeph. 1:7, 14.

sword:[5] "I will show portents in the heavens and on the earth, blood and fire and columns of smoke" (Joel 2:30 [Heb. 3:3]). YHWH's coming to judge is depicted as a theophany in which heaven and earth are shaken,[6] and sun and moon are darkened.[7]

The judgment of that day is almost always depicted as punishment, a kind of war of destruction and bloody carnage carried out by YHWH. Either it is directed at the nations and brings salvation for Israel,[8] or else it falls on Israel itself.[9] In Joel, both aspects are combined: the day of YHWH will first come upon Israel, and then will fall on the nations.[10]

This day can be conceived as a universal event, even when the judgment is proclaimed only for a particular nation. Thus Obadiah 1:15 concludes an oracle against Edom, "for the day of the Lord is near against all the nations." And Zephaniah closes a proclamation of judgment against Judah: "in the fire of his passion the whole earth shall be consumed; for a full, a terrible end he will make of all the inhabitants of the earth" (Zeph. 1:18).[11]

However, despite this apodictic proclamation, the prophet, with a "perhaps" like that of Amos (5:15), leaves open a possibility of salvation, for a call to repentance follows: "Seek YHWH! . . . seek righteousness, seek humility; perhaps you may be hidden on the day of YHWH's wrath" (Zeph. 2:3).[12] The apodictic proclamation of judgment appears to have a parenetical function. Zephaniah expects that there will be a "remnant of Israel" that, after the day of wrath, will dwell in Jerusalem with YHWH in its midst, righteous and free

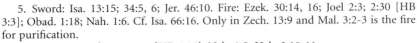

---

5. Sword: Isa. 13:15; 34:5, 6; Jer. 46:10. Fire: Ezek. 30:14, 16; Joel 2:3; 2:30 [HB 3:3]; Obad. 1:18; Nah. 1:6. Cf. Isa. 66:16. Only in Zech. 13:9 and Mal. 3:2-3 is the fire for purification.

6. Isa. 13:13; Joel 2:10; 3:16 [HB 4:16]; Nah. 1:5; Hab. 3:10-11.

7. Isa. 13:10; Joel 2:10; 2:31 [HB 3:4]. For the theophany motifs, see J. Bourke, "Jour," 23–28. For the metaphorical meaning of cosmic catastrophes within the scope of prophetic preaching, see A. Vögtle, *Zukunft des Kosmos,* 49–51.

8. Isaiah 13; 34; Jer. 46:10; Ezekiel 30; Zechariah 12–14.

9. Isa. 2:12-17; Ezekiel 7; Amos 5:18-20; Zeph. 1:2—2:3.

10. Joel 1:4—2:17; 2:18—3:21 [HB 4:17]; cf. Zechariah 14. H. W. Wolff, *Joel,* 12–15, 38–39.

11. Cf. Isa. 13:6-13; 34:2, 4; Ezek. 7:2; Joel 2:10. S. Mowinckel, *Psalmenstudien* 2: 248–50 and elsewhere emphasizes that this is poetic hyperbole; similarly A. Vögtle, *Zukunft des Kosmos,* 49–55. Cf. also H. Wildberger, *Jesaja* 2: 517; H.-P. Müller, *Ursprünge,* 80, 82.

12. For the compositional unity of Zeph. 1:7—2:3, see A. S. Kapelrud, *Zephaniah,* 27–33; G. Krinetzki, *Zefanjastudien,* 192–93. The appeal in 2:1-3 is logically consecutive with what precedes it (cf. M. Reiser, *Syntax,* 144). Cf. Joel 2:10-14; Mal. 3:1-7.

from fear of its foes (Zeph. 3:18-20), just as Joel also promises after the exile: "Then everyone who calls on the name of YHWH will be saved; for in Mount Zion and in Jerusalem there shall be those who escape, as YHWH has said, and among the survivors shall be those whom YHWH calls" (Joel 2:32 [Heb. 3:5]).[13] Without such a hope, a call to repentance would make no sense.

Malachi begins with a clear division, not between Israel and the nations, but between the righteous and the unrighteous. For the righteous, there is a "book of remembrance" (3:16); when the day of YHWH comes, the "sun of righteousness" will arise over them (4:2 [Heb. 3:20]), but the godless will burn up like stubble in a fiery oven (4:1 [Heb. 3:19]).

We find only incidental traces of a forensic judgment in connection with the "day of YHWH," as when (in Isa. 10:3) it is described with a phrase of juridical origin such as "day of visitation" (יוֹם פְּקֻדָּה, ἡμέρα τῆς ἐπισκοπῆς).[14] Ezekiel 7:27 employs what is clearly juridical language: "According to their way I will deal with them; according to their own judgments I will judge them" (וּבְמִשְׁפְּטֵיהֶם אֶשְׁפְּטֵם). In Mal. 3:5, YHWH appears as the accuser, and Joel speaks in 3:2, 12 [Heb. 4:2, 12] of a gathering and judging of the nations in the valley of "Jehoshaphat," but then shifts without transition to a different image of judgment: "Put in the sickle, for the harvest is ripe!" (3:13 [HB 4:13]). The image of a judicial proceeding is difficult to reconcile with that of the "day of ruin and devastation" (Zeph. 1:15).

YHWH's Judgment according to Isaiah 65–66

The two closing chapters of the book of Isaiah constitute, for the most part, a thematic and compositional unit,[15] usually dated in the early postexilic pe-

13. Cf. Zech. 13:8-9; 14:2. H. W. Wolff, *Joel*, 81–82. For the idea of the remnant, see J. Hausmann, *Israels Rest*, "Zur Erwartung der Rettung auf dem Zion"; H.-P. Müller, *Ursprünge*, 86–101; D. E. Gowan, *Eschatology*, 4–20. According to W. E. Müller, one may "simply call Zephaniah the prophet of the idea of a remnant" (*Rest*, 70). There is also a depiction of salvation including paradisiacal motifs in Joel 3:18-21 [HB 4:18-21] (cf. 2:14, 19-20, 25-27).

14. Cf. H. Wildberger, *Jesaja* 1: 199; H. S. Gehmann, art. "'Επισκέπτομαι," *VT* 22 (1972): 197–207.

15. J. Muilenburg, "Isaiah," 758; C. Stuhlmueller, "Deutero-Isaiah," 385; P.-E. Bonnard, *Isaïe*, 328–39, 462–63; O. H. Steck, "Beobachtungen." According to P. Volz (*Jesaja* 2: 296), however, the differences between chapters 65 and 66:7-24 are greater than their similarities. C. Westermann (*Jesaja*, 236–46) sees four different layers of tradition in Trito-Isaiah, but none of them contains chapters 65 and 66. P. D. Hanson regards Isaiah

riod.[16] These chapters present a brief eschatological compendium that, from many points of view, is closer to the eschatology of the apocalyptic writings than is the so-called Isaiah apocalypse (Isaiah 24–27). "Third Isaiah stems from the period of the dawn of apocalyptic, thus allowing us to observe the development of apocalyptic eschatology from its very beginnings."[17]

Isaiah 65–66 does not distinguish between Israel and the nations, but within the people itself between the "servants" of YHWH (65:8, 9, 13, 14, 15; 66:14) and YHWH's "enemies" (66:6, 14) who have not listened to the divine call and have done what is evil in God's sight (65:12; 66:4). They are reproached primarily with cultic offenses (65:3-4, 11-12; 66:3, 17), but they are still counted as "brothers and sisters" (66:5). Thus we do not find here an irreconcilable opposition between the "righteous" and the "evildoers," such as the Targum introduces.[18] However, the "servants" of YHWH, who will also constitute the community of the end time, are here called "the chosen" for the first time (בְּחִירַי, ἐκλεκτοί) in 65:9, 15, 22. This designation will be taken up later, especially by eschatologically oriented groups and the communities that preserved apocalyptic traditions.[19] But with this the idea of election is transferred from Israel as a whole to one or several groups within the people, an event whose significance for the history of this people and the ecclesiological self-interpretation of such groups and circles, for example, the Essenes of Qumran, can scarcely be overestimated. This development may have found its first literary expression in Trito-Isaiah.[20]

---

65 as a unit in itself and makes a division in Isaiah 66 between vv. 1-16 and 17-24. The latter, in his opinion, belong with Isa. 56:1-8 and Zechariah 14 (*Dawn,* 80–81; 134–35; 161–63; 388–89).

16. J. Muilenburg, "Isaiah," 745; C. Stuhlmueller, *Deutero-Jesaja,* 385; P.-E. Bonnard, *Isaïe,* 482–83. P. Volz (*Jesaja* 2: 280–81, 296–97) dates these chapters in the Hellenistic period, for reasons including their eschatology, which "brings us to the threshold of apocalyptic" (p. 281).

17. P. D. Hanson, *Dawn,* 21.

18. Cf. *Tg. Isa.* on 65:13; 66:24. On this, see B. D. Chilton, *Glory,* 81–86.

19. O this, see G. Schrenk, *TDNT* 4: 183–85; P. Volz, *Eschatologie,* 351; F. Dexinger, *Zehnwochenapokalypse,* 170–77.

20. P. D. Hanson, *Dawn,* 92–99, 150, 178–82, 209–79. He attempts a more precise historical dating and sees in the "servants" of YHWH the prophetic groups of the Deutero-Isaianic school, while their opponents are the ruling Zadokite priestly circles. For earlier theses, cf. J. M. Schmidt, *Apokalyptik,* 240–41. In a largely hypothetical manner, O. Plöger (*Theokratie,* 41–46) sketches the rise of this "conventicle type of differentiation" (p. 49) and "sectarian spirit" (p. 65) in connection with the development from prophetic to apocalyptic eschatology. These initiatives were carried further espe-

YHWH will make these chosen ones the "inheritors of [my] mountains," that is, of the land of Palestine (65:9).[21] Then God will create "new heavens and a new earth" (65:17). But in spite of this universal horizon, the subsequent description of eschatological bliss is limited to Jerusalem and remains quite earthly: people will rejoice and be glad; there will be no more weeping or crying (65:18-19). One who dies at a hundred years will be considered young (65:20), "for like the days of a tree shall the days of my people be" (65:22). People will build houses and plant vineyards, and not labor in vain (65:21, 23). YHWH will be so close to the chosen as to answer them before they call, and to hear them while they are still speaking (65:24). Only with the promise (in v. 25) of amity among the beasts, imported from Isaiah 11, does a truly paradisiacal feature enter the picture. The LXX and the Targum create another reference of that kind by interpreting the tree in v. 22 as the "tree of life."[22]

This description shows what the "new heavens and new earth" in 65:17 means: not a *totaliter aliter*, not a new creation after the destruction of the old, but a marvelous renewal of the world through God's removal of all evil from it.[23] Just as the day of YHWH can be presented as a universal event, even

---

cially by Martin Hengel (*Judaism* 1: 175–76) and F. Dexinger, *Zehnwochenapokalypse,* 45–57. For a critique, see G. W. E. Nickelsburg ("Social Aspects," 641–50) and E. Rau, *Kosmologie,* 23–27, 490–93. Rau writes: "It is necessary to affirm this point emphatically, namely, that there appear to have been a number of quite different groups that separated themselves, in a more or less thoroughly organized fashion, from the apostate people, in the consciousness of being the chosen remnant" (*Kosmologie,* 490). Hence the description of these groups as "Hasidim" is to be understood as an umbrella designation for circles that cannot be more precisely defined.

21. The LXX refers this promise to Zion: κληρονομήσει τὸ ὄρος τὸ ἅγιόν μου.

22. In 1 Enoch 25:5-6, then, the tree of life is actually growing in Jerusalem. See p. 54 below. Cf. also the paradise motif in the description of salvation in Joel 3:18-21!

23. Cf. C. Westermann, *Jesaja,* 324; idem, *THAT* 1: 528–29; A. Vögtle, *Zukunft des Kosmos,* 51–55. In distinction from Isa. 65:17, Westermann interprets Isa. 66:22 "apocalyptically": "Here for the first time is found the new thing that God creates, no longer in historical continuity to the present reality, but only as transcendent to it" (*THAT* 1: 528–29). However, I see the continuity with present reality also preserved in Isaiah 66, and surely there is nothing transcendent here. "The destruction of the world—to the extent that it has any place at all in Jewish eschatology—is a secondary and very late feature" (S. Mowinckel, *Psalmenstudien* 2: 247–48). As Augustine says: "*mutatione namque rerum, non omni modo interitu transibit hic mundus*" (For this world shall pass away by transmutation, not by absolute destruction: *De civ. Dei* 20, 14). For the motif of the "new creation" and the history of its reception, cf. N. Messel, *Einheitlichkeit,* 22–28; *Str-B* 3: 840–87; G. Dalman, *Worte,* 145–46; P. Volz, *Eschatologie,* 338–39; J. Bonsirven, *Judaïsme* 1: 511–16; M. Black, "New Creation"; U. Mell, *Neue Schöpfung.*

though the proclamation of judgment applies only to a particular nation,[24] eschatological salvation is here given a universal and cosmic horizon, even though Jerusalem alone is named as the place of salvation. The two events correspond and belong together.

In contrast to YHWH's "servants" are those "who forsake YHWH" (65:11). Their wickedness lies written before God (65:6), and God will not rest until they are repaid (LXX: ἀποδίδωμι) (65:7).[25] YHWH's parousia for the promised "slaughter" (65:7) is then described in 66:15-16:

> For YHWH will come in fire,
>   and his chariots like the whirlwind,
> to pay back his anger in fury,
>   and his rebuke in flames of fire.
> For by fire will YHWH execute judgment,
>   and by his sword, on all flesh;
>   and those slain by YHWH shall be many.

> ἰδοὺ γὰρ κύριος ὡς πῦρ ἥξει
>   καὶ ὡς καταιγὶς τὰ ἄρματα αὐτοῦ
> ἀποδοῦναι ἐν θυμῷ ἐκδίκησιν
>   καὶ ἀποσκορακισμὸν ἐν φλογὶ πυρός.
> ἐν γὰρ τῷ πυρὶ κυρίου κριθήσεται πᾶσα ἡ γῆ
>   καὶ ἐν τῇ ρομφαίᾳ αὐτοῦ πᾶσα σάρξ·
>   πολλοὶ τραυματίαι ἔσονται ὑπὸ κυρίου.[26]

The LXX thus translates consistently in the future tense. Just as in the tradition of the "day of YHWH," which in its motifs is closely related to this description, here also the sentence on the evildoers in Israel is described as YHWH's judgment on the whole world.[27]

The concluding section of the book (66:18-20) then offers a further purpose for YHWH's coming:[28] "I am coming to gather all nations and tongues; and they shall come and shall see my glory" (66:18). From among those who have "survived" the judgment YHWH will send missionaries to the nations to pro-

---

24. See p. 27 above.
25. Targum: "Their punishment will be in Gehenna, where the fire of all the days burns" (65:5). In the Targum for 65:6 this punishment is called a "second death."
26. C. Westermann (*Jesaja* 332) regards the readings of the LXX as original.
27. See pp. 26–28 of this chapter.
28. "The introductory 'but I am coming . . .' refers directly to the 'he is coming . . .' of the epiphany for world judgment in v. 15" (C. Westermann, *Jesaja*, 337).

claim YHWH's glory among them (66:19).[29] They will then bring the dispersed people back to Zion (66:20), to which "all flesh" will come to participate in the worship at the temple, "from new moon to new moon, and from sabbath to sabbath" (66:23).

Finally, the eternal adoration of the redeemed in the temple is contrasted with the eternal damnation of the rebels: "And they shall go out [i.e., to the Hinnom valley] and look at the dead bodies of the people who have rebelled against me; for their worm shall not die, their fire shall not be quenched, and they shall be an abhorrence[30] to all flesh" (66:24).[31] The places of blessedness and damnation are thus very near to one another. However, this gloomy conclusion of the prophetic book appeared so offensive at a later time that the Masoretes directed that v. 23 be read a second time after v. 24.[32]

In Isaiah 65–66 all the essential elements and motifs of apocalyptic eschatology are laid down, to the extent that it is a historical eschatology and not an eschatology of the hereafter: the division of the people into the wicked and the chosen, the end of the age brought about by a judgment of punishment on the wicked and their final elimination, the gathering of all the scattered faithful throughout the world at Zion, the coming of the pious Gentiles, the new sanctuary, the renewal of heaven and earth, the dwelling of God with God's people, and their living in perfect happiness. Apocalyptic took up these elements and motifs, frequently by means of quotations from and plays on Isaiah 65 and 66, and gave them further development.[33]

YHWH's Judgment in the Psalms

The Psalms give manifold expression to the belief in YHWH's judgment. This includes the idea of a court proceeding: YHWH ascends the throne as a righ-

---

29. "This is the first absolutely clear mention of mission in our sense of the word" (C. Westermann, *Jesaja*, 337).

30. The word דֵּרָאוֹן appears in the OT only here and in Dan. 12:2!

31. The image of the worm and the fire refers first of all only to "an unceasing process of torment and corruption" (F. Lang, *TDNT* 6: 937). The worm that does not die is "a sign of eternal perdition and its pains" (F. Lang, *TDNT* 7: 454). "Here for the first time, quite on the margin of the Old Testament . . . destruction as God's judgment is no longer a unique action, but an eternal condition: everlasting damnation. Here for the first time hell is thought of as a condition of eternal perdition" (C. Westermann, *Jesaja*, 340). In Jdt. 16:17 this image is applied to the punishment of Israel's enemies on the "day of judgment."

32. C. Westermann, *Jesaja*, 340.

33. Cf. P. D. Hanson, *Dawn*, 160.

teous judge and judges the wicked (7:9[10]), the nations (9:4-8[5-9]), and their gods (82:1). "He judges (שפט) the world with righteousness; he judges (דין) the peoples with equity" 9:8[9]. There is also a demand for this judgment: "Rise up, YHWH! Do not let mortals prevail; let the nations be judged before you" (9:19[20]).[34] These verses were certainly not intended in an eschatological sense to begin with. They appeal to YHWH who, as ruler of all nations, is also their judge, to repay the "proud" for their lawless actions and to restore order.[35] However, the overwhelmingly future tense translations in the LXX already indicate an eschatological interpretation.[36]

The case may be different with the three hymns to YHWH as king (Pss. 96, 97, 98) where it is said twice that YHWH "is coming to judge the earth" (96:13; 98:9). This epiphany of YHWH for judgment is described in detail in Ps. 97:2-6. Because these three psalms make use of many motifs and images from Deutero- and Trito-Isaiah, an eschatological interpretation has been suggested for them.[37] The description of YHWH's epiphany in Ps. 97:2-6 is followed by the judgment of the idols and idolaters, who are "put to shame" (97:7). This judgment makes possible the blessedness of the righteous, with a description of which the psalm closes:

> Zion hears and is glad, and the daughters of Judah rejoice,
>   because of your judgments, YHWH.
> For you, YHWH, are most high over all the earth;
>   you are exalted far above all gods.
> YHWH loves those who hate evil;
>   he guards the lives of his faithful;
>   he rescues them from the hand of the wicked.
> Light dawns for the righteous,
>   and joy for the upright in heart.
> Rejoice in YHWH, O you righteous,
>   and give thanks to his holy name! (Ps. 97:8-12)

34. Cf. Ps. 7:8[9]; 82:8; 94:2.

35. Cf. Ps. 94; J. Jeremias, *Königtum*, 128–30. In Ps. 9:8[9], however, Jeremias interprets the judgment eschatologically. In that verse he sees "the hope for a destroying, condemnatory judgment through which the nations (like earlier political powers), because of their unrighteous deeds, will sink into eternal oblivion" (p. 144).

36. LXX Ps. 7:8-9; 9:9; 57:11-12; 66:5; 93:14-15. On the other hand, cf. 57:12; 75:9-10.

37. H.-J. Kraus, *Psalmen* 2: 665–66, 671, 674–75, 677; H. D. Preuß, *TDOT* 2: 48–49. Mitchell Dahood also calls Psalm 97 "an eschatological hymn" (*Psalms* 2: 361). Cf. L. Jacquet, *Psaumes* 2: 805–8. He also interprets Ps. 97 eschatologically (pp. 817, 822), as does J. Jeremias, *Königtum*, 136–43.

The schema of a theophany, judgment on the wicked, and blessedness for the righteous, as we find it here in Psalm 97, recalls Isa. 66:15-24. It will recur frequently in future.[38] However, the plural "judgments" (v. 8) speaks against an originally eschatological significance for Psalm 97—or does מִשְׁפָּטִים here mean "ordinances, commandments" (cf. Ps. 48:11[12])?[39] In any case, the fact that this psalm was later interpreted eschatologically is indicated by an apocryphal psalm fragment (B) from the Qumran caves (4QPs^f), in which the tradition of the three hymns (Pss. 96–98) is taken up and developed:[40]

> [...] many [...] and they shall praise the name of YHWH,
> for he comes to judge every deed,
> to root out the wicked from the earth,
> [and the children] of unrighteousness will no longer be found there.
> Heaven will [drop down] dew,
> and there will be no more ruin in its borders.
> The land will [yield] its fruit in due season
> and its yield will not be fickle.
> The fruit-bearing trees . . . their vines,
> and its fountains will not deceive.
> The poor will eat
> and those who fear YHWH will be filled.

In contrast to Ps. 97:10-11, here the description of the eschatological bliss is not indicated by abstract concepts such as "light" and "joy," but is painted in concrete examples (cf. Zech. 8:12).

Psalm 50 (49) is unique. This is the only place in the psalms in which judgment is explicitly announced for Israel itself (v. 7). YHWH appears for this judgment, much as in Psalm 97, in an extensively described epiphany which the LXX consistently interprets as future: God will come (ἥξει) from Zion preceded by a consuming fire and surrounded by a tempest; heaven and earth will be called to witness; the heavens will proclaim God's righteousness "for God is the judge" (ὅτι ὁ θεὸς κριτής ἐστιν) (vv. 2-6). Then, in vv. 8-23, YHWH speaks, "testifying" against Israel and "convicting" them (vv. 7-8).[41]

38. L. Hartman, *Prophecy,* 55–60.
39. J. Jeremias, *Königtum,* 137, translates "executions of judgment" (Gerichtsvollzüge).
40. Text from J. Starcky, *Psaumes apocryphes,* 356–57. For the translation, cf. ibid., 366–68, and M. Delcor and P. García Martínez, *Introducción,* 279–80.
41. The verb ἐλέγχω (יכח) is often translated "rebuke." However, where possible I prefer to translate it as "convict," in order to make the juridical background quite clear. Cf. P. Volz, *Eschatologie,* 302.

YHWH is thus both accuser and judge.[42] YHWH's address is cast altogether along the lines of a prophetic judgment speech.[43] It treats two themes: sacrifices (vv. 7-15) and YHWH's ethical commands, especially as laid down in the Ten Commandments (vv. 16-22). The renewed address in v. 16 ("but to the wicked God says") is apparently of little significance. The real addressees are still those named in v. 7: Israel.[44]

The future tenses show that the Greek translator of the psalm already understood it as eschatological: ἐλέγξω σε (v. 8), ἐξελοῦμαί σε καὶ δοξάσεις με (v. 15), ἐλέγξω σε καὶ παραστήσω κατὰ πρόσωπόν σου (v. 21), θυσία αἰνέσεως δοξάσει με, καὶ ἐκεῖ ὁδός, ᾗ δείξω αὐτῷ τὸ σωτήριον τοῦ θεοῦ (v. 23).

The Targum interprets the psalm entirely from the perspective of rabbinic eschatology. Before the description of the theophany is the phrase: "The righteous will say on the day of the great judgment (ליום דינא רבא)." In v. 10 it inserts: "For the righteous I will prepare clean animals in the Garden of Eden. . . ." And v. 21c is paraphrased: "But I will take revenge on you with burning anger; I will convict you in this age and prepare the judgment of Gehenna for you in the age to come." We also find an interpretation in terms of the "day of rebuke" in a saying that is traced to the Tannaite Abba Cohen ben Delaja.[45]

Psalm 1 also has a particular significance with regard to the idea of judgment. Here, as in Psalm 97, we find the contrast, so typical of early Jewish judgment texts, between the "righteous" (צַדִּיקִים, δίκαιοι) and the "wicked" (רְשָׁעִים, ἀσεβεῖς) or "sinners" (חַטָּאִים, ἁμαρτωλοί). The righteous are like fruitful trees planted by the water, while the wicked are like chaff that the wind drives away.[46] The psalm culminates in the statement of v. 5:

---

42. This is typical of the fundamental form of רִיב. Cf. J. Harvey, *Plaidoyer*, 23–24, 55.

43. H.-J. Kraus, *Psalmen* 1: 372, 379. E. Beaucamp, "La Théophanie du Psaume 50," interprets the theophany in this psalm as occurring on behalf of Israel. Against this are the parallels in Micah 1:2-4, to which Kraus (*Psalmen* 1: 375) refers. Cf. also L. Jacquet, *Psaumes* 2: 128.

44. According to H.-J. Kraus, *Psalmen* 1: 379–81, who also considers the address in v. 16 as secondary, vv. 7-15 are addressed to Israel as a nation, while those in vv. 16-22 have as their object "the behavior of individual persons" (p. 381). However, this distinction appears very artificial. L. Jacquet also says that the introductory address in v. 16 is a gloss (*Psaumes* 2: 131).

45. *Gen. Rab.* 45:3, quoted below, p. 135.

46. The LXX has "dust" instead of "chaff" (1:4).

> Therefore the wicked will not stand in the judgment,
> nor sinners in the congregation of the righteous.

What kind of judgment is intended here, and why can the wicked not "stand" before it? Or does קוּם ב mean "enter," as in Ps. 24:3?[47] In that case, the wicked would not come to judgment at all, "because their life, like the chaff before the wind, has been blown away beforehand"[48] and they have thereby been judged already. According to *m. Sanh.* 10.3, Rabbi Nehemiah understood the verse in this sense, because he concluded from it that neither the generation of the flood nor the inhabitants of Sodom would stand before the judgment. However, Rabbi Jehoshua, according to *'Abot. R. Nat.* A 36.1, used the same verse to prove that they would stand before the judgment, and thus must have understood קוּם as "stand," or "endure," in the sense of the translation still common today. In the background is probably the custom of ancient Hebrew court procedure, in which the auditors are seated and the speaker rises.[49] Thus if the wicked "do not stand" for judgment, this means that their guilt is so evident that any defense is superfluous.

H.-J. Kraus reads this psalm eschatologically,[50] which is certainly plausible if it is dated in the third or even the first century B.C.E.[51] In any case, the Greek translator was surely thinking of the last judgment when he rendered v. 5a with διὰ τοῦτο οὐκ ἀναστήσονται ἀσεβεῖς ἐν κρίσει. This οὐκ ἀναστήσονται—the Vulgate has *non resurgent*—would have caused Greek-speaking readers to think of the final resurrection for judgment; according to the idea most commonly held in early Judaism, only the righteous would take part in it.[52]

47. Thus H.-J. Kraus, *Psalmen,* 1: 7–8. He criticizes the usual translation with "stand" as "careless" (p. 7). L. Köhler suggests that the accused remains kneeling or lying on the ground while his or her guilt is dealt with (*Mensch,* 149). But according to Zech. 3:1 the accused stands. E. Haag interprets קוּם ב as "appear against someone (before a court, as a witness for the prosecution)" ("Psalm 1," 167-68). But that would yield the absurd statement: "Therefore the wicked will not stand (before the judgment seat) against the judgment."

48. H.-J. Kraus, *Psalmen* 1. Cf. J. A. Soggin, "Zum ersten Psalm," 94; M. Dahood, *Psalms* 1: 4.

49. P. Bovati, *Giustizia,* 217–19.

50. H.-J. Kraus, *Psalmen* 1: 7–8; so also L. Jacquet, *Psaumes* 1: 216; differently J. A. Soggin, who sees the Vulgate and the Targum as supplying an eschatologizing interpretation ("Zum ersten Psalm," 87–88, 94).

51. On the question of dating, see H.-J. Kraus, *Psalmen* 1: 3.

52. See 2 Macc. 7:14! Cf. W. Bousset and H. Gressmann, *Religion,* 272; P. Volz, *Eschatologie,* 247; E. Schürer, *Geschichte* 2: 643; E. Schürer and G. Vermes, *History* 2: 543; Marie-Thérès Wacker, *Weltordnung,* 269; R. Martin-Achard, *DBSup* 10: 484.

The עֲדַת צַדִּיקִים is then the end time community of the righteous, from which sinners are excluded.[53] The Targum interprets the psalm in the same way, translating literally but paraphrasing בַּמִּשְׁפָּט in v. 5 with ביום דינא רבא, "on the day of the great judgment." In Qumran the contrast between "righteous" and "wicked" in this psalm was interpreted in terms of the contrast between their own community and the rest of Israel (4QFlor 1, 14–17).

Finally, Psalm 37 (36) deserves our notice with regard to the later preaching of judgment. It reveals a number of parallels to Psalm 1, and it was undoubtedly interpreted eschatologically by the LXX. This is clear not only from the many future, and especially future passive forms,[54] which were especially frequent later in eschatological contexts,[55] but also from the motif of "inheriting" the land (vv. 9, 11, 29, 34), which we also find in an eschatological sense in Trito-Isaiah (57:13; 60:21; 65:9).[56]

In this psalm the righteous[57] and the wicked[58] are enemies. The wicked are also called "enemies of YHWH" (אֹיְבֵי יְהוָה, οἱ ἐχθροὶ τοῦ κυρίου) in v. 20, as in Isaiah 65–66, and the LXX uses the word ἀσεβεῖς twice (vv. 28, 38). The righteous are also called "poor" (עֲנָוִים, עֶבְיוֹן, πραεῖς, πτωχὸς καὶ πένης) in vv. 11 and 14, and "faithful" or "pious" (חֲסִידִים, ὅσιοι) in v. 28. They apparently constitute a community separate from the rest of the people, called in Ps. 149:1 the "assembly of the faithful" (קְהַל חֲסִידִים, ἐκκλησία ὁσίων) and probably identical with the עֲדַת צַדִּיקִים in Ps. 1:5.[59] Their opponents are rich (v. 16) and powerful (v. 35), and they seek to kill the righteous (v. 14). Sinners are described in similar terms later, in the book of Enoch.[60] As punishment, they will be "cut off" (כרת, ἐξολεθρευθήσονται): vv. 9, 22, [34], 38; they will perish (יֹאבֵדוּ, ἀπολοῦνται): v. 20. Later readers would necessarily think of the eternal ἀπώλεια in Gehenna, and the Targum makes explicit mention of it at this point.[61]

53. H.-J. Kraus, *Psalmen* 1: 8. It is surprising that the LXX does not translate עֵדָה with συναγωγή, but with βουλή.
54. In vv. 2, 3, 9, 17, 19(2x), 22, 28(3x), 31, 38(2x).
55. See below, pp. 44–45, 60.
56. For early Judaism see W. Foerster, *TDNT* 3: 779–81; Matt. 5:5.
57. Verses 17, 29, 39; in the singular, vv. 12, 16, 21, 25, 30.
58. Verses 14, 16, 17, 20, 34, 40; in the singular, vv. 10, 12, 21, 32.
59. On this, see J. Morgenstern, "HASÎDIM." According to him, this term went through the same process of development as that of the "chosen" (see above, chap. 1. 2). Cf. also Martin Hengel, *Judentum*, 322–23; F. Dexinger, *Zehnwochenapokalypse*, 20–21.
60. See pp. 62–65.
61. In '*Abot. R. Nat.* 21. 5, Rabbi Meir is quoted as explaining the punishment of sinners in Ps. 37:9 by a reference to Mal. 3:19.

The righteous, in contrast, will "inherit the land" (יִירְשׁוּ אָרֶץ, κληρονομή-σουσιν γῆν): vv. 9, 11, 22, 29, as an eternal heritage (v. 18). They will enjoy abundance of peace (שָׁלוֹם, εἰρήνη): v. 11, and salvation (תְּשׁוּעָה, σωτηρία): v. 39. These concepts later became fixed topoi for the description of the eschatological happiness of the righteousness. Finally, the "day [that] is coming" in v. 13, the וּבֹא יוֹמוֹ, ἥξει ἡ ἡμέρα αὐτοῦ[62]—as well as the "evil times" (עֵת רָעָה, καιρὸς πονηρός), v. 19 and the "time of trouble" (עֵת צָרָה, καιρὸς θλίψεως), v. 39, can easily be interpreted as the day of YHWH, the day of judgment. The well-known *pesher* from Qumran (4QpPs 37) gives this psalm an eschatological interpretation for the writer's own time.

Judgment in the Book of Daniel

The book of Daniel was written ca. 165–164 B.C.E.[63] In the famous vision in chapter 7, the visionary sees four beasts arising out of the sea, symbolizing four world empires. The vision culminates in the appearance of a being that, unlike the previous four, comes from heaven and resembles a human being. To this being everlasting dominion is given, but the precondition for it is the judgment on the "beasts" described in vv. 9-10:[64]

> As I watched,
> thrones were set in place,
>   and an Ancient One took his throne,
> his clothing was white as snow,
>   and the hair of his head like pure wool;
> his throne was fiery flames,
>   and its wheels were burning fire.
> A stream of fire issued
>   and flowed out from his presence.
> A thousand thousands served him,
>   and ten thousand times ten thousand stood attending him.
> The court sat in judgment,
>   and the books were opened.

62. The personal pronoun can refer to God or to the sinners.
63. O. Eissfeldt, *Einleitung*, 705–7; M. Delcor, *Daniel*, 15; H. Gese, "Bedeutung," 374.
64. Cf. 1 Kgs. 22:19-22; Ezekiel 1.

This depiction of the heavenly court is dependent, from the point of the history of traditions, on the throne scene in 1 Enoch 14:15-23.[65] God presides over this college of judges, and apparently the angels are thought of as the associate members. The books of judgment, unlike the "book of remembrance" in Mal. 3:16, apparently contain not the names of the saved, but the list of the sins of the accused. The latter, however, are not even mentioned, much less heard: they are, so to speak, condemned *in contumaciam*. There is no proclamation of judgment or even any kind of description of a proceeding, so that the scene gives the impression of being fragmentary. It ends as suddenly as it began, and the imposition of sentence follows immediately.[66] The fourth beast is put to death, "and its body destroyed and given over to be burned with fire," while the other beasts' dominion is taken away and a limit placed on their lifetimes (7:11-12).

After this, Daniel sees "one like a human being" coming with the clouds of heaven; this figure is led before the Ancient One and receives everlasting dominion (7:13-14). In the first part of the book, that dominion belongs to God alone (2:44; 4:3 [Aram. 3:33]; 4:34 [Aram. 4:31]; 6:26 [Aram. 6:27]).

At his request, the seer's vision is interpreted for him by an angel, "one of the attendants" (7:16): The court has assembled to take away the dominion of the last of the violent rulers (7:26). Then the everlasting dominion will be given to the "holy ones of the Most High" (7:18, 22, 25) or "the people of the holy ones of the Most High" (7:27).[67] This is a reference to the eschatological people of God, the Israel of the end time, "that is, the faithful 'remnant' of the people."[68] The author was probably thinking primarily, in concrete terms, of

65. P. Grelot, "Histoire," 97; T. F. Glasson, "Son of man Imagery," 89; H. S. Kvanvig, "Henoch," 115; see idem, 127–30, against the idea that Daniel 7 and 1 Enoch 14 are both dependent on a third source. Matthew Black ("1 Enoch," 151–52) inclines to that opinion.

66. The literary-critical problem in these verses need not be discussed here, since we are interpreting the definitive text. Cf., most recently, U. B. Müller, *Messias,* 19–30; J. J. Collins, *Vision,* 127–32; H. Gese, "Bedeutung," 375–78; H. S. Kvanvig, "Struktur."

67. Theodotion has "the holy ones of the Most High" also in v. 17. On this, see C. C. Caragounis, *Son of man,* 65–66; see idem, 61–81, for the question of the relationship of the one like a human being in 7:13 to the "holy ones of the Most High" in the interpretation. Although Caragounis rejects the usual identification, he also sees the "Son of man" as "the leader or representative of the saints in their humiliation and suffering" (p. 76).

68. H.-W. Kuhn, *Enderwartung,* 92, with further examples of this use of the term "the holy ones."

the group to which he himself belonged: the Hasidim. These, or rather their spiritual leaders, he calls "the wise" (מַשְׂכִּילִים) in 11:33, 35; 12:3, 10.[69] They expect that, after judging their oppressors, God will establish an eternal reign and confer on them dominion over the earth.[70]

The accumulation of passives in the description of the vision in 7:2-14 is striking: there are 13 in all. Thrones "were set in place" (רְמִיו) in 7:9; books "were opened" (פְּתִיחוּ) in 7:10; the beast "was put to death" (קְטִילַת) in 7:11. Apparently in most cases the author thinks of heavenly beings, either God or the angels, as the active subjects.[71] Consequently, one may reasonably speak of divine passives here. Three times (7:5, 12, 13) the third person plural is used in place of a passive; in 7:12 both expressions occur together: "As for the rest of the beasts, *they took away* their dominion, but their lives *were prolonged* for a season and a time." Passives like these occur otherwise as eschatological passives primarily in the future tense. In Daniel 7:2-14 that future is anticipated in vision; consequently, the passives are in the perfect tense.[72]

G. W. E. Nickelsburg sees Dan. 12:1-3 also as the depiction of a forensic judgment scene.[73] Those verses climax the overview of history that begins in 11:2 with the last Persian kings and ends in 11:45 with the death of Antiochus IV. Since his death is not related in accord with historical events, we may suppose that Antiochus was still alive when this section was written. However, the

---

69. M. Hengel, *Judaism* 1: 180. For the origins of chs. 7–12 among the Hasidim, see M. Delcor, *Daniel,* 15–19. Nevertheless, Delcor rejects an identification of the "holy ones of the Most High" with the Hasidim and points to 7:21, 22, 25, which speak of the whole people (pp. 156–57). Some exegetes interpret the "holy ones of the Most High" as angels, but they often include the people faithful to YHWH among them: thus, for example, J. J. Collins, *Vision,* 144, 146; idem, *Apocalyptic Imagination,* 83–84. Collins interprets the "one like a human being" as the angel Michael (ibid., 84–85). On the contrary, Martin Hengel writes: "Therefore the eternal kingdom in Daniel is to be understood as the rule of the people of God—perhaps in conjunction with the angels" (*Judaism* 2: 122 n. 501). On this problem, cf. also U. B. Müller, *Messias,* 25–26 (the reference is to "the faithful in Israel," "the eschatological Israel"); A. Deissler, "'Menschensohn'"; K. Koch, *Daniel,* 234–39; J. J. Collins, "Apocalyptic Eschatology," 32; O. Camponovo, *Königtum,* 124–25 n. 241. Their common origin among the Hasidim led J. C. Trever to the suggestion that the final redactor of the book of Daniel and the Teacher of Righteousness in Qumran were one and the same person ("Qumran Teacher").

70. P. Grelot, "Histoire," esp. 94–100 offers some appealing remarks on the topic of judgment and salvation in the book of Daniel.

71. *Tanh. B Lev* VII § 1 speaks explicitly of angels (see below, p. 137).

72. For more detail on these passives and the so-called "*passivum divinum,*" see the corresponding excursus in chap. 8.

73. G. W. E. Nickelsburg, *Resurrection,* 11–27.

author believed that his death would introduce the end time. The genuinely eschatological events thus follow in 12:1-3. Nevertheless, we cannot really speak of a description of a "forensic judgment scene" in these verses. Neither the "arising" of the angel prince Michael nor the book in verse 1 indicates a forensic situation: Michael does not "arise" as a defense counselor before a court, but for the judgment of Israel's enemies, a tradition we find also in Dan. 8:11 LXX; *As. Mos* 10.2, and 1QM 17,6–7 (cf. 1QS 3, 20, 24). The "book" does not contain the register of the sins of Israel's enemies, like the books of judgment in 7:10, but explicitly the names of those who will be saved "at that time." Therefore it cannot be regarded as indicating a forensic judgment. In 12:2 ("Many of those who sleep in the dust of the earth shall awake, some to everlasting life, and some to shame and everlasting contempt"),[74] according to Nickelsburg the resurrection is "the means by which these persons are brought to judgment and, after that, to the fate meted out to them."[75] But the text does not by any means say that the resurrection leads first of all to judgment; instead, it immediately brings "everlasting life" or "everlasting contempt." Who will belong to the one or the other group appears to be determined from the outset, so that the division does not have to be made through any judicial process. In early Jewish literature until the first century C.E. this is never the work of the judgment, not even when, in contrast to Dan. 12:1-3, it is explicitly depicted as a court proceeding. Therefore in Dan. 12:2 the idea of an eschatological judgment is only "implicitly present."[76]

The reticence with which Dan. 12:1-3 speaks of eschatological salvation and damnation is noteworthy. The lot of the damned is "shame" and "everlasting contempt,"[77] while the lot of those "who [are] found written in the book" is "everlasting life" (12:2); the "wise" will "shine like the brightness of the firmament . . . , like the stars forever and ever" (12:3). Thus there is an absence of any fantastic elaboration, just as in chapter 7, where the exercise of the eschatological judgment, the final destruction of Israel's enemies (7:26), is indicated by the image of burning with fire (7:11), and it is said of God's eschatological reign only that it is universal and everlasting (7:14, 27; cf. 2:44).[78]

74. For the problem of resurrection in this passage, see K. Koch, *Daniel*, 239–43; K. Schubert, "Auferstehungslehre," 189; Marie-Theres Wacker, *Weltordnung*, 267–69 (and at p. 279 n. 55 on Nickelsburg's thesis); R. Martin-Achard, *DBSup* 10: 452–58.

75. G. W. E. Nickelsburg, *Resurrection*, 23.

76. Thus, rightly, K. Schubert, "Auferstehungslehre," 189 n. 50.

77. This is a play on Isa. 66:24 (see p. 32 above).

78. Cf. P. Grelot, "Histoire," 95–96, 100–4, with reference also to Dan. 9:24.

This vague and abstract conceptual language should not, however, deceive us into speaking of a "transcendent world" in Daniel.[79] More appropriate is a comparison with contemporary concepts in the book of Enoch, especially the book of dream visions (1 Enoch 83–90).[80] After the judgment of Israel's enemies, the world's history continues, although it is different in quality. What the author of the book of Daniel expects is a kind of *metahistory,* "a state of things in which the traits that mark the fate of sinful humanity have been effaced."[81] The "hereafter" that is expected in the visions of the book of Daniel is not an "otherworldly, spiritual, and timeless 'hereafter' as alternative to the present, earthly, and material 'here,'" but rather "the victorious alteration in the sphere of earthly conditions, coming from and ultimately with God."[82]

79. G. von Rad, *Theologie* 2: 334, as only one example among many others. Cf. C. Barth, *Diesseits,* 87–88.

80. P. Grelot, "Histoire," 96–100.

81. Ibid., 95, with reference to Dan. 2:44; 7:22b, 27; 9:24; 12:1-3, 13.

82. C. Barth, *Diesseits,* 100.

CHAPTER THREE

Judgment in Other Early Jewish Literature

The Book of Wisdom

The strongly Hellenistic book of Wisdom was composed, probably in Egypt, in the first century B.C.E.[1] Particularly in chapters 1–5, just as in Psalms 1 and 37, the righteous (δίκαιοι), twice designated ἐκλεκτοί as well,[2] are contrasted with the impious (ἀσεβεῖς) or sinners (ἁμαρτωλοί).[3] The righteous have a great deal to suffer during their lifetime, not least from the ridicule of the godless, but as a result their souls (ψυχαί) after death are preserved from "torment" (βάσανος) in Sheol;[4] instead, they are then "in the hand of God" (3:1),[5] "at peace" (3:3),[6] "at rest," (4:7).[7] The godless, on the other hand, "who disre-

---

1. O. Eissfeldt, *Einleitung,* 815; C. Larcher, *Sagesse* 1: 114–18, 138–39, 141–61. For chs. 1–5, Larcher proposes an origin ca. 31–30 B.C.E. (p. 159). As historical background, he posits the events in Palestine after Herod's seizure of power. M. Gilbert, *DBSup.* 10: 93, argues that the whole book was written during the reign of Augustus.
2. Wis. 3:9; 4:15, each time with the variant ὅσιοι.
3. Cf. J. Vílchez, "El binomio justicia—injusticia en el libro de la Sabiduría," esp. 8–10. For the use of Psalm 37 by the author of Wisdom, see H. Hübner, "Ethik," 181–86.
4. It is true that C. Larcher (*Sagesse* 1: 274) attempts, in light of 2:19, to refer βάσανος to earthly testing. But in a context where the dead are concerned that would produce only a banality. Cf. 1 Enoch 25:6, a passage that Larcher himself refers to 3:3 (ibid., 278); *T. Ash.* 6:5; *T. Abr.* B 8.11.
5. Cf. Deut. 33:3: "all his holy ones were in your charge." This receives an eschatological interpretation in 4 Macc. 17:19. According to an interpretation in *Sipre Devarim* 344 (Bietenhard, 839) this sentence refers to the souls of the righteous "that have been laid in his treasury." A reference to 1 Sam. 25:29 follows. Cf. also M. Delcor, "L'immortalité," 616–18; C. Larcher, *Sagesse* 1: 274.
6. Cf. Isa. 57:1-2; 1 Enoch 105:2. For the eschatological significance of this peace, see C. Larcher, *Sagesse* 1: 277–78. The wish that ἐν εἰρήνη ἡ κοίμησις αὐτοῦ is frequently found on Jewish epitaphs and is undoubtedly eschatological in intention: U. Fischer, *Eschatologie,* 217–19; A. Schmitt, *Weisheit,* 57.
7. Cf. 1 Enoch 99:14; *Jos. Asen.* 8.9(11); 15.7; 22.13(9); *Bib. Ant.* 28.10; *Paralip. Jer.* 5.32. A Schmitt, *Weisheit,* 66; idem, "Tod," 340–41.

garded the righteous and rebelled against the Lord," will not escape their punishment (3:10). God will hurl them headlong into the abode of the dead, where
eternal agony (ὀδύνη) awaits them; they will be the objects of eternal scorn
among the dead forever, and their memory will perish (4:19).[8]

This author therefore expects an individual reckoning immediately after
death, but, to all appearances, this reckoning is only preliminary. The ultimate
fate of the dead will only be decided "on the day of judgment" (ἐν ἡμέρᾳ
διαγνώσεως) (3:18); that day is characterized as the "time of . . . visitation"
(καιρὸς ἐπισκοπῆς) for the righteous (3:7; cf. 3:13), because on that day the
righteous and the wicked will again stand "face to face" (κατὰ πρόσωπον) with
one another (5:1) to receive their sentence (4:20—5:14).[9] The judicial inquiry
that, according to 6:3, God will conduct in person, will cover every word, and
even the most secret thoughts (1:9-10; 6:3). A register of sins (συλλογισμὸς
ἁμαρτημάτων) has been prepared (4:20); witnesses are mentioned (4:6), as
well as a defense (6:10). Typically forensic terminology is applied to this event:
ἐξέτασις / ἐξετασμός (1:9; 4:6) ἐξετάζειν (6:3), ἔρευνα (6:8), ἔλεγχος (1:9),
ἐλέγχειν (1:8; 4:20) μάρτυρες (4:6), ἀπολογία (6:10), διάγνωσις (3:18),
κρίσις (5:18; 6:5; 12:26).[10] "Nevertheless, it is a very special judgment, with no
explicit mention of a judge, no real confrontation between the parties, no verdict, and the case even appears already to have been judged, inasmuch as the
just are saved (v. 2b) and admitted into the heavenly society (v. 5)."[11] Thus we
have the same result as in Dan. 7:9-10.

The author repeatedly speaks of the judgment with the aid of eschatological
passives such as εὐεργετηθήσονται (3:5) or ἀφανισθήσεται (3:16).[12] After the
judgment the righteous will receive their reward (μισθός) "in the Lord," they

8. On this, see C. Larcher, *Sagesse* 2: 346–51. Cf. also P. Volz, *Eschatologie*, 266. For
the altered concept of Sheol presupposed here, in contrast to the old Hebrew idea of it,
see C. Larcher, *Études*, 309–10; D. S. Russell, *Apocalyptic*, 353–66. P. Grelot proposes,
on the basis of the parallels to the letter of Enoch (1 Enoch 91–105), that the souls of
the righteous also enter Sheol after death and, in a kind of holy sleep, await the day of
judgment for which they will then arise ("L'eschatologie de la sagesse," 173–74). But
that is improbable. The author of Wisdom, however, seems deliberately to choose vague
formulations (C. Larcher, *Études*, 310–15; R. A. Pfeiffer, *History*, 336).

9. This could imply a resurrection: R. A. Pfeiffer, *History*, 338–39; R. Schütz, *Idées*,
187–95; P. Grelot, "L'eschatologie de la sagesse," 174–75; R. J. Taylor, "Meaning,"
135–36; C. Larcher, *Études*, 321–27. Cf. also idem, *Sagesse* 1: 285–86; to the contrary
H. C. Cavallin, "Leben," 287.

10. Cf. G. Ziener, *Begriffssprache*, 104–5; C. Larcher, *Études*, 316.

11. C. Larcher, *Sagesse* 2: 351, on the judgment scene proper in 4:20—5:14.

12. Cf. 3:14, 17; 4:4(2x), 5, 19; 6:20, 25. Of course, not all future passives refer to
the final judgment; cf., for example, 2:4; 8:11.

will live forever and will receive from the hand of the Lord "a glorious crown and a beautiful diadem" (τὸ βασίλειον τῆς εὐπρεπείας καὶ τὸ διάδημα τοῦ κάλλους) (5:15-16);[13] they will be welcomed into the company of the angels (5:5).[14] On the other hand, the hope of the wicked is quenched forever, like the memory of a guest who stays but one day (5:14).

Nevertheless, it remains unclear to what extent this reward and punishment represent a change in the situation of the dead *before* the day of judgment.[15] But that poses the fundamental question why there is any need for a last judgment, if sinners and righteous, whose division is already fixed, enter into eternal bliss or eternal damnation immediately after death. The last judgment, after that, can only consist of a subsequent justification or confirmation of the fate assigned to them. R. A. Pfeiffer proposes that this difficulty arose out of the combination of two irreconcilable eschatological concepts in the course of the history of the tradition: the Jewish idea of a single day of judgment and the Greek notion of the assignment of reward and punishment to souls immediately after death.[16] We will return to this problem because it is not confined to the book of Wisdom.[17]

G. W. E. Nickelsburg's interpretation (*Resurrection*, 88–89), in agreement with Dieter Georgi ("Hymnus," 272–75), is unfounded. According to him, the death of the righteous in Wisdom is thought of as a "rapture" or assumption, and the "day of judgment" is seen as an individual judgment immediately after death. This interpretation does not do justice to the material. It is not possible to read out of 3:2 that the death of the righteous is only apparent (cf. 4:7!), nor to find in 4:10-11 a rapture of the righteous instead of their death, even though there is some play on assumption terminology in those verses (cf C. Larcher, *Sagesse* 2: 330–32): ἁρπάζω is not only a term for assumption, but is also "frequently used in the sense of 'taking away' by death, as many burial inscriptions attest. Unquestionably, this verb in 4:11 is not a term for assumption; it refers to the death

13. For the translation of βασίλειον, cf. O. Camponovo, *Königtum*, 369; A. Schmitt, *Weisheit*, 73; C. Larcher, *Sagesse* 2: 384. Larcher, however, decides in favor of "royalty" ("royauté"). For the crowns of the righteous in the world to come, cf. *b. Ber.* 17a (Str-B 4: 1132–33); D. E. Aune, *Realized Eschatology*, 187.

14. This is a striking parallel to Qumran. Cf. C. Larcher, *Études*, 122, 320–21; A. Schmitt, *Weisheit*, 72.

15. R. Schütz, who deals with this question, can only speak of an increased reward of the righteous and a heightened punishment of the sinners after the day of judgment (*Idées*, 76–95, 102, 168–69); likewise M. Delcor, "L'immortalité," 620: "a new blaze of glory." Cf. also C. Larcher, *Sagesse* 2: 380.

16. R. A. Pfeiffer, *History*, 339–40.

17. Cf. the summary below (chap. 4).

of the righteous" (A. Schmitt, *Entrückung,* 188; cf. idem, "Tod," 334–39). The interpretation of 3:13, 18; 4:6 in terms of a judgment immediately after death contradicts the judgment scene in 4:20—5:14, in which it is not the individual who is judged, but sinners and righteous are assembled in groups. The idea of an individual judgment after death would be unique in the Judaism of the first century B.C.E., even under Hellenistic influence. It appears in Judaism only near the end of the first century C.E.

In light of this eschatology of the hereafter, the depiction of the final judgment as a court of punishment and destruction on earth, as it appears in 5:17-23 with an asyndetic connection immediately after the description of the everlasting reward of the righteous, seems like a foreign body.[18] Very much as in the tradition of the day of YHWH and related texts like Isa. 26:21; 59:17-20; 66:5-16, God enters the fray in person. God raises the elements against the "frenzied foes" until the whole world is laid waste; this sets a period to the history of evil. Is it the absolute end of history? The text does not tell us.

What can have caused the author to conclude the eschatological portion of his book with such an apparently inappropriate description of YHWH's wrathful judgment?[19] C. Larcher attempts an answer to this question: "Earlier, his insistence on individual destiny and transcendent punishments seemed to make a final intervention of God on earth unnecessary. However, he is determined to integrate the final ends of the individual and of humanity in a kind of synthesis."[20]

However, there is a second point to be made. The author of this book is not the first to have presented historical eschatology and eschatology of the hereafter side by side without creating a genuine system of ideas to connect the two. The same side-by-side presentation is found in the letter of Enoch (1 Enoch 91–104), a writing that demonstrates so many similarities and parallels to the book of Wisdom that it would be easy to suppose that the author of Wisdom knew the letter of Enoch, perhaps already in its Greek form.[21] This example

---

18. Cf. R. A. Pfeiffer, *History,* 338; C. Larcher, *Sagesse* 2: 397–98. The fact that it really is the final judgment is apparent from the location of the section and the consistent use of the future tense.

19. Cf. the key words κρίσις (5:18) and ὀργή (5:20).

20. C. Larcher, *Sagesse* 2: 398. It is difficult to say whether 5:16c-d was written with a view to what would follow, and whether the shielding of the righteous by the arm of God is the same as their protection in face of the wrathful judgment on earth, so that a bridge is created to what follows (idem, 385–86, 398).

21. On this, see C. Larcher, *Études,* 103–12.

shows how strong the lines of literary communication must have been between the diaspora and the Palestinian homeland.[22]

The Psalms of Solomon

The Psalms of Solomon, with its obvious reference to Pompey, originated, like the book of Wisdom, in the first century B.C.E.[23] But while the book of Wisdom is strongly marked by Hellenism and was originally written in Greek,[24] the Psalms of Solomon has undoubtedly been translated from Hebrew and is usually regarded as "the expression of a Pharisaic mentality and point of view."[25]

Like Psalms 1 and 37 and Wisdom 1–5, the Psalms of Solomon is concerned primarily with the righteous[26] and sinners, and their fate on the day of judgment. For the sinners, that day, "when God oversees the earth at his judgment" (ὅταν ἐπισκέπτηται ὁ θεὸς τὴν γῆν ἐν κρίματι αὐτοῦ) is a "day of the Lord's judgment" (ἡμέρα κρίσεως κυρίου) (15:12), when God will requite them according to their deeds (2:34; 17:8. Cf. 2:7, 16).[27] Then they will receive their "inheritance" (κληρονομία): "Hades and darkness and destruction" (ἄδης καὶ σκότος καὶ ἀπώλεια) (14:9; cf. 15:10). Sheol, as in the book of Wisdom, has

---

22. Cf. also C. Larcher, *Études*, 112–29, "Sagesse et les écrits de Qumran." On the intellectual contacts between Alexandria and Palestine, as demonstrated in scriptural interpretation, see G. Delling, "Begegnung," 34–36.

23. O. Eissfeldt, *Einleitung*, 829–30; A.-M. Denis, *Introduction*, 64; J. Schüpphaus, *Psalmen Salomos*, 105–6, 115–16, 155–58 (between 63 and 42 B.C.E.); M. Delcor, *DBSup.* 9: 232–36 (between 69 and 47 B.C.E.).

24. C. Larcher, *Sagesse* 1: 91–95.

25. J. Wellhausen, *Die Pharisäer*, 113. J. Klausner calls the *Ps. Sol.* "this marvelous Pharisaic book" (*Messianic Idea*, 317). Despite some reservations, this judgment is still valid: J. Schüpphaus, *Psalmen Salomos*, 5–11; G. Maier, *Mensch*, 282–301; M. Delcor, *DBSup.* 9: 236–42; E. Schürer and G. Vermes, *History* 3/1: 194–95.

26. The righteous are also called ὅσιοι (2:36; 4:6, 8; 8:23, and frequently) and πτωχοί (10:6; 15:1). They are the φοβούμενοι τὸν κύριον (2:33; 3:12; 4:23; 5:18; 15:13), the πορευόμενοι ἐν δικαιοσύνη προσταγμάτων αὐτοῦ, ἐν νόμῳ, ᾧ ἐνετείλατο ἡμῖν εἰς ζωὴν ἡμῶν (14:2); they constitute a συνέδριον ὁσίων (4:1) and συναγωγαὶ ὁσίων (17:16). This description fits the Pharisees well. Cf. also M. Delcor, *DBSup.* 9: 230–32; to the contrary E. P. Sanders, *Paul*, 398–409.

27. J. Becker believes that nothing is said in the *Ps. Sol.* about God's punishing sinners in response to their sins. "God does not destroy the wicked on the day of judgment, but rather they perish of themselves because their evil deeds pursue them" (*Heil*, 28). He thinks that God is concerned only with the preservation of the relationship of cause and effect (p. 31). The passages cited speak against this idea, as does 15:4-5. It is true that the *Ps. Sol.*, in order to avoid anthropomorphisms, do not represent God as personally engaged in battle.

been transformed into Hades. In 15:4-5 the text speaks of "the flame of fire" (φλὸξ πυρός) and ὀργὴ ἀδίκων, the wrath that goes forth from the face of the Lord to destroy the sinners' whole existence. Their memory will be extinguished forever (3:11; 13:11).

For the righteous, on the other hand, both the living and the dead, that day is a "day of mercy" (ἡμέρα ἐλέους) (14:9).[28] They alone will find mercy (ἐλεηθήσονται) on that day, and will rise to everlasting life (ἀναστήσονται εἰς ζωὴν αἰώνιον),[29] a life "in the Lord's light" (ἐν φωτὶ κυρίου) (3:12). These psalms avoid any concrete description of that life; however, we should avoid inserting our Christian ideas about eternal life into them. The author of the Psalms of Solomon probably thinks of this eschatological life in the future time of salvation as something earthly, but without the evils that are now associated with it.[30] The contrast between ζωή (ζωὴ αἰώνιος) for the righteous and ἀπώλεια (ἀπώλεια εἰς τὸν αἰῶνα) for the sinners is a fixed topos in these psalms.[31] The division between the two groups on the day of judgment is made on the basis of a sign that sinners and righteous bear on their foreheads (15:6, 9; cf. Ezek. 9:4). Thus the judgment is understood here purely as a judgment for punishment and applies only to sinners. The "visitation of the righteous" (cf. 3:11; 11:1, 6) consists in a demonstration of God's merciful kindness.[32]

It is true that God also judges "Israel," but this is accomplished "in discipline" (ἐν παιδείᾳ) (8:26; cf. 8:29; 13:7-10). That, of course, is no more eschatological in intent than is the talk about God "who judges the whole earth in his righteousness" (8:24; cf. 2:32; 4:24; 9:2), and about God's "judgments" (2:15; 5:1; 8:24, 32, 34, and frequently). Typical of these noneschatological sayings about judgment is the forensic language found also, for example, in 2:18; 4:24.

28. For the concept of "mercy," which is central in the Ps. Sol., see H. Braun, "Vom Erbarmen Gottes." For Braun, these psalms reveal an "optimism of works" that could not yet attain to the idea of God's unconditional goodness, and therefore restricts God's mercy to the righteous. On this, see J. Schüpphaus, Psalmen Salomos, 13–14; E. P. Sanders, Paul, 392–97.
29. Cf. 2 Macc. 7:9, 14; T. Jud. 25:1.
30. Cf. J. Lindblom, Das ewige Leben, 29–38. For their apocalyptic, see idem, 48–66; G. Dalman, Worte, 127–31; W. Bousset and H. Gressmann, Religion, 275–77; P. Volz, Eschatologie, 341, 363–64. N. Messel (Einheitlichkeit, 130–37) disputes that "everlasting life" means a life after death, and finds here a present eschatology, because he completely overlooks the role of the day of judgment.
31. See 3:11-12; 9:5; 13:11; 14:9-10; 15:12-13.
32. H. Braun, "Vom Erbarmen Gottes," 25-32, 35.

In contrast to this eschatology we find a very different, messianic type, especially in the last two psalms.[33] It is not based on the distinction between righteous and wicked as two groups within Israel, but on the contrast between Israel and the nations. The hope of the one praying is not directed to resurrection and everlasting life, but to God's eternal reign, which means "judgment" for the nations (ἡ βασιλεία τοῦ θεοῦ ἡμῶν εἰς τὸν αἰῶνα ἐπὶ τὰ ἔθνη ἐν κρίσει) (17:3), and to the blessings of the messianic age: the gathering of a holy people, the coming of the nations to them, the rule of the Messiah, and his righteous reign over Israel (17:26-32).

But before this time of salvation can begin, the Messiah must impose judgment on Israel's oppressors (17:21-25). Their violent overthrow or destruction "with a rod of iron" (17:24) is described, finally, as "condemning sinners" (ἐλέγξαι ἁμαρτωλούς) (17:25). Destruction and "condemnation" are placed as unceremoniously alongside one another here as they are in 1 Enoch 1:9.[34] This "judgment" of the Messiah, otherwise carried out by God alone, must be kept strictly distinct from his office as judge, which he exercises as ruler of the eschatological people of God (17:26, 29).

Psalm 17 appeals for the coming of the messianic king in the near future (17:21, 45), while the author of Psalm 18 expects this to happen only for a future generation, which he therefore calls blessed: "Blessed are those born in those days, to see the good things of the Lord which he will do for the coming generation" (μακάριοι οἱ γενόμενοι ἐν ταῖς ἡμέραις ἐκείναις / ἰδεῖν τὰ ἀγαθὰ κυρίου, ἃ ποιήσει γενεᾷ τῇ ἐρχομένῃ) (18:6; cf. 17:44).[35] The Messiah will lead (καταστήσει) that generation before the Lord as a "good generation [living] in the fear of God, in the days of mercy" (γενεὰ ἀγαθὴ ἐν φόβῳ θεοῦ ἐν ἡμέραις ἐλέους) (18:9).[36] In this conception, it appears that the earlier generations are excluded from salvation; at any rate, nothing is said in Psalms 17 and 18 about an opportunity for them to participate in it through resurrection.

---

33. It is true that J. Schüpphaus makes a clear distinction between two groups of psalms and their differing thematic orbits (*Psalmen Salomos*, 76–117), but he too easily obliterates the differences in the eschatology of the two groups (idem, 81, 92–93, 124–26). Cf., on the other hand, P. Volz, *Eschatologie*, 26–27.

34. For this passage, see p. 52 below. In contrast, cf. 4 Ezra 12:32-34; 13:37-38, where the conviction comes first, followed by destruction (see below, pp. 120–22).

35. Cf. J. Schüpphaus, *Psalmen Salomos*, 70, 124–25. The motif of salvation reserved for a "future generation" (דּוֹר אַחֲרוֹן) may be taken from Ps. 102:19 (cf. 1 Enoch 1:2). The Essenes understood themselves to be this "last generation" (see p. 83 below).

36. Cf. Sir. 48:10.

Thus in these two psalms we encounter for the first time a situation in which it is not God, but another figure who carries out the eschatological judgment and thus inaugurates the time of salvation. But even when the Messiah is explicitly described as the king of the eschatological people of God, the author leaves no doubt that he acts entirely on God's commission; the purpose of the messianic rule is to glorify God (17:30-31); it is therefore summarized in the phrase βασιλεία τοῦ θεοῦ (17:3). The final verse, 17:46, reads: "The Lord Himself is our king forevermore!" (cf. 17:1). As God's representative, the Messiah in the Psalms of Solomon resembles another eschatological judging-figure: the "chosen one" or "son of humanity" in the pictorial passages of Enoch (1 Enoch 37–71), which were probably written at the same time as the Psalms of Solomon.[37]

First Enoch

The Book of Watchers

The book of Enoch is a "colorful collective mosaic"[38] of texts of differing origins and periods of composition. Aramaic fragments of all its books, with the exception of the "Book of Parables," have been found at Qumran.[39] Large portions of the "Book of Watchers" and the "Epistle of Enoch" have been retained in Greek translation. Beyond these, we are almost entirely dependent on the Ethiopic version.

Apart from the "Astronomical Book" (chs. 72–82), the central idea and principal theme—namely, the end time judgment of the wicked, to be followed by the salvation of the righteous—is common to all the sections within the book of Enoch that are immediately obvious or can be distinguished by literary-critical methods.[40] This theme is introduced immediately in the superscription and dominates the whole of the Book of Watchers (chs. 1–36). It stems from the pre-Maccabean period and thus originated even before the

37. See below, pp. 66–69.
38. Emil Schürer, *Geschichte* 3: 273.
39. Edition: J. T. Milik, *Fragments*. These are also easily available now in K. Beyer, *Texte*, 231–38.
40. Cf. F. Corriente and A. Piñero, "Henoc," 16; M. Black, *Enoch*, 8, 12. The astronomical book contains eschatological material only in chs. 80–81. On this, see J. C. VanderKam, *Enoch*, 106–9.

book of Daniel. Its oldest texts go back to the third century B.C.E.[41] Within this book, chapters 1, 2–5 constitute a literary unit that now also serves as an introduction to the whole book. Its theme is announced by the superscription:

> Λόγος εὐλογίας Ἐνώχ,
> καθὼς εὐλόγησεν ἐκλεκτοὺς δικαίους
> οἵτινες ἔσονται εἰς ἡμέραν ἀνάγκης
> ἐξᾶραι πάντας τοὺς ἐχθρούς,
> καὶ σωθήσονται δίκαιοι.[42]

> The blessing of Enoch:
> with which he blessed the elect and the righteous
> who would be present on the day of tribulation
> at (the time of) the removal of all the ungodly ones
> [and the righteous will be saved].

The "day of tribulation" spoken of here is then depicted in 1:3b-9 as a mighty theophany revealing Old Testament models, especially Mic. 1:3-4: "The Holy and Great One" emerges from his dwelling and treads upon Mount Sinai; in that presence the mountains tremble and melt like wax (or honeycomb) before a flame, the earth is split open, and everything on earth is destroyed (1:3b-7).[43] The purpose of the theophany is "judgment upon all" (κρίσις κατὰ πάντων) (1:7), leading to blessedness for the "righteous" and "chosen." God will give them peace (εἰρήνη), mercy (ἔλεος), and light (φῶς) (1:8).[44]

41. Marie-Theres Wacker, *Weltordnung,* 11–12; F. Corriente and A. Piñero, "Henoc," 21; S. Uhlig, *Henochbuch,* 506; J. C. VanderKam, *Enoch,* 111–14; K. Beyer, *Texte,* 227–30; E. Schürer and G. Vermes, *History* 3/1: 256.

42. The added conclusion, καὶ σωθήσονται δίκαιοι, which is syntactically awkward even in Greek, is lacking in the other textual witnesses, but its content is entirely suitable to the context (cf. 99:10). In addition, according to the Greek text it is the righteous themselves who will eliminate the godless (cf. 38:5; 91:12; 95:3; 98:12). The Ethiopic text has a passive construction that leaves open the question who destroys the wicked. Matthew Black's translation (*Enoch,* 25) follows G. For the use of εἰς, cf. 1 Thess. 4:15. The whole superscription is inspired by Deut. 33:1. [The English translation is based on that of E. Isaac in *OTP* 1:13-89, with alterations as required by the author's interpretation.—Trans.]

43. For the Old Testament models of this judgment-theophany, see J. C. Vander-Kam, "Theophany"; L. Hartman, *Meaning,* 22–24; E. Rau, *Kosmologie,* 42–66. Rau emphasizes the vividness of these traditions in post-Old Testament times (cf. especially pp. 62–64). Cf. also F. Schnutenhaus, "Das Kommen und Erscheinen Gottes im Alten Testament."

44. For contacts with the blessing of Aaron (Num. 6:24-26), see E. Rau, *Kosmologie,* 50–53; L. Hartman, *Meaning,* 25–28, 46–47.

Then, in 1:9, there is a renewed description of the judgment-theophany as if no such depiction had preceded it:[45]

ἰδοὺ[46] ἔρχεται σὺν ταῖς μυριάσιν αὐτοῦ
    καὶ τοῖς ἁγίοις αὐτοῦ
ποιῆσαι κρίσιν κατὰ πάντων,
καὶ ἀπολέσει πάντας τοὺς ἀσεβεῖς
καὶ ἐλέγξει πᾶσαν σάρκα
    περὶ πάντων ἔργων τῆς ἀσεβείας αὐτῶν ὧν ἠσέβησαν
    καὶ σκληρῶν ὧν ἐλάλησαν λόγων . . .[47]

Behold, he will arrive with ten million of the holy ones
in order to execute judgment upon all.[48]
He will destroy the wicked ones
and rebuke all flesh
on account of everything that they have done,
    that which the sinners and the wicked ones committed
        against him.

Here the text speaks both of a "destruction" and a "rebuking" (ἐλέγχειν) of the impious. The sequence indicates that the "destruction" is not thought of as a consequence of the "rebuke," as it is, for example, in 4 Ezra 12:32-34; 13:37-38.[49] Thus passing of sentence and forensic judgment are found immediately alongside one another.[50] The author of the letter of Jude, who quoted this passage in vv. 14-15, may have omitted καὶ ἀπολέσει for that reason, but then replaced the πᾶσαν σάρκα of the second part with the object of the omitted part, so that the judgment now consists solely of the "conviction of all the

45. E. Rau (*Kosmologie,* 49) sees the structure of 1:7-9 as reflecting a chiasm in content. But 1:9 clearly represents a new beginning, which G smoothes over (see n. 46 below).

46. For the text, cf. Jude 14–15; E. Isaac, *OTP* 1. Cf. R. H. Charles, *Enoch,* 8; C. D. Osburn, "Christological Use," 335–36; S. Uhlig, *Henochbuch* 509; M. Black, *Enoch,* 108; R. J. Bauckham, *Jude,* 94–96; B. Dehandschutter, "Pseudo-Cyprian." Probably G replaced ἰδού with ὅτι in order to obtain a better connection with what went before (A. Lods, *Hénoch,* 99; B. Dehandschutter, "Pseudo-Cyprian," 118).

47. Cf. Deut. 33:2 (LXX!); Zech. 14:5 (LXX!); Jer. 25:31 (LXX 32:31).

48. Behind ποιεῖν κρίσιν κατά is Aramaic עבד דין מן: cf. 22:4; 91:12 (see below, chap. 7).

49. See below, pp. 57–58.

50. This is completely ignored by L. Hartman (*Meaning,* 13–26). For him, the scene is "exactly one of a tribunal" (p. 129). But it was Jude 14–15 that made it such.

godless" (ἐλέγξαι πάντας τοὺς ἀσεβεῖς).[51] Therefore in Jude 15 ποιῆσαι κρίσιν κατὰ πάντων should not be translated, as in 1 Enoch 1:9, as "to execute judgment on all," but as "to judge all." Thus in Jude 15, in contrast to 1 Enoch 1:9, the forensic aspect is primary.

In spite of the twofold emphasis on a "judgment on all" (1:7, 9), this judgment appears to fall only on sinners; the righteous are excused from it.[52]

This last observation is also confirmed by chapters 2–5, in which sinners are confronted with the marvelous order of nature in which "everything functions in the way in which God has ordered it" (5:2), whereas *they* violate God's law and blaspheme God (5:4).[53] But they will reap destruction (ἀπώλεια), their name will be a curse to the righteous,[54] and they will find neither mercy nor peace (5:5-6). The "elect," on the other hand, will "inherit the earth" (κληρονομεῖν τὴν γῆν) (5:6, 7, 8);[55] they will sin no more and they will not die "through plague or wrath" (ἐν ὀργῇ θυμοῦ). Instead, they will complete their lives in the light and peace of God (5:7-9).[56] This "life" is still, just as in Isaiah 65, a long lifetime, as in the time of the patriarchs (cf. also 10:17; 25:6),[57] not an "everlasting" life as in the book of Wisdom and the Psalms of Solomon.

The remaining parts of the Book of Watchers are as devoid of any description of the actual judicial process as are chapters 1–5. In 25:3 the text speaks of Zion as a high mountain like a throne, on which "the Holy and Great Lord" will sit "when he descends to visit the earth with goodness" (ὅταν καταβῇ ἐπισκέψασθαι τὴν γῆν ἐπ᾽ ἀγαθῷ), that is, for "the great judgment when he shall take vengeance on all and conclude (everything) forever" (25:4). But

---

51. Cf. A. Lods, *Hénoch*, 99; R. J. Bauckham, *Jude*, 94–95. The text of Jude is uncertain at this point, however. The reading as quoted, πάντας τοὺς ἀσεβεῖς, is found, among other witnesses, in manuscripts A, B, and C, but only the 25th ed. of Nestle-Aland follows them. Other manuscripts read πᾶσαν ψυχήν, which Kurt Aland has adopted in the 26th edition—rightly?

52. "'All' in v. 7b is a very common exaggeration (cf., for example, *Jub.* 5:4; [4] Ezra 3:9-10) occurring again in 7c (since the righteous do not come before the judgment)" (N. Messel, *Einheitlichkeit*, 11). Cf. A. Lods, *Hénoch*, 96; P. Volz, *Eschatologie*, 17; J. Bonsirven, *Judaïsme* 1: 488–89; L. Hartman, *Meaning*, 129.

53. Cf. M. Limbeck, *Ordnung*, 63–72; L. Hartman, *Meaning*, 28–30; O. Betz, *Paraklet*, 46–51.

54. Cf. Isa. 65:15.

55. On this, see M. Black, *Enoch*, 115.

56. L. Hartman (*Meaning*, 14–15) sees in chs. 2–5 the ἔλεγχος of God that is spoken of in 1:9. There is no basis for this in the text. But Hartman rightly emphasizes that this text is deeply inspired by Deuteronomy 27–30 and Num. 6:24-26 (*Meaning*, 22–38).

57. R. H. Charles, *Enoch*, 53, on 25:4-5; P. Grelot, "Histoire," 97–98. Cf. *Jub.* 23:27; 2 Bar. 73:3.

there, as in chapter 5, what follows is only a description of the happiness of
the righteous (25:5-7) and the damnation of the "accursed" (26/27). For the
righteous, the fruit of the tree of life, which will be transplanted to Jerusalem,
makes possible a long life without sorrow or pain (25:5-6); but as for the "accursed," they will be subjected, before the eyes of the righteous, to punishment
in Gehenna (27:3).[58] It is obvious that here the tradition of Isa. 66:23-24 has
been adopted and developed.[59]

The promises and threats of judgment from the Book of Watchers discussed
thus far apply only to the generation of righteous and sinners living at the end
of time. What happens to the dead? We learn more of them in the narrative
of the "watchers" (6–16), and in chapter 22. The watchers—the angels who,
according to Gen. 6:1-4, begot giants through intercourse with human
women—for their wicked deed are bound and "thrown into the darkness"
until the "great day of judgment" (10:4-6, 12). Then they will be led "into the
bottom of the fire—and in torment (βάσανος)—in the prison [where] they
will be locked up forever" (10:13).[60] According to 10:14, the same fate will
overtake all sinners.[61] The righteous, on the other hand, will then dwell on a
cleansed earth as fruitful as Paradise (10:14—11:2).[62]

We find a very similar concept and parallel motifs in 1 Enoch 22. There
Enoch is shown, in the west, a "great and high mountain" with many caves in
which the souls [or spirits] of the dead are gathered: these places have been
prepared to house the spirits "until the day of their judgment and the appointed time of the great judgment upon them" (יתעבד עד זמן יום קצא דינ[י]
דינא רבא די מנהון (22:4).[63] The first cave is for the righteous; it is light[64] and
contains a spring, while the others are dark. The second cave is for the sinners
who were not judged during their lifetimes. For them, the day of judgment is
a day of retribution, of "plague and pain" (τῶν μαστίγων καὶ τῶν βασάνων),
when they will be bound forever (22:11). They will thus meet the same fate as

58. For this topographical designation, see esp. M.-T. Wacker, *Weltordnung*, 245–50.
59. Cf. idem, 251–52.
60. Cf. Isa. 24:22. On this, see Wacker, *Weltordnung*, 197–98.
61. Cf. ibid., 198. Wacker speaks very cautiously of "certain (guilty) persons." A.
Lods, *Hénoch*, 122; M. Black, *Enoch*, 138; L. Hartman, *Meaning*, 144; R. Rubinkiewicz,
Eschatologie, 111, on the other hand, see this as applying to all sinners.
62. For a detailed discussion, see R. Rubinkiewicz, *Eschatologie*, 72–94.
63. For the text, see Wacker, *Weltordnung*, 49–50, 95. For the meaning of עבד דין מן,
cf. 91:12 (see pp. 57–58 below).
64. Differently M. Black, *Enoch*, 167; but here he himself is uncertain, as his translation (p. 37) and the careful formulation on p. 17 shows: "The latter may also have
been dark."

the angelic watchers and the sinners in 1 Enoch 10:13-14.[65] The only element not mentioned here is the "fiery abyss." The third cave is for murdered righteous persons like Abel, the fourth for a group of sinners whose special character is not clear. It is possible that they differ from those in the second group by the fact that "they have already been judged by their violent death,"[66] and therefore on the day of judgment they will receive no further punishment; they will simply not be permitted to leave their cave (οὐ τιμωρηθήσονται ἐν ἡμέρᾳ τῆς κρίσεως, οὐδὲ μὴ μετεγερθῶσιν ἐντεῦθεν) (22:13).[67]

The Old Testament idea of Sheol as the dark realm of shadows, silence, and oblivion, from which there is no return, has clearly undergone a change here.[68] As a consequence of belief in a fixed, future day of judgment, Sheol has become a temporary abode of the dead, or rather of the souls of those who have died, until that day, while for some of the dead it has also become the definitive place of their punishment.[69]

The idea of judgment in this text is also indistinct and lacking in unity. While, according to 22:4, the final judgment will apparently be imposed on all sinners, in 22:8-13 it falls only on sinners who have died unpunished, and others are explicitly exempted from it. Perhaps this is a sign that at this point two originally independent traditions or literary units have been combined, as has been posited on the basis of other indications.[70] In that case, the original basis of 22:1-4 may have been the idea of a forensic judgment on all souls, both righteous and sinners. But that is improbable. In any case, vv. 8-13 presuppose a judgment of condemnation which, however, will fall only on those sinners of whom it can be said that "judgment has not been executed upon them in their lifetime" (22:10).

---

65. For the analogy between these two passages, see Wacker, *Weltordnung*, 199.

66. Wacker, *Weltordnung*, 106. M. Black thinks, on the basis of a somewhat different reconstruction of the text, that these are collaborators with pagan oppressors (*Enoch*, 168).

67. I follow Wacker, *Weltordnung*, 105–6, in accepting four, rather than three divisions. Thus previously G. Beer, "Henoch," 252, and M. Black, *Enoch*, 166.

68. On this, see Wacker, *Weltordnung*, 132–44; see the same location for the religious-historical origins of the motif of the western mountain and its prison caves. For the development of the idea of Sheol, see also R. H. Charles, *Enoch*, 127–28; D. S. Russell, *Apocalyptic*, 353–66.

69. R. H. Charles (*Enoch*, 128) regards belief in the resurrection as the occasion of this alteration. But that belief is probably secondary to belief in the day of judgment, or perhaps derived from it.

70. For detailed discussion of this point, see Wacker, *Weltordnung*, 110–31; on p. 131 she offers a reconstructed original text of 22:1-4.

Marie-Theres Wacker interprets 22:5-7, 8-13 differently, seeing in it "a scenario of preparation for the trial" that finds its "immediate development" in 1
Enoch 26–27.[71] This can scarcely be correct.

> Marie-Theres Wacker gives the greatest emphasis to the nature of the caves as
> prisons, and understands the "complaining" or "making suit" in 22:4-12 as a
> clamor by which the righteous demand a decision in "their case." "Their separa-
> tion is not an imprisonment; instead, it means that their being gathered together
> gives them an opportunity to present their complaint in an orderly fashion"
> (Weltordnung, 231). But there is no trace of an orderly presentation of this com-
> plaint to be found in 1 Enoch 27. Moreover, Wacker's supposition that the "ac-
> cursed" in 1 Enoch 26–27 are not identical with the dead sinners in 1 Enoch 22,
> but that these are only the wicked still alive at the end (pp. 258–59) contradicts
> this notion. Also incompatible with her interpretation is the proposition that
> neither of the two groups of sinners in 1 Enoch 22 is to leave its prison. "The
> functional description of the mountain of the dead in [1] Enoch 22 as an abode
> 'until the judgment' does not compel the conclusion that the sinners who have
> not yet been judged will leave their caves for judgment; it indicates only that on
> the 'day of judgment' there will be a change in their destiny" (p. 258). This asser-
> tion is connected with the fact that Wacker disputes the presence of a twofold
> resurrection of righteous and sinners in 1 Enoch 22. We need not go into that
> question in detail here.

However, Matthew Black also finds juridical vocabulary (ἐντυγχάνειν =
קבל and ἐμφανίζειν = Hebrew הגיד, Aramaic אחוי) in 22:12, and interprets:
"These spirits of men who have been violently slain have, like Abel, accusations
to bring and information to lay before the court at the last judgment with
regard to their deaths—accusations and information about their murderers."[72]
Is the author then really thinking of a judicial process, perhaps with a subsequent imposition of punishment? This seems very doubtful on the basis of the
other statements in the text. There is very little in chapter 27, either, to indicate
a judicial process. Some commentators suppose that the Ethiopic text in 27:2,
ὧδε ἔσται τὸ οἰκητήριον, had "κριτήριον" rather than "οἰκητήριον."[73] But
the underlying tradition from Isa. 66:23-24 gives us more reason to think of a
judgment purely for condemnation.

A further problem concerning the idea of judgment underlying 1 Enoch 22
is the division of the souls or spirits of the dead into different groups. This

71. Wacker, Weltordnung, 230, 234.
72. M. Black, Enoch, 167–68.
73. A. Lods, Hénoch, 190; S. Uhlig, Henoch, 563–64; M. Black, Enoch, 174.

division seems to suppose some kind of "first" judgment by which the dead
are assigned to one of the four caves as an abode until the final judgment.
However, there is not a word about such a preliminary judgment; the four
groups are simply represented as given. At the end of each individual life it is
already determined to which group of righteous or sinners he or she belongs;
there is no need for a special court of judgment. The idea of an individual
judgment immediately after death is quite foreign to the author of 1 Enoch
22.[74] But just as there is a distinction among souls, the very idea of retribution
beginning immediately after death introduces a contradiction in the eschatological concept that is not easily resolved: for in such a case, what need is there
for a final judgment? A. Lods has written, with regard to 1 Enoch 22: "It is
quite obvious that such a concept makes resurrection unnecessary, and with it
the whole final drama."[75] Lods presupposes the influence of Hellenistic Greek
ideas of Hades,[76] as does R. A. Pfeiffer with regard to the book of Wisdom,
where we encountered the same problem.[77] At the time the latter book was
written, then, the problem was at least 150 years old, and yet it had never been
experienced as a problem in Judaism.

The Ten-Week Apocalypse

The so-called Ten-Week Apocalypse (1 Enoch 93:[1-2], 3-10; 91:11-17) is now
part of the Epistle of Enoch (92–105), but from a literary-critical point of
view it has long been acknowledged as an originally independent unit, poorly
integrated into its context. It may be only slightly more recent than the Book
of Watchers.[78]

This miniature apocalypse divides history from creation to the end of the
world into twelve periods, called "weeks" (cf. Dan. 9:24!). The author, who is
probably one of the "elect" of Israel, the Hasidim, the "eternal plant of righ-

---

74. Against S. G. F. Brandon, *Judgement*, 69–70. Cf. also T. F. Glasson, "Last Judgment," 534: "There must be a postmortem judgment or separation of some kind to
determine which division of Sheol the soul is to occupy, but there is no description of
such a judgment."

75. A. Lods, *Hénoch*, lxiv.

76. Ibid., lxv. Cf. A. Dieterich, *Nekyia*, 218–20; M. Hengel, *Judaism* 1: 198; Wacker,
Weltordnung, 211–19, 281–88; T. F. Glasson, "Last Judgment," 537; N. Walter, "'Hellenistische Eschatologie.'"

77. See above, p. 45.

78. For dating, see below. I base my remarks essentially on the text reconstructed
by F. Dexinger with the aid of the Aramaic fragments from Qumran (*Zehnwochenapokalypse*, 178–79).

teousness" (93:10),[79] sees his own age as the end of the seventh and beginning of the eighth week. At this point, the threshold of the end time has been reached, and even passed. For now occurs what Enoch prophesies for the end of the seventh week: "And they [that is, the elect] will have rooted out[80] the foundations of violence and the structure of falsehood therein [namely, in the eternal plant of righteousness] to execute judgment."[81] However, this process can scarcely be distinguished from the bestowal of the sword on "the righteous one" at the beginning of the eighth week, "to execute a righteous judgment on sinners" למעבד דין קשוט מן כול רשיעין (91:11). The author has in mind the beginning of the Maccabean revolt, at the time when he is writing.[82]

But with this, the first act of the final judgment has begun. At first it touches only Israel's oppressors, but in the ninth week it will be extended to the whole world. Then the wicked will disappear from the earth and "they"—undoubt-

---

79. For this expression, cf. *Jub.* 1:16; 16:26; 36:6; 1QS 8,5; 11,8; 1QM 6,15; 8,6; also F. Dexinger, *Zehnwochenapokalypse,* 164–169; R. Borig, *Weinstock,* 188–92; S. Fujita, "Metaphor of Plant."

80. The Aramaic text reads ולהון עקרין. For imperfect forms of הוה, constructed with ל, see K. Beyer, *Texte,* 560–61. F. Dexinger translates: "For their sake the foundations will be uprooted" (*Zehnwochenapokalypse,* 179. Cf. idem, 114 n. 22). K. Koch, "Sabbatstruktur," 411, also considers this possibility. But who would be the new subject, to be distinguished from the "elect"?

81. 1 Enoch 91:11. The conclusion, למעבד [דין], is augmented following J. T. Milik, *Books,* 265; F. Dexinger, *Zehnwochenapokalypse,* 135, 179; K. Beyer, *Texte,* 248. This augmentation recommends itself because the same expression occurs again two lines below. The objection of Matthew Black that this is "stylistically clumsy" (*Enoch,* 292) is simply incomprehensible in view of the rest of the text, and of the book of Enoch as a whole, for it prefers to produce repetitions rather than avoid them. The expansion also fits precisely within the logical structure of the apocalypse, especially as presented by G. W. E. Nickelsburg: "The judgment of the wicked of Week 7 is fully executed in Week 8" ("Apocalyptic Message," 314. Cf. F. Dexinger, *Zehnwochenapokalypse,* 135). [The English translation given is based on Isaac's note y, *OTP* 1:73, rendering the text of 4QEn^e. Trans.]

82. Therefore "ca. 166 B.C.E." (F. Dexinger, *Zehnwochenapokalypse,* 139). "The 'sword' has already been given; success has not yet been obtained, but it is hoped for as something sure" (ibid.). Cf. U. B. Müller, *Messias,* 63–64. Therefore the events prophesied in 91:11 are not purely future for the author; the end time has begun. K. Müller (*TRE* 3:218) thinks that the Ten-Week Apocalypse awards no special mention to the Maccabean revolt and regards it as a failure. K. Koch also thinks of this text as originating at the time of John Hyrcanus (135–105 B.C.E.) ("Sabbatstruktur," 419–20). For dating, cf. Wacker, *Weltordnung,* 9; S. Uhlig, *Henochbuch,* 709; M. Black, *Enoch,* 288; E. Schürer and G. Vermes, *History* 3/1: 255–56. According to J. C. VanderKam, the Ten-Week Apocalypse originated between 175 and 167 B.C.E. and refers to pre-Maccabean events, especially the appearance of the Hellenists. Even the events described in 91:11 are in the future, from the point of view of the author (*Enoch,* 145–49; idem, *Studies,* 521–23).

edly the avenging angels—will throw them into the "everlasting pit," that is, Gehenna (91:14). Finally, in a third act, in the tenth week the "eternal judgment" (דין עלמא) will take place, at the "time of the great judgment" (קץ דינא רבא) on the Watchers (91:15). Then the first heaven will vanish and a new will appear, and "they," the righteous and chosen, will live forever in goodness and righteousness; sin will vanish completely (91:16-17).[83] Whether at the end of the apocalypse, in the Aramaic text, the resurrection of the righteous who have died is announced, as Matthew Black supposes, is very uncertain in light of the confused fragments.[84]

As the conclusion clearly shows, this apocalypse and its concept of judgment are very close to Isaiah 65–66. Much as in those chapters, and in the traditions of the Book of Watchers, judgment is conceived as a sentencing of the wicked (and the Watchers), in order that the "chosen" may live in righteousness beneath (or in?) a new heaven. The judgment is therefore seen explicitly as analogous to the destruction of sinful humanity in the Flood, which is described in 93:4 as the "first consummation."[85] In 1 Enoch 10:2, also, the Flood is called τέλος (cf. Gen. 6:13), and serves the author of 1 Enoch 9–11 as a model for the eschatological punishment, which is also called the "consummation" (συντελεσμός) (10:12).[86] It is disputed whether the Flood was explicitly called "judgment" in 93:3, because this sentence is differently interpreted and translated.[87]

83. Cf. Isa. 65:17; 66:22. Apparently there is no expectation of a new earth here (R. H. Charles, *Enoch*, 233, on 91:17, and 260, on 104:2). Then where are the righteous? F. Dexinger (*Zehnwochenapokalypse*, 143) is somewhat unclear in his expressions. He seems to think that the mention of a renewal of the earth in 91:16 was superfluous, since this had already occurred in 91:14. On the other hand, Matthew Black writes: "The apparent assumption at 1 En. 91:16 is not that the earth will be transformed with the heavens, but that a new heaven will appear and become the abode of the righteous forever" ("New Creation," 18).

84. Matthew Black, *Enoch*, 294–95. He uses 1 Enoch 91:10a; 92:3a to augment the text.

85. Cf. F. Dexinger, *Zehnwochenapokalypse*, 122–23. K. Müller (*TRE* 3:240) rejects this interpretation. But even in Nahum 1:7-8 the Flood appears as an image for the terrors of the Day of YHWH. In 1 Enoch 84:4, on the other hand, the Flood is described as the "day of the great judgment," an expression that otherwise is reserved for the final judgment. Cf. also 1 Enoch 91:5-7, and 1 Enoch 106:18—107:1. In Wis. 5:22 the final judgment is described in the guise of a new Flood (cf. C. Larcher, *Sagesse* 2: 395, ad loc.). Further instances of this idea are *Vit. Ad.* 49, 2 Enoch 70:10; Str-B 3: 773. Cf. also below, pp. 95–107, on *Sib. Or.* 1, 273–74.

86. R. Rubinkiewicz, *Eschatologie*, 35, 69–70. He supposes that קץ was originally found in both passages. Cf. also O. Betz, *Paraklet*, 55.

87. Cf. G. Beer's translation ("Henoch," 299) and M. Black's commentary (*Enoch*, 289); F. Dexinger, *Zehnwochenapokalypse*, 121.

Another striking feature of this short text is the frequent usage of eschatological passives, the active subjects of which are intended to be God or the angels: The elect "will be chosen" (תבחרו[ן]י); sevenfold wisdom and knowledge "will be given to them" ([תתיהב]ן); a sword "will be given" (תתיהב[ל]) to the righteous; the wicked will "be given" (יתיהבון) into their hand; to all the children of the earth the righteous judgment or right statutes[88] "will be revealed" (יתגלא); the Temple of the end time "will be built" (יתבנא) (93:10; 91:12-14). In this last instance, the elect could also be considered as the active subjects. Once or twice, in place of and immediately following an eschatological passive, there is a third person plural with the same function: [א]וירמון לבור, "they will cast them [that is, the wicked] into the pit."[89] In this case, the active subjects are undoubtedly the avenging angels.

The Vision of the Animals

The vision of the animals from the Book of Dreams (83–90) originated at about the same time as the Ten-Week Apocalypse[90] and, like it, in the circles of the Hasidim.[91] It tells the history of Israel in an allegory. In it, as in the Ten-Week Apocalypse, the eschatological judgment begins with the sheep (= Israel) being given a "great sword," with which they go forth against their enemies and oppressors (90:19). But according to 90:18 it is God who destroys them.[92] Here, as in the Ten-Week Apocalypse, the Maccabean revolt is seen as an eschatological event introducing the end time judgment.[93] Then God will be seated on the throne that is set up in the "pleasant land" of Palestine, and the archangel Michael will open the books of judgment (90:20). In these books Michael has recorded the misdeeds of the "seventy shepherds," that is, the angels of the nations under whose rule Israel lived in the diaspora (89:59-64, 68-71, 76-77). In a first act, the Watchers will be brought forth bound, to be

88. On this, see F. Dexinger, *Zehnwochenapokalypse,* 150–70.
89. 1 Enoch 91:14; text from K. Beyer, *Texte,* 248. J. T. Milik (*Books of Enoch,* 267), M. Black (*Enoch,* 86), and F. Dexinger (*Zehnwochenapokalypse,* 179) translate imprecisely with the passive here. Undoubtedly the preceding gap in the text contained a verb in the third person plural (K. Beyer, *Texte,* 248–49).
90. M. Hengel, *Judaism* 2: 116–17 n. 458; Wacker, *Weltordnung,* 9; S. Uhlig, *Henochbuch,* 673–74; J. C. VanderKam, *Enoch,* 161–63; E. Schürer and G. Vermes, *History* 3/1: 255.
91. They are the "lambs" in 90:6. Cf. R. H. Charles, *Enoch,* 182, 206–7; M. Hengel, *Judaism* 1: 187–88; U. B. Müller, *Messias,* 66–67; K. Müller, *TRE* 3:213.
92. On the difficulties and possibly necessary rearrangements in 90:13-19, see R. H. Charles, *Enoch,* 209–11; U. B. Müller, *Messias,* 67.
93. Cf. M. Hengel, *Judaism* 1: 187–88.

condemned and cast into a fiery abyss (90:24; cf. 10:13). Then the "seventy shepherds" will be judged and thrown into the same abyss (90:25).[94] Finally, the "blinded sheep" will be brought, condemned, and thrown into another abyss full of fire that will open in Gehenna (90:26). Then the new Jerusalem will be created (90:28-29), and to it will return "all those which had been destroyed and dispersed,"[95] and the Gentiles with them (90:34). The Messiah[96] appears, and with him God's people lives in purity and righteousness (90:37-38).[97]

The description of the judgment in the vision of the animals does contain forensic elements (throne, books of judgment, bringing forward of the accused, condemnation, carrying out of the sentence), but there is no formal procedure that might include, for example, a hearing of the accused. The guilt of the accused is already established beforehand. The similarity with the scene in Dan. 7:9-10, in which animals are also judged, is obvious, even though the tradition-historical relationships are difficult to determine since both texts originated at about the same time.[98] The inclusion of the "Watchers" and the place of their punishment indicate a tradition-historical connection with the Book of Watchers.[99]

Enoch's Admonition

Editors of the book of Enoch usually attach the admonitory speech in 91:1-10, 18-19 to the "Epistle of Enoch."[100] It may originally have been independent, as was the Ten-Week Apocalypse. The *terminus ad quem* for dating is then the writing of the "Epistle of Enoch" ca. 100 B.C.E.[101]

94. According to *Mekh Y* on Exod. 15:1 (Lauterbach 2: 20), also, in the final judgment God will first judge the angels of the nations, and then punish their empires.

95. This, therefore, implies a resurrection: P. Grelot, "Histoire," 99; M. Black, *Enoch*, 279.

96. According to M. Black (*Enoch*, 279–80), this is the new Adam. J. C. VanderKam also rejects the interpretation of the "white bull" as the Messiah (*Enoch*, 168).

97. U. B. Müller considers vv. 37-39 a later interpolation by a glossator (*Messias*, 68–72).

98. G. K. Beale (*Daniel* 67–88) considers Dan. 7:9-13 the model for 1 Enoch (90:20-27).

99. On this, see R. H. Charles, *Enoch*, 179–80.

100. S. Uhlig differs (*Henochbuch*, 705–7), placing it at the end of the Book of Dreams (see also idem, 674). However, its content is not appropriate for that arrangement. Matthew Black also (*Enoch*, 83–84) excludes it from the "Epistle" (see also idem, 11–12, 21). E. Rau, *Kosmologie*, 437–44, establishes a close connection between chs. 83–90 and 91:1—94:5.

101. See p. 62 below.

In this short discourse, Enoch admonishes his children to walk in righteousness and to avoid the company of those "with a double heart" (91:3-4, 18-19). He gives reason for his warning by referring to the coming judgment: first the Flood (91:5), then the final judgment that will occur after iniquity has prevailed "once more" (91:6-7). Then "the holy Lord shall emerge with wrath and plague in order that he may execute judgment upon the earth" (91:7). The wicked will be destroyed, and with them the Gentiles; they will be thrown "into the judgment of fire" (91:9). Then "the righteous one shall arise from his sleep [that is, the sleep of death], and the wise one [or: wisdom] shall arise; and he shall be given unto them" (91:10).

In addition to the parallel between Flood and final judgment, which we also found in the Ten-Week Apocalypse and elsewhere,[102] what is especially worth noting here is the expressly parenetic function of the proclamation of judgment.

The Epistle of Enoch

Enoch's letter (92–105) is a word of consolation for the righteous and a preaching of judgment for sinners, very much in the spirit of the superscription of the Book of Watchers in 1:1. It was probably composed about 100 B.C.E., in any case earlier than the book of Wisdom.[103] In it, sinners (ἁμαρτωλοί) are described as rich (94:8; 96:4) and powerful; they oppress the poor and the righteous (96:5, 8) and twist the law (99:2). They desire nothing except "food and drink, robbing and sin, impoverishing people and gaining property, and seeing good days" (102:9).[104] The "righteous and kind" (δίκαιοι καὶ ὅσιοι) (103:9; 104:12), on the other hand, are those "who accept the words of wisdom and understand them, to follow the commands of the Most High, and walk in the path of his righteousness and not go astray with those who go astray"

---

102. See p. 59 above.

103. R. H. Charles, *Enoch*, 221–22, 259; Wacker, *Weltordnung*, 11; S. Uhlig, *Henochbuch*, 709; J. C. VanderKam, *Enoch*, 142–44; G. W. E. Nickelsburg, "Epistle," all suppose a pre-Essene origin in Hasidic circles. S. Uhlig (idem) does not exclude the same conclusion for "some parts." This is true, of course, especially of the Ten-Week Apocalypse, which remains out of consideration in what follows here. For the author of Wisdom's knowledge of the book of Enoch, see above, p. 46. M. Sato, *Q*, 349–54, offers an interesting literary-critical analysis. He dates the traditions in this work primarily in the first quarter of the second century B.C.E. (idem, 358). In his opinion, a prophetic speaker stands behind the origins of the work.

104. For a further description of this group, see R. H. Charles, *Enoch*, 221–22; P. Volz, *Eschatologie*, 18–19; G. W. E. Nickelsburg, *Resurrection*, 112–13; idem, "Apocalyptic Message," 311.

(99:10).[105] R. H. Charles sees in this group the Pharisees, and in their opponents the Sadducees and the ruling class.[106]

The sinners will be requited according to their works (95:5; 100:7) on the "day of (the great) judgment."[107] That day will be a "day of spilling blood and . . . of darkness" (94:9; cf. 99:6), a "day of hard anguish" (ἡμέρα ἀνάγκης) (100:7; cf. 96:2), and a "day of destruction" (ἡμέρα ἀπωλείας) (98:10; 99:4).[108] The righteous should be ready to raise their "prayers as a memorial" (ἐν-τεύξεις); they are to present them to the angels as a testimony (διαμαρτυρία) in order that they may remind the Most High of the sinners' deeds (99:3). But what follows is not, as one might expect, a description of a trial; instead, there is an immediate imposition of sentence, consisting in the destruction of the sinners (99:9). According to 95:3; 98:12, they will be delivered into the hands of the righteous, who will show no mercy. But according to 99:16 it is God who will put them all to the sword (cf. 100:4). The righteous he will give into the protection of the angels, who will guard them "as the apple of the eye" (100:5).[109]

In another passage, God judges with fire: ". . . when he hurls out against you the terror of the fire, where shall you flee, and where shall you find safety?" (καὶ ὅταν ἐκβάλῃ ἐφ᾽ ὑμᾶς τὸν [κ]λύδωνα τοῦ πυρὸς τῆς καύσεως ὑμῶν, ποῦ ἀποδράντες σωθήσεσθε;) (102:1). Still another verse speaks of frost, ice, and snow that will come upon sinners (100:13).[110] The terrors of the end time, as we are familiar with them from the synoptic apocalypse in Mark 13 and parallels, are also to be found in the description of that day, or those days

105. Translation according to the Greek text.

106. R. H. Charles, *Enoch*, 221–22. Similarly Bo Reicke, "Elements," 149. According to J. T. Milik, the background is instead the milieu of a Hellenistic city in which the Jews constitute an oppressed minority (*Henoch*, 49–51). J. C. H. Lebram ("Piety," 194) proposes the same solution, apparently without knowledge of Milik's work. J. C. Van-derKam also rejects Charles's identification and an interpretation in terms of particular groups (*Enoch*, 143–44). G. W. E. Nickelsburg sees the "righteous and kind" as pre-Essene Hasidim (*Epistle*, esp. 347–48).

107. "Day of Judgment," 97:3; 100:4; "day of the great judgment," 94:9; 98:10; 99:15; 104:5.

108. Cf. above, p. 26, esp. Zeph. 1:15.

109. It is difficult to say what the "restful sleep of the righteous" that follows this is meant to signify. This passage is usually interpreted as the preservation of the righteous dead until the final judgment (P. Grelot, "L'eschatologie de la Sagesse," 173; S. Uhlig, *Henochbuch*, 730, 5e; M. Black, *Enoch*, 307 ad loc). But the context does not fit. Cf. also P. Hoffmann, *Die Toten*, 122; G. Stemberger, *Leib*, 40–41.

110. Cf. T. *Lev.* 3:2. There, "fire, snow, and ice" are already prepared for the day of judgment.

(99:4-5; 100:1-2; 102:2-3). Judgment, as pure condemnation, applies here only to sinners. "In those days, at the time of your condemnation, many and good days shall come for the righteous ones" (96:8). For this reason they are also called blessed (99:10), while myriad woes are proclaimed over sinners.[111]

Alongside this historical eschatology, which is part of the tradition of the "day of YHWH," we also find an eschatology of the hereafter, especially in chapters 102–4. It reveals many contacts with the eschatology of the book of Wisdom.[112]

The evil deeds of sinners are written down each day until the day of their judgment (98:8; 104:7).[113] Then the register that has been prepared ([πάντες] οἱ λόγοι τῶν ἀνομιῶν ὑμῶν)[114] will be read out, to their shame, before the "Great and Holy One," who will reject all their unrighteous works (97:6).[115] The righteous, on the other hand, need have no fear, for they will not be found to be sinners (104:5). These are the only passages in the Epistle of Enoch that presuppose a forensic judgment scene, with no further description given.[116] It is not clear whether the text here has in mind a judgment of living or dead, but the context of 97:6 suggests that we should more probably think of the historical "day of judgment."

As regards the fate of the dead and the influence of the last judgment on that fate, much remains unclear here, as in the book of Wisdom. The sinners are told that their souls will be brought down into Sheol after death.[117] There

111. 1 Enoch 94:6-8; 95:4-7; 96:4-8; 97:7-8; 98:9-15; 99:1-2, 11-16; 100:7-9; 103:5-8. There are 32 woes in all. By comparison, the book of Isaiah contains 20 examples. On this, see G. W. E. Nickelsburg, "Apocalyptic Message," 310–11; R. A. Coughenour, "Woe-Oracles."

112. P. Grelot, "Eschatologie," 168, 173–77; G. W. E. Nickelsburg, *Resurrection,* 128; C. Larcher, *Études,* 103–12.

113. It appears that angels do the writing (cf. 99:3; 100:10). Cf. G. Beer's translation of 104:7; however, the text is uncertain. Cf. R. H. Charles, *Enoch,* 261 ad loc; S. Uhlig, *Henochbuch,* 723 ad loc.

114. Matthew Black (*Enoch,* 90) correctly translates: "the complete account of your iniquities." Similarly F. Corriente and A. Piñero, "Henoc," 130: "toda la historia de vuestra iniquidad [all the history of your iniquity]." The Ethiopic has "all the speech of your unrighteousness," which S. Uhlig (*Henochbuch,* 721, 6a) wrongly equates with the Greek reading.

115. The Ethiopic has a passive construction; see S. Uhlig, *Henochbuch,* 721, 6e.

116. On 99:3, see above, p. 63. Cf. G. W. E. Nickelsburg, *Resurrection,* 120–22, where, however, the forensic elements are overemphasized.

117. In the active voice in the Greek text: "εἰς ᾅδου [κα]τάξουσιν τὰς ψυχὰς ὑμῶν (103:7). It appears that the angels will carry this out.

"they shall experience evil and great tribulation—in darkness, nets and burning flame" (καὶ ἐκεῖ ἔσονται ἐν ἀνάγκῃ μεγάλῃ καὶ ἐν σκότει καὶ ἐν παγίδι καὶ ἐν φλογὶ καιομένῃ) (103:7-8). That will be the place of their punishment "in all the generations of the world" (103:8). This place of punishment is also what is meant by the "fiery furnace" (98:3; 54:6). In other places the sinners are simply promised "destruction" (ἀπολεῖσθαι) (98:16; 99:1, 9). Once it is said that they will be slain in Sheol (99:11). A constantly recurring formula is: "you will not have peace!" (οὐκ ἔστιν ὑμῖν χαίρειν).[118]

To the righteous, on the other hand, Enoch offers consolation for their suffering,[119] which is described in detail (103:9-15), a mystery (μυστήριον) (103:2) that Enoch has read on the "heavenly tablets":[120] many good things (ἀγαθά), joy (χαρά), and honor (τιμή) are prepared for the souls of the righteous dead, and "their spirits shall not perish nor their memorial from before the face of the Great One unto all the generations of the world" (103:3-4).[121] Their names are written down before God (104:1), bright light will shine upon them (96:3), they will receive salvation (σωτηρία) (98:14; 99:1; 103:10), and they "shall be saved" (σωθήσονται) (99:10).[122] In a formula from Dan. 12:3, they will "shine like the lights of heaven,"[123] and the gates of heaven will be opened to them (αἱ θυρίδες τοῦ οὐρανοῦ ἀνοιχθήσονται ὑμῖν) (104:2).[124]

The sentence just quoted contains an eschatological passive, and there are other examples in the Epistle of Enoch: The sinners will be handed over to the "great curse" and given (παραδοθήσεσθε) into the hands of the righteous (97:10; 98:12); their sins will be read aloud ([ἀναγνωσθήσ]ονται) (97:6); they will be "poured out like water" (ὡς ὕδωρ ἐκχυθήσονται) (98:2). The righ-

118. 1 Enoch 94:6; 98:11, 16; 99:13; 101:3; 102:3; 103:8; (5:4!). It is true that one ought to translate the Greek version as "you have nothing to laugh about," but the formula is derived from LXX Isa. 48:22; 57:21, where χαίρειν translates שלום. Cf. 1 Enoch 12:5: οὐκ ἔσται ὑμῖν εἰρήνη (13:1; 16:4).

119. G. W. E. Nickelsburg correctly emphasizes this aspect of consolation ("Apocalyptic Message," 312, 317–18, 323–36); cf. J. C. H. Lebram, "Piety," 196.

120. For these tablets, on which the whole history of humanity is written, see also 81:1-2; 106:19. On this, cf. E. Rau, Kosmologie, 346–53.

121. This is formulated as an antithesis to 103:7-8.

122. Cf. 1:1; 98:10; 102:1, 7.

123. ὡσεὶ φωστῆρες τοῦ οὐρανοῦ ἀναλάμψετε καὶ φανεῖτε: a combination of the texts of Theodotion and the LXX in Dan. 12:3.

124. According to Ethiopic Enoch 104:6, the righteous will enter into the company of the angels. The Greek text omits this sentence, but G. W. E. Nickelsburg considers it original ("Enoch," 97–104, 133).

teous, on the other hand, will be guarded (τηρηθήσονται) (100:5)—by angels, as the context indicates—and their cries will be heard (ἀκουσθήσεται) (104:3).[125]

Thus in the Epistle of Enoch the reward and happiness of the righteous are only vaguely indicated in abstract concepts and images, much as in the book of Daniel and the book of Wisdom. It is striking that this author never takes up the motif of "life" or "everlasting life."[126] Correspondingly, Sheol is here definitively understood as the place of eternal punishment for sinners who have died. The characteristic of fire (98:3; 100:9; 103:8), which is now present there together with darkness, has been taken over from Gehenna, so that Sheol and Gehenna have become one.[127] But in this way Sheol has lost its purpose as an abode for souls until the final judgment. That judgment has in fact become superfluous if it is not conceived as a judgment immediately after death, and such an idea is nowhere suggested in the Epistle of Enoch. We here encounter the same problem as in the eschatology of the hereafter in the book of Wisdom.[128]

1 Enoch 92:3 speaks of a resurrection of the righteous, and so, indirectly, does 102:8; but in the overall conception, resurrection plays no part at all.[129]

The Book of Parables

The Book of Parables (37–71) represents the latest section of the book of Enoch, but ordinarily it is still dated in the first century B.C.E.[130] According

---

125. The examples can be multiplied on the basis of the Ethiopic text. One example of a noneschatological future passive is δοθήσεται in 104:12.

126. It is found only in 103:4, in an addition to the Ethiopic text that is not present in G.

127. Cf. R. H. Charles, *Enoch*, 256–57, on 103:7; J. Bonsirven, *Judaïsme* 1:330–31; S. Uhlig, *Henochbuch*, 737, 8b. Already in 1 Enoch 22, Sheol is a place of punishment for sinners, or at least some of them. See above, pp. 54–55.

128. See above, p. 45.

129. Cf. K. Schubert, "Auferstehungslehre," 196–97; G. Stemberger, *Leib*, 40–44.

130. R. H. Charles, *Enoch*, 67; Marie-Thérès Wacker, *Weltordnung*, 7–8; M. Delcor, "Paraboles"; S. Uhlig, *Henochbuch*, 574–75; C. C. Caragounis, *Son of man*, 85–94; G. Bampfylde, "Similitudes" (50 B.C.E. at the latest). Matthew Black prefers to date the Book of Parables in the early Roman period, before 70 C.E. (*Enoch*, 183–84; 187–88). F. Corriente and A. Piñero, "Henoc," 21–23, date them between the middle of the first century B.C.E. and the end of the first century C.E. E. Schürer and G. Vermes, *History* 3/1: 259, point to the last quarter of the first century C.E. In the following discussion we will not treat the Noachite sections that were inserted at a later date. For literary criticism, see U. B. Müller, *Messias*, 36–38.

to R. H. Charles, behind the contrast of "righteous" and "elect" on the one side and "sinners," "kings and mighty ones" on the other is, just as in the Epistle of Enoch, the opposition of the Pharisees toward the Sadducees, who were in league with the Hasmonean rulers.[131] These parables repeatedly depict an eschatological judgment scene (45:3-6; 47:3-4; 51:3-5; 61:8; 62–63; 69:27-29), but each time with different, partly contradictory features, so that no unified picture emerges. All contain one common motif: the throne on which the judge is seated. According to 47:3 the judge is God, but elsewhere it is always the "Elect One" (45:3; 51:3; 61:8; 62:2), the "Son of man" (62:5, 7, 9; 63:11; 69:27).[132]

The most extensive description of judgment is offered by chapters 61–63. Because it is not God, but the "Son of man" or "Elect One" who will judge, the day of judgment is called the "day of the Elect One" (61:5). On that day the righteous will rise (61:5),[133] the "Lord of the Spirits" will seat the "Elect One on the throne of his glory; and he [the Elect One] shall judge all the works of the holy ones in heaven above, weighing in the balance their deeds" (61:8). Here for the first time we hear explicitly of a judgment of the righteous and the weighing of their deeds.[134] But that there is no danger for the righteous in this judgment is shown by the thanksgiving song of the elect and the whole heavenly host that follows, and in which God's goodness and mercy are praised (61:9-13).

After this, in chapter 62, the judgment on "the kings, the governors, the high officials, and the landlords" (62:1) is described. It is true that they, like the elect, put their hope in the Son of man and petition him for mercy (62:9), but he judges justly; no "nonsensical talk" can be uttered before him (62:3), and "the word of his mouth will do the sinners in" (62:2). "The Lord of the Spirits" drives them away and hands them over to the angels of punishment, "in order that vengeance shall be executed on them—oppressors of his children and his elect ones" (62:11)—to the satisfaction of the righteous, who rejoice that "the wrath of the Lord of the Spirits shall rest upon them and his

---

131. R. H. Charles, *Enoch*, 72–73. Cf. also P. Volz, *Eschatologie*, 22–23; Volz, however, does not take a definite position.

132. For the figure of the "Elect One" or "Son of man" in the Book of Parables, see U. B. Müller, *Messias*, 38–47; C. C. Caragounis, *Son of Man*, 94–119.

133. The well-known passage at 51:1, on the other hand, presumes a general resurrection of the dead.

134. The latter is also in 4:1 and 38:2 (on which see S. Uhlig, *Henochbuch*, 576, 2c).

sword (shall obtain) from them a sacrifice" (62:12).[135] The remaining verses of this chapter contrast all this with the happiness of the elect, whose community is then "planted" (62:8).[136] They will be clothed with the robe of glory, the unchanging garment of life (62:15-16), "the Lord of the Spirits will abide over them; they shall eat and rest and rise with that Son of man forever and ever" (62:14).[137]

Chapter 63 turns again to the punishment of the mighty who have not honored the Lord and have placed their trust only in their own power, whose souls are "satiated with exploitation money" (63:7-8, 10). They implore the angels of punishment to grant them some respite, but all their sins are counted exactly (63:9), and so they go down "into the flames of the burden of Sheol" (63:10).

Thus we once again find forensic features in this judgment, but there is no genuine judicial process; instead, the verdict is determined beforehand. God's mercy is only for the righteous, and sinners are condemned with implacable justice to the punishment they have earned, to the great satisfaction of the elect.

The remaining judicial scenes and statements merely vary the theme with other motifs—for example, the books of the living (47:3)—or different descriptions of the punishment of sinners "who denied the name of the Lord of the Spirits" (38:2, and frequently elsewhere), and of the happiness of the righteous. According to 38:5 and 48:9, the kings and rulers will be delivered into the hands of the righteous. In chapter 54 the valley of judgment, Gehenna, is described. It is also called a "fiery furnace" (54:6) and equated with Sheol (56:8). According to 69:28 sinners "shall be bound with chains; and their ruinous congregation shall be imprisoned." The names of the angels of punishment are given: Michael, Gabriel, Raphael, and Phanuel (54:6).

The blessedness of the righteous as an entirely earthly phenomenon is also indicated by the use of familiar formulas and motifs.[138] They will "inherit eternal life" (40:9), they will be in the light of the sun and of eternal life (58:3),[139]

---

135. The sword motif seems out of place in this passage. It appears again in 63:11. For the rejoicing of the righteous over the punishment of the wicked, see Str-B 4: 1113–14.

136. According to 38:1, it then becomes "visible." The expression "community of the righteous" goes back to Ps. 1:5. Cf. M. Black (*Enoch*, 194) with Qumran parallels.

137. In 48:4 the Son of man is described as "a staff for the righteous," "light of the gentiles," and "hope of those who are sick in their hearts."

138. Cf. C. Barth, *Diesseits*, 56.

139. For the motif of light, see R. H. Charles, *Enoch*, 71–72, on 38:4.

they will have (eternal) peace (58:4; 71:15), heaven and earth will be changed (cf. Isa. 65:17; 66:22), and the righteous will dwell on earth, while the sinners will disappear from its face (45:4-5; 51:5). A vision, difficult to render in concrete terms, of the "dwelling places of the righteous" appears in 1 Enoch 39.[140] It is almost surprising that the text speaks once of a possible repentance, and of the mercy of the Lord of the Spirits (50:2-3). But on the day of judgment it will be too late (39:2; 50:5).

Thus we find in the Book of Parables both the motifs we previously observed and also some new ones, such as the weighing of deeds, or eating with the Son of man. Nevertheless, the description of the judgment, its function, and its consequences remains essentially the same. Even the person of the "Son of man" changes nothing in it; moreover, that figure alternates easily with God, as is evident from 47:3-4. The Son of man acts and "judge[s] . . . in the name of the Lord of the Spirits" (55:4), just as does the Messiah in the Psalms of Solomon, which originated at the same time.[141]

The Book of Jubilees

The book of Jubilees originated in the second century, probably about 150 B.C.E., in Hasidic or early Essene circles.[142] The complete text has survived only in an Ethiopic translation, with major portions also retained in Syriac and Latin. All these versions, with the possible exception of the Syriac, rest on a Greek translation of the Hebrew original. Hebrew fragments have been found

140. On this, see R. H. Charles, *Enoch*, 74–75: "The chief inference that we can legitimately draw is that the Messianic community will one day be composed of both angels and men, under the rule of the Messiah and the immediate protection of the Lord of Spirits" (p. 75).

141. See above, p. 49.

142. [The English translation is based on that by O. S. Wintermute in *OTP* 1.—Trans.] For the problem of the origins and time of writing, see M. Testuz, *Idées*, 25–39; A.-M. Denis, *Introduction*, 161–62; J. C. VanderKam, *Studies*, 206–85; A Díez Macho, *Introducción general*, 59–62; K. Berger, *Jubiläen* 298–301; O. S. Wintermute, "Jubilees," 43–44; E. Schürer and G. Vermes, *History* 3/1: 311–14. For J. Klausner, Jubilees is an early Pharisaic work, "the most ancient Midrash that we have" (*Messianic Idea*, 302). R. H. Charles also regards this writing as a Pharisaic work, but at the earliest from the period 135–105 B.C.E. (*Jubilees* xiii, li-lvi, lviii-lxvi, lxxiii). A. Caquot now dates Jubilees in the same period ("Eléments aggadiques") and regards it as an Essene writing. J. A. Goldstein ("Date"), on the other hand, regards it as falling between the autumn of 169 and the spring of 167 B.C.E.; similarly G. W. E. Nickelsburg in M. E. Stone, ed., *Jewish Writings*, 101–3.

at Qumran.[143] The book offers a midrashic retelling of the biblical story from creation to the time of Moses, and reveals striking agreements especially with Essene literature from Qumran.[144]

Future history up to the end time is sketched twice: in 1:5-26, 27-29; and in 23:9-32. The two sections are in some ways mutually enhancing: In chapter 1 the events leading up to the beginning of the end are narrated in detail, and the end time is treated rather briefly (vv. 23-26, 27-29); in chapter 23 the generations to the end time are merely summarized, while the eschatological events are described at length (vv. 16-31). In the description in chapter 1 it is striking that the end time begins immediately with the conversion of the people to God and God's commandments (1:23; cf. 1:15). This motif of end time conversion of the people is derived from Deut. 4:30: "In your distress, when all these things have happened to you at the end of days (בְּאַחֲרִית הַיָּמִים, LXX: ἐπ᾽ ἐσχάτῳ τῶν ἡμερῶν), you will return to the Lord your God and listen to his voice."[145] Thus Israel enters immediately, without judgment, into eternal blessedness made available by God's parental love and Holy Spirit (1:23-25). Then God will dwell with the people forever (1:26). In the following verses, 27-29, after a new beginning ("And he said . . .") there are references to the building of the eschatological Temple, God's royal rule on Zion, the sanctity of Jerusalem, and the renewal of heaven and earth.[146] According to v. 28, everyone will then acknowledge that God is "father of all the children of Jacob and king upon mount Zion forever and ever"; but according to v. 29 it is only "the elect of Israel" who will receive "healing and peace and blessing" forever.

The presentation in chapter 23 is different. After the Flood, human lifetimes decrease and in the period "henceforth [that is, from the generation of Moses]

143. K. Berger, *Jubiläen*, 285–93.
144. Ibid., 295–98.
145. Cf. 2 Chr. 6:38; Hos. 3:5, and the Temple Roll from Qumran, 59.9-11. Isa. 10:20-23 speaks of the conversion of a "remnant" before the "decreed destruction."
146. Cf. Isa. 65:17; 66:22-23. According to G. L. Davenport these verses, which are poorly integrated and are in tension with what precedes them, are the insertion of a redactor (*Eschatology*, 29–31). But the emphasis on the end time sanctuary corresponds exactly to the significance assigned to the Temple in 1:10, 15. In 1:16-18, moreover, the postexilic period is described in eschatological terms. The parallelism with the motif of conversion in vv. 15 and 23 should also be considered here. All this speaks rather for the original unity of chapter 1, although a redaction cannot be excluded, as the difference in the recipients of salvation in vv. 28 and 29 indicates. For an analysis, cf. also E. Rau, *Kosmologie*, 365–66. The eschatological sanctuary is also mentioned in 25:21; cf. 4:26 as well.

until the day of the great judgment" (23:11) they attain a maximum of 70 years, or 80 for the very strong (23:15; cf. Ps. 90:10). The people of that time— this may refer only to the last generation before the end—are lumped together as "an evil generation" or "this evil generation" (Latin: *generatio quae est iniqua, generatio illa pessima*) (23:14, 15). "And in this generation children will convict (Latin: *arguere*) their parents and their elders on account of sin, and on account of injustice," and for having forsaken God's law (23:16).[147] This introduces the end time. But the conversion does not result, as in chapter 1, in immediate blessedness; instead, it leads first to bloody wars in which the young are ranged against the old, the poor against the rich, and the lowly against the powerful "concerning the law and the covenant" (23:19). This is undoubtedly a reference to the Maccabean revolt, as are the words in vv. 22-25 about captivity, plunder, and Gentile attacks against the land.[148]

In this description, kept rigorously within realistic bounds, by means of which the author interprets his own time as the beginning of the end, v. 18 stands out oddly: "Behold, the land will be corrupted on account of all their deeds, and there will be no seed of the vine, and there will be no oil, for their works are entirely faithless. And all of them will be destroyed together: wild beasts, cattle, birds, and all of the fish of the sea on account of the sons of man." Much as in the traditions of the "day of YHWH," we find judgment represented here, in contradiction to the context, as a universal day of destruction encompassing all creation.

After the conversion of the "children" in v. 16 and the description of the sufferings of the Maccabean period, it is surprising to find a second reference to a conversion of the "children" to "the way of righteousness" and their "search[ing] the commandments" in v. 26. This verse can scarcely be interpreted as referring to a historical event *after* the Maccabean wars.[149] The conversion of the "children," however, immediately introduces the blessedness of the eschatological time, just as in 1:23. The lifetimes of human beings increase until they approach 1,000 years (23:27). A time of blessing and healing comes,

147. "This verse points most probably to the rise of the Chasids" (R. H. Charles, *Jubilees*, 146).

148. R. H. Charles, *Jubilees*, 146, 147–48; M. Testuz, *Idées*, 167; M. Hengel, *Judaism* 1: 54; G. L. Davenport, *Eschatology*, 41–43, 45–46. Verse 21 refers to the Maccabees' failure (M. Hengel, *Judaism* 1: 226; he speaks, however, of "23:21ff."). G. L. Davenport therefore regards this as a later insertion (*Eschatology*, 43–44). J. C. VanderKam sees this as a reference to Alcimus and his party (*Studies*, 253–54).

149. The Essenes may have referred it to the founding of their community.

a time when there is no Satan (23:29).[150] "And then the Lord will heal his servants, and they will rise up [or be raised?] and see great peace. And they will drive out his [or their] enemies, and the righteous ones will see and give praise, and rejoice for ever and ever with joy; and they will see all of their judgments and all of their curses among their enemies. And their bones will rest in the earth, and their spirits will increase in joy, and they will know that the Lord is an executor of judgment; but he will show mercy to hundreds, and thousands, to all who love him" (23:30-31).[151]

The doubling of the conversion motif (vv. 16 and 26) indicates that in vv. 26-31 (or 24-31) we are dealing with a description of the end time that originally was not associated with vv. 16-25 (or 16-23), but follows very well after v. 15.[152] As in Isa. 66:18-24, the salvation of the "servants" of God and the punishment of their enemies, which they witness, form the crucial contrast.[153] Beyond this, the text remains vague. Verse 30 wastes not a word on the "day of great judgment," to which v. 11 refers in connection with the shortening of life spans. Its temporal location within the course of the eschatological events remains indeterminate, but in any case it does not fall at the end of the period of salvation, but before it.[154]

Besides these extensive eschatological overviews in chapters 1 and 23, there are eschatological statements scattered throughout the entire book, from which we can derive other ideas about the final judgment. Several times we find the formula ". . . until the day of the (great) judgment."[155] Thus the "Watchers" (10:5) are bound in the depths of the earth, just as in 1 Enoch 10:12, "until the day of great judgment" (5:10). That day is also called "the day of wrath and anger" (Latin: *dies irae et indignationis*), and similar expressions (24:28, 30; 36:10). On that day God will judge evildoers "with a sword and with fire" (9:15; cf. Isa. 66:16) and will burn up their land just as Sodom was

150. Cf. 40:9, where Joseph's rule in Egypt is described in terms recalling the eschatological time of salvation. According to 50:5, the eschatological healing includes complete purification.

151. For the problem of whether and in what sense the text here speaks of a resurrection, see M. Hengel, *Judaism* 1: 198–99; H. C. Cavallin, "Leben," 277–78; K. Berger, *Jubiläen*, 446, on 30c, e.

152. According to G. L. Davenport, vv. 24-31 were once an eschatological poem that a redactor interpreted to apply to his own time by means of the prose description in vv. 16-23 (*Eschatology*, 33–35).

153. For a comparison with Isaiah 65–66, see G. W. E. Nickelsburg, *Resurrection*, 21–22.

154. F. Martin, "Livre," 529–30; N. Messel, *Einheitlichkeit*, 25–27.

155. *Jub.* 4:19, 24; 5:20; 9:15; 10:22; 23:11.

burned (36:10).[156] It is written on the heavenly tablets that no Philistine shall survive (24:30,33). The same is true of the descendants of Lot, the Moabites and Ammonites (16:9).

However, not only is the whole of history until the "last days" written on the heavenly tablets,[157] but also the whole of the Law,[158] and thereby also "the judgment" on all who do not act according to it (5:13).[159] "Judgment" is here to be understood in the sense of "sentence" or "punishment."[160] This sentence written in the Law is probably to be thought of in terms of Deuteronomy 27–30. Good and evil deeds are immediately registered in books, or on the heavenly tablets (30:19,23; 39:6), and human beings are written down as friends or enemies of God (19:9; 30:20,21,22). According to 4:6 it is angels who tell God about sins; in 4:23-24 it is Enoch who writes "condemnation and judgment of the world, and all of the evils of the children of [humanity]," because he was given as "a sign" to bear witness and "so that he might relate all of the deeds of the generations until the day of judgment" (cf. 10:17).

The motif of books of deeds points to an idea of a forensic judgment, and in fact God is described in various places as a just judge who cannot be bribed, and who judges without respect to persons (5:16; 21:4; 33:18), "the great one according to his greatness and the small one according to his smallness, and each one according to his way" (5:15). This is explicitly true of all human beings (5:15). "And for the children of Israel it has been written and ordained, 'If they return to him in righteousness, he will forgive all of their sins and he will pardon all of their transgressions'" (5:17). According to the next verse, the annual repentance on the Day of Atonement is sufficient.[161] The opportunity for the forgiveness of every sin that is here emphasized contradicts what has

156. For the exemplary function of the judgment on Sodom and Gomorrah, cf. also 16:5-6,9; 22:22. In 20:5-6 Abraham tells his children about the judgment on the giants and on Sodom and Gomorrah as cautionary examples. Abraham no doubt functions here as a pedagogical model.

157. Cf. *Jub.* 1:4-5,27; 31:32; 32:21.

158. Cf. *Jub.* 4:32; 15:25; 28:6; 30:9; 32:10.

159. For the heavenly tablets in Jubilees, see R. H. Charles, *Jubilees*, 24–25; E. Rau, *Kosmologie*, 359–77; C. Münchow, *Ethik*, 44–49; F. García Martínez, "Las Tablas." The last author emphasizes that these tablets also contain some new *halakhot* that are not written in the Torah (3:31; 4:32; 15:25; 28:6; 30:9; 32:10-15). They thus have the same function as the oral Torah of the rabbis (idem, 348–49).

160. Cf. E. Littmann's translation of 5:13-14.

161. This corresponds to later rabbinic teaching whereby a person can reverse the verdict of salvation or damnation passed on the day of New Year through repentance on the Day of Atonement (E. K. Dietrich, *Umkehr*, 375, 410–16).

gone before, as well as the warnings about a "mortal sin" that can exclude even the children of Israel from salvation (21:22; 26:34).[162]

The place of punishment associated with this judgment is also named: According to 22:22 there is "no hope in the land of the living" for idolaters and the perverse on the day of judgment,[163] "because they will go down into Sheol. And in the place of judgment they will walk, and they will have no memory upon the earth" (cf. 7:29). In this "place of judgment" the demons will also be imprisoned (10:5,9). The same punishment is intended when it is said of the Philistines that they will "walk in an eternal curse" (24:32). In 36:10 the same thing is described as "not be[ing] written in The Book of Life, [but rather] in the one which will be destroyed."[164] The following sentence then speaks of the ever-renewed torment of this punishment, which threatens everyone "who seeks evil against his brother" (36:9).

Thus the historical day of judgment in the book of Jubilees appears sometimes as a judgment of punishment and destruction in the tradition of the "day of YHWH," and sometimes as a judgment with forensic features. In the second concept, Sheol functions as a place of eternal punishment. It is striking that the contrast between righteous and sinners plays no role in any part of the book. It is true that the "elect of Israel" are mentioned in 1:29, but they are not antithetical to the wicked, nor are the "righteous ones" in 23:30. This author is concerned not merely with the righteous and the elect, but with all the "children of Israel." Still, he makes it clear that, even of these, only those will be saved who adhere to the Law written in the Torah and on the heavenly tablets, and who do penance at least once a year, on the Day of Atonement (5:18). Hence there is no hope for the uncircumcised (15:26). On the day of judgment they will be destroyed, or else they, together with the sinners of Israel, will go into Sheol, the place of eternal torment. Of the fate of the dead until the day of judgment, we learn nothing from the book of Jubilees.

---

162. Cf. also 15:34. On this, see E. P. Sanders, *Paul,* 367–74; A. Díez Macho, *Introducción general,* 185–86.

163. For "the land of the living," see Pss. 27:13; 116:9; 142:5.

164. The fact that in each case this refers to the same thing is shown by the formula "the land of the living," which is repeated in each of these passages (22:22; 36:9), as well as the description of this punishment as a "curse" (24:32; 36:10; cf. 1 Enoch 5:5-6, 27; 97:10). Still, such formulas can also refer to the historical judgment of destruction as well. Thus 30:23 (Latin): *Si autem transgressi fuerint testamentum et fecerint ex omnibus viis abominationum quaecumque scripta sunt in tabulis caeli, inimici Dei erunt et delebuntur de libro vitae et scribentur in libro perditionum inter eos qui eradicantur a terra.*

Qumran

The Psalms

In the psalms of the Teacher of Righteousness,[165] written after his break with the temple in Jerusalem, thus probably ca. 140 B.C.E.,[166] we encounter the familiar division between "wicked" (רְשָׁעִים) (II, 10, 12; IV, 34) and "elect of righteousness" (בְּחִירֵי צֶדֶק) (II, 13).[167] The former are also called "sons of iniquity" (VI, 30; VII, 11), "lying prophets deceived by error" (IV, 20); "children of mischief" (V, 25), and so on. They have gone astray from God's covenant (IV, 19), trespassed against God's word (IV, 27), seek God with divided hearts and do not stand firm in God's truth (IV, 14), for "a counsel of Belial is in their heart" (VI, 21–22). But for all this God will "destroy them in judgment" (תִּכְרַת בַּמִּשְׁפָּט) (IV, 20, 26) with fire (VI, 18–19) and sword, when the "sons of his truth" arise to destroy the "sons of iniquity" (VI, 29–30). Then the survivors will stand before God forever (IV, 21) in the company of the "Angels of the Face" (VI, 13).[168] The ultimate judgment and accomplished salvation are in the future, but even now the lot of the one and the other group is being decided. Hence the present is seen completely in its eschatological aspect.[169]

All these are strongly traditional topoi and motifs. What is new and unheard-of, however, is the role in which the Teacher sees himself: "For thou wilt condemn in judgment all those who assail me, distinguishing through me (or: in me, בִּי) between the just and the wicked" (VI, 12; cf. Mal. 3:18). "I have been a snare to those who rebel, but healing to those of them who repent" (II,

---

165. [The English translations of the Qumran texts are based substantially on those in Geza Vermes, *The Dead Sea Scrolls in English*, 3rd ed. (London: Penguin, 1987). — Trans.] In these psalms I include, in agreement with G. Jeremias (*Lehrer,* 171) and P. Schulz (*Autoritätsanspruch,* 5), 1QH II, 1–19; II, 31–39; III, 1–18; IV, 5–V, 4; V, 5–19; V, 20–VII, 5; VII, 6–25; VIII, 4–40. The same list, without II, 31–39; III, 1–18, is in H.-W. Kuhn, *Enderwartung,* 23. For the eschatology of Qumran, compare throughout E. Puech, *La croyance des Esséniens en la vie future.*

166. For the dating of the Teacher's life, see M. Hengel, *Judaism* 1: 224–27; H. Bardtke, "Literaturbericht," Part 10. J. C. Trever sees him as the final redactor of the book of Daniel (see above, chap. 2).

167. On this, see S. Holm-Nielsen, *Hodayot,* 290–93.

168. On the last two passages, see M. Delcor, *Hymnes,* 144, 176. The company of the angels I interpret here, differently from III, 22, as future-eschatological. This is indicated by VI, 12 and the broader context (vv. 6, 8). On this problem, cf. H.-W. Kuhn, *Enderwartung,* 74–75.

169. J. Becker, *Heil,* 72.

8–9). In and through his own person, that is, through their attitude toward his preaching,[170] Israel is divided into righteous and wicked, and in this sense God has "established him . . . for justice" (לְמִשְׁפָּט יְסַדְתַּנִי) (V, 8–9)[171] and "as a banner to the elect of righteousness" (II, 13).[172]

The Teacher's consciousness of mission can only be compared with that of Jesus.[173] It is also the foundation of his community's confidence that it is the "shoot" of the "everlasting plant" (VI, 15; VIII, 6) in contrast to the "horde of Belial" (II, 22), for "all those who observe the Law in the House of Judah" God will "deliver from the House of Judgment[174] because of their suffering and because of their faith in the Teacher of Righteousness" (1QpHab VIII, 1–3). Hence they know that they live already the life of salvation, even though its complete realization is still in the future.[175]

The eschatological framework presented by the Teacher's psalms is augmented by a few other features in the remaining psalms. Most striking is the idea of predestination, as expressed in XV, 14–20. According to this passage, God has destined the righteous from their mother's womb for the "time of goodwill" (מוֹעֵד רָעוֹן), for "eternal salvation (יְשׁוּעָה), . . . perpetual and unfailing peace (שָׁלוֹם)" (XV, 15–16). Correspondingly, God has destined the wicked from their mother's womb for the "day of massacre" (יוֹם הֲרֵגָה)[176] and for "great chastisements" (XV, 17, 19). Hence the duty of human beings can only be to recognize the end for which they are destined.[177] The expression "execute judgment on" appears in the Old Testament, especially in Ezekiel, and there refers to God's punishments within history, especially the catastrophe of 587

170. G. Jeremias correctly emphasizes this (*Lehrer*, 188–89). For this self-interpretation of the Teacher, cf. also ibid., 197–99, 266–67.

171. G. Jeremias (*Lehrer*, 219), E. Lohse and others translate מִשְׁפָּט here as "law" because of the parallelism with "counsel of truth" in the next line, but I am more inclined to see a parallel to VII, 12 (with J. Maier, *Texte* 2: 82, ad loc.). On this problem, cf. P. Schulz, *Autoritätsanspruch*, 65. He also decides for the interpretation "law."

172. Cf. M. Delcor, *Hymnes*, 97; G. Jeremias, *Lehrer*, 199–200.

173. G. Jeremias, *Lehrer*, 334–35.

174. The reference is to the final judgment: 1QpHab X, 3–4. G. Jeremias, *Lehrer*, 48.

175. This tension between present and future eschatology may no more be resolved in favor of the present than it is for Jesus or Paul, even though this is what P. Schulz does. According to him, the Teacher is not awaiting the inbreaking of the end time salvation, but sees it already realized in the covenant of Qumran (*Autoritätsanspruch*, 101). Against this position, cf. H.-W. Kuhn, *Enderwartung*, 188; C. Barth, *Diesseits*, 76–77. For present eschatology in Qumran, see also D. E. Aune, *Realized Eschatology*, 29–44.

176. Jer. 12:3.

177. Cf. D. Dimant in M. E. Stone, ed., *Jewish Writings*, 536–38.

B.C.E.[178] Here it is applied to the final judgment (cf. 1QM XI, 16; 11QMelch XIII). The parallels in construction and formulation between the two series of statements[179] make the correlation between judgment (on sinners) and salvation (for the righteous) especially clear.

> H.-W. Kuhn, who treats this section at length (*Enderwartung,* 38–39, 104–14), emphasizes that the "time of God's pleasure" is not seen here as purely future. It is true that "eternal salvation," "lasting peace" and "abundance" are unmistakably future-eschatological in conception, but he thinks that the preceding statements, especially about preservation in the covenant, refer to the present existence of the faithful, and that a sharp distinction between eschatological and noneschatological statements is not possible here. "The yawning gap between present and future, as seen in apocalyptic, is thus not present here. The song rather says that the coming eschaton is already happening" (p. 107. Cf. also 115–16 and the summary on 179–80). This is undoubtedly correct; however, it must be emphasized that early apocalyptic, in particular, does not recognize a "yawning gap between present and future" in a temporal sense. Consider only the Ten-Week Apocalypse! The crucial difference is rather, as Kuhn correctly observes elsewhere, that "for apocalyptic the present was empty of salvation, and here salvation can only be hoped for in future," while for the faithful of Qumran "God's present salvation was already a reality in the community" (p. 182).

According to another psalm, the "time of wrath" (קֵץ חָרוֹן) will come upon "all Belial" (III, 28) with a torrent of fire (III, 29–35) and the "war of the heavenly warriors" that hastens over the earthly sphere, until all that is at enmity with God is destroyed forever (III, 35-36).[180] Then God's righteousness will be revealed before the eyes of all creatures (XIV, 16).

Alongside these statements that apply to the future "judgment [of punishment] of the wicked" (מִשְׁפַּט רְשָׁעִים) (II, 24), we also find noneschatological sayings about judgment that employ the image of a forensic situation. They are in the tradition of the Old Testament doxology of judgment.[181] "I [am] a shape of clay . . . , an edifice of sin . . . and fearful of righteous judgments, and

178. Exod. 12:12; Num. 33:4; Ezek. 5:10, 15; 11:9; 16:41; 25:11; 28:22, 26; 30:14, 19. Cf. Ezek. 5:8.
179. On this, see S. Holm-Nielsen, *Hodayot,* 230. It is expressed even better in a text that is printed in verses and sense-lines. Cf. J. Maier's translation and H.-W. Kuhn, *Enderwartung,* 38–39, 104–5.
180. Cf. M. Delcor, *Hymnes,* 61–62. On the "little apocalypse" in III, 26–36, see M. Delcor, *Hymnes,* 131; H.-W. Kuhn, *Enderwartung,* 40–43, 61; J. J. Collins, "Patterns," 370–72.
181. J. Becker, *Heil,* 135.

what can I utter that is not foretold . . . All things are graven before Thee on a written Reminder for everlasting ages . . . What shall a man say concerning his sin? And how shall he plead concerning his iniquities? And how shall he reply to righteous judgment (מִשְׁפַּט הַצֶּדֶק)?" (I, 21–26). "No one can be just in Thy judgment, or [righteous in] Thy trial" (IX, 14–15).[182] Therefore the one praying trusts that God will judge the righteous graciously, "in . . . great lovingkindness and in the multitude of [God's] mercies" (VI, 9). As the context shows, such statements are to be understood against the background of the anthropology of these psalms; their intent, as with the Old Testament psalms (for example, Pss. 51:6; 130:3), is only to emphasize the frailty and sinfulness of human beings.[183] It is striking that the motif of the book of deeds in I, 24 is thus employed in a completely noneschatological context and is not intended, as it is elsewhere, to call the attention of sinners to the threat of judgment, but to alert the righteous to their nothingness.[184]

The Damascus Document

In the Damascus Document as well,[185] the idea of judgment presupposes a difference between the "covenant of repentance" (XIX, 16) established by the Teacher of Righteousness (I, 11) and the "congregation of traitors" (I, 12). God "has a lawsuit (רִיב) with all flesh and exercises judgment on all those who despise him" (I, 2).[186] God has begun this "lawsuit" with Israel because "they were unfaithful" (I, 3), and has punished them through Nebuchadnezzar's conquest of Jerusalem (I, 3), the "first visitation" (VII, 21; XIX, 11).[187] Now a

182. Cf. also VII, 28; XII, 28–31; fragment 4.10. F. Nötscher, *Terminologie*, 161–62, who, however, understands these sayings as eschatological. Against this position, see J. Becker, *Heil*, 142.

183. S. Holm-Nielsen, *Hodayot*, 275. See the extensive treatment in J. Becker, *Heil*, 135–62; H. Lichtenberger, *Menschenbild*, 73–93.

184. Cf. S. Holm-Nielsen, *Hodayot*, 25.

185. I cannot and need not enter in detail here into the difficult tradition-historical, literary-critical, and historical problems connected with this document. It is true that it reflects a later stratum of tradition than 1QH, 1QM and 1QS (Peter von der Osten-Sacken, *Gott und Belial*, 190–96), but it may contain pre-Qumran material. There is a review of research in P. D. Davies, *Covenant*, 3–47. Cf. also M. Delcor, *DBSup.* 9: 845–48; M. Delcor and F. García Martínez, *Introducción*, 77–81; E. Schürer and G. Vermes, *History* 3/1: 389–96.

186. Cf. Jer. 25:31; Hos. 4:1. On this sentence, see P. R. Davies, *Covenant*, 65–67. "Lawsuit" and "judgment" refer here first of all to the history of Israel summarized in 1.3–7, but the sentence is certainly gnomic in intent.

187. For this identification of the "first visitation," see P. R. Davies, *Damascus Covenant*, 153–54; cf. O. H. Steck, *Israel*, 166.

second, final "visitation" is about to happen; with it comes "retribution of the wicked" (VII, 9; XIX, 6), and in it God will also execute judgment on the backsliding members of the "covenant" (VIII, 1–2; XIX, 13–14). Then comes the word of the prophet Isaiah (Isa. 7:17): "The Lord will bring upon you, and upon your people, and upon your ancestral house, days such as have not come since the day that Ephraim departed from Judah" (VII, 11–12). The words of Zechariah are fulfilled (Zech. 13:7): "Awake, O sword, . . . strike the shepherd, that the sheep may be scattered" (XIX, 7–8), and also those of Hosea (Hos. 5:10): "The princes of Judah have become like those who remove the landmark; on them I will pour out my wrath like water" (XIX, 15–16).[188] That will be the time of "the coming of the Messiah of Aaron and Israel" (XIX, 10–11). However, he[189] is not assigned an active role in judgment.[190] That is carried out, rather, by the "Angels of Destruction," who will go forth with flames of fire against those who despise the Law (II, 5–6).

On the other hand, God has already determined the names of the "remnant"[191] (II, 11, 13). For them a "book of remembrance"[192] has been written (XX, 19). They are "those called by name who shall stand at the end of days" (IV, 4), the "remnant" that God has left in Israel (I, 4–5). The list of their names, according to IV, 5–6, also contains biographical information. They are destined for "everlasting life" (חַיֵּי נֶצַח) (III, 20), and to them will be revealed "salvation and righteousness" (יֶשַׁע וּצְדָקָה) (XX, 20). That this salvation is expected here on earth is indicated by I, 8 and II, 11–12.[193]

The War Scroll

The War Scroll gives an extensive description of the war, at the end of time, of the "sons of light" against the "sons of darkness" and the army of Belial (Satan) (I, 1) on the "day of destruction" and "vengeance" (II, 11; VII, 5), and it makes predictions about it. This war will last forty years[194] and will bring with it

188. For the original unity of VII, 9–13b with XIX, 7–14, and thus of the three prophetic citations as well, see J. Murphy-O'Connor, "Original Text." P. R. Davies essentially agrees: *Damascus Covenant,* 145–47.

189. For the singular, see M. Delcor and F. García Martínez, *Introducción,* 84–85.

190. Cf., on the contrary, VII, 20–21, where it is said of the Davidic Messiah that "when he comes, he shall smite all the children of Seth."

191. Cf. Isa. 66:19; Ezek. 14:22; Joel 3:5; Obad. 14, 17. Cf. 1 Enoch 83:8; 90:30; 4 Ezra 6:25; 7:28; 9:8; 12:34; 13:24, 26; *2 Bar* 29:4; *Sib. Or.* 5.384. For the idea of the "remnant" in Qumran, see J. Schmitt, "Les écrits," *RevSR* 30 (1956): 59–62.

192. Cf. Mal. 3:16.

193. J. Becker, *Heil,* 187. Cf. C. Barth, *Diesseits,* 73–74.

194. Cf. 1QM II, 6; CD XX, 14–15; 4QpPs 37. 2,6.

destruction for "all the nations of wickedness" (XV, 2). The struggle against Belial and his army will be led by God in person (I, 4–5, 14–15; cf. XVIII, 1–3), and it will end, for the sons of darkness and "all the company of Belial" with "everlasting destruction" (I, 5; IX, 5–6), but for the sons of light its end is "peace, blessing, glory, joy, and long life" when "at the season appointed by God, His exalted greatness shall shine eternally" (I, 8–9).[195]

According to another tradition in the War Scroll, as in Dan. 12:1, God sends the angel Michael to assist God's own "lot" in the struggle, but also to "enlighten with joy [the children] of Israel; peace and blessing shall be with the company of God. He will raise up the kingdom of Michael in the midst of the gods, and the realm of Israel in the midst of all flesh" (XVII, 7–8).[196] That this tradition, although more recent than the one previously mentioned,[197] must be very old is evident from the fact that here, in contradistinction to the other texts from Qumran, the contrast between Israel and the nations still has a part to play.[198]

The Community Rule

The Community Rule's eschatology combines material, motifs, and concepts especially from the War Scroll and the community psalms. This is particularly evident in the catalogs of good and evil.[199] God created human beings "to govern the world, and has appointed for them two spirits in which to walk until the day of their visitation" (עַד מוֹעֵד פְּקוּדָּתוֹ) (III, 17–18), "until the appointed time of judgment" (עַד קֵץ נֶחֱרָצָה וַעֲשׂוֹת חֲדָשָׁה) (IV, 25).[200] For those

195. "Salvation is thus a condition of earthly happiness based on a theophanic presence of God" (J. Becker, *Heil,* 82). Cf. C. Barth, *Diesseits,* 70–71.

196. Cf. also XIII, 10. Michael, the "prince of light," as leader in the struggle against the "angels of darkness" is also found in 1QS III, 20, 24. According to G. Bampfylde ("Prince"), Michael is, however, not identical with the "prince of light."

197. Peter von der Osten-Sacken, *Gott und Belial,* 99.

198. For this and associated problems in the War Scroll, see Peter von der Osten-Sacken, *Gott und Belial,* 108.

199. Ibid., 121–23, 158–63; M. Delcor and F. García Martínez, *Introducción,* 290–91.

200. For this terminology, cf. also IV, 16–17: ". . . until the final age;" IV, 19–20: ". . . until the appointed time of judgment;" X, 19: ". . . until the day of revenge." All of them mean the same thing (cf. E. Rau, *Kosmologie,* 177, 388–91). Cf. also *Jub.* 4:19, 24; 5:10; 9:15; 10:22; 23:11; *T. Levi* 1:1; *Adam and Eve* 12.1; 26.4. Cf. *As. Mos.* 1.18; *Sib. Or.* 1.273; *Bib. Ant.* 3.9 (*donec compleantur tempora*); 23.13 (*quousque compleatur tempus saeculi*); *Adam and Eve* 37.5; 43.2. For the term "until the new creation" cf. 1 Enoch 72:1: ". . . till the new creation which abides forever is created" (on this, cf. E. Rau, *Kosmologie,* 174–83; S. Uhlig, *Henochbuch,* 638; M. Black, "New Creation," 13–14); 4 Ezra 7:75: *donec veniant tempora illa in quibus incipies creaturam renovare* (see below). This kind of terminology is also associated with other eschatological gifts and events,

who walk in the spirit of truth, this visitation will lead to "healing, great peace in a long life" (אוֹרֶךְ יָמִים), and "fruitfulness, together with every everlasting blessing and eternal joy without end, a crown of glory and a garment of majesty in unending light" (IV, 6–8). "Life without end" here means nothing more than "a long lifetime." "Forever" must still be understood in the Old Testament sense of an immeasurably long time. Thus the idea of the time of salvation has not moved essentially beyond Isaiah 65.[201] However, the "sons of truth" must also be purified before this time of salvation, and cleansed with the "spirit of holiness" (IV, 20–22).[202]

For those who walk in the spirit of wickedness, on the other hand, the appointed visitation leads to "a multitude of plagues by the hand of all the destroying angels, everlasting damnation by the avenging wrath of the fury of God, eternal torment and endless disgrace together with shameful extinction in the fire of the dark regions" (IV, 12–13). In II, 7–8 the text also speaks of the "shadowy place of everlasting fire" for "those who are cursed forever" (II, 17). Darkness and fire, of course, are the characteristics of Sheol in 1 Enoch 103:7-8; there the souls of sinners who have died are brought down to eternal suffering. This has tempted many interpreters to suppose that they could find hints of this kind of eschatology of the hereafter also in 1QS II, 7–8; IV, 13.[203] However, in doing so they overlook the context of these passages. The motif of darkness combined with fire appears in 1QS not in the context of an eschatology of the hereafter that is concerned, as in 1 Enoch 103:7-8, with the fate of the individual dead *before* the day of visitation; instead, it is incorporated into historical eschatology as an image for the punishment that will be executed on the wicked on the day of visitation, "eternal destruction, . . . leaving no remnant" (V, 12–13).

Like the community psalms, the community rule contains a present eschatology in which the author sees himself already enjoying the gifts of salvation

---

for example, *Jub.* 1:26 (until God descends and dwells among the children of God); 1:29 (". . . until the day when the sanctuary of the Lord is created in Jerusalem on mount Zion"); Dan. 9:27; 11:36 (". . . until the period of wrath is completed"). A corresponding formula refers to the coming of the Messiah or another figure of the end time: 1QS IX, 11; CD VI, 10–11; XII, 23–24; XX, 1; 4Qpatr 3–4; 1 Macc. 4:46; 14:41. Cf. Gen. 49:10; Ezra 2:63; Neh. 7:65; Ezek. 21:32; Hos. 10:12. On this, see N. A. Dahl, "Eschatologie," 7.

201. Cf. C. Barth, *Diesseits*, 66.

202. The background is Ezek. 36:25–27. Cf. *Jub.* 1:23; 50:5. Peter von der Osten-Sacken, *Gott und Belial*, 177–79; B. Janowski and H. Lichtenberger, "Enderwartung und Reinheitsidee," esp. 54–57. For possession of the Spirit as eschatological gift in the Qumran writings, see also R. Schnackenburg, "Anbetung," 89–92.

203. Thus, for example, M. Philonenko, "L'apocalyptique qoumrânienne," 214.

that are, in essence, promised only for the time after the "visitation"—for example, the community of the angels (XI, 7), or purification from all human uncleanness, by which he sees himself as "justified" (XI, 14–15).[204]

11Q Melch

The role assigned to the angel Michael in 1QM and 1QS is given in a document of which we unfortunately possess only a few scraps, difficult to decipher (11Q Melch)[205] to Melchizedek.[206] In the end time, at the end of the tenth Jubilee (7),[207] Melchizedek will "avenge the vengeance of the judgments of God" (יקום נק[מ]ת מישפטי אל[ל)[208] on Belial and the spirits of his "lot," to seize the righteous from their hand (13);[209] in this the angels help him (14). The expression "vengeance of the judgments of God" is a variation on the "day of vengeance of our God" in Isa. 61:2.[210] We already saw, with regard to a corresponding expression in 1QH XV, 19, that the plural "judgments," which we encounter in the Old Testament only with reference to God's punishments within history, was applied in Qumran to the final judgment.[211]

However, Melchizedek's judgment coincides with the inbreaking of the "year of grace for Melchizedek" (9; cf. Isa. 61:2) and for all the members of the

204. On this, see H.-W. Kuhn, *Enderwartung*, 170–73.
205. First published by A. S. van der Woude, "Melchizedek." Cf. also M. de Jonge and A. S. van der Woude, "11Q Melchizedek"; J. A. Fitzmyer, "Melchizedek"; J. Carmignac, "Document"; J. T. Milik, "Milkî-ṣedeq"; F. L. Horton, *Melchizedek Tradition*, 64–82; P. J. Kobelski, *Melchizedek*, 3–23; C. Gianotto, *Melchisedek*, 64–86; M. Delcor and F. García Martínez, *Introducción*, 261–64; E. Puech, "Notes."
206. Cf. A. S. van der Woude, "Melchizedek," 369–70. According to Peter von der Osten-Sacken, one should not speak of an identification of the two figures (*Gott und Belial*, 208–9). On the contrary, P. Kobelski thinks that "[i]n all probability, this identification was explicitly made in 4Q ʿAmramᵇ 3:2" (*Melchizedek*, 71; cf. 71–74). Cf. also C. Gianotto, *Melchizedek*, 79–81; E. Puech, "Notes," 411.
207. On this, see J. T. Milik, "Milkî-ṣedeq," 103–4, 110, 124.
208. However, J. Carmignac thinks that the first two words are illegible, or at any rate should not be reconstructed as given here ("Document," 354–55). Against this, see J. T. Milik, "Milkî-ṣedeq," 106: "unfounded objections."
209. F. Laubscher's reconstruction of these lines reads: "And Melchizedek will exact the ve[nge]ance of the judg[m]ents of Go[d, and he will help all the Children of Light from the power of Be]lial and from the power of all [the spirits of] his [lot]" ("God's Angel of Truth," 50). P. J. Kobelski also accepts this reconstruction (*Melchizedek*, 18–19). Cf. A. S. van der Woude, art. "Melchizedek," *IDBSup.*, 585. J. T. Milik's reconstruction is slightly different ("Milkî-ṣedeq," 99, 106).
210. Thus A. S. van der Woude ("Melchizedek," 365, 368) and J. A. Fitzmyer, "Melchizedek," 38. The whole text is marked by plays on Isa. 61:1-2: M. P. Miller, "Function"; J. A. Sanders, "Isaiah 61," 90–91.
211. See above, pp. 76–77.

"covenant" (25). This is the day of which Isaiah said (Isa. 52:7): "How beautiful upon the mountains are the feet of the messenger who announces peace, who brings good news, who announces salvation, who says to Zion, 'Your God reigns'" (15–16). Next, the messenger of good news is identified as the Messiah (18). Whether he is also identical with Melchizedek is impossible to say.[212] J. T. Milik wishes to see in him the Teacher of Righteousness, and therefore dates this text to the period ca. 120 B.C.E., "at the height of the activity of the Teacher of Righteousness."[213]

There is disagreement about the extent to which the psalm passages (Ps. 82:1 and 7:8-9) cited in lines 10–11 are applied to Melchizedek. Does כתוב עליו in the introduction to the citation mean "written about him" (= Melchizedek)[214] or "about it" (= the judgment)?[215] In any case, the author interprets the first אלוהים in Ps. 82:1 as referring to Melchizedek.[216] David Flusser's proposal that Melchizedek's role as eschatological judge is derived from Psalm 110 is quite suggestive.[217]

Despite the remaining uncertainties, the text makes clear the correlation between salvation and judgment by its association of the day of judgment on Belial and his "lot" with the "year of favor" for the "lot of Melchizedek."

The Commentary on Habakkuk

According to the commentary on Habakkuk, God places in the hands of God's "elect" the task of judging all the nations and all the wicked among God's own people (V, 4–5). This will happen soon, because the author regards his own as "the final generation" (הַדּוֹר הָאַחֲרוֹן)[218] before "time [comes] to an end" (גְּמַר הַקֵּץ) (VII, 2) and the "day of judgment" (יוֹם הַמִּשְׁפָּט) arrives (XII, 14; XIII, 2-3).

212. J. A. Fitzmyer, "Melchizedek," 30–31, 40. P. J. Kobelski (Melchizedek, 61–62) and C. Gianotto (Melchizedek, 74) express themselves in opposition, while S. Sabugal is for the identification ("1Q Regla," 420–23).

213. J. T. Milik, "Milki-ṣedeq," 126 ("à l'époque de la pleine activité du Maître de Justice").

214. M. de Jonge and A. S. van der Woude, "11Q Melchizedek," 353; D. Flusser, "Melchizedek," 25; J. T. Milik, "Milki-ṣedeq," 99.

215. J. A. Fitzmyer, "Melchizedek," 28, 37; J. Carmignac, "Document," 353.

216. M. de Jonge and A. S. van der Woude, "11Q Melchizedek," 304; D. Flusser, "Melchizedek," 25; J. A. Fitzmyer, "Melchizedek," 37; P. J. Kobelski, Melchizedek, 59–60; C. Gianotto, Melchisedek, 70–73. Against: J. Carmignac, "Document," 366.

217. D. Flusser, "Melchizedek," 27. Cf. P. J. Kobelski, Melchizedek, 52–55; C. Gianotto, Melchisedek, 84; LXX Ps. 109:6!

218. The expression "the final generation" is also found in 1QpMi XVIII, 5; CD I, 11–12. It is taken from Ps. 102:19.

It thus appears that the Essene writings from Qumran reveal an essentially unified conception of the eschatological judgment that lies well within the tradition of the prophetic proclamation of the day of YHWH. All that is really new in contrast to the expressions we have treated previously is that the contrast between righteous and wicked is now interpreted in terms of the opposition between the community and "all Israel" (CD 3.14), and the proclamations of judgment and salvation in the Old Testament and other religious writings are read accordingly.[219] The commentary on Psalm 37 is a vivid example of this. An eschatology of the hereafter, with statements about the lot of those who die before the day of judgment, such as we have encountered in the book of Wisdom or the Epistle of Enoch, was not to be found in the writings from Qumran.[220]

The Testament of Moses (= *Assumptio Mosis*)

The text of the Testament of Moses, better known as the "Assumption of Moses" (*Assumptio Mosis*),[221] is retained only in a Latin palimpsest from the sixth century c.e. It is partly illegible, full of mistakes, and carelessly written. The Latin version is apparently a translation from Greek, but whether the original was written in a Semitic language, such as Hebrew or Aramaic, is uncertain.[222]

The work pretends to be a prophetic overview of history written by Moses shortly before his death and handed over to his successor, Joshua (1). It appears to have no literary unity. In chapter 5 the Seleucid period up to Antiochus IV is described, while chapters 6–7, after a brief introduction, turn to the Hasmonean and Herodian era. Chapter 8 suddenly returns to Antiochus

219. Cf. W. S. La Sor ("Interpretation"), with some striking conclusions for the present time.

220. On this, see the careful comparison in C. Larcher, *Études,* 112–29. Cf. H. Lichtenberger, *Menschenbild,* 227–30. For the question of belief in resurrection at Qumran, cf. H. C. Cavallin, *Leben,* 274–77; E. Schürer and G. Vermes, *History* 2: 582–83; H. Lichtenberger, *Menschenbild,* 219–24; M. Delcor and F. García Martínez, *Introducción,* 310–14; R. Martin-Achard, *DBS* 10: 478–81. 4Q521 now appears to offer clear evidence for this belief. Cf. E. Puech, *La croyance des Esséniens en la vie future* 2: 623–92.

221. [English translation based on J. Priest's in *OTP,* with adaptation as specified by the author (cf. n. 241 below).—Trans.] For the problem of genre and identity of this writing, see E.-M. Laperrousaz, *Testament,* 26–62; O. Camponovo, *Königtum,* 143–44. The most recent edition, with commentary, is by J. Tromp, *The Assumption of Moses. A Critical Edition with Commentary,* SVTP 10 (Leiden, 1993).

222. Cf. E. Schürer and G. Vermes, *History* 3/1: 284. A. Hilgenfeld, who argues for a Greek original, offers a Greek retroversion (*Messias,* 437–61). R. H. Charles prefers to posit a Hebrew original (*Assumption,* xxxviii-xlv).

IV and his religious persecutions. Near the end of this persecution, in chapter 9, appears the puzzling figure of Taxo, with his sons, who prefer to die rather than disobey God's commandments (9:6). After this appears God's reign (*regnum*) over all creation (10:1). Since chapters 8–10 belong together and would follow appropriately after chapter 5, the literary-critical problems are probably best resolved by the assumption that chapters 6–7 were inserted by a redactor. This insertion appears to have happened in the early post-Herodian period, which the redactor regards as the end time (7:1: *ex quo facto finientur tempora* ...). The basic document thus originated, like the book of Daniel, the Ten-Week Apocalypse, and the Vision of the Animals, in the period of the Maccabean wars, perhaps in Hasidic circles.[223]

We find a reference to the final events as early as the end of the first chapter, in a formulaic time reference we have often encountered elsewhere:[224] "... until the day of recompense [in the visitation] with which the Lord will visit them in the consummation of the end of days" (*usque in diem paenitentiae in respectu*,[225] *quo respicit illos dominus in consummatione exitus dierum*) (1:18). This "visitation" is described in chapter 10:

Et tunc parebit regnum illius in omni creatura illius
et tunc zabulus[226] *finem habebit*
et tristitia cum eo adducetur.[227]
Tunc implebuntur manus nuntii,
qui est in summo constitutus,
qui protinus vindicavit[228] *ab inimicis eorum.*

223. This opinion seems to be achieving increased acceptance. Cf. E. Schürer and G. Vermes, *History* 3/1: 281–84; O. Camponovo, *Königtum*, 144–62, with remarks on the history of research. Unfortunately, there are a number of typographical errors in these pages: on p. 152, third line from the bottom, one should read "chapter 5," not "chapter 7"; on p. 156, n. 40, the sequence should be "n. 32" rather than "n. 31" and "n. 33" rather than "n. 32." Worth noting also is the judgment of J. Klausner, who dates the whole work traditionally in the years ca. 4–6 c.e.: "This book . . . was composed, in my opinion, by one of the survivors of the sect of the Hasidim ('the first Hasidim'), from which the Essenes branched off; or by a member of that sect of the Essenes from which came the 'Dead Sea Scrolls'" (*Messianic Idea*, 325). K. Haacker ("Assumptio") advocates a Samaritan origin for the document and dates it to the second century c.e.

224. See above, 80–81.

225. Here *respectus* represents ἐπισκοπή, פְּקֻדָּה (cf. A. Hilgenfeld, *Messias*, 440). The object of the visitation is Israel. Hence in this passage the meaning is positive; it is not to be understood here in the sense of "punishment" (R. H. Charles, *Assumption*, 8).

226. *Zabulus = diabolus*. E.-M. Laperrousaz, *Testament*, 127.

227. *Adducetur = abducetur*.

228. *Vindicavit = vindicabit*.

> Then his kingdom will appear throughout his whole creation.
> Then the devil will have an end.
> Yea, sorrow will be led away with him.
> Then will be filled the hands of[229] the messenger, who is in the highest
>   place appointed.
> Yea, he will at once avenge them[230] of their enemies. (10:1-2)

Here the contrasted parties are not the righteous and the wicked, but Israel and its enemies. The "angel" or "messenger" who receives the commission to take vengeance on these enemies may well be the angel Michael.[231] This figure is correctly compared with that of Melchizedek in 11Q Melch.[232]

After this summary introduction, the theme is developed in more detail, according to a common ancient narrative technique (vv. 3-10). In the "parousia"[233] God is described as appearing in a mighty epiphany like that in 1 Enoch 1:3b-7. Its purpose is God's punishing judgment on the Gentile nations:

> . . .
> *et palam veniet, ut vindicet gentes,*
> *et perdet omnia idola eorum.*

> . . .
> In full view will he come to work vengeance on the nations.
> Yea, all their idols will he destroy. (10:7)

The fact that here, in contrast to 10:2, it is God who appears as judge should not be seen as contradictory; it furnishes no basis for a literary-critical division such as R. H. Charles proposed between vv. 1-2 and 3-10.[234] We find this kind of juxtaposition elsewhere as well. When the elect or a special figure such as the Messiah (*Psalms of Solomon* 17), the Son of man (1 Enoch 37–71), Michael (1QM), or Melchizedek (11Q Melch) appears as judge alongside God,[235] they

229. "To fill someone's hands" means to place that one in office, to give an assignment to. Cf. Exod. 28:41; 29:9; Lev. 21:10 and frequently; *Jub.* 32:3; *T. Levi* 8:10.

230. Israel.

231. Cf. Dan. 12:1; 1QM XVII, 6–7; 1QS III, 20, 24; *T. Dan* 6:1-7. E.-M. Laperrousaz, *Testament*, 127.

232. A. Y. Collins, "Composition," 181.

233. In 10:12 God's coming at the end is described as *adventus* .

234. R. H. Charles, *Assumption*, 39–41. On this, see O. Camponovo, *Königtum*, 169–70.

235. The Pauline letters even speak of God's judgment seat (Rom. 14:10) as well as of Christ's judgment seat (2 Cor. 5:10).

are, after all, only carrying out *God's* judgment. In our text, this judgment furnishes the precondition for Israel's salvation, which is the true purpose of the judgment:

> *Tunc felix eris tu, Istrahel,*
> *et ascendes supra cervices et alas aquilae*
> *et inplebuntur.*
> *Et altavit*[236] *te deus*
> *et faciet te herere caelo stellarum,*
> *loco habitationis eorum*[237]
> *et conspiges*[238] *a summo*
> *et vides inimicos tuos in terram*
> *et cognosces illos et gaudebis*
> *et agis gratias et confiteberis creatori tuo.*

> Then will you be happy, O Israel!
> And you will mount up above the necks and the wings of an eagle.[239]
> Yea, all things will be fulfilled.[240]
> And God will raise you to the heights.
> Yea, he will fix you firmly in the heaven of the stars,
>   in the place of their habitations.
> And you will behold from on high.
> Yea, you will see your enemies on earth.
> And recognizing them, you will rejoice.
> And you will give thanks.
> Yea, you will praise your Creator.[241] (10:8-10)

We find "you will be lifted up to the stars" as the expression of the hubris of a tyrant or a nation in LXX Dan. 8:10 and *Ps. Sol.* 1:5.[242] In this passage the

236. *Altavit* = *altabit.*
237. *Eorum* = *earum.*
238. *Conspiges* = *conspicies.*
239. The image is probably drawn from Exod. 19:4; Deut. 32:11. Cf. O. Campo-novo, *Königtum,* 168.
240. It is not clear to what this refers.
241. Not: ". . . and confess your Creator" (C. Clemen in E. Kautzsch, *Apokryphen und Pseudepigraphen* 2: 311–31; E. Brandenburger in *JSHRZ* 2 [1976]: 57–84). The same error is found in the English translations I have seen, e.g., J. Priest: ". . . you will confess your creator" (*OTP* 1: 932). In Christian Latin, *confiteri* with the dative means "praise" (*ThLL* 4: 231), like the underlying ἐξομολογεῖσθαι + dative (cf. A. Hilgenfeld, *Messias,* 452). For the meaning, see *BAGD* 277, 2c. Cf. also 1 Enoch 27:4, where precisely the same motif occurs.
242. Cf. also Isa. 14:13; Jer. 51:53; Amos 9:2; *Sib* 5.72.

metaphor has a positive application: Oppression will be followed by Israel's eschatological salvation, its elevation to God. It is noteworthy that this change in the situation after 10:1 can also be described as the "appearance" of God's "kingdom" or "reign" (*regnum* = βασιλεία). Thus the coming of God's reign is here an event that brings with it judgment and salvation: salvation for Israel, judgment for its enemies. It is God alone who elevates Israel into heaven, to God. This elevation can scarcely be regarded here as a mere image, because the earth remains only as a place of punishment for Israel's enemies, to which Israel looks down "from on high."[243] The metaphor is, so to speak, taken literally at this point.

The Testament of Moses is thus an example of a purely national, historical eschatology in which the purpose of judgment is the destruction of the enemy nations and the exaltation of Israel to the heavens. We learn nothing of the way in which this exaltation and subsequent salvation are to be imagined in concrete terms.

The Testaments of the Twelve Patriarchs

The language and style of the Testaments of the Twelve Patriarchs as we now have them point to the first or second century C.E.[244] The language is very close to that of the New Testament, and the semitizing-biblical style has its closest parallel in the Gospel of Luke and the Acts of the Apostles. In contrast to Greek Enoch, the fluid language of the Testaments does not, in general, give

243. N. Messel (*Einheitlichkeit*, 72) and C. Barth (*Diesseits*, 42) regard this elevation as merely an image. Barth writes: "Finally, the lapidary statement about the appearance of God's royal reign 'over all his creation' (10:1) may show clearly enough where, according to *As. Mos.*, the accomplishment of salvation is to be expected" (ibid.). I think this observation only points out one more example of the paucity of attention the apocalyptic writers paid to coherence of description and visual portrayal in their eschatological depictions.

244. The urgently necessary studies of this topic are unfortunately still lacking. Cf. to the present especially R. H. Charles, *Greek Versions*, xl-xlii; R. Eppel, *Piétisme*, 13–20. The selections in J. Becker, *Untersuchungen*, 169–72, 188, 192–93, 204–5, 209–10, 221–22, 241–42, 251–52, 280, 305–6, 325, 334, 356, 368 are valuable. A. Hultgård (*Eschatologie* 2: 74–79, 164–87), like Charles, supposes a Semitic original, but his remarks are methodologically very unsatisfying. Cf. M. de Jonge's review of Hultgård, *JSJ* 14 (1983): 78–79; H. W. Hollander and M. de Jonge, *Testaments*, 27–29; Marius Reiser, *Syntax*, 1–45, esp. 13. [The English translation follows H. C. Kee's in *OTP*, with modifications.—Trans.]

the impression of being a translation. Nevertheless, we must reckon with a long literary and tradition-historical development of this document and its sources, a history that remains difficult to trace.[245] The oldest elements may stem from the first quarter of the second century B.C.E., but *T. Benj.* 10:8 presupposes Dan. 12:2. R. H. Charles dates the presumed original work to the years 109–107 B.C.E.,[246] A. Hultgård only a little later.[247] Toward the end of the first or in the course of the second century C.E. the work underwent a Christian redaction, but as far as the content is concerned this consisted for the most part of interpolations.[248]

It is true that H. W. Hollander and M. de Jonge have a different opinion on this point. While they also believe there was a process of collection and compilation of widely different kinds of materials before the final version of the twelve testaments was prepared (*Testaments*, 2), they do not think that sources and early phases can be reconstructed using literary-critical methods (ibid., 8, 83. For corresponding attempts, including especially the contribution of J. Becker, cf. ibid., 2–8). They conclude their introduction with this statement: "*A fortiori*, it is practically impossible to answer the question whether there ever existed Jewish Testaments in some form. If they existed, we shall never be able to reconstruct them with any degree of certainty. In any case, our first and foremost task is to try to interpret the Testaments as they lie before us" (p. 85). The commentary is written from this standpoint. Although I also believe that J. Becker has overestimated the value of literary criticism in the case of the Testaments, I cannot share de Jonge's and Hollander's excessive skepticism. The competing descriptions in *T. Jos.* 1:3—10:4 and 10:5—16:8, for example, cry out for a literary-critical division (cf. R. H. Charles, *Testaments*, 172; J. Becker, *Untersuchungen*, 228–30; H. D. Slingerland, "The Testament of Joseph," positing a redactor who manipulated two sources).

245. A history of research and a good survey of the manifold and extremely difficult problems presented by this document, beginning with the text-critical level, is offered by H. D. Slingerland, *Testaments*. He ends with J. Becker's *Untersuchungen* of 1970. Important essays are collected in M. de Jonge, ed., *Studies*. Cf. now also the commentary by H. W. Hollander and M. de Jonge, which contains an extensive introduction (1–85).

246. R. H. Charles, *Testaments*, liii.

247. A. Hultgård, *Eschatologie* 2: 225–27. For the question of dating, cf. also E. Schürer, *Geschichte* 3: 348–50; E. Schürer and G. Vermes, *History* 3/2: 774–75; O. Eissfeldt, *Einleitung*, 858–62; K. Schubert, "Auferstehungslehre," 199–200; A.-M. Denis, *Introduction*, 58–59; J. Becker, *Untersuchungen*, 374–76.

248. On this, see A. Hultgård, *Eschatologie* 2: 228–38; also E. Schürer and G. Vermes, *History* 3/2: 770–72.

It is difficult to establish a place of origin. Palestine has been suggested,[249] and so has Egypt.[250] Egyptian origin seems especially likely in the case of *T. Jos.* 1:3—10:4, a narrative that apparently stems from a milieu quite similar to that which gave rise to *Joseph and Aseneth.*[251]

In some of the Testaments there are prominent sections that follow a particular salvation-historical schema known to us as the deuteronomistic view of history.[252] The patriarchs prophesy Israel's falling away from God and turning to sin and wickedness "in the last days."[253] This formula, usually to be interpreted eschatologically, is displaced here because the judgment that is the consequence of this wickedness is not meant to be eschatological. God's "righteous judgment," God's δικαιοκρισία (*T. Levi* 15:2) is instead effected, in this schema, through the scattering and imprisonment of the people, the destruction of the temple, disease, plague, and famine (λιμὸς καὶ λοιμός) (*T. Jud.* 23:3). But when the people repent, God will have mercy, gather the scattered people once again, and lead them back into their land. This saving action of God is described three times as "visitation" (ἐπισκέπτεσθαι) (*T. Levi* 16:5; *T. Jud.* 23:5; *T. Ash.* 7:2). Thus even though eschatological formulas and motifs are employed here, it is difficult to speak of a genuine eschatology in these sin-exile-return passages. However, the fact that they can easily be redacted and expanded to yield that sense is shown by *T. Zeb.* 9:5-9 and *T. Dan* 5:4-13.[254]

"The eschatology of the Testaments is a rather confused collection of heterogeneous elements."[255] It is scarcely possible any longer to determine when each of these elements entered the text, nor can the extent of Christian redac-

---

249. A. Hultgård (among others) suggests Galilee (*Eschatologie* 2: 223–25).

250. J. Becker, *Untersuchungen,* 374. On this question, cf. A.-M. Denis, *Introduction,* 57–58.

251. J. Becker, *Untersuchungen,* 235–38. For the origins and writing of *Jos. Asen.* in Egypt ca. 38 C.E., see D. Sänger, "Erwägungen," 185–200.

252. *T. Levi* 10:1-4, 14-15, 16; *T. Jud.* 18:1; 23:1-5; *T. Iss.* 6; *T. Zeb.* 9:5-9; *T. Dan* 5:4-9; *T. Naph.* 4:1-3; 4:4-5; *T. Ash.* 7:2-4, 5-7. On this, see J. Becker, *Untersuchungen,* 172–77; A. Hultgård, *Eschatologie* 1: 82–199; H. W. Hollander and M. de Jonge, *Testaments,* 39–41, 53–56.

253. *T. Jud.* 18:1; *T. Dan* 5:4. Cf. *T. Levi* 10:2; 14:1; *T. Iss.* 6:1. *T. Zeb.* 8:2; 9:5; *T. Jos.* 19:5 (10) are eschatological in intent.

254. On this, see below. Cf. also *T. Benj.* 9:1-2, where the motif of the eschatological gathering of the twelve tribes of Israel and "all the nations" around the Temple is reprised. On this, see R. H. Charles, *Testaments,* 211; A. Hultgård, *Eschatologie* 1: 157–59.

255. "L'eschatologie des Testaments est un assemblage assez confus d'éléments hétérogènes." R. Eppel, *Piétisme,* 90. According to A. Hultgård this is true only at first glance (*Eschatologie* 1: 230). But Hultgård inclines to harmonize (e.g., ibid., 254, 260, 262, 265–66).

tion of the passages in which those elements occur be precisely established in every case.

According to *T. Sim.* 6:3-5, the eschatological judgment will fall on the gentile nations, followed by God's end time epiphany. "Then all the spirits of error shall be given over to being trampled underfoot. And [human beings] will have mastery over the evil spirits" (6:6).[256] The contrast between Israel and the nations otherwise plays no part in the eschatology of the Testaments.

We encounter an entirely different concept of judgment in the Testament of Levi. In 2:6 Levi sees the heavens opened, and in the second heaven "fire, snow, and ice, ready for the day determined by God's righteous judgment" (ὁ δεύτερος ἔχει πῦρ, χιόνα, κρύσταλλον, ἕτοιμα εἰς ἡμέραν προστάγματος κυρίου ἐν τῇ δικαιοκρισίᾳ τοῦ θεοῦ) (3:2).[257] Also there are "all the spirits [winds] of those dispatched to achieve the punishment of the wicked" (πάντα τὰ πνεύματα τῶν ἐπαγωγῶν εἰς ἐκδίκησιν τῶν ἀνόμων) (3:2). It is difficult to decide whether the πνεύματα here are spirits or winds.[258] In the third heaven are the "armies" (δυνάμεις τῶν παρεμβολῶν) "arrayed for the day of judgment to work vengeance on the spirits of error and of Beliar" (3:3). Here, then, we find indications of the same idea as in Qumran: God's judgment leads, at the end, to a twofold war of destruction that eliminates the wicked from the earth and, in the realm of the spirits, destroys Beliar and his train.

T. Levi 4:1 also speaks of the destruction of the wicked: According to this passage, they will be punished (ἐν κολάσει κριθήσονται) because, even in view of God's appearance at the end time, which is described in similar terms to those used in 1 Enoch 1:3b-9,[259] they persist in their wrongdoing. According to *T. Zeb.* 10:3, they will be destroyed in eternal fire.

In addition to *T. Levi* 3:3., Beliar is mentioned four (possibly three) times in connection with descriptions of the time of salvation. One of these is *T. Dan* 5:10b-13, originally an independent poetic fragment that now follows a sin-exile-return passage:[260]

256. On the whole, see J. Becker, *Untersuchungen*, 330–32; A. Hultgård, *Eschatologie* 1: 248–53.

257. Cf. Sir. 39:28-30. H. W. Hollander and M. de Jonge, *Testaments*, 137. For the differing enumeration of the heavens in the MSS, see J. Becker, *Untersuchungen*, 260; M. de Jonge, "Notes," 248–51. Instead of ἡμέραν προστάγματος, n c h i j read ἡμέραν κρίσεως.

258. Cf. Sir. 39:28; Wis. 5:23; 1 Enoch 100:13.

259. On this, see A. Hultgård, *Eschatologie* 1: 257–59.

260. For the reconstruction and the text, see J. Becker, *Untersuchungen*, 352–54; idem, *Testaments*, 95–96. Becker considers the eighth line a gloss.

> [God] will make war against Beliar;
> [and] grant the vengeance of victory as our goal.
> And he shall take from Beliar the captives, the souls of the saints;
> and he shall turn the hearts of the disobedient ones to the Lord,
> and grant eternal peace to those who call upon him.
> And the saints shall refresh themselves in Eden;
> the righteous shall rejoice in the New Jerusalem,
> which shall be eternally for the glorification of God.
> And Jerusalem shall no longer undergo desolation,
> nor shall Israel be led into captivity,
> because the Lord will be in her midst [living among human beings].
> The Holy One of Israel will rule over them in humility and poverty,
> and [the one] who trusts in him shall reign in truth in the heavens.

There is a similar description, with motif-parallels, in *T. Zeb.* 9:8, also following a sin-exile-return passage: "And thereafter the Lord himself will arise upon you, the light of righteousness with healing and compassion in his wings.[261] He will liberate every captive of the [children of humanity] from Beliar, and every spirit of error will be trampled down. He will turn all nations to being zealous for him (ἐπιστρέψει πάντα τὰ ἔθνη εἰς παραζήλωσιν αὐτοῦ). And you shall see [God in a human form], he whom the Lord will choose: Jerusalem is his name."[262]

Another related and also originally independent poem or poetic fragment is found in *T. Levi* 18:10-14. It first speaks, in its present context, of a priestly Messiah, but undoubtedly God was the original subject.[263]

> And he shall open the gates of paradise;
> he shall remove the sword that has threatened since Adam,
> he will grant to the saints to eat of the tree of life.
> The spirit of holiness shall be upon them.
> And Beliar shall be bound by him.
> And he shall grant to his children the authority to trample on wicked
>   spirits.
> And the Lord will rejoice in his children;

261. Cf. Mal. 3:20.
262. The text is apparently not quite correct and also presents the kind of linguistic difficulties that cause me to suspect a Semitic original in this case. It has been subjected to Christian redaction at the end. For the originality of the longer text, see M. de Jonge, "Textual Criticism," 151–52; to the contrary A. Hultgård, *Eschatologie* 2: 24–26, 257. Cf. also J. Becker, *Untersuchungen,* 210–13; A. Hultgård, *Eschatologie* 1: 163–66.
263. For the reconstruction and the text, see J. Becker, *Untersuchungen,* 297–99; idem, *Testaments,* 61. A. Hultgård speaks somewhat vaguely on this point: *Eschatologie* 1: 282–83, 287–88.

he will be well pleased by his beloved ones forever.
Then Abraham, and Isaac, and Jacob will rejoice
and I shall be glad, and all the saints shall be clothed in righteousness.

While God's war against Beliar in *T. Dan* 5:10-11 recalls the War Scroll from Qumran (1QM I, 4–5, 14–15; XVIII, 1–3), the binding of Beliar seems more reminiscent of the fate of Azazel and his companions in 1 Enoch 10:4, 12.[264] This also resembles *T. Jud.* 25:3, according to which Beliar at the end "will be thrown into eternal fire" (cf. 1 Enoch 10:6, 13). Then there will be but "one people of the Lord, with one language" (*T. Jud.* 25:3).[265]

As in the War Scroll from Qumran, we also find in the Testament of Dan both the tradition that God leads the struggle against Beliar in person, and the tradition that an angel, probably Michael, assists Israel and opposes the "kingdom of the enemy," Beliar (6:1-7; cf. 1QM XVII, 6–7).[266] It comes to its end on the day when Israel repents (ἐν ᾗ ἡμέρᾳ ἐπιστρέψει Ἰσραήλ) (6:4).[267] The leader and *angelus interpres* in Levi's vision also presents itself in 5:5-6 as the angel upon whom Israel can call "on the day of distress" (ἐν ἡμέρᾳ θλίψεως) so that it may not be completely destroyed. This angel is undoubtedly Michael.[268]

Statements about judgment occur twice in connection with the resurrection of the patriarchs.[269] Thus in *T. Zeb.* 10:1-3 we read: "And now, my children, do not grieve because I am dying, ... I shall rise again in your midst, as a leader among your sons, and I shall be glad in the midst of my tribe—as many as keep the Law of the Lord and the commandments of Zebulon, their father. But the Lord shall bring down fire on the impious, and will destroy them to all generations."

We find a clearly related tradition in *T. Benj.* 10:6-10. This section is available without Christian interpolations only in the Armenian translation.[270] It is

---

264. Cf. A. Hultgård, *Eschatologie* 1: 285–86.

265. A. Hultgård sees an Iranian origin for the motif of one language (*Eschatologie* 1: 267). For the further description of the end time in *T. Jud.* 25:4-5 and its motifs, see ibid., 241–46.

266. Both traditions are combined in 1QS III, 24–25.

267. For the text, see J. Becker, *Testamente*, 97, ad loc.; R. H. Charles, *Testaments*, 132. Cf. A. Hultgård, *Eschatologie* 2: 260. For this theological topos, see Str-B 1: 164–65; 4: 992–93; P. Volz, *Eschatologie*, 103–4.

268. On this, see the extensive commentary by R. H. Charles, *Testaments*, 38–40; cf. H. W. Hollander and M. de Jonge, *Testaments*, 145.

269. For these, see P. Volz, *Eschatologie*, 267; A. Hultgård, *Eschatologie* 1: 260–63; H. W. Hollander and M. de Jonge, *TestXII*, 61–63.

270. J. Becker, *Untersuchungen*, 48–49; A. Hultgård, *Eschatologie* 2: 40. To the contrary M. de Jonge, *JSJ* 14 (1983): 73; H. W. Hollander and M. de Jonge, *Testaments*,

preceded by a call to keep God's commandments "until the Lord reveals his salvation to all the nations" (10:5). Then follows an eschatological instruction whose dry, schematic style recalls the Ten-Week Apocalypse: First Enoch, Seth, Abraham, Isaac, and Jacob will arise "at the right hand in great joy" (ἐκ δεξιῶν ἐν ἀγαλλιάσει); then the twelve patriarchs as leaders of their tribes; then all human beings, "some destined for glory, and others for dishonor" (οἱ μὲν εἰς δόξαν, οἱ δὲ εἰς ἀτιμίαν).[271] For God will first judge (κρινεῖ) Israel for the evil it has done, and then all the nations. "Then he shall convict Israel by the chosen gentiles as he convicted Esau by the Midianites. . . . You, therefore, my children, may your lot come to be with those who fear the Lord!" (10:10).[272] Noteworthy here, in addition to the parenetic framing and the insistence on the sequence of eschatological events, is especially the image evoked by the concept of "conviction" (ἐλέγχειν) of a forensic situation in which Israel will be exposed before "the chosen gentiles." That this can by no means be a Christian interpolation is shown by the allusion to a *haggadah* on Esau and the Midianites that is not otherwise known to us.

The passages thus far adduced all belong within the framework of a historical eschatology, but we also find alongside them, in the Testaments of the Twelve Patriarchs, traces of an individual eschatology of the hereafter according to which the soul of the individual, immediately after death, enters into eternal suffering or eternal bliss. The most extensive passage is found in the Testament of Asher, where it forms the conclusion of the teaching on the two ways: The two different paths and attitudes of human beings also lead to two different "ends" or "outcomes" (τέλη) (*T. Ash.* 1:3). The description of these τέλη is introduced, as in *T. Benj.* 10:6-10, with a commandment-parenesis: "You also, my children, give attention to the Lord's command. . . . For the ultimate end of human beings displays their righteousness, since they will be made known to the angels of the Lord and of Beliar.[273] For when the

---

412. According to them, the Armenian translation can make no claim to originality. A Greek retroversion of the Armenian text is offered by R. H. Charles, *Greek Versions*, 229–30.

271. Cf. Dan. 12:2.

272. For the originality of A in this last sentence as well, see R. H. Charles (*Testaments*) against J. Becker (*Testamente*) and A. Hultgård, *Eschatologie* 2: 271. The Greek MS 1 has the same reading.

273. I read γνωρίζοντες τοὺς ἀγγέλους, with M. de Jonge. J. Becker reads καὶ γνωρίζονται τοῖς ἀγγέλοις with c h i j and translates: "And they will be known by the angels of the Lord. . ." (*Testamente*, 116). The translation should, however, read: "And they will be made known to the angels of the Lord." R. H. Charles makes an interesting conjecture (*Greek Versions*, 179; *Testaments*, 169) and translates: ". . . when they meet the angels of the Lord and of Satan."

evil soul departs, it is harassed (βασανίζεται) by the evil spirit which it served through its desires and evil works. But if anyone is peaceful with joy he comes to know the angel of peace and enters eternal life" (*T. Ash.* 6:1, 4-6).[274] *T. Ash.* 5:2 also speaks of "eternal life." *T. Benj.* 4:1 mentions "crowns of glory" (στέ-φανοι δόξης),[275] *T. Rub.* 5:5 and *T. Gad* 7:5 the "eternal punishment" of sinners. *T. Jos.* 2:2 belongs here, also: "I struggled with a shameless woman who kept prodding me to transgress with her, but the God of my father rescued me from the burning flame (φλὸξ καιομένη)." As the parallel in 1 Enoch 103:8 shows, "the burning flame" refers to the fire of hell.[276]

Thus the opinion of R. Eppel cited above about the eschatology of this document is confirmed: It offers a colorful mixture of different eschatological concepts and traditions that cannot be reduced to any kind of orderly system. This impression would only be strengthened by introducing the messianic concepts to be found here. However, we have scarcely found an orderly eschatological system in any of the early Jewish writings we have examined. We could hardly have expected to find one here.

The Sibylline Oracles

As with the texts collected in the book of Enoch, the collection of Sibylline Oracles is also dominated by the theme of eschatology.[277] "The Sibyl foretells the fortunes of the world from the beginning to the time of the individual authors, then attaches threats and promises for the near future; in ominous words she accuses the gentile nations of idolatry and depravity and warns them to do penance while there is still time; for hideous punishments will fall on those who are unrepentant."[278] The schema of an overview of history up to the time of the author, with an eschatological outlook, is familiar to us from Dan. 11:1—12:3, the Ten-Week Apocalypse, the Vision of the Animals, the

274. The text of the last part of the sentence is from c h i j. Rabbinic parallels to these statements are collected in R. H. Charles, *Testaments*, 168–69. See further in H. W. Hollander and M. de Jonge, *Testaments*, 357.

275. Cf. Wis. 5:16 (see above, pp. 44–45); 1QS IV, 7; 1QH IX, 25; 1 Pet. 5:4.

276. Cf. *Jub.* 39:6 and *Tg. Neof.* on Gen. 39:10: "And he did not listen to her and lie with her in this world, in order not to have to be beside her in the world to come." So also *Ber. R.* 87:6, ad loc. Cf. also J. Bowker, *Targums*, 244–45. H. W. Hollander and M. de Jonge (*Testaments*, 370–71) see "burning flame" as a poetic expression for the seductress and her "burning" desire. They do not take note of the parallel in 1 Enoch 103:8 and the underlying tradition.

277. J. J. Collins, "Sibylline Oracles," *OTP* 1: 323.

278. E. Schürer, *Geschichte* 3: 567.

Book of Jubilees (1:23) and the Testament of Moses. Yet, because of their audience, the Sibylline Oracles incorporate the history of the Gentile nations, including mythical ones (3:110-55). Since the eschatological passages in the seventh and eighth books are certainly Christian in origin, we will treat here only the oracles in the first five books.

The Third Book

The third book of the Sibylline Oracles (without vv. 1-96, which originally belonged to the lost second book),[279] except for a few oracles and verses, was written around the middle of the second century B.C.E.[280] Its origins are Egyptian.[281] It can be loosely divided into two parts: the first (vv. 97-544) contains historical prophecies, and oracles about cities and nations, the tenor of which is formulated in 517–19: "Why indeed should I proclaim each one according to its fate? For on all peoples, as many as inhabit the earth, will the Most High send a terrible affliction (δεινὴν ἐπιπέμψει πληγήν)." This refers to the final judgment which, together with descriptions of the time of salvation, constitutes the principal subject of the eschatological oracles of the second part (vv. 545-807). These are introduced with a parenesis addressed to the Greeks and are separated by three other parenetic sections (545–72, 624–31, 732–40, 762–66). The Sibyl concludes with a few verses *pro domo* (808–28). J. J. Collins proposes that the eschatological oracles do not stem from different sources, but instead represent varying formulations from the one group from which the third book of Sibylline Oracles came.[282] But because the differences and contradictions among the individual oracles are not unimportant, I will treat each one separately.

The parenesis that introduces the second part warns the Greeks, as idolaters, against the coming "wrath of the great God" (θεοῦ χόλος) (556, cf. 561) on the "fated day" (αἴσιμον ἦμαρ) (569). There follows, by way of contrast, a praise of the Jews, "a sacred race of pious men" (573). This in turn leads, by

279. J. J. Collins, "Sibylline Oracles," *OTP* 1: 359–60; E. Schürer and G. Vermes, *History* 3/1: 639–40.
280. The precise dating depends primarily on the identification of the "seventh king of the race of the Greeks" (191–93, 316–18, 608–10). J. J. Collins ("Sibylline Oracles," *OTP* 1: 354–55) and E. Schürer and G. Vermes (*History* 3/1: 635–36) argue for Ptolemy Philometor, while earlier authors opted for Physcon (E. Schürer, *Geschichte* 3: 574–76; A. Rzach, "Orakel," 2127–28).
281. J. J. Collins, "Sibylline Oracles," *OTP* 1: 355–56; E. Schürer and G. Vermes, *History* 3/1: 638 consider another place of origin possible for some of the oracles.
282. J. J. Collins, *Sibylline Oracles*, 37.

means of a condemnation of the pederasty of other nations who thereby tres-
pass against "the holy law of immortal God" (600), to the first eschatological
oracle (601–23).

When the seventh Greek king rules in Egypt,[283] a great king from Asia will
cover the land with troops, plunder it, and pass on over the sea (608–15). Then
people will bend the knee before God, who will give them "great joy," because
then the land and the flocks will produce "the true fruit" of wine, honey, milk,
and grain (616–23).

Although this first eschatological oracle (601–23) concentrates on Egypt
alone, the others reveal a universal horizon. The second is the most elaborate
(632–731). The redactor of the book apparently wants it to be seen as a coherent piece, but originally vv. 632–56 and 657–731 were probably two different
oracles. According to the first of these, "the wrath of the great God" (τοῦ μεγά-
λοιο θεοῦ μήνιμα) (632) brings on war among nations, which will be ended
by a king whom God sends "from the sun" (ἀπ' ἠελίοιο) (652),[284] by "killing
some, imposing oaths of loyalty on others" (654).

In the next oracle the horizon is also universal, but attention is wholly fo-
cused on the Temple, around which the events are centered.[285] The kings of
the nations will attack it, but "judgment (κρίσις) will come upon them from
the great God, and all will perish at the hand of the Immortal" (670–72).[286]
Fiery swords will fall from heaven (672–73), the earth will be shaken by the
hand of the Immortal (675–76), before whose face fear will fall on every crea-
ture (675, 679). The ravines will be filled with corpses, and the rocks will
stream with blood (682–84).

> καὶ κρινεῖ πάντας πολέμῳ θεὸς ἠδὲ μαχαίρῃ
> καὶ πυρὶ καὶ ὑετῷ τε κατακλύζοντι· καὶ ἔσται

283. For this king, see J. J. Collins, *OTP* 1: 354–55; E. Schürer and G. Vermes, *History* 3/1: 636. Probably the reference is to Ptolemy Philometor, but perhaps it is to
Physcon.

284. On the basis of parallels with the oracle of the potter, J. J. Collins sees here an
allusion to Egyptian mythology in which the king was regarded as the son of the sun
god. He identifies this king with the "seventh king from the race of the Greeks" (*Sibylline Oracles*, 40–41; *Between Athens and Jerusalem*, 68–70). V. Nikiprowetzky differs
(*Troisième Sibylle*, 136–37). Cf. also J. G. Griffiths, "Apokalyptic," 290. For the oracle of
the potter, see also A. Hultgård, *Eschatologie* 1: 363–64.

285. It is mentioned in 657 (where, with nearly all editors and translators, we must
conjecture ναός rather than λαός), 665, 587, 702, 718.

286. This very common motif of the attack of the nations is found even in the
Psalms, esp. Pss. 2 and 46. Cf. S. Mowinckel, *He That Cometh*, 140, 145, 147; P. Volz,

θεῖον ἀπ᾽ οὐρανόθεν, αὐτὰρ λίθος ἠδὲ χάλαζα
πολλὴ καὶ χαλεπή· θάνατος δ᾽ ἐπὶ τετράποδ᾽ ἔσται.
καὶ τότε γνώσονται θεὸν ἄμβροτον, ὃς τάδε κρίνει.

God will judge all [humankind] by war and sword
and fire and torrential rain. There will also be brimstone from heaven
and stones and much grievous hail.
Death will come upon four-footed creatures.
Then they will recognize the immortal God who judges these things.
(689–93)

The whole section is based on Ezek. 38:14-23, a prophecy of judgment
against Gog, with other, individual motifs derived from Ps. 11:6; Isa. 29:6;
30:30; 66:15-16. The description, however, is reminiscent of Wis. 5:17-23,
which demonstrates the spread of this idea of judgment, according to which
God unites with the forces of nature in fighting against the godless until they
are vanquished. Only then can salvation be finally established: "The sons of
the great God" will dwell peacefully around the Temple (702–3), God will personally protect them, and there will be no war ever again. "And then all islands
and cities will say, 'How much the Immortal loves those men! . . . Let us send
to the Temple, since he alone is sovereign and let us all ponder the Law of the
Most High God!'" (710–11, 718–19).[287] Behind this is again a prophecy against
Gog in Ezek. 39:1-8. The oracle ends with a reprise of Ezek. 39:9-10.

It is thus evident that the whole text of vv. 657-731 is built on two prophecies against Gog, Ezek. 38:14-23; 39:1-10.[288] Particular to this text, in fact, is
only the central position assumed by the Temple. The author took this motif
from the tradition of the pilgrimage of nations, especially in Isa. 2:2-4; 66:18-
20, 23.

In light of the central role of the Temple in this oracle, J. J. Collins has posited
that the whole of the third book of the Sibylline Oracles originated in circles
surrounding Onias IV, the founder of the temple at Leontopolis ("Sibylline Oracles," OTP 1: 355–56; Between Athens and Jerusalem, 71–72). These groups expected one of the Ptolemaic house as Messiah, the "seventh king of the race of
the Greeks" (191–93, 316–18, 608–10), to be identified with the "king from the

---

Eschatologie, 149–52; L. Hartman, Prophecy, 77–101; E. Schürer and G. Vermes, History
2: 525–26.
287. For this motif, resting on Isa. 2:2-4, see A. Causse, "Myth," P. Volz, Eschatologie, 171–72; D. Zeller, "Völkerwallfahrt" (1971): 225–37.
288. L. Hartman, Prophecy, 91–94.

sun" (652–56) (*Between Athens and Jerusalem*, 69). "The king from the sun should establish universal peace. Then, when the 'sons of the great God' are allowed to 'live peacefully around the temple' (702–3), God himself will shield them (705) and 'the hand of the Holy One will be fighting for them' (708–9)" (*Between Athens and Jerusalem*, 70). This interpretation oriented to the facts of history proceeds on the assumption that vv. 632-731 are a unified whole, something that cannot simply be presumed, and it overestimates the importance of the Messiah in these oracles. For those reasons, I find the interpretation too speculative.

The next oracle (741-61) presents a description of the time of salvation that, in vv. 744-49, is similar to that in 619-22, but with the addition of some paradisiacal features: Honey comes from heaven, milk from fountains that break forth from the earth. Peace rules over the whole earth, and there is but *one* law. This salvation follows the "fated day" (741) and is called μεγάλη κρίσις ἠδὲ καὶ ἀρχή (743, also 784). Here κρίσις is practically synonymous with ἀρχή, "rule." Only the last verse quite inappropriately mentions God's fiery judgment on "a race of grievous men" (761).

The last oracle also depicts the time of salvation: God will "establish a kingdom forever over all humanity" (ἐξεγερεῖ βασιλήιον εἰς αἰῶνας / πάντας ἐπ᾽ ἀνθρώπους) (767-68), and open for the faithful "the gates of the blessed and all joys and immortal intellect (νοῦς) and eternal cheer" (770-71). The nations bring incense and gifts to the Temple in Jerusalem. Peace will reign, "prophets of the great God will take away the sword, for they themselves are judges of [mortals], and righteous kings" (781-82).

Who are the "prophets of the great God?" Emil Schürer thought of "the Israelites, 'the saints of the Most High' as they are called in Daniel,"[289] that is, the εὐσεβεῖς in v. 769 and the ἀγαθοί in v. 780. We may have here the first instance of a tradition that we receive in *Midr. Tanh.* B. Num III § 28: "The Holy One, blessed be he! said: In this world prophesy (only) a few, but in the world to come all Israelites will be prophets."[290] Schürer's proposal is further confirmed by the parallel in Wis. 3:8: (The righteous) κρινοῦσιν ἔθνη καὶ κρατήσουσιν λαῶν (will govern nations and rule over peoples). As in this

289. E. Schürer, *Geschichte* 2: 596; E. Schürer and G. Vermes, *History* 2: 502. Similarly P. Volz, *Eschatologie*, 358. J. J. Collins ("Sibylline Oracles," *OTP* 1: 379) takes "prophets" in the usual sense and therefore has difficulty in explaining this "unusual idea."

290. From the translation by H. Bietenhard, 2: 278. The foundation given is Joel 3:1. Cf. Str-B 2: 615–16.

Sibylline Oracle, in context this is about the eschatological time of salvation, and here also judging is connected with ruling.[291]

Then Isaiah's prophecy about the peaceable kingdom is fulfilled as well (788-95; cf. Isa. 11:6-8; 65:25).

Somewhat awkwardly placed at the conclusion of the eschatological oracles is a listing (796-807) of apocalyptic portents that announce "the end of all things . . . on earth" (πάντων τὸ τέλος γαίηφι) (797).

The eschatology of the third book of the Sibylline Oracles thus remains, on the whole, within the framework of what we already know from Isaiah 65–66, even though the oracle in 657-731 rests more obviously on Ezekiel 38–39.[292] The principal difference is that the Sibylline Oracles start with the contrast between Israel and the Gentiles, while in Isaiah 65–66 the separation runs through Israel itself.

The Fourth Book

The fourth book of the Sibylline Oracles contains a basic fund of pagan oracles. The Jewish version (that the redactor was Jewish in origin is no longer in doubt since the work of Emil Schürer)[293] was produced about 80 C.E.[294] The place of origin is generally presumed to have been Syria or the Jordan valley.[295]

The oracles against nations and cities in this book are framed by two warnings about the eschatological judgment (vv. 40-46, 152-92); the first of these represents a sometimes literal anticipation of the depiction of the last judgment in vv. 183-91. The Sibyl sees piety fading from among human beings,

---

291. Cf. above, *Sib. Or.* 3:743, 784. The same tradition is found in *Jub.* 32:18-19. Cf. also Dan. 7:22; 1 Cor. 6:2. P. Volz, *Eschatologie,* 275; M. Delcor, *Testament d'Abraham,* 60–61.

292. J. Klausner writes: "No other Jewish apocalyptist rose to this high plane of Isaianic universalism" (*Messianic Idea,* 379).

293. "As regards the Jewish nationality of the author of this book, no doubt can prevail" (A. Rzach, "Orakel," 2132).

294. E. Schürer, *Geschichte,* 3: 580–81; J. J. Collins, "Sibylline Oracles," *OTP* 1: 382; E. Schürer and G. Vermes, *History,* 3/1: 642–43. The eruption of Vesuvius in 79 C.E. is mentioned in 4:130-36.

295. J. J. Collins, "Sibylline Oracles," *OTP* 1: 382. The reason for this is the reference to a baptism in v. 165. E. Schürer argues for Asia Minor as the place of origin (*Geschichte* 3: 581). E. Schürer and G. Vermes, *History* 3/1: 643: "Nothing is known of its place of origin." Because of the eruption of Vesuvius in 79, mentioned in 4:130-36, H. Lichtenberger argues for Italy, probably Rome itself, as the place of writing ("Täufergemeinden," 41, 42–43).

their pleasure in evil deeds and shedding of blood, and she calls them to repent: μετάθεσθε (162). "Wash your whole bodies in perennial rivers . . . and ask forgiveness (συγγνώμη) for your previous deeds. . . . God will grant repentance[296] . . . and will . . . stop his wrath. . . ." (165-69).[297] She then continues: "But if you do not obey me, . . . there will be fire throughout the whole world . . . ; He will burn up the whole earth, and will destroy the whole [human] race" (171-76).[298] While the formulation here is conditional, the author is scarcely serious in supposing that the catastrophe being announced can be averted. In any case, thereafter "God himself" will create humanity anew out of ashes and bone, just as they were before (181-82).

καὶ τότε δὴ κρίσις ἔσσετ᾽, ἐφ᾽ ᾗ δικάσει θεὸς αὐτός
κρίνων ἔμπαλι κόσμον· ὅσοι δ᾽ ὑπὸ δυσσεβίῃσιν
ἥμαρτον, τοὺς δ᾽ αὖτε χυτὴ κατὰ γαῖα καλύψει
Τάρταρά τ᾽ εὐρώεντα μυχοὶ στύγιοί τε γεέννης.
ὅσσοι δ᾽ εὐσεβέουσι, πάλιν ζήσοντ᾽ ἐπὶ γαῖαν
πνεῦμα θεοῦ δόντος ζωήν θ᾽ ἅμα καὶ χάριν αὐτοῖς
εὐσεβέσιν· πάντες δὲ τότ᾽ εἰσόψονται ἑαυτούς
νήδυμον ἠελίου τερπνὸν φάος εἰσορόωντες.
ὢ μακαριστός, ἐκεῖνον ὃς ἐς χρόνον ἔσσεται ἀνήρ.

And then there will be a judgment over which God himself will preside,
judging the world again. As many as sinned by impiety,
these will a mound of earth cover,
and broad Tartarus and the repulsive recesses of Gehenna.
But as many as are pious, they will live on earth again
when God gives spirit and life and favor

296. For δοῦναι μετάνοιαν, "give [opportunity for] repentance," cf. Wis. 12:19; Acts 5:31; 2 Tim. 2:25. J. Thomas, *Mouvement baptiste*, 52–53; M. Dibelius, *Pastoralbriefe*, 85–86; H. Conzelmann, *Apostelgeschichte*, 47.

297. The baptism the Sibyl calls for here recalls the baptism of John (J. Thomas, *Mouvement baptiste*, 52–57; J. J. Collins, "Sibylline Oracles," *OTP* 1: 388 n. ad loc.; H. Lichtenberger, "Täufergemeinden," 40–41). Its onetime character is expressed by the aorist λούσασθε. The possibility that this refers to proselyte baptism (E. Schürer, *Geschichte* 3: 184, 580; E. Schürer and G. Vermes, *History* 3/1: 174; differently ibid., 642; A. Rzach, "Orakel," 2132) in my opinion cannot be excluded; the context even makes it probable. In addition, it appears to be a matter of self-baptism, as the middle voice, λούσασθε, shows.

298. For this idea of the burning of the earth, see N. Messel, *Einheitlichkeit*, 15–22; P. Volz, *Eschatologie*, 335–36; J. J. Collins, "Sibylline Oracles," *OTP* 1: 381, 388 n. ad loc.; idem, *Sibylline Oracles*, 101–10.

to these pious ones. Then they will all see themselves
beholding the delightful and pleasant light of the sun.
Oh most blessed, whatever man will live to that time.[299] (183-92)

In this concept, then, there is a twofold judgment, or rather two judgments,
one after the other: first a historical judgment of destruction, described here
as the burning of the world, and then, after the general resurrection of the dead
(or rather the re-creation of those who have gone to dust), a last judgment in
forensic forms. At this judgment God alone is judge over "impious *and* pious"
(42). This means not only the ungodly and the pious of Israel, but all humanity, which is now to be judged (41, 184).

The last judgment is here consistently described as universal. Even the contrast between Israel and the Gentiles appears to be eliminated. It plays no part
at all in the fourth book. The author addresses all humanity and distinguishes
only the impious and the pious. It is true that we may suppose, especially in
connection with the call to baptism, that the "faithful" or "pious" also include
God-fearers and proselytes from among the Gentiles, but this is not clear at
any point.[300] This reservation is possibly connected with the genre and purpose
of these oracles, for they seem to serve the purpose of missionary propaganda.

The punishment of the godless will be a second death,[301] the reward of the
faithful a renewed, blissful life on earth. Oddly enough, nothing is said of a
new creation of the earth, which has been reduced to ashes in the consuming
fire. This example again shows that the "apocalypticists" had little concern for
consistency, logic, or pictorial conception in their depiction of the "last
things."

> J. J. Collins thinks that the description in vv. 173-92 could well have a pagan
> basis, since both the idea of a world conflagration and that of the resurrection
> of the dead can come from Persian sources ("Sibylline Oracles," *OTP* 1: 381;
> "Place," 374–75). Apart from the question of the tradition-historical origins of
> the two ideas, however, it seems to me that a pagan substratum for this passage
> is improbable.

299. The last verse is also in 3:371 and could have been inserted from there. Since
it is preceded by a general re-creation, it is quite out of place in this location.
300. For Jewish universalism after 70 c.e., see M. Simon, *Verus Israel,* 52–86; idem,
"Aspects," 231. We find the same universalism in *T. Abr.,* in 2 Enoch, and in 3 Baruch
(E. P. Sanders, "Testament of Abraham," *OTP* 1: 876–78).
301. At most, ἐν πυρί in v. 43 hints at the pains of hell, but this is only in Lactantius.
The MSS have ἔμπαλι(ν).

Books One and Two

The first two books of the Sibylline Oracles constitute a single unit. The basic Jewish document, probably written in Phrygia around the turn of the era, underwent a Christian redaction about 150 C.E. The redaction cannot be isolated with certainty at every point.[302] Unmistakably, 1:1-323 (story of creation and history of the first seven generations) belong to the Jewish Sibyl, as does the eschatological oracle in 2:154-76, culminating in Israel's rule over the nations. The oracles about the last judgment in 2:214-20 and 2:221-37 contain nothing that could be pointed out as not Jewish.[303] But the motif of God's βῆμα, before which the dead are to be brought (2:218, 235, 237), is otherwise found primarily in Christian writings.[304] The long oracle in 2:252-338, with its extensive description of the punishments of hell and the joys of paradise, I consider entirely Christian.[305]

Before the Flood, God commands Noah to preach repentance to "all the peoples": "Proclaim repentance, so that all may be saved" (κήρυξον μετά-νοιαν, ὅπως σωθῶσιν ἅπαντες) (1:129).[306] But Noah's preaching (1:150-98), warning about the "wrath of the great God" that will come upon them from heaven (1:165), falls on deaf ears, and the threatened catastrophe occurs. After the Flood, Noah is to take care that humanity again increases and practices righteousness, generation after generation, "until the whole [human] race comes to trial, when there will be judgment for all" (ἄχρις εἰς κρίσιν ἥξει/ πᾶν γένος ἀνθρώπων, ἐπεὶ κρίσις ἔσσεθ' ἅπασιν) (1:273-74). With this designation of the time, which we have already encountered frequently in the same or similar form,[307] the Flood and the final judgment are clearly paralleled. The time between is understood as one *single* period.

---

302. J. J. Collins, "Sibylline Oracles," *OTP* 1: 330–32.

303. Ibid., 330, 333.

304. Rom. 14:10 (2 Cor. 5:10: βῆμα τοῦ Χριστοῦ. Cf. also Pol. *Phil.* 6:2); *Sib. Or.* 8:82, 222, 242, 372. The Jewish examples using this loan-word are all, as far as I know, late, e.g., *Midr. Tanh. B.* Exod. III § 13. It is also found in a parable in *Midr. Tanh. B.* Lev. I § 15; Num. IV § 22.

305. J. J. Collins does not come to a firm conclusion ("Sibylline Oracles," *OTP* 1: 323, 333).

306. For Noah as an unsuccessful preacher of repentance, cf. Jos. *Ant.* 1.74; *1 Clem.* 7:5-6; Theophilus, *Autol.* 3.29; *Apoc. Pauli* 50; *b Sanh.* 108a/b; *Qoh. R.* on Qoh 9:25 (IX, 15, 1) (quoted by A. Schlatter, *Matthäus,* 56). In 2 Pet. 2:5 he is called κήρυξ δικαιο-σύνης. Cf. also *Ber. R.* 30:7; *Mek. Y* on 15:6 (Lauterbach 2: 39–40); *Tg. Neof.* Gen. 6:3. J. P. Lewis, *Noah,* 102–3; E. Lövestam, "Eschatologie," 290–94; R. J. Bauckham, *2 Pet.* 250–51.

307. See above, pp. 80–81.

The final judgment is the subject of 2:154-76. It is announced by portents, "famines, pestilence, and wars" (λιμοὶ λοιμοὶ πόλεμοί τε) (2:156). Women bear no more children (2:163-64), false prophets appear (2:165-66), Beliar appears and performs many signs (σήματα πολλὰ ποιήσει) (2:167-68).[308] Thus one may recognize that this is the time of the "last generation" (ὑστατίη γενεή) (2:162); "the harvest of articulate men has come"; "the gathering together is near" (ἔφυ τὸ θέρος μερόπων ἀνθρώπων./ἡ δὲ συναίρεσις ἐγγύς) (2:164-65). Then the ten lost tribes will return (2:171-73) and "a terrible wrath" (170) will come upon Israel; nations will perish (2:173). But after this "the faithful chosen Hebrews" (ἐκλεκτοὶ πιστοὶ Ἑβραῖοι) will make the powerful their slaves "as of old" (2:174-76). Especially striking in this text are the importance of portents and the purely political and national conception of eschatology, which is apparently shaped by the ancient ideal of the Davidic empire. If the oracle were not written in Greek hexameters, one would unquestionably posit that it originated in Palestine.

In 2:187-213, after the return of Elijah, the destruction of the earth by a flood of fire from heaven is described. But because the extent of Christian redaction is difficult to determine (200-213 should be compared with 8:337-50), we will not examine these verses in detail.

Sib. Or. 3:1-96 and Fragment 3

Verses 3:1-96 from the lost second book[309] contain two oracles announcing the eschatological judgment: 46-62 and 75-92. According to the latter, "the judgment of the great God" (91) consists in the burning of the world, and it will occur "when a widow reigns over the whole world" (77). The "widow" is probably meant to be Cleopatra.[310]

According to the other oracle, the "bitter day" of judgment (59) coincides with the "manifestation" of the reign of God (47-48: τότε δὴ βασιλεία μεγίστη /ἀθανάτου βασιλῆος ἐπ᾽ ἀνθρώποισι φανεῖται).[311] Then a "holy prince" will come and reign forever over the whole earth (49-50). This ruler is probably intended to be the Messiah, rather than God. The instruments of

---

308. For Beliar and his signs, cf. also 3:63-74. There are literal echoes of our passage there. For the role of Beliar, see V. Nikiprowetzky, "Troisième Sibylle," 138–43; J. J. Collins, *Sibylline Oracles*, 86–87.

309. See p. 96, above.

310. J. J. Collins, *Sibylline Oracles*, 66–70; E. Schürer and G. Vermes, *History* 3/1: 641.

311. Cf. *As. Mos.* 10:1.

judgment are a fiery cataract from heaven and brimstone (54,60-61). Its time is also appointed: "When Rome will also rule over Egypt" (46). That happened in 31 B.C.E. with the battle of Actium. This oracle must have been written shortly thereafter.[312] It thus attests to an immediate eschatological expectation on the part of Egyptian Jews, and presumes an antipathy against Rome that expanded into irreconcilable hatred by the time of the revolt under Trajan in the years 115–117 C.E.

The two longer fragments, 1 and 3, quoted by Theophilus (*Autol.* 2.36), belong to the lost second book or the original beginning of the third. They indicate no Christian influence of any kind.[313] At the end of a speech about the greatness of God and the foolishness of idolatry, the Sibyl turns to those who have not come to their senses and are unwilling to acknowledge God as king (3:41-42):

> τοὔνεκεν αἰθομένοιο πυρὸς σέλας ἔρχετ᾽ ἐφ᾽ ὑμᾶς,
> λαμπάσι καυθήσεσθε δι᾽ αἰῶνος τὸ πανῆμαρ
> ψευδέσιν αἰσχυνθέντες ἐπ᾽ εἰδώλοισιν ἀχρήστοις.
> οἱ δὲ θεὸν τιμῶντες ἀληθινὸν ἀέναόν τε
> ζωὴν κληρονομοῦσι, τὸν αἰῶνος χρόνον αὐτοί
> οἰκοῦντες παραδείσου ὁμῶς ἐριθηλέα κῆπον
> δαινύμενοι γλυκὺν ἄρτον ἀπ᾽ οὐρανοῦ ἀστερόεντος.

> Therefore the gleam of blazing fire comes upon you.
> You will be burned with torches throughout eternity,
> shamed by lies on account of useless idols.
> But those who honor the true eternal God
> inherit life, dwelling in the luxuriant garden of Paradise for the time of
> eternity,
> feasting on sweet bread from starry heaven.
> (Fragment 3:43-49)

This whole passage and its motifs recall 4 Ezra 7:36-38.[314] The oracle may have been written at about the same time, roughly the end of the first century C.E. The two writings may rest on a common basic tradition.

---

312. J. J. Collins, "Sibylline Oracles," *OTP* 1: 360; idem, *Sibylline Oracles*, 64–66; E. Schürer and G. Vermes, *History* 3/1: 640.

313. J. J. Collins, "Sibylline Oracles," *OTP* 1: 360, 469; E. Schürer and G. Vermes, *History* 3/1: 638–39.

314. See below, pp. 115–16.

The Fifth Book

The oracles in the Fifth Book of the Sibylline Oracles originated in Egypt between 70 and 132 C.E., most of them probably before the revolt under Trajan in 115–117 C.E.[315] They may be regarded, in fact, as an expression of the intellectual atmosphere among the Egyptian Jews and the ideological background of the rebels.[316]

The author's starting point is the sharp conflict between Israel and the nations. He cries "woe" over the gentile cities, especially Rome (168-78), and has at his disposal "the whole arsenal of apocalyptic visions of horror."[317] According to these oracles (361-74), judgment will be introduced by a murderous war brought upon the world by the end time tyrant who "will come from the ends of the earth" (ἐκ περάτων γαίης) (363).[318] Accompanied by a "wintry blast" (375), judgment will go forth with a rain of fire (274, 377), with darkness, lightning (378), and cosmic catastrophes (344-50, 476-83, 512-31). According to 302-5, God in person will destroy the wicked with lightning; according to 414-19, a "blessed man" (ἀνὴρ μακαρίτης) will come from heaven, with a scepter bestowed by God in his hands, and will go forth with fire against the enemy cities and peoples.[319] After this he will make Jerusalem glorious and will build a tower "touching even the clouds and visible to all, so that all faithful and all righteous people could see the glory (δόξα) of eternal God" (425-27). Then the land will flow with milk and honey (281-83), and the remnant of the people that is left will enjoy the peace they have earned after the evils formerly suffered (εἰρήνην δ᾽ ἕξει λαὸς σοφός, ὅσπερ ἐλείφθη, / πειραθεὶς κακότητος, ἵν᾽ ὕστερον εὐφρανθείη) (384-85).

Like the oracle in 3:46-62, most of the oracles in the Fifth Book are inspired by a burning eschatological expectation.[320] They also show that apocalyptic

315. J. J. Collins, "Sibylline Oracles," *OTP* 1: 390; M. Hengel, "Hoffnung," 668; E. Schürer and G. Vermes, *History* 3/1: 644–45.

316. J. J. Collins, "Sibylline Oracles," *OTP* 1: 390; idem, *Sibylline Oracles,* 94–95; idem, *Between Athens and Jerusalem,* 122–28; M. Hengel, "Hoffnung," 668–79.

317. M. Hengel, "Hoffnung," 668.

318. The reference is to Nero *redivivus,* who was expected to come from the Parthian east. On this, see J. J. Collins, *Sibylline Oracles,* 81–87; M. Hengel, "Hoffnung," 669.

319. Cf. also 155-61. For the Messiah in *Sib. Or.* 5, see J. J. Collins, *Sibylline Oracles,* 87–92; M. Hengel, "Hoffnung," 674–78. Here he resembles the figure of Michael in Dan. 12:1 and 1QM XVII, 6-7, the *nuntius* in *As. Mos.* 10:2, and Melchizedek in 11Q Melch.

320. M. Hengel, "Hoffnung," 670.

eschatology descended from the idea of the "day of YHWH" and texts like Isaiah 65–66 were as vivid in the diaspora as in the Palestinian homeland.[321] Moreover, it is striking that these oracles, as even the language in which they are written shows, come from educated circles,[322] whereas the revolt under Trajan was more the work of the lower classes.[323] The division within the people with regard to messianic and political hopes, of which Martin Hengel speaks,[324] should therefore not be overemphasized.

The *Liber Antiquitatum Biblicarum*

Pseudo-Philo's *Liber Antiquitatum Biblicarum* presents a midrashic retelling and embellishment of the biblical story from Adam to the death of Saul, comparable to the Book of Jubilees or the Genesis Apocryphon from Qumran.[325] Numerous parallels to 4 Ezra and *2 Baruch* point to a common intellectual milieu, namely, Pharisaic or rabbinic Judaism.[326] The Latin text, as in the case of 4 Ezra, rests on a Greek translation of a Hebrew original.[327] The *Bib. Ant.* is usually dated in the period after 70 c.e., but P.-M. Bogaert, with good reason, posits a date not long before that year.[328]

The eschatology of the document is summarized in a kind of miniature apocalypse (3:10). In context, it represents the second expansion of God's

---

321. Thus correctly M. Hengel, "Hoffnung," 657–58, 663, against U. Fischer, *Eschatologie*, 255–56. One may also refer here to Wis. 5:17-23.

322. M. Hengel, "Hoffnung," 668.

323. Ibid., 666–67.

324. Ibid., 666.

325. L. Cohn, "Apocryphal Work," 314–22; M. Delcor, *DBSup* 7: 1364–66; C. Perrot (and P.-M. Bogaert), *Les Antiquités Bibliques* 2: 22–28; L. H. Feldman, "Prolegomenon," lii–liv. For parallels to the targums and midrash, ibid., lxvi–lxx.

326. M. R. James, *Biblical Antiquities*, 46–58; L. H. Feldman, "Prolegomenon," liv–lv; C. Perrot (and P.-M. Bogaert), *Les Antiquités Bibliques* 2: 28–39. We can probably not posit any direct literary dependence. J. Hadot ("Milieu d'origine") represents the point of view that this work was written at the time of Hyrcanus II (63–40 b.c.e.) in a marginal Essene group. But the eschatology of the work speaks against an Essene origin (a point of view that was represented in previous scholarship); this eschatology is fundamentally different from that of the Qumran writings. Cf. also L. Feldman, "Prolegomenon," xxxviii–xliii.

327. L. Cohn, "Apocryphal Work," 307–14; M. Delcor, *DBSup* 7: 1367–69; D. J. Harrington in C. Perrot and P.-M. Bogaert, *Les Antiquités Bibliques* 2: 75–77. L. H. Feldman expresses some doubt ("Prolegomenon," xxv–xxvii).

328. (C. Perrot) and P.-M. Bogaert, *Les Antiquités Bibliques* 2:66–74. Cf. L. H. Feldman, "Prolegomenon," xxviii–xxxi.

speech to Noah after the Flood, which is otherwise closely related to Gen. 8:21-22. The speech begins in 3:9:[329]

> And God said: I will never again curse the earth on [humanity's] account, for the tendency of [the human] heart is foolish from youth; and so I will never destroy all living creatures at one time as I have done. But when those inhabiting the earth sin, I will judge them (diiudicabo) by famine or by the sword or by fire or by death; and there will be earthquakes, and they will be scattered to uninhabited places. But no more will I destroy the earth by the water of the flood. And in all the days of the earth, seedtime and harvest, cold and heat, spring and fall will not cease day and night, until I remember those who inhabit the earth, until the appointed times are fulfilled (donec compleantur tempora).

Thus the initial expansion of the biblical text already has God's judgment as its theme, although not the final judgment; these are the punishing judgments of God that recur again and again throughout the nation's history, and that will cease with the last judgment—for the last words form a transition to the depiction of the final events. The formula "donec compleantur tempora" is taken up immediately afterward with the phrase "cum autem completi fuerint anni saeculi [but when the years appointed for the world have been fulfilled]." A very similar formula is found also in 23.13: "quousque compleatur tempus saeculi [until the time allotted the world be complete]." All three phrases refer to the same thing: a limit has been set to time (here meaning the time of this age, for in Bib. Ant. αἰών is always stereotypically translated with saeculum),[330] and when that limit has been reached, the end will come:[331]

> Cum autem completi fuerint anni saeculi,
> tunc quiescet lumen
> et extinguentur tenebrae,
> et vivificabo mortuos
> et erigam dormientes de terra.
> Et reddet infernus debitum suum,
> et perditio restituet paratecem suam,
> ut reddam unicuique secundum opera sua
> et secundum fructus adinventionum suarum,
> quousque iudicem inter animam et carnem.

329. In the following quotation the parts that parallel the biblical text are italicized.
330. Cf. G. Delling, "Zeit," 306.
331. Cf. G. Delling, "Zeit," 310–11, 313–14, 317. The text of the following quotation, like the others, follows D. J. Harrington, with some slight orthographic changes.

Et requiescet saeculum
et extinguetur mors,
et infernus claudet os suum.
Et non erit sine fetu terra,
nec sterilis habitantibus in se:
et non coinquinabitur ullus, qui in me iustificatus est.
Et erit terra alia et caelum aliud,
habitaculum sempiternum.

But when the years appointed for the world have been fulfilled,
then the light will cease
and the darkness will fade away.
And I will bring the dead to life
and raise up those who are sleeping from the earth.
And Sheol will pay back its debt,
and Abaddon[332] will return its deposit
so that I may render to each according to his works
and according to the fruits of his own devices,
until I judge between soul and flesh.
And the world will cease,
and death will be abolished,
and Sheol will shut its mouth.
And the earth will not be without progeny
or sterile for those inhabiting it;
and no one who has been pardoned by me will be tainted.
And there will be another earth and another heaven,
an everlasting dwelling place. (3:10)

All the remaining eschatological statements in the *Bib. Ant.* can be discussed as commentary on this little "apocalypse."[333] The general resurrection of the dead is described in words that echo Isa. 26:19 and Dan. 12:2, very similar to those in 1 Enoch 51:1, 4 Ezra 7:32, and *2 Bar.* 42:8.[334] To this point, the abode of the deceased sinners is in darkness (15:5; 16:3; 51:5) and "inextinguishable

332. For *perditio* (v. l. *perditum*) / ἀπώλεια / אֲבַדּוֹן, cf. M. Delcor, *DBSup* 7: 1358; G. Delling, "Zeit," 317 n. 1; M. Black, "1 Enoch," 214. Cf. also Rev. 9:11 and R. H. Charles, *Revelation* 1: 245–46.

333. At most, 6:1 might constitute an exception. There the nations of the earth say of the building of the tower: ". . . *et in novissimis diebus alterutrum erimus expugnantes nos.*" This apparently indicates an eschatological war among nations. For the expression "*in novissimis diebus*" in *Bib. Ant.*, see G. Delling, "Zeit," 317–18.

334. Cf. also Rev. 20:13. On this, see the comparative synopses of G. Stemberger (*Leib*, 119–20) and H. C. Cavallin, "Leben," 262–63. For resurrection in the *Bib. Ant.*, see G. Stemberger, *Leib*, 105–13.

fire" (63:4),[335] where Balaam gnashes his teeth (18:12). In contrast, God has prepared light for the righteous after death (51:5); they will be like the stars in heaven (33:5)[336] and will achieve "the repose of the just" (*requies iustorum*) (28:10); their lot is eternal life and God preserves their souls in peace "until the time allotted the world be complete."[337] Till then, the souls of both groups are kept in "chambers" (*promptuaria*) (32:13) or "chambers of darkness" (*thesauri tenebrarum*) 15:5).[338]

This state of things ends with the resurrection to judgment, when God judges the whole world according to the "eternal law" given to Moses on Sinai.[339] Thus, although this judgment is imagined as forensic, the author of *Bib. Ant.* can speak of it as a "visitation" (*visitare*) of God (19:12,13; 26:13). He uses the same expression in 1:20 for the judgment of the Flood.

After the last judgment, the sinners will be subject to final and definitive death (16:3), while for the righteous begins the "new age," the "age without measure"[340] on a renewed, fruitful earth.[341] Perhaps those sinners who, after a confession of their guilt on earth, have done penance through an early death may also find mercy (25:7). The designation of those who have survived the judgment as pardoned or "justified" by God (3:10) is striking. The eschatological time is once called the time of God's "just judgments."[342]

It is surprising to find that in an early Jewish writing of this extent Pseudo-Philo employs only a single eschatological conception, one whose fundamental

---

335. Cf. Isa. 66:24; *Tg. Neof.* on Gen. 38:25. The *locus ignis* was already shown to Abraham (*Bib. Ant.* 23:6).

336. Cf. Dan. 12:3.

337. *Bib. Ant.* 23:13: *Erit autem et in finem uniuscuiusque omnium vestrum sors in vita aeterna vobis et semini vestro, et accipiam animas vestras et reponam eas in pace quousque compleatur tempus saeculi.* M. Delcor (*DBSup* 7: 1372) sees here an indication of an individual judgment after death, to be distinguished from the judgment in 3:10. But there can be no question of that, as the final phrase indicates (cf. 3:9). The righteous receive "life eternal," in contrast to the sinners, whom definitive death awaits after the last judgment (16:3: *et tunc morientur et non vivent*).

338. Cf. G. Stemberger, *Leib*, 101–4.

339. *Bib. Ant.* 11:2: ... *dedi in manus tuas legem sempiternam, et in hac omnem orbem iudicabo. Erit enim haec in testimonium.*

340. *Bib. Ant.* 23:8: *Novum saeculum;* 23:3: *immensurabile tempus;* 34:3: *immensurabile saeculum.*

341. *Bib. Ant.* 3:10: *terra alia et caelum aliud* (cf. Isa. 65:17; 66:22); 16:3: *ero innovans terram;* 32:17: *in innovatione creaturae.*

342. *Bib. Ant.* 32:17: ... *quia tempus praeparabitur iustificationibus* (v. l. *iustificatis*) *suis.*

features we also find in the Book of Wisdom. According to it sinners and righteous can expect a preliminary reward after death: suffering for the one group, "peace" (Wis. 3:3; *Bib. Ant.* 23:13) and "rest" (Wis. 4:7; *Bib. Ant.* 28:10) for the other; only at the last judgment is their lot finally determined: eternal life for one group (cf. Wis. 5:15; *Bib. Ant.* 23:13), and ultimate death for the other (cf. Wis. 5:14; *Bib. Ant.* 16:3).

However, the eschatology of the *Bib. Ant.* is even more like that behind 4 Ezra 7:32-38 (cf. *Bib. Ant.* 3:10).[343] Common to both writings is the schema of two ages in which "this age" (*hoc saeculum*) (*Bib. Ant.* 19:7; 30:2; 4 Ezra 8:1), described as corruptible (*Bib. Ant.* 28:10) or corrupt (4 Ezra 4:11), is followed by the "age without measure" (*Bib. Ant.* 34:3) or the "immortal age" (4 Ezra 7:113).[344] In addition, the explicitly parenetic purpose is common to both writings: Since, after death, there is no further opportunity for repentance and no prayer of intercession is of any more avail, one should mend one's ways while one still has "the time of life and the light of the Law."[345]

The eschatological conception of the *Bib. Ant.* corresponds entirely to the Pharisaic and rabbinic ideas we will encounter at the conclusion of this chapter. With the eschatology of the Qumran writings, on the other hand, it has nothing in common.

Fourth Ezra

So-called 4 Ezra, included as an appendix to the Latin Vulgate, was written ca. 100 C.E., probably in Palestine.[346] In literary quality and theological content it surpasses all the comparable writings of early Judaism, and for that reason

343. See below, pp. 115–16.

344. For the schema of two ages, see pp. 112–13 below, on 4 Ezra. However, we should not fail to note the differences in the ideas in *Bib. Ant.* and 4 Ezra. A sharp opposition between the two ages, as revealed in 4 Ezra, is unknown to Pseudo-Philo. His conception is more like that of the rabbis than that of 4 Ezra.

345. *Bib. Ant.* 33:1–5. On this, see E. Reinmuth, "Ps.-Philo," 17–28. Cf. 4 Ezra 9:7–12; 14:34–35. For the impossibility of repentance hereafter, see Str-B 2: 233; 4: 1047–48. On the prayer of intercession, see 4 Ezra 7:102-15. P. Volz, *Eschatologie*, 290; C. Dietzfelbinger, *Pseudo-Philo*, 199, 5b; C. Perrot and P.-M. Bogaert, *Les Antiquités Bibliques* 2: 177.

346. Josef Schreiner, *4. Esr*, 301–2. [The English translation relies in part on B. M. Metzger, "The Fourth Book of Ezra," *OTP* 1: 517–59.—Trans.]. Compare now, throughout, the commentary by M. E. Stone, *Fourth Ezra*.

among others is "the most sympathetic of the apocalypses."[347] The received versions, the most important of which is the Latin, rest on the Greek translation of a Semitic original.[348] The author has redacted a variety of more or less well-formed traditions, so that one can call the work "almost a compendium of the world of eschatological thinking."[349] It is divided into seven sections, called "visions," but visions in the proper sense are found only in the second part (visions 4–7 = chaps. 9:26—14:47). The first part (visions 1–3 = chaps. 3:1—9:25) consists essentially of dialogues between Ezra and the angel Uriel, who also speaks on behalf of God. Chapters 1–2 and 15–16 are Christian books that were not originally part of this writing.

The author's eschatology is shaped by the schema of two ages or two periods of the world: The Most High "has made not *one* age [or: world], but two" (7:50). This is the answer to the troubling question of the promise of salvation to Israel and the righteous in light of their undeserved sufferings. Behind the contrast between "this age/world" (*hoc saeculum*) and "the age/world to come" (*futurum saeculum*) (8:1) is the rabbinic conceptual pair of העולם הזה and העולם הבא.[350] However, the contrast between the two ages received far less emphasis from the rabbis, and this age was not regarded so negatively as in the eyes of the author of 4 Ezra.[351] It is true that the author concedes that God

347. Hermann Gunkel, "4. Esr," 348. On style, idem, 349–50. For the artistic composition and thought structure of the book, see E. Brandenburger, *Verborgenheit*.

348. J. Schreiner, *4. Esr*, 294–95. There is a Greek retroversion in Adolf Hilgenfeld, *Messias*, 36–113.

349. H. Gunkel, "4. Esr," 348. For the literary-critical question, see J. Schreiner, *4. Esr*, 297–301. Here Gunkel's opinion ("4. Esr," 350) has prevailed. His work is still the best introduction to this document.

350. On the two-world teaching in 4 Ezra, cf. N. Messel, *Einheitlichkeit*, 44–60; H. Sasse, *TDNT* 1: 206; M. E. Stone, *Features*, 44–83; W. Harnisch, *Verhängnis*, 89–106; C. Barth, *Diesseits*, 26–34; P. Schäfer, "Lehre." Harnisch emphasizes (*Verhängnis*, 95), as do Messel and Sasse, that the concepts of "this" and "the future" age in 4 Ezra are primarily used in a temporal sense, which is concealed by the translation "world"—which J. Schreiner, for example, uses throughout. Cf. also C. Barth, *Diesseits*, 30–31. See the rabbinic material in Str-B 4: 815–57, 968–76; G. Dalman, *Worte*, 122–23; P. Volz, *Eschatologie*, 65–66; J. Bonsirven, *Judaïsme* 1: 310–32; H. Sasse, *TDNT* 1: 206–7; E. Schürer and G. Vermes, *History* 2: 537-38; P. Schäfer, "Lehre." Instead of עולם הבא, the rabbinic texts often write simply העתיד לבא, "the time to come," "the future."

351. P. Schäfer has demonstrated this difference ("Lehre," 264–74): "The teaching about the two worlds in 4 Ezra is dualistic and antagonistic and thus stands in sharp contrast to the continuing and linear model of rabbinic Judaism" (ibid., 274). Is the contrast too sharply drawn here?—for the rabbis' concept of history is also dualistic.

created this age for Israel's sake; but when Adam transgressed God's commands the creation was subjected to judgment (*iudicatum est quod factum est*) (7:11). Since then, this age is filled with hardship and danger, but the one to come contains the fruit of immortality (7:12-13).[352]

The day of judgment has an important function in this scheme: *Dies enim iudicii erit finis temporis huius et initium futuri immortalitatis temporis* (But the day of judgment will be the end of this age and the beginning of the immortal age to come: 7:113; cf. 12:34). The day of judgment brings the transition between the ages. Thus it is absolutely clear that the two-ages schema serves to conceptualize an idea, the substance of which has long existed and been expressed in formulas like ". . . until the day of judgment," ". . . until the new creation," and so on.[353] This concept, in which the course of history will at one point be sharply interrupted and this era replaced by a "new creation," belongs to that moment when the day of YHWH became an eschatological day of judgment—thus, at the latest, with Trito-Isaiah. The antagonistic two-ages schema in 4 Ezra, which even Pseudo-Philo did not know in this extreme degree, is the final culmination of the dualistic conception of history developed in the early postexilic period.

The schema of two ages is combined, in the first part of the document, with various eschatological concepts that we have already encountered in other early Jewish writings. The author of 4 Ezra adopted them from the tradition and applied them in the service of his own train of ideas. Here, however, we are less interested in the author's way of thinking than in the traditions and concepts he adopted.

In 6:7-10 we find a pesher-type interpretation of Gen. 25:26 (Jacob's hand holding the heel of Esau at their birth): "For Esau is the end (Syriac: the hand) of this age, and Jacob is the beginning (Syriac: the hand) of the age that follows" (6:9). This explanation apparently presumes a usage common in rab-

---

In their understanding as well, the day of judgment divides this era of the world from the one to come.

352. See the detailed discussion of this point in W. Harnisch, *Verhängnis*, 106–42.

353. For these examples, see above, pp. 80–81. W. Harnisch writes: "In the apocalypses of 4 Ezra and [*2 Bar.*] the dualistic conception of history whose initial stages can be demonstrated as early as the book of Daniel, and which is already present also in the older works of late [*sic*] Jewish apocalyptic acquires its full conceptual and substantial expression" (*Verhängnis*, 123). So also P. Vielhauer, "Einleitung," 412. However, the initial stages of this dualistic conception of history are in fact to be sought as early as the immediate postexilic period. Cf. P. D. Hanson, *Dawn*, 155–60.

binic literature, in which "Esau" symbolizes Rome, and "Jacob" is the symbol for Israel.[354] Israel's eschatological rule will replace that of Rome.[355] "When Esau goes down to the underworld, Jacob alone remains."[356]

This "pesher," however, is located within a section in which the subject is God's end time appearance for judgment. Previously, Ezra had asked through whom God would "visit" (*visitare*) the creation (5:56) and was answered that the end (*finis*) comes through God alone (6:6). The key word *visit* is then taken up again after the "pesher," in 6:18-20:

> [The voice] said: Behold, the days are coming,
> and it shall be that when I draw near to visit the inhabitants of the earth,
> and when I require from the doers of iniquity the penalty of their iniquity,
> and when the humiliation of Zion is complete.
> and when the seal is placed upon the age which is about to pass away,
> then I will show these signs: . . .

There follows a listing of typical signs accompanying the end, and then a description of the time of salvation: "It shall be that whoever remains after all that I have foretold to you shall be saved and shall see my salvation and the end of my world (*finem saeculi mei*). And they shall see those who were taken up, who from their birth have not tasted death; and the heart of the earth's inhabitants shall be changed and converted to a different spirit" (6:25-26).[357]

According to this, then, only the survivors of the last generation of Israel will enjoy eschatological salvation. What about those who have already died?

354. M. E. Stone cites *Ber. R.* and *Yalqut Shim'oni* (so already B. Violet, *4. Esr* 2: 47) as well as *Pirqe R. El.* and *Midr. HaGadol* on Gen. 25:26 (*Features*, 48–49). Cf. also S. Schechter, "Aspects," 3: 205; P. Volz, *Eschatologie*, 280; E. Schürer and G. Vermes, *History* 3/1: 298, n. 5. G. D. Cohen doubts that 4 Ezra 6:7-10 presupposes this usage and deliberately makes the identification ("Esau as Symbol in Early Medieval Thought," 21). "As far as I can determine, the first Rabbi to have clearly identified Rome with Esau and Edom was none other than Rabbi Akiba ben Joseph" (ibid., 22). Cf. recently F. Avemarie, "Esaus Hände, Jakobs Stimme."
355. Cf. M. E. Stone, *Features*, 48–53; P. Schäfer, "Lehre," 261–62. So previously H. Gunkel, "4. Esr," 365; Str-B 4: 813–14; J. Keulers, *Eschatologische Lehre*, 47–48, 107.
356. *Midr. Tanh. B.* Lev II, 1, § 4 (Bietenhard 2: 28). The whole passage is also in Str-B 3: 154–55.
357. For the Old Testament background of 4 Ezra 6:13–28, see L. Hartman, *Prophecy*, 132–37.

The author of 4 Ezra saw this problem (5:41) and "solved" it in his own fashion. Ezra receives this answer: "I shall liken my judgment to a crown [Ethiopic:
circle]; just as for those who are last there is no slowness, so for those who
are first there is no haste" (*sicut non novissimorum tarditas, sic nec priorum
velocitas*) (5:42).[358]

We find a different but equally historical conception in 7:26-44. Here the
new age begins with the general resurrection: ". . . the earth shall give up those
who are asleep in it; and the chambers shall give up the souls which have been
committed to them" (7:32).[359] Then the Most High appears on the throne of
judgment and judges without favor or mercy, but solely according to works
(7:33-35). Then "the pit of torment"[360] will appear, and opposite it the place
of rest (*locus requietionis*); the furnace of Gehenna will appear opposite the
Paradise of delight (*iucunditatis paradisus*). And then the Most High will say
to the nations that have been raised from the dead: "Look now, and understand whom you have denied, whom you have not served, whose commandments you have despised! Look on this side and on that; here are delight and
rest, and there are fire and torments" (7:36-38).

Thus vv. 32-38 are based on a concept of the course of events like the one
we encountered in 1 Enoch 51:1-5, *Bib. Ant.* 3:10, and *Sib. Or.* 4:181-91:[361] The
general resurrection is followed by a forensic judgment whose sentence decides
each person's blessedness or damnation. But since it is already determined,
before the judgment, who are the righteous and who the sinners, there is no
need for a judicial process as such, and consequently there is never any description of such a process.

358. Cf. W. Harnisch, *Verhängnis,* 293–94. This sentence has produced, it seems to
me, unnecessary difficulties for interpreters (see J. Schreiner, *4. Esr* 329, ad loc.). The
author only wants to say that the problem proposed does not exist for him. He is probably thinking of his "solution" in 14:35 (see below).

359. Cf. Isa. 26:19; Dan. 12:2; 1 Enoch 51:1; *2 Bar.* 42:8; *Bib. Ant.* 3:10. The author
here juxtaposes two different ideas of the state of the dead. J. Keulers thinks that he
"has the body arise from the earth and the soul return from its chamber, so that the
reunion of the two causes the human being to exist once more" (*Eschatologische Lehre,*
151). Similarly M. E. Stone, *Features,* 143–47. K. Schubert ("Auferstehungslehre," 207)
is somewhat reserved: "one gets the impression . . . "; so also H. C. Cavallin, "Leben,"
264. G. Stemberger, *Leib,* 74–84, treats the matter in detail: "This idea is apparently not
far removed, but it is not yet fully developed here" (ibid., 82). For later rabbinic teaching on the union of soul and body in the resurrection, see G. Stemberger, "Auferstehungslehre," 247–54.

360. *Lacus* (MSS: *locus*) *tormenti.* Behind this is Greek λάκκος τῆς βασάνου (cf.
Luke 16:28). B. Violet, *4. Esr* 2: 77.

361. See above, pp. 109–10 on *Bib. Ant.* 3:10.

The author has now joined this eschatological concept to a quite different, messianic idea in such a way that the messianic time is made to precede the new age, as a preliminary time of salvation lasting four hundred years (7:26-30).[362] This sacred time begins, after the portents, with the appearance of the "invisible city," that is, the heavenly Jerusalem, and the "hidden land" (7:26).[363] The meaning of this last item is disputed: is it the eschatological Paradise, as in 7:36 (4:7-8; 7:123; 8:52), or the Palestine of the time of salvation (cf. 9:8; 12:34; 13:48)? Perhaps the author deliberately left it ambiguous. The enjoyment of the good things and happiness that the Messiah gives is conveyed, as in the conception represented by the preceding section, 5:56—6:28, only to the "survivors" of the last generation (7:28). However, before the beginning of the new age even they, including the Messiah, will die (7:29). That the Messiah here, differently, for example, from *Ps. Sol.* 17, does not impose sentence on the nations nor exercise any other judicial functions is probably determined, like the idea that the Messiah will die, by the combination with the concept that follows. The author apparently wanted to avoid any appearance of a twofold judgment.

The yardstick for the last judgment, which follows the resurrection, is, as we have seen, nothing but the keeping of the Law. The author explains this in the description of the dialogue between Ezra and the angel that immediately precedes the last events (7:17-25): God determined in the Law that only the righteous would "inherit" the good things of the future, while the ungodly must perish (*peribunt*) (7:17). God declared to all, as soon as they were born, "what they should do to live, and what they should observe to avoid punishment" (7:21). The great majority of people, however, denied the existence of the Most High, scorned God's law, and therefore are subject to the punishment that was threatened (7:22-25). Here there is a clear allusion to passages like Deut. 8:1 and Deut. 30:15-20, whose promises ("life") and threats ("death") are interpreted eschatologically, as we have frequently observed elsewhere.[364]

362. Cf. U. B. Müller, *Messias*, 86–92. However, I do not think that vv. 26-27 must be connected to vv. 32ff., and that only vv. 28-31 represent an insertion. The "hidden land" need not be the "paradise" of v. 36; it could originally have referred to Palestine (see below). For the rabbinic concepts that acknowledge a preliminary messianic period of salvation, see Str-B 3: 823–30; P. Volz, *Eschatologie*, 71–72; J. Bonsirven, *Judaïsme* 1: 419–28. For its length, see also W. Bacher, *Agada* 1: 139–40.

363. For both of these, see N. Messel, *Einheitlichkeit*, 85–101; J. Keulers, *Eschatologische Lehre*, 78–79; M. E. Stone, "Features," 101–3; "J. Schreiner, *4. Esr*, 344–45 ad loc.

364. Cf. N. Messel, *Einheitlichkeit*, 120–29; W. Harnisch, *Verhängnis*, 148–49, 163–64. On *2 Bar.*, see ibid., 201–8. There is an express reference to Deut. 30:19 in 4 Ezra 7:129. Cf. *Sipre Devarim* § 53, on Deut. 11:26.

This "works righteousness" and the mercilessness of the judgment that is not only connected with it, but explicitly emphasized, led E. P. Sanders to draw a sharp division between 4 Ezra and the rest of early Jewish and rabbinic literature, and to declare that its teaching is not representative of the Judaism of its time.[365] This is not entirely correct, for the idea that there will be no mercy for sinners at the final judgment was an undisputed principle in early Judaism and among the rabbis.[366] There is, however, a difference between this writing and the rabbis to the extent that the latter assume the salvation of all Israel, while the author of 4 Ezra expects only a few to be saved.[367] Yet the Ezra of this document suffers so much from this and so stubbornly questions the principle enunciated that the angel at length sharply refuses to let him grumble anymore (8:51,55; 9:13), but not without having explained once again: "For the Most High did not intend that anyone should be destroyed; but they themselves who were created have defiled the name of him who made them, . . . Therefore my judgment is now drawing near" (8:59-61).[368]

The reason given for God's stern judgment in 9:7-12 is especially impressive. After a listing of portents and accompanying signs of the end, when "the most High is about to visit the world (saeculum) which he has made" (9:2), we read: ". . . it shall be that all who will be saved and will be able to escape on account of their works, or on account of the faith by which they have believed, will survive the dangers that have been predicted, and will see my salvation in my land and within my borders, which I have sanctified for myself from the beginning. Then those who have now abused my ways shall be amazed, and those who have rejected them with contempt shall dwell in torments. For as many as did not acknowledge me in their lifetime, although they received my benefits, and as many as scorned my Law while they still had freedom, and did not understand but despised it while an opportunity of repentance was still open to them, these must in torment acknowledge it after death" (9:7-12).[369]

---

365. E. P. Sanders, *Paul,* 409–18, 421–22, 427–28. "All that is left is legalistic perfectionism" (409). This interpretation is too one-sided. J. Klausner's judgment of this book is completely different (*Messianic Idea,* 349–65).

366. Cf. *Bib. Ant.* 33:2-3. E. Sjöberg, *Gott,* 105–9, 117; M. Limbeck, *Ordnung,* 108–16. On the measure of judgment, cf. P. Volz, *Eschatologie,* 289–96, and the same work, pp. 293–94, on "mercy in judgment": in rabbinic opinion there is mercy and consideration given only to the faithful; they do have need of it, because otherwise no one could withstand judgment (cf. ibid., 109–13, and the remarks there on 4 Ezra also).

367. On this, cf. P. Schäfer, "Lehre," 274–84.

368. For the approach of judgment in 4 Ezra, see H. Gunkel, "4. Esr," 337; J. Keulers, *Eschatologische Lehre,* 57–61; W. Harnisch, *Verhängnis,* 318–21.

369. With regard to the sinners referred to here, see P. Volz, *Eschatologie,* 284. For the freedom (*libertas*) of sinners in this age, cf. also 8:56. On this, see P. Volz, *Eschatolo-*

The section just quoted, with its slogan about God's "visitation" of the world, the listing of signs of the end, and description of salvation for the "survivors," at first glance reflects the same eschatological conception as was found in the section 5:56—6:28, discussed above. However, the expression "after death" in 9:12 does not fit within such a historical conception; it points, instead, to an eschatology of the hereafter. Thus vv. 9-12 are based on a quite different eschatological conception from the one underlying vv. 1-8.

We learn more about this eschatology of the hereafter in 7:62-131.[370] Here it appears at first, as in 9:12, that the judgment takes place immediately after the death of the individual. Ezra calls the animals blessed "for they do not look for a judgment, nor do they know of any torment or salvation promised to them after death. . . . And if we were not to come into judgment after death, perhaps it would have been better for us" (7:66, 69). But the eschatology of the hereafter is not carried through consistently; instead, as we have already seen above, it is combined with historical eschatology by means of the notion of chambers of rest in which the souls of the dead are preserved until the day of judgment. Then "the chambers shall give up the souls which have been committed to them," so that they can appear before God's judgment seat (7:32-33).[371] This intervening time between their death and the renewal of creation (7:75)[372] is spent by the souls of those "who have not kept the way of the Most High, and who have despised his Law, and who have hated those who fear God" (7:79) in a sevenfold torment (7:80-87), while the others will spend it in sevenfold bliss (7:88-99).

This gives rise to precisely the same systematic problem as in the Book of Wisdom: namely, that the day of judgment in this conception has lost its

---

gie, 307; W. Harnisch, *Verhängnis,* 142–78. The section is headed: "History as the limited time for decision." On the rabbinic teaching that there is opportunity for repentance until death, but not afterward, see E. K. Dietrich, *Umkehr,* 378–79; D. Sjöberg, *Gott,* 136.

370. The phrase "after death" appears there in 7:66, 69, 75, 117, 126. Cf. Heb. 9:27. There, too, the thought is not of the special, but of the general or "last" judgment (see below, chap. 4).

371. According to this passage and 7:101, all souls after death enter chambers; according to 7:80 it is only the souls of the righteous that do so. The contradiction is not resolved. On this, see M. E. Stone, *Features,* 144–45. On the chambers for souls, see also H. C. Cavallin, "Leben," 264–66.

372. For this expression, "*donec veniant tempora illa in quibus incipies creaturam renovare*" (7:75), M. E. Stone quotes as a parallel *b. Sanh.* 92b (*Features,* 78). Further examples are in G. Dalman, *Worte,* 145–46; P. Volz, *Eschatologie,* 338–39; J. Bonsirven, *Judaïsme* 1: 514–15.

meaning, because verdict and punishment or reward are anticipated, and that day can bring no decisive change for souls.[373] The author of this document saw this problem, too, and again attempted to "solve" it in his own fashion. This is evident in 14:34-35, the conclusion of the "brief summary of the theological solution offered by the author":[374]

> If you, then, will rule over your minds
> and discipline your hearts,
> you shall be kept alive,
> and after death you shall obtain mercy.
> For after death the judgment will come,
> when we shall live again;
> and then the names of the righteous will become manifest,
> and the deeds of the ungodly will be disclosed.

Here the day of judgment is apparently conceived, as in 7:66,69; 9:12, as following immediately after the individual's death; the intervening time between the death of an individual and the general resurrection ("when we shall live again"), a time that the dead are elsewhere said to spend in their "chambers," is simply ignored in this passage.[375] It is, of course, questionable whether the author of 4 Ezra really intends in this way to hint at an individual judgment immediately after death; still, the idea is not remote at this point. While the author does not succeed in proposing a systematic solution to the problem he rightly recognizes with the "intervening time" and "intermediate state"[376] of the dead, he apparently had a sense of the direction in which that solution could be found. He probably had this vague idea of a judgment "after death" in mind wherever we are in doubt about his underlying conception: for example, in 7:17-25 and 7:48, where he employs the traditional antithesis of "perishing" or "perdition" (*perditio*, ἀπώλεια, Hebr. אֲבַדּוֹן)[377] and "life" (*vita*, ζωή).[378]

---

373. "The lost are virtually in the position of condemned felons awaiting definitive sentence. This would appear to make the Last Judgment redundant" (F. T. Glasson, "Last Judgment," 531).

374. E. Brandenburger, *Verborgenheit*, 187.

375. J. Keulers, *Eschatologische Lehre*, 154. Cf. P. Volz, *Eschatologie*, 259.

376. See pp. 21–22 above.

377. M. E. Stone, *Features*, 196. See above, p. 109.

378. Other passages in which the underlying conception is unclear include 7:45-61; 8:18; 8:38-39; 9:18-22.

The palette of eschatological concepts is further enhanced by the dream-visions in chapters 11–12 and 13 (Visions 5 and 6). In both cases the author appears to have had written models that he supplied, in each instance, with a messianic interpretation.[379]

In the first dream-vision, the eagle stands for Rome, and its final, flaming destruction represents the collapse of the Roman world empire at the end of time. The figure of the lion, who proclaims its destruction to the eagle in a thoroughly conventional prophetic judgment speech (11:38-46), was inserted into the source document by the author of 4 Ezra: "This is the Messiah (*unctus*) whom the Most High has kept [on their account[380] and because of their godlessness] until the end of days. . . ."[381] He will denounce (*arguet*)[382] them for their ungodliness and for their wickedness, and will cast up before them their contemptuous dealings. For first he will set them living before his judgment seat, and when he has reproved them, then he will destroy them. But he will deliver in mercy the remnant of my people, those who have been saved throughout my borders, and he will make them joyful until the end comes, the day of judgment, of which I spoke to you at the beginning" (12:32-34). With this last remark, which sets a temporal limit to the messianic reign, the author tries to harmonize this concept with that in 7:26-44. The result is that he produces what he had tried to avoid, namely, a twofold judgment: a first, in which the Messiah is "accuser, judge, and executioner of judgment in one person,"[383] and a second, final judgment after the general resurrection, in which God judges the nations (cf. 7:32-38). The author had already pointed toward this judgment within the vision itself, in 11:46, at the end of the material he inserted into the source document.[384]

In the next dream-vision, Ezra sees "something like the figure of a human being come up out of the heart of the sea. And I looked, and behold, that [figure] flew with the clouds of heaven" (13:3). Then "an innumerable multi-

---

379. U. B. Müller, *Messias*, 94. I will adopt his analysis also in the following discussion (cf. ibid., 93–134). For the influence of Daniel on these chapters, see G. D. Beale, *Daniel*, 112–44.

380. Does this refer only to the Romans, or to all the nations? (cf. 13:37).

381. This is from the Latin text. The Syriac (and others) add: "who will arise from the offspring of David, and will come . . . ." The Latin text is usually augmented accordingly.

382. The underlying word here is the Greek ἐλέγξει (A. Hilgenfeld, *Messias*, 95; U. B. Müller, *Messias*, 100).

383. U. B. Müller, *Messias*, 101.

384. Cf. M. E. Stone, "Concept," 299.

tude of people were gathered together from the four winds of heaven" to make war against the figure who came up out of the sea (13:5). The one like a human being burns them to ashes with a stream of fire (*fluctus ignis*), a flaming breath (*spiritus flammae*), and a storm of sparks (*scintillae tempestatis*)[385] from its mouth (13:10). Then it calls a "multitude that was peaceable" to itself. "Then many people came to him, some of whom were joyful and some sorrowful; some of them were bound, and some were bringing others as offerings" (13:13).[386]

The appearance of the one like a human being is described in the vision with motifs from a theophany of judgment: In its presence everything trembles and melts like wax before a flame (13:3-4).[387] In the author's otherwise rather violent depiction, this judgment is sometimes interpreted forensically, quite obviously in imitation of the Messiah's judgment in 12:32-33: The one through whom God will "deliver creation" (13:26) will reprove (*arguet*) the nations for their sins, and finally destroy them (13:37-38). On the other hand, this same figure will defend "the people who remain" and show them many wonders (13:49-50). Thus, as in 12:34, judgment is followed by salvation for the end time remnant.[388] Then the ten lost tribes of Israel will be gathered to the Messiah (13:39-47). Nothing is said here about a second judgment after the resurrection of the dead, nor does the author refer to 7:32-44, as he did in 12:34. The messianic salvation of the eschatological people of God is presented here without any kind of explicit temporal limit.

Thus God's eschatological judgment appears in 4 Ezra in three different conceptions: that of the end time "visitation" of sinners by God, that of a resurrection for final judgment, and that of an eschatology of the hereafter with a judgment "after death." In the first of these conceptions, judgment is conceived purely as the imposition of punishment, while in the other two it is a forensic judgment followed by the execution of the punishment imposed. In the messianic conceptions in the fifth and sixth visions the Messiah takes the role of judge. Here also, the dominant contrast is between Israel and the nations, which plays no part in the eschatological conception of the first three

385. Cf. Isa. 11:4; 66:15; Ps. 18:8[9].
386. Cf. Isa. 66:20. This represents the return of the Jews from the diaspora (J. Klausner, *Messianic Idea*, 360–61; U. B. Müller, *Messias*, 118).
387. Cf. Mic. 1:4; 1 Enoch 1:6 (where both motifs are found!).
388. Cf. U. B. Müller, *Messias*, 104–5, 125–27. The parallel to *Ps. Sol.* 17:21-32 is obvious: there, too, we first have the destruction and "reproof" of the nations by the Messiah, then the time of salvation under the Messiah's righteous rule.

visions, except for the tradition in 6:7-10 (a "pesher" on Gen. 25:26). In a number of places we find evidence of the author's effort to unify the various eschatological conceptions and at least to take steps toward resolving the systematic problems that result. He can also make unexpected shifts from one conception to another (9:1-12). This shows that he unconsciously considered the concepts and traditions he employed to be somehow compatible and complementary.[389] Ultimately, he was concerned only with the idea of the judgment that awaits everyone, and in which blessedness or damnation will be determined. But even this idea of the future judgment functions in service of something else: It provides the reason for the primary, parenetic purpose of the book, the call to the people to "rule over your minds and discipline your hearts" and to follow "the law of life" (*lex vitae*), for it is according to these that they will be judged "after death." This is the substance of Ezra's last words to the people (14:28-35), what we may call his theological testament.[390]

We saw in the case of the schema of two ages, the messianic reign as a preliminary time of salvation before the coming age, and the interpretation of Esau and Jacob as representing Rome and Israel that 4 Ezra, like the *Liber Antiquitatum Biblicarum,* is indebted to the rabbinic world of ideas.[391] Let me add just three more points.

1. Expressions like "evil heart" (*cor malignum*) and "evil root" (*malignitas radicis*) (3:21-22) are based on rabbinic ideas about the "evil drive" or "evil inclination" (יצר הרע).[392]

2. When it is said of Behemoth and Leviathan (6:52) that they have been kept by God "to be eaten by whom you wish, and when you wish," this is an obvious allusion to the eschatological meal of the righteous, for which, according to rabbinic teaching, these two ancient beasts were to be slaughtered.[393]

---

389. On this, see M. E. Stone, "Coherence," esp. 241–43. Cf. also the judgment of P. Volz, *Eschatologie,* 272.

390. On this, see E. Brandenburger, *Verborgenheit,* 186–93.

391. Cf. also the references in J. Klausner, *Messianic Idea,* 349–65.

392. Cf. W. Bousset and H. Gressmann, *Religion,* 402–5; W. Harnisch, *Verhängnis,* 45–50, 165–75; J. Schreiner, *4. Esr,* 314; J. Schmid, *LThK*² 618–20; A. L. Thompson, *Responsibility,* 49–63, 332–39. See also the rabbinic material in Str-B 4: 466–83; E. E. Urbach, *Sages,* 471–83. According to K. Koch, however, the "evil heart" in 4 Ezra has nothing to do with the "evil drive" of the rabbis ("Esras erste Vision," 60–61).

393. Cf. *2 Bar* 29:4; 1 Enoch 60:7-24; Str-B 4: 1156–63; W. Bousset and H. Gressmann, *Religion,* 285; P. Volz, *Eschatologie,* 389; J. Bloch, *Apocalyptic,* 97–100; A. Caquot, "Léviathan," esp. 115; M. Delcor, "Mythologie," esp. 159–67, 177.

3. In order to give adequate emphasis to the supreme importance of the last judgment, the author writes in 7:70 that God, even before creating the world, "first prepared the judgment and the things that pertain to the judgment" (*primum praeparavit iudicium et quae sunt iudicii*). The background of this is the rabbinic theologoumenon about the things that were created before the world. These include the Torah as most important, repentance, the Garden of Eden (the eschatological paradise), and Gehenna.[394]

The Testament of Abraham

The so-called "Testament" of Abraham, which has little in common with the genre of testaments, has been received in two quite different Greek versions, one longer (A) and one shorter (B).[395] The literary and tradition-historical relationship of the two versions is unusually complicated and difficult to determine. In general, the longer version A is regarded as more recent in its language, but revealing a tradition history that is longer than that of B. However, in some details B reveals itself as closer to the original than A.[396] The language of A points to the Byzantine period: for example, forms of address like τὸ σὸν κάλλος (2:5); τὸ σὸν κράτος (4:6), ἡ σὴ ἐνδοξότης (16:10), late words like ὀψικεύω (10:3; 20:12) or θεούφαντος (20:10)[397] or the frequency of ἐν in place of εἰς. It is true that the linguistic form of the earlier recension of B appears to be older than that of A, but even there we find late words like ληθαργέω (10:15). In particular, manuscript E, which is the basis for the text in F. Schmidt's edition, presents a strongly semitizing style comparable to that in the Gospel of Luke. However, there is no translation Greek here either.[398]

---

394. Cf. Str-B 4: 1083–85; P. Volz, *Eschatologie*, 114–16. For a detailed discussion of this midrash, see G. Schimanowski, *Weisheit*, 233–89.

395. B, in turn, is found in two recensions: the first is represented by MSS E A C D H J (text in F. Schmidt, *Test. Abr.*, 83–95), the second and later by MSS B F G (text in F. Schmidt, *Test. Abr.*, 83–95). In what follows, only the first will be considered. [The English translation depends in part on E. P. Sanders, "Testament of Abraham," *OTP* 1: 871–902.—Trans.]

396. For the tradition-historical relationship of the versions, see M. Delcor, *Test. Abr.*, 5–14; E. Rau, *Kosmologie*, 317–22; G. W. E. Nickelsburg, "Eschatology"; idem, "Structure"; F. Schmidt, "The Two Recensions"; R. A. Kraft, "'Recensional Problem.'"

397. Cf. M. Delcor, *Test. Abr.*, 129, 172. For the vocabulary in general, idem, 28–32. The "book" in *TestAbr* A 12.7 is apparently a codex; this also points to a late dating. In B 10.11 at least one MS (C) still speaks of "unrolling" the book.

398. Cf. E. P. Sanders, "Testament of Abraham," 873–74.

The original work was probably written in Egypt in about 100 c.e.[399] Egyptian influence is evident especially in the depiction of the judgment.[400] We may exclude any suggestions of an origin among the Essenes or Therapeutae.[401] The longer version has undergone only a light Christian redaction,[402] the older recension of the shorter version apparently none at all. The echoes of New Testament passages found also in A are lacking there.

According to the longer version A, Abraham desires, before his death, to see the whole world (9:6). Thereupon he is carried through the air in a chariot of cherubim by Michael, the "commander of the [heavenly] hosts" (ἀρχι-στράτηγος)[403] and finally brought "toward the east, to the first gate of heaven" where he is to see "the judgments and the recompenses" (τὰς κρίσεις καὶ ἀνταποδόσεις)[404] in order that he may learn mercy for sinners (11:1; 10:15). Having arrived there, he sees two ways, one of them strait and narrow, the second broad and spacious, each with its corresponding gate (11:2-3).[405] Angels are driving many souls through the broad gate, which leads to destruction (ἀπώλεια) and eternal punishment (κόλασις αἰώνιος); only a few souls are being led through the narrow gate of life (ζωή) and Paradise (παράδεισος) (11:10-11).[406] Abraham and Michael follow the damned souls through the broad gate, but they do not arrive, as we would expect, in the place of eternal punishment; instead, they find themselves at the place of judgment.[407]

Between the two gates stands a crystalline throne,[408] "flashing like fire." On it sits "a wondrous man, bright as the sun, like unto a son of God." He judges souls and sentences them (ἔκρινεν καὶ ἀπεφήνατο τὰς ψυχάς). Before him stands "a table like crystal, all of gold," and on it lies a book, "whose thickness was six cubits, while its breadth was ten cubits." To the right and left of the

399. E. P. Sanders, "Testament of Abraham," 874–76. E. Schürer and G. Vermes even consider an origin in the 2nd–1st c. b.c.e. possible (*History* 3/2: 764).

400. M. Delcor, *Test. Abr.*, 61–62, 67–69; F. Schmidt, "Recensions," 78–79.

401. E. P. Sanders, "Testament of Abraham," 875–76. The *T. Abr.* "represents a kind of lowest-common-denominator Judaism" (ibid., 876). Cf. also the remarks of B. Schaller on the Testament of Job (*Test. Hiob*, 309–11). There is a strong tendency especially in French scholarship to assign early Jewish literature to Essene circles.

402. M. Delcor, *Test. Abr.*, 63–67.

403. Cf. Jos. 5:14; Dan. 8:11. E. P. Sanders, "Testament of Abraham," 882, on *T. Abr.* 1:4.

404. The plural shows how individualistically the judgment is here understood.

405. Here there are literal echoes of Matt. 7:13-14. These are absent in B 8:4, 10-11.

406. Cf. Matt. 7:13; 25:46. According to *T. Abr.* A 11:12, of 7,000 damned souls scarcely one will be saved.

407. The literary seam is very evident here: G. W. E. Nickelsburg, "Eschatology," 41.

408. Cf. 1 Enoch (Greek) 14:18!

table stand—precisely like the scribes in the Sanhedrin (*m. Sanh.* 4:3) and the two *notarii* in a Roman judicial court[409]—two angels with papyrus, ink, and pen; one records the sins, the other the good deeds. Before the table sits an angel with a scale in its hand to weigh the souls, and alongside, a fiery angel with a trumpet "which contained within it an all-consuming fire (for) testing the 'sinners'" or "'human souls'" (12:4-14). Michael explains, when Abraham questions him, that this is "judgment and recompense" (ἡ κρίσις καὶ ἀνταπό-δοσις) (12:15; cf. 10:15; 15:12). Then an angel brings a soul and places it before the judge, who has one of the serving angels open the book with the register of sins, and since the sins and good deeds are "equally balanced," "he neither turned it over to the torturers nor (placed it among) those who were being saved, but he set it in the middle" (οὔτε ταῖς βασανισταῖς ἐξέδωκεν αὐτὴν[410] οὔτε τοῖς σῳζομένοις, ἀλλ᾽ ἔστησεν αὐτὴν εἰς τὸ μέσον) (12:16-18).

In the following chapter, 13, in response to a corresponding plea on the part of Abraham, and in spite of the previous detailed explanation in 12:11-15, Michael gives a further interpretation of the scene, which at times overlaps word for word with the previous one, but contradicts it in detail. According to this interpretation the judge is Abel. "He sits here to judge the entire creation, examining (ἐλέγχειν) both righteous and sinners. For God said, 'I do not judge you, but every man is judged by man'" (13:3).[411] This first judgment will be followed, "at the second parousia," by another carried out by the twelve tribes of Israel, and finally, before the end, by still a third judgment by God in person. "And thus the judgment and recompense of the world is made through three tribunals" (καὶ λοιπὸν διὰ τριῶν βημάτων γίνεται ἡ κρίσις τοῦ κόσμου καὶ ἀνταπόδοσις) (13:4-8).

We have no parallels for this remarkable idea of Abel as judge.[412] The conception of the final judgment as having three stages is also unique. Here it appears that a variety of traditions have been combined, "although there is no clear combination of ideas as a result."[413]

---

409. Cf. P. Petitmengin and B. Flusin, "Livre," 253.
410. Cf. Matt. 18:34. Cf. *T. Abr.* B 10:16: καὶ ἐβασάνισαν αὐτήν.
411. The origin of the quotation is unknown.
412. M. Delcor attempts an explanation (*Test. Abr.,* 142–45). For the targumic traditions to which Delcor refers (the quarrel between Cain and Abel over the last things), see below.
413. E. Rau, *Kosmologie,* 310. Cf. G. W. E. Nickelsburg, "Eschatology," 41, 46. M. Delcor sees in the concept of a three-stage judgment a reflection of the three levels of jurisdiction in Egypt in the Roman period (*Test. Abr.,* 61–62, 146–47). For the individual traditions, see M. Delcor, *Test. Abr.,* 145–46; E. P. Sanders, "Testament of Abraham," 890, nn. a–d; E. Janssen, "Test. Abr.," 234, nn. 204–6.

The activity of the two angelic scribes is described in chapter 13 in almost identical words to those in 12:12: the angel on the right writes down the good deeds, the one on the left records the sins (13:9). The other two angels are given the expressive names Dokiel and Purouel. But in 12:13-14 it is souls that are weighed and tested, while in 13:10-11 it is their deeds.

Eckhard Rau is probably correct in regarding the whole of chapter 13 as "a secondary expansion, from the point of view of the history of tradition."[414] But even in chapters 11 and 12 traditions have come together that are difficult to harmonize. In the scene regarding the two ways, judgment is presumed or implied; the souls are separated and are already on the way to reward or punishment. Thus the judgment scene would make better sense *before* the two-ways scene. In fact, in version A the two scenes are only superficially connected.[415]

In the judgment scene in chapter 12 we should distinguish the following traditions:

1. The throne scene with judge and book of deeds. This tradition goes back to Dan. 7:9-10.[416] The angelic scribes have been added, but they are out of place in the throne scene, since "their recording of the deeds, in fact, precedes the judgment."[417] In the present context, at any rate, their precise activity is unclear: How did the sins get into the book?

The judge, in this tradition, is God. The identification with Abel in chapter 13 is secondary, as we have seen. It may have been created by the author of the Testament of Abraham.

2. The angel with the scales and the angel with the fiery trumpet. The motif of weighing souls (12:13) or of "good deeds and sins" (13:10) is Egyptian in origin.[418] The motif of testing human beings in fire or in a furnace is found in Ps. 66[65]:10-12, in an eschatological context in Mal. 3:2 and Wis. 3:6.[419]

---

414. E. Rau, *Kosmologie*, 318. For the difficulties posed by this chapter, see also G. W. E. Nickelsburg, "Eschatology," 44.

415. The redactor of B apparently tried to come to the rescue here, but with only partial success.

416. Cf. 1 Enoch 47:3; 90:20; Rev. 20:11-12.

417. E. Rau, *Kosmologie*, 320. Cf. 1 Enoch 89:61-64, 68-71, 76-77; *Apoc. Zeph.* 3.6-9. G. W. E. Nickelsburg ("Eschatology," 30) has not taken note of this.

418. F. Schmidt, "Recensions," 78–79; E. P. Sanders, "Testament of Abraham," 889, n. f. For this motif in Jewish tradition, see P. Volz, *Eschatologie*, 293. I think it improbable that, as regards its religious-historical origins, a distinction needs to be drawn between the weighing of souls and the weighing of deeds, as Sanders supposes. Both variations can be derived from the same Egyptian idea. Cf. also *Apoc. Zeph.* 8.5.

419. Cf. also Jer. 6:29; Zech. 13:9. E. P. Sanders, "Testament of Abraham," 889 n. g.

Concretely, however, it is difficult to imagine a testing "by fire *and* balance" (ἐν πυρὶ καὶ ζυγῷ) (13:14).

3. The judgment of individual souls, whose good deeds and sins balance one another. This scene, in contrast to the previous one, shows the judgment in action. From a tradition-historical point of view, it constitutes "a narrative elaboration of the traditional saying that the books will be opened."[420] The petition of Abraham ultimately replaces the one good deed that the soul still needs to be saved (14:1-9).

In the B version there is no depiction of the throne scene like the one we find in A 12:4-15, and consequently the explanations in A 13 are lacking also. All that remains, besides the scene of the two ways (B 8–9), is the strongly altered and dialogically expanded portrayal of the judgment of individual souls, with the judge again identified with Abel (B 10–11).[421]

Abraham is carried on a cloud by Michael to the "place of judgment," which is near Paradise (10:1-2). The angel of death brings a soul who is then, in a dialogue with the judge, convicted of her guilt. The judge has two books brought forward; in one of them a man wearing three crowns and with a golden pen in his hand, Enoch, "the scribe of righteousness" (11:3), records the sins of the accused, who must be brought to acknowledge that their sins are not forgotten here, even if they themselves have forgotten them. "Therefore the servant of wrath took them away and tortured them" (or: "Then they took her too and handed [her] over to the torturers") (10:16).[422]

In this scene the function of the judgment, which clearly occurs immediately after death,[423] is more than obvious: It is not a proper judicial process (prosecutor and defense attorney are lacking); its only purpose is the conviction of the sinner and the justification of the sentence that has already been fixed. There are two possibilities for sentencing: If the sins tip the balance, what follows is a condemnation to "torture" or "destruction," but if the good

420. E. Rau, *Kosmologie,* 321. The motif of opening the books is found in Dan. 7:10; 1 Enoch 47:3; 90:20; 4 Ezra 6:20; *2 Bar.* 24:1; Rev. 20:12.

421. In the Arabic, Coptic, and Ethiopic version, however, the judge is God (G. W. E. Nickelsburg, "Eschatology," 51).

422. Version B F G has παρέδωκα τοῖς βασανισταῖς, creating an allusion to Matt. 18:34 (10:16). A 12:18 is similar. The identification of this soul with the one mentioned in B 9:8, whose good and bad deeds balance each other (B 10:3), is "an (unsuccessful) attempt to combine two different traditions" (E. Rau, *Kosmologie,* 328).

423. It is the angel of death who brings the soul to judgment (B 9:11). Cf. A 14:15. It is a puzzle to me how E. Rau (*Kosmologie,* 326) cannot see in this judgment (with reference to A, also) the individual judgment hereafter, following the person's death, but instead regards it as referring to the general, historical judgment at the end of time.

deeds are in surplus, the soul will be released to "life" or enter into "Paradise." If there is a balance of sins and good deeds, the soul is left in an "intermediate place" (τόπος μεσότητος) (B 9:8) that is not further described.[424] According to A 14:2, their fate will be determined when "the judge [and God] of all shall come." Until then, however, it can still be saved by petitionary prayers. What is new in this conception, in fact, is only this third possibility and the narrative enhancement of the judgment scene, something unique in early Jewish literature. Moreover, according to A 14:15 the "special judgment" after death awaits only those who were not already judged during their lifetime. Souls are judged, but according to B 7:16 the body remains in the earth until the resurrection of the flesh: in Abraham's case, this will be six thousand years.

Rabbinic influence is indicated by, among other things, the separation of human beings into three classes and the tradition that Abraham is shown the last things in a vision.[425] We have already mentioned the Egyptian influences. However, there are similar scenarios, and even the motif of the book of deeds, in Greek religion.[426]

Thus we find that the eschatology of the Testament of Abraham offers a conglomerate of the most varied motifs and traditions, with only a faulty literary or thought connection—if any—established among them. Even apparent inconsistencies and contradictions in the narrative have been allowed to stand. From this point of view, the author is far inferior to the author of 4 Ezra.

The principal purpose of the book is the description of the righteous judgment that awaits every human being who has not already been judged during his or her lifetime. Noteworthy in this is the universalism of the idea of judgment, ignorant of any contrast between Israel and the Gentiles and only distinguishing between the righteous and sinners. In this, the Testament of Abraham

424. For the "three classes" in rabbinic literature, see the last section of this chapter.
425. M. Delcor (*Test. Abr.*, 39–42) quotes, among others, *Bib. Ant.* 23:6; 4 Ezra 3:14; *Tg. Neof.* on Gen. 15:17; *Apoc. Abr.* 15,19,27; *Ber. R.* 44:22. For the use of a Palestinian targum in *T. Abr.*, see ibid., 76–77. Cf. also J. Bonsirven, *Judaïsme* 1: 504.
426. G. H. Macurdy, "Platonic Orphism." He points especially to the myth of Er in Plato's *Republic* (X, 614–21), where judgment and the two-ways scene are combined, as well as to Euripides, *Fragm.* 506 (book of deeds), as well as the myths in Plato's *Gorgias* (523a–524a) and *Phaedo* (113rd–114c). In the last, just as in *T. Abr.*, people appearing before the judgment in the underworld are divided into good, evil, and middle. A description of judgment, the place of the blessed and the place of the damned is also found in the myth of the pseudoplatonic Axiochos, 371–72. A. Dieterich (*Nekyia*, 126–27) had already pointed to parallels with *T. Abr.* Cf. also L. Ruhl, *De mortuorum iudicio;* M. P. Nilsson, *Geschichte* 1: 821–26; 2: 233–42, 304–5; 492–93; 549–58.

is in remarkable agreement with the fourth Sibylline Oracle. Only sins and good works are weighed and counted, but without any reference to the Torah and its commands. "Judaism is depicted here as a religion of commonplace moral values, which nevertheless insists both on the strictness of God's judgment and on his mercy and compassion."[427] Of course, in this writing also, God's graciousness and compassion endure only as long as the sinner lives; for only during that time is there the opportunity for repentance (A 10:14; B 12:13). After that, nothing remains but the righteous judgment.

The ethical universalism and the analogy to Egyptian and Greek ideas of judgment after death may well have contributed a great deal to the broad circulation of this book in the Hellenistic world.

The Writings of the Tannaim

The following survey of tannaitic ideas of judgment does not claim to be a complete treatment of the material. However, the different conceptions found there, at least, should become clear. Apart from the lack of critical editions and translations, our sources for these writings present special methodological problems with regard to the dating of individual texts and channels of tradition, not to mention the assignment of sayings to particular rabbis.[428] Jacob Neusner writes: "Someone, perhaps everyone, produced pseudepigraphic dicta, and that is all we shall ever know for certain."[429] Still, the names of the rabbis are not entirely valueless even for him: "I may nonetheless suggest that sayings and stories clearly attributed to Tannaim are apt to be earlier than similar materials attributed to Amoraim, or not specifically assigned to any authority at all."[430] One aid in the temporal arrangement of particular ideas, concepts, and motifs is provided by parallels in early Jewish writings that are more easily dated. Fortunately, for our topic there are a considerable number of these.

427. E. P. Sanders, *Testament of Abraham,* 877. Sanders mentions 2 Enoch and *3 Baruch* as the closest parallels to this universalism, but one should not forget the fourth Sibyl, if only because of its temporal proximity.

428. Cf. H. L. Strack and G. Stemberger, *Einleitung,* 55–71; K. Müller, *Judentum,* 74–75, 89–95; idem, "Datierung"; P. S. Alexander, "Rabbinic Judaism."

429. J. Neusner, *Development,* 5. Cf. idem, "Verwendung"; K. Müller, "Datierung," 559–62.

430. J. Neusner, *Development,* 9. To the contrary: K. Müller, "Datierung," 584–85.

The idea of individual judgment plays an important part in the parenesis of the Tannaim. A frequently quoted saying of Akabiah ben Mahalaleel[431] reads: "Apply thy mind to three things, and thou wilt not come into the power of sin: Know whence thou comest, and whither thou art going, and before whom thou art destined to give an account and reckoning (ולפני מי אתה עתיד לתן דין וחשבון). Whence camest thou? From a fetid drop. Whither art thou going? To a place of dust, of worm and of maggot. Before whom art thou destined to give an account and reckoning? Before the king of the kings of kings, the Holy One, blessed be he!" (*m. 'Abot* 3.1). This dictum is quoted in a slightly variant form also in *'Abot R. Nat.* A 19.1 and *'Abot R. Nat.* B 32 as a saying of Akabiah, as well as in *Wayiqra Rab.* 18.1 on Lev. 15:1-2 and *Qoh. R.* on Qoh. 12:1. In *y. Sot.* 2.2 (18a ll. 26-27) and *Midr. Tanh.* B Gen V § 7 (Bietenhard 1: 127) a mention of the author and the first words are enough to recall the saying. The first part is found in *Der. 'Er. Zut.* 4.5 (Higger 1: 103; 2: 44) as an anonymous proverb: "Keep these words in your heart: Know whence thou camest, and whither thou art going, and before whom thou art destined to give an account and reckoning."

Although we may be inclined at first reading of Akabiah's saying to think of the individual judgment immediately after death, a closer examination shows that he can only be thinking of the last judgment after the general resurrection, as Paul Billerbeck has already noted: "Among other things, the sequence of the last two points favors this: first decay, and only then the judgment on the last day."[432] According to Billerbeck[433] there is a difference in the version of Akabiah's saying transmitted in *Der. 'Er. Rab.* 3.1 under the name of Ben Azzaiah. There it begins: "Whoever keeps the following four things in mind and takes them to heart will never commit a sin: Whence he comes, and where he is going, and who is his judge, and what must become of

431. Akabiah ben Mahalaleel "cannot be precisely located historically. Attempts at dating range from the first century B.C.E. to the time of Gamaliel II in Yavneh" (H. L. Strack and G. Stemberger, *Einleitung,* 74). However, he is usually located within the first generation of the Tannaim, especially because he does not yet bear the title "rabbi."

432. Str-B 4: 1038 n. 2. In agreement with L. Finkelstein, A. J. Saldarini finds in Akabiah's saying a hint of denial of the resurrection (*'Abot R. Nat.* B 189; idem, "Adoption," 554–56). It is true that there is no mention of the resurrection to judgment, but it is undoubtedly implied. I cannot see any denial of it in the mention of the "maggots and worms." W. D. Davies sees an antignostic point in Akabiah's saying ("Reflexions," 149–51), but there can be no question of that either.

433. Str-B 4: 1038 n. 2.

him. . . ."[434] In this version the "maggots and worms" come only *after* the judgment. Yet that must not mean that judgment is thought of as following immediately after death. Such a sequence does not make much sense, after all, because there are two possibilities after judgment: ultimate death *or* eternal life.[435]

Rabbi [Judah ha-Nasi] also takes up the saying of Akabiah and explains the third part: "Apply thy mind to three things and thou wilt not come into the power of sin: Know what there is above thee: an eye that sees, an ear that hears, and all thy deeds written in a book" (*m. 'Abot* 2.1).[436]

Of the book here mentioned, Rabbi [Judah ha-Nasi] says in another place: "[The human being] sins, and the Holy One, blessed be He, records it against him for death; he does penance, (and) the writing is erased. Had he not done penance, what is written would remain."[437] Rabbi Akiba speaks, in a striking image, of the ledger that is opened and the hand that writes what will serve as documentation at the judgment.[438]

The fourth chapter of the sayings of the fathers ends with a homiletic speech of Rabbi Eleazar ha-Qappar, a contemporary of Rabbi [Judah ha-Nasi]: "The born [are destined] to die, the dead to be brought to life, and the living to be judged; [it is, therefore, for them] to know and to make known, so that it become known, that he is God, he the fashioner, he the creator, he the discerner, he the judge, he the witness, he the complainant, and that he is of a certainty to judge, blessed be he, before whom there is no unrighteousness, nor forgetting, nor respect of persons, nor taking of bribes, for all is his. And

---

434. Cf. M. Higger, *Derek Erez* 1: 155–58; 2: 59; M. Ginsberg in A. Cohen, *Minor Tractates* 2: 543.

435. *Der. 'Er. Rab.* 3.1 reveals parallels to *'Abot R. Nat.* A 19.1 and apparently presumes *b. Ber.* 28b (Yohanan ben Zakkai's last words), as the characterization of the judge, in particular, indicates.

436. Cf. *'Abot R. Nat.* 5. 32 (Saldarini, 191).

437. *Midr. Tanh.* B Lev II 1 § 7 (Bietenhard 2: 30). A further saying of Rabbi [Judah ha-Nasi] on this book is found in *Qoh. R.* on 12:14 (Str-B 1: 639). Cf. also *Ber. R.* 81.1 on Gen. 35:1; *y. Yeb.* 12.6 (13a, 15ff.); Str-B 2: 171–72; 3: 628.

438. *m. 'Abot* 3.16. On this, see K. Marti and G. Beer, *'Abot*, 83–85; Str-B 1: 583; 2: 171; 4: 1041; W. Bacher, *Agada* 1: 335–36; P. Volz, *Eschatologie*, 125; A. J. Saldarini, *Rabbi Nathan* B 275. According to a later tradition, the human being will hereafter have the list of his or her deeds presented for signing and sealing, with reference to Job 37:7: "He has a seal from everyone's hand, so that all human beings may recognize his deed." Thus *b. Ta'an* 11a; *Midr. Tanh.* B Gen I 3 § 29 (Bietenhard 1:32); *Sipre Deut.* § 307 on Deut. 32:4 (Bietenhard, 740); Str-B 2: 171; 3: 135; 4: 1041.

know that all is according to the reckoning. And let not thy [evil] inclination assure thee that the grave is a place of refuge for thee; for without thy will wast thou fashioned, without thy will wast thou born, without thy will livest thou, without thy will wilt thou die, and without thy will art thou of a certainty to give an account and reckoning before the king of the kings of kings, blessed be he!" (*m. 'Abot* 4.22). The explicit mention of the resurrection clearly shows that here, as in Akabiah's saying, the thought is not yet of a judgment after death, but of the last judgment. Still, it is the individual who is to be judged, not the group of "sinners" or "righteous." Each person is taken as an individual. This is expressed primarily in the formula about giving "an account and reckoning," which we find both here and in Akabiah's saying. With the same formula, the targum on Gen. 3:19 refers to the one judgment.[439]

According to the words quoted, this judgment is not to be feared by sinners alone, but even by the righteous, as Rabbi Eliezer ben Hyrcanos said: "If the Holy One, blessed be he, wished to enter into judgment with Abraham, Isaac or Jacob, not [even] they could stand before his reproof (תוכחה)" (*b. 'Arak.* 17a).[440] According to a well-known midrash on 1 Sam. 28:15, Samuel believed, when Saul "called him up" by the medium's summoning, that the last day had come, and he was afraid. "But if Samuel, the teacher of the prophets, of whom it is written, 'And all Israel from Dan to Beer-sheba knew that Samuel was a trustworthy prophet of the Lord' (1 Sam. 3:20), feared the day of judgment (יום הדין), how much more we!"[441] This explanation also shows that it was possible to imagine the awakening of the dead for the last judgment in full analogy to the summoning of the dead portrayed in 1 Samuel 28. The midrash certainly comes from the tannaitic period, because even Pseudo-Philo knew it.[442]

The motif of fear of judgment leads us to the oldest rabbinic witness to belief in an individual judgment immediately after death. According to *b. Ber.* 28b, Eliezer's teacher, Rabbi Yohanan ben Zakkai, when he was dying, was so

439. Cf. *Tg. Neof.*, TJ I, TFrag. J. Bowker, *Targums*, 123; A. Rodriguez Carmona, *Targum*, 13–15. The last author derives the formula from Greek λόγον διδόναι.

440. Cf. Str-B 3: 156–57. Here we have the motif of the ". . . *cum vix iustus sit securus*" from the "Dies Irae," where it is taken from 1 Pet. 4:18 (= LXX Prov. 11:31).

441. *y. Hag.* 2.77a, 29-35. Cf. *b. Hag.* 4b; *Wa. R.* 26.7 on Lev. 20:27; *Tanh. Emor* 171b; *M. Shem* 24 § 5; Str-B 1: 816; 3: 220.

442. In *Bib.Ant.* 64.7 Samuel says, "Why have you disturbed me and called me up? I thought that the time of retribution for my works had come" (*putavi quod appropinquasset tempus reddendi merces operum meorum*).

terrified of the judgment to come that he began to weep.[443] "His disciples said to him: 'Lamp of Israel, pillar of the right hand, mighty hammer! Wherefore weepest thou?' He replied: 'If I were being taken today before a human king who is here today and tomorrow in the grave, whose anger if he is angry with me does not last for ever, who if he imprisons me does not imprison me for ever and who if he puts me to death does not put me to everlasting death, and whom I can persuade with words and bribe with money, even so I would weep. Now that I am being taken before the supreme King of Kings, the Holy One, blessed be He, who lives and endures for ever and ever, whose anger, if He is angry with me, is an everlasting anger, who if He imprisons me imprisons me for ever, who if He puts me to death puts me to death for ever, and whom I cannot persuade with words or bribe with money—nay more, when there are two ways before me, one leading to Paradise and the other to Gehinnom, and I do not know by which I shall be taken, shall I not weep?'"[444] In the apparently secondary parallel tradition in 'Abot R. Nat. A 25,1 the contrast "forever—not forever" has been replaced by "in this world—in the world to come" (בעולם הבא—בעולם הזה), and a series of scriptural references is added at the end, beginning with Ps. 22:30[29]: "Before him shall bow all who go down to the dust."[445] Since Yohanan's terrified words are not mentioned in the tradition about his death, preserved by y. Abod Zar. 3.1/y. Sot. 9.16 in the name of Rabbi Joshua ben Levi, Jacob Neusner considers them "late inventions, coming long after the very simple account of Joshua b. Levi."[446] The oldest extrarabbinic witness to the idea of an individual judgment immediately after death is the Testament of Abraham.[447] Therefore the tradition in b. Ber. 28b could easily have arisen in the second century c.e.

443. Something similar is reported of the Curé of Ars. Cf. W. Nigg, Große Heilige (10th ed., Zürich and Munich, 1981), 467.

444. Cf. Str-B 4: 1034. There is a striking parallel in 2 Enoch 39:8: "Frightening and dangerous it is to stand before the face of an earthly king, terrifying and very dangerous it is, because the will of the king is death and the will of the king is life. How much more terrifying [and dangerous] it is to stand before the face of the King of earthly kings and of the heavenly armies [the regulator of the living and of the dead]. Who can endure that endless misery?"

445. Cf. S. Schechter, 'Abot R. Nat. 79; Str-B 1: 208-9; J. Neusner, Development, 130–31. Ps. 22:30[29] is cited in Bemidbar Rab. 14.22 on Num. 7:89 with regard to seeing God at the hour of death.

446. J. Neusner, Development, 224. However, the brief note in y. Abod Zar. 3.1/y. Sot. 9.16 (J. Neusner, Development, 134, 141) can scarcely be called an "account."

447. Further rabbinic examples of this idea are provided by J. Bonsirven, Judaïsme 1: 336–40; Str-B 4: 1037–38.

The whole scene as given in *b. Ber.* 28b was apparently shaped, together with the preceding story of the death of Eliezer ben Hyrcanus, within his own school.[448] The two narratives were carefully collated. Eliezer's students ask him about the "paths of life," and he answers with three maxims. The third deals with prayer, and reads: "When you pray know before whom you are standing. . . ."[449] The subsequent words of Yohanan constitute a commentary on "before whom": it is the Judge in this world and the next, before whom even a man like Yohanan ben Zakkai is overcome with fear and trembling.[450]

That God is not only the creator, but also the judge of the world, whose word holds the final decision for eternity, is a genuinely fear-inspiring thought and an indication of the truly unconditioned power and majesty of God expressed in the title "supreme king of kings."[451] The application of this title to God, precisely as eschatological judge (in addition to this passage, also in *m. 'Abot* 3.1 and 4.22 in the words of Akabiah ben Mahalaleel and Rabbi Eleazar ha-Qappar), has a basis in reality, inasmuch as judging is an essential feature of the office of king, and that "judging" can stand for "ruling," and "judge" for "king."[452]

The idea contained in the sayings quoted thus far was that the individual human being must appear before God's throne, either immediately after death or at the last judgment, to give "an account and reckoning" of his or her life. But alongside this we find the idea that God *comes,* in person, to impose judgment. This parousia of God for judgment is spoken of in a saying that has been transmitted in several variants under the name of Eleazar ben Azariah or Abba Cohen ben Delaja.[453] It was inspired by Gen. 45:3: "Joseph said to his brothers,

448. J. Neusner, *Development,* 88, 223.

449. Cf. also the parallels in *'Abot R. Nat.* A 19.4. W. Bacher, *Agada* 1: 97–98, 103.

450. J. Neusner, however, thinks that "In this instance, there is no homiletical relationship between Eliezer's last words and those of Yohanan" (*Development,* 88).

451. "In order that God's majesty be exalted over all, he is called not only king of kings, as the high kings of the Orient called themselves (for example, Dan. 2:37), but 'king of all kings of kings'" (K. Marti and G. Beer, *'Abot,* 62). The earliest instance of this rare title is Hebrew Sirach 51:12(14). For God as king, cf. also Str-B 3: 656; W. Bousset and H. Gressmann, *Religion,* 375–77.

452. Cf., for example, Ps. 2:10; Amos 2:3; Mic. 4:14; 1 Kgs. 3:9; 2 Chr. 1:10-11; Sir. 45:26; Wis. 1:1; 3:8; 6:4; *Ps. Sol.* 17:26-32; 1 Macc. 9:73; *Sib. Or.* 3:743, 781,783. D. Winston, *Wisdom,* 100–101; O. Betz, *Paraklet,* 37–38; L. Morris, *Judgment,* 8–11; H.-J. Kraus, *Psalmen* 1: 197–200; G. Liedke, *THAT* 2: 1002–3; H. Niehr, *Herrschen,* passim.

453. For Abba Cohen ben/bar Delaja and the collection of traditions quoted under his name, see W. Bacher, *Tradition,* 232. In *Agada* 2: 548–49, Bacher calls him "Abba Cohen from Bardala." He appears under this name mainly in older literature.

'I am Joseph. Is my father still alive?' But his brothers could not answer him, so dismayed were they at his presence." "R. Simeon ben Eleazar quoted in the name of R. Eleazar b. 'Azariah what he used to say in the name of Abba Kohen the son of Dalyah:[454] 'Woe to us for the day of judgment, woe to us for the day of rebuke (אוי לנו מיום דין, אוי לנו מיום תוכחה)! Balaam was the wisest of the heathens, yet he could not withstand his ass's rebuke: "Was I ever wont to do so unto thee?" And he said: "Nay" (Num. 22:30). Joseph was the youngest of the tribal ancestors, yet his brethren could not withstand his rebuke, as it says: "And his brethren could not answer him." How much more then when the Holy One, blessed be he, comes and rebukes each man according to his deserts, as it says, "But now I will reprove thee, set the cause before thine eyes" (Ps. 50:21[455])!'"[456] The example of Balaam and his donkey is unknown to all the other versions transmitted in the name of Eleazar ben Azariah, including the second in Ber. R. (93.11, on Gen. 45:4). That one lacks the psalm quotation, too, but the saying is also introduced with the cry, "Woe to us for the day of judgment, woe to us for the day of rebuke!" This in turn is missing in the version in Midr. Tanh. B Gen XI § 7 (Buber, 207; Bietenhard 1: 241); the psalm quotation is there replaced by Amos 4:13.[457]

Thus according to this saying also, each individual will be judged on the "day of judgment," "when God comes."[458] God's parousia for judgment is a theme with a long tradition, going as far back as Pss. 96:13; 98:9. But while in

454. Some MSS and editions read אבא כהן בארדלא. But Codex Vat. Ebr. 60 has אבא כהן בן דלייה.

455. For Ps. 50, see above, chap. 2; discussion there also of the translation of יכח.

456. Ber. R. 93.10 on Gen. 45:3 (Theodor and Albeck 3: 1159–60). There is a very similar conclusion in the midrash on 1 Sam. 28:15 quoted above (see at n. 456). In b. Hag. 4b this comparison follows immediately after the one inspired by Gen. 45:3. Both are there ascribed to "Rabbi Eleazar" and give the reason why he was accustomed to weep when reading those verses in Scripture.

457. For the different versions, cf. Str-B 3: 220; 4: 1108; W. Bacher, Agada 1: 220–21; J. Theodor and C. Albeck, Bereschit Rabba 3: 1159–60; T. Zahavy, Eleazar Ben Azariah, 199–202. An anonymous echo of these words is found also in Midr. Tanh. B Deut 1 § 2 (Bietenhard 2: 437–38). In Tanh. Gen XI on Gen. 45:3 (Singermann, 267) it is attributed to "Rabbi Johanan," and instead of the psalm quotation, Mal. 3:2 and Exod. 33:20 are introduced. The "woe to us . . . " apparently circulated as an independent formula, for in Midr. Tanh. B Deut V § 7 (Buber, 30; Bietenhard 2: 481) Rabbi Johanan ben Zakkai uses it to introduce a commentary on Mal. 3:5 (cf. b. Hag. 5a, where the "woe to us" formula is lacking. J. Neusner, Development, 145).

458. "When the Holy One comes" is found both in Ber. R. 93.10 and in Midr. Tanh. B Gen XI § 7.

that tradition the judgment was almost entirely considered as a judgment for punishment—e.g., Isa. 66:15-16; 1 Enoch 1:3b-9; 4 Ezra 6:18-20—it proceeds here, as in Psalm 50, in forensic forms.

Thus when we read in the well-known passage *m. Sanh.* 10.1: "All Israelites have a share in the world to come, as it is said: 'Your people also shall be all righteous, they shall inherit the land forever' (Isa. 60:21)," this is simply a fundamental principle, as the subsequent exceptions demonstrate (*m. Sanh.* 10.1-4).[459] "All" and "everyone" are here, as frequently elsewhere, to be understood as hyperbole.[460] Neither "the generation of the Flood" nor the inhabitants of Sodom have a share in the world to come, and it is only consistent when Rabbi Nehemiah, with reference to Ps. 1:5, considers it not even necessary that they be present at the last judgment (*m. Sanh.* 10.3).[461]

Between the sinners and the righteous stand the "middle" people. The schools of Hillel and Shammai were at odds on whether they would have to endure a kind of "purgatory" in Gehenna or whether God's grace would prevail.[462]

There was a further discussion regarding the salvation of the Gentiles. "'R. Eliezer said: "The wicked shall be turned into hell, and all the nations that forget God" (Ps. 9:18[17]). "The wicked shall be turned into hell"—this refers to transgressors among Israel; "and all the nations that forget God"—to transgressors among the heathen.' This is R. Eliezer's view. But R. Joshua said to him: 'Is it stated, and [those] *among* all the nations? Surely "all the nations that forget God" is written. But [interpret thus]: "The wicked shall be turned into hell," and who are they? "All the nations that forget God."'"[463] Both Rabbi Eliezer and Rabbi Joshua interpret Psalm 9 eschatologically and refer the judgment that is spoken of in vv. 6-9, 17, 20 to the last judgment. Verse 18[17] then naturally speaks of the dead. They draw that conclusion from the word *return*

459. Cf. *'Abot R. Nat.* A 36. For rabbinic discussion of the eschatological fate of sinners in Israel, see P. Volz, *Eschatologie,* 348–50; E. Sjöberg, *Gott,* 117–24; P. Schäfer, "Lehre," 276–79. Also noteworthy is the modern interpretation of *m. Sanh.* 10.1 given by S. Bamberger: He understands "all Israelites" to mean "all Israelites who deserve the name and attempt to follow the call of Israel, as well as all non-Israelites who observe the seven Noachic commandments" (*Sprüche der Väter,* 1). This point of view corresponds to that of Rabbi Joshua in *t. Sanh.* 13.1, 2 (see below).

460. See above, p. 53.

461. For Ps. 1:5 and its rabbinic interpretation, see above, pp. 35–36.

462. *b. Roš. Haš.* 16b-17a; *t. Sanh.* 13.3; *'Abot R. Nat.* A 41.15; Str-B 4: 1033–34. Cf. W. Bacher, *Agada* 1: 15–16; P. Volz, *Eschatologie,* 296–98, 315, 326–27.

463. *b. Sanh.* 105a. Cf. the parallel passages in *t. Sanh.* 13.2 (with B. Salomonsen's commentary 203–4, esp. n. 17) and *Midr. Tehillim* on Ps. 9:15; Str-B 4: 1180.

(שוב): The dead will rise to judgment, the wicked among them will "return" to Sheol after sentence has been pronounced, which then continues as their place of eternal punishment. But while Rabbi Eliezer sees two different groups addressed in the two halves of the verse (the wicked in Israel and the Gentiles), Rabbi Joshua interprets the second half of the verse in apposition to the first and also understands the attribute "that forget God" not as explanatory, as does Rabbi Eliezer, but as restrictive:[464] Only those Gentiles who forget God will be condemned to Gehenna, but not the יראי שמים, the God-fearers among them.[465] Thus while Rabbi Eliezer here places Israel's sinners and the Gentiles on *one* single level, Rabbi Joshua apparently wishes not only to see God-fearing Gentiles excluded from eternal damnation, but the sinners of Israel as well. He probably proceeds on the basis of the rabbinic principle "that God deals with human beings 'measure for measure' (מדה כנגד מדה), i.e.,: If a person is fundamentally wicked, God judges him or her with the full severity of the Law; but if he or she is fundamentally righteous, God in turn will be gracious to him or her. . . . With those who are evil, God acts according to מדת הדין (also called מדת הפורענות); with those who are (otherwise) righteous and with penitents, God acts according to מדת הרחמים."[466]

In addition, a tannaitic midrash on Dan. 7:9, "thrones were set in place," deals with the judgment of "the nations of the world." "Our rabbis say: What does (the plural) 'thrones' mean? In the time to come the Holy One, blessed be he, will take his seat, and the angels will set up thrones for the Great Ones of Israel, and they will be seated and judge with the Holy One, blessed be he, the nations of the world, as it says: 'the Lord enters into judgment with the elders and princes of his people' (Isa. 3:14)."[467] Here the עם in Isa. 3:14, בְּמִשְׁפָּט יָבוֹא עִם זִקְנֵי עַמּוֹ, "he enters into judgment *with* the elders of his people" is not interpreted adversatively, as the original context and the construction of

---

464. For this difference in determinative attributes, cf. K. E. Heidolph, W. Flämig, and W. Motsch, *Grundzüge*, 5.3. §§ 106–10 (pp. 828–32).

465. For characterization of the Gentiles in the early Jewish and rabbinic writings, see P. Volz, *Eschatologie*, 83–85. For the eschatological fate of the Gentiles, ibid., 356–59; E. Sjöberg, *Gott*, 72–76; D. S. Russel, *Method*, 297–303. The forensic judgment of the Gentiles is described at length in a later tradition: *Midr. Tanh.* B Deut V § 9 (Bietenhard 2: 483–84). The parallels *b. 'Abod Zar.* 2b are in Str-B 3: 84, 675–76, 4: 1203–4.

466. B. Salomonsen, *Die Tosefta* 4: 3.202–3 on *t. Sanh.* 13.1. There it is a matter of the interpretation of Mal. 3:19, a passage that, according to Rabbi Joshua, also does not imply the exclusion of sinners from the world to come.

467. *Midr. Tanh.* B Lev VII § 1 (Buber, 72; Bietenhard 2: 104; Str-B 4: 1103–4, 1210; P. Volz, *Eschatologie,* 276; A. Schlatter, *Matthäus,* 583).

the phrase עִם בְּמִשְׁפָּט בּוֹא demand,[468] but in the sense of "together with." This interpretation is connected with that of the preceding verses: "YHWH rises to argue his case; he stands to judge the peoples" (Isa. 3:13). Many of the newer translations and commentaries, with reference to the LXX, correct M's עַמִּים to עַמּוֹ, "his people."[469] But the rabbis read with M and therefore applied the whole saying in Isa. 3:13-15 to the eschatological judgment of the Gentiles and the "coming" of YHWH at the parousia for that judgment.[470] Hence they are forced to understand the עִם in v. 14 as "together with" and to derive from it a cooperation of the "great ones of Israel" in the judgment of the Gentiles. Given such a reading, this passage is, in fact, admirably suited to the purpose of answering the question of the identity of those who are seated with God for judgment of the Gentile kingdoms in Dan. 7:9-12.[471]

The question why the righteous must suffer, while sinners live happily, received a new answer from Rabbi Akiba. The solution in 4 Ezra was that the balance would be redressed in the future age, when sinners will be punished and the righteous rewarded. The sufferings of the righteous in this world are explained by Adam's sin.[472] Rabbi Akiba expands on this idea when he interprets God's צְדָקָ in Ps. 36:7 as the צְדָקָה that God shows the faithful in the world to come, because they have already done penance for their sins through the "judgments" endured in this world. On the other hand, the sinners receive the reward of their good deeds in this world and can consequently expect nothing but punishment in the world to come.[473]

Since, after all this, belief in a future accounting before God's judgment seat appears purely a matter of course, we are quite surprised to find indications

---

468. Cf. Job 14:3. H. Niehr, *Herrschen,* 198–200; E. Jenni, *Kommen,* 258; P. Bovati, *Giustizia,* 200–201.

469. For this problem, cf. H. Wildberger, *Jesaja* 1: 131.

470. In addition, H. Wildberger (*Jesaja* 1: 132) also refers this coming to YHWH's parousia for judgment, because he appears to misunderstand the phraseology of the expression עִם בְּמִשְׁפָּט בּוֹא.

471. Wis. 4:16, a passage that P. Volz sees as related (*Eschatologie,* 175–76), should not be read eschatologically. Cf. C. Larcher, *Sagesse* 2: 340.

472. See above, on 4 Ezra.

473. *Midr. Tanh.* B Gen II § 8 (Buber, 34; Bietenhard 1: 45), with the parallels in *Ber. R.* 33 on Gen. 8:1 and *Wa. R.* on Lev. 22:27. Cf. *'Abot R. Nat.* B 44 (Saldarini, 275–76); *Sipre Devarim* § 307 on Deut. 32:4 (Bietenhard, 739–40, with n. 3b); *b. Ta'an* 11.1; P. Volz, *Eschatologie,* 101–2, 128–30, 295–96; E. P. Sanders, "Rabbi Akiba's View of Suffering." In *b. Qidd.* 40b, a corresponding parable is ascribed to Rabbi Eleazar ben Zadok (W. Bacher, *Agada* 1: 49).

of a denial of this very judgment. "R. Akiba cited: 'Wherefore doth the wicked condemn God, and say in his heart, "Thou wilt not require"' (Ps. 10:13)? meaning that there is no judgment or judge. [In truth] there is judgment and there is a Judge!"[474]

The statement: "There is no judgment or judge!" is frequently found in the rabbinic tradition as a heretical sentence and is also handed down in an expanded version in the targum on Gen. 4:8. The biblical text of this passage leaves it unclear for the reader why Cain killed Abel. The targum gives an answer: The occasion was a discussion of the last things. "Cain answered and said to Abel: 'There is no judgment or judge, and there is no other world; there is no reward for the righteous and no retribution for the wicked in the world to come.' They quarreled about this in the open field. And Cain rose up against his brother and killed him."[475] The historical background of this haggadah could have been anti-Sadducee polemic—Cain represents the opinion of the Sadducees—so that we would have to suppose an origin before 70 C.E.[476] But H. A. Fischel shows that it is probable that the sentence "there is no judgment or judge" is more likely to be aimed at Epicurean doctrine.[477] This also fits better with a Sitz im Leben after 70 C.E.

To this point we have only seen examples of a forensically conceived individual or general final judgment. But the Tannaim also maintain the tradition of the day of YHWH as the day of the great judgment on sinners, especially the Gentile nations. For this, we find the expression "day of Gog" or "day of Gog and Magog."[478] "Rabbi Eliezer says: If you have gained merit by keeping the Sabbath, you will be saved from three disasters (פורעניות): the day of Gog

---

474. *Ber. R.* 26.6 on Gen. 6:2 (Theodor and Albeck 1: 252, ll. 6–7; parallels in the commentary ad loc.). Cf. *Pesiq. R. Kah.* 24.14 (C. Thoma and S. Lauer, *Gleichnisse* 1: 281–86).

475. *Tg. Neof.* on Gen. 4:8. The parallels in *TJI* may be found in S. Isenberg, "Polemic," 436–37. See B. Chilton, "Comparative Study"; M. McNamara, *Targum Neofiti 1: Genesis* (The Aramaic Bible 1 A), 65–67.

476. S. Isenberg, "Polemic," 440–44. It is also said in 4 Ezra 9:9 that the wicked deny that there will be future punishment. Perhaps *m. 'Abot* 1.7 also belongs here: "Do not give up hope of retribution (הפרענות)."

477. H. A. Fischel, "Epikurean Sententia." G. Stemberger is also in agreement with this position (*Judentum,* 191).

478. On this, see Str-B 3: 831–40; J. Klausner, *Vorstellungen,* 99–103 (*Messianic Idea,* 497–501); W. Bousset and H. Gressmann, *Religion,* 219–20; P. Volz, *Eschatologie,* 150–51; K. G. Kuhn, *TDNT* 1: 790–92. 1QM XI, 16 also speaks of God's "judgments" (שפטים) on "Gog and his whole assembly."

[and Magog], the travails associated with the Messiah, and the great day of judgment (יום הדין הגדול)."[479] This seems to presume an eschatological conception like the one we encountered in 4 Ezra 7:26-44: this age will be replaced by the messianic era, and only then will come the "great day of judgment" as the beginning of the new age. In contrast to 4 Ezra 7:26, the messianic era is here introduced by the "day of Gog" and the messianic "travail." On the other hand, this text also illustrates something that is true of the tannaitic period overall: "The great majority of texts make no precise distinction between the days of the Messiah and the world to come; a clear separation into three periods is the exception."[480]

Rabbi Akiba counts "the judgment on Gog and Magog in the days to come" (משפט גוג ומגוג לעתיד לבא) among the five things that last twelve months (m. 'Ed. 2.10).[481] "This saying can perhaps also be referred to the wars of Hadrian, because a whole year had to elapse from the revolt in the year 132 c.e. to the minting of the Hebrew coins with the inscription לגאלת ישראל (for the redemption of Israel), as the whole war falls within the years 132–135, but Bar Kochba's coins have survived from only *two* of those years. In any case, this saying of Akiba is politically colored, because it tells of a prolonged struggle with Israel's enemies that will last a whole year."[482]

It is understandable that in the tannaitic period people mainly thought of Rome when they referred to the end time judgment of "Gog." As a rule, however, other symbols were used for Rome, such as Edom, Esau, or Amalek.[483] Thus also Exod. 17:14: "I will utterly blot out the remembrance of Amalek from under heaven" was interpreted to refer to the destruction of Rome at the

---

479. *Mek. Y* on Exod. 16:25 (Lauterbach 2: 120). The same saying is quoted soon afterward with regard to Exod. 16:30 (Lauterbach 2: 123). In both places the manuscripts and editions vary from "R. Eliezer" to "R. Eleazar" to "R. Eleazar from Modiim." Lauterbach has "R. Eliezer" in the first passage and "R. Eleazar" in the second. Horowitz and Rabin have "R. Eliezer" in both (p. 169, l. 10; p. 170, l. 13). The person intended is undoubtedly R. Eliezer ben Hyrcanus (W. Bacher, *Agada* 1: 111–12), who also mentions the "day of Gog" in *Pesiq. R.* 23.1. J. Neusner has not included the saying in his collection (*Eliezer ben Hyrcanus*) and accidentally omits the "day of Gog" in quoting *Pesiq. R.* 23.1 (1: 496). In *Mek. Sh.* (Epstein and Melamed, 113, ll. 21–23) the saying is attributed to Rabbi Joshua.

480. P. Schäfer, "Lehre," 256.

481. On this, see W. Bacher, *Agada* 1: 329.

482. J. Klausner, *Vorstellungen*, 8 (*Messianic Idea,* 398). For a full discussion of this saying, see also P. Volz, *Eschatologie,* 326–27. He considers Klausner's interpretation "quite aberrant" (327). For the coins minted under Bar Kochba, cf. E. Schürer and G. Vermes, *History* 1: 606; L. Mildenberg, *The Coinage of the Bar Kokhba War.*

483. P. Volz, *Eschatologie,* 280; cf. Str-B 4: 862–64.

end of time, and Eliezer ben Hyrcanus (?)[484] says on the subject: "When will the name of these (people) vanish? When idolatry and its servants are rooted up and the place (i.e., God) will be one in the world and his kingdom (מלכותו) established forever. Then "'Y" will go forth and fight against those nations' etc. (Zech. 14:3) 'and "Y" will become king'" (Zech. 14:9), and further: 'Pursue them in anger and destroy them' etc. (Lam. 3:66)."[485] The reference to Zechariah 14, an extensive depiction of the day of YHWH, is significant and shows how vivid and compelling this tradition was, even for the rabbis.[486] Here again, the end time destruction of Rome is not the beginning of the preliminary messianic kingdom, but of the eternal rule of God. As far as I am aware, the work quoted represents the oldest rabbinic example of the description of the eschatological time of salvation as "God's reign,"[487] and that part of the sentence is missing in the parallel tradition in *Ekha Rab.* on Lam. 3:66. There the whole saying is: "When will the name of these (people) vanish from the world and idolatry and its servants be rooted out from the world and the Holy One, blessed be he, rule alone in all the world, as it says: 'and "Y" will become king over all the earth; on that day the Lord will be one and his name one' (Zech. 14:9)? When you will 'pursue them in anger and destroy them from under heaven' (Lam. 3:66)."[488]

The survey thus shows that the most important eschatological traditions we have found in early Jewish literature were taken up and expanded by the rabbis of the tannaitic period. They expect the historical judgment as an end time war of destruction and as last judgment. Warning of this final judgment

484. The MSS and editions of *Mek. Y* on Exod. 17:14 here vary between "Eleazar," "Eleazar from Modiim," and "Eliezer": Lauterbach 2: 158, l. 155 prints "Eleazar." Horovitz and Rabin, 186, l. 4 have "Eliezer." The parallel *Ekha Rab.* on Lam. 3:66 attributes the saying to Eliezer (cf. Pesaro, and Z. M. Rabinovitz, *Ginzé Midrash*, 150, l. 32). W. Bacher also decides for Eliezer ben Hyrcanus (*Agada* 1: 141–42). Referring to him, G. Dalman incorrectly writes "Jehoschua ben Chananja" (*Worte*, 81).

485. *Mek. Y* on Exod. 17:14 (Horovitz and Rabin, 186, ll. 407; Lauterbach 2: 158–59. Cf. Str-B 4: 862–63, 897, 915). For the historical day of judgment cf. also *Mek. Y* on Exod. 14:21; 15:1, 6, 7; *Midr. Tanh.* B Ex III § 6; Lev II § 4, III 3 § 14; Deut VII § 4.

486. There is reference to Zech. 14:4 in '*Abot R. Nat.* A 34.6, where the coming of God "in the days of Gog and Magog" is counted among God's ten "descents."

487. Rabbinic examples of the description of the eschatological time of salvation as God's reign are extremely rare, except for a few prayers and the targums. Paul Billerbeck is able to present a half dozen (Str-B 1: 179–80), and most of them are late. Not all of them use the abstraction מלכות for God's royal character, including the other instance in *Mek. Y* (on Exod. 15:18), a saying of Joseph the Galilean, quoted below.

488. Text from Pesaro, 1519 (repr. Berlin, 1926). Cf. the text in Z. M. Rabinovitz, *Ginzé Midrash*, 150, ll. 32–34, with slight variants.

plays an important part in their parenesis. The idea, for the most part, is that after the resurrection of the dead each individual must appear before God's judgment seat and give an account of his or her life, in order either to be admitted to the life of the world to come (Garden of Eden, Paradise) or to be damned to Gehenna. Fear of this judgment, from which not even a person like Samuel is excepted, should keep people from sin and lead them on the way of life, on which they will then be held steady by the words of Torah, just as the ox is held to the furrow by the driver's goad.[489] This fear is impressively grounded in the words said to have been spoken by Johanan ben Zakkai shortly before his death (*b. Ber.* 28b, par. *'Abot R. Nat.* A 25.1). This tradition also represents the earliest rabbinic witness to the expectation of an individual judgment immediately after death. That notion thus appears to have acquired no especially broad circulation in the tannaitic period. But since the last judgment was considered by the Tannaim primarily as an individual judgment of each person, the transition to the idea that this judgment would occur immediately after the death of each individual may have come to dominate almost without being noticed, especially since it appears that there was the greatest possible lack of clarity about the condition and location of the dead until the day of judgment.[490]

But as long as no judgment was anticipated immediately after death, there is no reason to expect that the concept of the "world to come," the עולם הבא, would be applied to the world beyond death or, as Paul Billerbeck says, to the "world of souls."[491] There is no instance of this in tannaitic usage.[492] We find only one passage in which the contrast between "this world" and "the world to come" corresponds to the contrast between here (the present world) and hereafter (the world after death): significantly enough, it is the secondary parallel to *b. Ber.* 28b (Johanan ben Zakkai's deathbed saying) in *'Abot R. Nat.* A 25.1.

In some of the passages cited, and in countless other rabbinic exegeses, we are struck by the ever-present inclination to eschatological interpretation of Scripture. This type of interpretation is a part of the rabbis' hermeneutic that

489. The comparison of Torah with the goad of an ox-driver is taken from a saying of Eleazar ben Azariah, *b. Hag.* 3b parr. (Str-B 1: 461). It is inspired by Qoh. 12:11.

490. P. Schäfer, "Lehre," 263.

491. Cf. Str-B 4: 819–21.

492. P. Schäfer, "Lehre," 253–54 (against Paul Billerbeck). J. Bonsirven had already observed: "We must admit that there is no abundance of conclusive texts" (*Judaïsme* 1: 314).

is simply taken for granted.[493] Not only passages that are already understood eschatologically in the Old Testament, such as the prophetic sayings about the day of YHWH quoted in the first chapter, are applied to the "time to come" (הֶעָתִיד לָבֹא) or "the world to come" (הָעוֹלָם הַבָּא), but also many that, read against the background of current eschatological ideas, suggest such an interpretation or even demand it. This is especially true when the passage in question contains concepts that had long been understood eschatologically, such as "life," formulas such as, among others, לְעוֹלָם, עַד עוֹלָם, or the key word *judgment* (מִשְׁפָּט, דִּין).

This tendency was further supported by the clear distinction between preterite and future in the verbal system of mishnaic Hebrew, which was also introduced into the Old Testament passages and thus brought into consideration by the rabbis in their translation of Old Testament quotations. Wherever the context permits or invites it, an imperfect form tends to be understood as an eschatological future. This is explicitly the case in the interpretation of the Song at the Sea (Exod. 15:1-18) in the Mekilta. There the explanation of v. 6, "your right hand shattered the enemy," reads: "It does not say רָעֲצָתָ אוֹיֵב, 'thou hast shattered the foe,' but rather תִּרְעַץ אוֹיֵב, 'thou wilt shatter the foe'—in the Age to Come (לֶעָתִיד לָבוֹא)! As it is said: 'In fury you will tread the earth, in anger you will trample the nations' (Hab. 3:12)."[494] The individual phrases of the subsequent verses are then eschatologically interpreted along the same lines.[495] At the concluding verse of the song the Mekilta introduces the well-known interpretation of Rabbi Jose the Galilean: "If only at the Sea Israel had proclaimed: יְיָ יִמְלוֹךְ לְעוֹלָם וָעֶד, 'The Lord *is* king for ever and ever!' Not a nationality or empire would ever after have ruled over them! Alas, they said: יְיָ יִמְלוֹךְ לְעוֹלָם וָעֶד, 'The Lord *will* be king for ever and ever,' in the Age to Come."[496] This interpretation of the Song at the Sea indicates once again what great importance the rabbis assigned to the end time judgment of punishment and destruction on Israel's enemies: only in that judgment will God's kingdom be brought to its full and complete triumph, and only then will Israel's salvation come.

493. Cf. R. Kasher, "Interpretation of Scripture," 573–74.

494. *Mek. Y* on Exod. 15:6 (Lauterbach 2: 42).

495. *Mek. Y* on Exod. 15:7 "you throw down those who rise up against you" (Lauterbach 2: 47); "you send out your fury," with a reference to Ps. 69:25 (Lauterbach 2:48); "it consumes them like stubble," with a reference to Obad. 1:18 and Zech. 12:6 (Lauterbach 2: 48).

496. *Mek. Y* on Exod. 15:18 (Lauterbach 2: 80; Horovitz and Rabin, 150, ll. 14–16); Str-B 1: 179. Cf. also S. Schechter, "Aspects" 3: 199.

CHAPTER FOUR

Summary and Conclusion

Following the Law and awaiting the judgment is, if we would briefly summarize it, the *summa* of Jewish devotion. (W. Bousset and H. Gressmann, *Religion*, 202)

The doctrine of the last judgment is the most characteristic doctrine of Jewish apocalyptic. (D. S. Russel, *Method*, 380)

Nec me revocabat a profundiore voluptatum carnalium gurgite nisi metus mortis et futuri iudicii tui, qui, per varias quidem opiniones, numquam tamen recessit de pectore meo. (Augustine, *Conf.* VI, 16, 26)

As we are approaching the hidden end with increasing speed; as each, at his or her own death, reaches the end of history—for on the last day, the day of judgment on history, he or she will awaken, and from death until that day there is no more time—so we must absorb the end and our responsibility in face of it with growing intensity into our awareness of history. To live in history means to live in light of the end. (R. Schneider, *Verhüllter Tag*, 31–32)

The selection of documents and texts with eschatological content drawn from the Old Testament, the early Jewish literature of Palestine and the diaspora, as well as tannaitic traditions treated here, may well serve as representative for our purposes. The texts and traditions in this selection come from a period of time covering some seven hundred years, from the early postexilic period to the Bar Kochba rebellion. They reveal, as their *basic eschatological model,* the expectation of a judgment that leads to the damnation of some and the salvation of others. This basic model underlies both *historical eschatology* (with the judgment as the definitive turning point of history) and *eschatology of the hereafter* (with reward and punishment after death). Variations and expansions on this basic model result

(*a*) from the combination of historical eschatology and eschatology of the hereafter. This combination ultimately leads to the acceptance of the idea of two judgments, the special judgment after death and the general, last judgment.

(b) from the acceptance of a resurrection of the dead that makes it possible for those who have died to participate in eschatological salvation (or eschatological damnation), even within historical eschatology.

(c) from differing definitions of those who are destined for salvation or damnation. However, there are only two basic models for this: in the first, the contrasting pair consists of Israel and the Gentiles; in the second, it is the righteous and sinners. A corresponding contrast in the realm of spirits and angels may be added.

(d) from the introduction of a messianic figure who can sometimes function also as judge. The messianic reign is either identical with the eschatological time of salvation, or precedes it.

(e) from different forms of judgment. In essence, two forms can be distinguished: the judgment of punishment and destruction, and the juridical-forensic judgment. Portents and accompanying signs (of a cosmic nature) may be added to the idea of judgment.

(f) from different ideas of damnation and salvation. In historical eschatology they tend to be conceived as earthly, while in eschatology of the hereafter they are nonearthly. Otherwise, eschatological joy and pain tend to be much the same in both conceptions.

In the following pages I will recapitulate, in summary, the most important eschatological conceptions and traditions, with special attention to the historical origins and development of the individual conceptions, and to the type and function of judgment in each.

1. The oldest conception of eschatological judgment in Judaism expects *judgment as the imposition of punishment on Israel's enemies at the end of time.* This conception rests on the prophets' proclamation of the day of YHWH, which was a determining influence for the origin and development of Jewish eschatology as a whole.[1] This is indicated, for example, by the numerous expressions containing the word *day,* which we have encountered in almost all of the writings discussed, for example, "day of wrath," "day of trouble," "day of destruction," "day of Gog and Magog," "day of conviction," "day of the (great) judgment," and so on.[2] The judgment of that day consists in a violent action with which God and God's faithful utterly destroy the gentile nations. Charac-

---

1. Cf. D. S. Russell, *Method,* 94–95.
2. Cf. P. Volz, *Eschatologie,* 163–64.

teristic motifs in this context are "wrath," "fire," and "sword." Natural forces like storm, lightning, water, ice, and snow may be conceived as cooperating powers.[3] Some passages draw a parallel with the Flood.[4] Thus, ultimately, the history of the world is divided into three periods: the original world that was destroyed in the Flood, the present and again spoiled world that will end with the "day of judgment," and the "new creation" that will endure forever.[5] More common, however, is a twofold division that regards the period from creation to the "day of judgment" as a *single* age.[6]

The concept of an historical, punitive judgment is also found, however, in texts that are not based on the contrast between *Israel* and the *Gentiles,* but between *righteous* and *sinners.* In this case the division runs through Israel itself, with the punishment falling primarily on the sinners in Israel. Examples are found as early as Malachi and Isaiah 65–66. In later texts, especially those from Qumran, the rooting out of sinners is accompanied, in the realm of angels and spirits, by the destruction of Beliar and his array.

It is seldom possible to give a precise historical identification of the groups and circles that, in the texts based on this conception, are distinguished from the rest of Israel as "elect," "righteous," "faithful," and so on, and who expect salvation for themselves alone.[7] In the texts from the Maccabean period, these circles are usually equated with the Hasidim of 1 Macc. 2:42; however, we know very little about them. Better known to us are the Essenes of Qumran, who probably emerged from the Hasidim, as did the Pharisees. In texts from the second to first centuries B.C.E., R. H. Charles regularly saw Pharisees and Sadducees as standing behind the opposition of "righteous" and "sinners," but his position has found little agreement. Only in the case of the Psalms of Solomon has Pharisaic origin been accepted as the *opinio communis.*[8]

Of *the ultimate punishment of sinners* after the end time judgment we learn little in detail. Often it appears to consist simply in destruction and death, but as early as Isa. 66:24 ("their worm shall not die, their fire shall not be quenched") it is connected with the idea of enduring suffering in the valley of

---

3. *Sib. Or.* 3:689-93; Wis. 5:17-23; 1 Enoch 100:13; *T. Levi* 3:2.
4. See above, pp. 58–59.
5. Cf. 2 Pet. 2:5; 3:5-7, 13.
6. See no. 11 below.
7. See no. 11 below.
8. See above, p. 47.

Gehenna.[9] This passage is the source of the "fire" that becomes the epitome of the pains of hell; from this time on it describes Gehenna and then burns in Sheol after the latter was identified with Gehenna and became the place of eternal punishment for sinners.[10] The torments of the sinners, however, are never portrayed; at most they are alluded to in motifs like "torture," "bonds," "chains." In the main, however, the texts content themselves with abstract concepts like "shame," "everlasting contempt" (Dan. 12:2), "destruction," "curse,"[11] or "eternal destruction."[12] According to *Bib. Ant.* 16:3 and *Sib. Or.* 4:184-86, sinners, after resurrection and judgment, will be punished with final death.

The eschatological salvation of Israel, or of the righteous contrasts with the punishment of the gentile nations, or sinners. At least in the older texts[13] this is described somewhat more colorfully and in a quite earthly manner: Those who have "survived" the judgment enjoy a long life, a fruitful earth, milk from fountains, and honey from heaven; they live in the new Jerusalem and God dwells in their midst; peace reigns, and all the nations of the earth are subject to Israel.[14] Later texts are generally more reserved in their descriptions, but for the most part they continue to envision the earth as the place of salvation (*Bib. Ant.* 3:10!). The texts could be separated into those that tend to paint the time of salvation in the tones of Paradise,[15] and those that describe it more in political and social categories.[16] Many texts, however, do not fall within this scheme, since they either combine the two aspects, as do Isaiah 65 or Joel 4:18-21, or else they content themselves with generalized concepts like "peace," "joy," "light," "mercy," "salvation," "righteousness," "healing," "blessing."[17] Daniel

9. See above, p. 32. In Jdt. 16:17 this image describes the punishment of Israel's enemies on the "day of judgment."

10. Cf 1 Enoch 22; 63:10; 99:11; 103:7-8; *Jub.* 7:29; 22:22; *Ps. Sol.* 14:9; 15:10. Str-B 4: 1075, 1095; C. Milikowsky, "Which Gehenna?"

11. 1 Enoch 5:5, 7.

12. Psalms of Solomon (see above, p. 48); 1QM I, 5; IX, 5–6; 1QS V, 12–13.

13. Cf. Joel 4:18-21; 4QPs^f; 1 Enoch 10:15—11:2; *Sib. Or.* 3:616-23, 741-61.

14. Dan 7:14; *Sib. Or.* 2:174-76. This, of course, presumes that the Gentile nations have not been eliminated by the judgment.

15. 1 Enoch 10–11; 1 Enoch 25; *T. Levi* 18:10-14; *Sib. Or.* 3:601-23; 741-61; *Sib. Or.* Fragm. 3. For the notion of the end time Paradise, see J. Jeremias's article, *TDNT* 5: 765–68.

16. Isaiah 66; Daniel 7; *Ps. Sol.* 17, 18; 1 Enoch 83–90; 1QM; 11Q Melch; *T. Dan* 5:10b-13; *Sib. Or.* 3:657-731; *Sib. Or.* 2:154-76; *Sib. Or.* 3:46-62; *Sib. Or.* 5; 4 Ezra 13.

17. Ps. 97:11; 1 Enoch 1:8; 5:6-8; *Jub.* 23:30; *T. Zeb.* 9:8; CD XX, 20; 1QH XV, 15–16. There is a notable "depiction" containing all the important motifs in 4 Ezra 8:52-54.

12:3 says of the salvation of the "wise" only that they "shall shine like the brightness of the sky . . . like the stars forever and ever."[18]

In all the texts, salvation is essentially conceived as *here*, as earthly; there is no suggestion of anything like "transcendence." It is true that in the Testament of Moses the salvation of Israel is described as an exaltation to the heavens (10:9-10), but the same thing is described at the beginning of the chapter as the "appearance" of the "reign of God" over all creation. This information is as impatient of concretization as that in the Ten-Week Apocalypse.[19] The vagueness of the description in these texts is undoubtedly deliberate. The rabbis of the tannaitic period are similarly vague in their depiction of the "world to come."[20] Early Jewish expectation was thus directed "entirely to the renewal of the concrete, historical world, in the midst of which is a particular land, a particular city, and a particular people with an irreplaceable and unending history. Ruined by human guilt and judged by the coming of God, it is the 'old,' the passing world, the world of yesterday. But as the world that, in God's coming, will be changed and renewed from the roots upward, it does not cease to be the same concrete, historical world. *Mutata eadem resurgit:* it remains also the new world, in different circumstances, but identical with itself. On this side of the expected reversal lies the ruined earth; on the other side is the earth renewed. Although the validity of this presupposition may appear doubtful in some texts, it can by no means be demonstrated that it was ever abandoned in principle."[21]

2. If we now cast a glance over *the eschatology of the hereafter* in texts like 1 Enoch 22, 1 Enoch 92–105 (Epistle of Enoch), Wisdom, the Testaments of the Twelve Patriarchs, the Testament of Abraham, the *Liber Antiquitatum,* and 4 Ezra 7, we notice first of all that in the sources prior to the first century C.E. a special act of judgment is totally lacking. The texts do speak of a different lot for sinners and righteous (or for their "souls" or "spirits") after death—1 Enoch 22 even distinguishes four different groups—but nowhere do we learn how the separation of the groups and their direction to their different places of abode was accomplished. The separation of the dead presumes a judgment that has already taken place during their earthly lives. Until death, sinners had

---

18. Cf. Wis. 3:7; *2 Bar.* 51:10, and the *reditura ad lumina* in the Regina inscription (in A. Deissmann, *Licht,* 387; U. Fischer, *Eschatologie,* 233–34; G. Delling, "Speranda futura"). For eschatological salvation in Daniel, see above, pp. 41–42.

19. See above, pp. 58–59.

20. Cf. P. Schäfer, "Lehre," 270–71.

21. C. Barth, *Diesseits,* 101–2.

the opportunity to repent; God's patience lasts that long. But with the death of each individual it is firmly established to which group he or she belongs, and therefore what lot is reserved for him or her. From this point of view, all of life is a long period of probation concluding with death, a kind of process of judgment that is decided at the end, with no need for a special act of judgment or sentencing; death is followed immediately by sentencing, by reward or retribution. Only some 300 years after 1 Enoch 22, toward the end of the first or beginning of the second century c.e., does the idea of a *special judgment* seem to have arisen in Judaism.[22] The first literary witnesses are the Testament of Abraham and *b. Ber.* 28b.[23] But even in the Testament of Abraham, whose extensive depiction of the special judgment is unique in early Jewish literature, that judgment does not serve the purpose of reaching a verdict: it merely functions as a "conviction" (ἐλέγχειν) of sinners and justification of the sentence that is already determined.

As far as eschatological destiny is concerned, early Jewish conceptions comprehend only a twofold division of humanity: sinners and righteous. A striking novelty in the Testament of Abraham and among the rabbis, therefore, is the dissolving of this purely black/white picture and the separation of people, or rather the souls of the dead, into *three groups: sinners, righteous, and "middle."* With the "middle" sort, good and evil deeds are in balance. Their fate after death is uncertain; it can be turned toward the good either through petitionary prayer or by a kind of purgatory in Gehenna.[24]

Nowhere is *the different lot of sinners and righteous after death* really described. The elaborate description of hell and its punishments is Greek in origin.[25] The description in 1 Enoch 22 has also been influenced by Greek ideas:

22. The first Christian author who explicitly mentions the special judgment is Lactantius (*Div. Inst.* 7.21), but only in order to reject it. The next certain, and now affirmative, witnesses do not appear until the fourth century, with John Chrysostom: *In 1 Cor. Hom.* 42.3 (PG 61, 366–68); *De Laz. Hom.* 2.2–3 (PG 48, 984–86), and Jerome: *In Joel* 2.1 (PL 25, 965). Augustine also offers a single instance (*De Anima* II, 4, 8 [PL 44, 498–99]). *Sib. Or.* 2:93-94 is difficult to judge. Cf. J. Rivière, *DThC* 8: 1765–1828, with the passage in question at 1790–91, 1797, 1800. The Apocalypse of Paul 14–18 gives a description of the special judgment. It has many similarities with the description in *T. Abr.* That Heb. 9:27 does not, as is still occasionally asserted, refer to an individual judgment immediately after death is shown both by the parallel drawn to the death and parousia of Christ and by the exact parallels in 4 Ezra, especially 4 Ezra 14:34-35. Cf. also *m. 'Abot* 3.1.

23. See above, pp. 132–34.

24. See above, p. 136.

25. Cf. A. Dieterich, *Nekyia*. M. P. Nilsson describes hell as a "Greek invention" (*Geschichte* 2: 558). Cf. M. Hengel, *Judaism* 1: 201.

According to this, the souls of sinners are in dark caves, those of the righteous in bright caves with springs of water. According to *Bib. Ant.* 15:5, also, the chambers for the souls of sinners are dark. Otherwise, the texts give only passing hints, often using abstract concepts and images derived from historical eschatology. Sinners go into Sheol: "their distress will be great; and in darkness and in chains and in burning flames" (1 Enoch 103:7-8). In a clear allusion to Isa. 66:24, *Bib. Ant.* 63:4 speaks of a "fiery worm" and of abiding in "inextinguishable fire." Other designations for this punishment are "torment,"[26] "destruction,"[27] "eternal punishment" (*T. Abr.* A 10:11), "death" (*T. Abr.* B 8:11).

The souls of the righteous, on the other hand, are "in the hand of God" (Wis. 3:1) after death; they are "in peace" (Wis. 3:3),[28] "at rest" (Wis. 4:7; *Bib. Ant.* 51:5), "joy" (1 Enoch 103:3), and "salvation."[29] In the image of Dan. 12:3 they shine like the stars[30] and possess "(eternal) life,"[31] and according to *T. Abr.* A 10:10 they enter into Paradise.[32]

3. As is already evident from the nature of the punishment, which even in its terminology resembles that in historical eschatology, this eschatology of the hereafter really requires no augmentation. Nevertheless, from the very beginning it appears to be combined in contradictory fashion with historical eschatology. Even the Testament of Abraham mentions, in addition to individual judgment after death, two other collective-historical judgments, although without creating any systematic connection among them or even hinting at the function of the last two.

From a tradition-historical point of view, the two conceptions have different roots: Historical eschatology is genuinely Jewish and rests on the idea of the day of YHWH. Eschatology of the hereafter, on the other hand, is apparently the product of Hellenistic influence.[33] It is understandable that Jewish thinkers clung to the first idea, even when eschatology of the hereafter had triumphed in Judaism; it is equally understandable that from the outset attempts were made to combine the two.

---

26. Wis. 3:1; *T. Ash.* 6:5; *T. Abr.* B 10:16.

27. *Bib. Ant.* 3:10; *T. Abr.* A 10:11. Cf. *Ps. Sol.* 14:9; 15:10.

28. Cf. *Bib. Ant.* 23:12. *T. Ash.* 6:5 speaks of the "angel of peace" who receives the souls of the righteous. This is also the source of the prayer for peace frequently found in Jewish gravestone inscriptions (cf. U. Fischer, *Eschatologie*, 217–19).

29. 1 Enoch 98:14, and frequently.

30. 1 Enoch 104:2; *Bib. Ant.* 33:5; 4 Ezra 7:97, 125.

31. *T. Ash.* 5:2; 6:5; *Bib. Ant.* 23:12; *T. Abr.* A 10:10.

32. Cf. *b. Ber.* 28b.

33. See above, on Wisdom and 1 Enoch.

The customary *combination of historical eschatology and eschatology of the hereafter* represents the conception underlying 1 Enoch 22, Wisdom, *Bib. Ant.*, and 4 Ezra 7, and presumed by the rabbis. In this conception, retribution or reward after death is only provisional, and the "chambers" of which the *Liber Antiquitatum* and 4 Ezra speak serve only for the retention of souls until the day of the general, last judgment. But the actual content of this judgment, its function, and what if any change it brings in the lot of the dead remain altogether unclear. As far as the lot of the dead is concerned, it can only consist in an intensified punishment for sinners and an increased happiness for the righteous.

The clearest description is in 4 Ezra 7. According to this, the souls of the dead spend the intervening time between death and the day of judgment in "chambers," the sinners in sevenfold anguish, the righteous in sevenfold bliss (7:80-99). On the day of judgment they will be released from their chambers; God will appear on the judgment seat and show them their new abodes: "the pit of torment" or "the furnace of Gehenna" on the one side, and "the place of rest" or "the paradise of delight" on the other side (7:32-38). In this presentation, the judgment consists of nothing except the direction of the dead to their places. There is not a trace of a verdict or a judicial process, for the righteous and sinners have long since been identified and separated.

Even so, we can scarcely explain it as merely a clinging to tradition when Judaism, as well as later Christianity, maintains the idea of a general, last judgment in combination with an eschatology of the hereafter.[34] Since human beings are not merely individuals, but also members of society, in the end judgment must not be passed simply on each individual's personal life, but also on the history of the community or society to which he or she belongs, and ultimately that means the history of humanity as a whole.[35] The historical aspect cannot be neglected in any eschatology. The conviction of sinners, and especially humanity's great sinners, must occur before all the world and in irrevocable fashion.[36] The appearance of truth, the disclosure of the negative as nega-

---

34. For Christian dogma, the constitution *Benedictus Deus* of Benedict XII (1336) has been of particular importance (*DS* 1002).

35. Cf. *STh* Suppl. 88, 1 ad 1; Karl Rahner, *Prinzipien*, 422–23; idem, *Foundations of Christian Faith* (transl. William V. Dych; New York: Seabury, 1978), 444–47.

36. Cf. G. Greshake, *Heil*, 63–66. On the relationship between the special and general judgment, see above, p. 21. Perhaps the most profound thinking about the meaning of Christian teaching on judgment is found in the work of Romano Guardini: cf. especially *Freiheit, Gnade, Schicksal*, 243–59; idem, *Der Herr*, 397–404; idem, *Theologische Briefe*, 29–31.

tive, and the destruction of what is negative along with its claims to be positive—all this is necessarily a cosmic and universal event.[37]

4. The idea of history underlying the eschatological conceptions we have been discussing can also be graphically represented. The usual conception of history, as most often presented in these texts, would look something like this:

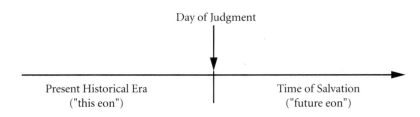

In this depiction, the day of judgment brings the decisive break in history. It dramatically and definitively closes the present period of history and inaugurates the time of salvation, the goal of history established by God. History continues after the day of judgment—the tenth week of the Ten-Week Apocalypse is followed by countless weeks without end (1 Enoch 91:17)—but with a different quality.[38] This new quality is determined in the first place by the fact that there are no more sinners, and the enemies of Israel have been rooted out or conquered, with the result that the conditions of Paradise are reestablished. The new quality has been indicated, since Isa. 65:17; 66:20, by use of the motif of the "new heaven" and "new earth," or as new creation or renewal of the world, without respect to the character of the depiction of salvation—in concrete and earthly, or in vague and abstract terms.[39]

37. Cf. Paul Tillich, *Systematic Theology* (Chicago: University of Chicago Press, 1963) 3: 406–9. Reinhold Schneider also interprets the eschatological event as the disclosure of the truth, and this "disclosure is also judgment, punishment, and grace" (*Weltgericht*, 6).

38. That this is true not only for prophetic eschatology, but also for apocalyptic was already indicated by Gerhard von Rad (*Theologie* 2: 124). He also refers (ibid., 117 n. 16) to 1 Enoch 91:17. However, in spite of this insight, von Rad also speaks of a "view toward the end of history" as "the best attested specific feature of apocalyptic" (ibid., 329). Cf. also ibid., 330, 334. K. Koch also emphasizes that apocalyptic does not anticipate an "end" to history (*TRE* 12 [1984]: 583). For prophetic eschatology, cf. also A. Vögtle, *Zukunft des Kosmos*, 49.

39. See above, pp. 30–31. For the motif of new creation, cf. 1 Enoch 45:4-5; 91:16; *Jub.* 1:29; 4:26; 1QS IV, 25; 11QT XXIX, 9; *Bib. Ant.* 3:10; 4 Ezra 7:25; 2 Pet. 3:13; Rev. 21:1, 5; *Mek. Y* on Exod. 16:25 (Lauterbach 2: 120); *b. Sanh.* 92b, 97b.

Out of this conception of history, which can rightly be called dualistic, we can abstract a subtype that can be graphically portrayed in this way:

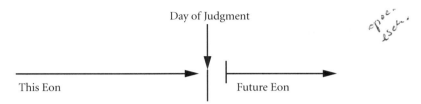

Day of Judgment

This Eon   Future Eon

This model is the final culmination of the dualistic conception of history. It is regarded among scholars even today as typical of apocalyptic and as the essential characteristic that distinguishes apocalyptic from earlier, prophetically influenced eschatology.[40] In this view, history is absolutely interrupted by the day of judgment; there is no longer any continuity between "this eon" and the "future eon." The difference between this and the previous conception was classically formulated by Emil Schürer: "The older hope for the future remained within the framework of the present condition of the world. People expected the destruction of Israel's enemies, a purification of the nation, and its glorious future. However ideal this future bliss was imagined to be, it remained within the scope of present conditions, except that they were idealized. In a later view, present and future increasingly became complete opposites, the cleft between them sharper, the conception more and more dualistic. With the arrival of the messianic era there begins a new way of the world, a new עוֹלָם. This future way of the world (עוֹלָם הַבָּא), however, is in every aspect the pure opposite of the present way (עוֹלָם הַזֶּה). The present is ruled by powers opposed to God, belonging to Satan and his angels, and therefore is sunk in sin and evil. The future is subject to the rule of God and God's anointed: therefore in that era only righteousness and happiness reign. There is scarcely any connection between the two. Through a marvelous act of God, the one is destroyed and the other is called into being."[41]

The fundamental error in this description is that the conception characterized by Schürer as a "later view" was formulated entirely under the influence

40. Cf. J. M. Schmidt, *Apocalyptik,* 194, 225–27, 283–84. P. Vielhauer writes: "This eschatological dualism of the two ages is the most essential characteristic in the content of apocalyptic; it distinguishes it fundamentally even from texts that have a formal resemblance to apocalyptic, and that have [used it to] enrich their language and imagery (e.g., Ezekiel)" (*Einleitung,* 413; P. Vielhauer and G. Strecker, *Einleitung,* 498).

41. E. Schürer, *Geschichte* 2: 586. Cf. D. S. Russell, *Method,* 264–71.

of the two-age doctrine of 4 Ezra and, if we are to be precise, can be found only there and somewhat in *2 Baruch*. It cannot be equated with the two-age teaching of the rabbis, as Peter Schäfer has shown,[42] nor even with that of Pseudo-Philo. Both Pseudo-Philo and the rabbis represent the first model, and it is that, and not the second model, that must be regarded as representative for postexilic-prophetic as well as "apocalyptic" Judaism.

The eschatology of the hereafter can be graphically depicted somewhat like this:

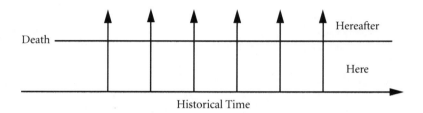

Of course, as we have seen, in Judaism this model was always combined with historical eschatology, so that at the end of the present period of history, after the day of judgment, the hereafter and the earthly time of salvation coincide. Or should we not say instead that in this conception even the hereafter will be dissolved, after the day of judgment, by the time of salvation, and will cease to function? This is true at least in the sense that there is no more death after that day. In this conception, in fact, the purpose of the resurrection is to make it possible for those who have died to participate in salvation, which is conceived as earthly and physical. This is the precise conception of *Bib. Ant.* 3:10, but also of 4 Ezra 7 and the rabbis, even though they do not give such concrete descriptions of salvation. But it is probably no accident that 4 Ezra 7:36 calls the salvation of the future age *iucunditatis paradisus*. The rabbis use the terms "Garden of Eden" and "Gehenna" both for the places of abode of departed souls and for the places of final damnation or blessedness after the last judgment.[43] Here again, then, the historical and concrete, here-and-now thinking of Judaism prevails.

5. Let us now turn once more to the *forms of judgment* as hinted or described in the texts. Essentially, there are two: *judgment as punishment* and *forensic judgment*. The judgment as punishment can consist in a military ac-

42. P. Schäfer, "Lehre."
43. Cf. P. Schäfer, "Lehre," 263.

tion against Israel's enemies that either eliminates them completely or brings
them forever under the rule of Israel. But it can also be directed against Israel's
sinners and either destroy them or hand them over to eternal torment in Sheol
or Gehenna. This is the oldest form of eschatological judgment.

Alongside it, however, the idea of judgment in judicial and forensic forms
acquires increasing importance. It is undoubtedly inspired by the word *judgment* (מִשְׁפָּט, κρίσις) itself. Even in connection with the "day of YHWH" we
find individual juridical expressions and initiatives toward a forensic depiction
of the final judgment.[44] However, in the beginning these features of a forensic
judgment stand immediately alongside or even within the depiction of the
judgment as punishment: for example, in 1 Enoch 1:9, where "destroy" and
"convict" are placed in *parallelismus membrorum*. The author of the Letter of
Jude, who quotes this passage at vv. 14-15, achieves the impression of a purely
forensic judgment by omitting the "destruction."[45] In any case, then, we must
take great care to note whether מִשְׁפָּט / κρίσις refers to the judicial process or
the imposition of punishment. The latter is far more frequent than the former.

We then find *graphic depictions of a court of judgment* (*throne scenes*) in the
framework of eschatological events in Dan. 7:9-10, approximately contemporary with the Vision of the Animals in 1 Enoch 90:20-26, and a century later
in the Book of Parables, in 1 Enoch 47:3-4.[46] However, these depictions are
fragmentary in each passage; the scenes feel stiff, and there is in no case any
genuine trial; such a thing is impossible, because the guilt of the accused is
established from the outset. In the Vision of the Animals, the guilty are only
brought forward to receive their sentence, and it is put into effect immediately.
In Daniel they are not even brought forth, to say nothing of any defense.

Something similar is the case with the judgment scene in the Book of Wisdom (4:20—5:14). It is not accuser and accused who appear in opposition to
each other, but "righteous" and "sinners." The verdict is already determined; a
trial is unnecessary, and consequently none is described. The legal terminology
for which the author of the Book of Wisdom shows a particular partiality, and
the idea of the eschatological judgment in some sense as a forensic judicial
process reveal quite clearly that this idea is an imaginative aid, a metaphor—
and it must always have been sensed that this is what it is.

Finally, the depiction of the special judgment in the Testament of Abraham
shows the kinds of contradictions and inconsistencies that this image brings

44. Mal. 3:5; Joel 4:2, 12.
45. See above, on 1 Enoch.
46. See above, on Daniel and 1 Enoch. Cf. also Rev. 20:11-12.

to eschatology.[47] However, in spite of its inadequacy, the image of a forensic last judgment has proved to be the most accurate and impressive representation of what the authors have in mind. The Psalms certainly contributed to its growing popularity, especially from the time when they began to be interpreted eschatologically.[48] Hence in the tannaitic period the יוֹם [הַ]מִּשְׁפָּט became the יוֹם [הַ]דִּין.[49]

6. The image itself, in turn, gave rise to *the idea of a judgment over the righteous as well.* At first, of course, judgment is imposed only on sinners; the righteous are released from it. Only near the end of the first century c.e. do indications of a judgment on sinners *and* righteous appear.[50] At this point even those for whom hitherto the judgment was nothing but a consolation and satisfaction, a λόγος εὐλογίας (1 Enoch 1:1), begin to fear it.[51]

7. In all these conceptions *the judge* is, essentially, God. But as in Zech. 3:1-7, where "the angel of YHWH" represents YHWH as judge of the heavenly court, in early Jewish writings other judge figures could function as God's representatives, especially the archangel Michael (Dan. 12:1; 1QM XVII, 6-7; *As. Mos.; T. Dan* 6:1-7), but also Melchisedek (11Q Melch), the Son of man (1 Enoch 37-71; 4 Ezra 13), the Messiah (*Ps. Sol.* 17; 4 Ezra 11-12; *Sib. Or.* 5), even Abel (*T. Abr.*). It is frequently the "elect" also who carry out the sentence of destruction by war, or at least participate in that action: for example, in texts from the period of the Maccabean wars such as the Ten-Week Apocalypse and the Vision of the Animals in 1 Enoch, or the texts from Qumran (1QM). When the judgment is imagined as forensic, God is sometimes the head of a group of judges. This tradition rests on Daniel 7, where the original idea was probably that angels participated, but a tannaitic midrash interprets it, with the aid of Isa. 3:14, to refer to the "great ones of Israel."[52]

8. Frequently, to avoid the necessity of directly naming the judge or those who carry out the judgment, some texts such as Daniel 7 and the Ten-Week Apocalypse repeatedly make use of the *passive,* usually in the future as an eschatological passive. In general, God is to be thought of as the subject of these

47. See above, on *T. Abr.*
48. See above, pp. 33–36.
49. See above, on the Psalms, Qumran, and the Tannaim.
50. *Sib. Or.* 4:42; 2 Enoch 46:3. N. Messel, *Einheitlichkeit,* 183. In *Jub.* 5:13-18 there is reference to a judgment over all people and each individual.
51. Noteworthy in this connection is the formula: "Woe to us [that is, the faithful] for the day of judgment, woe to us for the day of rebuke."
52. Thomas Aquinas also adduces both Matt. 19:28 and Isa. 3:14 to demonstrate *quod etiam alii iudicabunt cum Christo* (*STh* Suppl. 89,1).

passives, but sometimes they include angels or the elect. For the most part, however, the purpose of the passive is simply to avoid pointing out a particular agent. Occasionally the third person plural replaces the passive.[53]

9. *God's parousia for judgment* constitutes an established tradition.[54] This parousia is described as a mighty theophany and leads to a dreadful judgment as punishment, sometimes called a "visitation."[55] The rabbis refer this "coming" of God, however, to God's coming for a forensic last judgment.[56]

10. *The standard for judgment* is, essentially, the Torah. Fidelity to Torah is the basis for hope of salvation, and infidelity to it brings judgment with it, entirely in accord with the promises in Deuteronomy 27–30, which were eschatologically interpreted in early Judaism.[57] In the fourth book of the Sibylline Oracles and in the Testament of Abraham, the Torah is apparently replaced by general ethical norms, but they are not concretely described.

11. At this point, then, we can summarize the *function of eschatological judgment.* That judgment creates the precondition for Israel's salvation by subjugating the gentile nations to Israel, or eliminating them entirely and consigning them to punishment in Gehenna. Only the God-fearers among them are spared; they then come to Zion, together with the scattered members of Israel, to live there forever in peace according to God's law.[58] Where the fundamental division is between righteous and sinners, judgment is the precondition for the salvation of the righteous, or the holy "remnant" of Israel. This close connection between salvation and judgment is already formulated in Isa. 10:22: "Destruction is decreed, overflowing with righteousness." "Judgment runs its course and *must* do so, because only in this way can righteousness be realized in history."[59] In all texts up to and into the first century, this judgment is imposed exclusively on sinners. The judgment never has the character of an examination or inquiry to determine who are the sinners and who the righteous; their separation is always presupposed.

---

53. See above, on Daniel and 1 Enoch, and the excursus in chap. 8.

54. Isa. 66:15-16; Zech. 14:5; Mal. 3:1-2; Ps. 50:3; 96:13; 98:9; 4Q Ps[f] (see above, p. 34); 1 Enoch 1:3b-9; *As. Mos.* 10; *T. Levi* 4:1; 4 Ezra 6:18-20; *Ber. R.* 93.10 on Gen. 45:3; *Midr. Tanh.* B Lev VII § 1.

55. Thus, for example, 1QS IV, 11; 4 Ezra 5:56; 6:18. Cf. Isa. 10:3. Usually, however, the "visitation" is a "visitation for good" (1 Enoch 25:3) accorded as a blessing to Israel or the righteous, for example, Wis. 3:7; *Ps. Sol.* 3:11; 1QS IV, 6; *As. Mos.* 1:18.

56. See above, pp. 134, 136–38.

57. See above, pp. 53–54, 110, 117.

58. See above, pp. 97–99.

59. H. Wildberger, *Isaiah 1–12,* 437-38.

Judgment is an instrument of retributive justice, inasmuch as it punishes sinners and rewards the righteous. It is therefore also an answer to the old question about the sufferings of the righteous and the happiness of sinners on earth. That answer received a striking formulation in the words of Rabbi Akiba: Those who are faithful do penance for their few sins through the "judgments" in this world, so that in the world to come they can expect nothing but reward. On the other hand, sinners receive the reward for their few good deeds in this world and consequently can expect only punishment in the world to come.[60] From this point of view, judgment remains an object of hope even in the rabbinic period, at least for the righteous.

The day of judgment separates "this age" from "the age to come." It means a sharp end to previous history, the time of "Belial's rule" (1QS II, 19), and introduces the eternal time of salvation in the "new creation." It is true that we find a full development of the terminology of the teaching about the two ages first in Pseudo-Philo and 4 Ezra, but the substance of the idea was present from the time when the day of YHWH became a day of eschatological judgment—that is, from the early postexilic period.[61] This is demonstrated by, among other things, the more or less fixed formula "until the day of judgment," in which past, present, and future history up to this point are regarded as a *single* period.[62]

From still another point of view, the eschatological judgment marks an end, a genuine ἔσχατον: It is the last in the long series of God's "judgments," that is, punishments imposed throughout history on God's own people, the Gentiles, or even individuals. We find the plural "judgments" (מִשְׁפָּטִים, שְׁפָטִים) in this sense even in the Old Testament,[63] especially in the expression "execute judgment on" (עָשָׂה שְׁפָטִים בְּ).[64] Ezekiel 14:21 speaks of YHWH's "four deadly acts of judgment: sword, famine, wild animals, and pestilence" (cf. 5:16-17) that will be sent against Jerusalem. For Ezekiel the catastrophe of 587 B.C.E. is only the "execution of the judgments" of YHWH. When later the plural, "judgments," appears with conspicuous frequency in the Psalms of Solomon

60. See above, pp. 138–39.
61. See above, p. 112.
62. See above, pp. 80–81.
63. שְׁפָטִים: Exod. 6:6; 7:4; Ezek. 14:21; Prov. 19:29. מִשְׁפָּטִים Isa. 26:8, 9; Zeph. 3:15. It is not clear whether Ps. 97:8 speaks of "punishments" or "judgments," that is, "rulings."
64. Exod. 12:12; Num. 33:4; Ezek. 5:10, 15; 11:9; 16:41; 25:11; 28:22, 26; 30:14, 19. Cf. also Ezek. 23:10; 2 Chr. 24:24; Tob. 3:5. עָשָׂה מִשְׁפָּטִים occurs in Exod. 5:8.

(14x),[65] this is certainly connected with the similarity of the situation: It is on the occasion of Pompey's seizure of Jerusalem that the author of the eighth psalm reflects on "the judgments of God since the creation of heaven and earth," and must recognize that they have always been righteous (8:7), serving only for the "disciplining" (παιδεία) of Israel.[66]

God's punishing judgments in history are a fixed element in the so-called Deuteronomistic view of history.[67] The primary judgments of God in this view of history are the catastrophes in 722 and 587 B.C.E., but the Old Testament never uses the word מִשְׁפָּט for them. For the most part, with regard to these and other historical judgments, the text speaks of YHWH's being angry, which ultimately led to the use of the word *wrath* (קֶצֶף) in an absolute sense to mean "judgment" in the sense of punishment.[68] We find this usage with reference to the Flood in 1 Enoch 106:15 and *Sib. Or.* 1:165, but it is also applied to eschatological judgment,[69] just as it is generally the case that the same terms are found to be used for historical punishing judgments and eschatological judgment.

Thus the Flood is also described in 1 Enoch 84:4 as the "day of the great judgment." On the other hand, in Qumran the expression "execution of judgments" is applied to the final judgment.[70] Pseudo-Philo speaks of a "visitation" by God both with regard to the Flood and in referring to the last judgment.[71] Similarly, the Damascus Document distinguishes a "first visitation," namely, the conquest of Jerusalem in 587 B.C.E., from the eschatological "visitation," in which the wicked will receive their definitive punishment.[72] In the Testament of Levi, God's δικαιοκρισία in 15:2 have reference to the Babylonian exile, but in 3:2 to the last judgment. Therefore when Pseudo-Philo, in *Bib. Ant.* 3:9–10, deliberately locates the final judgment as the last in a series of historical judgments "through hunger or sword or fire or death," he is only expressing the common opinion of early Judaism. Overall, the compact review

65. *Ps. Sol.* 2:10,15; 3:3; 5:1; 8:7(2x), 8,23,25,32,34; 11:5; 17:10; 18:3.
66. Perhaps these judgments may also be identified with the "lash of chastening" in *Ps. Sol.* 7:9.
67. On this, see O. H. Steck, *Israel*, 110–218; H. W. Wolff, "Kerygma."
68. Num. 1:53; 18:5; Josh. 9:20; 22:20; 1 Chr. 27:24; 2 Chr. 19:10; 24:18; 32:25. אַף is used in the sense of wrathful judgment in Isa. 13:3; similarly θυμός in Sir. 48:10. Cf. J. Fichtner, art. ὀργή, κτλ., *TDNT* 5: 395–97. For the absolute use of זַעַם "curse," which the LXX also translates ὀργή, see idem, 5: 393 n. 69.
69. 1 Enoch 5:9; *Ps. Sol.* 15:4; 1QH III, 28.
70. See above, pp. 76–77.
71. See above, p. 110.
72. See above, pp. 78–79.

of history from the Flood to the last judgment and the time of salvation to
follow it, as given in that passage, can be seen as representative for the opinion
of early Judaism as a whole.

12. In early studies of the eschatology of Second Temple Judaism, including
the "classic" works of Wilhelm Bousset and Hugo Gressmann, Emil Schürer,
Paul Volz, and Joseph Bonsirven, the concepts of *"nationalism," "universalism,"*
and "individualism," as well as contrasting pairs constructed on the basis of
these concepts, play an important part in the interpretation and evaluation
of Jewish eschatology.[73] In particular, the concept of "individualism" and the
contrast between national and individual eschatology contributed more to the
confusion of the subject than to its illumination. Historical eschatology, with
judgment as a pronouncement of punishment on Israel's enemies, was described as "national," while eschatology of the hereafter, with the contrast between righteous and sinners, was regarded as "individual" or "universal." A
historical development was traced from the first conception to the second, and
this was interpreted as "progress" and *praeparatio evangelii.*[74]

There is more of falsehood than of truth in this construction. The conception of historical eschatology proceeding on the basis of a contrast between
Israel and the nations may somewhat correctly be described as "national." But
it is also "universal" to the extent that the judgment touches all nations, and
can even be explicitly extended to include all creation.[75] Moreover, this conception survived with undiminished vitality throughout the entire period we have
investigated. And the contrast between Israel and the nations was retained by
the rabbis even in their conception of a forensic last judgment after the resurrection of the dead.[76]

On the other hand, the contrast between righteous and sinners appears
already in the eschatology of Trito-Isaiah and Malachi, and in this conception,
attention is concentrated much more sharply on Israel than in the other; to
this extent it is also thoroughly "national." This conception became truly universal only in the course of the first century c.e. in documents like the Testament of Abraham and the fourth Sibylline Oracle. In these writings all contrast

73. Cf. W. Bousset and H. Gressmann, *Religion,* 289–301, 469–75; E. Schürer,
Geschichte 2: 583–86, 646–48; P. Volz, *Eschatologie,* 63–77; J. Bonsirven, *Judaïsme*
1: 307–9; J. Keulers, *Lehre,* 142–43. A similar interpretation is still found, however, in
P. Vielhauer, *Einleitung,* 414.
74. W. Bousset and H. Gressmann, *Religion,* 301.
75. See above, pp. 27, 31–32, 71–72.
76. See above, pp. 136–38.

between Israel and the Gentiles appears to have been erased; the "faithful" and "godless" come from all nations, and judgment is not based on fidelity to the Torah and its precepts, but solely on general ethical norms, good and wicked deeds. This may in part be accounted for by the fact that this literature served as propaganda for Judaism in the gentile world.

Finally, the description of eschatology of the hereafter as "individual" is inaccurate, or at least very deceptive. In this conception, "sinners" and "righteous" always exist as contrasting groups, and the idea of an individual judgment immediately after death appears only near the end of the period under investigation. There is some preparation for this in the parenesis of the Tannaim, who repeatedly emphasize that at the last judgment every individual must appear before God's throne and give an account of his or her life.[77] Only when this idea comes to the fore does the eschatological judgment acquire "individualist" features, and only then is the individual as a person taken into account. Until that time, the eschatological judgment, in whatever conception, must be said to be collective; it is always imposed on groups.[78] An individual note enters early eschatology (whether historical or hereafter) in the contrast of righteous and sinners only to the extent that now it is not primarily birth, but attachment to the right group that determines one's eschatological lot, and thereby the decision of the individual for one or another group acquires greater significance; indeed, this is the first moment at which such a thing is demanded at all. Liberal Protestantism, however, saw precisely in this the unique character of Jesus' message.[79]

13. Most of the writings and authors we have treated use not just one, but several eschatological conceptions and traditions in combination. The only important exceptions are the Assumption of Moses and Pseudo-Philo. This phenomenon cannot simply be explained as the result of the compilation of different literary units and traditions leading not only to colorful collections like 1 Enoch or the Sibylline Oracles, but also to works as resistant to literary-critical dismantling as the Testaments of the Twelve Patriarchs. Even in these

---

77. An isolated early example of the statement that God judges "every individual" is *Jub.* 5:16.

78. N. Messel (*Einheitlichkeit,* 182–85) had already raised this objection against W. Bousset.

79. Cf., for example, W. Bousset and H. Gressmann, *Religion,* 301. The (supposed) contrast between the collective eschatology of the prophet and the individual eschatology of Jesus is most clearly formulated by Rudolf Bultmann, *Theology of the New Testament* 1: 25: Only in Jesus do judgment and salvation become "eschatological events in the strict sense; i.e., events in which the present world and all history cease to be."

cases the redactor or compiler, at least, must have regarded the different conceptions as somehow compatible or mutually complementary. But even within literarily homogeneous writings and isolated units like the Book of Jubilees or the Book of Wisdom, very different eschatological models are found together. Fourth Ezra represents a fairly complete compendium of eschatological conceptions and traditions, and there can scarcely be any doubt that the rabbinically educated author considered all of them in some sense compatible and complementary.[80] But as to how anyone imagined the concrete combination of historical eschatology and eschatology of the hereafter, punishing judgment and forensic judgment, judgment of the gentile nations and judgment of sinners, judgment by God and judgment by God's representative, the special judgment after death and the general, last judgment—of this we learn nothing at all.

A search for concretization of imagery and internal consistency, coherence of ideas, motifs, and conceptions, is foreign to the apocalyptic authors. That is clear from every one of their eschatological descriptions and may never be forgotten in interpreting them. The coexistence of what, from a logical point of view, are mutually exclusive eschatological conceptions, a situation apparently regarded as unproblematic—this is characteristic of Jewish and to a great extent of Christian intellectual history. This coexistence finds its most exalted expression in apparently nonsensical formulations such as the well-known paradox of Rabbi Akiba: "Everything is foreseen but the right of choice is granted, and the world is judged with goodness, and everything is in accordance with the preponderance of [human] deed[s]."[81]

14. We find no essential differences in texts from Palestine and those from the diaspora, as far as their eschatology is concerned.[82] Both types use different eschatological conceptions, often side by side. The eschatology of the hereafter that has been regarded as characteristic of diaspora literature is first attested for us in a writing from Palestine from the end of the third century B.C.E., 1 Enoch 22; we find it again in the Epistle of Enoch. The latter may well have been read by the author of the Book of Wisdom, perhaps already in Greek

80. See above, pp. 121–22.
81. *m. 'Abot* 3.15.
82. In this respect I come to a completely different conclusion from that of U. Fischer, *Eschatologie*, 255–56. This undoubtedly results from the choice of sources: Fischer left entirely out of account the writings from the diaspora discussed here (Wisdom, *Sib. Or.*, *T. 12 Patr.*, *T. Abr.*).

translation.[83] The religious and cultural and particularly the literary connections between the homeland and the diaspora were so close and many-sided
that there was no essential disagreement in a question as important as eschatology. And with only a few corrections and additions, this eschatology, with
its focus the judgment and its goal eternal salvation, also became part of Christian dogma.

83. See above, p. 46.

PART TWO

Judgment in the Preaching of John the Baptizer

—————— CHAPTER FIVE ——————

The Tradition and Message of John the Baptizer

The Tradition in Q

Unlike the "apocalypticists" whom we know only as literary figures, John the Baptizer appeared as a prophet.[1] But in his preaching, as in the writings of the "apocalypticists," eschatology stood in the foreground. The expectation of the final judgment in the immediate future was the basis of his call for repentance and the action that gave him his name: baptizing.

The Baptizer's eschatological preaching, as given in Q, can be reconstructed more or less as follows (cf. Matt. 3:7-12; Luke 3:7-9, 16-17):

γεννήματα ἐχιδνῶν,
τίς ὑπέδειξεν ὑμῖν φυγεῖν ἀπὸ τῆς μελλούσης ὀργῆς;
ποιήσατε οὖν καρπὸν ἄξιον τῆς μετανοίας.
καὶ μὴ δόξητε λέγειν ἐν ἑαυτοῖς·
"πατέρα ἔχομεν τὸν Ἀβραάμ."
λέγω γὰρ ὑμῖν, ὅτι δύναται ὁ θεὸς ἐκ τῶν λίθων τούτων
    ἐγεῖραι τέκνα τῷ Ἀβραάμ.

ἤδη δὲ ἡ ἀξίνη πρὸς τὴν ῥίζαν τῶν δένδρων κεῖται·
πᾶν οὖν δένδρον μὴ ποιοῦν καρπὸν καλόν
    ἐκκόπτεται καὶ εἰς πῦρ βάλλεται.

ἐγὼ μὲν ὑμᾶς βαπτίζω ὕδατι·
ὁ δὲ [ὀπίσω μου] ἐρχόμενος ἰσχυρότερός μού ἐστιν,
οὗ οὐκ εἰμὶ ἱκανὸς τὰ ὑποδήματα βαστάσαι·
αὐτὸς ὑμᾶς βαπτίσει ἐν [πνεύματι ἁγίῳ καὶ] πυρί.

---

1. Cf. C. H. H. Scobie, *John*, 117–30; J. Becker, *Johannes*, 41–62; J. Ernst, *Johannes*, 290–300.

οὗ τὸ πτύον ἐν τῇ χειρὶ αὐτοῦ
καὶ διακαθαριεῖ τὴν ἅλωνα αὐτοῦ,
καὶ συνάξει τὸν σῖτον αὐτοῦ εἰς τὴν ἀποθήκην,
τὸ δὲ ἄχυρον κατακαύσει πυρὶ ἀσβέστῳ.

You brood of vipers,
Who told you that you could flee from the wrath to come?
Bear fruits worthy of repentance!
Do not begin to say to yourselves:[2]
"We have Abraham as our ancestor."
For I tell you, God is able from these stones to raise up children to
    Abraham!

Even now the axe is lying at the root of the trees;
every tree therefore that does not bear good fruit is cut down and
    thrown into the fire.

I baptize you with water;
but [after me] one who is more powerful than I is coming;
I am not worthy to carry his sandals;[3]
he will baptize you with [holy spirit and] fire.

The winnowing fork is in his hand;
he will cleanse what he has threshed,
and gather the wheat into his granary,
but the chaff he will burn with unquenchable fire.

The reconstruction of the first, second, and fourth units presents no major problems.[4] It is a different matter with the saying about the Stronger One, because here we have a double tradition from Q and Mark 1:7-8, and it is not absolutely clear to what degree Matthew and Luke have merged the two. For the most part, scholars think that the wording of Q (except for the addition εἰς μετάνοιαν) has been better preserved by Matthew than by Luke.[5] However, it can no longer be determined whether ὀπίσω μου in ὁ δὲ ὀπίσω μου ἐρχό-

2. For the translation of the imperative aorist in this verse, see *BD* § 336,3 (appendix).
3. For the meaning of βαστάζω, see below.
4. Cf. P. Hoffmann, *Studien,* 17–19; S. Schulz, *Q,* 367–69.
5. Cf. P. Hoffmann, *Studien,* 18–25; S. Schulz, *Q,* 368–69; R. Laufen, *Doppelüberlieferungen,* 94–97; H. Fleddermann, "John," 377–80; S. von Dobbeler, *Gericht,* 45–52. Fleddermann, however, like Heinz Schürmann (*Lukas* 1: 173 n. 79), believes that the untying of the sandal straps is original ("John," 379). J. Ernst thinks that Luke has the better tradition (*Johannes,* 48).

μενος (Matthew) has been inserted from Mark 1:7[6] or whether Luke eliminated it from the text of Q.[7] In addition, ὀπίσω with the genitive in the temporal sense is otherwise attested only in the LXX, and there but once.[8]

The most difficult expression to judge is ἐν πνεύματι ἁγίῳ καὶ πυρί. Was
it thus in Q, or did Matthew and Luke, independently of one another, insert
the baptism with holy spirit on the basis of Mark 1:8?[9] Two reasons are given
for supposing that in Q or an earlier stage of Q the text spoke only of baptism
with fire: first, the strict parallelism between the first and fourth lines that
results, with the clear antithesis ("I baptize you with water, but he will baptize
you with fire"); second, the fact that in the preceding and following similitudes
fire alone appears as the instrument of judgment. Both observations, however,
tell us only that the historical Baptizer did not speak of a baptism with holy
spirit; they contribute nothing to the reconstruction of the textual history of
the logion itself.[10]

The history of the text becomes entirely opaque if we suppose that this
logion originally spoke of a baptism ἐν πνεύματι καὶ πυρί, with πνεῦμα being
understood in the sense of "wind" or "storm."[11] It is true that wind and storm
are found in the Old Testament and early Jewish literature as instruments of
judgment,[12] sometimes in combination with fire,[13] so that this kind of combination is thoroughly imaginable in the Baptizer's preaching of judgment; in a

6. Thus S. Schulz, Q, 368; S. von Dobbeler, Gericht, 49.

7. Thus P. Hoffmann, Studien, 25.

8. BAGD 575 s. v. 2b; E. Lohmeyer, "Überlieferung," 313; J. Ernst, "Jesus," 19–20.

9. The latter is the opinion of A. von Harnack, Sprüche, 7–8; T. W. Manson, Sayings,
41; idem, "John," 404; S. Schulz, Q, 368; P. Hoffmann, Studien, 30. C. H. H. Scobie
(John, 70 n. 1) and S. von Dobbeler (Gericht, 50–51) consider this improbable. H.
Fleddermann ("John," 381) attributes the insertion to the redactor of Q. But since we
cannot even reconstruct the text of Q with certainty at this point, it is completely impossible to say anything about a pre-Q text. R. Bultmann (History of the Synoptic Tradition, 111 n. 1, 246) rightly leaves open the question of the stratum of tradition at which
the insertion occurred. R. Laufen does not discuss this question, but considers the
baptism with holy spirit to be original and καὶ πυρί an addition by the Q redaction
(Doppelüberlieferungen, 117–20).

10. U. Luz correctly writes: that Q contained only πυρί is something that can "only
be postulated, not proved" (Matthew 1: 171 n. 28).

11. Thus H. Sahlin, Studien, 50–52; E. Schweizer, TDNT 6: 399; W. Grundmann,
Lukas, 105; O. Böcher, TRE 17 (1986): 175. See the listing of other authors in J. D. G.
Dunn, "Baptism," 82.

12. Thus, for example, Isa. 4:4; Ezek. 13:11, 13; Wis. 5:23; 1 Enoch 100:13; Mek. Y
on Exod. 14:21 (Lauterbach 2: 229–30).

13. Thus, for example, Ps. 11:6; Isa. 29:6; 66:15-16 (see above, p. 31); Sir. 39:28-29;
4 Ezra 13:10, 27.

certain sense it also fits the image of winnowing. But then either Mark and the redactor of Q, independently of one another—if ἐν πνεύματι καὶ πυρί was in a pre-Q text—or Matthew and Luke on the basis of Mark 1:8—if ἐν πνεύματι καὶ πυρί was the text of Q—would have transformed the "wind" into "holy spirit" by the insertion of ἁγίῳ. This hypothesis is certainly ingenious, but it is not very probable.[14] From the point of view of the history of the text, then, it is a simpler and therefore preferable solution to see the whole phrase about baptism with holy spirit as a Christian expansion. Whether Q already contained this expansion, or whether it was introduced into the history of our texts through the influence of Mark, can no longer be determined, nor is it very important. It is improbable that the Baptizer himself spoke of a baptism with (holy) spirit.[15]

The "report" in Q is our oldest and best reference for the Baptizer's preaching; for his preaching of judgment it is the sole source, for it is well known that Josephus, in his description of the Baptizer (*Ant.* 18. 116–19), completely suppressed the eschatological thrust of his preaching. The type and character of the "report" in Q are highly similar to the synoptic tradition of Jesus' preaching: It is a rather artistic composition of characteristic words, significant sayings, and similitudes. Apart from the identification of John's predicted judge with Jesus and the vision of the Baptizer as derived from that identification, the text reveals no Christian tendencies, and consequently it deserves our fundamental trust. We may take it as given that the crucial phrases ("the wrath to come," "repentance"), the tersely formulated sayings (like that about the raising of Abraham's children from the stones, and the proclamation of one who will baptize with fire), and the two similitudes (the axe and the winnowing fork) are authentic. Early Christian communities had sufficient opportunities and avenues of access to this tradition.[16]

The Wrath to Come and Judgment with Fire

In attempting to determine the Baptizer's spiritual and intellectual home and to locate his proclamation within the eschatological traditions and concep-

14. Cf. P. Hoffmann, *Studien,* 30.
15. See below, pp. 184–85.
16. Cf. C. H. H. Scobie, *John,* 15–17; J. Becker, *Johannes,* 109 n. 21; I. H. Marshall, *Luke,* 138; H. Schürmann, *Lukas* 1: 183. R. Bultmann's opinion that Matt. 3:7-10 // Luke 3:7-9 represented genuine Christian tradition, and that it was a mere accident that the Baptizer, and not Jesus, was the one who spoke these threatening words (*History of*

tions of formative Judaism, we will do best to start with the key phrase "the wrath to come," which Q also places at the beginning of its report of his preaching. This motif leads us directly to the principal source of Jewish eschatology, namely the prophetic preaching of the day of YHWH. In Ezekiel and Zephaniah it is also called the "day of YHWH's wrath" יְהֹוָה (יוֹם אַף יְהֹוָה יוֹם עֶבְרַת), as in the Book of Jubilees.[17] The motif of wrath is frequently found in the context of this idea.[18]

The absolute usage of the concept of "wrath" in the sense of a punishing judgment is worth noting.[19] "My wrath" (אַפִּי), already refers to YHWH's punishing future judgment in Isa. 13:3. Sirach 48:10 says of Elijah that he will come at the end of time "to calm the wrath of God before it breaks out in fury [for judgment]" (κοπάσαι ὀργὴν πρὸ θυμοῦ), and 1 Enoch 5:9 says of the righteous: "they shall not be judged all the days of their lives; nor die through plague or wrath . . . " (οὐ μὴ ἀποθάνωσιν ἐν ὀργῇ θυμοῦ).[20] On the contrary, according to 1QH III, 27–36 "a time of wrath" (קֵץ חָרוֹן) will come upon all that is called Belial; while "the rope beat[s] down in judgment (מִשְׁפָּט) and a destiny of wrath (גּוֹרַל אַף) upon the abandoned, and a venting of fury (מַתַּד חֵמָה) upon the cunning"; a flood of fire rages on earth and "the war of the heavenly warriors shall scourge the earth; and it shall not end before the appointed destruction which shall be for ever and without compare."[21] An association between the eschatological wrath and judgment with fire is also found in Ps. Sol. 15:4-5, which speaks of "the flame of fire and anger against the unrighteous" (φλὸξ πυρὸς καὶ ὀργὴ ἀδίκων),[22] that will go forth from God (ἀπὸ προσώπου κυρίου) "to destroy the sinners' every assurance."[23]

---

the Synoptic Tradition, 117, 247) is entirely unfounded. Matt. 3:12 // Luke 3:17, however, he considered original (ibid., 247).

17. Ezek. 7:19; Zeph. 1:18; 2:2, 3; *Jub.* 24:28, 30; 36:10. Cf. Rom. 2:5; Rev. 6:17.

18. See above, pp. 75–84.

19. On this, see above, p. 157.

20. Cf. Isa. 42:25 (LXX!).

21. On this "little apocalypse," see above, p. 77. For the expression כָּלָה וְנֶחֱרָצָה, "decreed end," cf. Isa. 10:23; 28:22; Dan. 9:27! C. H. H. Scobie (*John*, 68–69) has already pointed to this text because of the motif of the judgment with fire.

22. The second genitive is a *genitivus objectivus.*

23. Further instances of the motif of eschatological wrath are, for example, 1 Enoch 91:7; 99:16; 101:3; 1QS IV, 12; CD VIII, 3; XX, 15–16; 1QM IV, 1–2; Wis. 5:20; *As. Mos.* 10:3; *Sib. Or.* 2:170; 3:556, 561, 632; 4:160, 162, 169. Cf. also Eph. 5:6; Col. 3:6; Rev. 6:16; 11:18; 14:10; 16:19; 19:15.

This makes it abundantly clear where we are to locate the Baptizer and his eschatological message: in the tradition of historical eschatology, which represents the principal strand of early Jewish "apocalyptic" eschatology. This current begins with the prophetic preaching of the day of YHWH and related traditions like Isa. 10:20-23 and Isaiah 65–66, and is continually renewed from those sources.

This placement is confirmed by the motif of fire as a means by which the sinners are destroyed at the eschatological judgment. We have already encountered it in connection with the motif of wrath. In the few words of the Baptizer transmitted by Q we find it three times: in connection with the coming judge and in both similitudes. This motif appears also in the context of the proclamation of the day of YHWH (Joel 2:3; 3:3; Obad. 18), together with wrath in Ezek. 30:14-16 and Nahum 1:6, "his wrath is poured out like fire."[24] Because of the history of its influence, the image in Mal. 4:1 [Hebrew 3:19] should be especially emphasized. There the day of YHWH is compared with a fiery furnace, which burns up the evildoers like straw. The rabbis liked to introduce this saying as a scriptural basis for the coming eschatological judgment that would punish either the sinners of Israel or the gentile nations.[25] It probably contributed something to the Baptizer's inspiration for his similitude of the winnowing fork (the straw will be burned!).[26] The motif of the judgment fire that burns up the "stubble" is also found in Obad. 18: "The house of Jacob

24. For fire as an image of God's wrath in the OT, see J. Fichtner, *TDNT* 5: 399. The two motifs are also found together in Isa. 66:16 (see above, p. 31); 1QS IV, 12–13. Other examples of the eschatological judgment with fire are Ezek. 38:22; 39:6; *Jub.* 9:15; 36:10; 1 Enoch 102:1 (see above, chap. 3); CD II, 5–6; *T. Zeb.* 10:3 (see above, chap. 3); 4 Ezra 12:3. For the idea of the world consumed by fire, cf. 1QH III, 26–36 (see above, chap. 3); *Sib. Or.* 3:75-92; 4:171-76 (see above, chap. 3). *Sib. Or.* 2:196-97, 285-86; 3:54 speak of a storm of fire from heaven; *Sib. Or.* 5:274, 377 of a rain of fire. According to *Sib. Or.* 5:414-19, the Messiah goes forth with fire against the enemies of Israel (see above, chap. 3). Cf. 4 Ezra 13:10. On the whole subject, see P. Volz, *Eschatologie*, 318–19; F. Lang, *TDNT* 6: 936–37 (on the OT), 937–38 (on apocalyptic), 939 (on Qumran). This *fire of judgment* should not be confused with the *fire of hell* developed out of Isa. 66:24: see Dan. 7:11; 1 Enoch 63:10; 91:9; 98:3; 100:9; 103:8; 108:3-5; *T. Jos.* 2:2. 1 Enoch 54:6; 98:3 speaks of a "furnace of fire," 4 Ezra 7:36 of the "furnace of Gehenna."

25. Thus, for example, *t. Sanh.* 13.1; *Ber. R.* 21.9 on Gen. 3:24; *Ber. R.* 26.6 on Gen. 6:3; *Ber. R.* 78.5 on Gen. 32:32; *Shem. R.* 15.27 on Exod. 12:2; *Shir. R.* on Song 7:3; *'Abot R. Nat.* A 36, 1; *Midr. Tanh.* B Gen IV § 4 (Bietenhard 1: 88, 89 [2x!]); *Midr. Tanh.* B Deut. V § 10 (Bietenhard 2: 484); *Midr. Tehillim* 21.5 on Ps. 21:7; *Midr. Tehillim* 41.4 on Ps. 41:2.

26. Matt. 3:12 // Luke 3:17 ἄχυρον refers to the larger parts of the stalk, the stubble: in Mal. 4:1 the קַשׁ (G. Dalman, *Arbeit* 3: 138). See p. 176 below.

shall be a fire, the house of Joseph a flame, and the house of Esau stubble (קַשׁ); they shall burn them and consume them, and there shall be no survivor of the house of Esau."[27]

Fire as an instrument for purification is insignificant in the eschatology of early Judaism.[28]

The Parable of the Axe at the Root of the Trees

In this similitude the Baptizer takes up an image of Israel that was already familiar in the Old Testament: that of God's planting.[29] This image portrays Israel as a glorious nation created by God and "planted," and owing its growth to God alone. But since the empirical nation never corresponded to this ideal, the title "planting" (מַטָּע) in the postexilic period described the eschatological people of God: "Your people shall all be righteous; they shall possess the land forever. They are the shoot that I planted, the work of my hands, so that I might be glorified." "They will be called oaks of righteousness, the planting of the Lord, to display his glory" (Isa. 60:21; 61:3).[30]

In the Ten-Week Apocalypse it is the whole nation from the seed of Abraham that is described as "the eternal plant of righteousness" (1 Enoch 93:5). The eschatological people of God can thus consist only of a part of this planting, namely, the "elect ones of righteousness from the eternal plant of righteousness" (1 Enoch 93:10).[31]

The Book of Jubilees also emphasizes that "a righteous planting for eternal generations" comes from Abraham (16:26).[32] But according to 1:16 it first requires a "transplanting" or "removal,"[33] in order that the eschatological "upright plant," or "righteous planting" may emerge.

In the Psalms of Solomon, the faithful are called "the Lord's paradise, the trees of life" (ὁ παράδεισος τοῦ κυρίου, τὰ ξύλα τῆς ζωῆς) (14:3). They are

27. Cf. also Isa. 47:14.
28. Cf. Zech. 13:9; Mal. 3:2-3.
29. Cf. Exod. 15:17; Num. 24:6; 2 Sam. 7:10 (= 1 Chr. 17:9); Ps. 44:3; Isa. 5:7; 60:21; 61:3; Jer. 2:21; 11:17; 12:2; 18:9; 24:6; 31:28; 32:41; 42:10; 45:4; Amos 9:15. I am grateful to Gerhard Lohfink, *Jesus and Community* 8, for this information. Cf. idem, "Metaphorik der Aussaat," 219–20.
30. It appears that there is a reference here to Isa. 5:7. Cf. F. Dexinger, *Zehnwochenapokalypse*, 165–66.
31. Cf. above, on 1 Enoch; F. Dexinger, *Zehnwochenapokalypse*, 164, 169. Further examples of the image of the planting in 1 Enoch are at 10:16 and 84:6.
32. Cf. also *Jub.* 21:24; 36:6. The image is also in *Jub.* 7:34.
33. Cf. the translations of K. Berger, E. Littmann, and O. S. Wintermute, ad loc.

also the "trees of joy" (δένδρα εὐφροσύνης) that the wicked "cut down" (ἐκ-κόψαι) (12:3). "Their planting is firmly rooted forever; they shall not be up-rooted as long as the heavens shall last. For Israel is the portion and inheritance of God" (14:4-5). The concept of "Israel" is thus restricted here to the community of the faithful (cf. Rom. 9:6); the promise of enduring forever, associated with the image of planting since Isa. 60:21, is reserved for them.[34] The sinners are not part of Israel, as the text explicitly says: καὶ οὐχ οὕτως οἱ ἁμαρτωλοὶ καὶ παράνομοι . . . (14:6). Their "inheritance" is "Hades (= hell), and dark-ness and destruction; and they will not be found on the day of mercy for the righteous" (14:9).[35] The "day of mercy for the righteous" is nothing other than the "day of the Lord's judgment" (15:12) on sinners, who will then be de-stroyed with fire (15:4-5). Therefore we are not surprised to find that the com-munity at Qumran claimed the honored title of "everlasting plantation" for itself alone.[36]

A noteworthy further development of this image can be observed in Pseudo-Philo's *Liber Antiquitatum Biblicarum*. In *Bib. Ant.* 28:4 a speech of God is reproduced, that God is supposed to have spoken before creation (*ante saecula*). It reads: "And I will plant a great vineyard (*vinea*), and from it I will choose a plant (*plantatio*); and I will care for it and call it by my name, and it will be mine forever. But when I have done all the things I said, nevertheless my plant that is called by my name will not recognize me as its planter, but will destroy its fruit and not yield up its fruit to me (*et non reportabit mihi fructum eius*)."[37] Whereas otherwise in Pseudo-Philo *vinea* means Israel, and *vinea* and *plantatio* once even stand in a *parallelismus membrorum* (*Bib. Ant.* 18:10), the passage quoted makes a distinction between the two. Unfortu-nately, the distinction is not entirely clear: Does *vinea* refer to the world and *plantatio* to Israel, or is *vinea* Israel and *plantatio* only a part of Israel?[38] In any case we find here, just as in the words of the Baptizer, the motif of planting

34. Cf. 1 Enoch 93:5, 10; *Jub.* 16:26; 21:24; 36:6; 1QS VIII, 5; XI, 8–9; 1QH VI, 15; VIII, 6.

35. S. Fujita, "Metaphor of Plant," 31–33.

36. 1QS VIII, 5; XI, 8–9; 1QH VI, 15; VIII, 6. Cf. CD I, 7–8. F. Dexinger, *Zehnwo-chenapokalypse*, 166–69; S. Fujita, "Metaphor of Plant," 40–44.

37. The ms. group π reads "*ut non proferat fructum eius*" (D. J. Harrington, *Les Antiquités Bibliques* 1, ad loc.).

38. On the basis of the context—the creation of the world was mentioned in the previous sentence—and the usage elsewhere in *Bib. Ant.*, the second interpretation is more likely. Cf. C. Dietzfelbinger, *Pseudo-Philo*, 185 ad loc. For Israel as vineyard, ibid., 135, on *Bib. Ant.* 12:8; C. Perrot and P.-M. Bogaert, *Les Antiquités Bibliques* 2: 115; R. Borig, *Weinstock*, 94–128.

combined with the motif of bringing fruit, and undoubtedly the bringing of fruit means the same in both places: life according to God's law.[39]

We see, then, that in Old Testament and early Jewish tradition the image of planting describes Israel as the descendants of Abraham (1 Enoch 93:5; *Jub.* 16:26!). But since this positive image can only be associated with the holy community of God living according to God's law (*Ps. Sol.* 14:2-3) and bringing fruit in accordance with it (*Bib. Ant.* 28:4), we observe a continual inclination to reserve the title of honor "God's planting" for the people of God of the end time (Isa. 60:21; 61:3; *Jub.* 1:16) or the (eschatological) community of the faithful (Psalms of Solomon, Qumran).[40]

The Baptizer could attach his own words to this tradition. He drew the consequence from the contradictory uses of the image—on the one hand for Israel as a whole, on the other for the faithful alone or the sacred remnant of Israel—by saying: In God's planting there are blighted trees that yield no fruit, but these will very soon be "cut down" (cf. *Ps. Sol.* 12:3!). Israel should, in fact, be "God's planting," God's holy people; but for that to be the case, it must first be cleansed.

With the motif of the cutting down of the bad trees, the Baptizer expanded the original image and thus created a genuine similitude not only pointing to the end time cleansing of Israel by the removal of sinners, but giving vivid expression to the immediate proximity of that event, and thus the urgency of repentance: the axe is already at work;[41] the woodcutter is preparing the initial blow, and it cannot be averted. As close as the first blow of the woodcutter after the axe has been laid on the point where the cut will begin—that is how close God's wrathful judgment is. That is the present situation. This temporal urgency is underscored still further in the Greek text by the present tenses of all three verbs.[42]

The Baptizer is evidently not thinking of a forest of conifers or deciduous trees, but of a fruit orchard.[43] Anyone who wants to cut down the blighted trees in an orchard has to get to their subterranean roots. Hence the roots

---

39. Cf. *Bib. Ant.* 12:8: *vinea ista emisit fructum suum et non cognovit cultorem suum.* Here the reference is to the forging of the golden calf. For the meaning of repentance and its "fruit" in the Baptizer's words, see the excursus in chap. 7.

40. R. Borig has also emphasized the eschatological aspect of this image, in contrast to that of the vineyard (*Weinstock*, 189).

41. Here κεῖμαι should be understood as the perfect passive of τίθημι.

42. Cf. E. Klostermann, *Matthäusevangelium*, 23–24.

43. E. Lohmeyer sees the trees as vines and the plantation, accordingly, as a vineyard, the ancient image for Israel ("Baum," 378–90).

must first be carefully uncovered. That is the situation presupposed by the similitude: The root has been laid bare, and the axe is ready for the first blow.

Who is the woodcutter? The Baptizer speaks in the passive throughout this similitude, as the "apocalypticists" are so fond of doing: κεῖται . . . ἐκκόπτεται . . . βάλλεται. God is usually implied as the subject of such eschatological passives, as we have seen, but sometimes heavenly beings or God's faithful are represented.[44] In general, however, the passive is chosen because the author does not want to settle firmly for any of these possibilities. Nevertheless, in this case the choice should not be difficult: The one who seeded the plantation also clears it of blighted trees. The woodcutter is God.[45]

The Parable of the Winnowing of the Chaff

The second similitude of the Baptizer in Q is a variation on the thought of the first. It is connected to the saying about the one who is to come by means of a relative clause, a connection that is undoubtedly the work of the redactor. Originally, it was an independent similitude.[46]

The material for the similitude is taken from agriculture and presumes knowledge of the process by which, throughout the ancient world, threshed grain was cleaned by winnowing.[47] The winnower used a shovel or winnowing fork to throw the threshed grain against the wind. The lighter chaff was blown away, while the heavier grain fell to the ground; the larger pieces of the stem, the straw or "stubble," fell a little farther away.[48] The grain was gathered up into containers or barns; the stubble was used for fodder, for the making of bricks, or for fires.[49] Thus what is to be burned, in the Baptizer's similitude, is

44. See above, pp. 156–57.
45. Cf. Isa. 10:33-34. However, I want at least to refer to the proclamation of judgment in Ezek. 20:45-49 [Hebrew 21:1-5]. Here Israel appears in the image of the forest ("forest of the Negeb [= south]"), containing green and dry trees. Both the green and the dry trees are to be burned in the fire of judgment that God personally kindles. The parallels with and differences from the Baptizer's similitude are immediately evident: In place of the fire that destroys indiscriminately, the Baptizer produces the image of the carefully selective axe of the woodcutter.
46. F. Lang proposes that the two similitudes at one time were placed next to each other ("Erwägungen," 466).
47. Cf., for example, Homer, *Iliad* 5, 499–502; 13, 588–590; Xenophon, *Oecon.* 18, 6–8; Colum. II, 9, 11; 20, 5. H. Blümner, *Technologie* 1: 7–9.
48. There is a more detailed description in G. Dalman, *Arbeit* 3: 126–32; P. Volz, *Altertümer*, 373–74; H. Weippert in K. Galling, *Reallexikon*, 64.
49. G. Dalman, *Arbeit* 3: 132–39, 188–206; P. Volz, *Altertümer*, 374–75.

not "chaff," as ἄχυρον is usually translated (for the chaff flies away on the wind), but "straw" or "stubble" (Hebrew קשׁ).[50] This also indicates the immediate motif-background for this feature of the similitude in Mal. 3:19 and Obadiah 18.[51]

Decisive for an understanding of the image is the phrase διακαθαρίζειν τὴν ἅλωνα. In many translations it is wrongly or misleadingly represented by "clear his threshing floor"[52] or "clean his threshing floor."[53] But the person with the winnowing shovel in hand is not interested in sweeping or clearing the threshing floor;[54] the task at hand is to winnow the threshed grain lying on it. That is the precise meaning of διακαθαρίζειν τὴν ἅλωνα: "cleanse (winnow) what he has threshed."[55] In fact, both in Greek and Hebrew, as well as in other Semitic languages to this day, "threshing floor" can refer to the grain lying on that floor,[56] and (δια)καθαίρειν, like the Latin expurgare, is a concise expression for "cleanse by winnowing" (for example, Xenophon, Oecon. 18.6: καθαροῦμεν τὸν σῖτον λικμῶντες, "we will cleanse the grain by winnowing").[57] There is an exact parallel to our passage in Alciphron 2, 23: ἄρτι μοι τὴν ἅλω διακαθήραντι καὶ τὸ πτύον ἀποτιθεμένῳ ὁ δεσπότης ἐπέστη ("As soon as I

50. G. Dalman, Arbeit 3: 138. Hellenistic examples of the burning of the ἄχυρον, which can only be stubble, are found in J. H. Moulton and G. Milligan, Vocabulary, 100, s. v.; BAGD 129, s. v. Unfortunately, Bauer only gives the meaning "chaff." To the contrary, see LSJ, s. v. or H. Menge (Langenscheidts Großwörterbuch), s. v. For the meaning "straw," see also LXX Isa. 11:7; 3 Kgs. 5:1; Sib. Or. 3:791. For the proverbial flying away of the chaff with the wind as an image for the punishing judgment, cf. Ps. 1:4; 35:5; Job 21:18; Isa. 17:13; Dan. 2:35; Hos. 13:3.

51. See above, pp. 172–73.

52. Thus Martin Luther, 1545, 1975; Zücher Bibel 1931 (1971); Jerusalem Bible 1968 [RSV, 1971; NRSV, 1989].

53. Martin Luther, 1984; J. Kürzinger, 1964; O. Karrer, 1963; U. Wilckens, 1977; U. Luz, Matthew 1: 165; E. Dietzfelbinger's interlinear version, 1986. The Einheitsübersetzung (1979) paraphrases: "He will separate the wheat from the chaff." It is properly translated by F. Stier, 1989: "He will cleanse the threshed grain of his threshing floor."

54. For this task, see G. Dalman, Arbeit 3: 96–97.

55. BAGD 41, s. v. ἅλων; ibid., 183, s. v. διακαθαίρω; E. Klostermann, Matthäusevangelium, 24; A. Schlatter, Matthäus, 82; G. Dalman, Arbeit 3: 73; H. Sahlin, Studien, 52–53. Cf. also J. Wellhausen, Ev. Matthaei, 6.

56. Thus, for example, Ruth 3:2: "he is winnowing [the barley-threshing floor]" (LXX: λικμᾷ τὸν ἅλωνα τῶν κριθῶν); Job 39:12; 4 Ezra 4:32 (quam magnam aream incipient facere). See further examples in BAGD 41, s. v. ἅλων; A. Schlatter, Matthäus, 82; G. Dalman, Arbeit 3: 67–68, 73.

57. Cf. ibid., 18. 8. J. Wettstein had already cited these two examples, ad loc. (NT 1: 267). Cf. also LSJ, s. v. J. H. Moulton and G. Milligan (Vocabulary, 310, s. v. καθαίρω) cite P. Teb. II, 373.10. Columella speaks of "thoroughly cleansing" (expurgare) the grain "with the winnowing shovel" (scaphisterio) or "with wings" (vannis) (II, 9, 11; II, 20, 5).

had finished cleansing the threshed grain and laid down the winnowing shovel, my master came to me").[58]

Heinz Schürmann (*Lukas* 1: 177–78), followed by Helmut Merklein (*Gottes-herrschaft*, 145), sees the material circumstances of the similitude somewhat differently. According to them, the similitude presupposes that the grain has already been winnowed. The winnowing shovel thus serves "on the one hand for shoveling the grain and stubble together, and on the other hand for scooping up the grain to be carried away to the storerooms" (H. Schürmann, *Lukas* 1: 177–78). For this interpretation, Schürmann refers to the following remark of Gustav Dalman: "A genuine winnowing shovel would probably be the Christian-Palestinian raḥtā and Syriac raphšā, reproduced in Matt. 3:12, Luke 3:17 with πτύον, although we must suppose that the same tool also served for cleaning off the threshing floor, as the Baptizer's saying presupposes" (*Arbeit* 3: 123). However, as Dalman's words show, the primary purpose of the winnowing shovel (in Palestine also) was winnowing, especially the second course (cf. ibid., 122, 124, 127; H. Weippert, in K. Galling, *Reallexikon*, 64). No other use is attested in antiquity. And Dalman himself (*Arbeit* 3: 73) denies the interpretation quoted as regards Matt. 3:12 // Luke 3:17: there it does *not* mean the "threshing floor," but the "grain lying on the threshing floor," "the threshed grain." Finally, what is decisive is that the essential meaning of (δια)καθαίρειν is synonymous with λικμᾶν (see above).

If the first similitude presented Israel in the image of an orchard, here it is represented by the threshed grain on the threshing floor. This was another image the Baptizer could derive from the Old Testament, for in Isa. 21:10a Israel is described as threshed grain: "O my threshed and winnowed one."[59] Both similitudes have the same theme: the end time cleansing of Israel by the action of God.

There is a striking parallel to the Baptizer's similitude of winnowing in an anonymous parable found in several versions in rabbinic literature.[60] According to *Shir. R.* on Song 7:3 it reads: "The straw, the chaff, and the stubble were quarreling. The one said: 'The field was sown for my sake!' The other

58. Cf. *BAGD* 183, s. v. διακαθαίρω. Unfortunately, A. R. Benner and F. H. Fobes (*The Letters of Alciphron, Aelian and Philostratus*, LCL [Cambridge, 1979], 121) also wrongly translate this "I had just finished sweeping the threshing floor. . . ."

59. For this passage, cf. G. Dalman, *Arbeit* 3: 73–74; H. Wildberger, *Jesaja* 2: 767, 784.

60. Because it is added to Rabbi Abin I (= Rabbi Abun) *Midr. Shir.* on Song 7:3, it is also attributed to him, for example, by Str-B 3: 140–41; 4: 852–53. See the parallel passages there also. Cf. as well J. Theodor and C. Albeck, *Bereschit Rabba* 2: 1000–1001; W. Bacher, *Amoräer* 3: 411–12.

said: 'The field was sown for my sake!' But the wheat said to them: 'Wait until the [time of] threshing comes, and then we will find out for whose sake the field was sown.' The [time of] threshing came, they were brought to the threshing floor, and the master of the house went out to winnow it [the threshing floor].[61] The chaff flew away on the wind, he took the straw and threw it on the ground, he took the stubble and burned it, but the wheat he took and piled it up. . . . So also the nations of the world. Some say: 'We are Israel, and the world was created for our sake.' Others say: 'We are Israel, and the world was created for our sake.' But Israel says to them: 'Wait until the day of the Holy One, blessed be he, and then we will find out for whose sake the world was created.' As it says: 'See, the day is coming, burning like an oven, when all the arrogant and all evildoers will be stubble; the day that comes shall burn them up . . . ' (Mal. 4:1[3:19]). And as it is written: 'You shall winnow them and the wind shall carry them away' (Isa. 41:16). But of Israel it says: 'Then you shall rejoice in the Lord; in the Holy One of Israel you shall glory' (ibid.)."[62]

In this parable, Israel is compared to the grain and the "nations of the world" to the remaining parts of the stalk, which are regarded as waste. That the "nations of the world" assert that they are Israel indicates that the phrase really refers to the Christian church and its internal conflicts.[63] Probably this feature, however, represents a contemporizing development of the original parable, for in the shorter versions in *Ber. R.* 83.5 on Gen. 36:43, and in *Pesiqta R.* 10.4, the "nations of the world" only assert that the world was created for their sake.[64]

The time of threshing is the eschatological day of judgment that is to bring salvation for Israel and destruction for the nations. Since that destruction is illustrated with the image of burning stubble (קַשׁ) the reference to Mal. 4:1[3:19] readily suggested itself. That passage may also have influenced the image, although in itself it corresponds very well to the reality.[65] The image of judgment as winnowing necessarily led to Isa. 41:16, especially since there— unlike Mal. 4:1!—the subject actually is the judgment of the nations and the triumph of Israel. The "you" in the first phrase ("you shall winnow them")

61. That is, the grain lying on it: see above; A. Schlatter, *Matthäus*, 82.
62. German translation based on the edition by S. Dunski (Jerusalem, 1980).
63. Str-B 3: 140; 4: 853; W. Bacher, *Amoräer* 3: 412. Cf. *Pesiqta Rab.* 5.1.
64. In *Ber. R.* 83.5 on Gen. 36:43 the quotation from Mal. 3:19 is also lacking. In *Pesiqta Rab.* 10.4 some very different scriptural passages are adduced, namely, Isa. 33:12 for the eschatological fate of the nations, and Deut. 32:12 and Joel 4:13 in reference to Israel.
65. See above, p. 177.

probably refers to God in the parable's interpretation of the verse, although in Isaiah it is Israel itself that will do the winnowing. The eschatological interpretation of this scriptural passage is taken for granted.

The correspondences with and differences from the Baptizer's similitude of winnowing are striking, and at the same time they make clear the unique features of the two. In both cases, the same material has been formed into an eschatological similitude. Both think of God as the one who does the winnowing (cf. Jer. 15:7; LXX Amos 9:9!), and the burning of the stubble or straw (Hebrew קַשׁ, Greek ἄχυρον)[66] is the image for the end time judgment of destruction; in contrast, the image of the gathering and storing of the grain represents eschatological salvation. Both similitudes were probably influenced by Mal. 4:1. The text of the Baptizer's similitude as we have received it, however, contains the expression πυρὶ ἀσβέστῳ: with this phrase it abandons the level of the original image. This is also an allusion to Isa. 66:24 and thus points not only to the end time punishing judgment of sinners, but also to their eternal sufferings in Gehenna.[67]

The crucial difference between the two similitudes lies in the definition of the groups: The rabbinic parable is based on the contrast between Israel and the nations; for the Baptizer, judgment brings division within Israel. Israel is not equated with the grain in the Baptizer's similitude, but with the whole threshed material, as in Isa. 21:10a. This threshed stuff must be "cleansed." The "grain" that goes into the storehouse is, in the Baptizer's thinking, the part of Israel that, after hearing his preaching, repents of its evil ways and brings "good fruit." To that part of Israel he promises eschatological salvation; to the rest of the people he announces the ultimate judgment. Thus here, still more clearly than in the similitude of the axe at the root of the trees, we find expression of the idea of the eschatological remnant.

The Baptizer does not seem to have given any special attention, in his preaching, to the eschatological fate of the Gentiles. This can only mean that on this question he shared the common conviction of early Judaism: The Gentiles, insofar as they were not converted to the God of Israel, would perish, or else live out their lives as slaves of Israel.

66. See above, p. 177.
67. See above, pp. 146–47.

The Baptizer's Baptism and the Baptism
of the "Stronger One"

We thus come to the difficult and disputed saying about the Stronger One. It must be interpreted on the basis of the two similitudes, and for that reason we must discuss them first.

The Baptizer announces the coming of a "Stronger One."[68] He illustrates his own unworthiness in relationship to this "Stronger One" by means of the image of the slave who must remove the master's sandals, carry them away, and bring them again.[69] He does not consider himself worthy to perform even this service for the one who is to come.

But is such a comparison in any way meaningful or imaginable in the historical situation of the Baptizer? Should we not rather look for its Sitz im Leben in the primitive Christian community? It identified the "Stronger One" with Jesus and would have used the image of the sandal-bearer to subordinate the Baptizer to Jesus.[70] No doubt the early Christian community did understand the comparison in that way. Nevertheless, one is reluctant to deny that the Baptizer was the author of the original image.[71] Why should he not have chosen it to divert attention from himself and turn it toward the "Stronger One"? After all, his activity took its meaning only from the actions of that other.

We must probably presume, as our starting point, that the saying about the "Stronger One," to which the image of the sandal-bearer belongs, was origi-

---

68. For the problem of ὀπίσω μου, its meaning and originality, see above, pp. 168–69.

69. For the meaning of βαστάζω in this passage, see *BAGD* 137, s. v.; A. Schlatter, *Matthäus*, 78–79. Bauer argues in this instance for the meaning "remove," but can give only a single example. In the papyri, the most frequent meaning of this verb is "carry away" (J. H. Moulton and G. Milligan, *Vocabulary*, 106, s. v.). In the Roman-Hellenistic cultural sphere it was customary to have a slave remove one's sandals when one reclined at table; the slave would take them away and bring them back later. One brought the slave with one for this purpose, *ad pedes* (Petronius, 31; Martial 12, 87) (cf. J. Marquardt, *Privatleben* 1: 322). In Plautus these slaves are called *sandaligerulae* (*Trin.* 252). Plutarch (*Moralia* 712 E, *Quaest. Conv.* VII, 8, 4) speaks of τὰ ὑποδήματα κομίζοντα παιδάρια. Κομίζω corresponds exactly to the colloquial βαστάζω in Matthew. For sandal-bearers in Egypt, see A. Erman, *Ägypten*, 253. Rabbinic examples are in Str-B 1: 121.

70. Thus P. Hoffmann, *Studien*, 21–22, 32–33; H. Merklein, *Gottesherrschaft*, 142–43; idem, "Umkehrpredigt," 32; J. Gnilka, *Matthäus*, 72; S. von Dobbeler, *Gericht*, 55.

71. Cf. R. Pesch, *Markus* 1: 85; J. Ernst, *Johannes*, 305.

nally an independent logion. Its combination with the saying about baptism is secondary.[72]

But who is this "Stronger One" for the Baptizer himself? Who is the judge he announces? In the early Jewish texts we treated in the first part of this investigation there were a variety of figures who could carry out the eschatological judgment: the archangel Michael (Dan. 12:1; 1QM XVII, 6–7; *As. Mos.* 10:2; *T. Dan* 6:1–7), the Messiah (*Ps. Sol.* 17; 4 Ezra 11-12; *Sib. Or.* 5), the Son of man (1 Enoch 37–71; 4 Ezra 13), but also Melchizedek (11Q Melch).[73] However, all these function only as representatives of God. In the proper sense, it is God who is the judge, and only by way of exception does another figure appear as judge alongside or in place of God. The "day of judgment" is the "day of the Lord," the "day of YHWH," which the prophets announced.[74] That was the starting point for the Baptizer's audience. This finding by itself strongly suggests that, in the Baptizer's "Stronger One," we should first of all see none other than God.[75]

This point of view is strengthened by the key word *coming*. The one who is announced "comes"—in fact, comes for judgment.[76] This points clearly to the old tradition of God's parousia for the final judgment that we have traced from the prophets' proclamation of the day of YHWH by way of some eschatologically interpreted psalms and early Jewish literature to the rabbis themselves.[77] The key word *coming* is encountered almost everywhere in these texts, and even in Mal. 3:2 the day of YHWH is called "the day of his coming."

72. On this question, cf. P. Hoffmann, *Studien*, 19–22; J. Ernst, *Johannes*, 13–16, 54–55.

73. See above, p. 156. The remarks of J. Becker on this theme (*Johannes*, 34–37) are very unsatisfying. Becker gives an inadequate survey of the early Jewish findings, and appears to overestimate the importance of the Son of man figure in early Jewish eschatology. However, his identification of the Coming One with the Son of man has found considerable acceptance. Becker did not even think of the archangel Michael or Melchizedek, who deserve equal consideration—to say nothing of God.

74. Only in 1 Enoch 61:5 is that day called the "day of the elect."

75. An extensive argument for identifying the Coming One with God is offered by J. H. Hughes, "John." Most recently, S. von Dobbeler (*Gericht*, 144–47) and J. Ernst (*Johannes*, 49–51) have advocated this interpretation.

76. J. Becker has overlooked this. He points to the "coming" of the Son of man in Dan. 7:13 (*Johannes*, 36). But there the Son of man does not come for judgment; he comes to assume rulership after judgment has already been accomplished. For the same reason, because what is at issue here is not the end time "coming" as such, but coming for judgment, the reference to the "coming" of the Messiah in P. Hoffmann, *Studien*, 29 n. 56, is inappropriate.

77. See above, p. 156.

The epithet "Stronger One" also points us toward God. Even in the LXX, ἰσχυρός is occasionally the translation for אֵל,[78] and Aquila acknowledges this in his translation.[79] In Pseudo-Philo's *Liber Antiquitatum Biblicarum*, the title *fortis* or *fortissimus* is used for God eighteen times, in 4 Esdras it is used six times, and the corresponding title appears in *2 Baruch* forty-seven times.[80]

Finally, we may recall Luke 1:16-17 and Luke 1:76 where, contrary to the usual Christian point of view, the Baptizer is expressly characterized as precursor and preparer of the way for God, in clear allusion to Mal. 3:1, 23-24. This tradition probably stems from the circles of the Baptizer's disciples and may well reflect the Baptizer's own understanding of himself. It appears that the book of the prophet Malachi played an important role in shaping that self-understanding.

Again and again, an objection is raised against this apparently obvious identification of the judge proclaimed by the Baptizer with God; as far as I can tell, the argument appeared for the first time in Adolf Schlatter's posthumously published dissertation. "Who this is (namely, the Coming One) John need not say. His hearers understand him, because the Coming One is also the one long awaited: naturally not God—who would speak of God's sandal straps?!—but God's anointed."[81] With "naturally not," Schlatter dismisses the most natural interpretation. For him, to speak of God's sandals is an insupportable anthropomorphism.[82]

Now it is certainly true that early Jewish literature ordinarily avoids anthropomorphisms in speaking of God.[83] But the notion of God's sandals was familiar to the Baptizer from Ps. 108:10, and we should not forget that the Baptizer's comparison is metaphorical speech, something he apparently loved. In using comparisons, however, the rabbis could also speak quite "anthropomorphically" about God, for example, in the metaphoric series of mourning cus-

78. LXX 2 Sam. 22:31, 32, 33, 48; 23:5. Cf. also Deut. 10:17; 2 Macc. 1:24. See J. Ernst, *Johannes*, 50.

79. D. Barthélemy, *Devanciers*, 83.

80. Cf. C. Perrot and P.-M. Bogaert, *Les Antiquités Bibliques* 2: 123; P. Bogaert, *Apocalypse de Baruch*, 393–95; G. Delling, "Morija," 7–8. Examples include: *Bib. Ant.* 11.8; 18.10, 11; 32.4, 8, 10, 13, 14; 4 Ezra 6:32; 9:45; 13:23. The *Apoc. Abr.* offers sixteen examples, mainly in the combination "eternal mighty one," for example, 8:1; 13:9; 27:4, 6.

81. A. Schlatter, *Johannes*, 103.

82. We find this argument, for example, also in C. H. H. Scobie, *John*, 66–67; J. Becker, *Johannes*, 34–35; F. Lang, "Erwägungen," 470; R. Pesch, *Markus* 1: 84.

83. Nevertheless, M. D. Johnson remarks of *Adam and Eve*: "God is pictured with a curious mixture of transcendent majesty and quaint anthropomorphism" (*OTP* 2: 253).

toms in which human practices (hanging sackcloth on the doors, putting out the lights, going barefoot, etc.) are attributed to God, and each of them confirmed by a scriptural verse.[84] Moreover, the same objection applies to any other heavenly being, such as the Son of man. The whole discussion is futile, of course, if one attributes the comparison with the Stronger One, and thus the whole image, to Christian redaction of the Baptizer's saying, because such a redaction would see Jesus of Nazareth as the Coming One. We must consider this as a possibility, but I think it is rather improbable.[85]

John's baptism "with water" is contrasted, in Matt. 3:11 // Luke 3:16, with the baptism of the Coming One "with holy spirit and fire." As we have already seen, it is no longer possible to be sure whether Q already contained baptism with holy spirit.[86] Many exegetes see it as an original element in the Baptizer's preaching and therefore speak of a double baptism by the Coming One: a baptism of purification with holy spirit for those who are to survive, and a baptism of judgment with fire for sinners. They base this on a correct idea, namely, that John's baptism with water demands "a positive counterpart at the final judgment."[87] The reference regularly introduced to demonstrate the idea of an end time purification with holy spirit is 1QS IV, 20–21.[88]

Against this idea, however, is the fact that the notion of a twofold baptism by the Coming One disturbs the clear antithesis to the Baptizer's simple baptism with water. In that case, what would be the meaning and purpose of John's

---

84. Cf. C. Thoma and S. Lauer, *Gleichnisse* 1: 224–27.

85. J. S. Kloppenborg also argues for tradition rather than redaction (*Formation of Q,* 104–5).

86. See above, pp. 155–56.

87. F. Lang, "Erwägungen," 466. Cf. H. Schürmann, *Lukas* 1: 176; R. Laufen, *Doppelüberlieferungen,* 101–3. Here and there, accordingly, the "fire" is interpreted as a purifying fire, for example, by P. Hollenbach, "Social Aspects," 867–68.

88. For this passage see above, p. 81. Cf. C. H. H. Scobie, *John,* 70–72; F. Lang, *TDNT* 6: 943; idem, "Erwägungen," 468–69; H. Schürmann, *Lukas* 1: 173; E. Cothenet, *DBSup.* 8 (1972): 1252; idem, *DBSup.* 9 (1979): 994; L. Goppelt, *Theologie,* 89; P. Hollenbach, "Social Aspects," 868; H. Braun, *Qumran* 2: 4; J. A. Fitzmyer, *Luke* 1: 474; J. Ernst, *Johannes,* 306–7. One could also have referred to *Jub.* 1:23. For the difficulties created by this purifying baptism with holy spirit for the equation of the Coming One with the Son of man or the Messiah, cf. F. Lang, "Erwägungen," 469–70; R. Laufen, *Doppelüberlieferungen,* 105–6. Laufen argues, following a suggestion of H. Schürmann (*Lukas* 1: 176–77), for an original contrast between water and spirit baptism, with no baptism of fire (*Doppelüberlieferungen,* 107–8). Against this is the motif of fire that already appears in both of the Baptizer's similitudes, quite apart from the reconstruction of the text's history that is presupposed by this.

baptism? It could be nothing but a symbolic pointer to the ultimately valid baptism of purification; in no event would it have any sacramental character, so that through it renewal would be "only promised, but not accomplished."[89] In that case, also, one would expect to find in the text, if not an ἤ in place of the καί, then at least a repetition of the preposition before πυρί. Without such a repeated preposition, the text seems rather to suggest that baptism "in holy spirit and fire" is a single action.[90]

That is probably also the reason why the idea that originally the text spoke of a baptism ἐν πνεύματι καὶ πυρί, "with wind" or "storm and fire," or "with a storm of fire," found so much agreement. But because this ingenious proposal can scarcely be made plausible on the basis of the history of the text itself, we should probably prefer the solution that assumes that baptism with holy spirit is an addition to the Baptizer's saying, acquired after it became part of Christian tradition.[91]

The Baptizer thus contrasts his baptism with water to the baptism with fire by the Coming One, whom he expects will be God. This simple antithesis reveals the full significance the Baptizer attributed to his own baptism: Whoever did not submit to his baptism with water would perish in the baptism of fire that God would pour out on sinners. But whoever was prepared to repent and undergo baptism with water would be preserved from the baptism of fire, because such a one belonged to the righteous, the holy remnant of Israel.[92] This is the "positive effect at the last judgment" to be expected from John's baptism with water.[93] Therefore there is no need to look for a special preaching of salvation by the Baptizer alongside his preaching of judgment in order to discover the aspect of salvation in his thought. The purpose of the judgment he announces is nothing other than salvation: the salvation of those who will escape judgment, namely, the baptized. They are the wheat that is gathered into the barn.

89. L. Goppelt, *Theologie*, 91. Cf. E. Lohmeyer, *Urchristentum*, 80; G. Beasley-Murray, *Baptism in the New Testament*, 43–44.

90. Thus previously A. Schlatter, *Johannes*, 108. Cf. J. D. G. Dunn, "Spirit-and-Fire Baptism," 83–84; J. S. Kloppenborg, *Formation of Q*, 106–7. For the subdividing function of the repeated preposition in Greek, see *KG* 1: 548–50; M. Reiser, *Syntax*, 15.

91. See above, pp. 169–70. Cf. S. von Dobbeler, *Gericht*, 56–57. For the early Christian interpretation of the saying, see P. Hoffmann, *Studien*, 30–31; U. Luz, *Matthew* 1: 171.

92. Cf. J. Jeremias, "Gedanke," 191: "Through baptism he gathers the remnant that will escape the wrathful judgment." Cf. also idem, *Theology* 45, 173.

93. See above, p. 184. This was correctly established by P. Wolf ("Gericht," 44).

The Baptizer's baptism can thus be described as an "eschatological sacrament," but it not only effects "repentance and forgiveness";[94] it also incorporates the baptized into the number of those who will constitute the eschatological community of salvation.[95] It thus has the same function as the mark with which, according to Ezekiel 9, the heavenly scribe signs those who will escape the coming judgment, the remnant of Israel, the eschatological people of God. According to *Ps. Sol.* 15:6 also, the righteous bear this mark on their foreheads on the day of judgment as σημεῖον εἰς σωτηρίαν, just as the sinners bear the σημεῖον τῆς ἀπωλείας (15:9). That this sign was important for the Qumran community also is shown by the quotation from Ezek. 9:4 in CD XIX, 12.[96]

Hence the saying about the future baptism of fire corresponds exactly to the two similitudes of the axe and the winnowing.

The Eschatological People of God

We find that those who were prepared to repent and had undergone John's baptism could already count themselves among the "remnant," those who had "escaped"[97]—who would avoid destruction in the final judgment that was immediately at hand, and afterward would constitute God's eschatological community of salvation. The ultimate gathering of the community of salvation after the day of judgment is described by the Baptizer in the image of the

94. Thus H. Thyen, *Studien*, 132. Cf. idem, "ΒΑΠΤΙΣΜΑ," 97–103.

95. Thus earlier A. Schweitzer, *Geschichte*, 424; R. Bultmann, *Jesus and the Word*, 23–24; idem, *Theology of the New Testament*, 1: 40. Cf. P. Vielhauer, *RGG³*, 3: 805; G. Lohfink, "Ursprung," 47. O. Böcher, "Initiationsritus für die Zugehörigkeit zum wahren, von Sündenschuld gereinigten Israel der Endzeit," *TRE* 17 (1986): 172. For a thorough discussion of the sacramental or "quasi-sacramental" character of John's baptism, see J. A. Sint, "Eschatologie," 76–83. For J. Becker, this characterization of John's baptism is "enigmatic and not very helpful" (*Johannes*, 39). J. Ernst also rejects it (*Johannes*, 335).

96. On this, see E. Dinkler, "Kreuzsymbol," 15–21; J. L. Teicher, "Sign X," 196–97. In Teicher's opinion CD XIX, 10–14 implies "that the members of the sect of the Fragments had their foreheads marked with the letter taw, which they regarded as an emblem guaranteeing their salvation on the day of the Last Judgment" (ibid., 196–97). Dinkler leaves open "whether there really was a widespread practice of sacramental stigmatization in Judaism, or whether the idea was more that of a spiritual mark" (ibid., 21); however, he does not consider it impossible that there was tattooing (cf. idem, "Kreuzzeichen," 33–34).

97. For the "survivors" and "escaped," the eschatological "remnant" of Israel, see above, pp. 27, 79, on the prophets and Qumran.

gathering of wheat into the barn; he expects God to be the one who gathers (Matt. 3:12 // Luke 3:17). But since it is already being decided who will then be "gathered," and thus the community of the end time is being constituted even before the day of judgment, it is true in some sense that the eschaton is already realized in the present. The work of the Baptizer and his disciples[98] thus implies a measure of present eschatology; it not only prepares for the eschatological fulfillment, but in a certain sense anticipates it, for the eschatological people of God is already present in the baptized, although to this point it remains dispersed and, we might say, "ungathered" among the unconverted remainder of Israel.

But is it really ungathered? What did the baptized and converted do when they returned home from the Jordan? Would they not have felt themselves separated from the rest of the people, who in their eyes were destined for destruction? And would that consciousness not of itself have led to a certain feeling of solidarity, and hence perhaps even to a closer form of community life among the baptized?

Our sources permit us to give only the most cautious answers to such questions. Apparently, those baptized by John did not form strictly organized communities with a *vita communis*, as did the Essenes, especially the Essenes of Qumran who, in fact, also regarded themselves as the eschatological people of God. On the other hand, it is difficult to join Jürgen Becker in seeing John's baptism as an "act of separation," and in no event was the purpose of his activity "a deep religious and social dislocation and isolation of individuals."[99] Quite apart from the fact that this is a much too modern idea, the notion contradicts the purpose of baptism as we have just described it. Adolf Schlatter is more judicious in his interpretation: "The Baptizer did not bring about a gathering of the converted to form a messianic community; he maintained his conviction that it was not he who revealed God's reign. It was only a beginning in that direction when those who had accepted baptism, and thereby had received the status of those who wait for the coming of [God's] rule, were separated from the unrepentant, who did not desire it, by a visible sign. But this did not yet create a new community, because the Baptizer sent those he baptized back into the existing situation with the counsel that they act as people

98. For the Baptizer's disciples, see M. Hengel, *The Charismatic Leader and His Followers*, 35–37. "It may well be that the task of his disciples was not least to assist him when he baptized and preached to the people" (ibid., 35).

99. J. Becker, *Johannes*, 40, 63.

of goodwill within it while awaiting the Christ. The result was not a union of the baptized; it was nothing like the founding of a church or sect."[100]

Consequently, it is customary to speak somewhat more cautiously of a Baptizer *movement*.[101] Joachim Jeremias even writes explicitly about a great "movement of repentance and revival."[102] And in fact the popular movement that emerged from the Baptizer's preaching may be compared sociologically, in many ways, to the movements of awakening and community building familiar to us in modern Christian history.[103] There are, for example, important common features such as the importance attached to the decision of the individual in response to the call to repentance, as well as the emphasis on a way of life corresponding to conversion, the "fruit" that befits "conversion" or "salvation."

We even find the key word *awakening* in the text of the Baptizer's preaching, if not in precisely the same sense: children are to be "awakened," or "raised

---

100. A. Schlatter, *Geschichte*, 72–73. A footnote adds: "This is not called into question, but rather confirmed, by the fact that, besides the great crowd of the baptized, there was also a group of the Baptizer's disciples. The formula 'disciples of the Baptizer,' certainly, does not of itself distinguish between those who obeyed his call to repentance and those who gathered around the Baptizer" (ibid., 73 n. 1).

101. Thus Martin Dibelius already spoke of a "popular movement that John aroused" (*Überlieferung*, 135). Cf. ibid., 135–39; R. Bultmann, *Jesus*, 20–21, where, however, he also speaks of the "Baptizer's sect"; G. Bornkamm, *Jesus of Nazareth*, 47, 50–51; J. A. Sint, "Eschatologie," 95; R. Pesch, *Markus* 1: 73; H. Lichtenberger, "Täufergemeinden," 54–55. For the period after the Baptizer's death people frequently speak of the "Baptizer community" or "Baptizer communities," but it is not always entirely clear whether these are thought to be gatherings only of the Baptizer's disciples, or more broadly of those baptized by John. Cf., for example, R. Bultmann, *History of the Synoptic Tradition*, 164–65; J. Becker, *Johannes*, 16, 64–65; H. Lichtenberger, "Täufergemeinden," passim. N. A. Dahl writes: "Those baptized by John were not brought together in an organized community life; it was simply that the well-known ethics of daily life were emphasized to them with the utmost seriousness (Luke 3:10-14). A closed circle was formed only by those who were his disciples in the narrower sense. . . . If this community was not the eschatological people of God, its aim nevertheless was toward the future, purified community, just as the baptism with water points to the baptism with spirit and fire" (*Volk Gottes*, 139). After the death of the Baptizer it appears, according to Dahl, that a certain "churchifying" of the disciple community ensued (ibid.). The concept of the "Baptizer circle" remains vague, but it is to be preferred as long as we know nothing more certain about the adherents and disciples of the Baptizer and their organization.

102. J. Jeremias, *Theology*, 45.

103. On Christian awakening movements, see E. Beyreuther, *RGG*³ 2: 621–29; G. A. Benrath, *TRE* 10 (1982): 205–20. On the community movements: H. Brandenburg, *RGG*³ 2: 1365–74; J. Cochlovius, *TRE* 12 (1984): 355–68.

up" for Abraham, even from the stones (Matt. 3:9 // Luke 3:8).[104] The Baptizer is *not* saying here that Israel has "squandered its prerogative of salvation over against the nations because of its own guilt;"[105] it has not squandered it, but it is about to. Thus the Baptizer is also not proclaiming "the transfer of salvation to the Gentiles."[106] For John does not say that God can awaken children for *God* out of the stones, but "God is able from these stones to raise up children to *Abraham*." "God has chosen Abraham, and his children constitute God's elect community. The promise to Israel remains in force."[107] But should it happen that those addressed, all of Israel, prove unworthy of being children of Abraham, God can awaken new children for Abraham, if necessary from "these" stones, that is, those lying about, which the Baptizer indicates with a sweep of the arm.[108] The hyperbole thus serves as a warning: As it is, Israel cannot expect salvation. Even calling on their Abrahamic ancestry will be of no help to them.[109]

Therefore the Baptizer calls all Israel to repentance and its fruits. His addressees are the same as those of the old prophets, who according to Dan. 9:6 "spoke in your name to our kings, our princes, and our ancestors, and to all the people of the land."[110] But he is certainly aware that he can move only a part of the people to repentance. Still, he places his entire hope in that portion, as did the postexilic prophets, for they will survive the judgment and after-

---

104. For the meaning of ἐγείρειν in this passage, see *BAGD* 214–15, s. v.; A. Oepke, *TDNT* 2: 334; A. Schlatter, *Matthäus*, 74.

105. J. Becker, *Johannes*, 32.

106. H. Lichtenberger, "Täufergemeinden," 42.

107. A. Schlatter, *Geschichte*, 64. Cf. idem, *Glaube*, 86–87.

108. This is indicated by the lack of a reference for τούτων in the text. T. Zahn, *Matthäus*, 138.

109. Cf. J. A. Sint, "Eschatologie," 76. Helmut Merklein writes: "Israel, as John finds it, can lay no further claim to its previous status as collectively chosen; instead, it represents a collective of evil" ("Jesus," 147. Cf. idem, *Botschaft*, 32–33). The expression "collective of evil," however, I consider subject to misunderstanding and ill suited to express what the author means. For Jewish appeal to the merits of Abraham, Str-B 1: 120 cites Justin, *Dial.* 140.2; A. Schlatter (*Matthäus*, 73–74) cites Jos. *Ant.* 11, 169. For the importance of Abraham in Second Temple Judaism, cf. also O. Schmitz, "Abraham."

110. The fact that the Baptizer addressed his message to all Israel is one of the correct elements in Josephus's description (*Ant.* 18, 116–19). Cf. Mark 1:5; Luke 3:8; A. Schlatter, *Geschichte*, 60; H. Schürmann, *Lukas* 1: 163; S. von Dobbeler, *Gericht*, 64–67. P. Hollenbach attempts a sharp distinction among the addressees ("Social Aspects," 856–75). He thinks that Matt. 3:7-10 is directed to the Jerusalem aristocracy (ibid., 860–61).

ward, as the holy remnant of Israel, will receive the gifts of eschatological salva-tion. For the time being this holy remnant must live scattered or, as we may at least surmise, in small, loose communities among the rest of the people; but soon, after God's punishing judgment in the immediate future on those who are unwilling to repent, they will be "gathered," and will be able to live together according to God's holy law and in the presence of God. This is impossible as long as sinners work their will. Therefore, even though neither the Baptizer's disciples nor the baptized as a whole are already living together in eschatologi-cal purity, holiness, and separation as the community of God, as the Essenes did at Qumran, still they live in the same consciousness of belonging to the eschatological people of God, not merely in the future, but now, in the pres-ent.[111] The difference lies in the practical consequences: While the Essenes at Qumran attempt to realize the eschatological life even now, the Baptizer and the children of Abraham who have been "awakened" through his assistance await that realization only in the future, after the judgment. This judgment could no more be averted than the blow of the woodcutter who has already laid the axe on the spot to be hewn (cf. Matt. 3:10 // Luke 3:9). But the laying on of the axe is happening already in the Baptizer's preaching.

Summary and Conclusion

The Baptizer proclaims to Israel God's immediately approaching and wrathful judgment. In light of this judgment he calls the people to repentance and ac-ceptance of his baptism, so that, like the marked people in Ezekiel 9, they may escape destruction at the eschatological judgment. It is not sufficient to belong to Abraham's descendants. What matters is that the people should prove them-selves worthy descendants of Abraham through repentance and its fruits: that is, through a right obedience to the Torah. "Repentance and good deeds are as a shield against punishment (הַפֻּרְעָנוּת)."[112]

Israel appears in the two similitudes of the Baptizer that have been retained in Q: once in the image of the planting that God has prepared for the divine

---

111. For the eschatological consciousness and present eschatology of the commu-nity at Qumran, see above, p. 76. The idea of the "remnant" is common to Qumran and the Baptizer, but the Baptizer, in contrast to Qumran, did not interpret it in a particularist fashion (J. Schmitt, "Les écrits," *RevSR* 30 [1956]: 57–62; H. Braun, *Qumran* 2: 18).

112. *m. 'Abot* 4.11. This saying is ascribed to Rabbi Eliezer ben Jacob (probably the younger).

glorification, and once in the image of the threshed grain that lies on the threshing floor, ready for winnowing. The Baptizer could have taken both images from the prophet Isaiah (Isa. 21:10; 60:21; 61:3). In both similitudes God, appearing once in the image of a woodcutter and once in that of a winnower, carries out a separation and purification: the blighted trees are cut down, and only the good remain standing; the straw is burned, and the grain gathered together.

The saying about the "Stronger One," in whom the Baptizer also sees God, is to be interpreted in corresponding fashion: Those who do not receive John's baptism of water as a sign of repentance will have to undergo God's baptism of fire, the eschatological judgment of divine punishment. The expressions about the "coming" of the "Stronger One" are a clear pointer to the well-attested tradition of God's parousia for eschatological judgment.

With this conception, as here sketched, the Baptizer stands entirely within the tradition of early Jewish eschatology that takes its starting point from the prophets' preaching of the day of YHWH. This is shown by the motifs of "wrath" and "fire" and their eschatological context. More narrowly, he stands within that tradition that starts from the perspective, not of a contrast between Israel and the Gentiles, but of a division between sinners and righteous within Israel. This conception of a historical eschatology that proclaims punishing judgment on Israel's sinners is attested in many places, beginning with Isaiah 65–66 and Malachi, by way of the various parts of the Book of Enoch, the writings of Qumran, the Psalms of Solomon, and the Book of Wisdom, to Pseudo-Philo and 4 Ezra.[113] In the Mishnah (*m. Sanh.* 10.1) it is said: "All Israelites have a share in the world to come, for it is written, 'Thy people also shall all be righteous, they shall inherit the land for ever' (Isa. 60:21)." But even this passage is followed immediately by a series of exceptions.[114]

Thus it is clear that the Baptizer does not regard Israel as a "*massa perditionis.*"[115] In his preaching, the anticipation of salvation is by no means to be found only "indirectly and in a concealed manner,"[116] as "a fragmentary image as auxiliary motif."[117] In that case, what would be the purpose of the call for

---

113. On this tradition, see above, pp. 145–48.

114. On this passage, see above, the final section of p. 136.

115. J. Becker, *Johannes,* 33. In his Habilitation, Helmut Merklein also employs the concept of "*massa damnata*" (*Gottesherrschaft,* 143; also idem, "Umkehrspredigt," 34).

116. J. Becker, *Johannes,* 21. Cf. H. Merklein, *Botschaft,* 29; S. von Dobbeler, *Gericht,* 75–76.

117. J. Becker, *Johannes,* 22.

repentance and baptism?[118] On the contrary: as in the whole early Jewish tradition before him, so also for the Baptizer judgment falls only on sinners; only the blighted trees that bear no fruit will be cut down, and only the straw will be burned, while the grain will be gathered into the granary.[119] Therefore Adolf Schlatter was correct when he wrote: "The positive statement of the Baptizer, not the negative, constitutes the principal content of his message, and it says that God is now creating the perfected community that is truly hallowed for God. The Christ's work with the axe is not his highest calling; he comes for the sake of the fruitful trees. The gathering of the wheat into the barns is the purpose of all his work."[120]

As the call to repentance of a Zephaniah or Joel was sustained by the hope for a "remnant of Israel" that would withstand the day of YHWH and afterward live in righteousness and peace,[121] so also the Baptizer's call to repentance. "Return to me, and I will return to you, says the Lord of hosts" (Mal. 3:7; cf. Zech. 1:3). John made this word of the prophet Malachi his own, and therefore the saying about the burning of the stubble on the day of YHWH, the "day of his coming" (Mal. 3:2), is followed by the saying about the "sun of righteousness" (Mal. 4:2). It is, in particular, the book of this prophet that seems to have played a major part in the Baptizer's preaching and self-interpretation. The salvation of the righteous (or of Israel) is the purpose of judgment. This statement is true of the whole of early Jewish eschatology, and

118. J. Becker himself saw this objection. Cf. H. Merklein, *Botschaft*, 30. Becker therefore speaks of a "tiny glimmer of hope" that is maintained, "concealed within the shadow of the words of judgment" and "not simply to be eliminated" (*Johannes*, 22). "One would not do wrong to lay claim to such a concealed possibility for salvation for those baptized by John, that is, for those who accepted the call to repentance. Otherwise there would be no reason for baptism" (ibid., 25). Nevertheless, according to Becker even the baptized can only "perhaps" escape the destroying judgment (ibid., 28, 40). With that kind of restriction, the Baptizer would scarcely have been able to appear in public! Becker correctly writes in his encyclopedia article, "Buße" (IV): "Baptism and repentance are understood as the last opportunity of rescue that God offers" (*TRE* 7 [1981]: 447). The saving aspect of the Baptizer's preaching is also correctly assessed by O. Böcher, *TRE* 17 (1986): 176.

119. J. Becker also saw this clearly, and he therefore quite rightly concludes: "Accordingly, we must suppose that the 'righteous' will continue to live on earth, without suffering detriment from the fire" (*Johannes*, 29).

120. A. Schlatter, *Geschichte*, 53. We must only read "God" instead of "Christ." To that extent H. Schürmann is also right in saying that the whole activity of the Baptizer "was to rescue and preserve from the coming judgment," and his interest in doing it "was ultimately directed entirely to salvation" (*Lukas* 1: 176; cf. idem, 171).

121. See above, pp. 27, 79.

it is true also for the Baptizer. Therefore Matthew and Luke were not entirely incorrect in saying that the Baptizer preached "good news" and the approach of the reign of God (Luke 3:18; Matt. 3:2), even though judgment stood in the forefront of his preaching, and in fact the whole of his preaching can be called "preaching of judgment." The judge has already laid on the axe, and has the winnowing shovel in hand. The day of the Lord is near.[122] Repent and be baptized by me, so that you may escape the punishing judgment! That is the message of the Baptizer.

122. See above, p. 26.

PART THREE

Judgment in the Preaching
of Jesus

CHAPTER SIX

Introduction

History of Research and Methodology

In spite of the great number of Jesus' sayings and parables in the tradition that speak of the subject of judgment, his preaching of judgment has received little attention in the scholarship of this century. There is no monograph on the subject, and comprehensive descriptions of Jesus' preaching, such as we find in Günther Bornkamm's *Jesus of Nazareth* or Leonhard Goppelt's *Theologie des Neuen Testaments,* while they treat his message about the reign of God at length, devote not a single chapter to his preaching of judgment.

> Günther Bornkamm treats Jesus' sayings and parables about judgment primarily under the title of "wisdom and watching" (*Jesus of Nazareth,* 87–89), but also in connection with the idea of reward (ibid., 139–40), and with the Son of man sayings (ibid., 175–78, 228). He gives a summary interpretation on p. 93: "The future of God is *salvation* to the [one] who apprehends the present as God's present, and as the hour of salvation. The future of God is *judgment* for the [one] who does not accept the 'now' of God but clings to his own present, his own past and also to his own dreams of the future." Leonhard Goppelt treats this theme in dealing with the terms for the eschatological future (*Theology,* 55–56), but especially in connection with the theme of "the order of retribution" (ibid., 122). According to Goppelt, Jesus expects both God's rule and God's judgment in the impending future; yet it is characteristic of him that he sees the content of what is to come not primarily as judgment, as it was in early Judaism, but as the salvation of God's reign (ibid., 61).

In contrast to these works, T. W. Manson's *The Teaching of Jesus* contains a separate chapter on "The Eschatological Teaching of Jesus," treating Jesus' preaching of judgment.[1] That chapter is prefaced by a survey of Old Testament and early Jewish eschatology.[2]

---

1. T. W. Manson, *Teaching,* 260–84.
2. Ibid., 244–60.

In the eschatological judgment, according to Manson's view, Jesus saw the form in which the reign of God would be established. "Jesus speaks of the final consummation of the Kingdom, which lies in the future, as the 'coming of the Son of man' or as 'the Day' or 'Parousia of the Son of man.'"[3] Manson refuses to rely on the synoptic apocalypse (Mark 13 and parallels) for the reconstruction of Jesus' eschatology; while the former contains authentic material, its present form reflects not the eschatology of Jesus, but that of the primitive church. Instead, he starts from the Son of man sayings that speak of the coming of the Son of man in the future, especially the saying about acknowledgment and denial (Luke 12:8-9 // Matt. 10:32-33), and the double saying about the Flood and the destruction of Sodom (Luke 17:24-30). According to these texts the reign of God will first be revealed, in its perfected form, as a judgment that arrives suddenly and without warning. The Son of man will appear in his glory and judge each individual according to the attitude of that person toward him. Manson does not understand the "Son of man" to be Christ alone; instead, he interprets this figure as a corporate personality and the head of the holy remnant constituted of those faithful to him. The promise to the Twelve in Matt. 19:28 // Luke 22:28-30 would also fit within this interpretation.

However, Manson interprets the judgment mentioned in these and other texts only as a prelude to the real judgment of the world that Jesus expected in the form described in Matt. 25:31-46. Manson sees a difference between this and the popular apocalyptic expectations of early Judaism in the universality of the judgment, which acknowledges no preference for Israel, as well as in the fact that Jesus, with reference to Dan. 7:9-14, has the present age end not in a violent battle, but in a violent scene of judgment.[4]

According to W. G. Kümmel, Jesus spoke not only of the approaching reign of God, but also of the eschatological "day" or "day of judgment," and expected it to coincide with the inbreaking of the reign of God, connected, in turn, with the appearance of the Son of man (Luke 17:24-27, 31-35).[5] According to the saying about acknowledgment and denial, Jesus expected that the Son of man on that day will judge each according to his or her attitude toward himself.[6]

3. Ibid., 140–41.
4. Ibid., 272–75. The first part of this study has already shown that this contrast does not do justice to the facts. Cf. especially pp. 145–48, 154–56, 160–61 above.
5. W. G. Kümmel, *Verheißung*, 29–42.
6. Cf. Luke 12:8-9 // Matt. 10:32-33; Mark 8:38. On this, see W. G. Kümmel, *Verheißung*, 38–40; idem, "Verhalten"; idem, *Jesus*, 175–76. According to this he has since come, like most exegetes, to regard the Q version of the saying as more original than the Markan version.

He saw the Son of man not as someone else, but as himself: "Jesus here lays claim to the authority of the final judge."[7] At the same time, it is again clear from this saying how firmly Jesus understood his own present as "the eschatological time of decision."[8] Kümmel sees this understanding confirmed also in the promise to the Twelve in Matt. 19:28 // Luke 22:28, 30. "According to this, the judgment will not be exercised solely by the Son of man when he appears, but Jesus' most intimate group of disciples will participate as accusers, witnesses, and co-rulers.[9] Moreover, there can be no doubt whatsoever that Jesus spoke frequently about judgment.[10]

Rudolf Bultmann gives an unsurpassed sketch of Jesus' preaching, including his proclamation of judgment, in his *Theology of the New Testament*. According to him, Jesus adopted the "apocalyptic picture of the future," although in a sharply reduced form. He expected the coming of the "Son of man" as judge and bringer of salvation, the resurrection of the dead, and the judgment; he shared the notion of a fiery hell into which the damned are thrown, and his simple term for the blessedness of the righteous was "life."[11] What is new and unique with Jesus is the assurance with which he proclaimed the inbreaking of the reign of God, and the way in which, in confident expectation of the beginning of the end, he calls for a decision in favor of love of God and neighbor. But in face of the factual attitude of the leaders of the people, and the greater part of the nation itself, confronted by their love for the world and their self-love, his preaching necessarily became a proclamation of woe and a call for repentance. The judgment will break upon those who are not prepared to repent, but "the promise of salvation" is for those "who await God's Reign aright, hungering and sorrowing, knowing how poor they are."[12]

Like T. W. Manson, Joachim Jeremias devotes a special chapter in his description of Jesus' proclamation to his preaching of judgment.[13] It follows immediately after the chapter on Jesus' message about the "dawn of the time of

7. W. G. Kümmel, *Jesus*, 176.

8. W. G. Kümmel, *Verheißung*, 40; idem, "Verhalten," 223.

9. W. G. Kümmel, *Verheißung*, 41. Cf. idem, *Jesus*, 173 n. 88: According to this, he is now inclined to regard the Lukan version, without "Son of man," as original.

10. W. G. Kümmel, *Verheißung*, 42. He refers, among other texts, to Matt. 7:13-14; 23:14; Luke 12:16-21, 57-59; 13:1-5, 6-9.

11. R. Bultmann, *Theology*, 6.

12. Ibid., 22. For Jesus' preaching of judgment, Bultmann looks primarily to Luke 11:31-32 par. (cf. ibid., 6, 21) and Matt. 23:24-36, 37-39 par.; Mark 8:38; Luke 6:24-26; 12:8-9 par.; 13:1-5.

13. J. Jeremias, *Theology*, 122–58. However, the Son of man sayings are left out of this chapter and are treated separately (ibid., 257–76).

salvation" and is entitled "The Period of Grace," because "the good news is announced in the final respite before the judgment."[14] Jeremias, like Manson and Kümmel, rests his reconstruction primarily on the so-called "little apocalypse" (Luke 17:20-37), but also includes reference to the "synoptic apocalypse" (Mark 13 and parallels), because it contains a good deal of genuine material.[15]

On the basis of these texts, he proposes the following image of Jesus' expectation regarding the end time: The ultimate arrival of the reign of God will be introduced by a catastrophe of unimaginable scope, comparable with the Flood. This catastrophe is in the immediate future; the generation now living is the last. But because they are living heedlessly as the day approaches, as if nothing could happen to them, they will encounter the coming catastrophe suddenly and unprepared. The "abomination of desolation" (Mark 13:14), the false Christ, will appear and reveal himself in the Temple. The Temple itself will be razed, but through God's intervention it will be restored within three days. Only those who survive those three days, until the Temple is rebuilt, will be saved. The last act in this time of tribulation is the separation of human beings by the angel of God, and the judgment that Jesus will carry out as Son of man, together with the Twelve as his assistants (cf. Matt. 19:28).[16] After this judgment, the few faithful will constitute the eschatological community of salvation, while the others will be devoured by the fiery hell of the end time. In light of this catastrophe, Jesus calls for repentance: "Take care, disaster is hanging over your head! before it is 'too late.'"[17]

Jürgen Becker treats Jesus' preaching of judgment in a running contrast to the judgment preaching of the Baptizer.[18] He begins with the double saying about the slaughtered Galileans and those felled by the tower (Luke 13:1-5), finding in it "a striking accumulation" of unmistakable elements from the Baptizer's preaching of judgment.[19] The parables of the rich farmer (Luke 12:16-20) and the unjust manager (Luke 16:1-7) also confirm, in his opinion, that

---

14. Ibid., 122.

15. Cf. ibid., 122–27.

16. It is not clear, of course, how the separation carried out by the angels, of which Jeremias also speaks on p. 129, relates to the judgment by the Son of man, which he describes on p. 272. Probably the angels are thought of as those who carry out the judgment.

17. Ibid., 139. Cf. also the chapters in his *Parables*, "The Imminence of Catastrophe" (pp. 160–69), "It May Be Too Late" (169–80), "The Challenge of the Hour" (180–98).

18. J. Becker, *Johannes*, 86–104.

19. Ibid., 87.

Jesus "in the substance [of his preaching]" stood "in immediate continuity with the Baptizer's preaching of judgment."[20]

Becker also finds corresponding elements in the Son of man traditions, especially the logia in Luke 17:24-35. There, however, he sees some differences between Jesus' preaching and that of the Baptizer. Thus Jesus, in contrast to the Baptizer, reveals no interest in the person who will judge or the nature of the act of judgment. "The Son of man is nothing but a linguistic indicator for portraying the approaching day of disaster as judgment (Luke 17:14, 26)."[21]

A further difference between Jesus and the Baptizer is said to consist in Jesus' explicit verbalizing of the opportunity for salvation.[22] For this, Becker refers to Matt. 7:13-14 par.; Matt. 7:24-27 par.; Mark 9:43-48; Luke 17:34-35, as well as the parables in Luke 15 and Luke 18:1-5, 9-14.[23] He concludes from the saying about the table companions of Abraham, Isaac, and Jacob in the reign of God (Matt. 8:11-12 par.) that Jesus also expected the Gentiles to share in eschatological salvation.[24] And with this, inasmuch as with Jesus the impending judgment no longer appears as "inevitable and unavoidable," the "frontal contrast to the Baptizer" is reached.[25] The *opus proprium* of the God of Jesus is said to be kindness and love, while judging is only his *opus alienum*.[26]

Becker treats the threat of judgment for those who reject Jesus' work as "a further development of the motif of judgment in the Jerusalem tradition."[27] He mentions the woes over the Galilean cities (Luke 10:13-14 par.), the saying about the Queen of the South and the Ninevites (Luke 11:31-32 par.), the parable of the unmerciful servant (Matt. 18:23-35), and the Son of man saying about acknowledgment and denial (Luke 12:8-9 par.). His concluding thesis is: "Jesus understands himself as a future criterion for judgment: that is, anyone who now rejects the graciousness of God as offered through him has lost it forever."[28]

Following Jürgen Becker very closely, Helmut Merklein also contrasts Jesus' preaching with that of the Baptizer.[29] While the Baptizer proclaimed judgment

20. Ibid., 89.
21. Ibid., 94.
22. For Becker's opinion that the Baptizer expresses the opportunity for salvation only indirectly, if at all, see above, pp. 191–92.
23. J. Becker, *Johannes*, 96–97.
24. Ibid., 99.
25. Ibid., 97.
26. Ibid., 97.
27. Ibid., 98.
28. Ibid., 106.
29. H. Merklein, *Gottesherrschaft*, 146–49; idem, *Jesu Botschaft*, 33–36.

"apodictically, unconditionally,"[30] and expressed the idea of salvation only in-directly, with Jesus "apodictic" words of salvation replace the "apodictic" words of judgment; for Jesus the judgment is simply "a consequence of salva-tion rejected."[31]

Peter Fiedler emphasizes the aspect of salvation in Jesus' preaching still more firmly. For Jesus, he thinks, the God who is willing to forgive is utterly dominant, so that the expectation of judgment is forced into the background.[32]

Hans Weder appears to want to deny altogether that Jesus threatened judg-ment, for: "The threat of judgment projects God's activity into my post-history. The forgiveness of sins, on the contrary, makes God's activity part of my prehistory. That is the difference between Jesus and the Baptizer: the Bap-tizer projects God into posthistory, while Jesus makes God, in his whole per-son, part of the prehistory of the human being (cf. Matt. 18:23ff.)."[33]

On the other hand, Heinz Schürmann writes: "The threatening Jesus re-ceived much more emphasis after Easter, but by no means can Jesus' preaching of judgment be entirely eliminated."[34] Whether, and in what sense, of course, the "threatening" Jesus was emphasized after Easter still needs some clarifi-cation.

According to Gerd Theißen, the prophet Jesus was also associated with a prophetic preaching of judgment. "This judgment will befall each individual, not particular groups or peoples."[35] He refers to Luke 17:26-30, 34-35 as docu-mentation. The single standard for this judgment is said to be "whether or not one had helped others."[36]

E. P. Sanders writes: "We find, as we would expect, the theme of judgment, but we do not find teaching or proclamation which depicts or predicts the

---

30. H. Merklein, *Gottesherrschaft*, 147. The unusual use of the word *apodictic* in the sense of "unconditional" is crucial for understanding Merklein's opinion. See below, ch. 9.

31. H. Merklein, *Jesu Botschaft*, 36. H. Schürmann also speaks in this sense (*Gottes Reich*, 34, 58–60). He emphasizes (ibid., 34 n. 44) that Jesus' sayings about judgment are in urgent need of a thorough study.

32. P. Fiedler, *Jesus*, 268.

33. H. Weder, "*Rede der Reden*," 243. Martin Hengel is critical of this position: "Berg-predigt," 399–400. For Weder's interpretation of the parable cited, see below, pp. 277–78. In order to understand it in his own sense, Weder has to explain the entire last scene (Matt. 18:31-34) as a secondary addition. Hence the "ff." is to be understood here only in a restricted sense.

34. H. Schürmann, *Gottes Reich*, 59.

35. Gerd Theißen, *The Shadow of the Galilean*, 136.

36. Ibid., 136, 137, with reference to Matt. 25:31-46.

impending judgment of the nation of Israel."[37] He considers the saying about acknowledgment and rejection, and the promise to the Twelve, to be authentic; Jesus' other judgment sayings he regards as more likely to be later constructions. Unlike the Baptizer, in his opinion, Jesus did not issue a call for repentance.[38]

This survey of scholarship reveals two primary *unresolved sets of problems:* (1) What is the relationship between Jesus' preaching of judgment and his proclamation of the reign of God?[39] and (2) To what extent is the judgment that is proclaimed connected with the person of the "Son of man" who is to come? Both sets of problems are associated with a third: the matter of sources. Which sayings and parables should serve as a basis for a reconstruction of Jesus' preaching of judgment?

Finally, the question of the location of Jesus' eschatological preaching within the eschatological conceptions of early Judaism deserves attention. New Testament scholarship has scarcely posed this question. To the present, only T. W. Manson has made a serious attempt to answer it.

First we must address the problem of sources and method. Most previous research was based on the so-called "little apocalypse" and the saying about acknowledgment and denial, and derived from these texts the basic framework of Jesus' preaching of judgment. Thus the principal texts by which it was established came from the Q tradition about the coming Son of man.[40] But it is well known that the interpretation of Jesus' sayings about the Son of man is one of the most difficult and disputed problems in New Testament exegesis, and there are still scholars who incline to the opinion that Jesus never spoke of the Son of man at all.[41] It therefore seems to me inadvisable to choose the sayings about the Son of man as the starting point for the investigation. In light of the multitude of texts available to us for the theme of Jesus' preaching of judgment, it is not even necessary. Therefore I will, for the present, leave the Son of man

37. E. P. Sanders, *Jesus,* 116.
38. Ibid., 91–119.
39. On this point, H. Stegemann remarks: "Apart from the special case of the 'Son of man' sayings of Jesus, this problem, oddly enough, has never yet been investigated consistently for the whole gospel tradition, at least not with a strict tradition-historical approach" (*Jesus,* 9 n. 32).
40. Luke 12:8-9 // Matt. 10:32-33; Luke 17:24 // Matt. 24:27; Luke 17:26-30 // Matt. 24:37-39; Luke 17:34-35 // Matt. 24:40-41.
41. Cf. A. Vögtle, "Bezeugt die Logienquelle die authentische Redeweise Jesu vom 'Menschensohn'?" However, W. G. Kümmel probably reflects the broad consensus of scholarship in his *Jesus der Menschensohn?*.

sayings aside, and will begin with some sayings and parables about judgment, the authenticity of which is generally acknowledged, or at least not readily subject to dispute.

Of course, there is probably no logion, or scarcely any, whose authenticity is above every doubt on the part of skeptics. And despite all the efforts of scholarship to establish criteria for the determination of authentic Jesus material, it is not rare for caprice to be the deciding factor in attributing or denying a particular saying or parable to Jesus. It is not necessary to enter into this problem in detail here; however, some fundamental remarks are in order.[42]

I start from the assumption that it is not the assertion of authenticity, but its denial that requires proof, and that a saying or parable, in the oldest form that can be reconstructed, may be regarded as authentic, at least in its content, if that content fits within the rest of Jesus' preaching and nothing speaks against its authenticity.[43] In my opinion, no other attitude is possible for a historian. Every historian must presume that his or her sources report reliably, within the limits of their possibilities, and to the extent that their unreliability either in detail or as a whole has not been proven. It is not the genuineness of a document that must be proven, but its falsity.[44]

> Thus in the historical researches, which just now came before us, it seems fair to say that no testimony should be received, except such as comes from competent witnesses, while it is not unfair to urge, on the other side, that tradition, though unauthenticated, being (what is called) in possession, has a prescription in its favour, and may, *prima facie*, or provisionally, be received. Here are the materials of a fair dispute; but there are writers who seem to have gone far beyond this reasonable scepticism, laying down as a general proposition that we have no right in philosophy to make any assumption whatever, and that we ought to begin with a universal doubt. This, however, is of all assumptions the greatest, and to forbid assumptions universally is to forbid this one in particular. (John Henry Newman, *Grammar of Assent*, 242–43. Cf. ibid., 234–39.)

42. For the criteria for authenticity of sayings of Jesus, cf. especially M. Lehmann, *Quellenanalyse*, 163–206; N. J. McEleney, "Criteria"; F. Hahn, "Überlegungen"; W. G. Kümmel, "Jesu Antwort"; idem, *Jesusforschung*, 28–31, 100–105; R. Latourelle, "Critères"; R. H. Stein, "Criteria"; R. Riesner, *Jesus*, 80–95; D. Polkow, "Method."

43. For the necessity of an overall conception and the hermeneutical circle that arises from the mutual relationship between the total picture and individual observations, see F. Hahn, "Überlegungen," 37–40.

44. Cf. N. J. McEleney, "Criteria," 445–48; R. Riesner, *Jesus*, 80–86; W. G. Kümmel, "Jesu Antwort," 186–87. Kümmel also quotes various historians.

This does not mean that I consider the search for criteria that can give positive proof of the authenticity of sayings of Jesus superfluous. That research has contributed a great deal to the understanding of the unique character of Jesus' preaching. Therefore I will carefully gather and present the indications of authenticity in each case. But since the question whether a saying or parable can be attributed to Jesus or not can normally be answered only after the reconstruction of the oldest version and its interpretation,[45] I will ordinarily treat them at the conclusion of each chapter.

---

45. Jacques Dupont, "Beaucoup . . . ," 158.

CHAPTER SEVEN

The Judgment of Israel

The Queen of the South and the Ninevites
(Matt. 12:41-42 // Luke 11:31-32)

Context and Tradition

The double saying about the Queen of the South and the people of Nineveh, in its present context, forms the conclusion of the pericope about the demand for signs, but it is not dependent on that context. On the other hand, the mysterious "sign of Jonah," according to the interpretation in Matt. 12:40 and Luke 11:30, really requires no further explanation, and it is difficult to find any explanation for it in this double saying. Hence an original connection with the proclamation of the sign of Jonah is improbable. But because that connection already existed in Q, it is likely that it was the redactor of Q who created it. First the redactor gave an interpretation for the enigmatic sign of Jonah, surviving in Luke 11:30, and apparently modeled on the Son of man sayings in Luke 17:24, 26-30 // Matt. 24:37-39.[1] The double saying followed easily, as a further word of warning to "this generation," especially because it also spoke about Jonah and the Ninevites.[2] But in spite of these common elements, the difference in content and theme is great: While the "commentary" in Luke

---

1. For creation by the redactor of Q, see D. Lührmann, *Redaktion*, 41–42; P. Hoffmann, *Studien*, 37. Cf. A. Vögtle, "Spruch," 131–34; idem, "Logienquelle," 81–84. H. Schürmann writes: "Probably Luke 11:30 was inserted as interpretation before Luke 11:29-30 par. Matt. was combined with Luke 11:31-32" (*Gottes Reich*, 164). Similarly D. Zeller, "Entrückung," 526. For the formal model: R. A. Edwards, *Sign*, 47–58; D. Schmidt, "Prophetic Correlative." Critical of the thesis of an "eschatological correlative" as a separate genre is M. Sato, *Q*, 278–87.

2. For the understanding of this saying as a "word of commentary," see J. Wanke, "*Bezugs- und Kommentarworte*," 59–60.

11:30, like its formal models, is intended to point to the parousia of the Son of man for judgment,[3] the double saying refers to the present work of the earthly Jesus, which will be a judgment for "this generation." The former is a Jonah-saying, because Jonah is both the subject of the comparison and the grammatical theme; in the second part of the double saying, however, we must speak of a Ninevite-saying, because here *they* constitute the theme.[4]

Matthew has replaced the explanation of the sign of Jonah in Q, which in itself is rather murky, with one of his own that nevertheless displays the same formal construction. But since it neither had the character of a warning nor contained the key words "this generation," Matthew made a rearrangement within the double saying, so as to achieve what at least amounts to a closer relationship among the key words.[5] In favor of the original character of the Lukan sequence is also the internal climax: The Queen of the South only listens, while the Ninevites repent. Thus the text of Q is easily determined, because Matthew and Luke otherwise present the double saying in the same words, apart from an unimportant expansion by Luke:

Βασίλισσα νότου ἐγερθήσεται
ἐν τῇ κρίσει μετὰ τῆς γενεᾶς ταύτης
καὶ κατακρινεῖ αὐτήν·
ὅτι ἦλθεν ἐκ τῶν περάτων τῆς γῆς
ἀκοῦσαι τὴν σοφίαν Σολομῶνος,
καὶ ἰδοὺ πλεῖον Σολομῶνος ὧδε.

ἄνδρες Νινευῖται ἀναστήσονται
ἐν τῇ κρίσει μετὰ τῆς γενεᾶς ταύτης
καὶ κατακρινοῦσιν αὐτήν·
ὅτι μετενόησαν εἰς τὸ κήρυγμα ᾿Ιωνᾶ,
καὶ ἰδοὺ πλεῖον ᾿Ιωνᾶ ὧδε.

3. A. Vögtle, "Spruch," 127–31; J. Schmid, *Lukas*, 207–8; D. Lührmann, *Redaktion*, 40; H. Schürmann, *Gottes Reich*, 164; D. Zeller, "Entrückung," 519–25; J. S. Kloppenborg, *Formation of Q*, 132–33. Some exegetes interpret Luke 11:30 as applying also to the Son of man as presently at work: thus, for example, P. Vielhauer, "Jesus," 112; S. Schulz, *Q*, 255–56; R. A. Edwards, *Sign*, 95; J. A. Fitzmyer, *Luke* 2: 933. Against this, however, are the future ἔσται, which is not weakened by the reference to the future δοθήσεται in Matt. 12:39 // Luke 11:29, as well as the formal models mentioned. And in that case, where would one look for the "sign"?
4. For grammatical "Thema" and "Rhema," see M. Reiser, *Syntax*, 60–63.
5. R. Bultmann, *History of the Synoptic Tradition*, 112–13; T. W. Manson, *Sayings*, 91; A. Vögtle, "Spruch," 117–19; S. Schulz, *Q*, 252. D. Lührmann (*Redaktion*, 38) declares Matthew's sequence to be the original and mistakenly adduces A. Vögtle in support of that position.

The queen of the South will rise
　　at the judgment with the people of this generation
　　and condemn them,
because she came from the ends of the earth
　　to listen to the wisdom of Solomon,
and see, something greater than Solomon is here!

The men of Nineveh will rise up
　　at the judgment with this generation
　　and condemn it,
because they repented at the proclamation of Jonah,[6]
and see, something greater than Jonah is here!

Diction and Phraseology

The diction and phraseology of this double saying are entirely Semitic. This is evident in the syntax: note the absence of the definite article before βασίλισσα νότου and ἄνδρες Νινευῖται;[7] the twofold καὶ ἰδού followed by a nominal phrase; the expression ἡ γενεὰ αὕτη;[8] the hyperbole of ἐκ τῶν περάτων τῆς γῆς;[9] and the designation "Queen of the South."[10] It is also striking that the Greek version of the double saying, despite its biblical material, is quite independent of the LXX, for there the "men of Nineveh" are called οἱ ἄνδρες Νινευη (with the definite article!: Jonah 3:5), while in the double saying they are ἄνδρες Νινευῖται. The adjective Νινευίτης occurs in the LXX only in some manuscripts of Tob. 1:19, especially A.[11] In the LXX the "repentance" of the Ninevites is described as ἀπέστρεψαν (3:8, 10), but in the double saying it appears as μετενόησαν. The description of the Queen of Sheba as "Queen of the South" cannot be derived either from the LXX or from the Hebrew text of 1 Kings 10 // 2 Chronicles 9.[12] The LXX translates 1 Kgs. 5:14 παρεγίνοντο . . . ἀκοῦσαι τῆς σοφίας Σαλωμων, but in the double saying we read ἦλθεν

6. For εἰς in the sense of "at" something, "on the basis of" something, see A. Plummer, *Luke,* 307–8. Cf. also εἰς τί, "why?" Sophocles, *Oedipus,* 524; Matt. 14:31; Mark 15:34.
7. Cf. *BD* § 259; H./v. S. § 133,4.
8. See below, pp. 215–17.
9. Cf. LXX Ps. 60:3, ἀπὸ τῶν περάτων τῆς γῆς; *Ps. Sol.* 8:15, ἀπ᾽ ἐσχάτου τῆς γῆς. Parallels in secular Greek are collected by J. Wettstein, *NT* 1: 396.
10. See below, pp. 212–13.
11. Cf. also Sinaiticus for Tob. 2:2.
12. On this, see below, pp. 212–13.

... ἀκοῦσαι τὴν σοφίαν Σολομῶνος. These findings speak against the double saying's having been created after Jesus.

The Form of the Symmetrically Constructed Double Saying

The two members of the double saying are constructed in strict parallel, both in form and content. Each member has two parts: the announcement of the sentence that will be imposed at the last judgment and the reason, introduced by ὅτι. Both parts, in turn, reveal a high degree of literal correspondence. In the first part, only the subject and the synonymous ἐγερθῆναι // ἀναστῆναι are reversed,[13] while the second part is each time attached, like a refrain, by means of a nominal phrase introduced by καὶ ἰδού, in which only the persons used for comparison are different. Each member of the double saying could exist on its own; both members vary the same idea, but in such a way that a climax is produced: we move from the mere listening of the Queen of the South to the repentance of the Ninevites.

The strict and catchy form of the saying facilitated its transmission, and probably was responsible for the almost word-for-word agreement of the versions in Matthew and Luke. We must suppose that Jesus spoke it not just once, but on a number of different occasions.

T. W. Manson has pointed out the striking form of such a complex, "strophic" parallelism in the received words and parables of Jesus.[14] The synoptic tradition offers a wealth of more or less strictly constructed examples of it, both in Q and in the Gospel of Mark, as well as in the Matthean and Lukan special material.[15] It is true that where pairs and triplets exist, as well as the parallelism that accompanies them, we can observe the tendency of the tradition to construct analogies,[16] but this in itself can only be explained by the

13. For the interchange of these synonyms, cf., for example, LXX Ps. 7:7; Isa. 26:19.

14. T. W. Manson, *Teaching*, 54–56. Unfortunately, no one took up his suggestion; there is still no thorough investigation of this parallelism.

15. Cf. Matt. 5:46-47 // Luke 6:32-34; Matt. 6:26-30 // Luke 12:24-28; Matt. 11:21-24 // Luke 10:13-15 (see below, pp. 221–23); Matt. 23:16-22; Mark 9:43-48 // Matt. 18:8-9; Luke 4:25-27; Luke 12:54-55; Luke 13:1-5 (see below, pp. 245–47); Luke 17:26-30 // (Matt. 24:37-39). For double metaphoric sayings and parables: Mark 2:21-22 // Matt. 9:16-17 // Luke 5:36-37; Matt. 13:31-33 // Luke 13:18-21 (cf. Mark 4:30-32); Matt. 13:44-46; Matt. 24:40-41 // Luke 17:34-35; Luke 14:28-32; Luke 15:4-10 (cf. Matt. 18:11-13).

16. R. Bultmann, *History of the Synoptic Tradition*, 81–86, 194–95. In particular, Matthew shows a tendency to create parallelisms: A. Denaux, "Spruch," 331–35; U. Luz, *Matthew* 1: 39–40.

original presence of double sayings and double parables with symmetrical form. These include the double metaphoric image in Mark 2:21-22:

Οὐδεὶς ἐπίβλημα ῥάκους ἀγνάφου ἐπιράπτει
    ἐπὶ ἱμάτιον παλαιόν·
εἰ δὲ μή, αἴρει τὸ πλήρωμα ἀπ᾽ αὐτοῦ
καὶ χεῖρον σχίσμα γίνεται.

καὶ οὐδεὶς βάλλει οἶνον νέον εἰς ἀσκοὺς παλαιούς·
εἰ δὲ μή, ῥήξει ὁ οἶνος τοὺς ἀσκούς
καὶ ὁ οἶνος ἀπόλλυται καὶ οἱ ἀσκοί.

No one sews a piece of unshrunk cloth
    on an old cloak;
otherwise, the patch pulls away from it,
and a worse tear is made.

And no one puts new wine into old wineskins;
otherwise, the wine will burst the skins,
and the wine is lost, and so are the skins.[17]

There can be as little doubt about the original pairing of these images, and their strophic parallelism, as of the authenticity of the saying.[18]

No matter how surprising it may seem, there are, to my knowledge, scarcely any genuine parallels to this form in the Old Testament or in early Jewish writings. The closest parallels are probably the two symmetrically constructed visions of judgment in Amos 7:1-6. One might also see a kind of model in the seven parallel threats in Amos 1:3—2:5. The double comparison in Micah 5:7-8[Heb. 6-7] also reveals this form of parallelism, but there it is not the same idea that is subject to variation. This is also true of the strictly constructed double parable by Rabbi Eleazar ben Azariah in *m. 'Abot* 3.17: here again, the strophic parallelism is not synonymous, but antithetical, and hence is comparable to the concluding parable of the Sermon on the Mount (Matt. 7:24-27 // Luke 6:47-49), which is not counted among the double parables.[19]

17. In the reconstruction, only the apparent insertion τὸ καινὸν τοῦ παλαιοῦ has been eliminated, along with the closing sentence. Cf. R. Pesch, *Markus* 1: 176; V. Taylor, *Mark,* 213–14; J. Wanke, *"Bezugs- und Kommentarworte,"* 83; M. G. Steinhauser, *Doppelbildworte,* 55–56. I see no reason to eliminate καὶ οἱ ἀσκοί.

18. Cf. R. Pesch, *Mark* 1: 177; J. Wanke, *"Bezugs- und Kommentarworte,"* 83; M. G. Steinhauser, *Doppelbildworte,* 60–64.

19. Cf. also 1QH XV, 14–21.

All this confirms T. W. Manson's conclusion: "Perhaps we should regard this strophic parallelism as the most distinctive characteristic of his [scil. Jesus'] poetry and his special contribution to the forms of poetry in general."[20]

The Scene of Judgment Obliquely Described

At the "last judgment," as Martin Luther's translation correctly paraphrases at this point, the Queen of the South and the Ninevites will "arise" "together with this generation" and "condemn" it. A forensic scene of judgment is thus obliquely sketched in a few words. The fact that it is a matter of something quite definite, and familiar to the hearers, namely, the last judgment, is evident from the use of the definite article: ἐν τῇ κρίσει. The image of a genuine trial is evoked especially by the mention of a concrete detail that has been an important part of judicial processes from of old: the rising of those taking part in the trial.[21] The fundamental rule is: "The judges are seated, and the contending parties stand before them."[22] The judge can permit the parties to be seated,[23] but whoever is speaking—complainant, defendant, or witness—stands up, and the judge or judges stand when delivering the verdict.[24] This practice is also presumed in the description of Jesus' trial in Mark 14:57,60. "Some stood up and gave false testimony against him. . . . Then the high priest stood up before them. . . ."

Therefore if "this generation" is to rise up at the last judgment because its case is being tried, it will be surprised to see the Queen of the South and the inhabitants of Nineveh also standing up to appear as witnesses against it. And their witness will lead to its condemnation.[25] The fact that these prosecutorial

20. T. W. Manson, *Teaching,* 56.
21. In particular it was older commentators who made this correct observation, for example, Hugo Grotius: "*Rursus iudicium Divinum ad humani iudicii formam describitur, in quo testes cum testimonium sunt dicturi surgere solent ex subselliis, quod ut apud Romanos ita et apud Judaeos moris fuisse ostendit Marc. 14,57. Adde Act. 6,13*" (*Annotationes zu Mt 12,41*). Cf. J. Wettstein, *NT* 1: 395 (with reference to Mark 14:57; Ps. 1:5, etc.); P. Schanz, *Matthäus,* 333 (with reference to Mark 14:57 and Job 16:8).
22. *t. Sanh.* 6.3. Cf. Zech. 3:1.
23. *t. Sanh.* 6.2.
24. *t. Sanh.* 6.2: "A judgment is only spoken while standing, and testimony is only given while standing." Cf. Deut. 19:15-16; Job 16:8; 30:12, 28; Ps. 1:5; 94:16; 109:6; Isa. 54:17; Mic. 6:1; 7:6, etc. In all these passages we find the verb קום. P. Bovati, *Giustizia,* 217–19. For the judge's standing when pronouncing sentence, cf. Isa. 3:13; Ezek. 44:24.
25. On the use of κατακρίνειν in this passage, H. Grotius remarked: "*Id est: efficient ut condemnetur; quomodo et supra dixit: 'Iudices vestri erunt*' [Matt. 12:27]. *Ita Cicero a se Verrem* [*Verr.* 6.177], *Tacitus a Domitio accusatore 'comdenatam' ait Claudiam* [*Ann.*

witnesses appear also agrees with what we know about Jewish judicial process: "The circle of witnesses was not restricted: besides witnesses in the strict sense, who spoke about the facts, anyone else present at the trial could speak and exercise influence for or against the accused."[26]

The judicial situation on the eschatological "day of visitation" (Wis. 3:7), as here indicated, corresponds exactly to that presupposed in Wis. 4:20—5:14, except that those involved in the process are different. Here in Jesus' saying, as in the other passage, the resurrection is implied.[27]

> Consequently, ἐγερθῆναι // ἀναστῆναι should not be translated "rise" (if this can be misunderstood to mean "rise from the dead"),* as sometimes happens, for example in E. Klostermann, *Matthäus*, 112; W. G. Kümmel, *Verheißung*, 37, 42; R. H. Gundry, *Matthew*, 246. On the contrary, and correctly: P. Schanz, *Matthäus*, 333. There is also no reason to see a Semitism in the expression ἐγείρεσθαι // ἀνίστασθαι μετά and therefore to understand μετά as adversative: "appear against (before the court)" (J. Jeremias, *TDNT* 3: 408 n. 15; idem, "Verheißung," 43; G. Dalman, *Worte*, 51), especially since the LXX represents the adversative עם in the Hebrew of this expression with ἐπί (cf. LXX Ps. 94:16). Matthew Black adduces two passages from the Talmud to clarify these verses, in which קום עם means "discuss with." He considers ἐν τῇ κρίσει an explanatory addition "to make an otherwise foreign idiom intelligible" (*Aramaic Approach*, 134). This interpretation of a supposed difficulty is quite improbable.

The Queen of the South and Solomon's Wisdom

The striking phrase "Queen of the South" for the "Queen of Sheba" (cf. 1 Kgs. 10:1-13, par. 1 Chr. 9:1-12) is found, apart from this passage, only in the so-called "Testament of Solomon," where she is twice called Σάβα ἡ βασίλισσα νότου,[28] and as in later legends is thought to be a witch or magician (γόης).

4.66]" (*Annotationes zu Mt 12,41*). Cf. *ThLL* 4: 125. The same metonymic expression is found also in Wis. 4:16: κατακρινεῖ δὲ δίκαιος καμὼν τοὺς ζῶντας ἀσεβεῖς. Cf. also John 12:48; Heb. 11:7. Underlying the double saying under discussion is probably the Aramaic חייב, "find to be in the wrong; effect condemnation" (J. Jeremias, *TDNT* 3: 408 n. 16). Cf. also Hebrew הִרְשִׁיעַ.

26. O. Betz, *Paraklet*, 36. For witnesses and accused at the last judgment, see P. Volz, *Eschatologie*, 303.

27. Cf. above, p. 44.

* [Translator's note: there is some ambiguity created here by the fact that English *rise* can mean both *stand up* and *rise* (from bed, from the dead, etc.), while German distinguishes between *aufstehen* (= stand up) and *auferstehen* (= rise from the dead). It is the latter against which the author wishes to caution.]

28. *T. Sol.* 19:3; 21:1. For the text in 19:3, cf. the reading of ms. N (in the edition by C. C. McCown [Leipzig, 1922], 120).

"Sheba" has here become a personal name. However, we also find a parallel to the designation "Queen of the South" in Daniel 11, where the Ptolemies are called "kings of the South" in contrast to the Seleucids, the "kings of the North." And since, according to a tradition attested by Josephus, the queen in 1 Kings 10 was not the queen of Sheba, but of Egypt and Ethiopia[29]—perhaps because, in the haggadah, Egypt is seen as the land of magic *par excellence,* as L. Ginzberg suggests[30]—we may well suppose that the designation "Queen of the South" stems from the same tradition.[31]

This, however, is without significance for the interpretation of the double saying, for here the queen appears only "to listen to the wisdom of Solomon." Jesus did not take the expression from the narrative in 1 Kings 10 // 2 Chronicles 9, for there the queen comes to Solomon "to test him with hard questions" (1 Kgs. 10:1 // 2 Chr. 9:1). Jesus instead derives his formulation from 1 Kings 4:34[Heb. 5:14]: "*People* came from all the nations *to hear the wisdom of Solomon;* they came from all the kings of the earth who had heard of his wisdom." Jesus apparently wants his citation to allude to this passage, and thus to the whole presentation of Solomon's wisdom in 1 Kings 4:29-34[Heb. 5:9-14]. The Queen of the South is only an example of the Gentiles as a whole, who came "to listen to the wisdom of Solomon."

According to the passage in 1 Kings 4:29-34, Solomon is regarded not merely as *the* wise person, but also as a teacher of wisdom surpassing all others, and not only in the Jewish tradition, but, growing out of it, in the Christian and Islamic traditions as well. Even the proverbial wisdom of the Egyptians, says Josephus in reference to 1 Kings 4:30[Heb. 5:10], was put in the shade by that of Solomon (*Ant.* 8, 42). The three thousand proverbs and 1,005 songs composed by Solomon, according to 1 Kings 4:32[Heb. 5:12], become in Josephus's account an equal number of books of songs and parables (*Ant.* 8, 44). ". . . he was not unacquainted with any of [Nature], nor omitted inquiries about [it], but described [it] all like a philosopher" (ἐν πάσαις ἐφιλοσό- φησε)" (ibid.).[32]

29. Josephus, *Ant.* 8, 165, 175. Josephus calls her Nikaule (8, 158–59) and identifies her with the queen of Egypt mentioned by Herodotus, *Hist.* II, 100, 2–4.

30. Cf. L. Ginzberg, *Legends* 6: 292. For the tradition Josephus is following, see the edition by H. St. J. Thackeray and R. Marcus (LCL), 5: 660–61 note.

31. Theodor Zahn thinks "Queen of the South" is a misunderstanding of מַלְכַּת תֵּימְנָא (*Matthäus,* 471 n. 7). This is improbable: (1) because of the parallels in *T. Sol.,* and (2) because even the phrase מַלְכַּת תֵּימְנָא instead of the biblical מַלְכַּת שְׁבָא is striking.

32. Cf. Wis. 7:15-21.

Josephus skips over the concluding verse of the biblical portrait that was so important for Jesus, but he goes beyond the biblical text to cite power over spirits and demons as a further sign of Solomon's wisdom; as proof he narrates the successful exorcism of a possessed man in which the demon was dragged out of the victim's nose by the use of a ring. The ring is supposed to have contained, under its seal, one of the roots given by Solomon for this purpose.[33] Jesus may well have known these traditions, but the fact that he speaks explicitly here of "listening to" Solomon's wisdom shows that in this saying he compares himself only with Solomon as a teacher of wisdom, not with Solomon the exorcist, as perhaps might have been expected.

The Ninevites and Jonah

The contrast between the repentant Ninevites and Israel, to which the prophets were sent in vain, is also found in the rabbinic writings.[34] This contrast is striking, because it does not exist in the biblical Jonah narrative. There is repeated attestation of a tradition, apparently old, that explains Jonah's flight from YHWH's commission with this consideration: "I will go out of the land to where the Shekinah is not revealed—for the Gentiles are close to repentance—that I may not be the occasion of Israel's condemnation."[35] This idea, which is probably derived from Jonah 4:1-2, like *Ekha Rab. Pet.* 31, assumes a contrast between Israel and the gentile nations that is not favorable to Israel—just as in this Jesus saying. In the version cited from the Mekhilta, we find

33. Josephus, *Ant.* 8, 45–49. The reference is probably to the Baaras root (= Alraun?) described in *Bell.* 7, 180–85. According to Wis. 7:20 also, God gave Solomon "the powers of spirits" (πνευμάτων βία) and δυνάμεις ῥιζῶν. For the corresponding apocryphal traditions, see K. Berger, "Messiastraditionen," 3–9; D. C. Duling, *T. Sol.* in *OTP* 1: 945–51.

34. *Ekha Rab. Pet.* 31; Str-B. 1: 651. On this, see now B. Ego, "'Denn die Heiden sind der Umkehr nahe,'" esp. 162–64.

35. *Mekhilta Y.* on Exod. 12:1 (Lauterbach, 1: 7). Further parallels are in Str-B. 1: 643–44; O. H. Steck, *Israel,* 95. For *y. Sanh.* 11.30b, see the translation by G. A. Wewers, 311. *Tanhuma Wayiqra* § 8 also offers an extended version: "Immediately 'great wrath came upon Israel' (2 Kgs. 3:27). Therefore Jonah said: 'The Gentile nations will very soon do penance, and the wrath of the Holy One, blessed be he, will come upon Israel. For the Holy One, blessed be he, will say: The Gentile nations, to whom I have given no statutes and ordinances—in the moment when I pronounce judgment on them and they learn of it, they immediately repent. But not so with Israel. For at every moment I send my prophets to them, but they are stubborn.' And therefore came 'a great wrath.'" I am indebted to Professor Dr. H. P. Rüger for the translation of this passage (letter of 11 June 1987).

not only the key word *repentance,* but also the key phrase חייב, "bring about judgment," which is probably behind the κατακρινοῦσιν in Matt. 12:42 // Luke 11:31.[36] The Gentiles' repentance leads to Israel's condemnation. This astonishing agreement suggests that Jesus knew the tradition we have described, and possibly even made a deliberate allusion to it.

We encounter a comparable tradition in *T. Benj* 10:10, where we read: "Then [God] will judge (ἐλέγξει) Israel by the chosen Gentiles as he tested Esau by the Midianites . . . ."[37] What is worth noting in this parallel is that, like the double saying under discussion, it speaks of a final judgment of a forensic nature, also following the general resurrection. There can thus be no doubt that Jesus is taking up an early Jewish tradition when he speaks of the contrast between the repentant Gentiles and unrepentant Israel in general, and uses the concrete example of the Ninevites as a particular instance.[38]

"This Generation"

Jesus describes his audience, to whom he announces the verdict of guilt in the final judgment to come, as "this generation." With this address, clearly negative in tone, he comprehends the whole nation of his contemporaries, all of Israel, as a unified opponent. The authenticity of this way of speaking is attested not only by this double saying, but also by Matt. 11:16 (par. Luke 7:31): "To what will I compare this generation?" and Luke 11:50-51, par. Matt. 23:35-36 (the blood of the prophets will be demanded of "this generation"), as well as Mark 8:12 and parallels: "Why does this generation ask for a sign?"[39]

With this address, Jesus takes up an expression found in the Old Testament, in early Jewish writings, and among the rabbis. Thus Gen. 7:1 reads: "Then the Lord said to Noah, 'Go into the ark, you and all your household, for I have seen that you alone are righteous before me in this generation (בַּדּוֹר הַזֶּה)." "This generation" refers to all the people living at the time of Noah. The rabbis call it "the generation of the Flood"; however, because this expression is not

---

36. See above, p. 212.

37. On this passage, see above, pp. 93–94.

38. *Midr. Tanh.* B Num IVa 2 § 9 (on Num. 14:27) also offers an example of the contrast between Israel and the Gentiles that is unfavorable to Israel (Bietenhard 2: 303): "The Holy One, praised be he, said: The nations of the world honor me (cf. Mal. 1:11), but you—how many signs have I done for you, but you have enraged me."

39. The remaining instances, some of them clearly redactional, are Matt. 12:45; Mark 8:38; 9:19 par.; 13:30 par.; Luke 11:30; 17:25. Cf. Acts 2:40.

purely temporal in its reference, but describes the people of that time as god-less, they do not count Noah among them.[40] Instead, he appears as a preacher of repentance to that "generation."[41]

Likewise, for the rabbis Moses did not belong to the "wilderness genera-tion."[42] In Deut. 1:35 they are called "this evil generation" (הַדּוֹר הָרָע הַזֶּה), and in Deut. 32:5 they are "a perverse and crooked generation" (cf. Deut. 32:20). In Ps. 95:10 they are simply "this generation,"[43] whom God loathed for forty years because they were "a people whose hearts go astray." "Therefore in my anger I swore, 'They shall not enter my rest'" (Ps. 95:11).

> This verse is quoted in Heb. 3:10-11. Jeremiah (7:29) uses the expression "the generation of his [= YHWH's] wrath" for his contemporaries. Yet the concept of "generation" need not be limited as to time. In Ps. 78:8 the "fathers" (= ances-tors) as a whole are called "a stubborn and rebellious generation." In a positive sense, as "generation of the righteous" and similar expressions, we find the term in Ps. 14:5; 24:6; 112:2. Here "generation" means "kind of people"—the modal meaning has completely suppressed the temporal. The same is true of Ps. 12:7[8], where "this generation" means the wicked in general. Cf. Prov. 30:11-14; Wis. 3:19; Luke 16:8.

The expressions "this generation" and "this evil generation" are found in an eschatological context in *Jub.* 23:14-16.[44] The rabbis also could occasionally address their contemporaries disparagingly as "this generation."[45]

With regard to a possible connection between Jesus and the talk of the "last generation" in the Qumran writings,[46] I see no more evidence for that than for a connection with the phrase "future generation" in Ps. 102:19; *Ps. Sol.* 18:6; and 1 Enoch 1:2.[47] Nor does the expression "this generation" mean *eo ipso* "the unrepentant Israel *of the last generation*."[48] It acquires eschatological significance only through its context. Jesus probably did adopt this manner of

40. E. Lövestam, "ἡ γενεὰ αὕτη," 407–8.
41. *Ber. R.* 30.7 on Gen. 6:9.
42. E. Lövestam, "ἡ γενεὰ αὕτη," 408.
43. In harmony with the LXX, we should read בַּדּוֹר הַהוּא in this verse (H. J. Kraus, *Psalmen* 2: 660).
44. See above, pp. 70–71.
45. A fine example is found in A. Schlatter, *Matthäus*, 554 (on Matt. 18:15). Cf. also ibid., 372, on Matt. 11:16, and 421, on Matt. 12:45; E. Lövestam, "ἡ γενεὰ αὕτη," 410.
46. See above, p. 83. H. Braun, *Radikalismus* 2: 47.
47. See above, p. 49.
48. Martin Hengel, "Kerygma," 334. Emphasis supplied. Cf. P. Hoffmann, *Studien*, 64, 169, 184.

speaking, which is not very widely attested, in order to compare the people he was addressing with the rebellious "wilderness generation" and the "generation of the Flood," to whom he, like Noah before him, preached repentance in vain, and who are therefore, like their ancestors, threatened by the wrathful judgment of God (cf. Luke 17:26-27; Matt. 24:37-39).

"More than Solomon," "More than Jonah"

"And see, more than Solomon is here," and also "more than Jonah." By saying πλεῖον, "more," and not πλείων, "a greater," Jesus withdraws from the foreground and places there the message that he brings in his word and works:[49]

> Blessed are the eyes that see what you see,
> and the ears that hear what you hear!
> For [Amen!] I tell you that
> Many prophets and kings
>   desired to see what you see,
>   but did not see it,
>   and to hear what you hear,
>   but did not hear it.[50]

As in this beatitude, so in the double saying here under discussion the concern is with the "hearing" of Jesus' message; it constitutes, in a sense, the "woe" corresponding to the beatitude. For "here," with Jesus, there comes to "this generation" something greater than Solomon's wisdom and Jonah's preaching. "As a teacher of wisdom, according to this logion, Jesus surpasses even the greatest, the universal Wise One of Israel, and indeed of the whole world, King Solomon; on the other hand, as a preacher of repentance his greatness is even beyond that of the most successful prophetic preacher, Jonah, who successfully called the great pagan city of Nineveh to repentance."[51]

---

49. Cf. A. Schlatter, *Matthäus*, 418–19; T. W. Manson, *Sayings*, 91–92; J. Gnilka, *Matthäus* 1: 466. "The message supports Jesus' 'self-concept,' not the other way around" (Martin Hengel, "Jesus," 152).

50. Matt. 13:16-17 // Luke 10:23-24. For the above reconstruction of Q, cf. H.-W. Kuhn, *Enderwartung*, 193–94; S. Schulz, *Q*, 419–20. Unlike Schulz, I do not consider the hearing with the ears a Matthean addition, but rather think it original. Cf. A. Harnack, *Sprüche*, 22–23; E. Klostermann, *Lukasevangelium*, 118; R. Bultmann, *History of the Synoptic Tradition*, 109; P. Hoffmann, *Studien*, 105; H.-W. Kuhn, *Enderwartung*, 194. For the interpretation, see M. Sato, *Q*, 260–61.

51. M. Hengel, "Jesus," 152.

The comparative statement also indicates "the difficulty of giving an adequate description of Jesus' claim of mission in a direct manner by use of an available category from the ancient biblical tradition, because that claim does not fit into any of the conventional patterns of Jewish eschatological expectation."[52] In that claim, which is so difficult to comprehend in conceptual categories of any kind, undoubtedly lies "the initial point for the construction of Christology, i.e., for the proclaimer becoming the proclaimed."[53] The fact that this claim, certainly outrageous in the ears of his hearers, is clearly expressed in this double saying without being formulated in a christological title is, in addition, a further sign of the authenticity of the saying.[54]

As for the Teacher of Righteousness at Qumran, who advanced a similar claim, so also for Jesus the ultimate judgment lies in the future. But by the same token, it was true for Jesus as for the Qumran teacher that the eschatological fate of the people and of each individual is being decided now, in his own person—in other words, in the position one adopts toward his own proclamation.[55] If one does not conceive the eschatological judgment as a unique action, but as an extended process, one may easily say that, in Jesus' understanding, the eschatological judgment began with his own appearance.

The Style of Argumentation

To make quite clear the guilt of "this generation," which consists in its rejection of his message and his claim, Jesus uses a kind of *qal wahomer* deduction (*a minori ad maius*): If even the Queen of the South (like many Gentiles) did not refuse to make a long journey merely to listen to Solomon's wisdom, how much more must "this generation" open its hearts and ears to his message, which surpassed even the wisdom of Solomon! And if the Ninevites, who were Gentiles, immediately repented at Jonah's preaching and did penance, "from the greatest to the least," from the king to the cattle (Jonah 3:5-10), how much more must "this generation" repent at his message about the reign of God! "The refusal to repent and do penance has now become inexcusable."[56] The climax, moving from mere hearing to actual repentance, was undoubtedly in-

---

52. A. Vögtle, "Jesus 'Christus,'" 44.

53. P. Vielhauer, "Gottesreich," 90. Cf. ibid., 88–90, on Jesus' claim. On this, see also F. Hahn, "Überlegungen," 49–50 (with bibliography).

54. F. Mußner, "Wege," 169–71.

55. See above, pp. 75–76. For the claims of the Teacher of Righteousness, see also below, pp. 311–12.

56. K. H. Schelkle, *Theologie* 3: 84.

tentional on the part of Jesus. In their refusal to repent now, when his message is being proclaimed, the eschatological fate of "this generation" is being decided. It will be condemned, and its condemnation will come as a result of the witness of Gentiles, which only deepens the shame.

We find a striking parallel to this argumentation, with the same reference to the last judgment, in a tradition of Rabbi Aqiba recorded in 'Abot R. Nat. A 6.2. According to it, the modesty of Rabbi Aqiba's needs will witness, at the last judgment, against poor people who did not concern themselves with the Torah: "In time to come [at the judgment], Rabbi Aqiba is going to impose guilt [for failing to study] on the poor [who use their poverty as an excuse not to study] (עתיד רבי עקיבא לחייב את כל העניים בדין). For if they say to them: 'Why did you not study the Torah,' if they say, 'Because of our children [whom we had to work to support],' they will say to them, 'Did not Rabbi Aqiba have sons and daughters?' "[57] In חייב בדין we have the exact Semitic equivalent of κατακρίνειν ἐν τῇ κρίσει in our saying.[58] And again the same kind of *qal wahomer* conclusion is employed: If even Aqiba, in spite of his poverty, and in spite of his children, found time to study Torah and to become such a learned man, how much more must those who are not as poor as he study Torah!

Parenetic purpose also links our double saying with the tradition just cited.[59] The proclamation of guilt at the last judgment may not be regarded in either case as the revelation of an unchangeable fate, any more than was Jonah's proclamation of judgment to Nineveh or the prophetic preaching of judgment as a whole.[60] Jesus' proclamation is not a prediction, but a deliberately provocative formulation of a warning designed, if possible, to move the addressees to repentance.

Conclusion

In all probability, there is scarcely a word in the Jesus tradition that we can more confidently regard as authentic, even to its easily reconstructed wording. It is not only that nothing speaks against it, but that everything favors it: the

57. Jacob Neusner, *The Fathers according to Rabbi Nathan. An Analytical Translation and Explanation* (Atlanta: Scholars Press, 1986), 52–53. Cf. P. Lenhardt and P. von der Osten-Sacken, *Rabbi Akiva*, 70–71. In Str-B. 1: 650–51 there is another variant of this tradition referring to Hillel instead of Akiba.

58. For κατακρίνειν / חייב, see above, pp. 211–12.

59. Regarding the tradition about Rabbi Aqiba, P. Lenhardt and P. von der Osten-Sacken speak of a "pedagogical-homiletic interest" (*Rabbi Akiva*, 80).

60. Cf. below, pp. 305–6.

Semitic diction and phraseology; the "rabbinic" argumentation; the strict form of symmetrically constructed double saying that has scarcely any parallels outside the Jesus tradition; the opposition between Jesus and "this generation," that is, the whole nation; the indirect, "open" Christology, reflecting the claim and self-understanding of the earthly Jesus; the importance of the present as the hour of decision concerning eschatological destiny, which is characteristic of Jesus' preaching.[61] This saying, more than almost any other, reveals Jesus' sense of unity both with the tradition of the Old Testament and with the living tradition of his own time, but on the other hand it shows the supreme ease with which he could give that tradition a twist that was devastating in its impact on his contemporaries. For even when he used "rabbinic" forms of argument and, like the teachers of his own time, drew his examples from the Old Testament, he nevertheless taught ὡς ἐξουσίαν ἔχων καὶ οὐχ ὡς οἱ γραμματεῖς (Mark 1:22).[62]

Jesus may have uttered this saying on more than one occasion. With it, he proclaimed to "this generation," that is, the whole nation of his contemporaries, their condemnation at the last judgment, in case they did not repent and accept his message. For if even Gentiles like the "Queen of the South" came "to listen to the wisdom of Solomon" (1 Kgs. 5:14), and the Gentiles of Nineveh repented at the preaching of Jonah, how much more must "this generation" listen to him, who brings more than Solomon's wisdom and Jonah's preaching. The key word about "hearing" Jesus' message unites this double saying with the blessing of the eye- and ear-witnesses in Matt. 13:16-17 // Luke 10:23-24. The double saying constitutes the logical supplement to the "blessing," because it shows what it means not to accept that "blessing."

In this saying, Jesus uses the traditional image of a forensic courtroom scene for the last judgment, with God as the judge, and the accused and witnesses

61. R. Bultmann, in his *Theology of the New Testament*, relies primarily on this double saying as a support for Jesus' expectation of judgment (pp. 6, 21–22. Cf. above, p. 199). In his *History of the Synoptic Tradition*, he was still wavering: on p. 113 he decided in favor of a community construction because of the formal parallels to Matt. 11:21-24 // Luke 10:13-15; but on p. 126 he lists it among the genuine sayings of Jesus. For the more recent discussion, see J. Becker, *Johannes*, 98–99. The saying is generally regarded as authentic: cf., for example, J. Gnilka, *Matthäus* 1: 469; D. R. Catchpole, "Law," 100. M. Sato writes: "Nothing speaks definitively against its genuineness" (*Q*, 151). He inclines, however, to the supposition that it is a saying of the Exalted One, because he considers the coupling of the proclamation of judgment for all Israel with the idea of Jesus as a teacher of wisdom to be a "late phenomenon" (ibid.). That is an unfounded hypothesis.

62. On this, see above, pp. 23–24.

present, as we have seen it presupposed, for example, in Wis. 4:20—5:14.[63] As
in that passage, the resurrection is implied. The "arising" of the Queen of the
South or the Ninevites refers to the posture of those who speak before the
court. In this case, the mere rising of the witnesses will be enough to establish
the guilt of "this generation." And then will occur what, according to a rabbinic
tradition, Jonah feared, and what drove him to flee from YHWH's commission: The repentance of the Gentiles will become an accusation against Israel,
and will bring about its condemnation. This shameful situation will come
about if "this generation" does not repent. Jesus sets it before the eyes of his
contemporaries in order to spare them from it.

The Woe over the Galilean Cities
(Matt. 11:21-24 // Luke 10:13-15)

Form, Tradition, and Text

The woe over the Galilean cities reveals, in Matthew, the form of strophic parallelism.[64] Each of the two strophes has three members: (1) the proclamation
of judgment, (2) the reason, and (3) the comparison with the gentile cities of
Tyre and Sidon, or with Sodom, for which it will "be more tolerable" on the
day of judgment than for the Jewish cities addressed. The Lukan text shows
broad agreement in wording with that of Matthew, but lacks the last two members of the second strophe, the one directed at Capernaum. Which of these
two versions was in Q? This is a question that must be answered in connection
with that of the context of the saying within Q.

    The most recent German scholarship mainly assumes that Luke has pre-
served the material and sequence of the sayings in Q in 10:2-15(16). According
to Dieter Lührmann, the woe over the Galilean cities followed the missionary
discourse in Q, which ended with Luke 10:12 // Matt. 10:15: "I tell you, on
that day it will be more tolerable for Sodom than for that town."[65] Lührmann
believes that this verse was created by the Q redaction as a transitional saying

63. See above, pp. 44–45.
64. See above, pp. 209–11.
65. Dieter Lührmann, *Redaktion*, 59, 62. This is a weakness in his analysis, because
the missionary discourse in Q undoubtedly concluded with Luke 10:16 // Matt. 10:40.
Cf. P. Hoffmann, *Studien*, 286, 288.

when the missionary discourse was combined with the warning, apparently in dependence on Luke 10:14 // Matt. 11:22.[66]

As regards the warning itself, the last two members of the second strophe (Matt. 11:23b, 24) are generally regarded by German scholars as an analogical construction by Matthew.[67] A repetition of the comparison with Sodom in the Capernaum saying did not disturb him because he had given it a different context and a separate introduction. On the other hand, there is said to be no discernible reason why Luke should have eliminated the corresponding members.[68]

English and American scholarship, on the other hand, starts with the observation that the warning to the Galilean cities does not fit within the missionary discourse, which both in Q and in Luke ended only at Luke 10:16 // Matt. 10:40. Thus in Q the woe either stood after v. 16 or in a very different place, and it was Luke who made the rearrangement.[69] English and American scholars generally regard the Matthean form of the saying as the original; Luke could have shortened it in order to avoid a repetition of the comparison with Sodom (Luke 10:12).[70]

It is not easy to decide between these two positions, but in my opinion there are three reasons for thinking it likely that Luke retained both the location and the form of the warning as found in Q: (1) the incongruency in Matt. 11:24 between the address, ὑμῖν, at the beginning of the verse and σοί at the end suggests Matthean redaction. The address λέγω ὑμῖν points back to the original context of the saying, the missionary discourse (cf. Matt. 10:15 // Luke 10:12).[71] (2) If Matt. 11:24 were original, we would have to posit three warn-

66. D. Lührmann, *Redaktion*, 62–63. P. Hoffmann agrees (*Studien*, 288, 303), as do L. Oberlinner, *Todeserwartung*, 88; J. S. Kloppenborg, *Formation of Q*, 196. This redaction need not have been the final redaction of Q. Cf. H. Schürmann, *Gottes Reich*, 96–97.

67. E. Klostermann, *Matthäus*, 101; J. Schmid, *Matthäus und Lukas*, 286–87; D. Lührmann, *Redaktion*, 62; P. Hoffmann, *Studien*, 284; S. Schulz, *Q*, 361; L. Oberlinner, *Todeserwartung*, 87; J. Gnilka, *Matthäus*, 427.

68. D. Lührmann, *Redaktion*, 62; S. Schulz, *Q*, 361.

69. T. W. Manson, *Sayings*, 77; I. H. Marshall, *Luke*, 424; J. A. Fitzmyer, *Luke* 2: 851.

70. According to J. A. Fitzmyer, the Matthean form of the saying "undoubtedly" reflects the original Q form (*Luke* 2: 851). Cf. T. W. Manson, *Sayings*, 77; I. H. Marshall, *Luke*, 424, 426; R. A. Edwards, "Matthew's Use of Q," 270. Thus also A. Schlatter, *Lukas*, 502.

71. E. Klostermann, *Matthäusevangelium*, 101; J. Schmid, *Matthäus und Lukas*, 287; idem, *Matthäus*, 195; P. Hoffmann, *Studien*, 285; S. Schulz, *Q*, 361. Cf. also T. Zahn, *Lukas*, 417.

ings, analogous in form and content, following closely on one another; two of them would have contained the comparison with Sodom. That is unlikely. (3) The parallelism in the Matthean version, which is so often emphasized by interpreters, is incomplete in the first and second member of each strophe. We need only contrast it with the double saying about the Queen of the South and the Ninevites treated in the previous chapter (Matt. 12:41-42 // Luke 11:31-32)! And whereas in the first strophe the proclamation of punishment is found only in the third member, in the second strophe it appears already in the first member. The third member of this strophe represents an unnecessary repetition.

Therefore Luke has retained the wording of the logion in Q, except for two small additions (καθήμενοι in v. 13 and the article before ᾅδου).[72]

Οὐαί σοι, Χοραζίν· οὐαί σοι, Βηθσαιδά·
ὅτι εἰ ἐν Τύρῳ καὶ Σιδῶνι
    ἐγενήθησαν αἱ δυνάμεις αἱ γενόμεναι ἐν ὑμῖν,
πάλαι ἂν ἐν σάκκῳ καὶ σποδῷ μετενόησαν.
πλὴν Τύρῳ καὶ Σιδῶνι
    ἀνεκτότερον ἔσται ἐν τῇ κρίσει ἢ ὑμῖν.

καὶ σύ, Καφαρναούμ,
    μὴ ἕως οὐρανοῦ ὑψωθήσῃ;
ἕως ᾅδου καταβιβασθήσῃ.[73]

Woe to you, Chorazin! Woe to you, Bethsaida!
For if the deeds of power done in you
    had been done in Tyre and Sidon,

72. Cf. P. Hoffmann, *Studien,* 284–85. The expression λέγω ὑμῖν (Matt. 11:22) is missing in Luke. When attested only by Matthew or Luke, it is usually redactional (F. Neirynck, "Developments," 69. On this passage, see ibid., 57–58).

73. In Luke 10:15 𝔓⁴⁵, ℵ A f ¹,¹³ and others read καταβιβασθήσῃ. The same variants are also found in Matt. 11:23. A. Huck and H. Greeven (*Synopse,* 63) accepted this reading into their text. The mss. 𝔓⁷⁵ B D and the edition of Nestle-Aland²⁶, on the other hand, have καταβήσῃ. A. Merk's 10th edition reads καταβήσῃ in Matt. 11:23, and καταβιβασθήσῃ in Luke 10:15. The reading καταβήσῃ offers a rhythmic easing and seems to be an assimilation to the LXX of Isa. 14:15. In Matt. 11:23 // Luke 10:15, however, there appears to be a reference to Isa. 14:15 independent of the LXX; this is also indicated by ἕως (LXX: εἰς). The passive, καταβιβασθήσῃ, corresponds to the *hophal* of תּוּרָד in Isa. 14:15. This text also yields two eschatological passives, as we should expect from the *parallelismus membrorum.* Cf. R. T. France, *Jesus,* 243; R. H. Gundry, *Use,* 81.

they would have repented long ago, sitting in sackcloth and
     ashes.[74]
But at the judgment
     it will be more tolerable for Tyre and Sidon than for you.

And you, Capernaum,
     will you be exalted to heaven?[75]
No, you will be brought down to Sheol!

Julius Wellhausen translates: "And you, Capernaum, since you will not be exalted
to heaven, you will be brought down to hell!" (*Das Evangelium Matthaei*, 56).
His reasoning: "The reading of ἕως οὐρανοῦ ὑψωθήσῃ, ἕως ᾅδου καταβήσῃ as
parallel questions is meaningless. If we suppose a Semitic original, we seem to
have here a negative parataxis in which the negation logically touches only the
second of the subjunctives" (ibid., 57). He is followed by Erich Klostermann
(*Matthäusevangelium*, 101) and Joachim Gnilka (*Matthäusevangelium* 1: 429).
But ὑψωθήσῃ and καταβήσῃ (or καταβιβασθήσῃ) are not subjunctives; they are
future forms, and μή is consequently not a negation, but an interrogative parti-
cle. Μή + indicative introduces doubtful questions to which ordinarily a negative answer is hoped for or expected: "Surely it is not true that . . . ?" (*KG* 2: 524;
H. W. Smyth, *Greek Grammar* § 2651b). However, such sentences can sometimes
also be understood as cautiously doubtful observations: "Perhaps it may be that
. . . (?)" (H. W. Smyth, *Greek Grammar* § 1772). Our case is unusual in that the
question introduced by μή is rhetorical. On this, see below, pp. 227–28.

As the unsuitable context in Q shows, this word of judgment was at one
time transmitted in isolation.

The Woe Proclaimed over Chorazin and Bethsaida

We find formally comparable woes over cities and countries in the Old Testament as well,[76] but they are not proclamations of judgment. The latter, however, are to be found in the Sibylline Oracles: *Sib. Or.* 3:303: αἰαῖ σοι, Βαβυλών
. . . 3:319: αἰαῖ σοι, χώρα Γὼγ ἠδὲ Μαγώγ . . . 3:323: αἰαῖ σοι, Λιβύη·/ αἰαῖ
δὲ θάλασσά τε καὶ γῆ·/ θυγατέρες δυσμῶν, ὡς ἥξετε πικρὸν ἐς ἦμαρ. "Woe
to you, Libya, / and woe, sea and land; / Daughters of the West, what a bitter

74. The German "Einheitsübersetzung" has "If *once* in Tyre and Sidon the miracles
had happened that have happened in you—people there would have repented in sackcloth and ashes." I do not know how this translation was obtained. For the meaning of
πάλαι, "long ago," see *BAGD* 605, s. v. 2 a; A. Schlatter, *Matthäus*, 379.
75. For the modal usage of the future, see H./V. S. § 202b; *KG* 1: 173–74; H. W.
Smyth, *Greek Grammar* § 1912.
76. Num. 21:29; Qoh. 10:16; Jer. 13:27.

day will come upon you!"[77] In the fourth book of the Sibylline Oracles we find a series of judgment oracles; two of them are tied to the preceding text, like the word to Capernaum, with καὶ σύ + vocative: *Sib. Or.* 4:99: καὶ σύ, Βάρις, πέσεαι καὶ Κύζικος . . . "And you, Baris, will fall, and Kyzikos . . ."; 4:105: καὶ σύ, τάλαινα Κόρινθε, τεήν ποτ᾽ ἐπόψει ἅλωσιν. "And you, unhappy Corinth, will one day see your conquest."

But while in the Jewish Sibylline Oracles it is always gentile cities and countries to which God's punishing judgment is announced, the threatening words here under consideration are addressed to three Jewish places. They presuppose that Jesus worked in those places and did miracles there. Here, exactly as in Matt. 11:4-6 // Luke 7:22-23 and Matt. 12:23 // Luke 11:20, those miracles are understood as eschatological signs, indissolubly connected with the proclamation of the reign of God. However, our gospels know very little of Jesus' work in those places. Chorazin is not mentioned anywhere except here; Bethsaida appears as the locus of a miracle only in Mark 8:22-26.[78] Only for Capernaum is there tradition of a considerable number of miracles: Matt. 8:5-13 par. (the centurion's servant), 17:24-27 (stater in the fish's mouth); Mark 1:21-28 (possessed man in the synagogue), 1:29-34 (Peter's mother-in-law and the healings at evening), 2:1-12 (the lame man), 3:1-6 (the withered hand).[79] Jesus also had a fixed residence in Capernaum; this is shown by the expression ἐν οἴκῳ, "at home" in Mark 2:1.[80] Probably this was Peter's house (cf. Mark 1:29-36). Matthew therefore rightly refers to Capernaum as "his own town" (Matt. 9:1).

Jesus sets up the two Jewish towns, Chorazin and Bethsaida, in contrast to the pair of gentile cities: Tyre and Sidon. He chooses those cities as examples not because of their economic significance, and not because hearers had come to him in large numbers from the hinterland of Tyre and Sidon (Mark 3:8), or because he himself had already passed through that region and healed the daughter of a Syrophoenician woman (Mark 7:24-31). Instead, Jesus here takes up a tradition from the prophetic books of the Old Testament. Several proph-

---

77. Cf. *Sib. Or.* 3:504, 507; 5:126, 289, 317, 434.

78. Luke 9:10-11 does not represent an independent ancient tradition. Matthew mentions Bethsaida, as well as Chorazin, only in this verse. The apocryphal Gospel of the Nazarenes sets the number of Jesus' miracles in Chorazin and Bethsaida at 53 (W. Schneemelcher, *New Testament Apocrypha* 1: 151).

79. Mark 5:21-43 (Jairus's daughter and the woman with the hemorrhage) probably belongs to Capernaum as well. Cf. also Luke 4:23: ". . . the things that we have heard you did at Capernaum."

80. Cf. *Arr. Epict.* 2: 21, 14.

ets had proclaimed divine judgment on those cities, or wrote ironic dirges describing catastrophes that had befallen them as God's punishment for their pride and wickedness. In those passages, Tyre and Sidon were always named together.[81]

So when Jesus asserts, in hyperbole, that if his miracles had been done there these cities would "long ago" have repented in sackcloth and ashes—as Nineveh once did (Jonah 3:5-9)—it is done with a provocative (or should we, in this case, rather say polemical?) intent: the saying is directed at Chorazin and Bethsaida. The provocation is made even sharper by the conclusion that it will be better for the gentile cities on the day of judgment than for the Jewish towns. This conclusion must have outraged Jesus' audience, for the damnation of the godforsaken Gentiles and their condemnation on the last day was a basic tenet of early Jewish and rabbinic tradition, never called into question;[82] a tenet, moreover, from which the despised and oppressed people derived more than a little hope and confidence. The conclusion, however, is based on Jesus' claim that the acceptance or rejection of his message would decide the eschatological destiny of each individual, and of the nation itself. The portion of Israel that was not prepared to repent in light of his message and miracles imposed greater guilt upon itself than the Gentiles, and therefore could expect a worse punishment on the last day. The saying presumes all that. It pronounces the verdict of the eschatological judge as if it were already fixed and unchangeable. "The confidence with which Jesus utters His judgments as being identical with the Divine judgments is all the more impressive from its being implied and not asserted."[83]

This claim, and the provocative contrast between Jews and Gentiles to the disadvantage of the Jews, recalls the double saying about the Queen of the South and the Ninevites. Common to that saying and the woes over the Galilean cities are the key words μετανοεῖν and ἐν τῇ κρίσει. Certainly, in Luke 10:14 // Matt. 11:22 Jesus does not formulate so much in terms of a forensic judicial process, but more with regard to a judgment of condemnation; κρίσις here, in contrast to the saying about the Queen of the South and the Ninevites, does not refer to the judicial process, but to the imposition of punishment. And while in the saying about the Queen of the South and the Ninevites Jesus' teaching and preaching were in the foreground, here it is explicitly his deeds

81. Isaiah 23; Jer. 47:4; Ezekiel 26–28; Joel 4:4-8; Zech. 9:2-4. See D. Lührmann, *Redaktion*, 62–63.

82. See above, pp. 136–41.

83. A. Plummer, *Matthew*, 165.

that are at issue. Thus if the other saying represented the counterpart, so to speak, to the blessing of the ear-witnesses, this one in a certain sense enhances the blessing of the eyewitnesses through the corresponding "woe."[84]

The Word of Judgment on Capernaum

The judgment-saying directed at Capernaum, attached with καὶ σύ, may once, in spite of its extreme brevity, have been an independent logion.[85] In this saying, Jesus again alludes to the Old Testament, this time to Isaiah's satirical song about the king of Babylon who says in his heart: "I will ascend to heaven," but is "brought down to Sheol" (Isa. 14:13, 15).[86] However, we find the metaphorical expression "to be exalted to heaven (or: to the stars)" or "ascend to heaven" elsewhere as well, as an expression of the desire to be exalted above all, the hubris that is punished with a fall.[87]

Especially enlightening for the interpretation of the Capernaum saying in particular, however, is the description of the eschatological events in the *Assumptio Mosis*. There this metaphor is, we might say, taken literally and given a positive twist: after the judgment on the nations, God will elevate Israel to the starry heavens, from which it will look down in triumph on its enemies (*As. Mos.* 10:9–10).[88] There, as here in the saying about Capernaum, "being elevated to the heavens" is an image for eschatological salvation. It is God alone who creates this salvation, something that is not directly asserted in the Capernaum saying as it is in *As. Mos.* 10:9, but is obliquely expressed in the eschatological passive ὑψωθήσῃ.[89]

In the two brief cola of this saying, the rhetorically posed question and the antithetically formulated response, there is a powerful drama at work. The question is rhetorical, which means that it takes the situation it formulates as already given; but it is introduced by μή, and therefore expects the one queried to answer "no," an answer that, of course, cannot be given. Therefore Jesus himself gives the answer. The saying does not tell us on the basis of what advantages the inhabitants of Capernaum expected the eschatological exaltation of their town, or at least could have held the kinds of expectations implied by

84. Cf. above, 217, 220–21.
85. Cf. M. Sato, *Q*, 131.
86. The targum explains "Sheol" with "the pit of destruction."
87. Cf. Jer. 51:53; Amos 9:2; Obadiah 4; LXX Dan. 8:10; *Ps. Sol.* 1:5; *Sib. Or.* 5:72. P. Volz, *Eschatologie*, 379. Secular parallels are in J. Wettstein, *NT* 1: 385.
88. See above, pp. 87–88.
89. For the eschatological passive, see the excursus below.

the question. The current context, however, suggests an answer similar to that in Luke 13:26 // Matt. 7:22: "We ate and drank with you, and you taught in our streets" and worked miracles.[90] Although this saying is very difficult to reconstruct in detail,[91] there is probably an authentic tradition behind it. Like the Capernaum saying, it stands within a context of eschatological judgment. At that judgment an appeal to acquaintance with Jesus, if it did not lead to repentance and a change in one's life, will be as useless as an appeal to descent from Abraham (cf. Matt. 3:9 // Luke 3:8). On the contrary, this advantage only makes the "case" worse. Therefore on the day of judgment Capernaum will not be "exalted to heaven," but will be "brought down to Sheol."[92]

Sheol, ᾅδης, here quite obviously refers to the eschatological place of punishment, as in 1 Enoch 103:7-8 or *Ps. Sol.* 14:9; 15:10, and frequently elsewhere. The context makes this clear. The antithesis to eschatological salvation, expressed in the image of exaltation to heaven, is necessarily eschatological damnation, expressed in the image of plunging into Sheol. The translation of ᾅδης as "hell" is therefore entirely appropriate to the sense of this passage.[93]

We should also take note of καταβιβασθήσῃ, which, if it is the original reading, represents an eschatological passive. But while in ὑψωθήσῃ God is to be regarded as the acting subject, in this case (as in 1 Enoch 103:7), it is probably God's avenging angels who act.[94] This contrast would further underscore the antithetical parallelism and the unsurpassable severity of this saying.

90. I. H. Marshall also refers to this saying in his commentary on the present passage (*Luke*, 425).
91. Cf. P. Hoffmann, "Πάντες," 200; U. Luz, *Matthew* 1:440–41.
92. Cf. the fine interpretation of M.-J. Lagrange, *Luc*, 300. He also adduces *As. Mos.* 10:9–10 for clarification.
93. The translation "hell" is offered, for example, by the Luther translation, edition of 1984; H. Menge; O. Karrer, 1954; U. Wilckens (5th ed., 1977); J. Wellhausen, *Das Evangelium Matthaei*, 225. Against J. Gnilka, who without offering any precise reasons writes: "The underworld (Sheol) is the realm of the dead, not hell" (*Matthäus*, 429). The identification of Sheol with Gehenna began as early as the third century B.C.E. (1 Enoch 22!). Cf. pp. 146–47; Str-B. 4: 1023, 1075, 1095; J. Bonsirven, *Judaïsme* 1: 530–31; F. Lang, *TDNT* 6: 937; U. Fischer, *Eschatologie* 82 (on *3 Bar.* 4:5). Josephus also speaks (*Bell* 2.165) of the καθ᾽ ᾅδου τιμωρίαι καὶ τιμαί. This idea is presumed by Luke 16:23. There can thus be no question of a "sharp distinction between ᾅδης and γέεννα" throughout the New Testament (J. Jeremias, *TDNT* 1: 148), nor can it be said that "throughout the New Testament" Hades "serves only an interim purpose" (ibid.). Substantially, it may be said that it was always regarded in early Judaism as the place of punishment. Cf. M. Reiser, art. "Hölle," *Neues Bibel-Lexikon* 2: 173–74.
94. Cf. above, pp. 64–65. There, rather than the passive, the text uses the third person plural.

Conclusion

The essential form and wording of the woe over the Galilean cities are retained in Luke 10:13-15. An origin in the situation of the post-Easter community, as reaction to the lack of success of the early Christian preaching in Chorazin, Bethsaida, and Capernaum, is highly unlikely.[95] "The later community had no further interest in these neighboring, utterly unimportant Galilean villages."[96] Against the background of Jesus' history, on the other hand, the allusion to these places is quite natural. Even a retrospective look at a period of his activity that had already concluded is not something that favors locating this saying in a period of "community building." It can be associated with a clearly discernible situation in the life of Jesus: namely, the time shortly before his departure for his last Passover in Jerusalem. Jesus probably knew that the decisive event would happen there;[97] he could regard his activity in Galilee as finished, and for the most part unsuccessful. Both these words of judgment reflect this situation.[98]

Favoring the authenticity of these sayings are also the evaluation of Jesus' miracles as eschatological signs,[99] the provocative reference to the Old Testament—the example of Tyre and Sidon, the allusion to the satirical song in Isa. 14:13-15[100]—and, finally, the connection between the woes and the sayings about the Queen of the South and the Ninevites.[101]

95. Representatives of this point of view include: J. Wellhausen, *Das Evangelium Matthaei*, 56; R. Bultmann, *History of the Synoptic Tradition*, 112–13; E. Käsemann, "Anfänge," 98; E. Haenchen, *Weg*, 226; D. Lührmann, *Redaktion*, 64; S. Schulz, *Q*, 362–64; L. Oberlinner, *Todeserwartung*, 90–93; M. Sato, *Q*, 199–200.

96. M. Hengel, *Jesus*, 151. Cf. F. Mußner, *Wunder*, 27.

97. Cf. H. Schürmann, *Tod*, 26–33.

98. Cf. F. Mußner, *Wunder*, 27: "Historically regarded, the logion belongs to that situation in Jesus' life when the 'Galilean spring' collapsed and Jesus set himself once and for all on the way of suffering."

99. Cf. Matt. 11:4-6 // Luke 7:22-23, and Matt. 12:28 // Luke 11:20. W. Grundmann, *Matthäus*, 313. The reference to the miracles is for L. Oberlinner "the most serious objection to the Jesuanic origin of these woes" (*Todeserwartung*, 91). That point of view fails to recognize the eschatological significance of Jesus' miracles and their close relationship to his proclamation of the reign of God.

100. Cf. F. Hahn, *Mission*, 27. Hahn speaks, with regard to the example of Tyre and Sidon, of an "antithetical reference to the Old Testament." But an antithesis to the Old Testament is just what Jesus does *not* offer here. Instead, the prophet's sayings about Tyre and Sidon are affirmed and employed to produce a provocative antithesis with regard to the attitude of the audience.

101. Also favoring authenticity are: P. Hoffmann, *Studien*, 303 n. 53; I. H. Marshall, *Luke*, 424; J. A. Fitzmyer, *Luke* 2: 852; J. Gnilka, *Matthäus* 1: 430. Cf. also A. Schlatter, *Geschichte*, 225–26.

The "woe" is related to the double saying through its provocative contrast between Jews and Gentiles, the accusation of failure to repent, and the explicit proclamation of the fate of the audience ἐν τῇ κρίσει. But while this statement in the double saying is located within the forensic situation of the last judgment, the woe refers instead to the eschatological judgment of condemnation, which will have a more horrible result for Chorazin and Bethsaida than for Tyre and Sidon because they, having seen Jesus' miraculous deeds within their own walls, still have not converted themselves to him and his message; hence they have laid on themselves greater guilt than the gentile cities.

What is true of Chorazin and Bethsaida is true also of Capernaum: On the day of judgment it will not be able to appeal to the fact that Jesus taught in its streets and did miracles there. Because it refused to repent, it will not be "exalted to heaven," but will be thrown down to Sheol, the place of eternal damnation.

Apparently we should read the sayings about the Queen of the South and the Ninevites as severe warnings and a last challenge to repentance; but in the case of the words of judgment on the Galilean cities, especially that over Capernaum, one has rather the impression of a settled condemnation. Here the sentence of the eschatological judge is proclaimed with absolute authority. The reign of God had come near to the cities of Galilee, but they remained far from it.[102] Thus they had pronounced the verdict on themselves.

Abraham, Isaac, and Jacob in the Reign of God
(Matt. 8:11-12 // Luke 13:28-29)

Form, Tradition, and Text

The saying about the table companions of Abraham, Isaac, and Jacob in the reign of God has been retained by Matthew and Luke in very different versions. In Matthew it constitutes an antithetical parallelism in which the Gentiles who come from east and west to recline at table with Abraham, Isaac, and Jacob in the reign of God are contrasted with the natural heirs of that realm, who are cast out into the darkness where there is weeping and gnashing of teeth. The clear form of the Matthean version, which constitutes an independent logion

---

102. A. Plummer, *Luke*, 276–77: "Of Chorazin and Bethsaida the paradox was true, that the Kingdom of God had come nigh to them, and yet they were far from the Kingdom of God." Cf. idem, *Matthew*, 165. Cf. Augustine, *Conf.* 10.27: *Mecum eras, et tecum non eram.*

capable of being handed down in isolation, has been completely shattered by Luke, and the individual parts have been rearranged in such a way that the unified logion falls into two independent statements apparently without internal connection. Although in this reformulation the wording has been only slightly changed, the content and meaning have shifted considerably. While for Matthew weeping and gnashing of teeth characterize the place of damnation, in the Lukan context these circumstances are evoked by the fact that those who are excluded from the eschatological banquet hall "see Abraham and Isaac and Jacob and all the prophets in the kingdom of God," but themselves are "thrown out" (Luke 13:28).[103] But by virtue of the fact that the ancestors and prophets are now in the reign of God, but the Gentiles are not, the original contrast has lost its force, and the point of the saying is removed. Nor is it entirely clear, on the basis of early Jewish eschatology, why it should be just the sight of the ancestors seated in the reign of God (the prophets are certainly secondary) that causes weeping and gnashing of teeth. It was a principle of faith, taken for granted, that the ancestors would be the first to enjoy the eschatological salvation; but it did not necessarily follow, even in the conceptions of Jews at that time, that salvation was reserved for all the descendants of Abraham, as those "thrown out" in Luke 13:28 appear to have believed.[104]

After v. 28 in the Lukan version a prophecy is attached with a simple καί: "[and] people will come from east and west, from north and south, and will eat in the kingdom of God"—although it is not quite clear what this sentence, vague and colorless in itself, adds to the context, or to what extent it is meant to expand or continue what precedes it. It is not even clear who these people who "will come" may be. The repetition of the expression "kingdom of God" from the preceding verse is also striking. As it is, the whole v. 29 appears superfluous.

This in itself suggests that we should regard the Matthean form of the saying as original. The conclusion is supported by the observation that Luke's shattering of the Matthean form and rearrangement of the parts can be easily explained by Luke's having attached this logion to the scene with the people locked out of the house (Luke 13:25-27). That is, by placing ἐκεῖ ἔσται ὁ

103. The excellent Greek of Luke 13:28 gives no occasion for the suggestion of an underlying Semitic original whose syntax the Greek translator is supposed not to have understood. Against J. Jeremias, *Verheißung*, 47 n. 185; M. Black, *Aramaic Approach*, 82, 92; K. Beyer, *Semitische Syntax*, 254–55; S. Schulz, *Q*, 324–25 n. 18; I. H. Marshall, *Luke*, 567; J. Schlosser, *Règne* 2: 613–14.
104. See above, pp. 79–80, 136–37.

κλαυθμὸς καὶ ὁ βρυγμὸς τῶν ὀδόντων at the beginning, Luke forged a close connection to the preceding scene; now ἐκεῖ refers back to v. 25 and describes the place of the excluded, "outside" the door that leads into the eschatological banquet hall.[105] However, the new connection has brought an inconsistency with it: The excluded are described as "thrown out," although they were never "inside."[106]

Apparently the repetition of ἐν τῇ βασιλείᾳ τοῦ θεοῦ in v. 29 was also brought about by the decomposition of the original unit and the rearrangement of its members. This repetition is used to create a rough connection to the preceding verse and to give the necessary clarification of the circumstances for ἀνακλιθήσονται.

Although, as we see, nothing appears to speak in favor of the originality of the Lukan version, not a few exegetes have argued for its priority and either consider Luke 13:28, 29 to be two originally independent logia,[107] or, because that is difficult to imagine, hold them to be two expansions of Luke 13:26-27, added one after the other in the course of the tradition-history of Q.[108] Matthew is supposed to have fused the two sentences, secondarily, to form a unit.

But what could have moved a redactor to add the superfluous and empty v. 29 after v. 28—unless it was fidelity to a tradition that attempted to retain all the basic elements of a rearranged saying of the Lord?[109] Thus it is easy to make a plausible case for how and why the original unity came to be deconstructed by Luke. On the other hand, a lucky combination of two logia as different as those in Luke 13:28, 29, which, moreover, originally may have had nothing to do with one another, into a shapely antithetical parallelism in

105. It is a very desperate solution to give ἐκεῖ a temporal sense and apply it to the following ὅταν, referring to the two or three doubtful instances thought to have been found in Greek literature for temporal ἐκεῖ: Soph. *Phil.* 395; Dem. *Or.* 22.28; Matt. 24:51. Thus J. Schlosser, *Règne* 2: 613. Cf., to the contrary, M.-J. Lagrange, *Luc,* 390–91.

106. I. H. Marshall, *Luke,* 568. This inconsistency was noted already by Theodor Zahn (*Lukas,* 534). It was probably for that reason that many mss. omitted the corresponding clause in Luke 13:28.

107. Thus, for example, H. J. Holtzmann, *Synoptiker,* 379; J. Schmid, *Matthäus und Lukas,* 255; W. Trilling, *Israel,* 88–89; G. Strecker, *Weg,* 100; I. H. Marshall, *Luke,* 567 (on the basis of the supposed Aramaism in v. 28); J. Schlosser, *Règne* 2: 603–14. M.-J. Lagrange also considered the Lukan order more natural (*Matthieu,* 166).

108. H. Schürmann, *Gottes Reich,* 117–22. Because Matthew contains the logia in Luke 13:24-29 not in unbroken sequence, but probably in the same order (Matt. 7:13-14, 22-23; 8:11-12), D. Marguerat also believes (*Jugement,* 244) that Luke has here retained the connection in Q, but thinks that Matthew's version of this logion is more original (ibid., 248–49). Cf. also J. Schlosser, *Règne* 2: 614.

109. Cf. P. Hoffmann, "Πάντες," 207.

which even being "thrown out" inadvertently acquired a meaning it previously lacked—all this is scarcely imaginable. Hence we must regard the Matthean form of the saying as original.[110] In any case, the context in which Matthew presents the saying, the pericope of the centurion of Capernaum, is certainly secondary.[111] Thus it is possible that Luke retained the context of the logion in Q, although not the form. This would explain his procedure, and the reconstruction of the saying, better than the supposition that he himself was the one who transferred it to this setting.

Consequently, the Q version of this saying can be reconstructed approximately as follows:[112]

πολλοὶ ἀπὸ ἀνατολῶν καὶ δυσμῶν ἥξουσιν
    καὶ ἀνακλιθήσονται μετὰ Ἀβραὰμ καὶ Ἰσαὰκ καὶ Ἰακὼβ
    ἐν τῇ βασιλείᾳ τοῦ θεοῦ,
οἱ δὲ υἱοὶ τῆς βασιλείας ἐκβληθήσονται ἔξω·
ἐκεῖ ἔσται ὁ κλαυθμὸς καὶ ὁ βρυγμὸς τῶν ὀδόντων.

Many will come from east and west
    and will eat with Abraham and Isaac and Jacob
    in the kingdom of God,
while the heirs of the kingdom will be thrown out
where there will be weeping and gnashing of teeth.

The Gentiles Come to the Eschatological Meal

The many who will come from east and west are contrasted with the "children of the kingdom," and must therefore be Gentiles.[113] The expectation that even the Gentiles will come to Zion when God establishes dominion there is attested

110. Thus, for example, A. Harnack, *Sprüche,* 56–57; E. Klostermann, *Lukas,* 147; P. Hoffmann, "Πάντες," 205–10; J. Dupont, "'Beaucoup,'" 153–58; D. Zeller, "'Völkerwallfahrt'" part 1, 222–24; S. Schulz, *Q,* 323–24; B. D. Chilton, *God,* 179–201; J. S. Kloppenborg, *Formation of Q,* 225–27.

111. J. Dupont, "'Beaucoup,'" 154–55; P. Hoffmann ("Πάντες," 205–6) leaves this question open.

112. For the reconstruction of the wording, cf. J. Dupont, "'Beaucoup,'" 156–57; D. Zeller, "'Völkerwallfahrt'" part 1, 223–24; S. Schulz, *Q,* 323–24; B. D. Chilton, *God,* 181–96; J. Schlosser, *Règne* 2: 603–8. It is difficult to decide whether Matthew's υἱοὶ τῆς βασιλείας or Luke's ὑμεῖς is the original, or whether both these formulations are secondary. In addition, πολλοί at the beginning of the saying could be Matthew's. I retain it, however, because it undoubtedly fits the sense, as does υἱοὶ τῆς βασιλείας. For this problem, see D. Zeller, "'Völkerwallfahrt'" part 1, 224.

113. Justin cites this saying: *Dial.* 120.5–6. He sees it as indicating a division within Israel.

in the Old Testament as well as in early Jewish and rabbinic literature.[114] It appears in several variations according to the impulse and purpose given for their coming. A conversion of the Gentiles is not always presupposed; in some texts they only come to bring tribute and homage, and to serve Israel. In the more extensive descriptions of the end time, the flocking together of the nations ordinarily precedes the judgment, so that only "the remnant of all nations" (Zech. 14:16) come to Zion.[115]

This saying does not describe the detailed circumstances of the Gentiles' coming. The purpose of their coming, however, suggests that we should not think of the "many" as representing the Gentiles as a whole, but only the righteous among them, the "survivors" of the judgment. They will be found worthy to recline at table with Abraham, Isaac, and Jacob at the eschatological banquet. This, of course, presumes that the patriarchs either are already living within the eschatological salvation, or else that they will be the first to rise from the dead. Both these ideas are attested.[116]

We find a combination of the motifs of the coming of the nations and the eschatological banquet elsewhere only in Isa. 25:6: "On this mountain [i.e., Zion] the Lord of hosts will make for all peoples a feast of rich food, a feast of well-aged wines. . . ." However, it is significant that this passage had no influence on the motif of the eschatological meal as developed especially by the rabbis. To my knowledge, no reference is made to it in any of the relevant texts. The usual references, instead, are Ps. 23:5: "You prepare a table before me in the presence of my enemies; you anoint my head with oil; my cup overflows," and Isa. 65:13: "Therefore thus says the Lord God: My servants shall eat, but you shall be hungry; my servants shall drink, but you shall be thirsty." The rabbis understood these passages eschatologically and applied them to the banquet in the age to come. Thus for example, *Midr. Tanh.* B Num VIII, 3, §

114. Cf. Isa. 2:2-4; 49:22-23; 60; 66:18,23; Jer. 3:17; Zech. 8:20-23; 14:16-19; Ps. 102:16,23; Tob. 13:11; 1 Enoch 90:33; *Sib. Or.* 3:710-24; *Ps. Sol.* 17:31; 1QM XII, 13-14; *'Abot R. Nat.* 35.9. Str-B. 3: 150-52; P. Volz, *Eschatologie,* 358; D. Zeller, "'Völkerwallfahrt'" part 1, 225-37.

115. Thus, for example, Isa. 66:15-21; Zechariah 14; 1 Enoch 90:19-33(see above, pp. 60-61); *Sib. Or.* 3:657-731; 1QM XII, 7-14; *Ps. Sol.* 17:21-31.

116. Cf., for example, 4 Macc. 7:19; 13:17; 16:25; *T. Benj* 10:6. P. Volz, *Eschatologie,* 267. Gerhard Lohfink believes that the patriarchs are mentioned in this saying only as *pars pro toto:* "With them all of Israel's just will have been raised" (*Jesus and Community,* 18; idem, "Kirche," 82). But the provocative point of this saying lies in the fact that those who recline at table with the tribal ancestors are not the righteous of Israel: they are Gentiles. A third component of the gathering is deliberately not mentioned.

12: "The Holy One, praised be he, said to the Israelites: In this world you bring me food offerings and show bread and sacrifices, but in the world to come I will prepare a great table for you, and the nations of the world will see it and be ashamed, as it says: 'You prepare a table before me' (Ps. 23:5). And it says: 'See, my servants shall eat' (Isa. 65:13)."[117] The submotif of the "table" and "reclining at table," found also in the saying under discussion, is thus derived from Ps. 23:5. "Reclining indicates that this is a festive meal."[118] In a number of passages the future age is even described as a "*triclinium*" (טרקלין),[119] for which the present age is the "anteroom."[120]

For the rabbis who cite Ps. 23:5 and Isa. 65:13, it appears that the contrast between the wicked and the righteous that is also integral to these passages is important; however, they are equally able to apply it to the contrast between Israel and the gentile nations, as in the passage cited above. Eschatologically interpreted, these scriptural passages express the idea of retribution once for all, and just compensation in the age to come, which meant so much to the faithful.[121] Thus the combination of the eschatological banquet with the coming of the (righteous) Gentiles, and with it the reference to Isa. 25:6, must in itself have seemed unusual; the explicit assertion that the Gentiles would recline at table with the ancestors was unheard of; but that this should occur to the exclusion of the "children of the kingdom" was for the Judaism of that era a completely unthinkable notion, as is demonstrated by Paul's exposition in Romans 9–11.[122] Therefore when Jesus said this, he could have intended nothing but provocation, with the intention of shaking up his hearers and warning them; by no means was he prophesying an event that must inevitably take place. This saying is not Jesus' promise to the Gentiles, but a warning for the "children of the kingdom": they alone are addressed, and the whole saying is for them.

117. From the German translation by H. Bietenhard, 2: 391–92. Isa. 65:13 is also adduced in *b. Shab.* 153a (Str-B. 1: 878–79); *Qoh. R.* 9.8; and *Shem. R.* 25.7 (on Exod. 16:4): Str-B. 4: 1157. For Ps. 23:5 see *Midr. Teh.* Ps. 23 § 7 (Str-B. 4: 1157). For the motif of the eschatological meal, cf. also 1 Enoch 62:14; *m. 'Abot* 3.16. P. Volz, *Eschatologie*, 367; Str-B. 4: 1146–47, 1154–65. For the two primeval beasts, Leviathan and Behemoth, which will be slaughtered for this meal, see above, p. 122. For the Essene expectations, cf. 1QSa II, 11–21.

118. A. Schlatter, *Matthäus*, 278.

119. *m. 'Abot* 4.16; *t. Ber.* 7.21; *y. Hag.* 77a; *b. Hag.* 14b.

120. *m. 'Abot* 4.16; *t. Ber.* 7.21.

121. See above, p. 138.

122. Cf. especially Rom. 11:1-2, 25-32.

Thus it is not permissible, as usually happens, to divide this saying into two parts, namely, (1) the promise to the Gentiles and (2) the proclamation of judgment for Israel, as though it were not one *single* saying, but—similarly to what happens in Luke 13:28-29—two separate, even though not equally important sayings, because according to the rule of the weighted end the principal emphasis would lie on the last part. On the contrary, it must be maintained that an antithetically constructed logion always has but *one* theme and therefore intends to make *one*, and not two different statements. Our saying has only one audience and only one point, as Dieter Zeller correctly emphasizes ("'Völkerwallfahrt'" part 2, 87–88), and therefore as a whole it represents a word of judgment addressed to Israel. Thus it is also impermissible to say that this saying contains or implies a promise. Certainly, it required only a shift in accent and a different audience for this threat directed at Israel to become a promise for the gentile nations—which is what happened to it in Matthew's hands.

The mention of the ancestors contains another special point, because their names were connected with "what is owing to the ancestors," which is to be credited to Israel, and specifically to sinful Israel—a conviction that Josephus puts on the lips of Nehemiah: "Men of Judah, you know that God has remained faithful to us for the sake of our fathers, Abraham, Isaac, and Jacob, and for the sake of their righteousness has not left off the eternal care (πρόνοια) of you."[123] It is unthinkable that the righteousness of the ancestors of Israel should be credited to the Gentiles!

The Place of Salvation and the Place of Damnation

"The children of the kingdom," Abraham's descendants and therefore his natural heirs, will be "thrown out (outside)."[124] Out where? What kind of "outside" is intended here, where there is "weeping and gnashing of teeth"? Matthew adds εἰς τὸ σκότος τὸ ἐξώτερον, indicating that he is thinking of the darkness of Sheol, or hell.[125] This interpretation certainly fits the sense, but it conceals the original thought of a quite specific place: the valley of Hinnom south of Jerusalem.[126] The preceding motifs of the "pilgrimage of the nations" and the

123. Jos. *Ant.* 11, 169, quoted by A. Schlatter, *Matthäus*, 73–74. For the credit owing to the ancestors, see also Str-B. 1: 117–21, especially the testimony in Justin, *Dial.* 140.2; *2 Bar.* 84:10, cited at Str-B. 1: 120.

124. Here, as frequently, ἔξω indicates the direction, and is often pleonastically added after composita with ἐκ-. (*BAGD*, 234, s. v. 1 b; LSJ 600, s. v. I, 1). Cf. Matt. 5:13; 13:48; 21:39; Mark 12:8; Luke 14:35; 20:15.

125. Cf. 1 Enoch 10:4; 103:8; *Jub.* 7:29; *Ps. Sol.* 14:9; 15:10. A. Schlatter, *Matthäus*, 279.

126. For the location of the valley of Hinnom between Ophel and the "mountain of bad counsel," see M.-T. Wacker, *Weltordnung*, 245–48 (on 1 Enoch 26).

eschatological banquet show that the reference must be to that valley: both these motifs point to Zion, but so especially does the scriptural passage here alluded to, namely, Isa. 66:24.[127]

The place of eschatological salvation, according to Isaiah 65–66, is Jerusalem, and Zion in particular. There, after the judgment "on all flesh" (Isa. 66:15-16), the nations will come to behold God's glory, bringing with them the dispersed of Israel (Isa. 66:18-20). After another reference to "the new heavens and the new earth" (Isa. 66:22; cf. 65:17), the description of salvation concludes with the proclamation: "From new moon to new moon, and from sabbath to sabbath, all flesh shall come to worship before me, says the Lord" (Isa. 66:23). From Zion, the place of salvation, the view turns to the place of damnation, the valley of Hinnom; to it the redeemed will "go out" (LXX: ἐξελεύσονται) to look at the dead bodies of the damned, whose worm does not die and whose fire is not extinguished (Isa. 66:24).[128]

This description exercised great influence on later apocalyptic. It is taken up in 1 Enoch 25–27 and developed with topographical detail.[129] On the basis of Isa. 66:24 an idea of Gehenna as the eschatological place of punishment for the damned is unfolded; it is located immediately opposite the place of blessedness.[130] We find a variety of allusions to this passage, such as this one in Jdt. 16:17:

> Woe to the nations that rise up against my people!
> The Lord Almighty will take vengeance on them in the day of
>   judgment;
> he will send fire and worms into their flesh;
> they shall weep in pain forever.[131]

Here we also encounter the motif of the "weeping" of the damned.[132] The combination with the Old Testament motif of "gnashing of teeth" as an expres-

127. It is worth nothing that Justin, in paraphrasing this saying in *Dial.* 120.5, describes the place of the damned by using a motif from Isa. 66:24, "unquenchable fire."

128. See above, p. 32.

129. See above, p. 54.

130. For Gehenna, see Str-B. 4: 1029–32; P. Volz, *Eschatologie*, 328–30. For the juxtaposition of the two places, derived from Isa. 66:23-24, in 1 Enoch 26–27, see M.-T. Wacker, *Weltordnung*, 253.

131. We find an allusion to the "inextinguishable fire" of Isa. 66:24 in *Bib. Ant.* 63:4. Rabbinic citations of this passage are in Str-B. 2: 19–20 (on Mark 9:43). In the targum on this passage we read: ". . . and the wicked will be judged in Gehenna, until the righteous shall say of them: 'We have seen enough.'" Cf. Str-B. 4: 1114.

132. For this motif, cf. also 1 Enoch 108:3, 5, 15.

sion of "despairing rage"[133] is not found outside the New Testament. It therefore appears that Matthew was the first to make this expression into a
formula.[134]

The people of God, including the Gentiles, on Zion—the damned "outside"
in the valley of Hinnom: That is the shape of the "last things" according to Isa.
66:18-24. The patriarchs alone with the Gentiles at the eschatological banquet
on Zion—"the children of the kingdom" "outside" in the valley of Hinnom:
That is Jesus' provocative antithesis to the ancient image.

The reference to the βασιλεία τοῦ θεοῦ fits within this context also; in fact,
one is tempted to find in it an allusion to a localizing of the reign of God on
Zion. One could appeal, for example, to Isa. 24:23: "the Lord of hosts will
reign on Mount Zion and in Jerusalem."[135] But we dare not forget that Jesus'
saying is not intended to make a statement about the place of God's reign, and
does not even expressly mention Zion; the latter is simply part of the traditions
alluded to, just as the valley of Hinnom is only hinted in ἐκβληθήσονται ἔξω,
which would remain incomprehensible apart from Isa. 66:24.

However, it is still less appropriate to disassociate the βασιλεία τοῦ θεοῦ
in this saying, as a "new age conceived as radically otherworldly" from the
"this-worldly eschatology" of the Old Testament Zion traditions, which are
incorporated in the saying together with the motifs of the "pilgrimage of the
nations" and the eschatological banquet from Isa. 25:6.[136] There can be no
question of a "heavenly," "apocalyptic," or certainly of an "apocalyptic-
transcendent" basileia in this saying.[137] Such an idea could not even be ex-

133. T. Zahn, Matthäus, 342. Cf., for example, Pss. 35:16; 112:10. However, it is
also found in Bib. Ant. 18:12. For its interpretation, cf. also B. Schwank, "Heulen und
Zähneknirschen." He understands it as an image of the self-reproaches of the damned,
as do K. H. Rengstorf, TDNT 1:642; A. Schlatter, Matthäus, 280. J. Schmid, Lukas, 239:
"Expression of regret and powerless rage."

134. Cf. Matt. 13:42, 50; 22:13; 24:51; 25:30.

135. For the eschatological description in Isa. 24:21-23, see H. Wildberger, Jesaja
2: 942–50.

136. F. Hahn, Mission, 27 n. 2; S. Schulz, Q, 325. Even Dieter Zeller, who correctly
refuses to eliminate Zion completely as the central goal, speaks of the motif of the
"coming of the many" as a "relic of a more this-worldly eschatology" ("'Völkerwallfahrt'" part 2, 86).

137. S. Schulz uses the expressions quoted (Q, 325, 326, 327). For him, it appears
that "apocalyptic" and "transcendent" are largely synonymous. J. Schlosser also considers it probable "that Jesus conceived the salvation of the kingdom in its fully perfected
state as a truly transcendent reality, belonging to a completely different mode of existence from that of this world and its history" (Règne 2: 641). Cf. I. H. Marshall, Luke,
567: "The Kingdom of God is here the transcendent future realm in which the righteous

pected on the basis of the historical eschatology of the apocalyptic writings, for, as we have seen in the first part of this study, that kind of apocalyptic was thoroughly oriented to this world; a truly transcendent conception of eschatological salvation after the day of judgment is not found in any early Jewish writing. The fundamental orientation to this world in early Jewish eschatology must be maintained, even if it very seldom paints eschatological salvation in the hues of earth and Paradise, and normally contents itself, in its descriptions, with abstract concepts and images—just as does this saying of Jesus.[138]

Conclusion

The form of the saying about the table companions of Abraham, Isaac, and Jacob in the reign of God, as it was recorded in Q, has been retained with its essential wording in Matt. 8:11-12. Luke, in order to create a better connection to the preceding scene about the excluded, has placed the last member of the saying at the beginning, and was thus forced to rearrange the whole saying. However, his touch was rather inept in this rearrangement: the antithetical parallelism of the original saying was lost, and it collapsed into two statements whose internal connection would scarcely be recognizable without the Matthean parallel. Moreover, the second sentence, Luke 13:29, has become so vague and empty that it appears positively superfluous. That the Lukan version was the original, and that it was Matthew who formed the two statements in Luke 13:28, 29 into a unified saying, is highly unlikely.

This saying shares the contrast between Israel and the Gentiles to the disadvantage of Israel with the two other sayings previously discussed. Its relationship with the double saying about the Queen of the South and the Ninevites (Luke 11:31-32 par.) is especially close. As in that saying, the provocative proclamation is directed to the whole people, the "children of the kingdom," who are the same as "this generation." They are positioned antithetically to the "many," the Gentiles, who in the end time, after the judgment, will come to Zion, where God's reign will be established. This was a familiar idea to the audience, but they must have found it intolerably impudent for Jesus to propose the idea that those Gentiles could recline at table with the ancestors of Israel in the eschatological banquet in the reign of God, while they, the descendants of those ancestors and therefore the natural heirs of that kingdom, would

---

dead are present." According to H. Schürmann, also, for Jesus "God's kingdom and rule are ultimately eschatological and transcendent" (*Gottes Reich*, 26).

138. See above, p. 148.

be "thrown out," thrust outside where there would be "weeping and gnashing of teeth"—into Gehenna. This must be what is meant, because of the clear allusion to Isa. 66:23-24. There the redeemed, including the Gentiles who have come in the "pilgrimage of the nations," go from Zion, the place of eschatological salvation, "out" to the valley of Hinnom to look upon the corpses of the damned. Because the end time "pilgrimage of the nations" leads to Zion, which, according to Isa. 25:6, will also be the site of the eschatological banquet "for all nations," our saying, like Isa. 66:24, can mean by "outside" nothing other than the valley of Hinnom, regarded on the basis of Isa. 66:24 as the eschatological place of punishment for the wicked and the godless Gentiles. Matthew has covered over this clear allusion by adding εἰς τὸ σκότος τὸ ἐξώτερον. In the Lukan version it was lost as a result of the new reference of "outside," acquired by the combination of this saying with the scene of those excluded from the house.

It is clear that this saying, even though it takes up the traditional motif of the "pilgrimage of the nations," was not originally concerned with a promise to the Gentiles, although Matthew himself wished to interpret it in that way. But that what is threatened in this saying could really happen—that is something that Jesus could not really have imagined, even in the sense given it by Matthew; in fact, this proclamation, even according to Matthew's Gospel, did not correspond to the actual course of salvation history, in which not the whole nation, but only a part—although the greater part—refused to be won over by Jesus.[139] Even for Paul, the idea of the final rejection of Israel was unthinkable.[140] But there is no promise to the Gentiles in this saying for the very reason that its original audience was not they, but the "children of the kingdom," that Israel to which Jesus addressed his message and that, as it is about to turn away from him, he seeks to shake up and bring to its senses with provocative words.

In this interpretation, there is no reason to doubt the authenticity of the saying.[141] Favoring our tracing it back to Jesus is also the close internal relationship to the two logia previously discussed, the double saying about the

---

139. Cf. G. Lohfink, "Kirche," 53–59.
140. Cf. Romans 9–11.
141. Cf. F. Hahn, *Mission*, 26. R. Bultmann (*History of the Synoptic Tradition*, 128) is uncertain. S. Schulz assigns it to the "newer layer of tradition in Q" (*Q*, 328–29). But the saying is usually regarded as genuine. Dieter Zeller, however, inclines to the "certainly rather isolated thesis of E. Käsemann ('Anfänge,' 98)," namely, that behind this logion are the words of an early Christian prophet ("'Völkerwallfahrt'" part 2, 91).

Queen of the South and the Ninevites (Luke 11:31-32 par.) and the woes over the Galilean cities (Luke 10:13-15 par.). It is connected to them not only by the provocative contrast between Israel and the Gentiles with regard to their eschatological destinies, but also by the original references to the Old Testament, which are given surprising and—for those addressed—scarcely flattering twists. This "unconventional" style of allusion and of reference to Sacred Scripture apparently was one of the original features of Jesus' preaching of judgment, and must be regarded as "typically Jesus."

The Parable of the Futile Invitation to the Feast (Luke 14:16-24 // Matt. 22:2-14)

The parable of the futile invitation to the feast has been preserved by Luke (14:16-24), by Matthew in a very different version (Matt. 22:2-14), and in the apocryphal Gospel of Thomas (logion 64).[142] Whether it was found in Q is, on the basis of the relatively few verbal agreements between the Matthean and Lukan versions, uncertain and rather improbable.[143] However, because the basic framework of the narrative is the same in both versions, there is undoubtedly a parable of Jesus behind it, the content of which must have approximated the Lukan version; only the double invitation of substitute guests in Luke 14:21-23 appears to be secondary,[144] and the closing saying in v. 24 can scarcely have been part of the original parable.[145] The formulation of the whole text of Luke 14:16-24 betrays the hand of the evangelist.[146]

The crucial statement of the parable on the lips of Jesus can be retrieved in connection with the simple narrative framework at the basis of both the synoptic versions: A wealthy man invites guests to a meal that has been prepared for them, but waits for them in vain. Enraged at their outrageous snub, he has

142. J. A. Fitzmyer regards the version in the Gospel of Thomas as earlier than those in the synoptic tradition, and incorrectly adduces in support of his opinion J. Jeremias and E. Haenchen (*Luke* 2: 1051). P. F. Beatrice also treats the Gospel of Thomas as an independent source ("Ev. Thom." 64, esp. 237–43).

143. A. Harnack, *Sprüche*, 84; A. Weiser, *Knechtsgleichnisse*, 59–60. Most authors, however, take it for granted, without further discussion, that there was a model in Q.

144. Cf. the reconstruction in R. Bultmann, *History of the Synoptic Tradition*, 175; F. Hahn, "Festmahl," 51–65; A. Vögtle, "Gastmahl," 171–90; M. Pesce, "Ricostruzione"; A. Weiser, *Knechtsgleichnisse*, 58–64; H. Weder, *Gleichnisse*, 177–86. All of them, in essence, reach the same conclusion.

145. A. Vögtle, "Gastmahl," 188–90.

146. J. Dupont, *Béatitudes* 2: 264–68. However, I cannot accept Dupont's method and individual examples without qualification.

people brought in at random from the street to sit as unanticipated guests at his table.

This parable, like the saying about the table companions of Abraham, Isaac, and Jacob in the reign of God (Matt. 8:11-12), uses the motif of the eschatological banquet, known to the rabbinic tradition as well, and employed there also in metaphors and parables describing the age to come. It was apparently inspired by Isa. 65:13 and Ps. 23:5.[147] On the basis of that tradition, Jesus' audience must immediately have understood the parable eschatologically and seen the host as an image of God.[148]

Crucial for interpreting this parable is understanding the two groups of guests, those first invited and the unusual substitute guests, as well as the audience's question that follows. Most interpreters see the Pharisees and the pious among the people as the addressees of the parable. Because they had closed their ears to Jesus' call, they could not participate in the eschatological banquet in the reign of God. Instead, it would be offered to the simple people they despised, the toll collectors and sinners in Israel.[149]

However, one essential element in the parable is the succession of invitations (in time) and the difference between the guests who were actually planned for and the substitute guests who were brought in because of the host's wrath. If we were to accept the interpretation of the groups given above, the parable would say that Jesus first addressed his message solely to the pious in Israel, its proper audience, and only turned to the toll collectors, sinners, and uneducated people when the first group rejected him. That, however, contradicts everything we know about him. It was, rather, the second group who from the beginning were his preferred audience.[150]

147. See above, p. 234.
148. Thus rightly Luise Schottroff, "Gastmahl," 197. But I cannot understand how she arrives at the conclusion that it is "inappropriate to the tradition to regard Israel or 'the Jews,' or any particular group of people ('the Pharisees,' 'the faithful') as reflected by the invited guests" (ibid., 198). Surely a brief glance at the tradition proves just the opposite!
149. Interpreting in this sense are, for example, T. W. Manson, Sayings, 130; J. Schmid, Lukas, 246; J. Jeremias, Parables, 179–80; E. Haenchen, "Gleichnis," 153–54; S. Schulz, Q, 400; G. Eichholz, Gleichnisse, 135; J. Dupont, "Invités," 682–91. F. Hahn sees a reference to Jesus' table fellowship with the sinners as model for the eschatological meal ("Festmahl," 69–70). However, such a reference is improbable, since Jesus was not the host at those meals (A. Vögtle, "Gastmahl," 192).
150. This objection to an interpretation in terms of two groups within Israel is old: cf. A. Jülicher, Gleichnisreden 2: 418; M.-J. Lagrange, Luc, 406. Since Ernst Haenchen apparently regards the interpretation here given as a matter of course, this objection is for him an argument against the authenticity of the parable ("Gleichnis," 153–54).

The character of the guests as substitutes who are only brought in out of anger, after those first invited have declined, is by no means a consequence of "modern sensibility," and is also contrary to Luise Schottroff's interpretation, according to which the parable is intended to proclaim God's one-sided preference for the poor ("Gastmahl," 204–5). However, the same reasoning refutes the psychological and existential interpretation of Hans Weder and Wolfgang Harnisch, according to which the two groups represent two aspects of the hearers of the parable, an old and a new attitude (Weder, *Gleichnisse*, 189; Harnisch, *Gleichnis-erzählungen*, 252). According to Harnisch, however, the old and the new attitude do not relate to the eschatological situation that has dawned with Jesus' message of the reign of God, "but to an alternative in concrete attitudes toward time, the loss or gain of present existence" (ibid., 252). Such an interpretation is quite stimulating in terms of a *sensus spiritualis* or *sensus plenior*, but can scarcely be entertained in relationship to the historical Jesus.

Therefore the addressees of the parable cannot be a particular group of people within Israel. Instead, Jesus speaks to the people as a whole. They, the descendants of Abraham, are the invited guests for God's eschatological banquet. In this belief, Jesus shows himself completely united with his people. But should the inconceivable happen, namely, that now, when everything is ready for the banquet, they decline the invitation like the boorish invitees in the parable, they must expect the wrath of God, who will bring in other guests—people they now look upon with scorn, such as the beggars in the streets. Should Israel remove itself, Gentiles will take its place.[151] "The parable is wholly and utterly intended as a word of warning directed to Israel, to bring it to a sense of the seriousness of the situation, with a decision now to be made. Jesus wishes to appeal to the people of Israel with the warning of a possibility that, to their sensibilities, is inconceivable, in order that they may open themselves to his call to salvation and repentance."[152]

In this interpretation, the parable follows admirably after the logia we have already discussed. Like them, it acquires its polemic sting through the provocative contrast between Jews and Gentiles. It is especially close to the word of warning about the table companions of Abraham, Isaac, and Jacob in the reign

151. Interpretations in this sense are given by, for example, M.-J. Lagrange, *Luc,* 407; A. Schlatter, *Lukas,* 338–39; H. Kahlefeld, *Gleichnisse* 1: 99–100; A. Vögtle, "Gastmahl," 194–95. According to Gerhard Lohfink ("Kirche," 81) Jesus formulates "still very indirectly" here and leaves open the question of the identity of the substitute guests. But if Israel is understood to be the first invited, the substitute guests can only be the Gentiles.

152. A. Vögtle, "Gastmahl," 195.

of God (Matt. 8:11-12), which also uses the image of the eschatological banquet. Like this parable, it addresses Israel as a whole, and places before its eyes the warning of a preference to be given to the Gentiles at that very banquet.

The image of the eschatological banquet is probably presumed also in Jesus' saying: "I have come to call not the righteous but sinners" (Mark 2:17; Matt. 9:13). Luke enhances the "call" in his parallel with "to repentance" (Luke 5:32); but in the original sense of this saying καλέω would have meant, quite simply, "call to a meal; invite."[153] The traditional context of the logion (the feast at the home of Levi the toll-collector) also suggests this meaning. With this word, then, Jesus summarizes all his saying and doing as an invitation to the eschatological banquet in the reign of God.[154] The old interpretation of the parable under discussion, which sees the messengers who "at the time for the dinner" call the invitees (Luke 14:17) as representing Jesus himself, is therefore not entirely inaccurate.[155] The saying: "Everything is ready! Come to the banquet!" (cf. Matt. 22:4; Luke 14:17) is an appropriate summary of Jesus' message, and in its content and structure corresponds exactly to the famous summary in Mark 1:15: "The time is fulfilled, and the kingdom of God has come near; repent, and believe in the good news!"[156]

In our parable, the invitees draw upon themselves the righteous wrath of the host, because they all "as if by agreement" (ἀπὸ μιᾶς, scil. γνώμης: Luke 14:18)[157] at the last minute withdraw their acceptance, which they apparently had already given, or which the host had at least firmly counted on.[158] The outrageous and even unreal nature of such a general rebuff cannot be sufficiently emphasized.[159] However improbable and even impossible it is that those invited to such a banquet should all withdraw at the last minute while pretending to be prevented from coming, it appeared to Jesus equally improb-

153. For this meaning of καλέω, attested since Homer, see BAGD 399, s. v. 1 b.

154. The word is interpreted in this sense, for example by A. Schlatter, Matthäus, 308–9; E. Klostermann, Markus, 27; W. Grundmann, Markus, 84; R. Pesch, Markus 1: 166–67; J. Gnilka, Markus 1: 109.

155. Cf. P. Schanz, Lukas, 385; L. Fonck, Parabeln, 395.

156. Special attention should be given here to the logical relationship of the clauses: A statement is followed asyndetically by an imperative. In such cases, in Greek as in German, this always produces a consecutive parataxis. (See M. Reiser, Syntax, 144–45.)

157. Cf. A. Plummer, Lukas, 361; T. Zahn, Lukas, 549 n. 43; BAGD 88, s. v. ἀπό VI.

158. "Apparet morem fuisse, qui nunc etiam multis in locis viget, ut vocati sub ipsam coenae horam iterum appellarentur: quod ipsum observare est apud Josephum in Estheris historia [Ant. 11.242]" (Hugo Grotius, Annotationes zu Lukas 14,17). Cf. Ter. Haut 169; Apul. Metam. III, 12; Luc. Merc. Cond. 14.

159. J. Jeremias, Parables, 178; W. Harnisch, Gleichniserzählungen, 247.

able, even impossible, that Israel, the chosen people, in the moment when "everything is ready," should refuse the invitation and reject the salvation that is offered. The parable apparently was composed and spoken at a time when this improbability threatened to become reality. In it, Jesus vividly illustrated for the people what was now at stake and what consequences a "no" to his invitation would necessarily bring. If they said "no," they would be refusing eschatological salvation, and would already have judged themselves.

> T. W. Manson writes, not inappropriately, at the conclusion of his interpretation of this parable: "Man cannot save himself; but he can damn himself. And it is this latter fact that makes the preaching of Jesus so urgent. For He sees the deepest tragedy of human life, not in the many wrong and foolish things that men do, or the many good and wise things that they fail to accomplish, but in their rejection of God's greatest gift." (*Sayings*, 130)

Thus there is no need for God's wrath to intervene and bring punishment, as happens in the Matthean version (Matt. 22:7); Israel carries out judgment on itself. In the Lukan version, and thus undoubtedly also in Jesus' original parable, the host's anger serves only to bring in substitute guests. This feature of the parable again clearly shows that Jesus' narrative is concerned with Israel alone, and is not intended, for example, as a promise to the Gentiles. Who would want to play the role of substitute guest?

The Slain Galileans and Those Struck by the Falling Tower (Luke 13:1-5)

Reconstruction and Authenticity

The double saying about the slain Galileans and those struck by the falling tower (Luke 13:1-5) is introduced by a narrator's note, according to which some people newly arrived report to Jesus about Pilate's massacre of some Galileans who were in the act of slaughtering animals for sacrifice. Jesus uses this event in the logion that follows as an urgent warning to repentance, underscoring it with a second example corresponding precisely to the first. If we look at the second part of the logion, it reveals a clear tripartite structure: the example is followed first by the rejection of a false lesson that could be drawn from it, and then by the lesson that should, instead, be derived. In the first part of the saying the example given in direct discourse in the second part is replaced by the narrator's note; only the second and third elements of the

saying are given in direct discourse, but formally they are exactly parallel to
the corresponding elements in the second part, and there is a strong verbal
agreement as well. Twice we find an exchange of synonyms (ἁμαρτωλοί/
ὀφειλέται, ὁμοίως/ὡσαύτως). The third element acts like a refrain.

This finding suggests that this logion was originally one of those symmetrically composed double sayings we must regard as unique to Jesus' way of
speaking, and in fact as his own special creation.[160] The evangelist has reformu-
lated the first element in the first part, or first strophe, into a transitional note,
but we can easily recover the original first element of the logion from it, because it must have matched the first element in the second strophe. If we carry
out that minor operation, we obtain the following double saying:

Ἐκεῖνοι οἱ Γαλιλαῖοι ὧν τὸ αἷμα
    Πιλᾶτος ἔμιξεν μετὰ τῶν θυσιῶν αὐτῶν,
δοκεῖτε ὅτι αὐτοὶ ἁμαρτωλοὶ ἐγένοντο
    παρὰ πάντας τοὺς Γαλιλαίους;
οὐχί, λέγω ὑμῖν,
ἀλλ᾽ ἐὰν μὴ μετανοῆτε
πάντες ὁμοίως ἀπολεῖσθε.

ἢ ἐκεῖνοι οἱ δεκαοκτὼ ἐφ᾽ οὓς ἔπεσεν
    ὁ πύργος ἐν τῷ Σιλωὰμ καὶ ἀπέκτεινεν αὐτούς,
δοκεῖτε ὅτι αὐτοὶ ὀφειλέται ἐγένοντο
    παρὰ πάντας τοὺς ἀνθρώπους
    τοὺς κατοικοῦντας Ἰερουσαλήμ;
οὐχί, λέγω ὑμῖν,
ἀλλ᾽ ἐὰν μὴ μετανοῆτε
πάντες ὡσαύτως ἀπολεῖσθε.

Those Galilieans whose blood
    Pilate mingled with their sacrifices,
do you think that they were worse sinners
    than all other Galileans?
No, I tell you;
but unless you repent,
you will all perish as they did.

Or those eighteen who were killed
    when the tower of Siloam fell on them,
do you think that they were worse offenders

160. See above, p. 208–10.

than all the others living in Jerusalem?
No, I tell you;
but unless you repent,
you will all perish just as they did.[161]

This symmetrically constructed double saying reveals a striking formal similarity to the double saying about the Queen of the South and the Ninevites (Matt. 12:41-42 par.). In both cases an idea is varied by the use of examples drawn from history, and the strophes, constructed in strictly parallel form, conclude with a refrain.

Thus the form itself points to the authenticity of the saying. Added to this are Semitisms in the semantics, syntax, and phraseology: "to mix the blood of someone with that of someone else" is an expression attested especially in the rabbinic writings; it does not occur in the LXX.[162] Luke and the early Christian authors, however, usually draw their Semitisms from the LXX. In addition, ὀφειλέτης in the sense of "sinner" is a translator's Semitism not yet encountered in the LXX, but appearing in 1 Enoch 6:3: ὀφειλέτης ἁμαρτίας μεγάλης.[163] The use of the positive instead of a comparative in combination with the preposition παρά in ἁμαρτωλοὶ παρὰ πάντας is apparently the result of Semitic influence.[164]

Finally, the two historical events to which the saying refers also favor its authenticity. An early Christian theologian would have chosen biblical examples.

Content and Meaning

The two events to which Jesus refers in this double saying are not otherwise known to us: Josephus, our principal source for the history of Palestine in the first century, does not mention them. Nevertheless, the events themselves are historically quite probable, and there is no reason to doubt their reality.[165]

---

161. This reconstruction was first presented and defended by G. Schwarz ("Lukas," 121–24). J. Becker indicates the same solution (*Johannes*, 113).

162. Cf. Bill 2: 193; A. Schlatter, *Lukas*, 323; J. Blinzler, "Niedermetzelung," 28–29.

163. Cf. Luke 11:4 // Matt. 6:12. F. Hauck, *TDNT* 5: 561, 565.

164. Cf. BD § 245,3. For παρά after the comparative, see BD § 185,3. I cannot accept the additional Semitisms adduced by G. Schwarz ("Lukas," 124–25).

165. For the slaughter of the Galileans, see M.-J. Lagrange, *Luc*, 378; J. Blinzler, "Niedermetzelung," 38–40; I. H. Marshall, *Luke*, 553; H. Merklein, *Gottesherrschaft*, 127; J. A. Fitzmyer, *Luke* 2: 1006–7.

The Galileans must have been cut down in the Temple, probably on the day before a Passover, while the sacrificial animals were being slaughtered. The note in Luke 13:1 gives the impression that the event had happened at the time it was reported to Jesus, or not long before. In that event, he himself would not have been in Jerusalem at that Passover festival. J. Blinzler deduces a Passover at which Jesus was not present in Jerusalem from John 6:4—7:2, and therefore dates this event to the 14th Nisan of the year 29 c.e.[166] If our reconstruction is correct, it cuts the ground out from under this hypothesis, because the reconstructed text neither presumes temporal proximity to the event mentioned, nor says anything about Jesus' personal presence or absence.

The tower near the pool of Siloam that fell and buried eighteen people was apparently part of the ancient city wall, which ran eastward above the pool and there bent southward.[167]

Jesus mentions these events, and first fends off a conclusion that apparently was often drawn from such occurrences: that the victims must have been particularly great sinners, since suffering and misfortune are thought to be the result of extraordinary guilt and sinfulness.[168] In a highly skilled and effective rhetorical turn, this conclusion is clothed in a question introduced by "Do you think. . . ." The rhetorical effect is further strengthened by the use of a *pendens* construction that permits the theme of the sentence to be placed at the beginning, for full impact.[169]

There follows the surprising and provocative lesson that Jesus himself wishes to have drawn from such events: Those who do not repent will perish just as these unfortunates did. Repentance, in fact, is demanded of everyone, without exception, be they great or little sinners, righteous or godless, and it is the same for all. Thus Jesus, with his "No, I tell you," is not interested merely in an utter rejection of the idea that misfortune must be the consequence of special guilt. Instead, he wants to say that the question of sins committed, their number and weight, has become meaningless in face of the decision that faces everyone. Every person is confronted with the same decision: to repent or not. But if they do not, they will "all perish just as did" the victims in the Temple and those crushed at Siloam.

---

166. J. Blinzler, "Niedermetzelung," 31–32.

167. Josephus, *Bell.* 5, 145. I. H. Marshall, *Luke,* 554.

168. For this idea, see Job 4:7; 22:4-5; Sir. 38:9-10; John 9:1-2. Str-B. 1: 495–96; 2: 193–97; A. Schlatter, *Johannes,* 222–23 (with examples from Josephus). J. A. Fitzmyer, *Luke* 2: 1007, also refers to 1QapGen XX, 16–29.

169. For *pendens* constructions in Greek, see M. Reiser, *Syntax,* 16. For the equivalent in Hebrew, see Walter Groß, *Pendenskonstruktion.*

This threatening statement used to be popularly referred to the catastrophe of 70 c.e., in which interpreters saw the warning fulfilled.[170] But apart from the fact that this interpretation does not take "all" seriously, a reference to perishing at the coming eschatological judgment of God is much more probable, especially since ἀπολεῖσθαι/ἀπώλεια is properly a *terminus technicus* with reference to that event.[171] Hence the conditional formula, "unless you repent . . ." does not represent merely a "tiny glimmer of hope,"[172] but explicitly says that those who repent will be preserved before the judgment that condemns. In this conviction, Jesus stands well within the tradition of prophetic preaching of repentance. But what did "repentance" mean for them, and what did it mean for Jesus? Why is it the same for "all," both righteous and sinners?

Excursus
Repentance in the Eschatological Thought of Formative Judaism, the Baptizer, and Jesus

---

For the preexilic prophets, repentance meant turning away from sinful deeds and returning to YHWH.[173] They demand this repentance from the nation as a whole, but also from each individual.[174] The rabbis, on the other hand, understand repentance concretely as turning away from violations of the law and returning to the Torah.[175] This interpretation should not be too quickly condemned as externalization and decline from the heights of the ancient prophetic idea of repentance; instead, it should be seen as a justified development

---

170. Cf., for example, Hugo Grotius, *Annotationes zu Lukas* 13:3, 5; P. Schanz, *Lukas*, 366; A. Plummer, *Luke*, 338–39; M.-J. Lagrange, *Luc*, 380.

171. Cf., for example, *Ps. Sol.* 15:12,13; 1 Enoch 98:9,16. For ἀπώλεια, see *Ps. Sol.* 14:9; 15:10 (see above, p. 47); 1 Enoch 5:5; 98:10; 99:4. Cf. above, pp. 109–10. This interpretation is supported also by J. Schmid, *Lukas*, 229; I. H. Marshall, *Luke*, 554.

172. J. Becker, *Johannes*, 88.

173. Cf. E. Würthwein, *TDNT* 4: 985; H. W. Wolff, "Umkehr," 145–49; J. A. Soggin, *THAT* 2: 888–89.

174. E. K. Dietrich, *Umkehr*, 117–19. However, it is worth noting that the earlier prophets generally presume "that repentance should occur, but has not" (H. W. Wolff, "Botschaft," 549). They almost never use the imperative "repent" (cf. ibid., 548–50). It is found in Isa. 31:6; Jer. 3:12,14,22; 18:11; Ezek. 18:32; 33:11; Hos. 14:2, and even in Jer. 25:5; 35:15; in Zech. 1:4 it summarizes the message of the prophets. The call for repentance is fundamentally associated with a promise (H. W. Wolff, "Umkehr," 141–45).

175. E. Würthwein, *TDNT* 4: 995–99.

of that idea; once the book of the Torah had been acknowledged as the revealed will of God, this was the necessary conclusion to be drawn. We can see the beginnings of this development even in the postexilic prophets, especially Ezekiel,[176] and just as in Neh. 9:26,29, so also for the author of the Book of Jubilees, repentance and turning to God "with all their heart and with all their soul and with all their might" (*Jub.* 1:15; cf. 1:23) and "returning to the way of righteousness" by seeking the laws and the commandments (*Jub.* 23:26) are one and the same.[177] The Book of Jubilees, like the rabbis, is familiar with the repeated repentance of individuals, which is to be carried out especially on the Day of Atonement (*Jub.* 5:17-18)[178]—what we would now be more inclined to call "doing penance"—as well as the end time repentance of a part of the nation before the arrival of eschatological salvation (*Jub.* 1:23; 23:16, 26). This motif is derived from Deut. 4:30.[179] "Repentance" is here distinguished from "doing penance" as a unique act of reorientation of one's whole life.

For the Essenes at Qumran, the motif of end time repentance acquired great significance. As in the Book of Jubilees, so in the Temple Scroll the (eschatological?) time of salvation begins with the nation's repentance and turning to the Torah (LIX, 9–10). This could also be connected with the fact that the Essenes knew the traditions found in the Book of Jubilees, and apparently emerged out of the Hasidic circles in which the Book of Jubilees also originated.[180] They call themselves the "converted of Israel,"[181] who have established the "covenant of repentance" (CD XIX, 16) by turning away from the "sin of Jacob" and thus preserving the "covenant of God" (CD XX, 17). For the Essenes of Qumran turning away from sin, "turning back to the Torah of Moses," and entry into the order of their community were all connected, and meant for them nothing other than the biblical "repentance and turning to God."[182] And of course,

176. Cf. ibid., 988–89.
177. Cf. 2 Kgs. 23:3,25. Therefore it is wrong (as frequently happens) to overemphasize the corresponding difference between the two versions of the fifth of the Eighteen Benedictions, "Bring us back to you, YHWH," and "Bring us back, our Father, to your Torah," as, for example, in E. K. Dietrich, *Umkehr,* 358–59; W. Schrage, *Ethik,* 44.
178. See above, p. 73.
179. See above, pp. 69–70.
180. Martin Hengel understands the Hasidim as a "penitential movement" (*Judaism and Hellenism* 1: 179–80).
181. CD IV, 2; VI, 5; VIII, 16; XIX, 29.
182. Cf. 1QS I, 16–17; II, 25—III, 1. G. Jeremias, *Lehrer,* 328–29; H.-J. Fabry, *Wurzel ŠÛB,* 25–68. "Turning back to the Torah of Moses" CD XV, 9, 12; XVI, 1–2, 4–5; 1QS V, 8. "Return to the covenant community": 1QS V, 22. Cf. CD XX, 5. "Repentance and turning to God": CD XX, 23; 1QH XVI, 17; 4QDibHam V, 13.

according to the conviction of the Essenes, on the "day of vengeance" God will preserve only those who have repented in this concrete and comprehensive sense.[183]

Apart from the Book of Jubilees and the writings of Qumran, the theme of repentance, especially that of unique, decisive repentance in view of the eschatological judgment or salvation, plays an astonishingly small role in early Jewish writings.[184] Only twice, and very much in passing, 4 Ezra mentions the possibility of repentance until the day of death.[185] The opportunity for Israel's end time repentance, or at least that of a part of the nation, is indicated by *As. Mos.* 1:18 ("day of repentance"), *T. Dan* 6:4, and 1 Enoch 50:2, but without any real clarity about how this repentance fits within the overall eschatological conception of the individual work.[186]

Especially noticeable is the lack of any direct demand for repentance such as we find, in connection with the proclamation of the day of YHWH, in Zephaniah, Joel, and Malachi.[187] The author of the Epistle of Enoch can scarcely get enough of woes pronounced over sinners,[188] but not once calls them to repentance. Only the fourth Sibyl issues a peremptory demand for repentance in view of the eschatological judgment with fire in the world holocaust, and calls for the washing of the whole body in the river.[189]

How can we explain these findings? First, we must certainly point to the purpose and the audience of a major portion of the early Jewish literary corpus. Like the Book of Enoch, these are intended to be consolatory writings, λόγοι εὐλογίας for the righteous,[190] and the proclamation of judgment serves also for the consolation and satisfaction of the righteous, because according to

---

183. Cf., for example, 1QS X, 19–21. H.-J. Fabry, *Wurzel ŠÛB*, 27–28, 69–71.

184. However, we also have only a handful of citations for repeated, constantly demanded penance. Cf. W. Bousset and H. Greßmann, *Religion,* 389–90; E. Sjöberg, *Gott,* 212–22.

185. 4 Ezra 7:82; 9:12 (see above, pp. 117–18).

186. See above, pp. 68–69, 85–86, 93. Cf. also R. J. Bauckham, *Jude, 2 Peter,* 312–13, with reference, in addition, to the well-known discussion between Eliezer ben Hyrcanus and Joshua ben Hananiah (Str-B. 1: 162–64). For the role of repentance in the Deuteronomistic conception of history, see above, pp. 89–90, on the Testaments. The preexilic prophets know that God will give another opportunity for repentance before the general judgment (cf. E. Würthwein, *TDNT* 4: 987); so do the rabbis. According to *Mekh. Y.* on Exod. 15:6 (Lauterbach 2: 39–40), God gave both the "generation of the Flood" and the "men of the tower" time for repentance, "but they did not repent."

187. Zeph. 2:1-3; Joel 2:10-14; Mal. 3:1-7.

188. See above, pp. 63–64.

189. *Sib. Or.* 4:162–70. See above, pp. 100–101.

190. Cf. 1 Enoch 1:1, quoted above, p. 51.

early Jewish conceptions that judgment would strike only the sinners.[191] It is true that these writings contain parenesis for the righteous, but apparently their authors had little interest in the repentance of sinners.

A second point may be added. The call for repentance is a typical element of prophetic proclamation and has its natural Sitz im Leben in the oral preaching of the prophets. In the writings of formative Judaism we are dealing with purely literary productions; unlike the prophetic books of the Old Testament, they have no oral preaching behind them. An indication of the fact that formative Judaism also assigned the theme of repentance and the call for conversion in view of the final judgment to oral preaching, and thought of it as entirely a prophetic concern, can perhaps be seen in the fact that it made Noah a prophet who, in face of God's imminent judgment, called "the generation of the Flood" to repentance.[192] This is all the more remarkable because the Flood served as the type of the eschatological judgment.[193]

This also explains the value acquired by the theme of repentance in the preaching of the Baptizer and of Jesus. The call to repentance belonged to their role as prophets of the end time who, each in his own way and with differing emphases, announced God's end time activity, bringing with it salvation and judgment.

Like Noah, in early Jewish tradition, in face of the approaching Flood, and like the Jewish Sibyl in view of the impending world holocaust, the Baptizer calls for repentance before "the wrath to come." He demands "fruit[194] worthy of repentance" (Matt. 3:8), and offers "a baptism of repentance for the forgiveness of sins" (Mark 1:4). Concretely, by "repentance" the Baptizer would have meant nothing other than that the whole early Jewish community, and thus his audience, should turn away from a sinful life and return to the Torah as the will of God, which it was their task to fulfill.[195] In this action, the "fruit" is the result of repentance.[196] The trees that will be cut down because they "do

191. See above, p. 157.
192. See above, p. 103.
193. See above, pp. 59–60.
194. The singular καρπός is to be read collectively in the sense of "yield," and is substantially equivalent to the plural in Luke (Luke 3:8). A. Schlatter, Matthäus, 72; H./ v. S., 173.
195. This is the interpretation also of E. Brandenburger, TRE 12 (1984): 469; O. Böcher, TRE 17 (1986): 176–77. Cf. also E. Lohmeyer, Urchristentum, 63–64.
196. Similarly, in 4 Ezra 6:28 the "fruit" of truth is the fulfillment of the law. Psalm 1:3, of course, also speaks of "fruit," but there the word does not refer to the doing of the Law, but to happiness and success. 4 Ezra 3:20; 9:31-32; 2 Bar. 32:1 speak of the

not bear good fruit" (Matt. 3:10 // Luke 3:9) are the part of Israel that does not live in obedience to the Torah as the will of God. Apparently the Baptizer can include the Pharisees within this accusation, which indicates that he is not satisfied with their interpretation and application of the Torah. The decision for repentance is sealed through baptism, combined with a confession of sins; therefore this is called a "baptism of repentance" (βάπτισμα τῆς μετανοίας).[197] Through this baptism, the converted person is received into the number of those who need not fear the coming judgment.[198]

> That the "fruit" of repentance demanded by the Baptizer was nothing other than "repentance itself" (Heinz Schürmann, *Lukas* 1: 182) is as unlikely as the thesis that his reference to fruit to be produced meant simply the acceptance of his baptism (Helmut Merklein, "Umkehrpredigt," 36–37). The fact that Merklein understands "repentance" in the Baptizer's sense not as a turning to God and God's law, but as "radical surrender of all assurance of salvation" (ibid., 37) results from his underestimation of the aspect of salvation in the Baptizer's preaching (see above, pp. 191–93).

In the Jesus tradition we find the key word *repentance* as a once-for-all, decisive act of reorientation only in three logia that can be regarded as authentic: the double saying about the slain Galileans and those struck by the falling tower (Luke 13:1-5), the woes over Chorazin and Bethsaida (Matt. 11:21 // Luke 10:13), and the saying about the Ninevites (Matt. 12:41 // Luke 11:32).[199] If even the Ninevites repented at the preaching of Jonah, how much more must Israel repent at his preaching! And if his miracles would have been enough to move cities like Tyre and Sidon to repentance, how much more should his Galilean homeland have allowed itself to be won over by those miracles to accept his message! Jesus uses the wicked slaughter of the Galileans in the Temple and the misfortune at the pool of Siloam as the occasion for an urgent call for repentance. The crucial question should not be: "What sins must those

---

fruit that the Law brings to the heart. It is not entirely clear what these passages mean by fruit. For the plantation of Israel and the fruit it brings in *Bib. Ant.* 28:4, see above, p. 174. For the metaphorical use of "fruit" generally, see F. Hauck, *TDNT* 3: 614–16; E. Lohmeyer, "Frucht," 391–95.

197. For the *genitivus qualitatis*, see BD § 165; H./v. S. § 162.

198. See above, pp. 185–86.

199. Cf. H. Merklein, "Umkehrpredigt," 39–41. A fundamental questioning of the authenticity of Jesus' call for repentance, as expressed by Meinrad Limbeck ("Verkündigung," 36–37) and E. P. Sanders (*Jesus*, 106–13), is thus unjustified.

unfortunates have committed?" but: "Will I perish in the same way before God's approaching judgment?" In light of the decision facing Israel as a whole, the difference between big and little sinners, and even the difference between the righteous and sinners, is meaningless. The repentance demanded is the same for all: "Unless you repent, you will *all* perish just as they did!"

These three logia show that Jesus interprets repentance differently from the Baptizer. While for the Baptizer repentance still meant turning back to the Torah, and thus received its concrete content from the Torah itself, Jesus' idea of repentance was turning to him and his message: it is this message, then, that supplies the content of the repentance he demands.

From a certain point of view, this interpretation of repentance is comparable to that of the community at Qumran. Just as, for them, repentance ultimately meant joining their community, so also for Jesus the ultimate consequence of repentance was discipleship.[200] Certainly it appears that Jesus, in contrast to Qumran, seldom used the word *repentance,* even in this sense. "'Repentance' is a collective term used by the evangelists primarily to summarize what Jesus wanted people to do. Jesus himself, however, spoke with differentiating concreteness about the life to which people were now being called, namely, to become poor as described in the Beatitudes and to invest themselves totally as described in the individual directives of the Sermon on the Mount."[201] Like the evangelists who could appeal to Jesus himself, however, we are also entitled to summarize Jesus' ethical demands in the word *repentance.*[202]

The call for repentance in the Old Testament and Second Temple Judaism is ordinarily grounded on a threatened catastrophe, or the eschatological judgment. The people's repentance averts the catastrophe and thus makes possible

200. Gerd Jeremias emphasizes the differences more sharply, because for Jesus, unlike the Teacher of Righteousness, repentance is said to be "a consequence of the promise of salvation" (*Lehrer,* 344). But, as we have seen, that is precisely *not* the case in the certainly authentic logia that contain this key word.

201. L. Goppelt, *Theology* 1: 77. Helmut Merklein also points to the Sermon on the Mount for the content of Jesus' concept of repentance ("Umkehrpredigt," 44). The interpretation in the corresponding chapter of Joachim Jeremias's *Theology* (1: 152–58) appears to me too vague and one-sided. Ultimately, according to him, repentance, for Jesus, was "simply trusting in the grace of God" (ibid., 156).

202. On this, see the fine discussion by L. Goppelt, *Theology* 1: 77–78. He entitles his third chapter "Repentance as Demand (The Ethics of Jesus)," and the fourth "Repentance as Gift of the Reign of God: The New Order of Salvation." See also the two chapters in A. Schlatter's *Geschichte des Christus:* "The Decision Jesus Demanded," and "The Repentance of the Faithful" (pp. 169–96).

the salvation God has planned for them.[203] In light of these three logia, the same seems to be true of Jesus' preaching of repentance. All three speak of repentance in view of the eschatological judgment. However, in his familiar summary (1:15) Mark founds Jesus' call for repentance not on his proclamation of judgment, but on his announcement of salvation: "The time is fulfilled, and the kingdom of God has come near! (Therefore:) Repent, and believe in the good news!"[204] Exegetes are agreed that Mark accurately summarizes Jesus' preaching in this verse. Must we, then, in Jesus' message separate the "demand for repentance" associated with the threat of judgment from the "call for decision" founded on the proclamation of salvation?[205]

This terminological distinction by Jürgen Becker undoubtedly contains an accurate observation. But it separates judgment and salvation as if they were not two sides of the same coin, two aspects of the one eschatological event that, according to early Jewish perception, always brings both things with it. Judgment is the obverse of salvation, and its necessary precondition. Certainly it makes a difference whether the call to repentance is founded on approaching judgment or approaching salvation. The warning about judgment appeals to fear, while the promise of salvation speaks to human hope. It is precisely the customary association of the call to repentance with the proclamation of judgment, which still constituted the basic framework of the Baptizer's preaching, that may have been the reason for Jesus to avoid the concept of "repentance" to some degree, although it was entirely apt for the description of what he demanded of Israel. Jesus' preaching was sustained by the conviction that the repentance of the individual and of the whole nation should not so much aim at avoiding catastrophe as at gaining God's salvation. Thus for him, in contrast to the Baptizer, the offer of salvation stands in the foreground of his preaching. The central focus of his speech and action is not judgment and the way to avoid it, but the reign of God and how to gain it; it is not fear of judgment that should move Israel to repentance, but the fascination of the reign of God. Therefore this message could not be better summarized than in Mark 1:15.[206] But when it met with rejection, Jesus had to point to the reverse of the medal.

---

203. Cf. E. K. Dietrich, *Umkehr*, 111–14, 127–33, 272–77, 418–25. For the association of the prophetic call to repentance with a promise of salvation (Jer. 3:12, 14, 22; Joel 2:13; Isa. 44:22), see H. W. Wolff, "Umkehr," 142–45.
204. For the logical structure of this sentence, see above, p. 244. Cf. Isa. 44:22.
205. Thus J. Becker, *TRE* 7 (1981): 448–49.
206. Cf. R. Schnackenburg, *Gottes Herrschaft,* 57–58.

The Harvest and the Laborers
(Mark 4:29; Matt. 9:37 // Luke 10:2;
Matt. 10:14 and parallels)

The similitude of the seed growing by itself (Mark 4:26-29) ends with the prospect of the harvest: "But when the grain is ripe, at once [the "person," that is, the farmer, cf. v. 26] puts in the sickle, because the harvest has come (ὅτι παρέστηκεν ὁ θερισμός)."[207] This similitude from Mark's special material is illuminated and explained by means of a logion from Q that also speaks about harvest: "The harvest is plentiful, but the laborers are few; therefore ask the Lord of the harvest to send out laborers into his harvest" (Matt. 9:37-38 // Luke 10:2).[208] Like Hebrew קָצִיר and English *harvest*, Greek θερισμός can describe the time for reaping, the work of reaping, and the yield that is expected or actually realized, that is, the fruit, grain, and so forth, to be harvested. Thus in Mark 4:29 it refers to the time for harvesting, but in the logion it refers first to the yield to be expected ("the harvest is great"), and then to the work of harvesting ("send out laborers into the harvest").

In the Old Testament harvest is an image for the destroying judgment on Israel or the nations.[209] In Joel 3:13 the harvest—apparently the grape harvest[210]—and the treading of the wine press is an image for the bloody judgment on the nations, on the day of YHWH, and it follows immediately after the image of the judgment scene in the valley of "Jehoshaphat."

In early Jewish literature the content of the image shifts. In accord with the twofold aspect of the eschatological event, 4 Ezra 4:28, 32 and *2 Bar.* 70:2 speak of the harvest of the evil and the good.[211] According to the eschatological oracle

207. For the authenticity of the similitude, see R. Stuhlmann, "Beobachtungen," 161–62; R. Pesch, *Markus* 1: 258.

208. This logion is preserved identically, except for a minute detail in the word order, in Matthew and Luke. There is no reason to doubt its authenticity (F. Hahn, *Mission,* 32 n. 3). J. Gnilka assigns it to the authors of Q, because it fits the situation of the Sayings Source (*Matthäus,* 353). It is true that it fits the conditions of the Sayings Source, but that is no reason to think that it was first spoken in that situation. It fits the situation of Jesus just as well (cf. S. Schulz, *Q,* 410; I. H. Marshall, *Luke,* 416). For the link between Mark 4:29 and Matt. 9:37 // Luke 10:2, see C. H. Dodd, *Parables,* 178–80; V. Taylor, *Mark,* 266; W. Grundmann, *Lukas,* 208.

209. Cf. Isa. 17:5; 18:4-5; 24:13; 63:1-6; Jer. 51:33; Hos. 6:11; Mic. 4:12-13; Joel 3:13 [Heb. 4:13].

210. Cf. H. W. Wolff, *Joel,* 97. Therefore the LXX correctly translates קָצִיר at this point with τρυγητός.

211. Cf. the rabbinic parable of the quarrel among straw, chaff, and stubble, *Midr. Shir.* on Song 7:3 par. (see above, pp. 178–80). According to *Midr. Shir.* on Song 8:14, the grain harvest is an image of the redemption of Israel. Joel 3:13 [Heb. 4:13] is adduced as scriptural evidence (see Str-B. 1: 672).

in *Sib. Or.* 2:154–76, "the [time of the] harvest of articulate men" is coming, when women will cease to bear children; "the gathering together is near," when false prophets will come forth, and Beliar will appear and do many signs.[212] Here the harvest (τὸ θέρος) and the gathering (ἡ συναίρεσις) are images for the eschatological event as a whole.

It also stands for this in the Baptizer's similitude of winnowing (Matt. 3:12 // Luke 3:17) and in the remainder of the New Testament.[213] And so this image appears in Jesus' similitude and logion as well for God's action at the end of time, which means both salvation and judgment. "The harvest is the gathering in of those human beings who are destined for the reign of God and have decided in its favor, and the removal of those others who have rejected it."[214] But while the Baptizer put the accent on the catastrophic aspect of the eschatological harvest, Jesus, in both the similitude and the logion, emphasizes only the salvific side. The other side of the matter should not be forgotten, but neither is it stressed. The call, παρέστηκεν ὁ θερισμός, is for him a joyful shout and corresponds exactly to πεπλήρωται ὁ καιρὸς καὶ ἤγγικεν ἡ βασιλεία τοῦ θεοῦ (Mark 1:15).[215] For Jesus, that time is no longer in the future, but has begun with his own activity. "See how the fields are ripe for harvesting!" (John 4:35). Now he needs helpers who will work with him to bring in the harvest.

As coworkers, not only as messengers, Jesus sends out his disciples[216] "to participate by confronting the whole people, along with him, with the offer of approaching salvation and with the proclamation of the final judgment."[217] Their task, like his, is "to proclaim the reign of God and to heal,"[218] but they are to abandon any place that rejects them and shake its dust from their feet.[219]

---

212. *Sib. Or.* 2:164–68. For more on this oracle, see above, p. 104.

213. Cf. Matt. 13:30, 39; John 4:35-38; Rev. 14:15.

214. W. Grundmann, *Lukas*, 208.

215. For the affective placement of the words in these clauses, see M. Reiser, *Syntax*, 69–70, 93.

216. F. Hahn, *Mission*, 32.

217. M. Hengel, *Charismatic Leader*, 73, where this is formulated as a question. Cf. R. Pesch, "Voraussetzungen," 26–28: "The pre-Easter mission of Jesus' disciples." For the historicity of the sending of the disciples, see M. Hengel, *Charismatic Leader*, 73–74; H. Schürmann, *Lukas* 1: 505; R. Pesch, *Markus* 1: 330–31; I. H. Marshall, *Luke*, 350; J. Gnilka, *Matthäus*, 370–71. P. Hoffmann considers a special, unique sending out of the disciples unlikely (*Studien*, 262–63).

218. Luke 9:2; cf. Matt. 10:7 (Q!); Mark 6:12-13.

219. Cf. Matt. 10:14; Mark 6:11; Luke 9:5; 10:10-11. For the reconstruction of the Q version from Matt. 10:14 and Luke 9:5, see P. Hoffmann, *Studien*, 268–72. S. Schulz, on the other hand, sees the Q version preserved instead in Luke 10:10, 11a (*Q*, 407).

The gesture of shaking off dust apparently means that all community is effectively broken off.[220] Thus the place itself is regarded as delivered over to judgment.

Unfortunately, there is no other record of this gesture that would shed further light on it. Since the work of John Lightfoot (*Horae Hebraicae,* on Matt. 10:14, pp. 331–32) it has been customary to point out that gentile land was regarded as unclean for Jews. Shaking off the dust meant that one equated the place in question with gentile territory (cf. Str-B. 1: 571; M.-J. Lagrange, *Marc,* 153–54; Rudolf Pesch, *Markus* 1: 329–30). But we have no example to show that the gesture was really practiced in this sense—for example, on leaving gentile territory. The gesture itself is not even clear. Adolf Schlatter sees it not as a shaking of the feet, but as a shaking off from one's clothes of the dust stirred up in departing (*Matthäus,* 334). However, that interpretation is not suggested even by the Matthean formulation τὸν κονιορτὸν τῶν ποδῶν (Matt. 10:14).

The Twelve as Judges of the Twelve Tribes of Israel
(Matt. 19:28 // Luke 22:28-30)

The logion about the eschatological judgment of the Twelve over the tribes of Israel (Matt. 19:28 // Luke 22:28-30) has been retained by Matthew in a preexisting context, while Luke has given it a new setting. The common source, at least for the last clause, was apparently Q. A synopsis gives the following picture:

Matthew 19:28	Luke 22:28, 30b
ἀμὴν λέγω ὑμῖν ὅτι ὑμεῖς οἱ ἀκολουθήσαντές μοι,	ὑμεῖς δέ ἐστε οἱ διαμεμενηκότες μετ᾽ ἐμοῦ ἐν τοῖς πειρασμοῖς μου·
ἐν τῇ παλιγγενεσίᾳ, ὅταν καθίσῃ ὁ υἱὸς τοῦ ἀνθρώπου ἐπὶ θρόνου δόξης αὐτοῦ, καθήσεσθε καὶ ὑμεῖς ἐπὶ δώδεκα θρόνους κρίνοντες τὰς δώδεκα φυλὰς τοῦ Ἰσραήλ.	καὶ καθήσεσθε ἐπὶ θρόνων τὰς δώδεκα φυλὰς κρίνοντες τοῦ Ἰσραήλ.

220. J. Jeremias, *Theology* 1: 238. Cf. H. J. Cadbury, "Dust," 269–71.

Amen, I tell you:

| You who have followed me, | You are those who have stood by me in my trials; |

at the renewal of all things,
when the Son of man is seated
on the throne of his glory,
you will also sit on twelve thrones,
judging the twelve tribes of Israel.

you will sit on thrones
judging the twelve tribes of Israel.[221]

In this synopsis, part of the Lukan text that has no counterpart in Matthew has been omitted: "and I confer on you, just as my Father has conferred on me, a kingdom, so that you may eat and drink at my table in my kingdom" (Luke 22:29-30a). This could once have been an independent logion. In any case, it was first introduced at this point by Luke, although it does not fit well, thematically speaking, with what follows.[222] Luke eliminated "twelve" before "thrones," probably because he did not wish to have Jesus speaking about "twelve" thrones at his last meal with his disciples, at a time when hints had already been given about the identity of the betrayer (Luke 22:21-23). Judas is to be excluded from the promise.

It is difficult to make a judgment about the tradition history of the first part of the logion. The only word common to the two versions is ὑμεῖς. One can see a certain commonality of meaning in "you who have followed me" and "you . . . who have stood by me in my trials," but on the whole the common features are restricted to the obvious underlying idea that the promise uttered here rests on the special relationship between Jesus and his disciples. Since, in addition, the first part of each version betrays, in vocabulary and phraseology, the hand of the individual evangelist, it is difficult to reject the suggestion that neither of them was in Q.[223] Thus for Q we can reckon with certainty only on the words: "you will sit on twelve thrones, judging the twelve tribes of Israel." This saying can also be imagined as a separate logion handed down in isolation, which Matthew and Luke provided with an introduction when incorporating it into their gospels in order to fit it into the individual context.

Thus, although we do not know the original context of this promise, it is clear that Jesus gave it to the group of twelve that he himself had created, and

221. Cf. J. Dupont, "Logion," 361. This fundamental study has received far too little attention in German-language literature.
222. Cf. J. Dupont, "Logion," 359-60.
223. J. Dupont, "Logion," 361-68, with more precise argumentation. For other suggestions for reconstruction, see M. Trautmann, *Zeichenhafte Handlungen*, 192-96.

through which he advances his claim over all of Israel.[224] The number twelve "looked back to the old constitution of Israel and also forward to the final shape of the messianic community.[225] The twelve messengers were appointed for the whole of Israel, for all its tribes, and the fruits of their labor will be the replacement of the present tiny and broken community by the complete, new Israel."[226] The cooperation of the Twelve in the eschatological "harvest," however, also meant, as we have seen above,[227] that they would have a role in the eschatological judgment, which is the unavoidable reverse side of the coming of eschatological salvation. Every place whose dust the disciples have shaken from their feet is subject to judgment; thus it is only right that Jesus should also promise the Twelve that they will cooperate in the eschatological judging of Israel. Their cooperation is only the final "official act" of a set of duties that they are now already carrying out, when they, like Jesus himself and under his authority, proclaim salvation and judgment.

This interpretation suggests that we should intimate that Jesus himself is the presider at the judgment here contemplated, but the logion says nothing about who presides. Strictly speaking, it does not even permit us to say that the Twelve "sit in" as members of the judicial panel. However, since its apparent intention is only to speak of the Twelve and their eschatological office, we need not strain our brains too greatly in imagining what role Jesus himself planned for them.

This interpretation presumes that κρίνειν is to be understood here not in an expanded sense as "ruling" or "reigning," but in its usual meaning as "judging," "passing judgment."[228] Against the meaning "rule" in this passage is a

224. For the earthly Jesus's having appointed the Twelve, see K. H. Rengstorf, *TDNT* 2: 325–26; J. Jeremias, *Theology* 1: 233–34; M. Trautmann, *Zeichenhafte Handlungen,* 179–85.

225. Instead of a "messianic community," we would do better to speak of the "eschatological" community (see above, Introduction). The eschatological reference of the number twelve was probably connected with the early Jewish idea about the ten lost tribes of Israel, who would return at the end of time (A. Schlatter, *Matthäus,* 583–84; J. Jeremias, *Theology* 1: 234–35). For this idea, see P. Volz, *Eschatologie,* 347–48, 378; W. Bousset and H. Gressmann, *Religion,* 237–38; C. Maurer, *TDNT* 9: 248.

226. A. Schlatter, *Geschichte,* 322. For the symbolic function of the Twelve, cf. also G. Lohfink, *Jesus and Community,* 9–12.

227. See above, pp. 257–58.

228. Among those who argue for the meaning "rule," "reign," in Matt. 19:28 // Luke 22:30 are Hugo Grotius, *Annotationes zu Mt* 19:28; F. Büchsel, *TDNT* 3: 923; T. Zahn, *Matthäus,* 604–5; M.-J. Lagrange, *Matthieu,* 382; E. Klostermann, *Matthäusevangelium,* 158–59; W. G. Kümmel, *Verheißung,* 41; G. Bornkamm, *Jesus,* 209–10 n. 13; R. H. Gundry, *Matthew,* 393; J. A. Fitzmyer, *Luke* 2: 1419. For the meaning "judge," see G.

basic rule of semantics, according to which a word ordinarily appears in its principal meaning. Another meaning deviating from the principal meaning must be indicated by the context.[229] Now, the principal meaning of κρίνω is undoubtedly "judge." Only in rare cases indicated by the context can it also take on the transferred meaning of "rule."[230] In the present case there is no reason to deviate from the principal meaning. On the contrary, collegial rule would be a highly unusual thing for Judaism, but groups of judges were part of the everyday picture of Jewish judicial procedure in the first century. We know of groups of three, seven, twenty-three, and—in the case of the Sanhedrin—seventy judges.[231]

It may be that in this logion Jesus even addresses a tradition that we encountered in the first part of this study.[232] We can summarize it in a tannaitic midrash on Dan. 7:9. There, as in this passage, there is talk of "thrones" in an eschatological context; on them sit a group of judges headed by the "Ancient of Days," to judge the world's empires.[233] The midrash interprets this judgment in terms of the eschatological judgment on the gentile nations, and on the basis of Isa. 3:14 it sees those associated with the "Ancient of Days" as "the great ones of Israel." We cannot exclude the possibility that Jesus knew this exegetical tradition on Dan. 7:9 and alluded to it.[234] In that case, his saying would acquire an additional acerbity through the contrast: Judgment will be imposed not on the gentile nations, but on Israel itself, and those associated with the highest judge will not be "the great ones of Israel," but the Twelve

---

Schrenk, *Weissagung,* 17–18; M. Trautmann, *Zeichenhafte Handlungen,* 197–98. According to J. Gnilka (*Matthäus* 2: 171–72) this is about cooperating in a judgment of condemnation. But the thrones do not fit that picture. Undecided are S. Schulz, *Q,* 333, and I. H. Marshall, *Luke,* 818. J. Schmid (*Matthäus,* 283; *Lukas,* 330) and J. Dupont ("Logion," 378, 381) propose for Matthew the reading "judge," and for Luke the meaning "rule." For Jesus, J. Dupont supposes that the meaning was "judge" ("Logion," 389).

229. For the problem of lexical and actual, principal and auxiliary meanings, see W. Schmidt, *Lexikalische und aktuelle Bedeutung,* esp. 22–30. He defines "principal meaning" as "the actual meaning which is initially apprehended as the socially most important meaning at a given time when the word appears in isolation, that is, at the level of the *langue,* in the consciousness of the majority of speakers of the language" (ibid., 26).

230. See above, p. 134.

231. Cf. *T. Sanh.* 7.1. E. Schürer and Geza Vermes, *History* 2: 186–88; G. Stemberger, *Judentum,* 69; G. Alon, "Those Appointed for Money," esp. 385–90.

232. See above, pp. 137–38.

233. See above, p. 38.

234. J. Dupont, in particular, has emphasized this point ("Logion," 381–86). He describes this suggestion, however, as "daring" ("téméraire") (ibid., 386).

chosen by Jesus! In any case, however, Jesus' saying may well represent an allusion to Dan. 7:9, for only there, or in reference to that passage, does the early
Jewish tradition speak of a group of judges at the last judgment.[235] There is a
verbal link through the plural "thrones," which was also the occasion for the
midrash just mentioned.[236]

There is no reason to doubt the authenticity of this saying.[237] "This promise
to the 'twelve disciples' could hardly have originated after Easter: after the betrayal by Judas it is hard to imagine that a promise would have been invented
which also assigns him rule over Israel as one of the Twelve."[238] As we have
shown, it fits the assignment Jesus had given his disciples in sending them out
to the "harvest." The eschatological judicial tribunal of the Twelve constitutes
the completion of their present task, and it will finally and undeniably reveal
the seriousness and scope of the decision involved in accepting or rejecting
Jesus' message.

235. The same is true of Rev. 20:4!
236. There may also be a motif parallel in Matt. 12:27 ("Therefore they will be your
judges") and in 1 Cor. 6:2-3 ("Do you not know that the saints will judge the world?").
In Wis. 3:8, κρίνειν apparently means "rule." For the judgment by the twelve tribes of
Israel at the "second parousia" in *T. Abr.* A, 13:6, see above, p. 125; J. Dupont, "Logion," 375–76.
237. Against R. Bultmann, *History of the Synoptic Tradition,* 163; idem, *Theology,*
37, 48; S. Schulz, *Q,* 333–34; M. Trautmann, *Zeichenhafte Handlungen,* 198–99, and
others. Among those who argue for authenticity are T. W. Manson, *Sayings,* 217; W. G.
Kümmel, *Verheißung,* 41; J. Dupont, "Logion," 386–91; I. H. Marshall, *Luke,* 815.
238. Gerd Theißen, *The Shadow of the Galilean,* 209 n. 41.

CHAPTER EIGHT

The Judgment of Individuals

Prohibition of Judging (Matt. 7:1-2 // Luke 6:37-38)

The prohibition on judging in both Matthew and Luke, as well as the remarks added to it (Matt. 7:1-2 // Luke 6:37-38), are drawn from Q. However, that source must have contained only the two sentences found in both Matthew and Luke: μὴ κρίνετε, ἵνα μὴ κριθῆτε· ἐν ᾧ γὰρ μέτρῳ μετρεῖτε μετρηθή-σεται ὑμῖν. "Do not judge, so that you may not be judged. For with the measure by which you measure will it be measured out to you."[1] The wording of this reconstruction follows Matthew for the most part. In the first sentence, Luke has a consecutive formulation in place of the purposive "so that." Luke's form has an equally good claim to be original.[2] The connection between the two sentences is secured with γάρ in both Matt. 7:2a and Luke 6:38. However, the connection of the two sayings is not original, as the isolated tradition of the second in Matt. 4:24 demonstrates. Still, the combination was suggested not only by the content, but also by the formal similarity between the two sayings.[3]

Matthew and Luke have given different meanings to the saying about the "measure" by means of the individual context. In Luke, it explains the preceding command to give, and promises a reward corresponding to the measure by which one gives; for him, μέτρον has its proper meaning of "measure of capacity," while μετρεῖν + dative means "measure out," "allocate."[4] Matthew precedes it with an analogously constructed saying: ἐν ᾧ γὰρ κρίματι κρίνετε

---

1. For this reconstruction of Q, cf. Dieter Zeller, *Mahnsprüche*, 113; S. Schulz, *Q*, 146. Schulz, however, wishes to retain Matt. 7:2a as part of Q also.
2. For the syntactic structure of the sentence in Luke 6:37-38, see M. Reiser, *Syntax*, 16–17, 120–22.
3. Dieter Zeller believes that there was an original unit of tradition containing both sayings (*Mahnsprüche*, 113–14).
4. *BAGD* 514, s. v. 2; K. Deißner, *TDNT* 4: 633; H. Schürmann, *Lukas* 1: 362–63.

κριθήσεσθε, thus appearing to interpret μέτρον as parallel to κρίμα as "measuring rod" or "standard," as in the saying of Epictetus: οἶδας γὰρ τὰ μέτρα, καθ᾽ ἃ κρίνεται ἄνθρωπος ὑπ᾽ ἀνθρώπου: "You know the standards by which one human being is judged by others" (*Arr. Epict.* II, 13, 16). However, a saying about "measuring out" (μετρηθήσεται ὑμῖν) does not match that idea very well. This unevenness appears to be an indication that Luke is more likely to have hit on the original sense of the saying than Matthew. The saying was originally conceived as a promise, but in Matthew—and probably already in Q—it had become a warning, and simply underscores the prohibition on judging.

In that prohibition κρίνειν, according to most exegetes, does not mean the activity of a judge, but the act of criticizing and judging fellow human beings in general.[5] Yet Jesus' sovereign attitude toward the Law and his notable lack of interest in halachic questions favor "not limiting the application of our sentence to the personal realm. [Like] the command to love one's enemies, . . . this demand probably should be understood in the context of Jesus' eschatology: The kingdom of God is coming; there must in principle be an end to the judging of human beings by others."[6] Luke appears also to have understood the saying in this sense, for he follows it with a series of analogically constructed clauses that remain within the juridical sphere: "Do not judge, and you will not be judged; do not condemn, and you will not be condemned. Reprieve, and you will be reprieved" (Luke 6:37b, c).

In almost all translations and commentaries, ἀπολύειν in Luke 10:37c is interpreted in the sense of "forgive" or "pardon," but in fact we have no examples of this meaning for ἀπολύω. Walter Bauer, after adducing many examples of the meaning "set free, release, pardon" [a prisoner], gives for Matt. 18:27 the meaning "release a debtor," and assumes this meaning for the present passage as well (*BAGD* 96, s. v. 1). But in Matt. 18:27 ἀπολύειν has its usual meaning of "release," "let go": the debtor is only introduced by the context. Since this applies to someone else in Luke 6:37, Bauer's interpretation is out of the question. Theodor Zahn gives the correct interpretation: "ἀπολύειν in combination with

5. Thus, for example, F. Büchsel, *TDNT* 3: 939; J. Schmid, *Matthäus*, 145; H. Schürmann, *Lukas* 1: 361; I. H. Marshall, *Luke*, 265–66; S. Schulz, *Q*, 148; J. A. Fitzmyer, *Luke* 1: 641. T. Zahn differs (*Matthäus*, 303): The disciples are warned "not to assume the position of judges." Similarly A. Schlatter, *Matthäus*, 240: "Jesus' rule commands the disciple not to take the fate of human beings into [his or her] own hands, to measure the punishment for their sins and the retribution for their godlessness."
6. U. Luz, *Matthew* 1: 416. Cf. J. Gnilka, *Matthäus* 1: 255–56.

the idea of a judicial act, and in contrast to καταδικάζειν, means to release from guilt and imprisonment or punishment by a judicial action." (*Lukas*, 294 n. 66).

We know of no genuine Jewish parallels for this radical prohibition on judging. Closest are the saying of Hillel preserved in *m. 'Abot* 2.4: "Judge not thy fellow-man until thou hast reached his place."[7] Even if the significance of this warning is ultimately that one should simply abandon all judging and condemning of others, it lacks the categorical tone and the eschatological correspondence that make this saying so typical of Jesus. Consequently, the saying is rightly "almost universally attributed to Jesus."[8]

We find a corresponding eschatological passage with the same verb in the primary and secondary clauses in a verse of Pseudo-Phocylides whose content is also related: ἢν σὺ κακῶς δικάσῃς, σὲ θεὸς μετέπειτα δικάσσει. "If you judge badly, God will judge you later" (Ps.-Phoc. 11 = *Sib. Or.* 2:63).[9] In a very general sense, *T. Zeb.* 5:3 reads: ὡς ἄν τις ποιήσῃ τῷ πλησίον αὐτοῦ, οὕτως καὶ ὁ κύριος ποιήσει αὐτῷ. "Whatever anyone does to his neighbor, the Lord will do to him."[10] Both examples, unlike our saying, are formulated actively in the second clause as well, so that the acting subject is explicitly named.

The Old Testament is already acquainted with this kind of correspondence between human action and God's response, and not only in sayings about judgment: "Return to me, and I will return to you" (Mal. 3:7; cf. Tob. 13:6).[11] ". . . those who honor me I will honor, and those who despise me shall be treated with contempt" (1 Sam. 2:30). "Because you have forsaken YHWH, he has also forsaken you" (2 Chr. 24:20; cf. 2 Chr. 12:5). "Forgive your neighbor the wrong he has done, and then your sins will be pardoned when you pray" (Sir. 28:2). The fundamental principle is formulated in Ezek. 7:27: "According to their way I will deal with them; according to their own judgments I will judge them (וּבְמִשְׁפְּטֵיהֶם אֶשְׁפְּטֵם)." The rabbis summarized it thus: "By the measure with which you measure, so they [that is, God] will measure you."[12] This

---

7. Cf. Str-B. 1: 441; U. Luz, *Matthew* 1: 416 n. 24.

8. U. Luz, *Matthew* 1: 413.

9. For the interpretation, see P. W. van der Horst, *Pseudo-Phocylides*, 119.

10. Cf. *T. Zeb.* 8:1, 3. H. W. Hollander and M. de Jonge, *Testaments*, 264; K. Berger, "Zu den sogenannten Sätzen heiligen Rechts," 21–22. For corresponding examples from 2 Enoch, see U. Fischer, *Eschatologie*, 45–47.

11. In sentences with this structure the imperative can represent a conditional clause: cf. M. Reiser, *Syntax*, 120–21.

12. This principle is also known in the brief form, "measure for measure." Str-B. 1: 444–45; A. Schlatter, *Matthäus*, 241.

fundamental principle is frequently attested in the rabbinic literature; some of those examples have a passive formulation in place of the third person plural. In two cases, the passive is eschatological in intent, as in this saying of Jesus.[13]

Jesus' saying: "Do not judge, so that you may not be judged" is therefore to be regarded, in both content and form, as an original variation of a common Jewish principle, according to which God's action, especially in punishing, corresponds exactly to human action. It also underlies the plea for forgiveness in the Our Father, and is illustrated in the parable of the unforgiving servant (Matt. 18:23-24). This principle, which in turn is to be classified within the broader field of similar statements that formulate a correspondence between action and reaction,[14] is formally underscored by the fact that the corresponding action of God is described with the same verb or expression as the human action. "So that you may not be judged" refers to the eschatological judgment, probably with a forensic last judgment in mind before which every individual must appear to give an account of his or her life. This idea is attested even in the earliest tannaitic traditions.[15]

The eschatological passive employed in our logion represents a special formal characteristic of this saying and the analogous expressions in Matt. 7:2 and Luke 6:37-38 that is very rare in comparable early Jewish and rabbinic sayings about corresponding actions. We have encountered these eschatological passives already in the word of judgment on Capernaum (Matt. 11:23 // Luke 10:15) and in the saying about the table companions of Abraham, Isaac, and Jacob (Matt. 8:12). The following excursus will explore the origins, meaning, and function of this kind of passive usage.

Excursus
The So-called *Passivum Divinum* or *Passivum Theologicum* and the Eschatological Passives

---

Gustav Dalman treats the passive construction, among others, under the heading, "Discreet Ways of Speaking about God,"[16] remarking: "At times the passive

---

13. H. P. Rüger, "'Maß,'" 181–82. For the early Jewish and rabbinic parallels, cf. also D. Zeller, *Mahnsprüche*, 115–17.
14. On this, see M. Sato, *Q*, 264–78.
15. See above, pp. 129–32.
16. G. Dalman, *Worte*, 167, 183–85, 382–83.

form of the verb is preferred when the use of an active verb would require God to be named as its subject."[17] The only examples Dalman cites are the future passives of fourteen verbs. Because similar passives are rare in the rabbinic writings, he posits that the underlying Aramaic for the most part had a "subjectless active" such as we find in Luke 6:38, δώσουσιν, "they will give" (that is, God will give).[18] He presents rabbinic examples of this way of speaking and asserts "that the reluctance to utter the divine name had its effect on style."[19]

According to Paul Billerbeck, the passive construction "for avoiding the name of God" is "unusually frequent" in the New Testament.[20] He provides examples and refers to the extensive discussion by Julius Boehmer, *Die neutestamentliche Gottesscheu und die ersten drei Bitten des Vaterunsers.* Under the title "Reticence before the Person of God," Boehmer also deals with the "silences," that is, "passages in which the name of God is suppressed altogether, while at the same time the reader (or hearer) is left to guess at it."[21] He includes here especially the "numerous" passive constructions listed and interpreted on pp. 20–34. Strangely enough, his examples also include the intransitive γενηθήτω (Matt. 6:10, and frequently elsewhere), which is only formally a passive.[22] Otherwise, his list includes practically all the passives for which God *must* be considered the active subject, or only *might* be thought to be. The result is that Dalman's modest list of examples is generously multiplied.

Joachim Jeremias introduced the concept of "*passivum divinum*" to describe this way of "[speaking] of the action of God by means of circumlocutions."[23] The term itself suggests a special form of passive usage. In gathering examples, Jeremias apparently proceeded on the same principle as Boehmer.[24] According to his list "the 'divine passive' occurs round about a hundred times in the sayings of Jesus,"[25] and although Jeremias deliberately attempts to bracket out intransive passives, he also includes γίνομαι in the examples Matt. 6:10; 9:29; 26:42; Mark 12:10.[26] The "*passivum divinum*" is said to be "a veiled hint at an

17. Ibid., 183.
18. Ibid.
19. Ibid., 184–85.
20. Str-B. 1: 443.
21. J. Boehmer, *Gottesscheu,* 20.
22. Ibid., 30.
23. J. Jeremias, *Theology* 1: 9. To my knowledge the term "*passivum divinum*" does not appear before Jeremias's work.
24. Cf. J. Jeremias, *Theologie* 1: 11–12. What is surprising is that Jeremias does not refer to Boehmer's work.
25. J. Jeremias, *Theology* 1: 11.
26. Ibid., 11.

action on the part of God" and the meaning of Mark 2:5 should be rendered "My son, there is one who forgives you your sins."[27] Dalman's proposal that these passives rest on Aramaic subjectless actives is rejected by Jeremias. In his opinion, the *"passivum divinum"* stems from apocalyptic literature. "It was not only used [in apocalyptic literature] out of reverence, to avoid uttering the name of God, but served above all as a way of describing in veiled terms God's mysterious activity in the end time."[28] Jesus is said to have taken up this usage, but given it a much broader scope by using the *"passivum divinum"* not only for future eschatological statements, but also to describe God's action in the present. It is thus "one of the clearest characteristics of his way of speaking."[29]

As early as 1961, ten years before the appearance of Joachim Jeremias's *Neutestamentliche Theologie,* Elpidius Pax, in an excursus on "the so-called *passivum theologicum,"* denied that it represented the model of a New Testament linguistic taboo, as was widely supposed.[30] Only in particular cases did it serve the purpose of concealment. Its primary function was to express "an event as such, without regard to the agent."[31]

The principal meaning Pax ascribes to the so-called *passivum divinum* or *theologicum* corresponds to the principal function of the passive as such:† "The passive is used primarily when the speaker desires to characterize an event explicitly without reference to an agent, or as independent of an agent."[32] By use of the passive, the naming of an agent, that is, the author of an action or the cause of an event or situation, is avoided. There can be any number of reasons for this avoidance: for example, because the agent is known from the context and therefore need not be named, or because the agent cannot or should not be named. It is possible that the speaker or author desires to leave the agent indeterminate or unmentioned because he or she is inessential to an understanding of the subject. The shift between active and passive forms can

27. Ibid., 10–11.
28. Ibid., 13.
29. Ibid., 14.
30. E. Pax, "Beobachtungen zum biblischen Sprachtabu," 92–110.
31. Ibid., 111–12. Similarly E. M. Sidebottom, "The So-called Divine Passive."
† [Translator's note: In what follows, the author's observations are based on German construction and are only partly representative of the relationships in English grammar.]
32. K. E. Heidolph, W. Flämig, and W. Motsch, *Grundzüge einer deutschen Grammatik,* 553. Hence L. Weisgerber has described the passive as "a diathesis [whose focus is] averted from the doer" (*Kräfte* 2: 332–35. Cf. K. Brinker, "Passiv," 14).

also be a matter of style, or suggested by the relationships of *thema* and *rhema*.[33] Under some circumstances, the passive also serves for the avoidance of the first person singular.[34] The passive shifts the focus from the acting subject to the action itself. In an active transformation, the subject is often to be constructed by an indefinite pronoun, such as "one." But there are also cases in which an active transformation is impossible because the agent is neither expressed nor implied. In such cases, passives approach very closely to the meaning of actives and are often the equivalent of reflexives.[35]

These insights drawn from German grammar are essentially true of Greek also, and of other Indo-European languages.[36] Originally, there was no passive in Greek; it developed later out of the middle voice. But in classical Greek as well, middle and passive can be formally distinguished only in the aorist and future. Greek never established a clear opposition between active and passive.[37]

Obviously, a discussion of *passiva divina* can deal only with passive forms that have a passive meaning. Deponent passives and passives with intransitive-middle significance[38] must be set aside. Thus γενηθήτω in Matt. 6:10 and elsewhere cannot be considered a *passivum divinum*.

A consideration of the passive in general also sheds light on the question of the so-called *passivum divinum*. It shows that we ought to avoid speaking of "the" *passivum divinum*, as if this were a way of using the passive voice that is different from other uses of the passive.[39] There is no specific passive usage that could be called "the *passivum divinum*."[40] It is sensible to see only those

33. For *thema* and *rhema*, see M. Reiser, *Syntax*, 60–63.

34. For the different motives for use of the passive, see K. Brinker, *Passiv*, 111–13; G. Stein, *Passive*, 140–45; S. Pape-Müller, *Textfunktionen*, 93–121; K. E. Heidolph, W. Fläming, and W. Motsch, *Grundzüge*, 553–55. Especially instructive are the examples and discussion in W. Schneider, *Stilistische Deutsche Grammatik*, 260–68. For the NT, see E. Pax, "Beobachtungen," 98–110.

35. K. Brinker, "Das Passiv in der 'Augsburgischen Konfession,'" 170; idem, *Passiv*, 33–34, 74–81, 114–16.

36. Cf. J. Wackernagel, *Syntax* 1: 143–44; E. Schwyzer, *Grammatik* 2: 238–39.

37. Cf. E. Schwyzer, *Grammatik* 2: 238; L. Pernée, "Passif." While modern Greek makes a formal distinction only between active and passive, the passive often has the same meaning as the ancient middle voice (A. Thumb, *Handbuch* § 175).

38. Cf. BD § 313.

39. In H./v. S. the *passivum divinum* appears, reflecting the work of W. Bühlmann and K. Scherer (*Stilfiguren*, 85), as a form of antonomasia (§ 296b).

40. This conclusion is found also in the article by C. Macholz, who adduces examples from the Old Testament ("Das 'Passivum divinum,' seine Anfänge im Alten Testament und der 'Hofstil,'" *ZNW* 81 [1990]: 247–53). But it is as much a mistaken procedure to look for the origins of this kind of expression in court style as it is to try

passives as *passiva divina* in which the intended agent or doer of the action is God, or whose subject would be God in the case of an active transformation. Whether in a given instance there is actually an intention to say that God is the agent—that is, whether this is really a *passivum divinum*—must be determined from the context. One must consider that in many cases even the effort to discover the supposed agent is out of place, because "the exclusion of the 'doer' should be regarded as the proper communicative function of the passive construction."[41] Thus an active transformation, even if formally possible, can go directly against the expressive intention of the speaker or author. This is the case, for example, with the active transformation that Joachim Jeremias suggests for Matt. 5:4: "Blessed are those who mourn, for there is one who will comfort them."[42] It is indeed *not* "according to the sense" of the text, for the author is less concerned here about who will do the comforting than about the fact that comfort is something certain. He chose the passive formulation παρακληθήσονται precisely for that reason. In this and many similar cases, however, the choice of the passive may also be conditioned by a further advantage it possesses: in this way, the agent—in this case, the one who comforts—need not be more exactly determined. Certainly, the author would have thought in the first place of God as the comforter, but especially in an eschatological interpretation of the passage one should probably think at the same time of the angels, the eschatological community of the righteous, and the whole eschatological environment as sources of comfort.[43]

This also makes it obvious that in this and similar cases, as Pax already saw, the passive is by no means employed to hint at the action of God in a "hidden" way, or because of reverent reticence about using the name of God. There is no such reticence in the New Testament, as the numerous active formulations with God as their subject demonstrate. Circumlocutions for God in the New Testament arise from other motives.

The case mentioned above: τέκνον, ἀφίενταί σου αἱ ἁμαρτίαι (Mark 2:5) must be judged somewhat differently. Here again, Joachim Jeremias sees the passive as a veiled indication of the action of God and paraphrases: "'My son,

---

to derive it from apocalyptic. It arises from the possibilities inherent in the passive form itself, which can serve a variety of purposes.

41. K. E. Heidolph, W. Fläming, and W. Motsch, *Grundzüge*, 547. E. Pax had already pointed this out with respect to the so-called *passivum divinum* ("Beobachtungen," 95).

42. J. Jeremias, *Theology* 1: 11. Cf. W. Bühlmann and K. Scherer, *Stilfiguren*, 85; H./ v. S. § 296b.

43. To this extent Gerhard Lohfink emphasized a genuine aspect of the matter in choosing to understand this passage also as "*passivum ecclesiasticum*" (*The Work of God Goes On*, 53–57).

there is one who forgives you your sins.'"[44] But, as the rest of the story shows, the scribes take it for granted that it is Jesus who is claiming the ability to forgive sins, and Jesus himself, by means of the miracle, demonstrates *his own* power to release from sin. This, then, may be a case in which the passive is chosen as a circumlocution for the first person singular, a technique known in German (and also in English). Nevertheless, this is probably not the real reason for the choice of a passive form at this point. Instead, here the passive is used to place full emphasis on the sins that are forgiven; the one who forgives remains in the background. There is a certain irony, probably intended by the narrator, in the fact that the scribes immediately make the principal issue out of the very question that was pushed into the background by means of this linguistic tool. Exegetes need not imitate them.

Thus it is not sufficient to say that a given passive represents a *passivum divinum*. Instead, even in the case of a passive whose intended agent is certainly God, we need to inquire, just as with every passive, on the basis of the context in which it is used, about the reasons why the author chose it and the way it functions in its context. In doing so, and in spite of the multitude of passive functions, we should never lose sight of the principal use of the passive: namely, to characterize an event explicitly as unrelated to or independent of an agent.

Joachim Jeremias saw the *passivum divinum* as a typical characteristic of apocalyptic literature.[45] In fact, we have noted the frequent appearance of passives, precisely in the eschatological descriptions in early Jewish literature.[46] Thus in the visions in Dan. 7:2-14 there are no fewer than thirteen passives, and in the Aramaic text of the Ten-Week Apocalypse at least six.[47] When the events are not, as in Daniel 7, depicted in a visionary manner as events beheld, such expressions and descriptions are usually presented in the future tense. Therefore in the words of Jesus as well, these passives are mainly future forms.[48] Scholarship has built on these, and they represent in the New Testa-

---

44. J. Jeremias, *Theology* 1: 11. This interpretation is accepted by Rudolf Pesch (*Markus* 1: 156); thus also M. Zerwick, *Biblical Greek* § 236.

45. See above: J. Jeremias, *Theology* 1: 13–14.

46. See above, pp. 40, 44–45, 60, 65–66, 156–57, cf. also p. 176.

47. See above, pp. 40, 60. The Greek text of 1 Enoch 22 offers fifteen passives, most of which corresponded to passives in the Aramaic text as well. This is evident from the Aramaic fragments of the chapter (cf. esp. 1 Enoch 22:4. Text in K. Beyer, *Texte*, 241).

48. Cf. Matt. 5:4,6,7,9 // Luke 6:21; Matt. 6:33 // Luke 12:31; Matt. 7:1 // Luke 6:37a; Matt. 7:2a; Matt. 7:2b // Luke 6:38c; Matt. 7:7-8 // Luke 11:9-10; Matt. 8:12 (cf. Luke 13:28); Matt. 10:26 // Luke 12:2; Matt. 11:23 // Luke 10:15; Matt. 12:32 // Luke 12:10; Matt. 12:37; 15:13; 21:43; Matt. 23:12 // Luke 14:11 // Luke 18:14; Mark 3:28 (par. Matt. 12:31); Mark 4:25 (par. Matt. 13:12; Luke 8:18); Mark 9:49; 13:13 (par. Matt.

ment, as in the rest of early Jewish literature, something like a fixed group of sayings that for the most part, if not always, have an eschatological content. We may therefore describe them as eschatological passives.

As active agent behind these passives, we should usually think of God or the angels, occasionally the righteous as well. However, the preference for passive formulations especially in eschatological statements and descriptions is apparently motivated primarily by the fact that in this form the agent can remain indeterminate. Thus it need not be said who sets up thrones at the final judgment, opens the books, and slays the beast (cf. Dan. 7:10-11); who places the sword in the hand of the righteous, and who builds the Temple at the end of days (cf. 1 Enoch 91:12-13); who destroys sinners, and who saves the righteous, preserves them, and has mercy on them (cf. *Ps. Sol.* 15:13). The variety of individual possibilities that may be implied is something we have already seen illustrated in the interpretation of Matt. 5:4. These statements are not at all concerned with the agent, who of course is always ultimately God. What is decisive is *that* all this will happen; how and through whom it will come about, the prophet of the end time events is happy to leave open. The passive, which relieves the prophet of the need to name the agent, is especially useful in such cases.[49]

Semitic languages also have the third person plural available for cases in which the agent is intended to remain indeterminate: it can be translated in German or English as "one" or "they." Gustav Dalman proposed that such third person plural forms in Aramaic were, for the most part, behind the future passives in Jesus-logia. But, as Daniel 7, 1 Enoch 22, and the Ten-Week Apocalypse (1 Enoch 93:3-10; 91:11-17) show, such a proposal is unnecessary. There, too, however, such forms can alternate with passives[50] and we repeatedly come across corresponding variations in text and translation. Thus Dan. 7:13 reads: "And he [the 'one like a human being'] came to the Ancient of Days, and they presented him before him [NRSV: 'and was presented before him'] (וּקְדָמוֹהִי הַקְרְבוּהִי)." The Theodotion text has καὶ προσήχθη αὐτῷ, but there is a variant reading, ἐνώπιον αὐτοῦ προσήγαγον αὐτόν.[51] In the same expres-

_____

24:13); Luke 6:37b, c, 38a; Luke 11:51 (cf. Matt. 23:36!); Luke 12:9 (cf. Matt. 10:33!); Luke 12:48; Luke 12:53 (cf. Matt. 10:35); Luke 14:14.

49. Cf. also the words of R. Schneider: "As we are torn, so shall we be torn; as we quarrel, so the quarrel will destroy us; as we tolerate betrayal, so we will be betrayed; as we contemplate destruction, so will we perish" ("Verloren haben die Christen!" 172).

50. See above, pp. 40, 60.

51. Cf. the Göttingen LXX, ad loc.

sion, the LXX can reproduce a third person plural (= "they" or "one") in the Hebrew text once with the same form in Greek, and another time as a passive: προσθήσουσίν σοι or προστεθήσεταί σοι (Prov. 3:2; 9:11). In *Jub.* 30:19, the Ethiopic text reads: "And so they will report. . . ." The Latin version reads: *Et sic refertur.* The following sentence, in the Ethiopic text, begins: "And we remember. . . ." The Latin version has: *Et memorabitur.* Two verses later, the Ethiopic and Latin texts provide still more *passiva divina.*

This use of the third person plural, which is foreign to secular Greek, occurs five times in the Gospel of Luke as well, apparently in imitation of Semitic style.[52] In 12:48 it is set in a *parallelismus membrorum* with a *passivum divinum.* The use of both forms of expression has the same motivation: the agent is not to be mentioned because the reader or hearer knows, in any event, who the subject is.

The Parable of the Unforgiving Servant (Matt. 18:23-35)

Structure and Imagery

The parable of the unforgiving servant is written in superb koiné Greek, free of Semitisms.[53] It was apparently composed by Matthew himself. Whether he had a written model or not cannot be determined.[54]

The parable is told neatly and carefully. It is subdivided into three scenes or "acts," such as we often find them in Jesus' parables and similitudes.[55] In the first scene a "servant" (δοῦλος) is brought before a "king." The servant is apparently a high official.[56] He owes the king "ten thousand talents." To the ears of Jesus' hearers, that sum had to sound like something out of a fairy tale; it would immediately carry them into the atmosphere of the level of society in

---

52. Luke 6:38; 12:20,48; 16:9; 23:31.
53. In the narrative itself, only the word σπλαγχνίζομαι (Matt. 18:27) can be considered a Semitism. The frame contains two examples of Semitic phraseology: ἡ βασιλεία τῶν οὐρανῶν (Matt. 18:23) and ἀπὸ τῶν καρδιῶν ὑμῶν (Matt. 18:35).
54. A. Weiser (*Knechtsgleichnisse*, 75–93), more than any other, has meticulously attempted to demonstrate that Matthew derived the essential text of the parable from the tradition. He calls v. 31 redactional (ibid., 85–86), as does H. Weder, *Gleichnisse*, 211. But that verse reveals no special features of vocabulary, phraseology, or syntax, and is no more "Matthean" than the rest of the narrative. Cf. R. H. Gundry, *Matthew*, 371–72.
55. W. Harnisch, *Gleichniserzählungen*, 23–24. Cf., for example, Matt. 25:14-30; Luke 15:11-32 (3 + 2).
56. Cf. R. Sugranyes de Franch, *Etudes*, 32–47.

which people played with such fantastic sums. Haman promised to contribute ten thousand talents to the royal treasury following the destruction of all the Jews in the Persian empire and the seizure of their property (Esth. 3:9). Darius tried to purchase peace from Alexander for ten thousand talents.[57] Alexander set aside ten thousand talents for the mausoleum of his beloved Hephaestion.[58]

Obviously, the servant can never produce such a sum. The king's intention to have him sold into slavery together with his wife and children was routine legal procedure in the ancient Near East.[59] Such a seizure of the person served "as a means of putting pressure on the debtor himself, his family, and his friends."[60] However, when the servant begs for indulgence, desperately promising to pay back "everything," the master has pity and not only releases him from being sold, but beyond that, with almost unbelievable generosity, forgives him the whole debt.

K. E. Bailey, *Poet,* 107 n. 91, offers some fine examples of comparable royal generosity from more recent times: "There is a wonderful story in the oral tradition of the Middle Eastern peasantry which tells of a condemned murderer during the days of the famous sultan Saladin. The killer was condemned to death and kept crying, 'I want to see the Sultan.' Finally he was taken into the presence of the great Sultan where he cried out, 'O most gracious Sultan, my sins are great but the mercy of the Sultan is greater.' He was released.

"A modern version of the same story was related to me in 1965 by one of the leaders of the Arab section of Jerusalem, a man named Abū Alfons. In 1960, the

57. Plutarch, *Mor.* 180B; *Alex.* 29.

58. Plutarch, *Alex.* 72.5. Cf. R. Sugranyes de Franch, *Etudes,* 48–51. The tetrarchy of Philip, according to Josephus, *Ant.* 17, 318–20, had a tax revenue of 100 talents, that of Antipas 200 talents, and that of Archelaus 600 talents. Cf. Josephus, *Bell.* 2, 95–97, according to which Archelaus's income was only 400 talents. When Crassus plundered the Temple at Jerusalem in 54 B.C.E., he seized 2,000 talents in silver and gold, to the value of 8,000 talents (Josephus, *Ant.* 14, 105). Further examples of large sums from antiquity can be found in C. Spicq, *Dieu,* 55–56; J. D. M. Derrett, "Unmerciful Servant," 36 n. 1. Derrett's interpretation on the level of imagery, however, is eccentric. Joachim Jeremias is too one-sided in his emphasis on the fantastic value of the sums Jesus names, and explains them as features of oriental narrative style (*Parables,* 30). The sum is really both: fantastic to the audience, but realistic for the social situation envisaged by the narrative. M. C. de Broer considers the mention of 10,000 talents to be Matthean redaction ("Ten Thousand Talents?"). Joachim Gnilka suspects the same thing (*Matthäus* 2: 144–45).

59. Cf. J. Jeremias, *Parables,* 211. Jewish law, however, did not permit the sale of a debtor; seizure of persons was countenanced only in cases of theft. The Law of the Twelve Tables does envision the sale of debtors into slavery, but it appears that the provision was never put into practice (M. Kaser, *Zivilprozeßrecht,* 101–2).

60. M. Kaser, *Zivilprozeßrecht,* 300.

wife of a condemned spy came to Abū Alfons for advice on how to free her husband. He told her to wait outside the palace for the king's motorcade to form and then throw herself in front of the king's car. He explicitly instructed the lady *not* to plead innocence, with the warning, 'You know he is guilty and so does the king. To offer excuses is to destroy all hope. Throw yourself on the mercy of the king!' The lady carried out the instructions. The Jordanian monarch knows full well how a noble king is expected to act and the spy was released."

The second scene forms a sharp contrast to the first. The same man who had just been forgiven a debt of "ten thousand talents" has scarcely left the king's presence when he encounters a fellow servant who owes him the sum of one hundred denarii, ridiculous in comparison. He seizes him by the throat[61] and demands: "Pay what you owe!"[62] We find this formula in Latin in Petronius's *Satyricon*, where one person boasts: "No one has ever said to me in the forum: 'Give back what you owe!' (*nemo mihi in foro dixit: 'Redde quod debes'*)" (57.7). The plea for a delay in payment, which the tormented servant utters in the same words that his creditor had just spoken on his own behalf, does not move him. He has him thrown into prison "until he would pay the debt."[63]

In the third scene, the king takes the unmerciful servant to task and, in his rage, hands him over to the torturers "until he would pay his entire debt."[64]

61. For this, see the parallels in J. Wettstein, *NT* 1: 445–46; A. Schlatter, *Matthäus*, 563.

62. Not ". . . if you owe anything," as if he were not sure (M.-J. Lagrange, *Matthieu*, 361). Εἴ τι for ὅ τι was common in popular koiné: BD § 376 appendix; H. Ljungvik, *Beiträge*, 9–18; E. Michevc-Gabrovec, *Etudes*, 47. Even the Old Latin translation even has *quod* for that reason.

63. Roman law, from early times, countenanced personal seizure and private imprisonment or enslavement for debt (M. Kaser, *Zivilprozeßrecht*, 101, 103–4, 300, 406, 513). In Egypt in the Ptolemaic and Roman periods, the execution of judgment on the person was not accomplished through private imprisonment by the creditor, but through incarceration in the public prison (ibid., 407 n. 11; L. Mitteis and U. Wilcken, *Grundzüge* II, 1: 44–45). This practice is also presupposed in the parable. It was unknown to Jewish law (J. Jeremias, *Parables*, 180, 211–12). It is true that G. Stemberger (*Judentum*, 72) and J. Juster (*Juifs* 2: 161) assert the contrary. But Juster refers incorrectly to J. L. Saalschütz, *Das Mosaische Recht* (2 vols., Berlin, 1853). There is nothing there about a Jewish practice of imprisonment for debt. Neither the Old Testament nor the Talmud knows such a practice.

64. Torture on personal initiative is well attested from late Roman times. "Extortion through the application of torture frequently appears to have been more effective for the creditors than the seizure of property, which, if the debtor was wealthy, was not always hopeless, but often complicated" (M. Kaser, *Zivilprozeßrecht*, 513 n. 18). R. Taubenschlag (*Law*, 540) cites an example from the year 50 B.C.E. (*BGU* 1847). Cf. also C. Spicq, *Dieu*, 60; R. Sugranyes de Franch, *Etudes*, 62–63. See the last also for the situation in Palestine.

There the story ends. In v. 35, Matthew has Jesus add a passing comment, the conclusion to the framing scene begun in vv. 21-22.[65]

The only reason why the second scene is so scandalous is that it is preceded by the first.[66] The relentless, rough insistence on collecting the debt would seem to us quite "in order," at least according to the rules of the world in which the story takes place, if an act of unlimited kindness and magnanimity had not just been described. Even if the one who implacably demands repayment of a debt of one hundred denarii were not the same person who had just been forgiven a debt of ten thousand talents, we would, after the first scene, consider such a person mean and unfeeling. But as it is, the contrast is too great, and the attitude of the servant appears to us inconsistent and inhuman.

That is the precise point the king strikes when he tells the servant: "You wicked servant! I forgave you all that debt because you pleaded with me. Should you not therefore have had mercy on your fellow servant, as I had mercy on you?" (Matt. 18:32-33).[67] It is not really his hardness and lack of mercy that are here held up as a reproach to the servant, but his thoughtlessness and lack of insight. The king expected the servant to draw the simple conclusion that the one who has experienced kindness and mercy should also allow kindness and mercy to prevail in his or her own relationships. That the servant did not draw that logical conclusion, and did not see, or refused to acknowledge, the inconsequence of his own behavior, brings the king to a state of righteous indignation; for the sake of justice he can do nothing else but withdraw his act of forgiveness and hand this blockhead over to the torturers. Thus the third scene brings the narrative to its logical and necessary conclusion.

Literary Integrity

The text of the parable (vv. 23-34) is fully consistent. At no point does it reveal logical or stylistic breaks that would give occasion for literary critical dissection. Nevertheless, some exegetes consider either the whole of the last scene (vv. 31-34), or at least v. 34, to be secondary additions by the evangelist or the

---

65. For the framing, cf. E. Linnemann, *Gleichnisse,* 111–13.

66. Cf. E. Linnemann, *Gleichnisse,* 117–18; H. Weder, *Gleichnisse,* 214–15; W. Harnisch, *Gleichniserzählungen,* 262–63.

67. For the consecutive relationship in asyndetic parataxis—hence the "therefore" in the translation—see M. Reiser, *Syntax,* 144–45.

pre-Matthean tradition.[68] Stylistic reasons are advanced for this proposal,[69] as well as the supposed contradiction between this and Matt. 5:45.[70] In v. 34, according to Hans Weder, we should expect the punishment originally envisioned in v. 25, rather than the handing over of the servant to the torturers; at any rate, the punishment of the servant now corresponds to the fate he had arranged for his fellow servant.[71] Wolfgang Harnisch even asserts that the motif of the torturers is "inadequately integrated in the milieu of the narrative world," gives the impression of being isolated, and lacks narrative plausibility.[72]

The principal reason for these literary incisions, however, is said to be a "twisting" of the original meaning of the parable, which appears to be accomplished at least by v. 34. The king's retraction of his amnesty is said to contradict his mercy in the first scene.[73] According to Weder, the parable describes the gracious, anticipatory mercy of God, which here, to the amazement of the hearers, does not produce results. Therefore the judgment that falls on the servant in v. 34 *cannot* be part of the narrative, because it relativizes that gracious mercy.[74]

There is, however, no contradiction between the king's dealings in the first and third scenes, since the behavior of the servant in the second scene has created a different situation requiring another decision. Moreover, the whole reasoning calling for the elimination of v. 34, or the whole last scene, rests on

68. The former is the choice of H. Weder (*Gleichnisse*, 210–12), A. Lindemann (*TRE* 15: 202), and P. Fiedler (*Jesus*, 197–99), the latter of W. Harnisch (*Gleichniserzählungen*, 259–62), I. Broer (*Parabel*, 152–57), and J. Gnilka (*Matthäus* 2: 144–45).

69. H. Weder, *Gleichnisse*, 211; rightly rejected by W. Harnisch (*Gleichniserzählungen*, 260). Cf. also above, p. 273.

70. P. Fiedler (*Jesus*, 197), following E. Fuchs, "Zeitverständnis," 361. On this, see A. Weiser, *Knechtsgleichnisse*, 96; D. O. Via, *Parables*, 143–44.

71. H. Weder, *Gleichnisse*, 211 n. 8.

72. W. Harnisch, *Gleichniserzählungen*, 261. The opposite is the case: see above, p. 276; M.-J. Lagrange, *Matthieu*, 362–63; E. Klostermann, *Matthäus*, 153.

73. H. Weder, *Gleichnisse*, 210–11; P. Fiedler, *Jesus*, 197–98; W. Harnisch, *Gleichniserzählungen*, 262 ("self-contradiction by the one in control of the action"); I. Broer, *Parabel*, 154. For Broer, however, what is "decisive" is that v. 34 is not integrated into the direct speech of v. 33 ("Parabel," 157). This argument, also advanced by J. Gnilka (*Matthäus* 2: 144 n. 6), is opaque to me. Nevertheless, Broer thinks that the secondary character of v. 34 "can scarcely be demonstrated in a compelling way" ("Parabel," 156).

74. H. Weder, *Gleichnisse*, 215. Cf. W. Harnisch, *Gleichniserzählungen*, 262. The idea "that God will not tolerate the abuse of his goodness," according to E. Fuchs, "scarcely does justice to the dignity of that goodness" ("Zeitverständnis," 361). Does that mean, to apply the well-known *bon mot* ascribed to Heinrich Heine or Voltaire, that God has to forgive because, after all, that is God's *métier*?

a *petitio principii:* First the original meaning of the parable is determined without regard to the final scene, or in the absence of v. 34; then the meaning thus determined is advanced as an argument for removing that very part. The parable is said to be "not a proclamation of judgment, but the promise of the Gospel,"[75] and therefore it must end, at the latest, with v. 33. And because the "threatening tone" is regarded as untypical of Jesus, and a punishing righteousness as incompatible with the goodness of God,[76] v. 34 could not come from Jesus. What first needs to be proven is presumed instead.[77]

But even apart from this, it is entirely unlikely that the parable ever ended with v. 33. On the narrative level, v. 33 only makes sense if it gives the reason for what happens in v. 34. For, at the narrative level, what would be the point of the king's obviously rhetorical question, without the subsequent punishment of the servant? It could only be understood as an astonished query or a sorrowful remark, an expression of impotent sadness. The narrative could not possibly end that way, and the servant's case could not be finished. "Every hearer asks: 'What will happen to him now? Will he be reproached, but retain the advantages he received from the immeasurable forgiveness of his debt?' This question must be answered if the story is not to remain only the torso of a narrative. The hearers themselves cannot answer *this* question. It can only be answered by the narrator. The conclusion that v. 34 is necessary to the integrity of the parable is as compelling as a conclusion based on form-critical observations can ever be."[78]

Interpretation

The parable contains a number of features we readily recognize as metaphorical. As in rabbinic parables about rulers, the king here stands for God. Another transparent metaphor is the servant's enormous monetary debt, for Semitic

---

75. H. Weder, *Gleichnisse,* 216 n. 32.

76. Cf. E. Fuchs, "Zeitverständnis," 361; H. Weder, *Gleichnisse,* 218; P. Fiedler, *Jesus,* 197.

77. Cf. A. Jülicher, *Gleichnisreden* 2: 311: "We must refuse to say that the idea that the refusal of the obligation of brotherly forgiveness threatens loss of eternal life cannot be what is meant, because that would thrust us outside the sphere of the Gospel, and place us under the rod of discipline, because it is from the Gospel itself, to which Matt. 18:21ff. belongs, that we must derive the correct idea of what the 'sphere of the Gospel' really is."

78. A. Weiser, *Knechtsgleichnisse,* 91. Cf. A. Jülicher, *Gleichnisreden,* 309: "Finally comes 34, as we expected after the severe words in 33."

חוֹב, חוֹבָה, like German *Schuld*, meant "debt of money," but also developed the meaning "debt of sin," that is, "guilt."[79] Therefore we find ὀφείλημα, meaning "sin," and ὀφειλέτης, meaning "sinner" in two certainly authentic Jesus sayings.[80] The similitude of the two debtors in Luke 7:41-42 also uses the image of release from monetary debt to teach about the forgiveness of sins. We find corresponding similitudes in the writings of the rabbis as well.[81]

However, the third scene also contains features that can easily be understood as metaphorical. The king's wrath in v. 34 suggests God's eschatological fury and wrathful judgment,[82] while the handing over of the servant to the torturers recalls the sufferings of the damned in hell, frequently described in ancient Jewish literature as βάσανος, "torture."[83]

Hence it is clear that the parable, in accordance with its triadic structure, first speaks of God's willingness to forgive even the greatest degree of guilt, then of the consequences that human beings must draw from that forgiveness, and finally of the punishment that anyone must expect if he or she fails to draw the consequences that are expected.

For Adolf Schlatter the parable—probably he means its first scene—"describes justification as the act of perfect grace, as powerfully as Paul did in Romans."[84] But for Paul also, the justification of the sinner by God's grace freely bestowed is the true reason why those not prepared to repent store up "wrath" for themselves on the "day of wrath" (cf. Rom. 2:5), for such people have received grace in vain and thus have forfeited it (cf. 2 Cor. 6:1). "Note then the kindness and the severity of God: severity toward those who have fallen, but God's kindness toward you, provided you continue in his kindness; otherwise you also will be cut off [again]" (Rom. 11:22). This parable illus-

79. Cf. F. Hauck, *TDNT* 5: 562. [Translator's note: English separates the two ideas as "debt" and "guilt" respectively; the identity of the two is preserved only in formal language such as that of the Our Father (Matthew): "forgive us our debts . . . ."]
80. Matt. 6:12 (cf. Luke 11:4b); Luke 13:4. Cf. 1 Enoch 6:3.
81. Cf. *Pesiq. K.* 14.7; 27.7 (C. Thoma and S. Lauer, *Gleichnisse*, 222, 267).
82. Cf. T. Deidun, "Parable," 212. For this motif, see above, pp. 170–72.
83. Thus, for example, 1 Enoch 10:13; 22:11; 25:6; Wis. 3:1 (see above, p. 43); 2 Macc. 7:17; 4 Macc. 9:9; 12:12; 13:15; 4 Ezra 7:36 (see above, pp. 115–16); 7:67; 9:12-13. The . . . ἐβασάνισαν αὐτήν (scil. τὴν ψυχήν) in *T. Abr.* B 10.16 apparently became παρέδωκαν τοῖς βασανισταῖς in the later recension of B under influence of Matt. 18:34; in *T. Abr.* A 12.18 it became ταῖς βασανισταῖς ἐξέδωκεν αὐτήν. Cf. also Luke 16:23, 28. Further examples are in P. Volz, *Eschatologie*, 322. Cf. A. Jülicher, *Gleichnisreden* 2: 309; L. Fonck, *Parabeln*, 643; E. Klostermann, *Matthäusevangelium*, 153.
84. A. Schlatter, *Matthäus*, 560.

trates the same line of thought: "The description of divine grace is the premise according to which the refusal of forgiveness will be judged."[85] For those who have received forgiveness, forgiving is an obligation; its nonfulfillment brings judgment in its wake.[86]

Therefore this parable does not say the same thing as Sir. 28:2: "Forgive your neighbor the wrong he has done, and then your sins will be pardoned when you pray."[87] It is true that the Matthean application in v. 35 appears to understand the parable in this sense; but in the parable itself the servant is not judged simply because he refused mercy; it is because he refused it after he himself had received it in lavish measure.[88]

For the same reason, the words of Jesus that formulate a correspondence between human actions and God's response to them can only be adduced as parallel with some reservations: "Forgive us our debts, as we also forgive our debtors" (Matt. 6:12; cf. Luke 11:4). "Do not judge, so that you may not be judged" (Matt. 7:1; cf. Luke 6:37). "The measure you give will be the measure you get" (Mark 4:24; cf. Matt. 7:2 // Luke 6:38).[89] Certainly the idea that God's attitude toward human beings corresponds to the attitude of human beings toward their fellow men and women plays an important part. But we should not explain the parable on the basis of the logion; instead, the logion should by interpreted on the basis of the parable.[90] The parable expresses the unspoken premise of the logion: Because we ourselves have received God's grace, we can and should give up judging; we should forgive and be generous. Otherwise, we have received grace in vain. But in the context of Jesus' message, that grace is nothing other than the reign of God that he brings with him.[91] Who-

---

85. Ibid., 561.

86. Cf. W. Grundmann, *Matthäus*, 425: "A person who has received God's mercy forfeits it by being unmerciful." One should not speak here of a "parable about the last judgment" (J. Jeremias, *Parables*, 213), for the theme of the parable is neither the final judgment nor the question of when, in that judgment, God will apply the measure of mercy and when the measure of judgment (ibid., 213–14). C. Dietzfelbinger ("Gleichnis") understands the release from debt as a gift of time and interprets accordingly. On this, see H. Weder, *Gleichnisse*, 215 n. 27.

87. Against A. Jülicher, *Gleichnisreden* 2: 314.

88. A. Weiser, *Knechtsgleichnisse*, 93. On Matt. 18:35, see ibid., 96, 100–103.

89. A. Weiser, like others before him, refers also to Matt. 5:7; Mark 11:25 (*Knechtsgleichnisse*, 95).

90. Thus, correctly, Helmut Merklein, *Gottesherrschaft*, 242.

91. Cf. ibid., 241–42. Merklein rightly sees the parable as confirming his thesis: "that Jesus' demands are nothing other than concretizations of the proclamation of the *basileia*, understood as a principle of action" (ibid., 241).

ever does not draw the appropriate consequences from the situation created by this fact falls victim to a self-chosen judgment.

The Injunction to "Accommodation" with the Accuser
(Matt. 5:25-26 // Luke 12:57-59)

Tradition and Form

Matthew and Luke derived the injunction to "accommodation" with accusers (Matt. 5:25-26 // Luke 12:57-59) from Q. The text of the source appears to have been preserved, in essence, by Matthew:[92] ἴσθι εὐνοῶν τῷ ἀντιδίκῳ σου ταχύ, ἕως ὅτου εἶ μετ᾽ αὐτοῦ ἐν τῇ ὁδῷ, μήποτέ σε παραδῷ ὁ ἀντίδικος τῷ κριτῇ καὶ ὁ κριτὴς τῷ ὑπηρέτῃ καὶ εἰς φυλακὴν βληθήσῃ· ἀμὴν λέγω σοι, οὐ μὴ ἐξέλθῃς ἐκεῖθεν, ἕως ἂν ἀποδῷς τὸν ἔσχατον κοδράντην. "Be accommodating [that is, pleasant, obliging] quickly with your accuser while you are on the way with him. Otherwise your accuser will hand you over to the judge, and the judge to the guard, and you will be thrown into prison. Amen, I tell you, you will never get out until you have paid back the last *quadrans*."

Luke has created a transitional question in v. 57, and introduced a number of changes and fine-tunings that betray his own hand, including the Latinism (already at home in the koiné before Luke) δὸς ἐργασίαν (= *da operam*),[93] the phrase κατασύρειν πρὸς τὸν κριτήν, "drag before the judge," in place of παραδιδόναι τῷ κριτῇ, "hand over to the judge," and λεπτόν in place of κοδράντης.[94] The phrase ἴσθι εὐνοῶν, "be of good will, pleasant, obliging," in the Matthean version is to be read as a euphemism, as the context indicates.[95] What is meant is: give in, that is, "pay what you owe" (Matt. 18:28), because your situation is hopeless! Luke makes no bones about it: δὸς ἐργασίαν ἀπηλλάχθαι ἀπ᾽ αὐτοῦ, "See to it that you get rid of him!" That can scarcely be understood as an injunction to flee,[96] or as advice to "bribe" the accuser or

---

92. S. Schulz, Q, 421–22; U. Luz, *Matthew* 1: 281. However, the Lukan version is usually seen as original, for example, by J. Schmid, *Matthäus und Lukas*, 226; Dieter Zeller, *Mahnsprüche*, 64; C.-P. März, "Vorgeschichte," 72–73.

93. Cf. BD § 5, 3; A. Deissmann, *Licht*, 93; T. Zahn, *Lukas*, 519 n. 65.

94. Cf. Luke 21:2, diff. Mark 12:42!

95. For the meaning of εὐνοεῖν, see E. Lohmeyer, *Matthäus*, 123–24 n. 1. He sees the strangeness of the word at this point, but scarcely can be said to interpret it rightly (cf. ibid., 124–25). [Translator's note: RSV translates "make friends," NRSV "come to terms," both in the sense of the real meaning rather than the euphemism.]

96. A. Jülicher, *Gleichnisreden* 2: 243. For this possibility, cf. *BAGD* 80, s. v. ἀπαλλάσσω, 2 b.

"talk him around" with dishonest offers.[97] The latter interpretation does not really suggest itself, nor has it any further support in the text, and the former would be foolish, because such flight would only set off a search by the police.[98] Even if it happened fairly often, in practice, that an accused escaped the judicial process by fleeing, such a suggestion is unthinkable as a piece of general advice given by a teacher of wisdom.[99]

This logion, especially in the Lukan version, is frequently referred to as a "similitude,"[100] but both in Matthew and in Luke its form is, first of all, that of a typical, wisdom-style exhortation.[101] Still, this classification is only superficially accurate; Jesus was not interested in giving banal advice about coming to terms with one's opponent in good time when a lawsuit threatens, or, more accurately, giving way in a hopeless legal dispute before there is a verdict and sentence is carried out. That is clear from the emphatic "Amen, I tell you," which is not appropriate for an exhortation in the wisdom tradition.[102] This interjection is a signal pointing to the underlying meaning of the saying, which Luke (or the redactor of Q) emphasizes still further by giving it an eschatological context. This aspect of ambiguity and suppressed meaning does, in fact, turn the injunction into a metaphor or similitude.[103] Thus we probably do best to describe the logion as a parabolic exhortation.[104]

The Legal Situation

There is a lack of clarity in the exegetical literature regarding the legal situation presupposed by this logion. Joachim Gnilka writes: "Everything accords with a Jewish legal process," and remarks a few lines later: "The threatened impris-

---

97. Thus T. Schramm and K. Löwenstein, *Unmoralische Helden,* 59–61.
98. There is an example of an official search warrant in J. Hengstl, *Papyri,* 125–26.
99. One must not forget that this logion, in contrast to Luke 16:1-8, is not simply a similitude. T. Schramm and K. Löwenstein paid too little attention to this point.
100. Thus, for example, E. Klostermann, *Lukas,* 141; T. W. Manson, *Sayings,* 122; J. Schmid, *Matthäus,* 99; idem, *Lukas,* 227; C. H. Dodd, *Parables,* 136; J. Jeremias, *Parables,* 180; W. Schrage, *Ethik,* 29; T. Schramm and K. Löwenstein, *Unmoralische Helden,* 59. According to Adolf Jülicher (*Gleichnisreden* 2: 245–46), what was originally a warning has been turned into a similitude, while according to Rudolf Bultmann (*History of the Synoptic Tradition,* 96, 172) what was originally a similitude has become a warning.
101. Dieter Zeller, *Mahnsprüche,* 65; U. Luz, *Matthew* 1: 281.
102. D. Zeller, *Mahnsprüche,* 65.
103. Cf. M.-J. Lagrange, *Matthieu,* 100: "The parable is implicit or insinuated."
104. Cf. H. Schürmann, "Eschatologie," 282–83.

onment for debt, which is unknown to Jewish law, presumes Greco-Roman legal arrangements."[105] Which is correct?

As the conclusion of the logion shows, the fictional addressee and the opponent are debtor and creditor. The exhortation presupposes that the creditor has made a complaint and is now with the (apparently delinquent) debtor on the way to the nearest large town, perhaps the capital city of Jerusalem, to appear before the judicial authorities at a time already fixed. The debtor is threatened with the civil penalty of incarceration in the public prison until he or his relatives and friends have repaid the whole debt.[106]

The saying therefore presumes a judicial process in which (1) the initiative comes entirely from the creditor—it is *he* who brings the debtor, and *he* hands him over to the judge, (2) a single judge, and not a court of judges, makes the decision, (3) there appears to be no question of a trial, and (4) there is practically no chance for the debtor to escape the imprisonment demanded by the creditor, so that he has only one choice: to give in and satisfy the creditor before a judicial decision is reached. Do we know of such a judicial procedure?

As we have already seen, imprisonment for debt is unknown to Jewish law, both in the Old Testament and in the Talmud.[107] Therefore, the jurisdiction presupposed by the logion cannot be a Jewish one. However, it corresponds surprisingly to what we know about the legal situation and judicial procedures in Ptolemaic and Roman Egypt.[108]

In addition to the proper judicial authorities of the Laocrites and Chrematistes, the higher civil authorities in Ptolemaic Egypt also exercised judicial functions. But while the former groups sat as *collegia*, a civil official passed judgment alone.[109] In the Roman period jurisdictional authority was essentially the prefect's prerogative, but he could also name a lower official as κριτής.[110] Since our logion speaks of an individual judge, we must suppose that,

105. J. Gnilka, *Matthäus* 1: 156–57.
106. For civil penalties, and their purpose, see above, p. 274.
107. See above, pp. 275–76. This is something that R. Sugranyes de Franch completely overlooks (cf. *Etudes*, 60)—even though he himself points it out (ibid., 106)! He thus obstructs his own access to a correct interpretation of the juridical situation. He presumes that this is a Jewish court proceeding.
108. We owe this knowledge to the papyri. Cf. L. Mitteis and U. Wilcken, *Grundzüge* II, 1: 1–22 (Ptolemaic period), 23–46 (Roman period); R. Taubenschlag, *Law;* H. J. Wolff, *Justizwesen.*
109. H. J. Wolff, *Justizwesen*, 113.
110. L. Mitteis and U. Wilcken, *Grundzüge* II, 1: 43; R. Taubenschlag, *Law,* 500, 511–12; H. J. Wolff, "Rechtspflege," 36–40.

if he were not the prefect himself, he must have been one of these civil officials installed as κριτής. Luke explicitly calls him an ἄρχων (Luke 12:58).

> A. N. Sherwin-White sees the judge in our text as definitely not the *iudex* of Roman civil law, installed *ad hoc,* but as a regular judge like the one who figures in the parable of the unjust judge (Luke 18:2-5). But since Roman practice and the hierarchy of magistrates was ignorant of such an office of judge as a continuing status, the scene has for him "a very un-Roman and un-Greek ring to it" (*Roman Society and Roman Law in the New Testament,* 133). Sherwin-White does not mention the quite un-Jewish punishment of imprisonment for debt, but in my opinion it is the most secure starting point for the interpretation of the judicial situation presupposed by this exhortation.

What we otherwise know from the Egyptian papyri about Ptolemaic and Roman judicial procedures before a civil official also fits the situation indicated by this logion. The process was introduced by a petition (ὑπόμνημα) from the plaintiff, and apparently it quite often represented a kind of speedy and superficial process without a thorough review of the matter. In such a process the creditor had the essential advantage; in spite of certain rights of challenge, the debtor was almost defenseless. The very content of the petitions in such cases gives evidence of this: "What was *requested* by those who turned to the *strategoi* or some other administrative or military tribunal, because of an injustice done to them, was neither a judicial decision nor simply an arbitration of the case. In the petitions recovered in great numbers from all three centuries of the Ptolemaic era, it appears instead that the weight of the petition lies, with persuasive unanimity, on the *power of office,* which the official to whom the petition is addressed is to apply in order to effect the required service, action, cessation of action, or behavior on the part of those opposing the petition. The official's required investigation of the case, and the process for decision that may, under some circumstances, have to be initiated play a thoroughly secondary role, even when there is explicit provision for them.[111] This type of petition for official action is also attested for the Roman period.[112]

Accordingly, this logion presupposes that the creditor has petitioned the official he has approached, or the civil officer appointed κριτής, for a civil

---

111. H. J. Wolff, *Justizwesen,* 127. It is true that Wolff remarks (ibid., 130 n. 28): "Of course it is self-evident, in such official actions, that the opponent could effect a cancellation of the decree or a contrary judgment." But according to our logion the debtor could have no such hope.

112. L. Mitteis and U. Wilcken, *Grundzüge* II, 1:34.

penalty to be imposed on the debtor in the form of imprisonment because of a failure to pay the debt. As the concluding sentence shows, it is presumed that the creditor is not making a demand contrary to law; in making the petition, he has the law on his side. It is all the more necessary for the debtor, if he wants to avoid incarceration, to do everything he can to satisfy the creditor and move him to withdraw his petition.

In the Roman period, a petition for execution of sentence was granted by means of a corresponding instruction from the judge to the πράκτωρ, who acted as bailiff—the Lukan version of the logion mentions this officer—or to the ὑπηρέτης, a subordinate of the πράκτωρ, of whom the Matthean version speaks.[113] Ὁ πράκτωρ ἢ ὁ ὑπηρέτης πραξάτω . . . ἐκ τοῦ σώματος: "The practor or the subordinate . . . shall carry out the civil punishment."[114] In this context, the expression παραδιδόναι τῷ πράκτορι or τῷ ὑπηρέτῃ is very common.[115]

What imprisonment in antiquity could mean emerges from the letter of a flute-player to Zeno; he begs Zeno to obtain his release from prison before the latter's departure: οὐ γὰρ ἔχω τὰ ἀναγκαῖα, "for I am lacking the necessities of life."[116]

Jesus and his audience must have been familiar with such processes of judgment and incarceration. In fact, the address in the second person singular, "be accomodating," forces us to suppose that the debtor threatened with the very un-Jewish punishment of imprisonment for debt is thought of as a Jew, for Jesus' hearers were almost exclusively Jews. But is it conceivable that, at the time of Jesus, a dispute among Jews under civil law could be argued before a Roman court?

We are poorly informed about the legal situation in Palestine before the year 70 C.E. It is true that civil disputes were in the hands of Jewish tribunals

---

113. For procedures between creditors and debtors in the first century C.E., see R. Taubenschlag, *Law*, 533–36. For the πράκτωρ ξενικῶν as bailiff, see ibid., 525. For the ὑπηρέτης as bailiff, see L. Mitteis and U. Wilcken, *Grundzüge* II, 1: 31, 44; K. H. Rengstorf, *TDNT* 8: 539. Therefore the assertion that the mention of a ὑπηρέτης points to a Jewish procedure, and that of a πράκτωρ to a Roman process (J. Jeremias, *Parables*, 43 n. 73) is false. It also contradicts the observation made by the same author that imprisonment for debt is foreign to Jewish law (see above, pp. 275–76).

114. *P. Hal.* 1, 116–17. Cf. ibid., 119–20 (3rd century B.C.E.). Quoted from *Dikaiomata* 19 (*Kommentar*, ibid., 80–81). At the passage cited it is not a question of creditor and debtor. The quotation is meant only to illustrate the wording.

115. Cf. *P. Col. Zen.* II, 83.8 (quoted in J. Hengstl, *Papyri*, 114); J. H. Moulton and G. Milligan, *Vocabulary*, s. v. ὑπηρέτης, 655; *BAGD*, 840–41.

116. Quoted, with commentary, in J. Hengstl, *Papyri*, 143–44.

when both parties were Jewish,[117] but I think it is highly probable that Jews could also appeal to the decision of Roman courts or Roman officials, as is attested for the period after 70 c.e.[118]

Another possible explanation for the legal situation presupposed by this logion is indicated by J. D. M. Derrett when he writes: "More efficient modes of execution lay with judge-magistrates, not bound by Jewish norms and customs."[119] However, that the freedom of those judges with respect to Jewish legal traditions was so great that they could impose the civil penalty of imprisonment for debt seems to me highly dubious.

The further question whether, for example, in the jurisdiction of Herod Antipas, Jews could turn to Greek courts in civil law cases, must remain open. We have to content ourselves with the established fact that this logion presumes a set of legal circumstances that is not Jewish, and a judicial process of the type we find in the Egyptian papyri.

Interpretation

The superficial sense of the exhortation is clear: Give in and satisfy your creditor before you are faced with a judicial decision and its unavoidable consequences! A similar warning is found in Prov. 17:14: "The beginning of strife is like letting out water; so stop before the quarrel breaks out." The rabbis saw this proverb as recommending an accommodation through arbitration.[120]

But what is the underlying meaning of the saying? Earlier interpreters for the most part read it as an allegory, following the opinion of the Latin fathers. Thus Paul Schanz sees the opponent as someone against whom one has offended, the road as the road of life, the judge as God, the guard as the angel of punishment, and the prison as hell.[121] In this reading, of course, the judgment is the particular judgment after death. The interpretation is unavoidable

---

117. For Jewish legal arrangements in Palestine, see *t. Sanh.* 7.1; J. Juster, *Juifs* 2: 92–182; G. Alon, "Those Appointed"; E. Schürer and G. Vermes, *History* 2: 184–88; G. Stemberger, *Judentum*, 69–73.

118. Cf. J. Juster, *Juifs* 2: 116–18; G. Stemberger, *Judentum*, 71.

119. J. D. M. Derrett, "Law and Society," 504. Cf. Luke 18:2-5. For the Jewish lay judges who were appointed in all the larger towns and were not bound to the rabbinic traditions, see G. Alon, "Those Appointed," 390–98.

120. *t. Sanh.* 1.6. In a Jewish court of arbitration the parties, by prior agreement, submitted to the decision of a college of judges, normally made up of three persons. Cf. E. Klingenberg, "I dina . . . ," 69–75.

121. P. Schanz, *Matthäus*, 188. Allegorization of the Lukan version is more difficult. On this, see idem, *Lukas*, 363–64. Essentially like that of Schanz is the interpretation of Dietrich Bonhoeffer, *Nachfolge* (ed. M. Kuske and J. Tödt, Munich, 1989), 125–26.

as long as one understands the road as the path of the individual's life.[122] Moreover, every interpretation that reads the saying as a demand for reconciliation must, like Schanz, see the opponent as the neighbor.[123] However, some interpreters have identified the opponent as God.[124] The difficulty that then arises, in that God is both plaintiff and judge, is set aside by appeal to *m. 'Abot* 4.22, according to which at the final judgment God is judge, witness, and accuser.[125] It is certain that the evangelist Matthew, at least, understood individual features of the saying allegorically.[126]

More recent interpreters join their predecessors in seeing the true meaning of the saying as implying a reference to the coming eschatological judgment, but they, for the most part, reject an allegorical interpretation of its individual features. "The meaning of the saying is that one should not simply await the outcome of the divine judgment, but make provision in advance to meet it.[127] But what provision can one make? What is the "challenge of the hour" in light of the "threat [that] 'it may be too late'"? Joachim Jeremias answers: "the hour . . . calls for resolute action."[128] In this interpretation, the saying is closely related to the parable of the unjust judge (Luke 16:1-8): "It warns us to consider the end and to understand the present on that basis; it advises us to use the time that is given us in order to escape unscathed from the future testing. In neither case is it spelled out what we have to do; it is a matter of everything that belongs to the fruit of repentance."[129] The logion is thus "a call to repentance, in view of the eschatological judgment, cloaked in parable form."[130] With this description, Josef Schmid encompasses both the form and the intention of the saying.

Can we give a more precise description of the meaning of the repentance that is demanded? The interpretation of ἴσθι εὐνοῶν τῷ ἀντιδίκῳ σου as a

---

122. Thus also, for example, Theodor Zahn (*Matthäus*, 232; *Lukas*, 518–19), and, if I understand him rightly, T. W. Manson, *Sayings*, 122.

123. Thus, for example, T. Zahn, *Matthäus*, 231–33; A. Schlatter, *Matthäus*, 175; H. Schürmann, "Eschatologie," 283. It is suggested also by W. Schrage, *Ethik*, 29–30.

124. Thus A. Plummer, *Matthew*, 80. W. Grundmann (*Lukas*, 274) wishes to see the opponent as both the neighbor *and* God.

125. The passage is cited above, p. 132.

126. Cf. A. Jülicher, *Gleichnisreden* 2: 241; E. Klostermann, *Matthäus*, 45; J. Schmid, *Matthäus*, 99; D. Marguerat, *Jugement*, 164–65.

127. M. Dibelius, *Formgeschichte*, 249.

128. J. Jeremias, *Parables*, 180. Cf. C. H. Dodd, *Parables*, 138–39.

129. H. Kahlefeld, *Gleichnisse* 2: 124–25. Cf. Rudolf Bultmann, *History of the Synoptic Tradition*, 96; W. Schrage, *Ethik*, 29.

130. J. Schmid, *Matthäus*, 99.

call for reconciliation with the neighbor, which has been repeatedly proposed or considered,[131] is certainly suggested by the Matthean context,[132] but can scarcely touch the original meaning of the saying on the lips of Jesus. The debtor is in the hands of the creditor. At that point, an exhortation to the debtor to offer reconciliation is scarcely appropriate. It is also improbable that Jesus would have the neighbor appear in the guise of the opponent at law, unless one joins Paul Schanz in regarding this person as the neighbor whom I have offended, and who therefore rightly stands before God as my accuser. However, what is owing to that person is not reconciliation, but apology and restitution.

This consideration opens up a further possibility for interpretation: Could it be that Jesus, with a certain irony, thought of himself as the ἀντίδικος, and the "debtor" he is addressing as Israel?[133] Jesus presents a case against his people before God's judgment seat, and accuses them of their "debt." Israel desires to receive the salvation that has come with him, and lauds him for his miracles, but refuses to pay the "debt" it has thereby incurred, namely, the obligation to repent. Those who have received salvation and accepted it, but have not, in consequence, paid the debt of repentance, will be subject to the coming judgment, which will treat them with as little consideration as is shown by a gentile court to a debtor unwilling to pay. That is also the funda-mental idea in the parable of the unmerciful servant in Matt. 18:23-34. Behind it all could be a motif from the prophetic preaching of judgment: the motif of the legal prosecution brought by God against God's people, in which God is both plaintiff and judge.[134] Jesus will plead this case for God and in God's place; but God remains the judge. "Be accommodating with your accuser" would then mean: "turn to me by fulfilling my 'demands' and paying your 'debt,' before God's judgment passes a just verdict on you and you can no longer avoid punishment!" It remains uncertain, however, whether this inter-pretation is accurate.

Conclusion

The Q version of this saying is essentially retained by Matthew. In form, it is a parabolic exhortation. The situation it supposes is that of a debtor who is on

131. See above, p. 287.
132. Cf. Matt. 5:24: "be reconciled to your brother or sister." D. Marguerat, *Juge-ment*, 160–61.
133. In that case, of course, the saying belongs in chap. 7.
134. Cf. Isa. 3:13-14 (see above, p. 137); 27:8; 57:16; Jer. 2:9; Hos. 4:1; 12:3; Mic. 6:2. This motif plays an important role in Psalm 50 (see above, pp. 34–35) and is also encountered in CD I, 2 (see above, p. 78).

the way with a creditor to appear before a judge. The creditor has accused the debtor of failure to pay, and has demanded the civil penalty of imprisonment for debt. The appearance of such imprisonment, which was unknown in Jewish law, shows that the underlying situation here is a proceeding before a non-Jewish, therefore probably a Roman court. The legal situation presupposed here corresponds exactly to what we know from Egyptian papyri about jurisdiction and legal procedure in the Roman period. In those circumstances the judge is either the prefect or an official designated by him. In light of the unavoidable imprisonment for debt, if sentence should be passed, the exhortation calls on the debtor to be "accommodating" with the opponent. This euphemism means that the creditor should be appeased by a proof of willingness to pay, so that the complaint may be withdrawn.

But the fact that the worldly wisdom of this advice does not exhaust the meaning of the saying, as Chrysostom and the Greek fathers indicate,[135] is shown by the emphatic "Truly (amen) I tell you," which does not fit the case of a wisdom-style exhortation. In Luke, and probably in Q, the saying is found in an eschatological context, and undoubtedly it was originally conceived as a warning about the eschatological judgment. In light of that judgment, toward which Israel is moving as surely as a debtor accused by a creditor, and in view of the short time allowed by the last stretch of road, the saying calls urgently for immediate action. In the context of Jesus' preaching, that action can be nothing other than the repentance he demands, the acceptance of his message and the readiness for perfection captured in the Sermon on the Mount.[136]

There is nothing to prevent us from regarding this as an authentic saying of Jesus.[137] Favoring it are not only the formal characteristics, but the ambiguity in its talk of "judgment." "Just for this reason it fits into the proclamation of Jesus."[138] A further indication of this is its kinship with the parable of the unjust judge (Luke 16:1-8), which makes a similar statement, for a similar purpose.

It is possible that Jesus even referred to himself in speaking of the ἀντίδικος, and saw his warning to "be accommodating with your accuser" in a somewhat ironic light as a challenge to his people to be "accommodating" with himself and to pay their "debt" to him by repenting. In that case we should

---

135. Johannes Chrysostomos, *In Mt.* 16.10–11. Cf. P. Schanz, *Matthäus*, 188.

136. On the subject of repentance, see the excursus, chap. 7. For the perfection embodied in the Sermon on the Mount, see Gerhard Lohfink, "Radikalität," esp. 69–75.

137. Because of the "commenting" use of the "I tell you" formula, S. Schulz assigns the saying to a later layer of the Q tradition (Q, 51, 423). That is a *petitio principii*.

138. U. Luz, *Matthew* 1: 281.

consider that Jesus is taking up the prophetic motif of the legal action that God, as plaintiff, brings against God's people. In place of God stands Jesus himself as the accuser. This very way of speaking and acting as if he stood in God's place is, in fact, characteristic of Jesus and the claim he advanced.

The Parable of the Clever Manager (Luke 16:1-8)

This parable has created a good deal of scandal, because it is very difficult to see it as an exemplary story and to conclude: "Go and do likewise!" (Luke 10:37). The example of a cunning rascal has seemed insupportable to many people, and even incompatible with the Gospel.[139] To this day, the parable continues to produce new difficulties for interpreters. For the most part, interpretation is oriented to the added parenetical commentary, especially v. 9. But here a new problem arises: Where does the parable itself end, and where does the commentary begin? Who is the κύριος in v. 8: Jesus, or the master in the parable? And do the comments in vv. 9-13, centered on the key word *mammon*, have anything to do with the theme of the parable? Another problem, much discussed since the beginning of this century, is the correct understanding of the story-image itself, especially the estimation of the deed of the "unrighteous" manager, which is pronounced "shrewd." Was it an illegal act? If so, why is he praised for it, whether by his own master or by Jesus? Or was it perhaps a praiseworthy action after all?

The authenticity of the parable is undisputed. It is demonstrated by the very difficulty that its interpretation presented to the oldest tradition, which led to the commentary in vv. 9-13.[140] However, the narrative was apparently formulated and shaped, like the other similitudes and parables in the Lukan special material, by the evangelist himself.[141] This is evident from the good literary koiné Greek of this passage, revealing scarcely any Semitisms or Septuagintalisms; in the present case, we may note also the use of a proverbial Greek expression in v. 3: σκάπτειν οὐκ ἰσχύω, "dig I cannot."[142]

The Ending of the Parable

Many exegetes regard v. 8a as part of the parable. The "master," who praises the manager here, would then have to be the manager's "master" mentioned

139. Cf. the survey in M. Krämer, *Rätsel*, 29–41.
140. Cf. T. Schramm and K. Löwenstein, *Unmoralische Helden*, 16–19.
141. G. Sellin shows this for Luke 10:25-37 ("Lukas," 35-37); E. D. Freed does the same for Luke 18:1-8 ("Parable").
142. Cf. *BAGD* 753, s. v. σκάπτω; J. Wettstein, *NT* 1: 762–63; E. Klostermann, *Lukasevangelium*, 162.

in vv. 3 and 5.[143] A shift in the meaning of κύριος at this point would be quite unexpected, and without v. 8a the parable would lack a conclusion. "Since the parable began with the fact that the master was settling accounts with his manager and had made known to him his unwillingness that he should continue, it would remain an unintelligible fragment if the last words did not express the master's judgment on the manager."[144] From this point of view it also seems probable that we should conclude that Jesus, with "And *I* tell you" in v. 9, in a certain sense agrees with the judgment of the master in the parable.[145]

However, the argument is frequently reversed: The formula "And (= but) *I* tell you . . ." is said to show that the "master" in v. 8 refers to the master in the parable, at least on the redactional level.[146] But καὶ ἐγὼ ὑμῖν λέγω, as the exact parallel in Luke 11:9 shows, is purely a sequential formula in which ἐγώ has no particular emphasis and thus need not express a contrast to what has gone before. Καί is not to be understood here adverbially in the sense of "also." Instead, as in Luke 11:9, it has a consecutive nuance: "And so I tell you. . . ."[147]

One difficulty in interpreting the "master" in v. 8 as the master in the parable is produced by the designation of the manager as οἰκονόμος τῆς ἀδικίας. An evaluative attribute like this fits better in a commentary by the narrator than within the narrative itself,[148] where its effect is disturbing. Add to this that the betrayed master's praise of the betrayer has always been hard to understand.[149] Even if it is emphasized that the master explicitly acknowledges only the manager's cleverness, this presupposes a complicated psychological profile that is quite foreign to the figures in Jesus' parables, and to popular narrative

143. L. Fonck, *Parabeln*, 599; T. Zahn, *Lukas*, 572–73; M.-J. Lagrange, *Luc*, 433–34; A. Schlatter, *Lukas*, 365; H.-J. Degenhardt, *Evangelist*, 116–17; C. Stuhlmueller, "Luke," 149; J. A. Fitzmyer, "Manager," 165–67; M. Krämer, *Rätsel*, 139–44, 166–73; L. J. Topel, "Injustice," 218; B. B. Scott, "Praise," 174–77; K. E. Bailey, *Poet*, 102–5; I. H. Marshall, *Luke*, 619–20.

144. A. Schlatter, *Lukas*, 365.

145. According to M. Krämer, this is "by far the majority opinion of exegetes" (*Rätsel*, 132).

146. H.-J. Degenhardt, *Evangelist*, 117; T. W. Manson, *Sayings*, 292; J. A. Fitzmyer, "Manager," 167; J. Jeremias, *Parables*, 45.

147. For consecutive parataxis with καί, see M. Reiser, *Syntax*, 123–26.

148. Cf. Luke 18:6.

149. E. Klostermann is not entirely wrong when he writes: "This would be easier to believe in a comedy" (*Lukasevangelium*, 163). Cf. P. Fassl, "'Verwalter,'" 115–17. This difficulty is eliminated by J. D. M. Derrett's interpretation (see below); its adherents, all of whom argue for Luke 16:1-8a as the scope of the parable, must have had their decision made much easier by it.

as a whole.[150] The judgment that the manager acted shrewdly, as well as the description of him as "unrighteous," fits better within a commentary than within the narrative itself.

This adds plausibility to the opinion that sees Jesus as the "master" and separates v. 8a from the parable.[151] Similitudes and parables can, as Rudolf Bultmann observed,[152] easily remain without conclusion if the ending is either obvious or irrelevant. Examples of this are the parables of the rich farmer in Luke 12:16-20, the banquet in Luke 14:16-24, the unrighteous judge in Luke 18:1-5, and the Pharisee and the toll collector in Luke 18:10-13. In three of these examples the parable ends, just as in this case, with a word of commentary by Jesus;[153] and with the possible exception of Luke 14:16-24, all of these parables are taken from Luke's special material.

The opinion that sees Jesus as the "master" in v. 8 also has the advantage that it need not explain how the manager's master found out about his tricks, and why he did not reverse his actions.[154] Moreover, one can really call the manager's activities "shrewd" only if his master in fact did not find out about them.[155]

The content of the two halves of v. 8 is closely connected: with φρόνιμος, v. 8b picks up the key word in the preceding clause. This observation also favors the interpretation of the "master" as Jesus, especially if we suppose that, after the narrator's commentary in v. 8a, the direct discourse begins immediately in v. 8b, which I consider highly probable.[156]

It is true that, if we adopt this position, the text presents a complicated structure: The parable, and thus Jesus' direct discourse, ends with v. 7. In v. 8a there follows, without any linguistic signal, a concluding phrase by the evange-

150. On this, cf. M. Reiser, "Alexanderroman," 147.
151. This opinion is defended by, for example, J. Wellhausen, *Lukas,* 86; R. Bultmann, *History of the Synoptic Tradition,* 175–76; E. Klostermann, *Lukasevangelium,* 163; J. Jeremias, *Parables,* 45–46; H. Preisker, "Lukas," 89; J. Schmid, *Lukas,* 258–59; G. Bornkamm, *Jesus,* 88, 203 n. 38; J. Dupont, "Exemple," 69–70; H. Weder, *Gleichnisse,* 262–64; C. Focant, "Mamon," 555–56—but often with reference to the supposed parallel in Luke 18:6. However, that verse does not help with our question, because there is no κύριος in that parable, and therefore no question of ambiguity.
152. R. Bultmann, *History of the Synoptic Tradition,* 190.
153. Luke 12:21; 18:6-8; 18:14.
154. See the speculations on this point in J. D. M. Derrett, "Parable," 72–73; K. E. Bailey, *Poet,* 101–2; J. A. Fitzmyer, "Manager," 177.
155. J. Schmid, *Lukas,* 258.
156. For unmarked shifts from indirect to direct discourse, see I. H. Marshall, *Luke,* 209 (on Luke 5:14); BD § 470, 2; M. Reiser, "Alexanderroman," 148.

list. Within the same verse, with the second ὅτι ("for"), or else with v. 9, the text goes back, without transition, from indirect to direct discourse. Even the exegetes who posit that originally the "master" meant Jesus, but that Luke understood this as referring to the master in the parable,[157] or vice versa,[158] thereby simply betray their indecision.

All this being said, one will still be better off in deciding to see Jesus in the κύριος of v. 8. Nevertheless, one can scarcely avoid reproaching the evangelist, who could easily have made this clear. *Quandoque bonus dormitat Homerus.*

The Socioeconomic Background

We must probably join the majority of exegetes in seeing the "rich man" as a large landowner. The very situation in Palestine suggests this: major portions of the plain of Megiddo, Galilee, and the Jordan valley were divided into *latifundia*. Some of them were in the hands of foreign owners, as the parable of the winegrowers in Mark 12:1-9 presupposes.[159] The property owner has a manager who is equipped with all the authority of a legal representative.[160]

It is more difficult to give a precise description of the debtors and their obligations to the landowner. We might well see them as tenants who, as usual, were required to deliver a fixed quantity of produce as their rent. However, in that case it is remarkable that the debtors are not called μισθωταί, the usual word for tenants, but instead are said to be χρεοφειλέται, the common word for borrowers.[161] It appears that Luke, at least, did not think of them as tenants, but originally the case may have been different.[162] Some exegetes leave it open whether the reference here is to tenants, or to wholesalers who have taken delivery of goods secured by notes of indebtedness.[163]

157. Thus A. Jülicher, *Gleichnisreden* 2: 504; R. Bultmann, *History of the Synoptic Tradition,* 175–76; G. Bornkamm, *Jesus,* 88, 203 n. 39; J. Jeremias, *Parables,* 45–46; A. Descamps, "Composition," 47.

158. W. Grundmann, *Lukas,* 320.

159. Cf. J. Jeremias, *Parables,* 74–75; M. Hengel, "Weingärtner," 11–16, 19–25.

160. For the Jewish law of representation, see G. Horowitz, *Jewish Law,* 538–68; J. D. M. Derrett, "Parable," 52–55; J. A. Bühner, *Der Gesandte,* 181–267. J. Hermann sees here only a kind of indirect representation ("Überlegungen," 396–97).

161. Cf. Luke 7:41. M.-J. Lagrange rejects the tenant theory for this reason (*Luc,* 432). L. Fonck sees the difficulty, but inclines nevertheless to the tenant theory (*Parabeln,* 598). It is rejected by E. Klostermann (*Lukasevangelium,* 162–63), and vigorously defended by K. E. Bailey, *Poet,* 86–94.

162. A. Schlatter, *Lukas,* 365.

163. Thus A. Jülicher, *Gleichnisreden* 2: 500; J. Jeremias, *Parables,* 181; J. Schmid, *Lukas,* 257; W. Grundmann, *Lukas,* 318. We find deliveries of wheat and oil together, also measured in *cors* and *baths,* as typical items of commerce in 1 Kgs. 5:11 [Heb. 5:25].

In any case, we must imagine the notes as acknowledgments of indebtedness, in analogy to the χειρόγραφα used in Egypt: this was a form of contract in the style of a private letter.[164] For such contracts, witnesses were not required; they received their attestation solely through the handwritten signature.[165] Therefore the legal dealings in vv. 5-7 require no other witnesses in order to be valid.

A correct understanding of the process described in these verses is essential for an interpretation of the parable. The manager makes use of the fact that the debtors are unaware of his firing, and so he acts quickly (v. 6: ταχέως). The ignorance of the debtors also makes his dispositions legally valid, even though he has already been relieved of his office.[166] He calls in his master's debtors and makes them a generous gift by sharply reducing their obligations. He hands back their old notes of indebtedness and has new ones prepared.[167] Probably he also has them backdated. Thus when he prepares his accounts, his master will not be able to tell what has happened, and in this case the manager has no need to fear betrayal.

The value of the discounted amounts of oil and wheat in both cases approaches some 500 denarii.[168] In this way, the manager secures the gratitude of the debtors.

At this point, Jesus breaks off his narrative; everything essential has been said. But instead of passing moral judgment on the man who has betrayed his master, as the audience expects, he praises him.[169] He praises him because he has acted φρονίμως: calculating cleverly and shrewdly, and acting with the greatest possible decision.[170] Jesus sincerely admires this characteristic of such

164. Cf. the reading *chirographum* in two Old Latin mss. for τὰ γράμματα in Luke 16:6! (T. Zahn, *Lukas*, 572 n. 85.)

165. P. M. Meyer, *Juristische Papyri*, 108ff.; J. Herrmann, *Studien*, 24. Cf. also J. D. M. Derrett, "Parable," 64. He points to the mention of a note of indebtedness without witnesses in *T. Job* 11.

166. J. Herrmann, "Überlegungen," 396–97. J. D. M. Derrett supposes that the firing only takes effect after the manager's final accounting ("Parable," 55). For this question, cf. also K. E. Bailey, *Poet*, 96–97.

167. T. Zahn, *Lukas*, 571–72; J. D. M. Derrett, "Parable," 72; J. A. Fitzmyer, "Manager," 176; J. Herrmann, "Überlegungen," 393, 398.

168. J. Jeremias, *Parables*, 181. It is noteworthy that in tenancy agreements for grain-growing land in Egypt the rent always consisted of a fixed amount of grain, never a sum of money (J. Herrmann, *Studien*, 98–101). The quantity, as in this parable, is usually given in a unit of capacity. Seldom is a fixed portion of the harvest set as the interest, but it would amount to half or two-thirds of the yield (ibid., 255–73, documents 6, 13, 44, 93, 158, 166, 173, 202).

169. J. Jeremias, *Parables*, 182.

170. Cf. K. E. Bailey, *Poet*, 105–6.

people, for it is a matter of life and death for anyone who has recognized the signs of the times.

J. D. M. Derrett's interpretation presents a completely different perspective on the parable.[171] The difference lies primarily in his view of the obligations of debtors and the events in vv. 5-7. He believes that the debts are not in produce, but in money. In the background are the Old Testament prohibition against taking interest from fellow Israelites,[172] the "fence" the rabbis drew around it, and a loophole they had left in that fence.

The biblical prohibition on interest could very easily be evaded by simply including the amount of the interest as part of the debt, so that no interest, as such, appeared on the note of indebtedness. Usury practiced in this way could not be verified by a court. But to stop such tricks or at least to pass a moral judgment on them, the rabbis developed the theory of the "dust of usury," which branded as illegal cases that could scarcely be contested in law. However, since the rabbis desired only to condemn the charging of exorbitant interest, and not dealings at interest that were to the advantage of both parties, they left a back door open. That is, they permitted the lending of any quantity of natural produce, even though the lender possessed only a small fraction of the stated amount. Notes of indebtedness made out in this way were not suspect as usurious, but this made it possible to convert a money debt, including the interest, into a debt in produce in order to exclude any suspicion of usury or even the "dust of usury." Oil and wheat were especially well suited to such manipulations, because who was there who did not possess at least a drop of oil or some wheat?

According to Derrett, just such a case is presented in this parable. The debtors have received a loan that they must repay with interest. The interest is included in the sum of the debt, and in order to avoid any appearance even of the "dust of usury," the debt has been converted into a quantity of oil or wheat and the notes of indebtedness made out accordingly. We even learn the amount of the interest, and that it was, in fact, usurious; for what the manager does when he summons his master's debtors is nothing other than to release them from the illegally calculated interest.[173] Therefore, in this interpretation,

---

171. J. D. M. Derrett, "Parable," 52–74. M. Krämer, *Rätsel*, 53–63, gives a good review of his remarks.

172. Cf. Exod. 22:24; Lev. 25:36-37; Deut. 15:7-8; 23:20-21.

173. J. D. M. Derrett, "Parable," 56–62, 66–69. Derrett explains the fact that the interest on the "oil" debt was 50 percent and that on the "wheat" debt only 25 percent by pointing to a parallel phenomenon in Indian legal practice. There the rate of interest rose with the risk, which in turn was connected with the kind of goods lent ("Parable," 69–72). He appears, however, to forget entirely that according to his own point of view

the manager does nothing unjust, even toward the master. On the contrary, he reverses an injustice.

In this way his precarious situation moves the manager to perform a genuinely praiseworthy deed, and the master could scarcely do anything but praise his action, even though it damaged him. It is true that he could have insisted on the sum legally due to him, but he was morally obligated to reduce the illegal, exorbitant interest—which, in fact, his manager may have demanded without his knowledge. And because, in doing so, he could acquire the reputation of being a pious man who revered the Law, he gave his blessing to the manager's action. For that, according to Derrett, is what ἐπῄνεσεν means in v. 8.[174]

Derrett's interpretation, which at first glance is highly impressive, has found considerable agreement.[175] Even Joseph Fitzmyer adopts it, but (and this he does not make quite clear) he introduces a change that is by no means trivial: Fitzmyer thinks that the interest belongs to the manager, and by reducing the amount he is simply foregoing his own profit, so that his master incurs no damage at all.[176] Thus Fitzmyer combines an older interpretation with that of Derrett. That older interpretation was based on an eastern practice in which a manager had to deliver fixed quantities or rents to the master, but, like the toll collectors, collected much higher sums from the debtors. The difference is the manager's profit. This practice is also presumed to have existed at the time of Jesus,[177] but we have no examples of it in our sources.[178] The combination of this idea with Derrett's theory, which regards the interest as profit, is completely arbitrary.

---

both of these are cases of money debts resulting from loans, not really of produce lent or to be delivered. The practice to which he alludes, therefore, even if it had been common in Palestine, could have no influence on the rate of interest. This apparently does not occur to M. Krämer either, for Krämer finds this very explanation to be "the securest starting point" for Derrett's line of argument (*Rätsel*, 60).

174. J. D. M. Derrett, "Parable," 64. But because the object of ἐπῄνεσεν is not a thing, but a person, this interpretation is wrong.

175. It was adopted, for example, by J. Herrmann, "Überlegungen," 399–402; H.-J. Degenhardt, *Evangelist*, 115–18; H. Zimmermann, "Botschaft," 157–58; M. Krämer, *Rätsel*, 63; I. H. Marshall, *Luke*, 617.

176. J. A. Fitzmyer, "Manager," 175–76; idem, *Luke* 2: 1098. Likewise C. Stuhlmueller, "Luke," 149.

177. For this interpretation and its advocates, see M. Krämer, *Rätsel*, 47–49; K. E. Bailey, *Poet*, 88. It is also found in O. Karrer, *NT*, 219–20. Cf. A. Plummer, *Luke*, 383.

178. I. H. Marshall, *Luke*, 615. See the further objections in K. E. Bailey, *Poet*, 88–90. J. Herrmann rightly questions whether the manager would have been acting shrewdly in setting aside these sums in exchange for the general good will of the debtors when he might need help in the future ("Überlegungen," 399).

But Derrett's interpretation of the parable is not sustainable. We have no evidence that the practices it presupposes were also in use in first-century Palestine.[179] Even if we were to suppose that they were, it is impossible that the parable presumes such manipulations and that knowledge of them is the key to understanding it. We find no indication in the parable that the amounts deducted were really illegal, usurious interest. If so, the narrator could easily have made it clear, for example, by having the manager ask not about the amount of the debt, but about the rate of interest, especially since the rate was different in the two instances.

In addition, it is highly unlikely that the rabbinic theory of the "dust of usury" and a loophole deliberately left open in Mishnaic and Talmudic law constitute the background for this parable, and that these are meant to explain the statement of the debt in produce although the debt is really a sum of money. According to Derrett, Jesus' very purpose in creating the parable was "to reveal the essential weakness of Pharisaic thinking and practice."[180] Could one possibly suppose that these not entirely uncomplicated legal connections—Derrett himself calls them "truly controversial and complex"[181]—were immediately and completely obvious to hearers or readers at the time?[182] And is the evangelist really supposed to have handed on the parable "without providing the key to the meaning"?[183] A debt of one hundred *baths* of oil and one hundred *cors* of wheat is much more naturally and simply explained as the amount to be delivered in return for goods actually received, or as a tenant's rent.

Moreover, as mentioned above, the "rich man" need not necessarily be thought of as a Jew. Derrett has to exclude the possibility that he is not, because otherwise his theory is invalid. Another rather serious difficulty for him is that the manager is explicitly called "dishonest" in v. 8. Since Derrett can no longer refer this judgment to the manager's "clever" deed, he has to apply it to the

---

179. In the example from Josephus (*Ant.* 18, 157), which Joseph Fitzmyer adduces ("Manager," 176), the total debt includes not the interest, but the principal of a previous debt, as K. E. Bailey correctly points out (*Poet*, 90). Still, Derrett can bring examples from the Egyptian papyri that go back to the second century B.C.E. ("'Take thy Bond . . .'"). But the Old Testament prohibition of interest is certainly not the background for those.

180. J. D. M. Derrett, "Parable," 51. He thinks it was not impossible that Jesus, in this parable, is objecting to the fact that "even the Pharisees permitted objectionable usurious contracts under colour of a possibly fictitious absence of necessity on the borrower's part" (ibid., 61 n. 1).

181. Ibid., 51.

182. Cf. ibid., 51, 59; idem, "'Take thy Bond . . . ,'" 440.

183. J. D. M. Derrett, "Parable," 51.

squandering of the property that is spoken of in v. 1.[184] This interpretation feels very forced.

Derrett's interpretation appears to be an attempt to rescue this offensive parable for the moral world by means of an innocuous reading.[185] In doing so, it misses the true intention of the parable.

Interpretation

Most of the earlier exegetes, but many more recent ones as well, see the theme of the parable as the correct use of earthly possessions, and find here a challenge to almsgiving. In this, they allow themselves—explicitly or implicitly—to be guided by the interpretation in v. 9 and the larger redactional context. A thematic connection with the parable of the rich glutton in Luke 16:19-31 and that of the wealthy farmer in Luke 12:16-21 is often posited.[186] "On the other hand, it ought to give us pause if we consider that Jesus' attitude toward wealth is not a matter of shrewdness."[187] "For Jesus, possessions and wealth are not primarily a means for doing good, but an obstacle to entry into the reign of God that is now being proclaimed and that requires absolute commitment."[188]

184. J. D. M. Derrett, "Parable," 73–74; H.-J. Degenhardt, *Evangelist,* 118; J. A. Fitzmyer, "Manager," 171. Fitzmyer sees a parallel in Luke 18:2-8, where the judge in v. 6 is also called "unjust" (ibid., 172–73). According to H. Kosmala, the word is merely intended to describe the manager as a child of this world, in contrast to the children of light ("Parable," 114–21). M. Krämer accepts this position (*Rätsel,* 149–50).

185. On this, see T. Schramm and K. Löwenstein, *Unmoralische Helden,* 117–19. They show that this represents a typical reaction to texts "that abandon the usual conventions of morality and custom" (ibid., 119).

186. For example, J. Wellhausen, *Lukas,* 86–87; A. Plummer, *Luke,* 380–81; M.-J. Lagrange, *Luc,* 430; E. Percy, *Botschaft,* 166–67; M. Krämer, *Rätsel,* 131–38; I. H. Marshall, *Luke,* 621–22; see the interpretation in v. 9. A thematic connection with Luke 16:19-31 (in part also with Luke 12:16-21) is proposed by M.-J. Lagrange, *Luc,* 430; A. Schlatter, *Lukas,* 363; H. Preisker, "Lukas," 88–89; J. A. Fitzmyer, "Manager," 163–64; idem, *Luke 2:* 1095. For the older interpretations, see H. Preisker, "Lukas," 87–88. W. Grundmann, *Lukas,* 317, also interprets in terms of the right use of possessions. Even J. A. Fitzmyer upholds this interpretation, but connects it with the eschatological theme: The crisis that the reign of God brings with it demands a shrewd use of wealth ("Manager," 164, 178; *Luke 2:* 1098–99).

187. H. Preisker, "Lukas," 88. In spite of this insight, however, he too sees mammon as the theme of the parable: The manager is driven by greed and thus becomes guilty. The parable is "a cry of warning in face of the humanly destructive danger of riches" (ibid., 92). This misses the point of the parable.

188. H.-J. Degenhardt, *Evangelist,* 124. He therefore correctly sees the point of the original parable exclusively in "shrewdness and decision when salvation is at stake" (ibid., 114).

Moreover, it is someone else's property that the manager is giving away, and he is doing it for an entirely selfish purpose.[189] Only a violently allegorical interpretation can derive from this story a moral about the right use of wealth.

J. D. M. Derrett derives from the parable a parenesis that is very widely accepted. Altogether in line with his interpretation of the imagery, he sees in it the story of a crook who is compelled, by adverse circumstances, to give heed to God's commandments.[190] The lesson we should draw from it is that those commandments are valid and are applicable in every area of life.[191] This interpretation makes the parable an innocuous example story, the moral of which is a banality. "But Jesus has something more on the agenda than merely to affirm a moral lesson that no one doubts; we can recognize his own method in the way he is able to draw the conclusion so as to offer an unexpected and very profound lesson."[192]

K. E. Bailey reads the parable as an allegory, finding the key to its interpretation in the grace experienced by the manager when his master only dismisses him without throwing him into prison. The manager counts on that kindness once again in his hour of need, and he is not disappointed.[193] In the same way, human beings should put their trust in God, who will pay the price for their redemption.[194] Thus a motif introduced into the text (the supposed graciousness of the master) becomes the key to interpretation. This reading entirely overlooks the fact that the manager does not rely on the kindness of his master only because of an unjust action he has already done, but also for one he is about to do. That is surely not the right way to practice trust.

An interpretation that means to do justice to the original meaning of the parable must ignore the redactional context and take its starting point entirely from the point of the parable as expressed in v. 8a: the shrewdness and resourcefulness of the manager, who secures his existence by his decisive action in the face of impending ruin. Almost all exegetes agree that this is the critical

---

189. Cf. A. Jülicher, *Gleichnisreden* 2: 509–10. A. Plummer (*Luke,* 381) and J. D. M. Derrett ("Parable," 74) interpret this feature allegorically: Our goods do not belong to us, but are only entrusted to us by God for our management.

190. J. D. M. Derrett, "Parable," 75. He sees here a parallel to the parable of the lost son in Luke 15:11-32.

191. Ibid., 76. In ibid., 49 n. 1, he places more emphasis on the right use of earthly goods.

192. J. Dupont, "Exemple," 69.

193. K. E. Bailey, *Poet,* 98.

194. Ibid., 107. Similarly allegorizing is the interpretation by L. J. Topel, "Injustice," 224.

point in the story. That the manager's decisive action extends to unscrupulous dealing cannot play a part in the interpretation: that feature is simply part of the material and belongs entirely to the imagery of the parable.[195] But what was the original theme of the parable, if not "mammon"? Why does Jesus tell this offensive example of the decisive action of a cunning scoundrel?

As in most of Jesus' similitudes and parables, the only possible theme is the eschatological event that is impending, or has already begun in his own work, and the consequences of that event for the present. "The story of the deceitful steward in Luke 16:1ff., who knows how to secure his future with a last act of betrayal before he is dismissed, contains an example of resolution; translated into eschatological terms, it offers teaching and warning for the community of disciples as it stands before the great transformation. It does not contain everyday parenesis."[196] Martin Dibelius speaks vaguely here of "the great transformation"; Joachim Jeremias characterizes that transformation as "catastrophe," "crisis," "imminent disaster." As cleverly and resolutely as the manager acts in face of his impending ruin, that is how clever and resolute Jesus' contemporaries should be in face of the coming eschatological catastrophe.[197]

In fact, it is difficult to assert that this parable speaks of the reign of God as something that brings salvation, but not judgment.[198] In an eschatological interpretation, the threatening character that the future bears for the manager must correspond to the threatening character of the impending event. Then Jesus is saying that just as the threat of ruin forces the manager to immediate and resolute action, so the impending judgment, as an unavoidable aspect of the eschatological event, must compel everyone to act immediately and decisively.[199] But by that action Jesus can mean nothing other than repentance in a concrete sense, such as he understands it and demands it. That is the pre-

---

195. Cf. T. Schramm and K. Löwenstein, *Unmoralische Helden,* 20–21.

196. M. Dibelius, *Formgeschichte,* 248. A. Jülicher for the most part restricted his interpretation to the single point of shrewdness and left the original context indeterminate: "The resolute exploitation of the present as precondition for a happy future is to be driven home by means of the story of the steward . . ." (*Gleichnisreden* 2: 511). G. Bornkamm, *Jesus,* 87–88, remains similarly vague.

197. J. Jeremias, *Parables,* 45–47, 182; idem, *Theology* 1: 152. Jeremias emphasizes the catastrophic character of the eschatological event much too one-sidedly. Cf., to the contrary, C. H. Dodd, *Parables,* 30; J. Becker, *Johannes,* 89; J. Dupont, "Exemple," 70–71; C. Focant, "Mamon," 567.

198. Against H. Weder, *Gleichnisse,* 266.

199. Cf. H. Kahlefeld, *Gleichnisse* 2: 91.

condition for escaping judgment and achieving the salvation of the reign of God.[200]

If this interpretation is accurate, we should also take one feature of the parable more seriously than usually happens: that is, the accounting that is demanded of the manager, which is what forces him to take swift action. The motif of giving an account, drawn from the world of business,[201] is found not only in the New Testament, but also in the rabbinic literature and the targums in eschatological contexts as a reference to the accounting that God will demand of every human being at the last judgment.[202] In two of Jesus' other parables as well we find stories of giving account: in the parable of the unmerciful servant (Matt. 18:23-27), and in that of the talents, or minas (Matt. 25:19-28 // Luke 19:15-24). The first of these cannot be referred to the eschatological judgment and it is certainly not a metaphorical feature of the parable, but in the second case it does seem to apply. The two parables of the unrighteous manager and the talents have a great deal in common. They have the same *skopus:* in both of them, Jesus calls for repentance in face of the impending "accounting," and for acting with the greatest possible commitment. The same kind of commitment that crooks and profiteers show on behalf of an evil purpose—that is what Jesus' disciples have to show for a good purpose: for the one thing that is really worth commitment, namely, the reign of God.

200. See above, the excursus in chap. 7.
201. Cf. R. Kittel, *TDNT* 4: 103.
202. Matt. 12:36; Rom. 14:12; Heb. 13:17; 1 Pet. 4:5; Str-B. 1: 640 (on Matt. 12:36); A. Rodríguez Carmona, *Targum,* 13–15. Cf. above, the final section of chap. 3. (*m. 'Abot* 3.1); 120 (*m. 'Abot* 4.22). In a noneschatological sense: Acts 19:40.

CHAPTER NINE

Summary and Conclusion

As the first part of this study has shown, judgment is not merely *one* element of early Jewish eschatology among others, but the most important element in that eschatology, and therefore the principal theme of many early Jewish writings in which prophetic preaching of judgment, especially the announcement of the day of YHWH, was taken up and developed. Those who speak of this judgment await it with longing, not so much because it will bring them recompense for their sufferings, but rather because it will create the necessary precondition for ultimate salvation in the presence of God and limitless happiness on earth, either for the righteous of Israel (if it is the judgment of sinners), or for the whole nation (if the judgment is pronounced against the gentile peoples). For that very reason, Jesus could not preach the reign of God without speaking of judgment. And that Jesus, who spoke with absolute certainty about the reign of God, also spoke with utter seriousness about judgment is something that, in the wake of this investigation, can no longer be doubted.

In the following pages my purpose is to give a summary description and interpretation of Jesus' preaching of judgment based on the texts examined, to shed some light on its function, and to determine the relationship between judgment and the reign of God in Jesus' eschatology. Only then will it be possible to show the relationship of that eschatology to early Jewish conceptions and also to the Baptizer's preaching, and thus to determine what is characteristic of Jesus in this regard.

1. For a *reconstruction of Jesus' preaching of judgment* this study has referred only to texts whose authenticity, at least as regards their content, can scarcely be doubted. They represent all the layers in the synoptic tradition: Q,[1] the

---

1. Matt. 5:25-26 // Luke 12:58-59; Matt. 7:1-2 // Luke 6:37-38; Matt. 8:11-12 // Luke 13:28-29; Matt. 9:37-38 // Luke 10:2; Matt. 10:14 // Luke 9:5; Matt. 11:21-24 // Luke 10:13-15; Matt. 12:41-42 // Luke 11:31-32; Matt. 19:28 // Luke 22:28-30. It is possible that Luke 14:16-24 // Matt. 22:2-14 also stems from Q (see above, p. 241).

Gospel of Mark,[2] the Matthean and Lukan special material.[3] The texts could easily have been increased in number, but I have placed greater value on a careful investigation of individual texts than on the piling up of supporting materials. However, to give some impression of the scope of the tradition on this theme, I will here list those texts in the synoptic tradition that speak of eschatological judgment. Sayings and similitudes that, in my opinion, could be regarded as authentic at least at the core are marked with an asterisk (*).

Q: *Matt. 5:25-26 // Luke 12:58-59; *Matt. 7:1-2 // Luke 6:37-38; Matt. 7:13-14 // Luke 13:23-24; *Matt. 7:22-23 // Luke 13:25-27; *Matt. 7:24-27 // Luke 6:47-49; *Matt. 8:11-12 // Luke 13:28-29; *Matt. 10:14 // Luke 9:5; Matt. 10:15 // Luke 10:12; *Matt. 10:28 // Luke 12:4-5; *Matt. 10:32 // Luke 12:8-9; Matt. 10:39 // Luke 17:33; *Matt. 11:6 // Luke 7:23; *Matt. 11:21-24 // Luke 10:13-15; *Matt. 12:27 // Luke 11:19; Matt. 12:32 // Luke 12:10; *Matt. 12:41-42 // Luke 11:31-32; *Matt. 19:28 // Luke 22:28-30; *Matt. 23:34-36 // Luke 11:49-51; Matt. 23:37-39 // Luke 13:34-35; *Matt. 24:37-39 // Luke 17:26-29; Matt. 24:40-41 // Luke 17:34-35; Matt. 24:45-51; Luke 12:42-46; *Matt. 25:11-12 // Luke 13:25; *Matt. 25:14-30 // Luke 19:11-27; Luke 11:30 (cf. Matt. 12:40); *Luke 14:16-24 // Matt. 22:2-14 (Q?).
Mark: 3:28-29 (cf. Matt. 12:31-32 // Luke 12:10); *4:24 (cf. Matt. 7:2 // Luke 6:38); 4:25; *4:29; *6:11 (cf. Matt. 10:14 // Luke 9:5); *8:38 (cf. Matt. 10:32-33 // Luke 12:8-9); *9:43-48; *9:49; *10:25; *10:31; *12:1-12; *12:40; 13:4; 13:13; 13:20; 13:24-27; 14:62.
Special material, Matt. 5:4; 5:7; 5:22; 7:19; 7:21 (cf. Luke 6:46); 8:29; 12:36-37; *13:24-30; 13:36-43; *13:47-50; 15:13; 18:14 (cf. Luke 15:7); *18:23-35; 21:43; 23:33; 25:31-46.
Special material, Luke 6:21b; 6:24-26 (Q?); 10:20; 12:48; 12:49; *13:2-5; *13:6-9; 14:11; *16:1-8; *16:19-31.

In Q, Jesus' logia and parables, numbered according to the Lukan text, comprise 223 verses; in Mark, they are 171 verses; in the Matthean special material 94 verses, and in the Lukan special material 132 verses.[4] The judgment sayings and parables of Jesus comprise, according to the above list in Q, 76 verses (= 35 percent of the oral discourse); in Mark, 37 verses (= 22 percent of the oral discourse); in the Matthean special material 60 verses (= 64 percent of the oral discourse); and in the Lukan special material 37 verses (= 28 percent of the oral discourse). It is true that these numbers can only be regarded as

2. Mark 4:29; 6:11 (with Q).
3. Matt. 18:23-35; Luke 13:1-5; 16:1-8.
4. In determining the scope of Q and the Matthean and Lukan special material I am following the lists in Georg Strecker and Udo Schnelle, *Einführung*, 53–59.

approximate guidelines, because it cannot always be clearly determined what should or should not be counted. Nevertheless, they indicate the weight accorded the theme of eschatological judgment in the synoptic tradition. What is most striking is the high percentage of judgment sayings and parables in the discourse material of the Matthean special source. In the other layers of tradition, Q shows the highest percentage, but the numbers are more equal if the parable of the banquet (Luke 14:16-24 // Matt. 22:2-14) is not assigned to Q.[5] In any case, more than a quarter of the traditional discourse material of Jesus is concerned with the theme of the final judgment.

Thus there can be no question of any sharp accentuation of the preaching of judgment that would be characteristic of the redaction of Q, and certainly not of a "'re-apocalypticizing' of Jesus' preaching in Q."[6] The assertion that the judgment sayings in the synoptic tradition, as well as the call for repentance associated with them in the tradition, resulted "mainly from the revision of the Jesus tradition or were new constructions by the (early) community"[7] cannot be sustained. The place assumed by the preaching of judgment in Q corresponds exactly to its importance in the preaching of Jesus. That preaching was taken up and developed in Q and the rest of the synoptic tradition.

2. The texts we have investigated yield an *astonishingly clear and consistent picture of Jesus' preaching of judgment*. It is directed both to individuals and to the nation as a whole. The role of individuals in Jesus' preaching is, in the context of early Judaism, nothing new, and it should by no means be overemphasized; the individual is not the proper addressee of Jesus' eschatological preaching, as liberal Protestantism in particular believed.[8] But even though the addressees change, what Jesus announces is always the same event, and the

---

5. For this problem, see above, p. 241.

6. Dieter Lührmann, *Redaktion*, 94. Lührmann, who counts Matt. 11:21-24 // Luke 10:13-15 and Matt. 12:41-42 // Luke 11:31-32 among the "community constructions" (ibid., 93 n. 4), writes of Q on p. 102 of his study: "Its special orientation to the preaching of judgment and its dissemination through the [work of the] disciples makes it a unique quantity within the synoptic tradition and the history of its genre."

7. E. Brandenburger, art. "Gericht Gottes III," *TRE* 12 (1984): 469. J. S. Kloppenborg formulates much more cautiously: "To say that the wisdom components were formative for Q and that the prophetic judgment oracles and apophthegms describing Jesus' conflict with 'this generation' are secondary is *not* to imply anything about the ultimate tradition-historical provenance of any of the sayings. It is indeed possible, [even] probable, that some of the materials from the secondary compositional phase are dominical or at least very old, and that some of the formative elements are, from the standpoint of authenticity or tradition-history, relatively young" (*Formation of Q*, 244–45).

8. See above, p. 161.

decision he demands in light of that event is always the same. Since all are threatened by destruction, he calls for all to repent.[9] This repentance is nothing other than the acceptance of his message and the willingness to do what he says, and it is urgently demanded, because the eschatological event, which brings salvation and destruction with it, is imminent: in fact, it has already begun in his work. The situation of Israel and of every individual is comparable to that of a debtor who is already on the way with the creditor to appear before the judge, or of a manager whose swindles have been discovered and who has only a short time before the final accounting.[10]

3. Some logia, and the parable of the banquet, draw their rhetorical and argumentative force from a *provocative contrast between Israel and the Gentiles*.[11] To understand the intention of these sayings and parables on the lips of Jesus, we must keep the original addressees in mind, namely, Israel. For Jesus, "Israel" means the rightful heirs of God's promises, the "children of the kingdom," the invited guests at the eschatological banquet, where they are to recline at table with Abraham, Isaac, and Jacob. But for Jesus, "Israel" is also "this generation," who will not remain true to their calling, and who oppose him especially in the Galilean towns, the scenes of his activity. Jesus contrasts "this generation" to the Gentiles: the "Queen of the South" and the repentant Ninevites; those who will come from east and west and recline at table with the ancestors in place of the unworthy "children of the kingdom"; the "poor and the crippled" whom the host in anger will summon as guests; the disreputable cities of Tyre and Sidon, who will have it easier at the judgment than Chorazin and Bethsaida.

The provocative intent of these contrasts is unmistakable. The proclamations of judgment connected with or resulting from them are not to be understood as the prediction or revelation of an unchangeable fate, but as serious warnings meant to shake up Israel and cause it to think. This is true not only of Jesus' preaching of judgment, but of that of the Baptizer as well, and of prophetic preaching of judgment as a whole.[12] That preaching announces what

9. Luke 13:1-5.
10. Matt. 5:25-26 // Luke 12:58-59; Luke 16:1-8.
11. Matt. 12:41-42 // Luke 11:31-32; Matt. 11:21-24 // Luke 10:13-15; Matt. 8:11-12 // Luke 13:28-29; Luke 14:16-24 // Matt. 22:2-14.
12. Cf. H. W. Wolff, "Botschaft," 555–56; M. Sato, Q, 120–21; Jer. 18:7-10! Reinhold Schneider speaks of the "immanent contradiction in all prophecy: by nature it is absolutely valid, and is therefore not dependent on justification by history, and yet it is pointed toward the course of history, as salvation or destruction; in an insupportable religious fire it melts the absolute into the temporal; it threatens as something certain

must infallibly occur as a consequence of present behavior, and at the same time it hopes that it can effect a change in that behavior.

From this point of view, the only exception seems to be the series of woes over the Galilean towns, in which Jesus looks back at his activity in those towns and, in retrospect, passes judgment on them. He does not say: "if miracles should occur," but "if miracles had occurred." Jesus appears, at this point, no longer to expect that his preaching could still effect repentance. Consequently, these words must have been spoken shortly before his last journey to Jerusalem.

But if the true purpose of the proclamation of judgment is to warn the audience and urgently summon them to repentance, we cannot speak of a "promise" to the Gentiles, not even when Jesus warns of the Gentiles' being given preference. Such a promise to the Gentiles has been found in the parable of the banquet, but even more so in the saying about the table companions of the ancestors in the reign of God, because it makes use of the motif of the "pilgrimage of nations." But this is to mistake the form and the original purpose of the saying. The word, as in all these contrasts, is addressed solely to the "children of the kingdom," and presents to their eyes an "impossible" situation: the ancestors alone with the Gentiles at the eschatological banquet on Zion, the goal of the "pilgrimage of nations," while they themselves are "thrown outside," namely, into the valley of Hinnom, south of Jerusalem.[13] This grotesque situation must come to pass if Israel does not repent; it would be, so to speak, the consequence of the reproachful contrast with the Queen of the South and the Ninevites at the last judgment, which must lead to the condemnation of "this generation."[14] The two sayings are related as passing of judgment and imposition of sentence. Jesus wants to spare his people both eventualities; for that reason, he confronts them now with both.

Thus these very words show how great is Jesus' concern for Israel and the "children of the kingdom," and how little for the Gentiles. Nothing either positive or negative is said in these words about the salvation of the Gentiles. Certainly, a shift in the audience is all that is required to change a warning for Israel into a promise for the Gentiles. That shift in audience had already been accomplished in the gospels. Both Matthew and Luke show, by means of the

---

what could still be turned aside—and, still more difficult to comprehend, it proclaims judgment and hopes that the arrival of the judge will be delayed" ("Jeremia," 270).

13. The basis is an allusion to Isa. 66:18, 24. See above, p. 237.

14. Matt. 12:41-42 // Luke 11:31-32.

context in which they place this saying, that they regard it as a final judgment on Israel and a promise for the Gentiles.

4. In the texts investigated we find a variety of *images and designations for the eschatological judgment.* As the suggestion of a judgment scene indicates, ἡ κρίσις in the saying about the Queen of the South and the Ninevites has a forensic sense and refers there to the last judgment. The prohibition on judging and the parabolic exhortation to "accommodation" with an opponent also have that reference, as does the saying about the Twelve as judges of the tribes of Israel, the last in clear allusion to Dan. 7:9-10.[15] Like the early Jewish tradition, Jesus also uses juridical vocabulary and images from the courts to make statements about the eschatological judgment.[16] The fact that the description of that judgment in forensic terms makes use of imagery drawn from earthly situations must have been evident from the outset to those who deliberately employed such imagery.

Related to the image of the forensic judgment is that of giving an account, which is derived from the world of business. It appears with reference to the eschatological judgment in the parables of the unrighteous manager and the talents.[17] This image, too, was applied not only by Jesus to the eschatological judgment; however, its use in this context does not appear to have been very ancient.[18]

Jesus also speaks of the eschatological event using the image of harvest. But whereas in the Old Testament harvest was always an image for the destroying judgment of condemnation (that is, the imposition of sentence), for Jesus, the Baptizer, and some early Jewish texts it stands for the eschatological event as a whole and encompasses both aspects of it: judgment and salvation. Jesus, in using this image, even puts the aspect of salvation in the foreground.[19]

This already brings us to the words and images for the imposition of sentence. That can also be the sense of ἡ κρίσις, as in the woes over the Galilean towns.[20] Other conventional images and words for eschatological punishment are "torture," "perishing," and "being brought down to Sheol."[21] The compari-

---

15. Matt. 12:41-42 // Luke 11:31-32; Matt. 7:1 // Luke 6:37; Matt. 5:25-26 // Luke 12:58-59; Matt. 19:28 // Luke 22:30.

16. Cf. above, pp. 154–56.

17. Luke 16:2; Matt. 25:19-28 // Luke 19:15-24.

18. See above, p. 301.

19. Cf. Mark 4:29; Matt. 9:37-38 // Luke 10:2. See above, pp. 256–57.

20. Luke 10:14. Cf. Matt. 11:22.

21. Matt. 18:34; Luke 13:3, 5; Luke 10:15 // Matt. 11:23.

son with a debtor being brought before the court by a creditor leads to the
image of imprisonment for debt.[22] According to the saying about the table
companions of the ancestors in the reign of God, the punishment consists in
being excluded from the eschatological meal and being cast out into Gehenna;
but the parable of the banquet also speaks of exclusion from the eschatological
banquet.[23] Again, Jesus adopts an inherited form of speaking when he uses
this imagery.

5. Especially noteworthy are the *references in the texts investigated to scriptural passages and traditions.* Almost all of them contain allusions to the Old
Testament, or motifs taken from it. However, we observe a thoroughly original
use of those motifs. Thus, while in the saying about the Queen of the South
and the Ninevites Jesus picks up the tradition about the Queen of Sheba from
1 Kings 10 // 2 Chronicles 9, he makes a verbal reference that combines it with
the description of Solomon's wisdom in 1 Kgs. 5:9-14. The queen does not
come to "test [Solomon] with hard questions" (1 Kgs. 10:1 // 2 Chr. 9:1), but
"*to listen to the wisdom of Solomon*" (1 Kgs. 5:14). Jesus apparently derived
the term "Queen of the South" from the post–Old Testament legends about
the queen.

Equally striking is the contrast of the repentant Ninevites with unrepentant
Israel in the second part of the double saying. This contrast, which leads to a
condemnation of Israel, is not founded on the biblical text of the book of
Jonah, but appears to be attested in the rabbinic tradition. This allows us to
suppose that Jesus knew that tradition, and may even have made a conscious
reference to it.

In the woes over the Galilean towns Jesus takes up the prophetic tradition
about the twin cities of Tyre and Sidon and the satirical song in Isa. 14:13-15
in provocative fashion. This makes it clear that Jesus himself takes the eschatological interpretation of the Old Testament for granted: he, like *As. Mos.* 10:9,
reads "being exalted to the heavens" as an image for eschatological salvation,
while Sheol is correspondingly understood as the place of eschatological punishment, that is, hell.

Jesus uses biblical motifs and traditions that were also alive in early Judaism
and among the rabbis in his saying about the table companions of the ances-

22. Matt. 5:25-26 // Luke 12:58-59; Matt. 18:34. For the formulation ἕως ἂν ἀποδῷς
τὸν ἔσχατον κοδράντην, "until you have paid the last penny" (Matt. 5:26), cf. ἕως οὗ
ἀποδῷ πᾶν τὸ ὀφειλόμενον, "until he would pay his entire debt" (Matt. 18:34).
23. Cf. Luke 13:28 // Matt. 8:12; Luke 14:16-24.

tors in the reign of God,[24] but in a way that must have seemed not only offensive, but insupportable to his contemporaries. While the rabbis took the motif
of the eschatological meal from Ps. 23:5 and Isa. 65:13, Jesus takes up Isa. 25:6,
where the meal is promised not to Israel alone, but to "all nations." Such an
idea did not fit within any of the eschatological conceptions of early Judaism,
in which eschatological salvation is reserved either for Israel or for the holy
remnant of the nation. Gentiles could take part in it only through conversion.
The idea that Gentiles would recline at table with the ancestors at the eschatological banquet, and that the "children of the kingdom" could be cast out, was
unheard of. But its enormity is only grasped when we understand the allusion
to Isa. 66:24 that was concealed by both the Matthean and Lukan redaction.
"Being thrust outside" in the original Jesus saying is only comprehensible as
an allusion to the Isaiah verse, out of which the idea of Gehenna as the place
of eternal punishment for the damned had developed. Jesus dares to give voice
to the notion that Israel could fall into Gehenna. Of course, he only expressed
the idea in order that it might not come true.

In the promise to the Twelve[25] there is a reference to the throne scene in
Dan. 7:9. We can no longer be certain whether Jesus was here also referring
antithetically to the midrash on this passage, which applied the judgment in
Dan. 7:9-10 to the eschatological judgment of the Gentiles and saw those associated with the judge as the "great ones of Israel."

We have already pointed to the motif of the harvest and its application.[26]

Thus the very way in which Jesus uses Scripture reveals his closeness to the
tradition and his independence in dealing with it. But that Jesus could also use
the events of the present as illustrations, in place of Old Testament examples,
is evident in the double saying about the slain Galileans and those felled by
the tower.[27]

6. Since Jesus does not explicitly name the *judge* in any of the logia we have
treated, we may suppose that for him, as for early Judaism as a whole, the
eschatological judge was obviously God. The "lord of the harvest" determines
when the sickle will begin its work; the host at the eschatological meal decides
who will be guests and who will be excluded. Every other judge-figure acts
only as representative or by cooperating at the master's command. Still, with

24. Matt. 8:11-12 // Luke 13:28-29.
25. Matt. 19:28 // Luke 22:28-30.
26. See above, p. 307.
27. Luke 13:1-5.

regard to the process of the eschatological judgment, Jesus was as little concerned as was early Judaism about a logically coherent conception;[28] thus he could promise the Twelve that they would participate in the last judgment without giving any indication of his own role in it.[29]

Like early Judaism, Jesus did not make a strict distinction between the passing of judgment (that is, the proceedings before the court and the imposition of sentence) and the execution of the judgment (or declaration of punishment and damnation). When he speaks of the eschatological "judgment," he sometimes means one and sometimes the other. He would have thought of the *execution of judgment,* entirely in accord with the ideas of early Judaism, as lying in the hands of the angels, but also like them he is fond of describing it by the use of a passive construction that permits the active subject to be left indefinite.[30]

7. The judgment Jesus announces for Israel as a whole and for every individual is closely *related to himself and his message.* The repentance he calls for is not, as in early Judaism and still for the Baptizer, a turning back to the Torah, but turning to him and his teaching, in which, of course, he fully affirms the Torah and thus sees it simultaneously elevated (*aufgehoben*) and given its full force. "In a sense he speaks God's final word, and it is in their attitude toward him and his proclamation that the fate of his contemporaries is decided."[31] This is especially evident in the saying about the Queen of the South and the Ninevites and in the woes over the Galilean towns.[32] The one emphasizes hearing his words, the other seeing his deeds; but words and deeds go together. As "this generation" will be condemned because it has not listened to Jesus' words, so will a terrible judgment fall upon the Galilean towns because they did not repent at the sight of his miracles.

These two judgment sayings constitute, so to speak, the "woe" corresponding to the beatitude pronounced over the eye- and ear-witnesses:[33] Blessed are those who hear his words and see his works, for they "behold the good" that is promised to the generation at the end of time[34]—in fact, they are that gifted

28. For Second Temple Judaism, see above, pp. 161–62.
29. Matt. 19:28 // Luke 22:28-30. Cf. above, pp. 260–61.
30. See the excursus in chap. 8.
31. R. Bultmann, "Verständnis," 98. The "in a sense," of course, is superfluous.
32. Matt. 12:41-42 // Luke 11:31-32; Matt. 11:21-24 // Luke 10:13-15.
33. Matt. 13:16-17 // Luke 10:23-24.
34. Cf. *Ps. Sol.* 17:44; 18:3; 1 Enoch 1:2. See above, p. 49.

end time generation! But woe to them if their ears hear and their eyes see, but their hearts remain closed: then will all those things be fulfilled in them that the prophets proclaimed over the wicked and sinners! The objects of judgment, then, are not sins and violations of the Torah in general. The object of judgment, according to the words of Jesus, is nothing but the refusal to repent in response to his message. At the last judgment, that message will take the place of the Torah.[35]

This represents an unusual *claim*, which many of Jesus' contemporaries experienced as outrageous presumption—and necessarily so. Jesus formulates it explicitly when he asserts that in him has appeared "more" than Solomon and "more" than Jonah.[36] By saying "*more* than Solomon," and not "*one greater than* Solomon," of course, he places the spotlight on his message; but that message is indissolubly connected with his person. After all, he says: "Here is more than *Solomon*," and not "more than *Solomon's wisdom*." That is a direct christological statement by Jesus about himself.[37]

8. The founder of the Qumran community, the Teacher of Righteousness, was like Jesus in that he took a stance "in his own environment with the claim that salvation or destruction would be decided by the acceptance or rejection of a message that *only* he embodied."[38] In one of his hymns he says: "Thou wilt condemn in Judgement all those who assail me, distinguishing through me between the just and the wicked."[39] "Thus in fact the Teacher is the only figure known to us from late [*sic*] Judaism whose consciousness of his high station could be compared to that of Jesus."[40] Both of them expect the eschatological event in the very near future; not only that, but in the eyes of both it has already begun in their own activity: in a certain sense it is already possible to experience the happiness of the eschatological time of salvation.[41] Even if the

35. For the early Jewish conception of the Torah as the standard to be applied at the last judgment, see above, p. 157.

36. Matt. 12:41-42 // Luke 11:31-32.

37. H. Schürmann has pointed to the inadequacy of the category of "implicit Christology" with regard to the historical-earthly Jesus (*Gottes Reich,* 43–44).

38. G. Jeremias, *Lehrer,* 334. Cf. ibid., 332–35.

39. 1QH VII, 12.

40. G. Jeremias, *Lehrer,* 335. Of course, in what follows Jeremias emphasizes that Jesus' claim went far beyond that of the Teacher, and to that extent was still unique.

41. G. Jeremias, *Lehrer,* 333–34. His remarks at this point, however, are somewhat contradictory to those on pp. 338, 347–48 of the same work. Here he says: "But the gifts [scil. of the end time] are not merely future, either for Jesus or for the Teacher." However, at the later pages cited he writes that although the Teacher knows that his

final judgment is still to come, it is now, in the acceptance or rejection of their message, that the decision about the verdict of that judgment is being made. The future judgment will thus consist only in the implementation of the verdict already determined, and is nothing other than the consequence of a decision made by each individual and the people as a whole. The verdict that will be implemented at the final judgment is imposed by each person on him- or herself, and that decision is being made even now.

Nevertheless, these common features are balanced by some characteristic differences:[42] these differences are found both in the concrete form of their preaching of judgment and salvation, and in the position accorded to each of them within the proclamation as a whole, as also in their attitudes toward the Torah, particularly its cultic and ritual ordinances. As a consequence of these differences, they diverge also in the content, and ultimately also in the motivation of the repentance each demands.[43] Despite all the formal parallels in the eschatology of the two men, these differences should not be overlooked. The question of the truth of the claim advanced by each is not to be answered by the historian, but by the believer, then and now.

9. *What unites Jesus with the Baptizer* is first of all a fondness for parables and metaphors as a way of pointing to the coming eschatological event and characterizing the present as a time of eschatological decision. In this, both reveal the same inventive gift and creative power; they know how to combine familiar motifs and images with new elements and thus to give them surprising twists.

Both describe eternal damnation by means of an allusion to Isa. 66:24.[44]

Both address their preaching exclusively to Israel, and give no separate attention to the eschatological fate of the Gentiles. Their eschatological thinking does not proceed from the contrast between Israel and the Gentiles, which had customarily served to assign salvation to Israel and destruction to the Gentiles. Instead, they reckon with a division running through Israel itself, with the result that it is not "all Israelites" who "have a share in the world to come,"[45]

---

preaching will lead to salvation, he is still awaiting the beginning of that salvation. For the present eschatology of the Qumran community, see above, p. 76. For Jesus, cf. especially Matt. 12:28 // Luke 11:20; Matt. 13:16-17 // Luke 10:23-24; Matt. 11:2-6 // Luke 7:18-23.

42. Cf. G. Jeremias, *Lehrer*, 336–51.

43. See the excursus in chap. 7.

44. Cf. Matt. 3:12 // Luke 3:17; Matt. 8:12 // Luke 13:28 (see above, p. 237); Mark 9:43-48.

45. Cf. *m. Sanh.* 10.1. See above, p. 136.

but only a part of the nation. Both thus stand within a broad tradition attested since the postexilic prophets.[46] But while the Baptizer combines the idea of this division with the resulting idea of the "remnant" at the end time, and is concerned to gather that "remnant" himself, namely, in those who accepted his baptism, this idea plays no part in Jesus' thinking. On the contrary: it seems that Jesus deliberately avoids it. He never surrendered his claim to the whole of Israel. Even when he had to know that the larger part of Israel had closed itself against his message, he was not prepared to reserve salvation for the remnant that did not. His refusal to be satisfied with this inviting solution ultimately led him not only to go deliberately to his death, but to regard it as "ransom for many," that is, for the unbelieving part of Israel.[47]

Thus it is only partly true that Jesus desired "to gather God's people of the time of salvation."[48] "Gathering" in ordinary language means "to remove certain individuals (people or things) from a larger group and to unite them anew," or "to bring together what is scattered." This intention, with regard to Israel, one can indeed attribute to the Teacher of Righteousness and, in a certain sense, to the Baptizer—the Baptizer's activity prepares for the eschatological "gathering" of the "wheat" (Matt. 3:12 // Luke 3:17)—but not to Jesus, unless one understands "gathering," with respect to Jesus' activity, not in its ordinary, concrete sense, but in a transferred meaning. Such an expanded sense appears to be indicated by the logion about gathering and scattering (Matt. 12:30 // Luke 11:23), and in the metaphor of the hen and her chicks (Matt. 23:37 // Luke 13:34), at least in their application to Jesus' intention and activity.

Both the Baptizer and Jesus proclaim the imminence of the eschatological event that brings with it salvation and destruction; they see it as their mission to make Israel ready for that event. Like the Teacher of Righteousness, they are convinced that the eschatological division is now being accomplished in their own work.

46. See above, pp. 145–48, 190–91.
47. Cf. Mark 10:45. For the problem of Jesus' interpretation of his death, see the two essays in H. Schürmann, *Gottes Reich*. On this, see also Martin Hengel, *Atonement*, 71–72; P. Stuhlmacher, *Jesus*, 54–55, and the criticism by A. Vögtle, "Grundfragen."
48. J. Jeremias, *Theology* 1: 170. Correctly opposed is L. Goppelt, *Theology* 1: 210. Cf. also R. Schnackenburg: "The idea of a 'sacred remnant' that he would gather from *out* of Israel is foreign to him" (*Gottes Herrschaft*, 66). It is true that Jeremias sharply distinguishes Jesus' gathering of the people of God from the assembly of the remnant in Qumran and by the Baptizer (*Theology* 1: 170–78), but the difference for him appears to lie only in the composition of the group assembled.

Both Jesus and John gathered disciples and appeared as prophets. These aspects of their work distinguish them both from the Teacher of Righteousness and from the authors of the major portion of early Jewish literature, who are often described with the vague term *apocalypticists*. While the latter, as far as we know, worked only as authors and proclaimed the final judgment in writing, the Baptizer and Jesus, like the ancient prophets, came bringing an oral message to the people. We need to keep this in mind when we interpret their preaching on the basis of "apocalyptic" literature. While that literature testifies to the thoughts, ideas, conceptions, motifs, terms, and images that were probably known, in large part at least, to the Baptizer and Jesus, we should take care not to try to make a direct comparison, for example, between the tenth chapter of the *Assumptio Mosis* and the description of the Baptizer's preaching in Matt. 3:7-12 // Luke 3:7-9, 16-17. The one is the work of someone at a desk, the other the echo of oral preaching.

Both the Baptizer and Jesus demand repentance from the people in light of the eschatological event. Readiness to repent or refusal to do so bring on the eschatological division of the people. But while the Baptizer still understood repentance as a return to the Torah, the revelation of God's will that was familiar to all and not in need of further interpretation—so that everyone knew what the "fruit of repentance" meant—Jesus interpreted repentance as a turning to him, and his message as the teaching in which, we might say, the Torah first found its own identity. And while the Baptizer was concerned to point away from himself to the "Stronger One," Jesus makes it clear that his message is bound up with his person.

Neither the Baptizer nor Jesus is content with oral preaching; they support it with attention-getting actions and signs. But just here they differ in a characteristic way. John baptizes; Jesus heals. The Baptizer's baptism is done with a view to the approaching judgment and is meant to preserve people from it; Jesus' healing miracles are done in light of the coming salvation that is already appearing in those very healings.

Here, then, we touch the crucial difference between the preaching of Jesus and that of the Baptizer. Jürgen Becker wishes to see it in the fact that Jesus, in contrast to the Baptizer, speaks explicitly of the possibility of salvation and no longer sees the impending judgment as "inevitable and inescapable."[49] But that interpretation does not do justice to either the message or the actions of the

49. J. Becker, *Johannes*, 97. See above, p. 201.

Baptizer. He does not depict the judgment as "inescapable." Quite the contrary: in his baptism he offers just what is needed: an "escape."[50]

Helmut Merklein tries to comprehend the difference by use of the adjective *apodictic,* understanding it differently from normal usage as meaning *unconditional.* The Baptizer preached judgment, and Jesus salvation, as "apodictic."[51] And as the Baptizer in turn promised salvation only conditionally, so Jesus preached judgment conditionally. But the term *apodictic,* even if one were to understand it in the sense Merklein proposes, is scarcely adequate to shed light on the subject. For Jesus, as also for the Baptizer, *both* salvation and judgment are certainly and unconditionally coming. It was unthinkable both for Jesus and for the Baptizer that one or the other should not happen. Both of them are aware of the possibility of salvation and also of the possibility of damnation as consequences of judgment, and therefore they call for repentance. But while the Baptizer sets the impending judgment in the foreground of his preaching and shows a way to avoid it, Jesus gives pride of place to the present and future salvation, and shows the consequences of rejecting it. At the center of the Baptizer's preaching is the concept, known already from the Old Testament, of ὀργή, God's wrathful judgment; but the center of Jesus' preaching is the concept of the βασιλεία τοῦ θεοῦ, which occurs only in widely scattered examples within early Jewish literature as a description of eschatological salvation.[52] And while the Baptizer motivates the decision he demands solely through fear of the judgment, Jesus first awakens hope for definitive salvation and expects repentance primarily as a consequence of the nearness, indeed the visible presence of this salvation in his own deeds: "The reign of God has come near: Repent!"[53] "Everything is ready: Come to the banquet!"[54]

The dialectic of salvation and judgment, or damnation, is inescapable; but it can be approached from different directions. The Baptizer says: Whoever escapes judgment will achieve salvation. Jesus says: Whoever rejects salvation will be subject to judgment. Judgment and salvation are two sides of the same

50. See above, pp. 191–93.
51. See above, pp. 201–2.
52. Cf. O. Camponovo, *Königtum,* esp. p. 57. For the rabbinic writings, see above, p. 141.
53. Mark 1:15.
54. Cf. Matt. 22:4 // Luke 14:17. See above, p. 244. Of course, as we have shown above (excursus, chap. 7), Jesus' call for repentance, where the key word *repentance* is explicitly found in authentic logia, is always founded on the approaching judgment, just as it is for the Baptizer.

coin. The Baptizer holds up the judgment side for the people to see, Jesus the salvation side; but both know what is on the other face, and they make no secret of it. Just as winnowing produces straw for burning as well as wheat to be gathered, so at the eschatological meal there are guests, but there are also those who are excluded.

10. Jesus thus shared the early Jewish expectation of the eschatological event that brings salvation and judgment with it. For him, too, judgment is the unavoidable precondition for the final salvation of the reign of God, and he also thinks of that salvation, in principle, not as other worldly and transcendent, but as this-worldly and earthly.[55] What was special and unique in his eschatological proclamation lay first of all in the message that the eschatological event was in the immediate future and had even begun, in a visible manner, in his own work; second, in the prominence given to the salvational aspect of the event, with the central position assigned to the idea of the reign of God; and finally in his claim that the decision about salvation and destruction for the whole nation and every individual must be made in terms of an attitude toward him and his message. Even though formal parallels to these characteristics can be found especially with the Baptizer and the Teacher of Righteousness, as a whole and in the concrete form they received through Jesus and the reference to his person and message, they constitute something completely new and never before seen in this form. Thus the *proprium*, the uniqueness of Jesus' message, is expressed in the simple statement: "Blessed is anyone who takes no offense at me!"[56] This saying implies another: But woe to the one who takes offense at me! It thus contains within itself Jesus' preaching of salvation and judgment in one, and again shows that the two belong together and are mutually conditioned.

11. The basic features of Jesus' preaching of judgment we have sketched have been derived purely from a few selected sayings and parables whose authenticity has proved to be undisputed or at least difficult to impeach. *Additional judgment sayings and parables of Jesus* can be introduced within the same framework without great difficulty. We should at least make reference to some of them, especially the saying about acknowledgment and denial, which is the logion most often mentioned in this context. We omitted it earlier because of

---

55. For the this-worldly idea of salvation in formative Judaism, see above, pp. 148, 152–54.

56. Matt. 11:6 // Luke 7:23.

the special problem of the "Son of man" sayings.[57] Its original wording was probably preserved, in essence, by Luke:

> Everyone who acknowledges me
>   before human beings,
> the Son of man also will acknowledge
>   before the angels of God.
> But whoever denies me
>   before human beings
> will be denied
>   before the angels of God.
> (Luke 12:8-9, par. Matt. 10:32-33)[58]

This saying, like the one about the Queen of the South and the Ninevites, with which it is in many ways comparable, deals with the last judgment. It clearly presupposes a forensic situation in which "the Son of man," as the single conclusive witness, determines the judge's decision.[59] The mention of the angels is also a reference to the tradition of eschatological judgment scenes stemming from Dan. 7:9-10.[60] The sole criterion for judgment is the acknowledgment of Jesus "before human beings." The saying "solicits" that acknowledgment. Thus there are two primary aspects of Jesus' preaching of judgment that reappear here: Jesus' claim that the verdict at the judgment will depend entirely on one's attitude to him and his preaching, and, connected with it, the emphasis on the fact that the decision is being made now. Thus, ultimately, each is her or his own judge.

Even if we should conclude that the confessional situation here addressed belongs to the post-Easter period, or that the Son of man sayings are absolutely not to be credited to Jesus, we must consider it established that this saying, in its imagery and expression, agrees completely with the preaching of Jesus that

---

57. See above, pp. 203–4.

58. Cf. Mark 8:38 // Luke 9:26. For the reconstruction of the oldest version, see Rudolf Pesch, "Autorität," 26–39; W. G. Kümmel, *Jesus,* 175–76; H. Fleddermann, "Confessing," 607–12.

59. It appears that God, and not the Son of man, is presumed to be the judge. Still, it is ultimately unimportant whether the Son of man is thought of as representative judge or as conclusive witness. For the figures of representative judges in early Jewish tradition, see above, p. 156.

60. For this tradition of scenic depiction of the last judgment, see above, pp. 154–56. For Jesus' appropriation of that tradition, see above, p. 307.

is certainly attested. The question of the extent to which Jesus identified with the "Son of man" can be left open.

The saying about the Flood (Luke 17:26-27 // Matt. 24:37-39) also speaks about the eschatological judgment. It takes up the early Jewish tradition that regarded the Flood as a paradigm for the eschatological judgment of condemnation, and which was fond of setting the two "judgments" in parallel:[61]

> Just as it was in the days of Noah,
> so too it will be in the days of the Son of man.[62]
> They were eating and drinking,
> and marrying and being given in marriage,
> until the day Noah entered the ark,
> and the flood came and destroyed all of them.
> (Luke 17:26-27)[63]

This logion reveals some striking parallels to the double saying about the slain Galileans and those crushed by the tower.[64] In both logia, sudden catastrophes are used as paradigms for the eschatological judgment of condemnation; there is even a common key phrase (πάντες ἀπολεῖσθε—ἀπώλεσεν πάντας). Moreover, the striking fact that Jesus, unlike the early Jewish tradition, lays no emphasis on the special sinfulness of the "generation of the Flood,"[65] but stresses only their thoughtless, carefree living, is explained by the double saying: In face of the decision that confronts everyone in the same way, the question of the individual's degree of sinfulness is simply meaningless; the repentance demanded is the same for all. And this, the call to reflection and repentance, is undoubtedly the intended effect of the saying about the Flood as well.

Closely related to this saying is also the closing parable of the Sermon on the Mount (Matt. 7:24-27 // Luke 6:47-49). Again a sudden catastrophe is cho-

---

61. See above, p. 59.
62. For the "days of the Son of man" as an expression for the eschatological day of judgment, cf. the "day of the elect (= Son of man)" in 1 Enoch 61:5 (see above, p. 67). The plural, "days," is conditioned by the *parallelismus membrorum,* but it is not unusual (cf., for example, 1 Enoch 27:4; 96:8; 4 Ezra 6:18).
63. After this, Luke introduces the corresponding example of the rain of fire on Sodom, achieving a strophic parallelism. (For this, see above, pp. 208–11). It is difficult to say whether it originally belonged here.
64. Luke 13:1-5. See above, pp. 245–49.
65. See above, pp. 215–17.

sen as image for the eschatological judgment: this time it is the collapse of a house in a storm. Once again, in view of this danger, Jesus asks only one thing: Repent. And he clearly says what that means: it consists in doing his words. Ulrich Luz points to the close relationship between this parable and the saying about acknowledgment and denial (Luke 12:8-9), which is also formulated both positively and negatively: Acknowledgment of Jesus corresponds to the hearing and doing of his words, and the acknowledgment of the Son of man before the angels of God corresponds to the survival of the "building" at the judgment.[66] These correspondences in form and content in turn show that the choice of the imagery for the judgment—forensic last judgment or judgment of condemnation—is pragmatically determined. Thus it is again and again the same demand that Jesus bases on and underscores through his references to the impending judgment and the approaching reign of God: the demand for repentance. But for Jesus, not the least among the aspects of repentance was a new attitude toward wealth and poverty, for "It is easier for a camel to go through the eye of a needle than for someone who is rich to enter the reign of God."[67] This statement was unthinkable in the whole Jewish tradition; it contradicts in the sharpest possible way the traditional high esteem for riches honorably acquired.[68] "Only someone who is able to separate from his or her riches can escape destruction."[69] However, according to this saying, "destruction" consists of nothing other than exclusion from the reign of God, "being thrown outside."[70]

The parable of the rich glutton and poor Lazarus (Luke 16:19-31) reads like a commentary on this logion. In it we find an eschatology of the hereafter that corresponds entirely to that found in early Jewish writings.[71] The principal characteristic of that eschatology of the hereafter is to be seen in the fact that, although it acknowledges retribution or compensation after death, and different abodes for sinners and the righteous, it does not provide for a special, individual judgment. It simply presumes that at the end of each individual's life, the group to which she or he belongs, and the place to which she or he

66. U. Luz, *Matthew* 1: 452.

67. Mark 10:25 // Matt. 19:24 // Luke 18:25. Cf. Luke 6:24-26.

68. No one has so clearly shown this as J. Schmid in his excursus on "Jesus' Attitude toward Riches" (*Markus*, 194–97).

69. Ibid., 195.

70. Cf. Matt. 8:11-12 // Luke 13:28-29. See above, pp. 239–40.

71. For an understanding of the concept of "eschatology of the hereafter," see above, p. 21.

accordingly must "be brought," is already determined.[72] There is no reason to deny that Jesus spoke this parable.[73]

One question could not be fully answered before this: If the unique center of Jesus' preaching is the reign of God, understood as impending and already present in his own work, what about the *presence of judgment?* For formative Judaism, the coming of the reign of God meant likewise the judgment of all the enemies of God, and the time of salvation cannot commence "as long as the dominion of Satan [Belial] endures."[74] But with the "appearing" of the "reign of God," according to *As. Mos.* 10:1, "the devil" will also "have an end."[75] For formative Judaism, the eschatological judgment is always both a judgment on Satan and his "lot."

For Jesus, that judgment had already begun. He had seen Satan fall like lightning from heaven (Luke 10:18). With that, the "rule of Belial" is ended; the stronger one has overcome the strong (Mark 3:27). Therefore the reign of God "has come" when he drives out demons (Matt. 12:28 // Luke 11:20). Thus, for Jesus, the judgment has already begun in his own work, not only in the sense that the eschatological fate of every individual and the whole people is being decided now, in their attitudes toward him and his message, but also in the sense that the completion of the end time event of judgment has begun, at least as far as Satan and the demons are concerned.

12. We find that, in his sayings and parables, Jesus not only uses the different forms of judgment (forensic and punishing or destroying judgment), but also images, concepts, and motifs that were available to him in early Jewish eschatology; he also uses both eschatological conceptions, namely, historical eschatology and eschatology of the hereafter. It is repeatedly asserted that Jesus "does take over the apocalyptic picture of the future, but he does so with significant reduction of detail."[76] It is said that, unlike apocalyptic, he did without

72. See above, pp. 148–49. For being "carried away by the angels" (Luke 16:22), cf. 1 Enoch 103:7 (see above, pp. 64–65) and *T. Ash.* 6:4–6 (see above, pp. 94–95).

73. This is true even if Luke formulated the parable and shows a special interest in the eschatology of the hereafter: J. Dupont "L'après-mort dans l'oeuvre de Luc"; idem, *Béatitudes* 3: 99–147. For the eschatology of the parable, see also E. Reinmuth, "Ps.-Philo," 28–38.

74. The formulation ". . . as long as the dominion of Satan endures" is found in 1QS II, 19.

75. See above, pp. 85–86. According to *Jub.* 23:29 also, the eschatological time of salvation is a time without Satan. Cf. K. Berger, *Jubiläen,* 445, n. ad loc. For the war against Belial at the end of time, see 1QM (pp. 79–80 above); 11Q Melch (pp. 82–83 above); *T. 12 Patr.* (pp. 90–93 above)

76. R. Bultmann, *Theology,* 6. Cf. idem, *Jesus,* 39–41.

any fantastic portrayal of the world to come.[77] But a fantastic portrayal of the world to come, whether of the joys of the righteous or the sufferings of the damned, is not at all typical of early Jewish literature of the time before Jesus. Examples like 1 Enoch 10:13-22 are extremely rare.[78] Moreover, the concept of "apocalyptic" is slippery and has not been adequately defined as yet.[79] As long as no such definition has been found, the question (usually answered in the negative) *whether Jesus was an apocalypticist* makes little sense. One must answer "no" if one associates apocalyptic primarily with speculation about the hereafter and advance calculation of the end, but one must answer "yes" if one understands apocalyptic, as it is used in this study, as simply the specific eschatology of early Judaism emerging from the eschatology of the prophets.

13. That Jesus' preaching of judgment, no matter how well rooted in apocalyptic eschatology, has its own characteristic uniqueness has surely been adequately demonstrated by this investigation. Here I wish only to point to one important point at which Jesus' preaching of judgment differs from the apocalyptic texts.

The depictions of judgment in early Jewish writings are quite often dictated by an unconcealed hatred and thirst for revenge: the hatred of the pious against the godless, of the righteous against the wicked, of the tortured against their torturers. In these texts, the eschatological judgment brings not only righteous punishment for sinners, but also serves for the final satisfaction of those who, against all obstacles, remained true to God and God's law. Therefore, at the end of the Book of Isaiah, the redeemed go "out" to the valley of Hinnom to feast their eyes on the corpses of those who have fallen away from YHWH (Isa. 66:24); and therefore, according to 1 Enoch 27, the judgment of condemnation falls on the "accursed" before the eyes of the righteous, and they rejoice when God's sword is bathed in the blood of the oppressors, or they take vengeance into their own hands.[80] The "prophets" who speak in texts of that kind reveal such a desire for revenge that they entirely forget the call to

---

77. Cf., for example, G. Bornkamm, *Jesus*, 67; R. Schnackenburg, *Gottes Herrschaft*, 63–64; L. Goppelt, *Theology* 1: 72. W. Zager, *Apokalyptik*, passim, offers a history of research on this problem (cf. esp. 254–56).

78. Cf. above, pp. 146–47, 149–50.

79. See above, pp. 22–23.

80. 1 Enoch 62:12 (see above, pp. 67–68); 98:12; *Jub.* 23:30 (see above, pp. 71–72); 4 Ezra 7:93. Cf. Str-B. 4: 1113–14; P. Volz, *Eschatologie*, 89–90, 316–17. For the elimination of sinners by the righteous on the day of judgment, see above, pp. 50–51.

repentance; in fact, one has the impression that they are not at all interested in the repentance of sinners.[81]

Nothing of that can be found in the preaching of Jesus. His words about judgment are not inspired by hatred of sinners, but solely by love for them. In fact, he has come especially to call them to the eschatological banquet.[82] Of course, a rejection of the invitation would mean nothing other than self-imposed judgment. Hence the call to repentance, which is equally valid for the righteous and for sinners, plays a central role in Jesus' preaching. The danger that is anticipated can still be averted. Jesus proclaims judgment to "this generation," because he wants to preserve them from it. Only in light of that purpose can we understand his preaching of judgment.

14. *How did Jesus arrive at his preaching of judgment?* What was it, ultimately, that caused him to undertake it? Did he simply take over the idea of judgment as an obvious component of early Jewish eschatology? Did his preaching of judgment merely continue the judgment preaching of the Baptizer, although from a different standpoint and with different accents? Or is his preaching of judgment only a reaction to the increasing rejection of his message in Israel? Each of these three possibilities has an aspect of truth. Jesus stands within the tradition of early Jewish eschatology; he has much in common with the Baptizer; and the rejection of his message undoubtedly led him to emphasize the idea of judgment more strongly. Thus the sayings about the Queen of the South and the Ninevites (Matt. 12:41-42 // Luke 11:31-32) and the parable of the futile invitation to the banquet (Luke 14:16-24) were apparently spoken at a time when it seemed his message might be rejected, while the woes over the Galilean towns (Matt. 11:21-24 // Luke 10:13-15) presuppose that the rejection has already happened. But even when taken together, these three points of view cannot really explain Jesus' judgment preaching. This is clear from the seriousness with which Jesus preached judgment, the originality of his judgment preaching that is evident in so many ways, but primarily from the goal his preaching is intended to achieve: the repentance of individuals and of the whole nation, consisting in turning to him and the resolute performance of his words. For only through that repentance is it possible to avoid the inexorably approaching judgment. We must therefore presume that from the beginning the proclamation of judgment was a fixed, and for Jesus a very important, part of his preaching.

81. See the excursus, chap. 7.
82. Mark 2:17. See above, pp. 243–44.

This opinion is also suggested by the dialectic we have described between judgment or damnation, on the one hand, and salvation on the other. The coming of the reign of God means the final restoration of God's good creation, and thus, at the same time, the destruction of all evil that opposes that restoration. Therefore judgment must come as inevitably as salvation, and the prayer that the reign of God may come (Matt. 6:10 // Luke 11:2) includes the plea that judgment come, too. But that judgment is not only *the precondition for the final coming of salvation;* to the extent that salvation is already present in Jesus' work, judgment is at the same time *the necessary consequence of salvation rejected or despised.* That is never more clear, in Jesus' preaching, than in the parable of the unmerciful servant (Matt. 18:23-34). Accordingly, the gift of undeserved grace and forgiveness is the word that God speaks to human beings. The word demands a response. And the refusal to respond leads inevitably to judgment.

Bibliography I
(for Part One)

Ancient Jewish Sources

Editions, Commentaries, and Annotated Translations (See also pp. 349–62.)

a. Collected Works

Beyer, Klaus. *Die aramäischen Texte vom Toten Meer samt den Inschriften aus Palästina, dem Testament Levis aus der Kairoer Genisa, der Fastenrolle und den alten talmudischen Zitaten. Aramaistische Einleitung, Text, Übersetzung, Deutung, Grammatik/Wörterbuch, Deutsch-aramäische Wortliste, Register.* Göttingen, 1984.

Charlesworth, James H., ed. *The Old Testament Pseudepigrapha. I: Apocalyptic Literature and Testaments. II: Expansions of the "Old Testament" and Legends, Wisdom and Philosophical Literature, Prayers, Psalms, and Odes, Fragments of Lost Judeo-Hellenistic Works.* New York, 1983, 1985.

Díez Macho, Alejandro, ed. *Apócrifos del Antiguo Testamento.* Madrid, 1982–.

Dupont-Sommer, André, and Marc Philonenko, eds., with Daniel Bertrand. *La Bible. Écrits intertestamentaires.* Paris, 1987.

Hilgenfeld, Adolf. *Messias Judaeorum, libris eorum paulo ante et paulo post Christum natum conscriptis illustratus.* Leipzig, 1869.

Kautzsch, Emil, ed. *Die Apokryphen und Pseudepigraphen des Alten Testaments. II: Die Pseudepigraphen des Alten Testaments.* Tübingen, 1900; repr. Darmstadt, 1975.

Kümmel, Werner G., ed., with Christian Habicht et al. *Jüdische Schriften aus hellenistisch-römischer Zeit.* Gütersloh, 1973ff. (= JSHRZ)

Sparks, H. F. D., ed. *The Apocryphal Old Testament.* Oxford, 1984.

b. Individual Writings and Groups of Writings

1. Ethiopic Enoch (= *1 Enoch*)

Beer, Georg. "Das Buch Henoch," 217–310 in Karl Kautzsch, ed., *Pseudepigraphen.* Tübingen, 1900; repr. Darmstadt, 1975.

Beyer, Klaus. "Henoch," in idem, *Die aramäischen Texte,* 225–72.

Black, Matthew. "Apocalypsis Henochi Graece," 5–44 in PVTG 3. Leiden, 1970.
Black, Matthew, with James C. VanderKam. *The Book of Enoch or 1 Enoch: A New English Edition with Commentary and Textual Notes.* SVTP 7. Leiden, 1985.
Bonner, C., and H. C. Youtie. *The Last Chapters of Enoch in Greek.* London, 1937; repr. Darmstadt, 1968.
Charles, R. H. *The Book of Enoch or 1 Enoch. Translated from the Editor's Ethiopic Text and Edited with the Introduction, Notes and Indexes of the First Edition. Wholly Recast, Enlarged and Rewritten Together with a Reprint from the Editor's Text of the Greek Fragments.* Oxford, 1912.
Corriente, F., and Antonio Piñero. "Libro 1 de Henoc," 13–143 in Alejandro Díez Macho, ed., *Apocrifos del Antiguo Testamento IV. Ciclo de Henoc.* Madrid, 1984.
Lods, Adolphe. *Le Livre d'Hénoch. Fragments grecs découverts à Akhmîm (Haute-Egypte), publiés avec les variantes du texte éthiopien, traduits et annotés.* Paris, 1892.
Milik, Jozef T., with Matthew Black. *The Books of Enoch. Aramaic Fragments of Qumrân Cave 4.* Oxford, 1976.
Uhlig, S. *Das Äthiopische Henochbuch.* JSHRZ V, 6. Gütersloh, 1984.

2. Jubilees

Berger, Klaus. *Das Buch der Jubiläen.* JSHRZ II, 3. Gütersloh, 1981.
Charles, R. H. *The Book of Jubilees, or, The Little Genesis.* Translated from the Editor's Ethiopic Text and Edited, with Introduction, Notes, and Indices. London, 1902.
Corriente, F., and Antonio Piñero. "Libro de los Jubileos," 66–193 in Alejandro Díez Macho, ed., *Apocrifos del Antiguo Testamento* II. Madrid, 1983.
Littmann, Enno. "Das Buch der Jubiläen," 31–119 in Karl Kautzsch, ed., *Pseudepigraphen.*
Rönsch, Hermann. *Das Buch der Jubiläen oder Die kleine Genesis. Unter Beifügung des revidierten Textes der in der Ambrosiana aufgefundenen lateinischen Fragmente sowie einer von Dr. August Dillmann aus zwei äthiopischen Handschriften gefertigten lateinischen Übertragung erläutert, untersucht und . . . herausgegeben.* Leipzig, 1874; repr. Amsterdam, 1970.
Wintermute, O. S. "Jubilees," *OTP* 2: 35–142.

3. The Qumran Writings

Delcor, Mathias. *Les Hymnes de Qumran (Hodayot). Texte hébreu, introduction, traduction, commentaire.* Paris, 1962.
Holm-Nielsen, Svend. *Hodayot: Psalms from Qumran.* AThD 2. Aarhus, 1960.
Lohse, Eduard. *Die Texte aus Qumran. Hebräisch und Deutsch, mit masoretischer Punktation, Übersetzung, Einführung und Anmerkungen.* Munich, 1964; 2nd ed., 1971.
Maier, Johann. *Die Texte vom Toten Meer.* 2 vols. Munich, 1960.

4. The Testament of Moses (= Assumptio Mosis) (As. Mos.)

Brandenburger, Egon. "Himmelfahrt Moses," 59–67 in JSHRZ II. Gütersloh, 1976.
Charles, R. H. *The Assumption of Moses. Translated from the Latin Sixth Century Ms., the Unemended Text of which is Published herewith, together with the Text in its*

Restored and Critically Emended Form. Edited with Introduction, Notes, and Indices. London, 1897.

Clemen, Carl. "Die Himmelfahrt Moses," 311–31 in Emil Kautzsch, ed., *Pseudepigraphen.*

———. *Die Himmelfahrt des Mose.* KlT 10. Bonn, 1904.

Hilgenfeld, Adolf. "Mosis Assumptio," 437–68 in idem, *Messias.*

Laperrousaz, Ernest-Marie. *Le Testament de Moïse (Généralement appelé "Assomption de Moïse").* Traduction avec introduction et notes. Sem. 19. Paris, 1970.

Priest, James E. "Testament of Moses," 919–34 in *OTP* 1.

5. The Testaments of the Twelve Patriarchs

Becker, J. *Die Testamente der Zwölf Patriarchen.* JSHRZ III, 1. Gütersloh, 1974.

Charles, R. H. *The Greek Versions of the Testaments of the Twelve Patriarchs. Edited from nine MSS together with the Variants of the Armenian and Slavonic Versions and some Hebrew Fragments.* Oxford, 1908; repr. Darmstadt, 1960.

———. *The Testaments of the Twelve Patriarchs. Translated from the Editor's Greek Text and Edited, with Introduction, Notes, and Indices.* London, 1908.

de Jonge, Marinus, et al. *The Testaments of the Twelve Patriarchs. A Critical Edition of the Greek Text.* PVTG I, 2. Leiden, 1978.

Hollander, Harm W., and Marinus de Jonge. *The Testaments of the Twelve Patriarchs. A Commentary.* SVTP 8. Leiden, 1985.

6. The Sibylline Oracles (*Sib. Or.*)

Collins, John J. "*Sibylline Oracles,*" 317–472 in *OTP* 1.

Gerrcken, J. *Die Oracula Sibyllina.* GCS. Leipzig, 1902.

Nikiprowetzky, Valentin. *La troisième Sibylle.* Etudes Juives 9. Paris, 1970.

Suárez de la Torre, E. "Oraculos Sibilinos," 240–396 in A. Díez Macho, ed., *Apocrifos del Antiguo Testamento* III. Madrid, 1982.

7. The *Liber Antiquitatum Biblicarum* (*Bib. Ant.*)

Dietzfelbinger, Christian. *Pseudo-Philo: Antiquitates Biblicae.* JSHRZ II, 2. Gütersloh, 1979.

Fuente Adónez, Alfonso de la. "Antigüedades Biblicos (Pseudo-Filon)", 195–316 in A. Díez Macho, ed., *Apocrifos del Antiguo Testamento* II. Madrid, 1983.

Harrington, Daniel J. *Pseudo-Philon: Les Antiquités Bibliques I: Introduction et texte critiques.* Traduction par Jacques Cazeaux, revue par Charles Perrot et Pierre-Maurice Bogaert. SC 229. Paris, 1976.

James, Montague R. *The Biblical Antiquities of Philo.* London, 1917; repr. New York, 1971, with a prolegomenon by Louis H. Feldmann, ix–clxix.

Perrot, Charles, and Pierre-Maurice Bogaert. *Pseudo-Philon: Les Antiquités Bibliques II: Introduction littéraire, commentaire et index.* SC 230. Paris, 1976.

8. 4 Ezra

"ΕΖΡΑΣ Ο ΠΡΟΦΗΤΗΣ," 36–113 in Adolf Hilgenfeld, *Messias.*

"Liber Ezrae Quartus," 1931–74 in Robert Weber, ed., *Biblia Sacra iuxta Vulgatam Versionem* 2. 2nd ed., Stuttgart, 1975.

Gunkel, Hermann. "Das 4. Buch Esra," 331–401 in Emil Kautzsch, ed., *Pseudepi-graphen.*
Klijn, Albertus F. J. *Der lateinische Text der Apokalypse des Esra. Mit einem Index Gram-maticus von G. Mussies.* TU 131. Berlin, 1983.
Myers, Jacob Martin. *I and II Esdras: Introduction, Translation and Commentary.* AncB 42. Garden City, N.Y., 1974.
Schreiner, Josef. *Das 4. Buch Esra.* JSHRZ V, 4. Gütersloh, 1981.
Violet, Bruno. *Die Esra-Apokalypse (IV Esra).* GCS 18. Leipzig, 1910.
———. *Die Apokalypsen des Esra und des Baruch in deutscher Gestalt.* GCS 32. Leip-zig, 1924.

9. The Testament of Abraham (*T. Abr.*)

Delcor, Mathias. *Le Testament d'Abraham. Introduction, traduction du texte Grec et com-mentaire de la recension Grecque longue suivi de la traduction des testaments d'Abra-ham, d'Isaak et de Jacob d'après les versions orientales.* SVTP 2. Leiden, 1973.
James, Montague R. *The Testament of Abraham. The Greek Text Now First Edited with an Introduction and Notes.* TaS 2. Cambridge, 1982.
Janssen, Enno. "Testament Abrahams," 193–256 in JSHRZ III, 2. Gütersloh, 1975.
Sanders, E. P. "Testament of Abraham," 871–902 in *OTP* 1.
Schmidt, Francis. *Le Testament grec d'Abraham. Introduction, édition critique des deux recensions grecques, traduction.* Texte und Studien zum Antiken Judentum 11. Tü-bingen, 1986.

10. Rabbinic Literature and Targums

Bamberger, S. פרקי אבות *Die Sprüche der Väter.* Basel, 1981.
Bietenhard, Hans. *Der tannaitische Midrasch Sifre Deuteronomium. Übersetzt und erklärt mit einem Beitrag von Henrik Ljungmann.* Judaica et Christiana 8. Bern and New York, 1984.
———. *Midrasch Tanhuma B: R. Tanhuma über die Tora, genannt Midrasch Je-lammedenu.* 2 vols. Judaica et Christiana, 5, 6. Bern and Las Vegas, 1980, 1982.
Blackmann, Philip. *Mishnayot IV: Order Nezikin* (Pointed Hebrew Text, English transla-tion, Introductions, Translation, Notes, Supplement, Appendix, Indexes, Ad-denda, Corrigenda). London, 1954; 2nd ed., New York, 1964.
Braude, William G. *Pesikta Rabbati. Discourses for Feasts, Fasts, and Special Sabbaths.* 2 vols. Yale Judaica Series 18. New Haven, 1968.
Buber, Salomon. *Midrasch Tanchuma. Ein agadischer Commentar zum Pentateuch.* Wilna, 1885. ET: *Midrash Tanḥuma (S. Buber Recension).* Translated into English with Introduction, Indices, and Brief Notes by John T. Townsend. Vol. I: Genesis. Hoboken, N.J., 1989.
Cohen, Abraham, ed. *The Minor Tractates of the Talmud.* 2 vols. London, 1965; 2nd ed., 1972.
Díez Macho, Alejandro. *Neophyti 1. Targum Palestinense. Ms. de la Biblioteca Vaticana.* 5 vols. (Introduction and text with Spanish, French, and English translations.) Madrid, 1968–1978.

Diez Merino, Luis. *Targum de Salmos. Edición Principe del Ms. Villa-Amil n. 5 de Alfonso de Zamora (Biblia Poliglota Complutense. Tradición sefardí de la Biblia Aramea IV, 1)*. BHBib 6. Madrid, 1982.

Epstein, Jacob N., and Ezra T. Melamed. *Mekhilta d'Rabbi Sim'on b. Jochai. Fragmenta in Geniza Cairensi reperta digessit apparatu critico, notis, praefatione instruxit*. Jerusalem, 1955.

Freedman, Harry, and Maurice Simon, eds. *Midrash Rabbah*. 13 vols. in 10. London, 1939; 2nd ed., 1951.

Goldschmidt, Lazarus. *Der Babylonische Talmud, herausgegeben nach der ersten, zensurfreien Bombergschen Ausgabe (Venedig, 1520–23)*. 9 vols. Haag, 1933–1935.

Hengel, Martin, et al., eds. *Übersetzung des Talmud Yerushalmi, Bd. II, 11: Hagiga (Festopfer)*. Translated by Gerd A. Wewers. Tübingen, 1983. *Bd. IV, 4: Sanhedrin (Gerichtshof)*. Translated by Gerd A. Wewers. Tübingen, 1981.

Herford, R. Travers. *Pirke Aboth. The Tractate "Fathers" from the Mishnah, Commonly Called "Sayings of the Fathers."* Edited with Introduction, Translation, and Commentary. New York, 1925; repr. 1962.

Higger, M. *The Treatises Derek Erez, Masseket Derek, Pirke Ben Azzai, Tosefta Derek Erez*. Edited from Manuscripts with an Introduction, Notes, Variants, and Translation. 2 vols. New York, 1935.

Hoffmann, David. *Mischnaiot. Die sechs Ordnungen der Mischna. Hebräischer Text mit Punktation, deutscher Übersetzung und Erklärung IV: Seder Nesikin*. Berlin, 2nd ed., 1924.

Horovitz, H. S. *Mechilta d'Rabbi Ismael cum variis lectionibus et adnotationibus, defuncti editoris opus exornavit et absolvit J. A. Rabin*. Frankfurt am Main, 1931; 2nd ed., 1970.

Lauterbach, Jacob. *Mekilta de Rabbi Ishmael. A Critical Edition on the Basis of the Manuscripts and Early Editions with an English Translation, Introduction and Notes*. 3 vols. Philadelphia, 1933–1949; repr. Philadelphia, 1976.

Marti, Karl, and Georg Beer. "'Abôt (Väter). Text, Übersetzung und Erklärung nebst einem textkristischen Anhang," in Georg Beer and Oskar Holtzmann, eds., *Die Mischna*. Gießen, 1927.

McNamara, Martin, et al., eds. *The Aramaic Bible*. Edinburgh, 1987ff.

Midrash Bereshit Rabba. Codex Vatican 60 (Ms. Vat. Ebr. 60). A Previously Unknown Manuscript, Recently Established as the Earliest and Most Important Version of Bereshit Rabba. A limited facsimile edition of 160 copies, by special permission of the Bibliotheca Apostolica Vaticana. Jerusalem, 1972.

Pollak, K. *Rabbi Nathans System der Ethik und Moral. Zum erstenmale übersetzt und mit Anmerkungen versehen*. Budapest, 1905.

Rabinovitz, Zvi Meir. *Ginzé Midrash. The Oldest Forms of Rabbinic Midrashim according to Geniza Manuscripts*. Tel Aviv, 1976.

Rengstorf, Karl Heinrich, ed. *Rabbinische Texte. Erste Reihe: Die Tosefta. IV, 3: Sanhedrin—Makkot, übersetzt und erklärt von B. Salomonsen*. Stuttgart, 1976.

Saldarini, Anthony J. *The Fathers according to Rabbi Nathan (Abot de Rabbi Nathan) Version B. A Translation and Commentary*. Studies in Judaism in Late Antiquity 11. Leiden, 1975.

Schechter, Solomon. *Aboth de Rabbi Nathan. Hujus libri recensiones duas collatis variis apud bibliothecas et publicas et privatas codicibus edidit. Prooemium notas appendices indicesque addidit.* Vienna, 1887; repr. Hildesheim, 1979.

Schwab, Moise. *Le Talmud de Jérusalem. Traduit pour la première fois en français.* 6 vols. Paris, 1871–90; repr. Paris, 1969.

Singermann, F. *Midrasch Tanchuma mit verbessertem hebräischem Text übersetzt und erläutert.* Berlin, 1927 (Genesis only).

Stenning, John Frederick. *The Targum of Isaiah.* (Aramaic text with English translation.) Oxford, 1949.

Talmud Yeruschalmi nach der Krotoschiner Ausgabe (1865/66). Jerusalem, 1960.

Theodor, Julius, and Chanoch Albeck. *Bereschit Rabba mit kritischem Apparat und Kommentar.* 3 vols. with a volume of introduction and indexes. Berlin, 1912–36.

Winter, Jakob, and August Wünsche. *Mechiltha, ein tannaitischer Midrasch zu Exodus. Mit Beiträgen von Dr. Ludwig Blau.* Leipzig, 1909.

Secondary Literature

Alexander, Philip S. "Rabbinic Judaism and the New Testament," *ZNW* 74 (1983): 237–46.

Althaus, P. S. *Die letzten Dinge. Lehrbuch der Eschatologie.* 7th ed. Gütersloh, 1957.

Aune, David E. *The Cultic Setting of Realized Eschatology in Early Christianity.* NT.S 28. Leiden, 1972.

Avemarie, F. "Esaus Hände, Jakobs Stimme. Edom als Sinnbild Roms in der frühen rabbinischen Literatur," 177–208 in Reinhard Feldmeier and Ulrich Heckel, eds., *Die Heiden. Juden, Christen und das Problem des Fremden.* WUNT 70. Tübingen, 1994.

Bacher, Wilhelm. *Die Agada der Tannaiten, I: Von Hillel bis Akiba. Von 30 vor bis 135 nach der gew. Zeitrechnung. II: Von Akiba's Tod bis zum Abschluß der Mischna (135 bis 220 nach der gew. Zeitrechnung).* Strasbourg, 1890; 2nd ed., 1903; repr. 1965, 1966.

———. *Tradition und Tradenten in den Schulen Palästinas und Babyloniens. Studien und Materialien zur Entstehungsgeschichte des Talmuds.* Leipzig, 1914; repr. Berlin, 1966.

Balthasar, Hans Urs von. *Theodramatik IV: Das Endspiel.* Einsiedeln, 1983.

Bampfylde, G. "The Prince of the Host in the Book of Daniel and the Dead Sea Scrolls," *JSJ* 14 (1983): 129–34.

Bardtke, Hans. "Literaturbericht über Qumran X. Teil: Der Lehrer der Gerechtigkeit und die Geschichte der Qumrangemeinde," *ThR* 41 (1976): 97–140.

Barr, James. "Jewish Apocalyptic in Recent Scholarly Study," *BJRL* 58 (1975): 9–35.

Barth, Christoph. *Diesseits und Jenseits im Glauben des späten Israel.* SBS 72. Stuttgart, 1974.

Bauckham, Richard J. *Jude, 2 Peter.* Word Biblical Commentary 50. Waco, Tex., 1983.

Bauer, Walter. *Griechisch-deutsches Wörterbuch zu den Schriften des Neuen Testaments und der frühchristlichen Literatur.* 6th ed. Edited by Kurt and Barbara Aland. Berlin, 1988. ET: *A Greek-English Lexicon of the New Testament and Other Early Chris-*

tian Literature: A Translation and Adaptation of the Fourth Revised and Augmented Edition of Walter Bauer's Griechisch-deutsches Worterbuch . . . by William F. Arndt and F. Wilbur Gingrich; 2nd ed. revised and augmented by F. Wilbur Gingrich and Frederick W. Danker from Walter Bauer's 5th ed., 1958. Chicago, 1979.

Beale, Gregory K. *The Use of Daniel in Jewish Apocalyptic Literature and in the Revelation of St. John.* London and Lanham, Md., 1984.

Beaucamp, Evode. "La Théophanie du Psaume 50 (49). Sa signification pour l'interprétation du Psaume," *NRTh* 81 (1959): 897–915.

Becker, Jürgen. *Untersuchungen zur Entstehungsgeschichte der Testamente der Zwölf Patriarchen.* Arbeiten zur Geschichte des antiken Judentums und des Urchristentums 8. Leiden, 1970.

Beckwith, Roger T. "The Pre-History and Relationships of the Pharisees, Sadducees and Essenes: A Tentative Reconstruction," *RdQ* 11 (1982): 3–46.

Betz, Otto. *Der Paraklet.* Leiden, 1963.

Black, Matthew. "The New Creation in 1 Enoch," 13–21 in Richard W. A. McKinney, ed., *Creation, Christ and Culture. Studies in Honour of T. F. Torrance.* Edinburgh, 1976.

Bloch, Joshua. *On the Apocalyptic in Judaism.* JQR MS 2. Philadelphia, 1952.

Bonnard, P.-E. *Le second Isaïe, son disciple et leurs éditeurs. Isaïe 40–66.* EtB. Paris, 1972.

Bonsirven, Joseph. *Le Judaïsme Palestinien au temps de Jésus-Christ. Sa Théologie. I: La Théologie dogmatique. II: Théologie morale. Vie morale et religieuse.* BTH. Paris, 1934, 1935. ET: *Palestinian Judaism in the Time of Jesus Christ.* Translated from the French by William Wolf. New York [1964].

Borig, R. *Der wahre Weinstock.* StANT 16. Munich, 1967.

Bourke, J. "Le Jour de Yahvé dans Joël," *RB* 66 (1959): 5–31, 191–212.

Bousset, Wilhelm, and Hugo Gressmann. *Die Religion des Judentums im späthellenistischen Zeitalter.* HNT 21. 4th ed. with a foreword by Eduard Lohse. Tübingen, 1966.

Bovati, Pietro. *Ristabilire la giustizia. Procedure, vocabolario, orientamenti.* AnBib 110. Rome, 1986.

Bowker, John W. *The Targums and Rabbinic Literature: An Introduction to Jewish Interpretations of Scripture.* Cambridge, 1969.

Brandenburger, Egon. *Die Verborgenheit Gottes im Weltgeschehen: das literarische und theologische Problem des 4. Esrabuches.* AThANT 68. Zürich, 1981.

Brandon, Samuel G. F. *The Judgement of the Dead: An Historical and Comparative Study of the Idea of Post-Mortem Judgement in the Major Religions.* London, 1967.

Braun, Herbert. "Vom Erbarmen Gottes über den Gerechten. Zur Theologie der Psalmen Salomos," *ZNW* 43 (1950/51): 1–54. (Also in idem, *Gesammelte Studien zum Neuen Testament und seiner Umwelt,* 8–69. Tübingen, 1962.)

Brooke, George J. "The Amos-Numbers Midrash (CD 7,13b—8,1a) and Messianic Expectations," *ZAW* 92 (1980): 397–404.

Bultmann, Rudolf. *Theologie des Neuen Testaments.* 9th ed. Tübingen, 1984. ET: *Theology of the New Testament.* Translated by Kendrick Grobel. 2 vols. New York, 1951–55.

Camponovo, Odo. *Königtum, Königsherrschaft und Reich Gottes in den frühjüdischen Schriften*. OBO 58. Fribourg and Göttingen, 1984.

Caquot, André. "Léviathan et Behémoth dans la troisième 'Parabole' d'Hénoch," *Semitica* 24 (1975): 111–22.

———. "Eléments aggadiques dans le livre des 'Jubilés,'" 57–68 in *La littérature intertestamentaire. Colloque de Strasbourg (17–19 octobre 1983)*. Paris, 1985.

Caragounis, Chrys C. *The Son of man: Vision and Interpretation*. WUNT 1st ser., 38. Tübingen, 1986.

Carlson, D. C. "Vengeance and Angelic Mediation in Testament of Moses 9 and 10," *JBL* 101 (1982): 85–95.

Carmignac, Jean. "La notion d'eschatologie dans la Bible et à Qumran," *RdQ* 7 (1969): 17–31.

———. "Le Document de Qumrân sur Melkisédeq," *RdQ* 7 (1970): 343–78.

———. "Les dangers de l'eschatologie," *NTS* 17 (1970/71): 365–90.

———. "Qu'est-ce que l'apocalyptique? Son emploi à Qumrân," *RdQ* 10 (1979/81): 3–33.

Causse, Antonin. "Le myth de la nouvelle Jérusalem, du Deutéro-Esaïe à la IIIᵉ Sibylle," *RHPhR* 18 (1938): 377–414.

Cavallin, Hans C. "Leben nach dem Tode im Spätjudentum und im frühen Christentum I: Spätjudentum," *ANRW* 19.1 (1979): 240–345.

Charles, R. H. *Eschatology. The Doctrine of a Future Life in Israel, Judaism, and Christianity. A Critical History*. Introduction by George W. Buchanan. First publication 1913. New York, 1963.

———. *The Revelation of St. John*. 2 vols. ICC. Edinburgh, 1920.

Charlesworth, James H. *The Pseudepigrapha and Modern Research with a Supplement*. SBL. SCS 7. Ann Arbor, 1981.

Chilton, Bruce D. "A Comparative Study of Synoptic Development: The Dispute between Cain and Abel in the Palestinian Targums and the Beelzebub Controversy in the Gospels," *JBL* 101 (1982): 553–62.

———. *The Glory of Israel: The Theology and Provenience of the Isaiah Targum*. JSOT Suppl. Ser. 23. Sheffield, 1983.

Cohen, Gerson D. "Esau as Symbol in Early Medieval Thought," 19–48 in Alexander Altmann, ed., *Jewish Medieval and Renaissance Studies*. Cambridge, Mass., 1967.

Cohn, Leopold. "An Apocryphal Work Ascribed to Philo of Alexandria," *JQR* 10 (1898): 277–332.

Collins, Adela Yarbro. "Composition and Redaction of the Testament of Moses 10," *HThR* 69 (1976): 179–86.

Collins, John J. *The Sibylline Oracles of Egyptian Judaism*. SBL.DS 13. Missoula, Mont., 1972.

———. "Apocalyptic Eschatology as the Transcendence of Death," *CBQ* 36 (1974): 21–43.

———. "The Place of the Fourth Sibyl in the Development of the Jewish Sibyllina," *JJS* 25 (1974): 365–80.

———. "Jewish Apocalyptic against the Hellenistic Near Eastern Environment," *BASOR* 220 (1975): 27–36.

————. *The Apocalyptic Vision of the Book of Daniel*. HSM 16. Missoula, Mont., 1977.

————. "Dualism and Eschatology in 1 QM. A Reply to P. R. Davies," *VT* 29 (1979): 212–15.

————. "Patterns of Eschatology at Qumran," 351–75 in Baruch Halpern and Jon D. Levenson, eds., *Traditions in Transformation: Turning Points in Biblical Faith*. Winona Lake, Ind., 1981.

————. "The Apocalyptic Technique: Setting and Function in the Book of Watchers," *CBQ* 44 (1982): 91–111.

————. *Between Athens and Jerusalem. Jewish Identity in the Hellenistic Diaspora*. New York, 1983.

————. "The Genre Apocalypse in Hellenistic Judaism," 531–48 in David Hellholm, ed., *Apocalypticism*.

————. *The Apocalyptic Imagination. An Introduction to the Jewish Matrix of Christianity*. New York, 1984.

————, ed. *Apocalypse. The Morphology of a Genre. Semeia* 14 (1979).

Conzelmann, Hans. *Die Apostelgeschichte*. HNT 7. 2nd ed. Tübingen, 1972. ET: *Acts of the Apostles: A Commentary*. Translated by James Limburg, A. Thomas Kraabel, and Donald H. Juel; edited by Eldon Jay Epp with Christopher R. Matthews. Hermeneia. Philadelphia, 1987.

Coughenour, Robert A. "The Woe-Oracles in the Ethiopic Enoch," *JSJ* 9 (1978): 192–97.

Dahl, Nils A. "Eschatologie und Geschichte im Lichte der Qumrantexte," 3–18 in Erich Dinkler, ed., *Zeit und Geschichte. Dankesgabe an Rudolf Bultmann zum 80. Geburtstag*. Tübingen, 1964.

Dahood, Mitchell. *Psalms*. 3 vols. AncB. New York, 1966, 1968, 1970.

Dalman, Gustav. *Die Worte Jesu. Mit Berücksichtigung des nachkanonischen jüdischen Schrifttums und der aramäischen Sprache erörtert*. 2nd ed. Leipzig, 1930.

Davenport, Gene L. *The Eschatology of the Book of Jubilees*. StPB 20. Leiden, 1971.

Davies, Philip R. "Dualism and Eschatology in the Qumran War Scroll," *VT* 28 (1978): 28–36.

————. "Eschatology in the Book of Daniel," *JSOT* 17 (1980): 33–53.

————. *The Damascus Covenant: An Interpretation of the "Damascus Document."* JSOT Suppl. Ser. 25. Sheffield, 1983.

Davies, William D. "Apocalyptic and Pharisaism," 19–30 in idem, *Christian Origins and Judaism*. Philadelphia, 1962.

————. "Reflexions on Tradition: The Aboth Revisited," 127–59 in William R. Farmer et al., eds., *Christian History and Interpretation. Studies Presented to John Knox*. Cambridge, 1967.

Dehandschutter, Boudewijn. "Pseudo-Cyprian, Jude and Enoch. Some Notes on 1 Enoch 1:9," 114–20 in Jan Willem van Henten et al., eds., *Tradition and Re-Interpretation in Jewish and Early Christian Literature: Essays in Honour of Jürgen C. H. Lebram*. StPB 36. Leiden, 1986.

Deissler, Alfons. "Der 'Menschensohn' und 'das Volk der Heiligen des Höchsten' in Dan 7," 81–91 in Rudolf Pesch and Rudolf Schnackenburg, eds., *Jesus und der Menschensohn. FS Anton Vögtle*. Freiburg, 1975.

Deissmann, Gustav Adolf. *Licht vom Osten: das Neue Testament und die neuentdeckten Texte der hellenistisch-römischen Welt.* 4th rev. ed. Tübingen, 1923.

de Jonge, Marinus. *The Testaments of the Twelve Patriarchs. A Study of Their Text, Composition and Origin.* Leiden, 1953.

―――. "Textual Criticism and the Analysis of the Composition of the Testament of Zebulun," 144–60 in idem, ed., *Studies on the Testaments of the Twelve Patriarchs* (1975).

―――. "Notes on Testament of Levi II–VII," 247–60 in idem, ed. *Studies on the Testaments of the Twelve Patriarchs* (1975).

―――. Review of Anders Hultgård, *L'eschatologie II, JSJ* 14 (1983): 70–80.

―――, and A. S. van der Woude, "11Q Melchizedek and the New Testament," *NTS* 12 (1965/66): 301–26.

―――, ed. *Studies on the Testaments of the Twelve Patriarchs. Text and Interpretation.* SVTP 3. Leiden, 1975.

Delcor, Mathias. "L'immortalité de l'âme dans le Livre de la Sagesse et dans les documents de Qumrân," *NRTh* 77 (1955): 614–30.

―――. *Le Livre de Daniel.* SBi. Paris, 1971.

―――. "Le livre des Paraboles d'Hénoch Ethiopien. Le problème de son origine à la lumière des découverts récents," *EstB* 38 (1979/80): 5–33.

―――. "Le Dieu des Apocalypticiens," 210–27 in idem, *Etudes bibliques et orientales de religions comparées.* Leiden, 1979.

―――. "Le milieu d'origine et le développement de l'apocalyptique juive," 193–209 in idem, *Etudes bibliques et orientales de religions comparées.* Leiden, 1979.

―――. "Le mythe de la chute des anges et de l'origine des géants comme explication du mal dans le monde dans l'apocalyptique juive. Histoire des traditions," 263–313 in idem, *Etudes bibliques et orientales de religions comparées.* Leiden, 1979.

―――. "Mythologie et Apocalyptique," 143–77 in Louis Monloubou and Henri Cazelles, eds., *Apocalypses et théologie de l'espérance.* (Also 228–62 in M. Delcor, *Etudes bibliques et orientales de religions comparées.* Leiden, 1979.)

―――, and Florentino García Martínez. *Introducción a la literatura esenia de Qumran.* Madrid, 1982.

Delling, Gerhard. "Speranda futura. Jüdische Grabinschriften Italiens über das Geschick nach dem Tode," 39–44 in idem, *Studien zum Neuen Testament und zum hellenistischen Judentum; gesammelte Aufsätze 1950–1968.* Edited by Ferdinand Hahn, Traugott Holtz, and Nikolaus Walter. Göttingen, 1970.

―――. "Die Weise, von der Zeit zu reden, im Liber Antiquitatum Biblicarum," *NT* 13 (1971): 305–21.

―――. "Die Begegnung zwischen Hellenismus und Judentum," *ANRW* II, 20.1 (1986): 3–39.

Denis, Albert-Marie. *Introduction aux pseudépigraphes grecs de l'Ancien Testament.* SVTP 1. Leiden, 1970.

Dexinger, Ferdinand. *Henochs Zehnwochenapokalypse und offene Probleme der Apokalyptikforschung.* StPB 29. Leiden, 1977.

Dibelius, Martin. *Die Pastoralbriefe.* HNT 13. 3rd ed. Tübingen, 1955. (See also *The Pastoral Epistles; a Commentary . . .* by Martin Dibelius and Hans Conzelmann.

Translated by Philip Buttolph and Adela Yarbro. Edited by Helmut Koester. Hermeneia. Philadelphia, 1972.)

Dieterich, Albrecht. *Nekyia. Beiträge zur Erklärung der neuentdeckten Petrusapokalypse.* 2nd ed. Leipzig and Berlin, 1913; repr. Darmstadt, 1969.

Dietrich, Erich K. *Die Umkehr (Bekehrung und Buße) im Alten Testament und im Judentum bei besonderer Berücksichtigung der neutestamentlichen Zeit.* Stuttgart, 1936.

Díez Macho, Alejandro, et al. *Introducción general a los Apócrifos del Antiguo Testamento.* Apócrifos del Antiguo Testamento I. Madrid, 1984.

Eissfeldt, Otto. *Einleitung in das Alte Testament unter Einschluß der Apokryphen und Pseudepigraphen sowie der apokryphen- und pseudepigraphenartigen Qumrān-Schriften.* 4th ed. Tübingen, 1976. ET: *The Old Testament: an Introduction, including the Apocrypha and Pseudepigrapha, and also the Works of Similar Type from Qumran: The History of the Formation of the Old Testament.* Translated by Peter R. Ackroyd. Oxford, 1965.

Eppel, Robert. *Le piétisme juif dans les Testaments des douze Patriarches.* EhPhR 22. Strasbourg, 1930.

Feldman, Louis H. "Prolegomenon," ix–clxix in Montague R. James, *The Biblical Antiquities of Philo.* London, 1917; New York, 1971.

Fischel, Henry A. "An Epicurean Sententia on Providence and Divine Justice," 35–50 in idem, *Rabbinic Literature and Greco-Roman Philosophy. A Study of Epicurea and Rhetorica in Early Midrashic Writings.* StPB 21. Leiden, 1973.

Fischer, Ulrich. *Eschatologie und Jenseitserwartung im hellenistischen Diasporajudentum.* BZNW 44. Berlin, 1978.

Fitzmyer, Joseph A. "Further Light on Melchizedek from Qumran Cave 11," *JBL* 86 (1967): 25–41. (Also 245–67 in idem, *Essays on the Semitic Background of the New Testament.* London, 1971.)

Flusser, David. "Melchizedek and the Son of man (A preliminary note on a new fragment from Qumran)," *CNFI* 17 (1966): 23–29.

Fujita, S. "The Metaphor of Plant in Jewish Literature of the Intertestamental Period," *JSJ* 7 (1976): 30–45.

García Martínez, Florentino. "Las Tablas Celestes en el Libro de los Jubileos," 333–49 in Antonio Vargas-Machuca and G. Ruiz, eds., *Palabra y Vida. Homenaje a José Alonso Díaz en su 70 cumpleaños.* Publicaciones de la Universidad pontificia comillas I, 28. Madrid, 1984.

———. "Encore l'Apocalyptique," *JSJ* 17 (1986): 224–32.

———. "Escatologización de los Escritos proféticos en Qumran," *EstB* 44 (1986): 101–16.

Geffcken, Johannes. *Komposition und Entstehungszeit der Oracula Sibyllina.* TU. NF 8,1. Leipzig, 1902.

Gehman, Henry S. "Ἐπισκέπτομαι, ἐπίσκεψις, ἐπίσκοπος, and ἐπισκοπή in the Septuagint in Relation to פקד and other Hebrew Roots—a Case of Semantic Development Similar to That of Hebrew," *VT* 22 (1972): 197–207.

Georgi, Dieter. "Der vorpaulinische Hymnus Phil 2,6-11," 263–93 in Erich Dinkler, ed., *Zeit und Geschichte. Dankesgabe an Rudolf Bultmann zum 80. Geburtstag.* Tübingen, 1964.

Gese, Hartmut. "Die Bedeutung der Krise unter Antiochus IV. Epiphanes für die Apokalyptik des Danielbuches," *ZThK* 80 (1983): 373–88.

Gianotto, Claudio. *Melchisedek e la sua tipologia. Tradizioni giudaiche, cristiane e gnos-
tiche (Sec. II a. C.—Sec. III d. C.)*. Supplementi alla Rivista biblica 12. Brescia,
1984.

Glasson, Thomas F. *His Appearing and His Kingdom: The Christian Hope in the Light of
Its History*. London, 1953.

———. *Greek Influence in Jewish Eschatology. With Special Reference to the Apocalypses
and Pseudepigraphs*. London, 1961.

———. "The Son of man Imagery: Enoch XIV and Daniel VII," *NTS* 23 (1977): 82–90.

———. "The Last Judgment in Rev. 20 and Related Writings," *NTS* 28 (1982): 528–39.

Goldstein, Jonathan A. "The Date of the Book of Jubilees," *PAAJR* 50 (1983): 63–86.

Gowan, Donald E. *Eschatology in the Old Testament*. Philadelphia, 1986.

Grelot, Pierre. "L'eschatologie des Esséniens et le livre d'Hénoch," *RdQ* 1 (1958):
113–31.

———. "L'eschatologie de la Sagesse et les apocalypses juives," 165–78 in *A la rencontre
de Dieu. Mémorial Albert Gelin*. Le Puy, 1961. (Also 187–99 in idem, *De la mort á
la vie éternelle. Etudes de théologie biblique*. LeDiv 67. Paris, 1971.)

———. "Hénoch et ses écritures," *RB* 82 (1975): 481–500.

———. "Histoire et eschatologie dans le livre de Daniel," 63–109 in *Apocalypses et
théologie de l'espérance. Congrès de Toulouse (1975)*. Présentation de Louis Monloubou. Préface de Henri Cazelles. LeDiv 95. Paris, 1977.

———. *L'esperance juive á l'heure de Jésus*. Collection "Jésus et Jésus-Christ" 6. Paris,
1978.

Greshake, Gisbert. "Heil *und* Unheil? Zu Bedeutung und Stellenwert von Strafe und
Sühne, Gericht und Hölle in der Heilsverkündigung," *Theologisches Jahrbuch*
(Leipzig), 1986.

Griffiths, John Gwyn. "Apocalyptic in the Hellenistic Era," 273–93 in David Hellholm,
ed., *Apocalypticism*.

Grönbæk, Jakob H. "Zur Frage der Eschatologie in der Verkündigung der Gerichts-
propheten," *SEÅ* 24 (1959): 5–21.

Guardini, Romano. *Freiheit, Gnade, Schicksal. Drei Kapitel zur Deutung des Daseins*.
Munich, 1948; 4th ed., 1956.

———. *Der Herr. Betrachtungen über die Person und das Leben Jesu Christi*. 10th ed.
Würzburg, 1951. ET: *The Lord*.

———. *Theologische Briefe an einen Freund. Einsichten an den Grenzen des Lebens*. Paderborn, 1976; 4th ed., 1985.

Haacker, Klaus. "Assumptio Mosis—eine samaritanische Schrift?" *ThZ* 25 (1969):
385–405.

Haag, Ernst. "Psalm 1. Lebensgestaltung nach dem alttestamentlichen Menschenbild,"
153–72 in Rudolf Mosis and Lothar Ruppert, eds., *Der Weg zum Menschen: zur
philosophischen und theologischen Anthropologie. Für Alfons Deissler*. Freiburg,
1989.

Habets, Goswin. "Eschatologie—Eschatologisches," 351–69 in Heinz-Josef Fabry, ed.,
*Bausteine biblischer Theologie. Festgabe für G. Johannes Botterweck zum 60. Geburts-
tag dargebracht von seinen Schülern*. BBB 50. Cologne and Bonn, 1977.

Hadot, Jean. "Le milieu d'origine du 'Liber Antiquitatum Biblicarum,'" 153–71 in *La Littérature Intertestamentaire*. Paris, 1985.

Hanhart, Robert. "Die Bedeutung der Septuaginta-Forschung für die Theologie," 36–64 in idem, *Drei Studien zum Judentum*. TEH 140. Munich, 1967.

Hanson, Paul D. *The Dawn of Apocalyptic: The Historical and Sociological Roots of Jewish Apocalyptic Eschatology*. Philadelphia, 1975; rev. 2nd ed., 1979.

———. "Prolegomena to the Study of Jewish Apocalyptic," 414–52 in Frank M. Cross et al., eds., *Magnalia Dei: The Mighty Acts of God. Essays on the Bible and Archeology in Memory of G. E. Wright*. New York, 1976.

Harnisch, Wolfgang. *Verhängnis und Verheißung der Geschichte. Untersuchungen zum Zeit- und Geschichtsverständnis im 4. Buch Esra und in der syrischen Baruchapokalypse*. FRLANT 97. Göttingen, 1969.

Hartman, Lars. *Prophecy Interpreted: The Formation of Some Jewish Apocalyptic Texts and of the Eschatological Discourse Mark 13 Par*. CB. NT 1. Lund, 1966.

———. *Asking for a Meaning: A Study of 1 Enoch 1–5*. CB. NT 12. Lund, 1979.

Harvey, Julien. *Le plaidoyer prophétique contre Israël après la rupture de l'alliance. Etude d'une formule littéraire de l'Ancien Testament*. Studia 22. Bruges and Paris, 1967.

Hausmann, Jutta. *Israels Rest: Studien zum Selbstverständnis der nachexilischen Gemeinde*. BWANT 124. Stuttgart, 1987.

Heidolph, K. E., W. Flämig, W. Motsch, et al. *Grundzüge einer deutschen Grammatik*. Berlin, 1981.

Hellholm, David, ed. *Apocalypticism in the Mediterranean World and the Near East. Proceedings of the International Colloquium on Apocalypticism, Uppsala August 12–17, 1979*. Tübingen, 1983.

Hengel, Martin. *Judentum und Hellenismus. Studien zu ihrer Begegnung unter besonderer Berücksichtigung Palästinas bis zur Mitte des 2. Jh.s. v. Chr.* WUNT 10. 2nd ed. Tübingen, 1973. ET: *Judaism and Hellenism: Studies in their Encounter in Palestine during the Early Hellenistic Period*. Translated by John Bowden. Philadelphia, 1974.

———. "Anonymität, Pseudepigraphie und 'Literarische Fälschung' in der jüdisch-hellenistischen Literatur," 229–308 in *Pseudepigrapha I. Pseudopythagorica—Lettres de Platon—Littérature pseudépigraphique juive*. Entretiens sur l'Antiquité classique publiée par Olivier Reverdin. Vandoeuvres-Genève, 1972.

———. "Messianische Hoffnung und politischer 'Radikalismus' in der 'jüdisch-hellenistischen Diaspora.' Zur Frage der Voraussetzungen des jüdischen Aufstandes unter Trajan 115–117 n. Chr.," 655–86 in David Hellholm, ed., *Apocalypticism*.

Hoffmann, Paul. *Die Toten in Christus: Eine religionsgeschichtliche und exegetische Untersuchung zur paulinischen Eschatologie*. NTA. n.s. 2. Münster, 1966; 3rd rev. ed., 1978.

Hollander, Harm W., and Marinus de Jonge. *The Testaments of the Twelve Patriarchs: A Commentary*. SVTP 8. Leiden, 1985.

Horton, Fred L. *The Melchizedek Tradition: A Critical Examination of the Sources to the Fifth Century A.D. and in the Epistle to the Hebrews*. MSSNTS 30. Cambridge and New York, 1976.

Hübner, Hans. "Zur Ethik der Sapientia Salomonis," 166–87 in Wolfgang Schrage, ed., *Studien zum Text und zur Ethik des Neuen Testaments. FS zum 80. Geburtstag von Heinrich Greeven*. BZNW 47. Berlin and New York, 1986.

Hultgård, Anders. *L'eschatologie des Testaments des Douze Patriarches, I: Interprétation des textes; II: Composition de l'ouvrage, textes et traductions.* AUU. HR 6, 7. Uppsala, 1977, 1981.

Isenberg, Sheldon R. "An Anti-Sadducee Polemic in the Palestinian Targum Tradition," *HThR* 63 (1970): 433–44.

Jacquet, Louis. *Les Psaumes et le coeur de l'homme: Etude textuelle, littéraire et doctrinale.* 3 vols. Gembloux, 1975–1979.

Janowski, Bernd, and Hermann Lichtenberger. "Enderwartung und Reinheitsidee. Zur eschatologischen Deutung von Reinheit und Sühne in der Qumrangemeinde," *JJS* 34 (1983): 31–59.

Jenni, Ernst. "'Kommen' im theologischen Sprachgebrauch des Alten Testaments," 251–61 in Hans Joachim Stoebe, ed., with Jakob Stamm and Ernst Jenni, *Wort, Gebot, Glaube. Beiträge zur Theologie des Alten Testaments. Walther Eichrodt zum 80. Geburtstag.* AThANT 59. Zürich, 1970.

Jeremias, Gert. *Der Lehrer der Gerechtigkeit.* StUNT 2. Göttingen, 1963.

Jeremias, Jörg. *Theophanie. Die Geschichte einer alttestamentlichen Gattung.* WMANT 10. 2nd ed. Neukirchen-Vluyn, 1977.

———. *Das Königtum Gottes in den Psalmen: Israels Begegnung mit dem kanaanäischen Mythos in den Jahwe-König-Psalmen.* FRLANT 141. Göttingen, 1987.

Kapelrud, Arvid S. *The Message of the Prophet Zephaniah: Morphology and Ideas.* Oslo, 1975.

Kasher, Rimon. "The Interpretation of Scripture in Rabbinic Literature," 547–94 in M. J. Mulder, ed., *Mikra: Text, Translation, Reading, and Interpretation of the Hebrew Bible in Ancient Judaism and Early Christianity.* CRINT II, 1. Assen and Philadelphia, 1988.

Keulers, J. *Die eschatologische Lehre des vierten Esrabuches.* BSt 20, 2.3. Freiburg, 1922.

Klausner, Joseph. *Die messianischen Vorstellungen des jüdischen Volkes im Zeitalter der Tannaiten kritisch untersucht und im Rahmen der Zeitgeschichte dargestellt.* Krakow, 1903; Berlin, 1904.

———. *The Messianic Idea in Israel, from Its Beginning to the Completion of the Mishnah.* Translated from the 3rd Hebrew edition by W. F. Stinespring. New York, 1955.

Knibb, Michael A. "Apocalyptic and Wisdom in 4 Ezra," *JSJ* 13 (1982): 56–74.

Kobelski, Paul J. *Melchizedek and Melchireša'* CBQ MS 10. Washington, 1981.

Koch, Klaus. *Ratlos vor der Apokalyptik. Eine Streitschrift über ein vernachlässigtes Gebiet der Bibelwissenschaft und die schädlichen Auswirkungen auf Theologie und Philosophie.* Gütersloh, 1970. ET: *The Rediscovery of Apocalyptic: A Polemical Work on a Neglected Area of Biblical Studies and Its Damaging Effects on Theology and Philosophy.* Translated by Margaret Kohl. London, 1972.

———. "Esras erste Vision: Weltzeiten und Weg des Höchsten," *BZ* n.s. 22 (1978): 46–75.

———, et al. *Das Buch Daniel.* EdF 144. Darmstadt, 1980.

———. "Sabbatstruktur der Geschichte. Die sogenannte Zehn-Wochen-Apokalypse (I Hen 93.1-19; 91,11-17) und das Ringen um die alttestamentliche Chronologie im späten Israelitentum," *ZAW* 95 (1983): 403–30.

———, and Johann Michael Schmidt, eds. *Apokalyptik.* WdF 365. Darmstadt, 1982.

Köhler, Ludwig. *Theologie des Alten Testaments.* 4th ed. Tübingen, 1966. ET: *Old Testament Theology.* Translated by A. S. Todd. Philadelphia, 1957.

―――. *Der hebräische Mensch.* Darmstadt, 1980. ET: *Hebrew Man.* Translated by Peter R. Ackroyd. Nashville, 1957.

Koep, L. *Das himmlische Buch in Antike und Christentum.* Theoph. 8. Bonn, 1952.

Kraft, Robert A. "Reassessing the 'Recensional Problem' in Testament of Abraham," 121–37 in G. W. E. Nickelsburg, ed., *Studies on the Testament of Abraham.*

Kraus, Hans-Joachim. *Psalmen.* BK XV/1.2. 4th ed. Neukirchen-Vluyn, 1972. ET: Vol. 1: *Psalms 1–59: A Commentary.* Translated by Hilton C. Oswald. Minneapolis, 1988. Vol. 2: *Psalms 60–150: A Commentary.* Translated by Hilton C. Oswald. Minneapolis, 1989.

Krinetzki, Gunter. *Zefanjastudien: Motiv- und Traditionskritik + Kompositions- und Redaktionskritik.* Regensburger Studien zur Theologie 7. Frankfurt am Main, 1977.

Kuhn, Heinz-Wolfgang. *Enderwartung und gegenwärtiges Heil. Untersuchungen zu den Gemeindeliedern von Qumran mit einem Anhang über Eschatologie und Gegenwart in der Verkündigung Jesu.* StUNT 4. Göttingen, 1966.

Kvanvig, Helge S. "Struktur und Geschichte in Dan 7, 1-14," *StTh* 32 (1978): 95–115.

―――. "Henoch und der Menschensohn. Das Verhältnis von Hen 14 zu Dan 7," *StTh* 38 (1984): 101–33.

La Sor, William S. "Interpretation and Infalliability: Lessons from the Dead Sea Scrolls," 123–37 in Craig A. Evans and William F. Stinespring, eds., *Early Jewish and Christian Exegesis. Studies in Memory of William Hugh Brownlee.* Atlanta, 1987.

Lagrange, Marie-Joseph. *Le Judaïsme avant Jésus-Christ.* EtB. Paris, 1931.

Larcher, C. *Etudes sur le livre de la Sagesse.* EtB. Paris, 1969.

―――. *Le livre de la Sagesse ou La Sagesse de Salomon.* 3 vols. EtB n.s. 1, 3, 5. Paris, 1983, 1984, 1985.

Laubscher, François. "God's Angel of Truth and Melchizedek: A Note on 11QMelch 13b," *JSJ* 3 (1972): 46–51.

Lebram, Jürgen C. H. "The Piety of the Jewish Apocalyptists," 171–210 in David Hellholm, ed., *Apocalypticism.*

Lentzen-Deis, Fritzleo. *Die Taufe Jesu nach den Synoptikern. Literarkritische und gattungsgeschichtliche Untersuchungen.* Frankfurter Theologische Studien 4. Frankfurt am Main, 1970.

Lévi, Israel. "La Pesikta Rabbati et le 4ᵉ Ezra," *REJ* 24 (1892): 281–85.

Lewis, Jack Pearl. *A Study of the Interpretation of Noah and the Flood in Jewish and Christian Literature.* Leiden, 1978, ©1968.

Licht, Jacob. "Taxo, or the Apocalyptic Doctrine of Vengeance," *JJS* 12 (1961): 95–103.

Lichtenberger, Hermann. *Studien zum Menschenbild in Texten der Qumrangemeinde.* StUNT 15. Göttingen, 1980.

―――. "Täufergemeinden und frühchristliche Täuferpolemik im letzten Drittel des 1. Jahrhunderts," *ZThK* 84 (1987): 36–57.

Limbeck, Meinrad. *Die Ordnung des Heils: Untersuchungen zum Gesetzesverständnis des Frühjudentums.* Düsseldorf, 1971.

Lindblom, Johannes B. *Das ewige Leben. Eine Studie über die Entstehung der religiösen Lebensidee im Neuen Testament.* Arbeten utgifna af Vilhelm Ekmans Universitetsfond 15. Uppsala, 1914.

Lövestam, Evald. "Eschatologie und Tradition im 2. Petrusbrief," 2: 287–300 in William C. Weinrich, ed., *The New Testament Age: Essays in Honor of Bo Reicke.* 2 vols. Macon, Ga., 1984.

Loretz, Oswald. *Regenritual und Jahwetag im Joelbuch. Kanaanäischer Hintergrund, Kolometrie, Aufbau und Symbolik eines Prophetenbuches.* Ugaritisch-Biblische Literatur 4. Altenberge, 1986.

Luck, Ulrich. "Das Weltverständnis in der jüdischen Apokalyptik, dargestellt an äthiopischen Henoch und am 4. Esra," *ZThK* 73 (1976): 283–305.

Macurdy, G. H. "Platonic Orphism in the Testament of Abraham," *JBL* 61 (1942): 213–26.

Maier, Gerhard. *Mensch und freier Wille. Nach den jüdischen Religionsparteien zwischen Ben Sira und Paulus.* WUNT 12. Tübingen, 1971.

Martin, François. "Le Livre des Jubilés. But et procédés de l'auteur. Ses doctrines," *RB* 8 (1911): 321–44, 502–33.

Martin-Achard, Robert. "L'espérance des croyants d'Israël face à la mort selon Esaïe 65,16c-25 et selon Daniel 12,1-4," *RHPhR* 59 (1979): 439–51.

Maser, Peter. "Darstellungen des olam hab-ba in der spätantik-jüdischen Kunst Roms?" 228–38 in *Jenseitsvorstellungen in Antike und Christentum. Gedenkschrift für Alfred Stuiber.* JAC. E 9 (1982).

Mell, Ulrich. *Neue Schöpfung. Eine traditionsgeschichtliche und exegetische Studie zu einem soteriologischen Grundsatz paulinischer Theologie.* BZNW 56. Berlin, 1989.

Messel, Nils. *Die Einheitlichkeit der jüdischen Eschatologie.* BZAW 30. Gießen, 1915.

Mildenberg, Leo. *The Coinage of the Bar Kokhba War.* Edited and translated by Patricia Erhart Mottahedeh. Monographien zur antiken Numismatik 6. Aarau, 1984.

Milik, Jozef T. "Milkī–ṣedeq et Milkī–reša' dans les anciens écrits juifs et chrétiens," *JJS* 23 (1972): 95–144.

Milikowsky, C. "Which Gehenna? Retribution and Eschatology in the Synoptic Gospels and in Early Jewish Texts," *NTS* 34 (1988): 238–49.

Miller, M. P. "The Function of Isa 61:1-2 in 11Q Melchizedek," *JBL* 88 (1969): 467–69.

Monloubou, Louis, and Henri Cazelles, eds. *Apocalypses et Théologie de l'espérance.* Association Catholique Française pour l'Etude de la Bible, Congrès de Toulouse 1975. LeDiv 95. Paris, 1977.

Morgenstern, Julian. "The HASĪDĪM—Who Were They?" *HUCA* 38 (1967): 59–73.

Morris, Leon. *The Biblical Doctrine of Judgment.* London, 1960.

Mowinckel, Sigmund. *Psalmenstudien.* 2 vols. Amsterdam, 1961; original publication 1921–1924.

———. *He That Cometh.* Oxford, 1956.

Müller, Hans-Peter. *Ursprünge und Strukturen alttestamentlicher Eschatologie.* BZAW 109. Berlin, 1969.

Müller, Karlheinz. *Das Judentum in der religionsgeschichtlichen Arbeit am Neuen Testament: eine kritische Rückschau auf die Entwicklung einer Methodik bis zu den Qumranfunden.* Judentum und Umwelt 6. Frankfurt am Main, 1983.

———. "Die religionsgeschichtliche Methode," *BZ* 29 (1985): 161–92.

———. "Zur Datierung rabbinischer Aussagen," 551–87 in Helmut Merklein, ed., *Neues Testament und Ethik. Für Rudolf Schnackenburg.* Freiburg, 1989.

Müller, Ulrich B. *Messias und Menschensohn in jüdischen Apokalypsen und in der Offenbarung des Johannes*. SNT 6. Gütersloh, 1972.

Müller, Werner E. *Die Vorstellung vom Rest im Alten Testament*. New edition reviewed and revised, with additions and an appendix by Horst Dietrich Preuß. Neukirchen-Vluyn, 1973.

Müller-Goldkuhle, Peter. *Die Eschatologie in der Dogmatik des 19. Jahrhunderts. Beiträge zur neueren Geschichte der katholischen Theologie* 10. Essen, 1966.

Münchow, Christoph. *Ethik und Eschatologie. Ein Beitrag zum Verständnis der frühjüdischen Apokalyptik mit einem Ausblick auf das Neue Testament*. Göttingen, 1981.

Muilenburg, James. "The book of Isaiah, Ch. 40–66," 381–773 in *IntB* 5. New York, 1956.

Muñoz, León Domingo. "El 4.° de Esdras y el Targum Palestinense," *EstB* 33 (1974): 323–55; 34 (1975): 49–82; 42 (1984): 5–20.

Murphy-O'Connor, Jerome. "A Literary Analysis of Damascus Document XIX.33–XX.34," *RB* 79 (1972): 544–64.

———. "The Original Text of CD 7:9—8:2 = 19,5-14," *HThR* 64 (1971): 379–86.

———. "The Damascus Document Revisited," *RB* 92 (1985): 223–46.

Neusner, Jacob. *A Life of Rabban Yohanan ben Zakkai, ca. 1–80 C. E.* StPB 6. Leiden, 1962; 2nd ed., completely revised, Leiden, 1970.

———. *Development of a Legend. Studies on the Traditions concerning Yohanan ben Zakkai*. StPB 16. Leiden, 1970.

———. *Eliezer ben Hyrcanus. The Tradition and the Man*. 2 vols. Studies in Judaism in Late Antiquity 3, 4. Leiden, 1973.

———. "Die Verwendung des späteren rabbinischen Materials für die Erforschung des Pharisäismus im 1. Jahrhundert n. Chr.," 93–111 in idem, *Das pharisäische und talmudische Judentum. Neue Wege zu seinem Verständnis*. Edited by Hermann Lichtenberger with a foreword by Martin Hengel. Tübingen, 1984. (First published in *ZThK* 76 [1979]: 292–309.)

Nickelsburg, George W. E. *Resurrection, Immortality, and Eternal Life in Intertestamental Judaism*. HThS 26. Cambridge, Mass., 1972.

———, ed. *Studies on the Testament of Moses*. Septuagint and Cognate Studies 4. Cambridge, Mass., 1973.

———, ed. *Studies on the Testament of Abraham*. Septuagint and Cognate Studies 6. Missoula, Mont., 1976.

———. "Eschatology in the Testament of Abraham: A Study of the Judgment Scene in the Two Recensions," 23–64 in idem, ed., *Studies on the Testament of Abraham*.

———. "Structure and Message in the Testament of Abraham," 85–93 in idem, ed., *Studies on the Testament of Abraham*.

———. "Enoch 97–104. A Study of the Greek and Ethiopic Texts," 90–156 in Michael E. Stone, ed., *Armenian and Biblical Studies. Sion*. Supplementary volume 1. Jerusalem, 1976.

———. "Apocalyptic and Myth in 1 Enoch 6–11," *JBL* 96 (1977): 383–405.

———. "The Apocalyptic Message of 1 Enoch 92–105," *CBQ* 39 (1977): 309–28.

———. "The Books of Enoch in Recent Research," *Religious Studies Review* 7 (1981): 210–17.

———. "Social Aspects of Palestinian Jewish Apocalypticism," 641–54 in David Hellholm, ed., *Apocalypticism*.

———. "The Epistle of Enoch and the Qumran Literature," *JJS* 33 (1982): 333–48.

———, and Michael E. Stone. *Faith and Piety in Early Judaism: Texts and Documents*. Philadelphia, 1983.

Niehr, Herbert. *Herrschen und Richten: Die Wurzel špṭ im Alten Orient und im Alten Testament*. FB 54. Würzburg, 1986.

Nilsson, Martin P. *Geschichte der griechischen Religion I: Die Religion Griechenlands bis auf die griechische Weltherrschaft; II: Die hellenistische und römische Zeit*. HAW V.2.1/2. 2nd ed. Munich, 1955, 1961.

Nötscher, Friedrich. *Zur theologischen Terminologie der Qumran-Texte*. BBB 10. Bonn, 1956.

Osburn, C. D. "The Christological Use of I Enoch I.9 in Jude 14,15," *NTS* 23 (1977): 334–41.

Osten-Sacken, Peter von der. *Gott und Belial. Traditionsgeschichtliche Untersuchungen zum Dualismus in den Texten aus Qumran*. StUNT 6. Göttingen, 1969.

Petitmengin, Pierre, and Bernard Flusin. "Le livre antique et la dictée. Nouvelles recherches," 247–62 in Enzo Lucchesi and Henri Dominique Saffrey, eds., *Mémorial André-Jean Festugière: Antiquité païenne et chrétienne: Vingt-cinq Etudes*. Cahiers d'orientalisme 10. Geneva, 1984.

Pfeiffer, Robert H. *History of New Testament Times: With an Introduction to the Apocrypha*. New York, 1949.

Philonenko, Marc. *Les interpolations chrétiennes des Testaments des Douzes Patriarches et les manuscrits de Qumrân*. CRHPhR 35. Paris, 1960.

———, "L'apocalyptique qoumrânienne," 211–18 in David Hellholm, ed., *Apocalypticism*.

Plöger, Otto D. *Theokratie und Eschatologie*. WMANT 2. Neukirchen, 1959; 2nd ed., 1962. ET: *Theocracy and Eschatology*. Translated from the 2nd ed. by S. Rudman. Oxford, 1968.

Preuss, Horst Dietrich, ed. *Eschatologie im Alten Testament*. WdF 480. Darmstadt, 1978.

Puech, Emile. "Notes sur le manuscrit de XIQMelkisédeq," *RdQ* 48 (1987): 483–513.

Rad, Gerhard von. *Theologie des Alten Testaments*. 2 vols. Munich, 1960; 8th ed., 1982, 1984. ET: *Old Testament Theology*. Translated by D. M. G. Stalker. New York, 1962–65.

Rahner, Karl. "Theologische Prinzipien der Hermeneutik eschatologischer Aussagen," 401–28 in idem, *Schriften zur Theologie* IV. Einsiedeln, 1960. (English series title: *Theological Investigations*.)

———. "Über den 'Zwischenzustand,'" 455–66 in idem, *Schriften zur Theologie* XII. Einsiedeln, 1975.

———. *Grundkurs des Glaubens. Einführung in den Begriff des Glaubens*. Freiburg, 1976. ET: *Foundations of Christian Faith: An Introduction to the Idea of Christianity*. Translated by William V. Dych. New York, 1978; 2nd ed., 1982.

Rau, Eckhard. *Kosmologie, Eschatologie und die Lehrautorität Henochs; Traditions- und formgeschichtliche Untersuchungen zum äth. Henochbuch und zu verwandten Schriften*. (Diss.) Hamburg, 1974.

Reicke, Bo. "Official and Pietistic Elements of Jewish Apocalypticism," *JBL* 79 (1960): 137–50.

Reinmuth, Eckart. "Ps.-Philo, Liber Antiquitatum Biblicarum 33,1-5 und die Auslegung der Parabel Lk 16:19-31," *NT* 31 (1989): 16–38.

Reiser, Marius. *Syntax und Stil des Markusevangeliums im Licht der hellenistischen Volksliteratur.* WUNT, 2nd ser. 11. Tübingen, 1984.

Rodríguez Carmona, A. *Targum y resurrección: estudio de los textos del Targum Palestinense sobre la Resurrección.* BT Gran 18. Granada, 1978.

Rowley, Harold Henry. *The Relevance of Apocalyptic: A Study of Jewish and Christian Apocalypses from Daniel to the Revelation.* London, 1944; 3rd ed. 1963; New York, 1964.

Rubinkiewicz, Ryszard. *Die Eschatologie von Henoch 9–11 und das Neue Testament.* Translated by Herbert Ulrich. Österreichische Biblische Studien 6. Klosterneuburg, 1984.

Ruhl, L. *De mortuorum iudicio.* RVV 2,2. Gießen, 1903.

Russell, David S. *The Method and Message of Jewish Apocalyptic: 200 BC–AD 100.* London and Philadelphia, 1964; 3rd ed., 1980.

Rzach, Aloisius. "Sibyllinische Orakel," *PRE* II (2) 4: 2103–69. Stuttgart, 1923.

Sabugal, Santos. "1Q Regla de la Comunidad IX,11: Dos ungidos, un Mesias," *RdQ* 8 (1972–75): 417–23.

Safrai, Shemuel, ed. *The Literature of the Sages.* CRINT Section 2, Volume 3 (3:1 of the whole series). Philadelphia, 1987.

Sänger, Dieter. "Erwägungen zur historischen Einordnung und zur Datierung von 'Joseph und Aseneth,'" 181–202 in *La Littérature intertestamentaire. Colloque de Strasbourg (17–19 octobre 1983).* Paris, 1985. (Also in *ZNW* 76 [1985]: 86–106.)

Saldarini, Anthony J. "The Uses of Apocalyptic in the Mishna and Tosepta," *CBQ* 39 (1977): 396–409.

———. "The Adoption of a Dissident: Akabya ben Mahalaleel in Rabbinic Tradition," *JJS* 33 (1982): 547–56.

Sanders, E. P. *Paul and Palestinian Judaism. A Comparison of Patterns of Religion.* Philadelphia, 1977.

———. "R. Akiba's View of Suffering," *JQR* 63 (1972/73): 332–51.

Sanders, James A. "From Isaiah 61 to Luke 4," 75–106 in Jacob Neusner, ed., *Christianity, Judaism and Other Greco-Roman Cults I. Studies for Morton Smith at Sixty.* Leiden, 1975.

Sato, Migaku. *Q und Prophetie. Studien zur Gattungs- und Traditionsgeschichte der Quelle Q.* WUNT, 2nd ser. 29. Tübingen, 1988.

Schäfer, Peter. "Die Lehre von den zwei Welten im 4. Buch Esra und in der tannaitischen Literatur," 244–91 in idem, *Studien zur Geschichte und Theologie des rabbinischen Judentums.* AGJU 15. Leiden, 1978.

Schaller, Berndt. *Das Testament Hiobs.* JSHRZ III, 3. Gütersloh, 1979.

Schechter, Solomon. "Some Aspects of Rabbinic Theology III," *JQR* 7 (1895): 195–215.

Schimanowski, Gottfried. *Weisheit und Messias: Die jüdischen Voraussetzungen der urchristlichen Präexistenzchristologie.* WUNT, 2nd ser. 17. Tübingen, 1985.

Schmaus, Michael. *Katholische Dogmatik* IV/2. 5th ed. Munich, 1959.

Schmidt, Francis. "The Two Recensions of the Testament of Abraham: In Which Way Did the Transformation Take Place?" 65–83 in G. W. E. Nickelsburg, ed., *Studies on the Testament of Abraham*.

Schmidt, Johann Michael. *Die jüdische Apokalyptik. Die Geschichte ihrer Erforschung von den Anfängen bis zu den Textfunden von Qumran*. Neukirchen-Vluyn, 1969; 2nd ed., 1976.

Schmitt, Armin. *Entrückung, Aufnahme, Himmelfahrt: Untersuchungen zu einem Vorstellungsbereich im Alten Testament*. FB 10. Stuttgart, 1973; 2nd ed., 1976.

————. *Das Buch der Weisheit: Ein Kommentar*. Würzburg, 1986.

————. "Der frühe Tod des Gerechten nach Weish 4,7-19. Ein Psalmthema in weisheitlicher Fassung," 325–47 in Ernst Haag and Frank-Luther Hossfeld, eds., *Freude an der Weisung des Herrn. Beiträge zur Theologie der Psalmen. Festgabe zum 70. Geburtstag von Heinrich Groß*. SBB 13. Stuttgart, 1986.

Schmitt, J. "Les écrits du Nouveau Testament et les textes de Qumrân. Bilan de cinq années de recherches," *RevSR* 30 (1956): 55–74.

Schnackenburg, Rudolf. "Die 'Anbetung im Geist und Wahrheit' (Joh 4,23) im Lichte von Qumrân-Texten," *BZ* 3 (1959): 88–94.

Schneider, Reinhold. *Verhüllter Tag* (*Gesammelte Werke* vol. 10). Frankfurt am Main, 1978.

————. *Das Weltgericht* (*Der Bilderkreis* 22). 2nd ed. Freiburg, 1958.

Schnutenhaus, F. "Das Kommen und Erscheinen Gottes im Alten Testament," *ZAW* 76 (1964): 1–21.

Scholem, Gershom. "Zum Verständnis der messianischen Idee im Judentum," *ErJb* 28 (2959): 193–239.

Schubert, Kurt. "Die Entwicklung der eschatologischen Naherwartung im Frühjudentum," 1–54 in idem, ed., *Vom Messias zum Christus: Die Füller der Zeit in religionsgeschichtlicher und theologischer Sicht*. Vienna, 1964.

————. "Die Entwicklung der Auferstehungslehre von der nachexilischen bis zur frührabbinischen Zeit," *BZ* 6 (1962): 177–214.

Schürer, Emil. *Geschichte des jüdischen Volkes im Zeitalter Jesu Christi*. 3 vols. Leipzig, 1970. ET: *The History of the Jewish People in the Age of Jesus Christ (175 B. C.– A. D. 135)*. Translated by T. A. Burkill et al. Revised and edited by Geza Vermes and Fergus Millar. 3 vols. in 4. Edinburgh, 1973–87.

Schüpphaus, Joachim. *Die Psalmen Salomos. Ein Zeugnis Jerusalemer Theologie und Frömmigkeit in der Mitte des 1. vorchristlichen Jahrhunderts*. ALGHL VII. Leiden, 1977.

Schütz, Rodolphe. *Les idées eschatologiques du Livre de la Sagesse*. Strasbourg, 1935.

Schulz, Paul. *Der Autoritätsanspruch des Lehrers der Gerechtigkeit in Qumran*. Meisenheim am Glan, 1974.

Schunck, K.-D. "Strukturlinien in der Entwicklung der Vorstellung vom 'Tag Jahwes,'" *VT* 14 (1964): 319–30.

————. "Der 'Tag Jahwes' in der Verkündigung der Propheten," *Kairos* 11 (1969): 14–21.

Siegert, Folker. "Gottesfürchtige und Sympathisanten," *JSJ* 4 (1973): 109–64.

Simon, Marcel. *Verus Israel. Etudes sur les relations entre Chrétiens et Juifs dans l'empire romain, 135–425.* Paris, 1948, 1964. ET: *Verus Israel: A Study of the Relations between Christians and Jews in the Roman Empire (135–425).* Translated by Henry McKeating. New York, 1986.

———. "Sur quelques aspects des Oracles Sibyllins juifs," 219–33 in David Hellholm, ed., *Apocalypticism.*

Sjöberg, Erik. *Gott und die Sünder im palästinischen Judentum, nach dem Zeugnis der Tannaiten und der apokryphisch-pseudepigraphischen Literatur.* BWANT 27. Stuttgart, 1938.

Slingerland, H. Dixon. "The Testament of Joseph. A Redaction-Critical Study," *JBL* 96 (1977): 507–16.

———. *The Testaments of the Twelve Patriarchs: A Critical History of Research.* SBL MS 21. Missoula, Mont., 1977.

Soggin, J. Albert. "Zum ersten Psalm," *ThZ* 23 (1967): 81–96.

Spiegel, Joachim. *Die Idee vom Totengericht in der ägyptischen Religion.* Leipzig, 1935.

Starcky, Jean. "Psaumes apocryphes de la grotte 4 de Qumrân (4 QPsᶠ VII–X)," *RB* 73 (1966): 353–71.

Steck, Odil Hannes. *Israel und das gewaltsame Geschick der Propheten; Untersuchungen zur Überlieferung des deuteronomistischen Geschichtsbildes im Alten Testament, Spätjudentum und Urchristentum.* WMANT 23. Neukirchen, 1967.

———. "Überlegungen zur Eigenart der spätisraelitischen Apokalyptik," 301–15 in J. Jeremias and L. Perlitt, eds., *Die Botschaft und die Boten. Festschrift für Hans Walter Wolff zum 70. Geburtstag.* Neukirchen, 1981.

———. "Beobachtungen zur Anlage von Jes 65–66," *BN* 38/39 (1987): 103–16.

Stegemann, Hartmut. "Die Bedeutung der Qumranfunde für die Erforschung der Apokalyptik," 495–530 in David Hellholm, ed., *Apocalypticism.*

Stemberger, Gunter. *Der Leib der Auferstehung. Studien zur Anthropologie und Eschatologie des palästinischen Judentums im neutestamentlichen Zeitalter (ca. 170 v. Chr.– 100 n. Chr.).* AnBib 56. Rome, 1972.

———. "Zur Auferstehungslehre in der rabbinischen Literatur," *Kairos* 15 (1973): 238–66.

———. *Das klassische Judentum. Kultur und Geschichte der rabbinischen Zeit (70 n. Chr. bis 1040 n. Chr.).* Munich, 1979.

Stiassny, M. J. "L'occultation de l'apocalyptique dans le rabbinisme," 179–203 in Louis Monloubou and Henri Cazelles, eds., *Apocalypses.*

Stiegman, E. "Rabbinic Anthropology," *ANRW* II, 19.2 (1979): 487–579.

Stone, Michael E. *Features of the Eschatology of IV Ezra.* Harvard Semitic Studies 35. Atlanta, 1989.

———. "Paradise in 4 Ezra 4,8 and 7,35; 8,52," *JJS* 17 (1966): 85–88.

———. "The Concept of the Messiah in IV Ezra," 295–312 in Jacob Neusner, ed., *Religions in Antiquity. Essays in Memory of Erwin Ramsdell Goodenough.* SHR XIV. Leiden, 1968.

———. "Coherence and Inconsistency in the Apocalypses: The Case of 'the End' in 4 Ezra," *JBL* 102 (1983): 229–43.

————, ed. *Jewish Writings of the Second Temple Period. Apocrypha, Pseudepigrapha, Qumran Sectarian Writings, Philo, Josephus.* Compendia Rerum Judaicarum ad Novum Testamentum II, 2. Assen, 1984.

Strack, Hermann L., and Gunter Stemberger. *Einleitung in Talmud und Midrasch.* 7th completely rev. ed. Munich, 1982.

Stuhlmueller, Carroll. "Deutero-Isaiah," 366–86 in *JBC.*

Taylor, R. J. "The Eschatological Meaning of Life and Death in the Book of Wisdom I–V," *EThL* 42 (1966): 72–137.

Testuz, Michel. *Les idées religieuses du Livre des Jubilés.* Geneva and Paris, 1960.

Thoma, Clemens, and Simon Lauer. *Die Gleichnisse der Rabbinen. I: Pesiqtā de Rav Kahanā (PesK).* Judaica et Christiana 10. Bern and New York, 1986.

Thomas, Joseph. *Le mouvement baptiste en Palestine et Syrie (150 av. J.-C.–300 ap. J.-C.).* Gembloux, 1935.

Thompson, Alden L. *Responsibility for Evil in the Theodicy of IV Ezra: A Study Illustrating the Significance of Form and Structure for the Meaning of the Book.* SBL, DS 29. Missoula, Mont., 1977.

Tigchelaar, E. J. C. "More on Apocalyptic and Apocalypses," *JSJ* 18 (1987): 137–44.

Tillich, Paul. *Systematische Theologie III: Das Leben und der Geist. Die Geschichte und das Reich Gottes.* Translated by Renate Albrecht et al. Stuttgart, 1966. English original: *Systematic Theology.* 3 vols. in 1. Chicago, 1967.

Trever, John C. "The Qumran Teacher—Another Candidate?" 101–21 in Craig A. Evans and William F. Stinespring, eds., *Early Jewish and Christian Exegesis: Studies in Memory of William Hugh Brownlee.* Atlanta, 1987.

Urbach, Ephraim E. *The Sages, Their Concepts and Beliefs.* Translated by Israel Abrahams. Jerusalem, 1975.

VanderKam, James C. "The Theophany of Enoch I, 3b-7,9," *VT* 23 (1973): 129–50.

————. *Textual and Historical Studies in the Book of Jubilees.* Harvard Semitic Museum, Harvard Semitic Monographs 14. Missoula, Mont., 1977.

————. *Enoch and the Growth of an Apocalyptic Tradition.* CBQ MS 16. Washington, 1984.

————. "Studies in the Apocalypse of Weeks (1 Enoch 93,1-10; 91,11-17)," *CBQ* 46 (1984): 511-23.

Vielhauer, Philipp. "Einleitung zu 'Apokalypsen und Verwandtes,'" 407–27 in Edgar Hennecke and Wilhelm Schneemelcher, *Neutestamentliche Apokryphen in deutscher Übersetzung II: Apostolisches. Apokalypsen und Verwandtes.* 4th ed. Tübingen, 1971. Revised by Georg Strecker, 491–515 in Wilhelm Schneemelcher, *Neutestamentliche Apokryphen in deutscher Übersetzung* II. Tübingen, 1989. ET: *New Testament Apocrypha.*

Vílchez, J. "El binomio justicia–injusticia en el libro de la Sabiduría," *Cuadernos Bíblicos* 7 (1981): 1–16.

Vögtle, Anton. *Das Neue Testament und die Zukunft des Kosmos.* Düsseldorf, 1970.

Volz, Paul. *Jesaja II.* KAT IX,2. Leipzig, 1932.

————. *Die Eschatologie der jüdischen Gemeinde im neutestamentlichen Zeitalter nach den Quellen der rabbinischen, apokalyptischen und apokryphen Literatur.* (2nd ed. of *Jüdische Eschatologie von Daniel bis Akiba.*) Tübingen, 1934.

Wacker, Marie-Theres. *Weltordnung und Gericht: Studien zu 1 Henoch 22.* FB 45. Würzburg, 1982.

Wahle, Hedwig. "Die Lehren des rabbinischen Judentums über das Leben nach dem Tod," *Kairos* 14 (1972): 291–309.

Walter, Nikolaus. "'Hellenistische Eschatologie' im Frühjudentum—ein Beitrag zur 'Biblischen Theologie'?" *ThLZ* 110 (1985): 331–47.

Wellhausen, Julius. *Die Pharisäer und die Sadducäer: Eine Untersuchung zur inneren jüdischen Geschichte.* Greifswald, 1874; 3rd ed., Göttingen, 1967.

Westermann, Claus. *Das Buch Jesaja Kapitel 40–66.* ATD 19. Göttingen, 1966. ET: *Isaiah 40–66: A Commentary.* Translated by David M. G. Stalker. Philadelphia, 1969.

Wildberger, Hans. *Jesaja.* BK X/1–3. Neukirchen-Vluyn, 1972, 1978, 1982. ET: *Isaiah: A Commentary.* Continental Commentaries. Minneapolis, 1990–.

Winston, David. *The Wisdom of Solomon: A New Translation with Introduction and Commentary.* AncB. New York, 1979; 3rd ed., 1982.

Wolff, Hans Walter. "Das Kerygma des deuteronomistischen Geschichtswerks," *ZAW* 73 (1961): 171–86.

———. *Dodekapropheton 2: Joel, Amos.* BK XIV/2. Neukirchen-Vluyn, 1969. ET: *Joel and Amos: A Commentary on the Books of the Prophets Joel and Amos.* Translated by Waldemar Janzen, S. Dean McBride, Jr., and Charles A. Muenchow; edited by S. Dean McBride, Jr. Philadelphia, 1977.

Woude, A. S. van der. "Melchizedek als himmlische Erlösergestalt in den neugefundenen eschatologischen Midraschim aus Qumran-Höhle XI," *OTS* 14 (1965): 354–73.

Zager, Werner. *Begriff und Wertung der Apokalyptik in der neutestamentlichen Forschung.* Europäische Hochschulschriften ser. XXIII, vol. 358. Frankfurt am Main and New York, 1989.

Zahavy, Tzvee. *The Traditions of Eleazar Ben Azariah.* Brown Judaic Studies 2. Missoula, Mont., 1977.

Ziener, Georg. *Die theologische Begriffssprache im Buche der Weisheit.* BBB 11. Bonn, 1956.

Bibliography II
(For Parts Two and Three)

Titles listed in Bibliography I are not repeated here. See also pp. 325–48.

Alon, Gedalia. "Those Appointed for Money. On the History of the Various Juridical Authorities in Eretz-Israel in the Talmudic Period," 374–435 in idem, *Jews, Judaism and the Classical World. Studies in Jewish History in the Times of the Second Temple and Talmud*. Jerusalem, 1977.

Bacher, Wilhelm. *Die Agada der palästinischen Amoräer*. 3 vols. Strasbourg, 1892, 1896, 1899.

Bailey, Kenneth E. *Poet and Peasant. A Literary Cultural Approach to the Parables in Luke*. Grand Rapids, Mich., 1976.

Barthélemy, Dominique. *Les Devanciers d'Aquila*. VT.S. 10. Leiden, 1963.

Beasley-Murray, George R. *Baptism in the New Testament*. London, 1962.

Beatrice, Pier Franco. "Il significato di Ev. Thom. 64 per la critica letteraria della parabola del banchetto (Mt. 22,1-14/Lc. 14,15-24)," 237–77 in idem, *La parabola degli invitati al Banchette. Dagli evangelisti a Gesù*. Brescia, 1978.

Becker, Jürgen. *Johannes der Täufer und Jesus von Nazareth*. BSt 63. Neukirchen-Vluyn, 1972.

Berger, Klaus. "Zu den sogenannten Sätzen heiligen Rechts," *NTS* 17 (1970/71): 10–40.

———. "Die königlichen Messiastraditionen des Neuen Testaments," *NTS* 20 (1974): 1–44.

Beyer, Klaus. *Semitische Syntax im Neuen Testament. I: Satzlehre Teil 1*. StUNT 1. Göttingen, 1962.

Black, Matthew. *An Aramaic Approach to the Gospels and Acts*. 3rd ed. Oxford, 1967.

Blinzler, Josef. "Die Niedermetzelung von Galiläern durch Pilatus," *NT* 2 (1958): 24–49.

Blümner, H. *Technologie und Terminologie der Gewerbe und Künste bei Griechen und Römern* I. 2nd ed. Leipzig, 1912.

Boehmer, Julius. *Die neutestamentliche Gottesscheu und die ersten drei Bitten des Vater-unsers*. Halle, 1917.

Bogaert, Pierre. *Apocalypse de Baruch. Introduction, traduction du Syriaque et commentaire*. 2 vols. SC 144, 145. Paris, 1969.

Bornkamm, Günther. *Jesus von Nazareth*. 1956. 9th ed., Stuttgart, ET: *Jesus of Nazareth*. Translated by Irene and Fraser McLuskey with James M. Robinson. New York, 1960.

Braun, Herbert. *Spätjüdisch-häretischer und frühchristlicher Radikalismus. Jesus von Nazareth und die essenische Qumransekte*. 2 vols. Tübingen, 1957.

———. *Qumran und das Neue Testament*. 2 vols. Tübingen, 1966.

Brinker, K. "Das Passiv in der 'Augsburgischen Konfession.' Mit einem Ausblick auf den Passiv-Gebrauch in theologischen Texten der Gegenwart," 162–88 in *Studien zur Syntax des heutigen Deutsch*. Sprache der Gegenwart. Schriften des Instituts für deutsche Sprache VI. Düsseldorf, 1970.

———. *Das Passiv im heutigen Deutsch. Form und Funktion*. Heutiges Deutsch I, 2. Munich, 1971.

Broer, Ingo. "Die Parabel vom Verzicht auf das Prinzip von Leistung und Gegenleistung (Mt 18,23-35)," 145–64 in *A cause de l'évangile. Etudes sur les Synoptiques et les Actes. Festschrift Jacques Dupont*. LeDiv 123. Saint-André, 1985.

Bühlmann, Walter, and Karl Scherer. *Stilfiguren der Bibel. Ein kleines Nachschlagewerk*. BiBe 10. Friburg, 1973.

Bühner, Jan-Adolf. *Der Gesandte und sein Weg im 4. Evangelium*. WUNT, 2nd ser., 2. Tübingen, 1977.

Bultmann, Rudolf. *Jesus*. Tübingen, 1926; repr. 1983. ET: *Jesus and the Word*. Translated by Louise Pettibone Smith and Erminie Huntress Lantero. New York, 1962.

———. *Die Geschichte der synoptischen Tradition*. FRLANT 29. 1921. 8th ed., Göttingen, 1970. ET: *The History of the Synoptic Tradition*. Translated by John Marsh. Oxford, ca. 1963; rev. ed. 1968.

———. "Das Verständnis der Geschichte im Griechentum und im Christentum," 91–103 in idem, *Glauben und Verstehen. Gesammelte Aufsätze* 4. Tübingen, 1965.

Cadbury, Henry J. "Dust and Garments," 5: 269–71 in Foakes Jackson and Kirsopp Lake, eds., *The Beginnings of Christianity*. 5 vols. London, 1920–33.

Catchpole, David R. "The Law and the Prophets in Q," 95–109 in G. F. Hawthorne and Otto Betz, eds., *Tradition and Interpretation in the New Testament. Essays in Honor of E. Earle Ellis*. Grand Rapids, Mich., 1987.

Chilton, Bruce D. *God in Strength. Jesus' Announcement of the Kingdom*. SNTU B 1. Linz, 1979.

Dahl, Nils A. *Das Volk Gottes. Eine Untersuchung zum Kirchenbewußtsein des Urchristentums*. Oslo, 1941. 2nd ed., Darmstadt, 1963.

Dalman, Gustaf. *Arbeit und Sitte in Palästina III: Von der Ernte zum Mehl. Ernten, Dreschen, Worfeln, Sieben, Verwahren, Mahlen*. 1933. Hildesheim, 1964.

de Broer, M. C. "Ten Thousand Talents? Matthew's Interpretation and Redaction of the Parable of the Unforgiving Servant (Matt 18:23-35)," *CBQ* 50 (1988): 214–32.

Degenhardt, Hans-Joachim. *Lukas, Evangelist der Armen. Besitz und Besitzverzicht in den lukanischen Schriften. Eine traditions- und redaktionsgeschichtliche Untersuchung*. Stuttgart, 1965.

Deidun, T. J. "The Parable of the Unmerciful Servant (Mt. 18,23-35)," *BTB* 6 (1976): 203–24.

Delling, Gerhard. "Von Morija zum Sinai (Pseudo-Philo, Liber Antiquitatum Biblicarum 32,1–10)," *JSJ* 2 (1971): 1–18.

Denaux, Adelbert. "Der Spruch von den zwei Wegen im Rahmen des Epilogs der Bergpredigt (Mt 7,13-14 par. Lk 13,23-24). Tradition und Redaktion," 305–35 in Joel Delobel, ed., *Logia. Les Paroles de Jésus; the Sayings of Jesus. Mémorial Joseph Coppens.* BEThL 59. Louvain, 1982.

Derrett, J. D. M. "The Parable of the Unjust Steward," 48–77 in idem, *Law in the New Testament.* London, 1970. (First published in *NTS* 7 [1960–61]: 198–219.)

————. "'Take thy Bond . . . and write Fifty' (Luke 16,6). The Nature of the Bond," *JThS* 23 (1972): 438–40.

————. "The Parable of the Unmerciful Servant," 32–47 in idem, *Law in the New Testament.* London, 1970.

————. "Law and Society in Jesus's World," *ANRW* II. 25.1 (1982): 477–564.

Descamps, Albert-Louis. "La composition littéraire de Lc 16,9-13," *NT* 1 (1956): 47–53.

Dibelius, Martin. *Die urchristliche Überlieferung von Johannes dem Täufer.* FRLANT 15. Göttingen, 1911.

————. *Die Formgeschichte des Evangeliums.* 3rd rev. ed. with an appendix by G. Iber; edited by Günther Bornkamm. Tübingen, 1959. ET: *From Tradition to Gospel.* Translated by Bertram Lee Woolf. New York, 1965.

Dietzfelbinger, Christian. "Das Gleichnis von der erlassenen Schuld. Eine theologische Untersuchung von Matthäus 18,23-35," *EvTh* 32 (1972): 437–51.

Dikaiomata: Auszüge aus alexandrinischen Gesetzen und Verordnungen. Edited by Graeca Halensis. PHal 1. Berlin, 1913; repr. Milan, 1972.

Dinkler, Erich. "Zur Geschichte des Kreuzsymbols," 1–25 in idem, *Signum Crucis. Aufsätze zum Neuen Testament und zur Christlichen Archäologie.* Tübingen, 1967.

————. "Kreuzzeichen und Kreuz. Tav, Chi und Stauros," 26–54 in idem, *Signum Crucis. Aufsätze zum Neuen Testament und zur Christlichen Archäologie.* Tübingen, 1967.

Dobbeler, Stephanie von. *Das Gericht und das Erbarmen Gottes. Die Botschaft Johannes des Täufers und ihre Rezeption bei den Johannesjüngern im Rahmen der Theologiegeschichte des Frühjudentums.* BBB 70. Frankfurt am Main, 1988.

Dodd, Charles Harold. *The Parables of the Kingdom.* 1935. 13th ed., London, 1953.

Dunn, James D. G. "Spirit-and-Fire Baptism," *NT* 14 (1972): 81–92.

Dupont, Jacques. "Le logion des douze trônes (Mt 19,28; Lc 22,28-30)," *Bib* 45 (1964): 355–92. Also 2: 706–43 in idem, *Etudes sur les Evangiles Synoptiques,* edited by Frans Neirynck. BEThL 70-B. Louvain, 1985.

————. *Les Béatitudes* I–III. EtB. Paris, 1969, 1973.

————. "L'après-mort dans l'oeuvre de Luc," *RTL* 3 (1972): 3–21.

————. "L'exemple de l'intendant débrouillard (Lk 16,1-13)," *ASeign* 56 (1974): 67–78.

————. "'Beaucoup viendront du levant et du couchant . . . '" (Matthieu 8,11-12; Luc 13,28-29)," *Sciences ecclésiastiques* 19 (1967): 153–67. Also 568–82 in idem, *Etudes sur les Evangiles synoptiques.*

————. "La parabole des invités au festin dans le ministére de Jésus," 667–705 in idem, *Etudes sur les Evangiles synoptiques.*

Edwards, Richard Alan. *The Sign of Jonah in the Theology of the Evangelists and Q.* SBT 2, series 18. London, 1971.

―――. "Matthew's Use of Q in Chapter Eleven," 157–75 in Joel Delobel, ed., *Logia. Mémorial Joseph Coppens.* BEThL 59. Louvain, 1982.

Ego, Beate. "'Denn die Heiden sind der Umkehr nahe.' Rabbinische Interpretationen zur Buße der Leute von Nineve," 158–76 in Reinhard Feldmeier and Ulrich Heckel, eds., *Die Heiden. Juden, Christen und das Problem des Fremden.* WUNT 70. Tübingen, 1994.

Eichholz, Georg. *Gleichnisse der Evangelien. Form, Überlieferung, Auslegung.* 3rd ed. Neukirchen-Vluyn, 1979.

Erman, Adolf. *Ägypten und ägyptisches Leben im Altertum.* New ed. by Hermann Ranke, Tübingen, 1923; repr. Hildesheim, 1981.

Ernst, Josef. *Johannes der Täufer. Interpretation, Geschichte, Wirkungsgeschichte.* BZNW 53. Berlin, 1989.

―――. "War Jesus ein Schüler Johannes' des Täufers?" 13–33 in Hubert Frankemölle and Karl Kertelge, eds., *Vom Urchristentum zu Jesus. Für Joachim Gnilka.* Freiburg, 1989.

Fabry, Heinz-Josef. *Die Wurzel ŠÛB in der Qumran-Literatur. Zur Semantik eines Grundbegriffes.* BBB 46. Cologne, 1975.

Fassl, Peter. "'Und er lobte den ungerechten Verwalter' (Lk 16,8a). Komposition und Redaktion in Lk 16," 109–43 in Rudolf Kilian et al., eds., *Eschatologie. Bibeltheologische und philosophische Studien zum Verhältnis von Erlösungswelt und Wirklichkeitsbewältigung.* Festschrift for E. Neuhäusler. St. Ottilien, 1981.

Fiedler, Peter. *Jesus und die Sünder.* Frankfurt am Main, 1976.

Fitzmyer, Joseph A. "The Story of the Dishonest Manager (Lk 16:1-13)," 161–84 in idem, *Essays on the Semitic Background of the New Testament.* London, 1971. (First publ. in *TS* 25 [1964]: 23–42.)

―――. *The Gospel according to Luke. Introduction, Translation, and Notes.* 2 vols. AncB 28. Garden City, N.Y., 1983, 1985.

Fleddermann, Harry T. "John and the Coming One (Matt 3,11-12/Luke 3,16-17)," *SBL Seminar Papers* Series 23 (1984): 377–84.

―――. "The Q Saying on Confessing and Denying," *SBL Seminar Papers* Series 26 (1987): 606–16.

Focant, Camille. "Tromper le mamon d'iniquité (Lc 16, 1-13), 547–69 in *A cause de l'évangile. Festschrift Jacques Dupont.* LeDiv 123. Paris, 1985.

Fonck, Leopold. *Die Parabeln des Herrn im Evangelium exegetisch und praktisch erläutert.* Innsbruck, 1902.

France, R. T. *Jesus and the Old Testament. His Application of Old Testament Passages to Himself and His Mission.* Grand Rapids, Mich., 1982.

Freed, Edwin D. "The Parable of the Judge and the Widow (Luke 18, 1-8)," *NTS* 33 (1987): 38–60.

Fuchs, Ernest. "Das Zeitverständnis Jesu," 304–76 in idem, *Zur Frage nach dem historischen Jesus. Gesammelte Aufsätze* II. 2nd ed. Tübingen, 1965. ET: *Studies of the Historical Jesus.* Translated by Andrew Scobie. Naperville, Ill., 1964.

Galling, Kurt. *Biblisches Reallexikon.* HAT 1, Series 1. 2nd ed. Tübingen, 1977.

Ginzberg, Louis. *The Legends of the Jews.* Translated by Henrietta Szold. 7 vols. Philadelphia, 1909–38.

Gnilka, Joachim. *Das Matthäusevangelium.* 2 vols. HThK 1/1, 2. Freiburg, 1986, 1988.

———. *Das Evangelium nach Markus.* 2 vols. EKK II. 2nd ed. Neukirchen-Vluyn, 1986.

Goppelt, Leonhard. *Theologie des Neuen Testaments.* Edited by Jürgen Roloff. 3rd ed. Göttingen, 1976; repr., 1981. ET: *Theology of the New Testament.* Translated by John E. Alsup; edited by Jürgen Roloff. 2 vols. Grand Rapids, 1981–82.

Grimm, Werner. "Zum Hintergrund von Mt 8, 11f/Lk 13,28f," *BZ* 16 (1972): 255–56.

Groß, Walter. *Die Pendenskonstruktion im Biblischen Hebräisch.* Arbeiten zu Text und Sprache im AT 27. St. Ottilien, 1987.

Grotius, Hugo. *Annotationes in Novum Testamentum* I–III. 1641. Groningen, 1826, 1827.

Grundmann, Walter. *Das Evangelium nach Matthäus.* ThHK 1. 5th ed. Berlin, 1981.

———. *Das Evangelium nach Markus.* ThHK 2. 8th ed. Berlin, 1980.

———. *Das Evangelium nach Lukas.* ThHK 3. 6th ed. Berlin, 1971.

Gundry, Robert H. *The Use of the Old Testament in St. Matthew's Gospel with Special Reference to the Messianic Hope.* NT.S 18. Leiden, 1967.

———. *Matthew. A Commentary on His Literary and Theological Art.* Grand Rapids, Mich., 1982.

Haenchen, Ernst. "Das Gleichnis vom großen Mahl," 135–55 in idem, *Die Bibel und wir. Gesammelte Aufsätze* II. Tübingen, 1968.

———. *Der Weg Jesu. Eine Erklärung des Markus-Evangeliums und der kanonischen Parallelen.* 2nd ed. Berlin, 1968.

Hahn, Ferdinand. *Das Verständnis der Mission im Neuen Testament.* WMANT 13. Neukirchen-Vluyn, 1963. ET: *Mission in the New Testament.* Translated by Frank Clarke. Naperville, Ill., 1965.

———. "Das Gleichnis von der Einladung zum Festmahl," 51–82 in Otto Böcher and Klaus Haacker, eds., *Verborum veritas. Festschrift Gustav Stählin.* Wuppertal, 1970.

———. "Methodologische Überlegungen zur Rückfrage nach Jesus," 11–77 in Karl Kertelge, ed., *Rückfrage nach Jesus. Zur Methodik und Bedeutung der Frage nach dem historischen Jesus.* QD 63. Freiburg, 1974.

Harnack, Adolf von. *Sprüche und Reden Jesu. Die zweite Quelle des Matthäus und Lukas.* Beiträge zur Einleitung in das Neue Testament. Leipzig, 1907.

Harnisch, Wolfgang. *Die Gleichniserzählungen Jesu. Eine hermeneutische Einführung.* Göttingen, 1985.

Hengel, Martin. *Nachfolge und Charisma. Eine exegetisch-religionsgeschichtliche Studie zu Mt 8,21f. und Jesu Ruf in die Nachfolge.* BZNW 34. Berlin, 1968. ET: *The Charismatic Leader and His Followers.* Translated by James Greig. New York, 1981.

———. "Das Gleichnis von den Weingärtnern Mc 12, 1-12 im Lichte der Zenonpayri und der rabbinischen Gleichnisse," *ZNW* 59 (1968): 1–39.

———. "Kerygma oder Geschichte," *ThQ* 151 (1971): 323–36.

———. "Jesus als messianischer Lehrer der Weisheit und die Anfänge der Christologie," 147–88 in Edmond Jacob et al., eds., *Sagesse et Religion. Colloque de Strasbourg Octobre 1976.* Paris, 1979.

———. *The Atonement. The Origins of the Doctrine in the New Testament.* London, 1981.

———. "Zur matthäischen Bergpredigt und ihrem jüdischen Hintergrund," *ThRv* 51 (1987): 327–400.

Hengstl, J. *Griechische Papyri aus Ägypten als Zeugnisse des öffentlichen und privaten Lebens.* Munich, 1978.

Hermann, J. *Studien zur Bodenpacht im Recht der Graeco-aegyptischen Papyri.* MBPF 41. Munich, 1958.

———. "Rechtsgeschichtliche Überlegungen zum Gleichnis vom ungerechten Verwalter (Lk 16, 1-8), *TRG* 38 (1970): 389–402.

Hoffmann, Paul. "Πάντες ἐργάται ἀδικίας. Redaktion und Tradition in Lk 13,22-30," *ZNW* 58 (1967): 188–214.

———. *Studien zur Theologie der Logienquelle.* NTA. NS 8. 3rd ed. Münster, 1982.

Hollenbach, P. "Social Aspects of John the Baptizer's Preaching Mission in the Context of Palestinian Judaism," *ANRW* II 19.1 (1979): 850–75.

Holtzmann, Heinrich Julius. *Die Synoptiker.* HC I. 3rd ed. Tübingen, 1901.

Horowitz, G. *The Spirit of Jewish Law.* New York, 1953.

Hughes, J. H. "John the Baptist: The Forerunner of God Himself," *NT* 14 (1972): 191–218.

Jeremias, Joachim. *Die Gleichnisse Jesu.* 1947. 9th ed. Göttingen, 1977. ET: *The Parables of Jesus.* Translated by S. H. Hooke from the 6th ed. of 1962. 2nd rev. ed. New York, 1972.

———. "Der Gedanke des 'Heiligen Restes' im Spätjudentum und in der Verkündigung Jesu," *ZNW* 42 (1949): 184–94. (Also 121–32 in idem, *Abba. Studien zur neutestamentlichen Theologie und Zeitgeschichte.* Göttingen, 1966.)

———. *Jesu Verheißung für die Völker.* 2nd ed. Stuttgart, 1959.

———. *Neutestamentliche Theologie. Erster Teil: Die Verkündigung Jesu.* Gütersloh, 1971. ET: *New Testament Theology.* Translated by John Bowden. London, 1971.

Jülicher, Adolf. *Die Gleichnisreden Jesu. Zwei Teile in einem Band.* 2nd ed. Tübingen, 1910; Darmstadt, 1976.

Juster, Jean. *Les Juifs dans l'Empire Romaine.* 2 vols. Paris, 1914; repr. New York, 1965.

Käsemann, Ernst. "Die Anfänge christlicher Theologie," 82–104 in idem, *Exegetische Versuche und Besinnungen.* Göttingen, 1964.

Kahlefeld, Heinrich. *Gleichnisse und Lehrstücke im Evangelium.* 1963. 2 vols. in one. Frankfurt am Main, 1981. ET: *Parables and Instructions in the Gospels.* Translated by Arlene Swidler. New York, 1966–.

Karrer, Otto. *Neues Testament. Übersetzt und erklärt.* Munich, 1954.

Kaser, M. *Das römische Zivilprozessrecht.* HAW X 3.4. Munich, 1966.

Klingenberg, E. " 'I dina ba' eto i peschara ba' eto.' Urteil, Schiedsspruch und Vergleich im römischen, griechischen und jüdischen Recht," 63–75 in Ernst Ludwig Ehrlich et al., eds., *"Wie gut sind deine Zelte, Jaakow . . ." Festschrift Reinhold Mayer.* Gerlingen, 1986.

Kloppenborg, John S. *The Formation of Q. Trajectories in Ancient Wisdom Collections.* Philadelphia, 1987.

Klostermann, Erich. *Das Markusevangelium.* HNT 3. 3rd ed. Tübingen, 1936.

———. *Das Matthäusevangelium.* HNT 4. 4th ed. Tübingen, 1971.

———. *Das Lukasevangelium.* HNT 5. 3rd ed. Tübingen, 1975.

Kosmala, Hans. "The Parable of the Unjust Steward in the Light of Qumran," *ASTI* 3 (1964): 114–21.

Krämer, Michael. *Das Rätsel der Parabel vom ungerechten Verwalter: Lk 16,1-13. Auslegungsgeschichte—Umfang—Sinn. Eine Diskussion der Probleme und Lösungsvorschläge der Verwalterparabel von den Vätern bis heute.* BSRel 5. Zürich, 1972.

Kümmel, Werner Georg. *Verheißung und Erfüllung. Untersuchungen zur eschatologischen Verkündigung Jesu.* 3rd ed. Zürich, 1956.

———. *Jesu Antwort an Johannes den Täufer. Ein Beispiel zum Methodenproblem in der Jesusforschung.* Sitzungsberichte der Wissenschaftlichen Gesellschaft an der Johann-Wolfgang-Goethe Universität XI, no. 4. Wiesbaden, 1974. Also 177–200 in idem: *Heilsgeschehen und Geschichte* 2. MThSt 16. Marburg, 1978.

———. "Das Verhalten Jesus gegenüber und das Verhalten des Menschensohns. Markus 8,38 par und Lukas 12,3f par Mattäus 10,32f," 210–24 in Rudolf Pesch and Rudolf Schnackenburg, eds., *Jesus und der Menschensohn. Festschrift für Anton Vögtle.* Freiburg, 1975. Also in idem, *Heilsgeschehen und Geschichte* 2: 201–17.

———. *Dreißig Jahre Jesusforschung (1950–1980).* BBB 60. Bonn, 1985.

———. *Jesus der Menschensohn?* Sitzungsberichte der Wissenschaftlichen Gesellschaft an der Johann-Wolfgang-Goethe Universität Frankfurt am Main 20,3. Wiesbaden, 1984.

Lagrange, Marie-Joseph. *Evangile selon Saint Matthieu.* EtB. 5th ed. Paris, 1941.

———. *Evangile selon Saint Luc.* EtB. 5th ed. Paris, 1941.

Lang, Friedrich. "Erwägungen zur eschatologischen Verkündigung Johannes des Täufers," 459–73 in Georg Strecker, ed., *Jesus Christus in Historie und Theologie. Festschrift Hans Conzelmann zum 60. Geburtstag.* Tübingen, 1975.

Latourelle, René. "Critères d'authenticité historique des Evangiles," *Gr.* 55 (1974): 609–38.

Laufen, Rudolf. *Die Doppelüberlieferungen der Logienquelle und des Markusevangeliums.* BBB 54. Königstein, 1980.

Lehmann, Martin. *Synoptische Quellenanalyse und die Frage nach dem historischen Jesus. Kriterien der Jesusforschung untersucht in Auseinandersetzung mit Emanuel Hirschs Frühgeschichte des Evangeliums.* BZNW 38. Berlin, 1970.

Lenhardt, Pierre, and Peter von der Osten-Sacken. *Rabbi Akiva. Texte und Interpretationen zum rabbinischen Judentum und Neuen Testament.* Arbeiten zur neutestamentlichen Theologie und Zeitgeschichte 1. Berlin, 1987.

Lichtenberger, Hermann. "Täufergemeinden und frühchristliche Täuferpolemik im letzten Drittel des 1. Jahrhunderts," *ZThK* 84 (1987): 36–57.

Lightfoot, J. B. *Horae Hebraicae et Talmudicae in omnes Evangelistas.* Leipzig, 1675.

Limbeck, Meinrad. "Jesu Verkündigung und der Ruf zur Umkehr," 35–42 in Otto Knoch et al., eds., *Das Evangelium auf dem Weg zum Menschen. Zur Vermittlung und zum Vollzug des Glaubens. Festschrift Heinrich Kahlefeld.* Frankfurt am Main, 1973.

Linnemann, Eta. *Gleichnisse Jesu. Einführung und Auslegung.* 7th ed. Göttingen, 1978. ET: *Parables of Jesus: Introduction and Exposition.* Translated from the 3rd German ed. by John Sturdy. London, 1966.

Ljungvik, H. *Beiträge zur Syntax der spätgriechischen Volkssprache.* SHVU 27,3. Uppsala, 1932.

Lövestam, Evald. "The ἡ γενεὰ αὕτη Eschatology in Mk 13,30parr.," 403–13 in Jan Lambrecht, ed., *L'Apocalypse johannique et l'Apocalyptique dans le Nouveau Testament.* BEThL 53. Louvain, 1980.

Lohfink, Gerhard. "Der Ursprung der christlichen Taufe," *ThQ* 156 (1976): 35–54.

―――. *Wie hat Jesus Gemeinde gewollt?* Freiburg, 1982. ET: *Jesus and Community: The Social Dimension of Christian Faith.* Translated by John P. Galvin. Philadelphia and New York, 1984.

―――. "Die Metaphorik der Aussaat im Gleichnis vom Sämann (Mk 4,3-9)," 211–28 in *A cause de l'évangile. Festschrift Jacques Dupont.* LeDiv 123. Saint-André, 1985.

―――. *Gottes Taten gehen weiter. Geschichtstheologie als Grundvollzug neutestamentlicher Gemeinden.* Freiburg, 1985. ET: *The Work of God Goes On.* Translation by Linda M. Maloney. Philadelphia, 1985.

―――. "Jesus und die Kirche," 49–96 in Walter Kern et al., eds., *Handbuch der Fundamentaltheologie* 3. Freiburg, 1986.

―――. "Worin besteht der Radikalität der Bergpredigt?" 65–98 in idem, *Wem gilt die Bergpredigt? Beiträge zu einer christlichen Ethik.* Freiburg, 1988.

Lohmeyer, Ernst. "Zur evangelischen Überlieferung von Johannes dem Täufer," *JBL* 51 (1932): 300–319.

―――. "Vom Baum und Frucht. Eine exegetische Studie zu Matth. 3,10," *ZThK* 8 (1932): 377–97.

―――. *Das Urchristentum. 1. Buch: Johannes der Täufer.* Göttingen, 1932.

―――. *Das Evangelium des Matthäus. Nachgelassene Ausarbeitungen und Entwürfe zur Übersetzung und Erklärung.* Edited by W. Schmauch. KEK Sb. Göttingen, 1956.

Lührmann, Dieter. *Die Redaktion der Logienquelle.* WMANT 33. Neukirchen-Vluyn, 1985.

März, Claus-Peter. "Zur Vorgeschichte von Lk 12,49-59," *SNTU* 12 (1987): 69–84.

Manson, T. W. *The Sayings of Jesus. As recorded in the Gospels according to St. Matthew and St. Luke arranged with introduction and commentary.* London, 1937; 4th ed., 1957.

―――. "John the Baptist," *BJRL* 36 (1953/54): 395–412.

―――. *The Teaching of Jesus. Studies of Its Form and Content.* Cambridge, 1955.

Marguerat, Daniel. *Le Jugement dans l'Evangile de Matthieu.* Geneva, 1981.

Marquardt, J. *Das Privatleben der Römer.* 2 vols. Leipzig, 1886; repr. Darmstadt, 1980.

Marshall, I. Howard. *The Gospel of Luke. A Commentary on the Greek Text.* The New International Greek Testament Commentary. Exeter, 1978.

McEleney, Neil J. "Authenticating Criteria and Mark 7:1-23," *CBQ* 34 (1972): 431–60.

Menge, Hermann. *Langenscheidts Großwörterbuch Griechisch-Deutsch.* Berlin, 1913; 23rd ed., 1979.

Merklein, Helmut. *Die Gottesherrschaft als Handlungsprinzip. Untersuchungen zur Ethik Jesu.* FB 34. 2nd ed. Würzburg, 1981.

————. "Die Umkehrpredigt bei Johannes dem Täufer und Jesus von Nazareth," *BZ* n.s. 25 (1981): 29–46. Also 109–26 in idem, *Studien zu Jesus und Paulus.* Tübingen, 1987.

————. *Jesu Botschaft von der Gottesherrschaft.* SBS 111. Stuttgart, 1983.

————. "Jesus, Künder des Reiches Gottes," 145–74 in Walter Kern et al., eds., *Handbuch der Fundamentaltheologie* 2. Freiburg, 1985. Also 127–56 in idem, *Studien zu Jesus und Paulus.* Tübingen, 1987.

Meyer, Paul M. *Juristische Papyri. Erklärung von Urkunden zur Einführung in die juristische Papyruskunde.* Berlin, 1920.

Michevc-Gabrovec, E. *Etudes sur la syntaxe de Joannes Moschos.* Ljubljana, 1960.

Mitteis, Ludwig, and Ulrich Wilcken. *Grundzüge und Chrestomatie der Papyruskunde 1: Historischer Teil; II: Juristischer Teil.* Leipzig, 1912.

Moulton, James Hope, and George Milligan. *The Vocabulary of the Greek Testament. Illustrated from the Papyri and Other Non-literary Sources.* 1930. Grand Rapids, Mich., 1976.

Mußner, Franz. *Die Wunder Jesu. Eine Hinführung.* SK 10. Munich, 1967.

————. "Wege zum Selbstbewußstsein Jesu: Ein Versuch," *BZ* n.s. 12 (1968): 161–72.

Neirynck, Frans. "Recent Developments in the Study of Q," 29–75 in Joel Delobel, ed., *Logia. Mémorial Joseph Coppens.* BEThL 59. Louvain, 1982.

Newman, John Henry. *An Essay in Aid of a Grammar of Assent.* Edited by J. T. Ker. Oxford, 1985.

Oberlinner, Lorenz. *Todeserwartung und Todesgewißheit Jesu. Zum Problem einer historischen Begründung.* SBB 10. Stuttgart, 1980.

Pape-Müller, S. *Textfunktionen des Passivs. Untersuchungen zur Verwendung von grammatisch-lexikalischen Passivformen.* Series "Germanistische Linguistik," 29. Tübingen, 1980.

Pax, Elpidius. "Beobachtungen zum biblischen Sprachtabu," *SBFLA* 12 (1961/62): 66–112.

Percy, Ernst. *Die Botschaft Jesu. Eine traditionskritische und exegetische Untersuchung.* Lund, 1953.

Pernée, L. "Passif et Moyen en Grec ancien," 93–102 in *Cercle linguistique d'Aix-en-Provence. Travaux 2: Le Passif.* Université de Provence, 1984.

Pesce, Mauro. "Ricostruzione dell' archetipo letterario commune a Mt. 22,1-10 e Lc. 14,15-24," 167–236 in *La parabola degli invitati al banchetto. Dagli evangelisti a Gesù.* Brescia, 1978.

Pesch, Rudolf. *Das Markusevangelium.* 2 vols. HThK II. Freiburg, 1976, 1977.

————. "Über die Autorität Jesu. Eine Rückfrage anhand des Bekenner- und Verleugnerspruchs Lk 12,8f par.," 25–55 in Rudolf Schnackenburg et al., eds., *Die Kirche des Anfangs. Festschrift Heinz Schürmann.* Freiburg, 1978.

————. "Voraussetzungen und Anfänge der urchristlichen Mission," 11–70 in Karl Kertelge, ed., *Mission im Neuen Testament.* QD 93. Freiburg, 1982.

Plummer, Alfred. *A Critical and Exegetical Commentary on the Gospel according to St. Luke.* ICC. Edinburgh, 1901; repr. 1977.

————. *An Exegetical Commentary on the Gospel according to St. Matthew.* 1915. Grand Rapids, Mich., 1982.

Polkow, D. "Method and Criteria for Historical Jesus Research," *SBL Seminar Papers Series* 26 (1988): 336–56.

Preisker, Herbert. "Lukas 16,1-7," *ThLZ* 74 (1949): 85–92.

Reiser, Marius. "Der Alexanderroman und das Markusevangelium," 131–61 in H. Cancik, ed., *Markus-Philologie. Historische, literargeschichtliche und stilistische Untersuchungen zum zweiten Evangelium*. WUNT 33. Tübingen, 1984.

Riesner, Rainer. *Jesus als Lehrer. Eine Untersuchung zum Ursprung der Evangelien-Überlieferungen*. WUNT, 2nd ser. 7. 3rd ed. Tübingen, 1988.

Rüger, Hans Peter. "'Mit welchem Maß ihr meßt, wird euch gemessen werden,'" *ZNW* 60 (1969): 174–82.

Sahlin, H. *Studien zum dritten Kapitel des Lukasevangeliums*. UUA 2. Uppsala, 1949.

Sanders, E. P. *Jesus and Judaism*. London, 1985.

Sato, Migaku. *Q und Prophetie. Studien zur Gattungs- und Traditionsgeschichte der Quelle Q*. WUNT, 2nd ser. 29. Tübingen, 1988.

Schanz, Peter. *Commentar über das Evangelium des heiligen Matthäus*. Freiburg, 1879.

———. *Commentar über das Evangelium des heiligen Lucas*. Tübingen, 1883.

Schelkle, Karl Hermann. *Theologie des Neuen Testaments*. 4 vols. Düsseldorf, 1968–76. ET: *Theology of the New Testament*. Translated by William A. Jurgens. 4 vols. Collegeville, Minn., 1971–78.

Schlatter, Adolf. *Johannes der Täufer*. (Diss. 1880). W. Michaelis, ed. Basel, 1956.

———. *Die Geschichte des Christus*. 2nd ed. Stuttgart, 1923; 4th ed., 1984.

———. *Der Evangelist Matthäus. Seine Sprache, sein Ziel, seine Selbständigkeit*. Stuttgart, 1929; 7th ed., 1982.

———. *Das Evangelium des Lukas. Aus seinen Quellen erklärt*. Stuttgart, 1931; 3rd ed., 1975.

———. *Der Evangelist Johannes. Wie er spricht, denkt und glaubt*. Stuttgart, 1930; 4th ed., 1975.

———. *Der Glaube im Neuen Testament*. Stuttgart, 1927.

Schlosser, Jacques. *Le règne de Dieu dans les dits de Jésus*. 2 vols. EtB. Paris, 1980.

Schmid, Josef. *Matthäus und Lukas. Eine Untersuchung des Verhältnisses ihrer Evangelien*. BSt[F] 23,2–4. Freiburg, 1930.

———. *Das Evangelium nach Matthäus*. RNT 1. Regensburg, 1956.

———. *Das Evangelium nach Markus*. RNT 2. 4th ed. Regensburg, 1958.

———. *Das Evangelium nach Lukas*. RNT 3. Regensburg, 1955.

Schmidt, D. "The LXX Gattung 'Prophetic Correlative,'" *JBL* 96 (1977): 517–22.

Schmidt, Wilhelm. *Lexikalische und aktuelle Bedeutung. Ein Beitrag zur Theorie der Wortbedeutung*. 4th ed. Berlin, 1967.

Schmitt, Joseph. "Les écrits du Nouveau Testament et les textes de Qumran. Bilan de cinq années de recherches," *RevSR* 29 (1955): 381–401; 30 (1956): 55–74, 261–82.

Schmitz, Otto. "Abraham im Spätjudentum und im Urchristentum," 99–123 in *Aus Schrift und Geschichte. Theologische Abhandlungen Adolf Schlatter zu seinem 70. Geburtstage dargebracht*. Stuttgart, 1922.

Schnackenburg, Rudolf. *Gottes Herrschaft und Reich. Eine biblisch-theologische Studie*. 4th ed. Freiburg, 1965.

Schneemelcher, Wilhelm, ed. *Neutestamentliche Apokryphen in deutscher Übersetzung.* 5th ed. of the collection begun by Edgar Hennecke. I: Evangelien. Tübingen, 1987. ET: *New Testament Apocrypha.* Translated by A. J. B. Higgins et al.; edited by R. McLean Wilson. 2 vols. Philadelphia, 1963–66.

Schneider, Reinhold. "Verloren haben die Christen!" 167–73 in idem, *Gesammelte Werke* 9. Frankfurt am Main, 1978.

———. "Jeremia (Prophetie in der Zeit)," 266–79 in idem, *Gesammelte Werke* 9. Frankfurt am Main, 1978.

Schneider, Wilhelm. *Stilistische Deutsche Grammatik. Die Stilwerte der Wortarten, der Wortstellung und des Satzes.* 1959. 4th ed., Freiburg, 1967.

Schottroff, Luise. "Das Gleichnis vom großen Gastmahl in der Logienquelle," *EvTh* 47 (1987): 192–211.

Schrage, Wolfgang. *Ethik des Neuen Testaments.* GNT 4. Göttingen, 1982.

Schramm, Tim, and Kathrin Löwenstein. *Unmoralische Helden. Anstößige Gleichnisse Jesu.* Göttingen, 1986.

Schrenk, G. *Die Weissagung über Israel im Neuen Testament.* Zürich, 1951.

Schürmann, Heinz. "Eschatologie und Liebesdienst in der Verkündigung Jesu," 279–98 in idem, *Ursprung und Gestalt. Erörterungen und Besinnungen zum Neuen Testament.* Düsseldorf, 1970.

———. *Jesu ureigener Tod. Exegetische Besinnungen und Ausblick.* Freiburg, 1975.

———. *Das Lukasevangelium. Erster Teil. (Kommentar zu Kap. 1,1—9,50).* HThK 3. 3rd ed. Freiburg, 1984.

———. *Gottes Reich—Jesu Geschick. Jesu ureigener Tod im Licht seiner Basileia-Verkündigung.* Freiburg, 1983.

Schulz, Siegfried. *Q. Die Spruchquelle der Evangelisten.* Zürich, 1972.

Schwank, Benedikt. "Dort wird Heulen und Zähneknirschen sein," *BZ* n.s. 16 (1972): 121–22.

Schwarz, Günther. "Lukas 13,1-5. Eine Emendation," *NT* 11 (1969): 121–26.

Schweitzer, Albert. *Geschichte der Leben-Jesu-Forschung.* Tübingen, 1913.

Schwyzer, E. *Griechische Grammatik I.* HAW II, 1, 1. 5th ed. Munich, 1977. *Griechische Grammatik II.* HAW II, 1, 2, completed and edited by Albert Debrunner. 4th ed. Munich, 1975.

Scobie, Charles H. H. *John the Baptist.* London, 1964.

Scott, Bernard Brandon. "A Master's Praise: Luke 16, 1-8a," *Bib* 64 (1983): 173–88.

Sellin, Gerhard. "Lukas als Gleichniserzähler. Die Erzählung vom barmherzigen Samariter (Lk 10,25-37)," *ZNW* 65 (1974): 166–89; 66 (1975): 19–60.

Sherwin-White, A. N. *Roman Society and Roman Law in the New Testament.* Oxford, 1963.

Sidebottom, E. M. "The So-called Divine Passive in the Gospel Tradition," *ET* 87 (1975/76): 200–204.

Sint, Josef A. "Die Eschatologie des Täufers, die Täufergemeinden und die Polemik der Evangelien," 55–163 in Kurt Schubert, ed., *Vom Messias zum Christus.* Vienna, 1964.

Smyth, Hubert W. *Greek Grammar.* 1920. 10th ed., Cambridge, Mass., 1976.

Spicq, Ceslas. *Dieu et l'homme selon le Nouveau Testament.* LeDiv 29. Paris, 1961.

Stegemann, Hartmut. "Der lehrende Jesus. Der sogenannte biblische Christus und die geschichtliche Botschaft Jesu von der Gottesherrschaft," *NZSTh* 24 (1982): 3–20.

Stein, G. *Studies in the Function of the Passive.* Tübinger Beiträge zur Linguistik 97. Tübingen, 1979.

Stein, Robert H. "The 'Criteria' for Authenticity," 1: 225–63 in R. T. France and David Wenham, eds., *Gospel Perspectives. Studies of History and Tradition in the Four Gospels.* 2 vols. Sheffield, 1980.

Steinhauser, Michael G. *Doppelbildworte in den synoptischen Evangelien. Eine form- und traditionskritische Studie.* FB 44. Würzburg, 1981.

Strecker, Georg. *Der Weg der Gerechtigkeit. Untersuchungen zur Theologie des Matthäus.* FRLANT 82. 2nd ed. Göttingen, 1966.

——— and Udo Schnelle. *Einführung in die neutestamentliche Exegese.* Göttingen, 1983.

Stuhlmacher, Peter. *Jesus von Nazareth—Christus des Glaubens.* Stuttgart, 1988.

Stuhlmann, Rainer. "Beobachtungen und Überlegungen zu Markus IV, 26-29," *NT* 19 (1972/73): 153–62.

Stuhlmueller, Carroll. "The Gospel According to Luke," *JBC* II: 115–64.

Sugranyes de Franch, Ramon. *Etudes sur le droit palestinien à l'époque évangelique.* Fribourg, 1946.

Taubenschlag, R. *The Law of Greco-Roman Egypt in the Light of the Papyri (332 B. C.–640 A. D.).* 2nd ed. Warsaw, 1955; repr. Milan, 1972.

Taylor, Vincent. *The Gospel According to St. Mark.* Hong Kong, 1980.

Teicher, J. L. "The Christian Interpretation of the Sign X in the Isaiah Scroll," *VT* 5 (1955): 189–98.

Theißen, Gerd. *Der Schatten des Galiläers. Historische Jesusforschung in erzählender Form.* Munich, 1986; 13th ed., 1993. ET: *The Shadow of the Galilean: The Quest of the Historical Jesus in Narrative Form.* Translated by John Bowden. Philadelphia, 1987.

Thumb, Albert. *Handbuch der neugriechischen Volkssprache.* 2nd ed. Strasbourg, 1910; repr. Berlin, 1974.

Thyen, Hartwig. "ΒΑΠΤΙΣΜΑ ΜΕΤΑΝΟΙΑΣ ΕΙΣ ΑΦΕΣΙΝ ΑΜΑΡΤΙΩΝ," 97–125 in Erich Dinkler, ed., *Zeit und Geschichte. Dankesgabe an Rudolf Bultmann zum 80. Geburtstag.* Tübingen, 1964.

———. *Studien zur Sündenvergebung im Neuen Testament und seinen alttestamentlichen und jüdischen Voraussetzungen.* FRLANT 96. Göttingen, 1970.

Topel, L. J. "On the Injustice of the Unjust Steward Lk 16,1-13," *CBQ* 37 (1975): 216–27.

Trautmann, Maria. *Zeichenhafte Handlungen Jesu. Ein Beitrag zur Frage nach dem geschichtlichen Jesus.* FB 37. Würzburg, 1980.

Trilling, Wolfgang. *Das wahre Israel. Studien zur Theologie des Matthäus-Evangeliums.* StANT 10. Munich, 1964.

van der Horst, Pieter Willem. *The Sentences of Pseudo-Phocylides. With Introduction and Commentary.* SVTP 4. Leiden, 1978.

Via, Dan Otto. *The Parables: Their Literary and Existential Dimension.* Philadelphia, 1967. German: *Die Gleichnisse Jesu. Ihre literarische und existentiale Dimension. Mit einem Nachwort von E. Güttgemanns.* Munich, 1970.

Vielhauer, Phillipp. "Gottesreich und Menschensohn in der Verkündigung Jesu," 55–91 in idem, *Aufsätze zum Neuen Testament.* TB 31. Munich, 1965. (First published as 51–79 in *Festschrift Günther Dehn,* Neukirchen, 1957.)

————. "Jesus und der Menschensohn. Zur Diskussion mit Heinz Eduard Tödt und Eduard Schweizer," 92–140 in idem, *Aufsätze zum Neuen Testament.* First published in *ZThK* 60 (1963): 133–77.

Vögtle, Anton. "Der Spruch vom Jonas-Zeichen," 230–77 in *Synoptische Studien. Alfred Wikenhauser zum 70. Geburtstag.* Munich, 1953. Also 103–36 in idem, *Das Evangelium und die Evangelien. Beiträge zur Evangelienforschung.* KBANT. Düsseldorf, 1971.

————. "Die Einladung zum großen Gastmahl und zum königlichen Hochzeitsmahl. Ein Paradigma für den Wandel des geschichtlichen Verständnishorizonts," 171–218 in idem, *Das Evangelium und die Evangelien.*

————. "Der verkündigende und verkündigte Jesus 'Christus,'" 27–91 in J. Sauer, ed., *Wer ist Jesus Christus?* Freiburg, 1977.

————. "Bezeugt die Logienquelle die authentische Redeweise Jesu vom 'Menschensohn'?" 77–99 in Joel Delobel, ed., *Logia. Memorial Joseph Coppens.* BEThL 59. Louvain, 1982. Also in idem, *Offenbarungsgeschehen und Wirkungsgeschichte. Neutestamentliche Beiträge.* Freiburg, 1985.

————. "Grundfragen der Diskussion um das heilsmittlerische Todesverständnis Jesu," 141–67 in idem, *Offenbarungsgeschehen.*

Volz, Paul. *Die biblischen Altertümer.* 2nd ed. Stuttgart, 1925.

Wackernagel, J. *Vorlesungen über Syntax mit besonderer Berücksichtigung von Griechisch, Lateinisch und Deutsch.* 2 vols. Basel, 1920, 1924.

Wanke, Joachim. *"Bezugs- und Kommentar-Worte" in den synoptischen Evangelien. Beobachtungen zur Interpretationsgeschichte der Herrenworte in der vorevangelischen Überlieferung.* EThSt 44. Leipzig, 1981.

Weder, Hans. *Die Gleichnisse Jesu als Metaphern. Traditions- und redaktionsgeschichtliche Analysen und Interpretationen.* FRLANT 120. Göttingen, 1978.

————. *Die "Rede der Reden." Eine Auslegung der Bergpredigt heute.* Zürich, 1985.

Weiser, Alfons. *Die Knechtsgleichnisse der synoptischen Evangelien.* StANT 29. Munich, 1971.

Weisgerber, L. *Von den Kräften der deutschen Sprache II: Die sprachliche Gestaltung der Welt.* Düsseldorf, 1962.

Wellhausen, Julius. *Das Evangelium Matthaei.* Berlin, 1904; repr. Berlin, 1987.

————. *Das Evangelium Lucae.* Berlin, 1904; repr. Berlin, 1987.

Wettstein, John Jacob. *Novum Testamentum Graecum.* 2 vols. Amsterdam, 1752; repr. Graz, 1962.

Wolf, P. "Gericht und Reich Gottes bei Johannes und Jesus," 43–49 in Peter Fiedler and Dieter Zeller, eds., *Gegenwart und kommendes Reich. Schülergabe Anton Vögtle zum 65. Geburtstag.* SBB. Stuttgart, 1975.

Wolff, H. J. "Organisation der Rechtspflege und Rechtskontrolle der Verwaltung im ptolemäisch-römischen Ägypten bis Diokletian," *TRG* 34 (1966): 1–40.

———. *Das Justizwesen der Ptolemäer.* 2nd ed. Munich, 1970.

Wolff, Hans Walter. "Das Thema Umkehr in der alttestamentlichen Prophetie," 130–50 in idem, *Gesammelte Studien zum Alten Testament.* TB 22. Munich, 1973.

———. "Die Eigentliche Botschaft der klassischen Propheten," 547–57 in Herbert Donner et al., eds., *Beiträge zur alttestamentlichen Theologie. Festschrift Walther Zimmerli.* Göttingen, 1977.

Zahn, Theodor. *Das Evangelium des Matthäus.* KNT 1. 4th ed. Leipzig, 1922; repr. Wuppertal, 1984.

———. *Das Evangelium des Lucas.* 4th ed. Leipzig, 1920; repr. Wuppertal, 1988.

Zeller, Dieter. "Das Logion Mk 8, 11f/Lk 13,28f und das Motiv der 'Völkerwallfahrt,'" *BZ* n.s. 15 (1971): 222–37; 16 (1972): 84–93.

———. *Die weisheitlichen Mahnsprüche bei den Synoptikern.* FB 17. Würzburg, 1977.

———. "Entrückung zur Ankunft als Menschensohn (Lk 13,34f.; 11,29f.)," 513–30 in *A cause de l'évangile. Festschrift Jacques Dupont.* LeDiv 123. Saint-André, 1985.

Zerwick, Max. *Biblical Greek.* Rome, 1963 (= *Graecitas Biblica,* 1960).

Zimmermann, Heinrich. "Die Botschaft der Gleichnisse Jesu IV. Die Forderung der Gleichnisse Jesu. Das Gleichnis vom ungerechten Verwalter Lk 16,1-9," *BiLe* 2 (1961): 254–61.

Index of Ancient References

3:14	26
3:18-21	28, 30
4:2	155
4:4-8	226
4:12	155
4:13	179
4:18-21	147

Amos

1:3—2:5	210
2:3	134
4:13	135
5:15	27
5:18-20	27
5:20	26
7:1-6	210
9:2	87, 227
9:9	180
9:15	173

Obadiah

4	227
12	26
14	26, 79
15	26, 27
17	79
18	27, 143, 172, 177

Jonah

3:5	208
3:5-9	226
3:5-10	218
3:8	208
3:10	208
4:1-2	214

Micah

1:2-4	25, 35
1:3-4	51
1:4	121
4:1	24
4:12-13	256
4:14	134
5:7-8	210

6:1	21
6:2	288
7:6	211

Nahum

1:5	27
1:6	26, 27, 172
1:7	26
1:7-8	59

Habakkuk

3:10-11	27
3:12	26, 143
3:16	26

Zephaniah

1:2—2:3	27
1:7	26
1:14-16	26
1:15	26, 28, 63
1:18	26, 27, 171
2:1-3	251
2:2	26, 171
2:3	26, 27, 171
3:15	158
3:18-20	28

Zechariah

1:3	192
1:4	249
3:1	36, 211
3:1-7	156
8:12	34
8:20-23	234
9:2-4	226
12—14	27
12:6	143
13:7	79
13:8-9	28
13:9	126, 173
14	29, 234
14:2	28
14:3	141
14:4	141

Old Testament Apocrypha and Pseudepigrapha

Qumran Writings, Dead Sea Scrolls

Rabbinic Literature

Midrash Tanhuma
B Gen. I, 3 § 29   131
B Gen. II § 8   138
B Gen. IV § 4   172
B Gen. V § 7   130
B Gen. XI § 7   135
B Exod. III § 6   141
B Exod. III § 13   103
B Lev. I § 15   103
B Lev. II, 1 § 4   114
B Lev. II, 1 § 7   131
B Lev. II § 4   141

B Lev. III, 3 § 14   141
B Lev. VII § 1   137, 157
B Num. III § 28   99
B Num. IVa, 2 § 9   215
B Num. IV § 22   103
B Num. VIII, 3 § 12 234–35
B Deut. 1 § 2   135
B Deut. V § 7   135
B Deut. V § 9   137
B Deut. V § 10   172
B Deut. VII § 4   141

New Testament

Matthew
3:2   193
3:7-10   170, 189
3:7-12   167, 314
3:8   252
3:9   189, 228
3:10   190, 253
3:11   184
3:12   171, 172, 178, 187, 257, 312, 313
4:24   263
5:4   270, 271, 272, 303
5:5   37
5:6   271
5:7   271, 280, 303
5:9   271
5:13   236
5:22   303
5:24   288
5:25-26   281, 302, 303, 305, 307, 308
5:45   277
5:46-47   209
6:10   267, 269, 323
6:12   247, 279, 280
6:26-30   209
6:33   271
7:1   271, 280, 307
7:1-2   263, 302, 303
7:2   266, 271, 280

7:7-8   271
7:13-14   124, 199, 201, 232, 303
7:19   303
7:21   303
7:22   228
7:22-23   232, 303
7:24-27   201, 210, 303, 318
8:5-13   225
8:11-12   2, 201, 230, 232, 239, 242, 244, 302, 303, 305, 309, 319
8:12   266, 271, 308, 312
8:29   303
9:1   225
9:13   244
9:16-17   209
9:29   267
9:37-38   256, 302, 307
10:7   257
10:14   256, 257, 258, 302, 303
10:15   221, 222, 303
10:26   271
10:28   303
10:32-33   198, 203, 303, 317
10:33   272
10:35   272
10:39   303
10:40   221, 222
11:2-6   312
11:4-6   225, 229

Other

Index of Modern Authors

Index of Subjects

Abba, God as, 1
Abel as eschatological judge, 125, 126,
  139, 156
abomination of desolation, 200
Abraham, 124, 125, 127, 128, 132, 168,
  230–41
  children of, 170, 173, 175, 188–89,
    190, 228, 243. *See also* Planting, Is-
    rael as God's; People of God, escha-
    tological
  table companions of in reign of God,
    201, 242, 243, 266, 305, 308, 309
abyss, fiery, 55, 61
accommodation with the accuser,
  281–91
Adam, 113
Amalek as symbol of Rome, 140
angels, 60, 63, 66, 73, 82, 94, 124, 125,
  126, 137, 146, 156, 157, 272, 317,
  319
  eschatological fellowship with, 45
  of destruction, 79, 81
  of peace, 95
  of punishment, 68, 286, 310
  See also Michael; Watchers
Antiochus IV, 40, 84, 85
apocalyptic, apocalyptics, 314, 320, 321
  circles, 146
  defined, 22
  Jesus and, 203
Azazel, 93

banquet, eschatological, 82, 83, 86, 233–
  36, 238, 239, 240, 242, 243, 244,
  305, 306, 308, 309, 315
baptism
  of John the Baptist, 181–86
  of the Stronger One, 181–86, 191
  with fire, 168, 169, 184, 185, 186, 191
  with Holy Spirit, 168, 169, 170, 184,
    185
  with water, 168, 184, 185, 191, 253
beasts, of Daniel, 38–39
Behemoth, 122
Belial (Beliar), 75, 76, 77, 79, 80, 82, 83,
  146, 158, 320
  God's war against, 91, 92, 93
  judgment on, 94, 171
  performs signs, 104, 257
  See also Satan
Bethsaida. *See* Woes, Jesus' over the Galilean cities
books, eschatological, 39, 41, 68, 73, 74,
  272
  of deeds, 124, 125, 126, 127, 128
  See also Tablets, heavenly

Cain, 139
Capernaum. *See* Woes, Jesus' over the
  Galilean cities
chaff as image of judgment, 176–80
Chorazin. *See* Woes, Jesus' over the Gali-
  lean cities

as image of final judgment, 59, 62, 146, 198, 200
forgiveness, 186, 279, 280, 323

Gabriel, 68
Gehenna, 37, 54, 59, 66, 101, 137, 142, 147, 154, 155, 157, 180, 237, 308, 309
and Paradise, 123, 133
and purgatory, 136, 149
furnace of, 61, 68, 115, 151
preexistence of, 123
See also Sheol
generation of the end time, 70–71, 83, 104, 114, 116, 121, 216–17, 311
Gog and Magog, 98
grace of God, 279, 280, 323
guilt, 279

Hades, 47, 57, 174
See also Sheol
hand of God, souls in, 150
harvest, eschatological, 256–58, 262, 307, 309
Hasidic, Hasidim, 57, 60, 69, 146
hell, 103, 147, 149, 174, 199, 279, 286.
See also Sheol
hellfire, 95, 147
hereafter, 42
defined, 21
Hinnom, valley of, 31, 236, 237, 238, 240, 306, 321. See also Gehenna

inheritance of the land, eschatological, 38, 53, 136, 191
intermediate state, 12, 119, 128

Jacob, as symbol of Israel, 113, 114, 122
Jerusalem, 158
conquest of, 159
eschatological, 106
new, 61, 116
Jesus
as Coming One. See Coming One
as Messiah. See Messiah
as Son of man. See Son of man, Jesus as
resurrection of. See Resurrection, of Jesus
Jesus Seminar, 3
Jesus' words, authenticity of, 3, 4, 202, 203, 204
John the Baptist, 9, 12–14, 167–93, 201, 202, 252, 253, 254, 255, 257, 305, 307, 310, 312, 313, 314, 315, 316, 322
Jonah, 206, 207, 214, 217, 218, 253, 308, 311
Josephus, 8, 170, 214, 247
judging, prohibition of, 263–66
judgment
according to works, 67, 115, 125, 126, 127, 128, 129, 138
after death, 44, 45, 57, 118, 119, 121, 122, 127, 130, 131, 134, 142, 150, 162, 286
as punishment, 22, 73, 74, 121, 136, 143, 145, 154, 155, 157, 159, 162, 171, 180, 225, 320
books of, 60, 124, 125, 126, 127
by fire, 104, 106, 170–73, 251
by others than God, 106, 162, 199, 263, 264, 265, 266. See also Judging, prohibition of; Twelve, the, as judges
by the Messiah, 13
day of. See Day of judgment
for sinners and righteous, 55, 56, 64, 68, 77, 111, 125, 132, 156
for sinners only, 162, 180, 252
forensic, 7, 8, 22, 41, 55, 56, 61, 64, 68, 73, 74, 115, 121, 145, 154, 155, 156, 157, 160, 162, 211, 214, 220, 226, 230, 266, 307, 317, 319, 320
images and designations of, 150, 162, 307, 308. See also Chaff as image of judgment; Winnowing as judgment imagery
individual, 22, 81, 94, 118, 119, 127, 128, 130, 132, 134, 142, 150, 151, 198, 202, 263–301, 319